Y0-BCE-407

$7⁹⁵

Perspectives on Personality

Perspectives on Personality

A Comparative Approach

Edited by
SALVATORE R. MADDI
UNIVERSITY OF CHICAGO

Little, Brown and Company, Boston

BF
698
M 3 372
1971

541 p.

VNYS BF 698 .M237
1971 c.1

CL122

Personality

COPYRIGHT © 1971 BY LITTLE, BROWN AND COMPANY (INC.)

ALL RIGHTS RESERVED. NO PART OF THIS BOOK MAY BE REPRODUCED
IN ANY FORM OR BY ANY ELECTRONIC OR MECHANICAL MEANS
INCLUDING INFORMATION STORAGE AND RETRIEVAL SYSTEMS WITH-
OUT PERMISSION IN WRITING FROM THE PUBLISHER, EXCEPT BY A
REVIEWER WHO MAY QUOTE BRIEF PASSAGES IN A REVIEW.

LIBRARY OF CONGRESS CATALOG CARD NUMBER: 74-160697

FOURTH PRINTING

Published simultaneously in Canada
by Little, Brown & Company (Canada) Limited

PRINTED IN THE UNITED STATES OF AMERICA

To my children, Karen and Christopher

Preface

This collection of readings should be representative and comprehensive concerning personality theorizing. Wherever possible, I have given preference to material written by the originator of a theory rather than his followers. When you find selections of recent origin, they reflect either the beginnings of a new personality theory or some discriminably new trend in an older tradition. I have taken care to include material concerning not only the overall, unlearned nature of man (e.g., Freud's sex instinct) but also the particular life-styles (e.g., Freud's oral, anal, and phallic character types) developed by men. Original source material from eighteen different viewpoints appears here. These eighteen viewpoints are classified under three broad models (each with two forms) for personality theorizing, and one frank alternative to, or substitute for, such theorizing.

The focus of this collection is on personality theory rather than research (though references to and summaries of research do appear in several of the papers). I believe it best to introduce neophytes into a field through its theories, as long as they are organized in a fashion that illuminates the concepts, problems, issues, and subject matter under consideration. Having gained a basic understanding, the student is then readily able to assimilate the more specific, detailed information of empirical studies. It is more than likely that separate research studies will cover only a tiny bit of the huge terrain of personality. One would have to include an impossible number of studies in a reader if one's aim was to introduce forests rather than trees (to sketch the shape of the field rather than give mere examples of its contents).

Separate research studies also go out of fashion and are superseded by others very rapidly. But I have discussed in a final chapter some themes in contemporary personality research. Also mentioned there are the diagnostic and psychotherapeutic activities of personologists.

This collection could well be used as the central reading of a course if the instructor prefers to assign original source material that he interprets, analyzes, and organizes in his own fashion. The classification of material that I offer is inclusive but does not require progression from first materials to last. The instructor can easily dissect and choose freely among the selections to suit his purposes. My organization could be held in the background or used only insofar as it coincided with the instructor's intent. The main value of the collection used in this way is that it includes diverse, penetrating (often "classical") writings, usually excerpted from longer works, and available to the reader in one place.

Many instructors may want to use this collection along with a textbook. A textbook has special value since only one voice is involved; thus, a tightly organized, intellectually convincing position on personality can be presented. Exclusive reliance upon secondary sources such as textbooks does not encourage the most vivid experience of the excitement and power of personality theorizing. Assigning this collection along with a textbook would ease this problem.

Actually, this collection was designed to be used along with my personality textbook (*Personality Theories: A Comparative Analysis*. Homewood, Ill.: Dorsey Press, 1968). The organization of theories in this book derives from arguments presented in that textbook. Also, the particular writings included here reflect the material most relied upon and quoted in framing the textbook. Using this collection permits the reader to check the various theorists' own words against the interpretations I develop in my textbook. Together, the books provide an interesting treatment of the personality field.

Of course, this collection could easily be used with other textbooks. So many viewpoints are represented here that articulation with any general textbook would present no difficulty. Even when a textbook is written from one particular viewpoint to the exclusion of others, a fair proportion of these readings will be relevant anyway, either to support, or to demonstrate parallel or opposing approaches. Since the readings are seminal, they might even be relevant in courses where the main emphasis is not on personality, such as psychopathology or motivation.

I especially want to thank Miss Jackie Bertoletti for diligent work in preparing the manuscript, and my students for helpful criticisms and suggestions that convinced me of the need for this collection.

Salvatore R. Maddi

Contents

Perspectives on Personality

I   Introduction

I have contended that two basic parts of personality theories are *core statements* and *peripheral statements* (Maddi, 1968). In the core statement, the theorist delineates the tendencies and characteristics he considers to be inherent in all men. In the peripheral statement, he considers the various personality types or life-styles that come to be learned through the interaction of the core and the developmental experiences the person encounters. For example, Freud assumed that all men have a sex instinct, but that whether one learns an oral, anal, phallic, or genital personality type stems from the parental reaction to one's expressions of this sex instinct in the oral, anal, phallic, and genital periods of early development. As much as possible, I have selected readings to include both the core and peripheral statements made by a theorist, even when these distinctions are not salient for him.

I have grouped the theories into three types, each with two sub-types (Maddi, 1968). These types and subtypes are defined primarily with regard to the core tendency assumed by the theorist. In *conflict theories,* man is construed as caught in the grips of two great forces that are inevitably opposed. Therefore, conflict is a ubiquitous experience, which can be minimized but never rendered absent. Life, for conflict theorists, is necessarily a compromise, which at best involves a dynamic balance of the two opposing forces, and at worst involves a foredoomed attempt to deny the existence of one of them. Theirs is a tragic view. In the *psychosocial version* of conflict theorizing, the source of one great force is in the person as an individual, whereas the source of the other great force is in groups or societies. In the *intra-psychic version*, both great forces arise from within the person, regardless of whether he is considered as an individual or as a social entity.

In *fulfillment theories*, man is seen in the grip of only one great force, without an inherent basis for conflict. Conflict can occur for a fulfillment theorist, but only if society fails to create the circumstances whereby the great force within individuals can be adequately expressed. But society need not fail in this manner, and therefore, there is no tragic view of life. At best, life is a gradually greater and more vigorous expression of the one great force. In the *actualization version* of fulfillment theorizing, the great force is in the form of a genetic blueprint determining the person's special capabilities. Living richly, then, is pursuing these capabilities. In contrast, the *perfection version* defines the great force as striving toward ideals of what is fine, excellent, and meaningful in life, regardless of a person's genetic capabilities.

Consistency theories emphasize not great forces but the formative influence of feedback from the external world. If the feedback is consistent with what was expected or had been customary, quiescence results. But if there is inconsistency, then pressure toward reducing this uncomfortable state of affairs develops. Life is to be understood as the extended attempt to maintain consistency. The consistency theory assumes no predetermined capabilities or ideals as guides to living, and is therefore different from fulfillment theorizing. And whereas conflict theorizing assumes conflict to be continuous, unavoidable, and set in content, consistency theorizing assumes none of these things. Inconsistency is avoidable, and can vary in content. In the *cognitive dissonance version* of consistency theorizing, the relevant aspects of the person in which there may or may not be consistency are cognitive (e.g., thoughts, perceptions, expectations). In contrast, the *activation version* emphasizes consistency or inconsistency between the degree of bodily tension or activation that is customary for the person and that which exists at a given time.

I have tried to include a wide range of theories in this book, so that they may be compared and contrasted. Some of the theories are old and others new; some emphasize psychopathology and others mental health; some emphasize core statements and others peripheral; some stress emotional phenomena and others are more intellectually oriented; some spring from the practice of psychotherapy, whereas others come out of the academy and research. Any omitted theories either derive from or are very similar to those included. There are, of course, a few general approaches which, though not formal personality theories in the previously mentioned sense, do have ties to and implications for the personality field. Foremost among these is behaviorism. I have included readings on the aspects of this approach most relevant to personology.

REFERENCES

Maddi, S. R. *Personality Theories: A Comparative Analysis*. Homewood, Ill.: Dorsey Press. 1968.

II Conflict Theory: Psychosocial Version

In these readings, one sees clearly the existence of the psychosocial version of the conflict model, stressing as it does a conception of life in which one great force is in individuals and the other is in societies. In varying degrees of explicitness, the authors describe personality as a dynamic balance of these two forces, the conflict of which can never be fully transcended.

In "Instincts and Their Vicissitudes," Freud sets forth his view of instincts as the constituents of the id, which is the part of the personality core that is present at birth in all persons. Freud details the components of an instinct as source, impetus, aim, and object, and clarifies its internal, basically biological character. In discussing the vicissitudes of instincts, he presents his view of defenses. This view is part of the distinction between pleasure-principle functioning, with its emphasis on unmitigated id expression, and reality-principle functioning, which tames the instincts to more socially appropriate and effective expression.

Much of this discussion is amplified and extended in "The Dissection of the Psychical Personality." Here are detailed the three major components of the personality core — id, ego, and superego. Though the latter two come into being as the result of experience and learning, they too are properly considered part of the personality core, because no person could grow into adulthood — indeed survive — without them. It also becomes quite clear that the id and superego are perpetually in conflict, and that the superego is the internalization of the great force localized in society. It is the ego's role to foster as much gratification of id instincts as possible while minimizing the punishment and guilt that arises from the superego and society itself. Here more than anywhere else it is clear that Freud's is a psychosocial conflict theory. For him, life is, even at best, a compromise between man as an individual and as a member of society. Also discussed are defensiveness and the resulting lack of consciousness of the true nature of the instincts. It is through these procedures that the ego engineers the compromise that stands at the basis of the successful life. Freud refers to this compromise by saying, "Where id was, there shall ego be." This indicates the necessity for translating pleasure-principle functioning into reality-principle functioning.

The other two papers by Freud are included to give some sense of the periphery of personality in psychoanalytic theory. Although the papers have special relevance to fixations in the anal period of psychosexual development and to the subsequent anal personality type, the personality types growing out of fixations at the oral and phallic psychosexual stages are certainly implied. In order to develop a genital, or ideal, personality type, the person will have had to negotiate childhood development without any fixations at all, a most unlikely possibility. The two papers included detail the traits and defenses marking the anal personality type.

In his paper with Kluckhohn, Murray gives evidence of his richly detailed distinctions and terminology on personality. In addition, he puts emphasis on describing the environment as it impinges on the person. We find also a hint of his views on needs and his general emphasis on motivation. Finally, his Freudian parentage is shown by the assumption of id, ego, and superego, though it is clear that his is a position in transition away from the strictly psychosocial conflict theory toward something more like a fulfillment theory. The ego, for example, is given many possibilities beyond the meager ones detailed by Freud, who used that component of personality merely as the architect of compromise through defense. In "Proposals for a Theory of Personality," Murray sets forth his taxonomy of needs, which has so profoundly affected personologists and test developers. Various beginnings for a classification of these needs are introduced. He properly considers needs at the periphery of personality, because each of them may or may not be strong in any person. All but the most obviously biological of them at least imply learning.

The paper by Rapaport is a sophisticated modern expression of ego psychology. In it, he delineates the ego as autonomous from id instincts, on the one hand, and even the pressure of external reality, on the other hand. Over the last twenty-five years there has been an accelerating tendency in psychoanalytic circles to consider the ego to have an inherent basis in man separate from the instincts. In this emphasis, the ego is only partially concerned with resolving conflict between id and society (or superego), being partially free to prompt development of rational, truly individualistic functioning.

Erikson's paper details a basis for conceptualizing peripheral personality that is quite consistent with the emphasis on conflict-free ego functioning seen in Rapaport. Although the first four developmental stages are similar to those put forth by Freud, in Erikson they are not so strictly determined by the biological maturation of the sex instinct. More important is the sociocultural pressure on the child. Further, the final four stages named by Erikson take the person through adulthood, and seem quite separate from sexual considerations. More relevant are the cognitive, perceptual, and social considerations consistent with a potent ego such as that described in Rapaport. The best possible outcome of Erikson's developmental stages is conceptualized as less of a compromise than is true in Freud. The selections included here from the writings of Murray, Rapaport, and Erikson document well the transition from classical Freudianism to modern ego psychology.

In "Basic Conceptions," Sullivan sets forth his major concepts associated with the core of personality. Included here are dynamic principles of the pursuit of satisfaction (which is mainly the assuaging of biological requirements) and the pursuit of security (which is mainly the easing of anxiety through approval). Several other important concepts are presented. Sullivan's selection on "Developmental Syndromes" details his views on the periphery of personality, with added description of the processes of development. Although there may well be disagreement as to whether Sullivan's theory is properly classified as a psychosocial conflict view, the pursuits of satisfaction and security, which are common to all men, do seem to be somewhat incompatible with one another. The self-system seems largely defensive, being formed out of the approvals received from significant others. As such, the self-system seems similar to Freud's superego.

SIGMUND FREUD

Instincts and Their Vicissitudes

The view is often defended that sciences should be built up on clear and sharply defined basal concepts. In actual fact no science, not even the most exact, begins with such definitions. The true beginning of scientific activity consists rather in describing phenomena and then in proceeding to group, classify and correlate them. Even at the stage of description it is not possible to avoid applying certain abstract ideas to the material in hand, ideas derived from various sources and certainly not the fruit of the new experience only. Still more indispensable are such ideas — which will later become the basal concepts of the science — as the material is further elaborated. They must at first necessarily possess some measure of uncertainty; there can be no question of any clear delimitation of their content. So long as they remain in this condition, we come to an understanding about their meaning by repeated references to the material of observation, from which we seem to have deduced our abstract ideas, but which is in point of fact subject to them. Thus, strictly speaking, they are in the nature of conventions; although everything depends on their being chosen in no arbitrary manner, but determined by the important relations they have to the empirical material — relations that we seem to divine before we can clearly recognize and demonstrate them. It is only after more searching investigation of the field in question that we are able to formulate with increased clarity the scientific concepts underlying it, and progressively so to modify these concepts that they become widely applicable and at the same time consistent logically. Then, indeed, it may be time to immure them in definitions. The progress of science, however, demands

Chapter IV of Volume 4 of *The Collected Papers of Sigmund Freud*, edited by Ernest Jones, M.D., Basic Books, Inc., Publishers, New York, 1959. First published in *Zeitschrift*, Bd. iii., 1915; reprinted in *Sammlung*, Vierte Folge. [Translated by Cecil M. Baines.]

a certain elasticity even in these definitions. The science of physics furnishes an excellent illustration of the way in which even those "basal concepts" that are firmly established in the form of definitions are constantly being altered in their content.

A conventional but still rather obscure basal concept of this kind, which is nevertheless indispensable to us in psychology, is that of an *instinct*. Let us try to ascertain what is comprised in this conception by approaching it from different angles.

First, from the side of physiology. This has given us the concept of *stimuli* and the scheme of the reflex arc, according to which a stimulus applied *from the outer world* to living tissue (nervous substance) is discharged by action *towards the outer world*. The action answers the purpose of withdrawing the substance affected from the operation of the stimulus, removing it out of range of the stimulus.

Now what is the relation between "instinct" and "stimulus"? There is nothing to prevent our including the concept of "instinct" under that of "stimulus" and saying that an instinct is a stimulus to the mind. But we are immediately set on our guard against treating instinct and mental stimulus as one and the same thing. Obviously, besides those of instinctual origin, there are other stimuli to the mind which behave far more like physiological stimuli. For example, a strong light striking upon the eye is not a stimulus of instinctual origin; it is one, however, when the mucous membrane of the oesophagus becomes parched or when a gnawing makes itself felt in the stomach.[1]

We have now obtained material necessary for discriminating between stimuli of instinctual origin and intention of warding off stimuli, for they maintain an incessant and unavoidable afflux of stimulation. So we may probably conclude that instincts and not external stimuli are the true motive forces in the progress that has raised the nervous system, with all its incomparable efficiency, to its present high level of development. Of course there is nothing to prevent our assuming that the instincts themselves are, at least in part, the precipitates of different forms of external stimulation, which in the course of phylogenesis have effected modifications in the organism.

Then when we find further that the activity of even the most highly developed mental apparatus is subject to the pleasure-principle, *i.e.* is automatically regulated by feelings belonging to the pleasure-"pain" series, we can hardly reject the further postulate that these feelings reflect the manner in which the process of mastering stimuli takes place. This is certainly so in the sense that "painful" feelings are connected with an increase and pleasurable feelings with a decrease in stimulation. Let us, however, be careful to preserve this assumption in its present highly indefinite form, until we succeed, if that is

---

[1] Assuming, of course, that these internal processes constitute the organic basis of the needs described as thirst and hunger.

possible, in discovering what sort of relation exists between pleasure and "pain," on the one hand, and fluctuations in the quantities of stimuli affecting mental life, on the other. It is certain that many kinds of these relations are possible, some of them by no means simple.

If now we apply ourselves to considering mental life from a biological point of view, an "instinct" appears to us as a borderland concept between the mental and the physical, being both the mental representative of the stimuli emanating from within the organism and penetrating to the mind, and at the same time a measure of the demand made upon the energy of the latter in consequence of its connection with the body.

We are now in a position to discuss certain terms used in reference to the concept of an instinct, for example, its impetus, its aim, its object and its source.

By the *impetus* of an instinct we understand its motor element, the amount of force or the measure of the demand upon energy which it represents. The characteristic of impulsion is common to all instincts, is in fact the very essence of them. Every instinct is a form of activity; if we speak loosely of passive instincts, we can only mean those whose aim is passive.

The *aim* of an instinct is in every instance satisfaction, which can only be obtained by abolishing the condition of stimulation in the source of the instinct. But although this remains invariably the final goal of every instinct, there may yet be different ways leading to the same goal, so that an instinct may be found to have various nearer or intermediate aims, capable of combination or interchange. Experience permits us also to speak of instincts which are *inhibited in respect of their aim*, in cases where a certain advance has been permitted in the direction of satisfaction and then an inhibition or deflection has occurred. We may suppose that even in such cases a partial satisfaction is achieved.

The *object* of an instinct is that in or through which it can achieve its aim. It is the most variable thing about an instinct and is not originally connected with it, but becomes attached to it only in consequence of being peculiarly fitted to provide satisfaction. The object is not necessarily an extraneous one: it may be part of the subject's own body. It may be changed any number of times in the course of the vicissitudes the instinct undergoes during life; a highly important part is played by this capacity for displacement in the instinct. It may happen that the same object may serve for the satisfaction of several instincts simultaneously, a phenomenon which Adler calls a "confluence" of instincts. A particularly close attachment of the instinct to its object is distinguished by the term *fixation:* this frequently occurs in very early stages of the instinct's development and so puts an end to its mobility, through the vigorous resistance it sets up against detachment.

By the *source* of an instinct is meant that somatic process in an organ or part of the body from which there results a stimulus represented in mental life by an instinct. We do not know whether this process is regularly of a chemical nature or whether it may also correspond with the release of other, *e.g.* mechanical, forces. The study of the sources of instinct is outside the scope of psychology; although its source in the body is what gives the instinct its distinct and essential character, yet in mental life we know it merely by its aims. A more exact knowledge of the sources of instincts is not strictly necessary for purposes of psychological investigation; often the source may be with certainty inferred from the aims.

Are we to suppose that the different instincts which operate upon the mind but of which the origin is somatic are also distinguished by different qualities and act in the mental life in a manner qualitatively different? This supposition does not seem to be justified; we are much more likely to find the simpler assumption sufficient — namely, that the instincts are all qualitatively alike and owe the effect they produce only to the quantities of excitation accompanying them, or perhaps further to certain functions of this quantity. The difference in the mental effects produced by the different instincts may be traced to the difference in their sources. In any event, it is only in a later connection that we shall be able to make plain what the problem of the quality of instincts signifies.

Now what instincts and how many should be postulated? There is obviously a great opportunity here for arbitrary choice. No objection can be made to anyone's employing the concept of an instinct of play or of destruction, or that of a social instinct, when the subject demands it and the limitations of psychological analysis allow of it. Nevertheless, we should not neglect to ask whether such instinctual motives, which are in one direction so highly specialized, do not admit of further analysis in respect of their sources, so that only those primal instincts which are not to be resolved further could really lay claim to the name.

I have proposed that two groups of such primal instincts should be distinguished: the *self-preservative* or *ego*-instincts and the *sexual* instincts. But this proposition has not the weight of a necessary postulate, such as, for instance, our assumption about the biological "purpose" in the mental apparatus (*v. supra*); it is merely an auxiliary construction, to be retained only so long as it proves useful, and it will make little difference to the results of our work of description and classification if we replace it by another. The occasion for it arose in the course of the evolution of psycho-analysis, which was first employed upon the psychoneuroses, actually upon the group designated transference neuroses (hysteria and obsessional neurosis); through them it became plain that at the root of all such affections there lies a conflict between the claims of sexuality and those of the ego. It is always possible that an exhaustive study of the other neurotic affections (especially of the narcissistic psychoneuroses, the schizophrenias) may oblige us to alter this formula and therewith to make a different classification of the primal instincts. But for the present we do not know what this new formula may be, nor have we met with any argument which seems likely to be prejudicial to the contrast between sexual and ego-instincts.

I am altogether doubtful whether work upon psychological material will afford any decisive indication for the distinction and classification of instincts. Rather it would seem necessary to apply to this material certain definite assumptions in order to work upon it, and we could wish that these assumptions might be taken from some other branch of knowledge and transferred to psychology. The contribution of biology on this point certainly does not run counter to the distinction between sexual and ego-instincts. Biology teaches that sexuality is not on a level with the other functions of the individual, for its "purposes" go beyond the individual, their content being the production of new individuals and the preservation of the species. It shows, further, that the relation existing between the ego and sexuality may be conceived of in two ways, apparently equally well justified: in the one, the individual is regarded as of prime importance, sexuality as one of his activities and sexual satisfaction as one of his needs; while in the other the individual organism is looked upon as a transitory and perishable appendage to the quasi-immortal germ-plasm bequeathed to him by the race. The assumption that the sexual function differs from other bodily processes in virtue of special chemical processes is, I understand, also a postulate of the Ehrlich school of biological research.

Since a study of the instincts from the side of consciousness presents almost insuperable difficulties, psycho-analytic investigation of mental disturbances remains the principal source of our knowledge. The development of this line of investigation, however, has necessarily produced hitherto information of a more or less definite nature only in regard to the sexual instincts, for it is this group in particular which can be observed in isolation, as it were, in the psychoneuroses. With the extension of psycho-analysis to other neurotic affections we may be sure that we shall find a basis for our knowledge of the ego-instincts also, though it would be optimistic to expect equally favourable conditions for observation in this further field of research.

An attempt to formulate the general characteristics of the sexual instincts would run as follows: they are numerous, emanate from manifold organic sources, act in the first instance independently of one another and only at a late stage achieve a more or less complete synthesis. The aim which each strives to attain is "organ-pleasure"; only when the synthesis is complete do they enter the service of the function of reproduction, becoming thereby generally recognizable as sexual instincts. At their first appearance they support themselves upon the instincts of self-preservation, from which they only gradually detach themselves; in their choice of object also they follow paths indicated by the ego-instincts. Some of them remain throughout life associated with these latter and furnish them with libidinal components, which with normal functioning easily escape notice and are clearly recognizable only when disease is present. They have this distinctive characteristic — that they have in a high degree the capacity to act vicariously for one another and that they can readily change their objects. In consequence of the last-mentioned properties they are capable of activities widely removed from their original modes of attaining their aims (sublimation).

Our inquiry into the various vicissitudes which instincts undergo in the process of development and in the course of life must be confined to the sexual instincts, for these are the more familiar to us. Observation shows us that an instinct may undergo the following vicissitudes: reversal into its opposite, turning round upon the subject, repression, sublimation.

Since I do not intend to treat of sublimation here and since repression requires a special chapter to itself, it only remains for us to describe and discuss the two first points. Bearing in mind that there are tendencies which are opposed to the instincts pursuing a straight-forward course, we may regard these vicissitudes as modes of defence against the instincts.

The *reversal* of an instinct *into its opposite* may on closer scrutiny be resolved into two different processes: a change from active to passive, and a reversal of the content. The two processes, being essentially distinct, must be treated separately.

Examples of the first process are met with in the two pairs of opposites: sadism-masochism and scoptophilia-exhibitionism. The reversal here concerns only the aims of the instincts. The passive aim (to be tortured, or looked at) has been substituted for the active aim (to torture, to look at). Reversal of content is found in the single instance of the change of love into hate.

The *turning round* of an instinct *upon the subject* is suggested to us by the reflection that masochism is actually sadism turned round upon the subject's own ego, and that exhibitionism includes the love of gazing at the subject's own body. Further, analytic observation leaves us in no doubt that the masochist also enjoys the *act* of torturing when this is being applied to himself, and the exhibitionist the exposing of someone in being exposed himself. So the essence of the process is the change of the object, while the aim remains unchanged.

We cannot fail to note, however, that in these examples turning round upon the subject's self and transformation from active to passive coincide or occur in one process. To elucidate the relation between the two processes, a more thorough investigation must be undertaken.

With the pair of opposites sadism-masochism, the process may be represented as follows:

A. Sadism consists in the exercise of violence or power upon some other person as its object.

B. This object is abandoned and replaced by the subject's self. Together with the turning round upon the self the change from an active to a passive aim in the instinct is also brought about.

C. Again another person is sought as object; this person, in consequence of the alteration which has taken place in the aim of the instinct, has to take over the original rôle of the subject.

Case C is the condition commonly termed masochism. Satisfaction follows in this case also by way of the original sadism, the passive ego placing itself in phantasy back in its former situation, which, however, has now been given up to another subject outside the self. Whether there is, besides this, a more direct masochistic satisfaction is highly doubtful. A primary masochism not derived in the manner I have described from sadism, does not appear to be met with.[2] That it is not superfluous to make the assumption of stage B is quite clear when we observe the behaviour of the sadistic impulse in cases of obsessional neurosis. In these we have the turning upon the subject's self, without the attitude of passivity towards another: the reversal has only reached the second stage. Self-torment and self-punishment have arisen from the desire to torture, but not masochism. The active voice is changed, not into the passive, but into the reflexive middle voice.

The conception of sadism is made more complicated by the circumstance that this instinct, side by side with its general aim (or perhaps rather, within it), seems to press towards a quite special aim: the infliction of pain, in addition to subjection and mastery of the object. Now psycho-analysis would seem to show that the infliction of pain plays no part in the original aims sought by the instinct: the sadistic child takes no notice of whether or not it inflicts pain, nor is it part of its purpose to do so. But when once the transformation into masochism has taken place, the experience of pain is very well adapted to serve as a passive masochistic aim, for we have every reason to believe that sensations of pain, like other unpleasant sensations, extend into sexual excitation and produce a condition which is pleasurable, for the sake of which the subject will even willingly experience the unpleasantness of pain. Where once the suffering of pain has been experienced as a masochistic aim, it can be carried back into the sadistic situation and result in a sadistic aim of *inflicting pain*, which will then be masochistically enjoyed by the subject while inflicting pain upon others, through his identification of himself with the suffering object. Of course, in either case it is not the pain itself which is enjoyed, but the accompanying sexual excitement, and this is especially easy for the sadist. The enjoyment of pain would thus be a primary masochistic aim, which, however, can then also become the aim of the originally sadistic instinct.

In order to complete my exposition I would add that pity cannot be described as a result of the reversal of the sadistic instinct, but necessitates the

---

[2] *Additional Note*, 1924. In later works (cf. "The Economic Problem of Masochism," 1924, *Collected Papers*, vol. ii) relating to problems of instinctual life, I have expressed the opposite view.

conception of a *reaction-formation* against that instinct (for the difference, v. *infra*).

Rather different and simpler results are afforded by the investigation of another pair of opposites, namely, those instincts whose aim is sexual gazing (scoptophilia) and self-display (the "voyeur" and exhibitionist tendencies as they are called in the language of the perversions). Here again we may postulate the same stages as in the previous instance: (a) scoptophilia as an activity directed towards an extraneous object; (b) abandonment of the object and a turning of the scoptophilic instinct towards a part of the subject's own person; therewith a transformation to passivity and the setting up of a new aim — that of being looked at; (c) the institution of a new subject to whom one displays oneself in order to be looked at. Here too, it is hardly possible to doubt that the active aim appears before the passive, that scoptophilia precedes exhibitionism. But there is an important divergence from what happens in the case of sadism, in that we can recognize in the scoptophilic instinct a yet earlier stage than that described as (a). That is to say, that at the beginning of its activity the scoptophilic instinct is auto-erotic: it has indeed an object, but that object is the subject's own body. It is only later that the instinct comes (by the way of comparison) to exchange this object for the analogous one of the body of another (stage (a)). Now this preliminary stage is interesting because it is the source of both the situations represented in the resulting pair of opposites, according to which element in the original situation is reversed. The following might serve as a scheme for the scoptophilic instinct:

α Subject's looking   Subject's own sexual organ
    at his <u>own sexual organ</u> =   being looked at by <u>himself</u>

β Subject's looking γ Subject's own sex-
    at an <u>extraneous object</u>   ual organ being
        (active scoptophilia)   looked at by <u>another person</u>
                                        (exhibitionism)

A preliminary stage of this kind is absent in sadism, which from the outset is directed upon an extraneous object, although it might not be altogether unreasonable to regard as such a stage the child's efforts to gain control of his own limbs.[3]

With regard to both these instincts just examined as examples, it must be said that transformation of them by a reversal from active to passive and by a turning round upon the subject never in fact concerns the whole amount of impelling force pertaining to the instinct. To some extent its earlier active direction always persists side by side with the later passive direction, even when the transformation is very extensive. The only correct description of

---

[3] Cf. footnote 2.

The King's Library

the scoptophilic instinct would be that all phases of its development, the auto-erotic, preliminary phase as well as its final active or passive form, co-exist alongside one another; and the truth of this statement becomes manifest if we base our opinion, not upon the actions which are prompted by the instinct, but upon the mechanism of its satisfaction. Perhaps yet another way of conceiving and representing the matter may be justified. We may split up the life of each instinct into a series of "thrusts," distinct from one another in the time of their occurrence but each homogeneous within its own period, whose relation to one another is comparable to that of successive eruptions of lava. We can then perhaps picture to ourselves that the earliest and most primitive instinct-eruption persists in an unchanged form and undergoes no development at all. The next "thrust" would then from the outset have undergone a change of form, being turned, for instance, from active to passive, and it would then, with this new characteristic, be superimposed upon the earlier layer, and so on. So that, if we take a survey of the instinctual tendency from its beginning up to any given stopping-point, the succession of "thrusts" which we have described would present the picture of a definite development of the instinct.

The fact that, at that later period of development, the instinct in its primary form may be observed side by side with its (passive) opposite deserves to be distinguished by the highly appropriate name introduced by Bleuler: *ambivalence*.

These considerations regarding the developmental history of an instinct and the permanent character of the intermediate stages in it should make instinct-development more comprehensible to us. Experience shows that the degree of demonstrable ambivalence varies greatly in individuals, groups and races. Marked ambivalence of an instinct in a human being at the present day may be regarded as an archaic inheritance, for we have reason to suppose that the part played in the life of the instincts by the active impulses in their original form was greater in primitive times than it is on an average to-day.

We have become accustomed to call the early phase of the development of the ego, during which its sexual instincts find auto-erotic satisfaction, *narcissism*, without having so far entered into any discussion of the relation between auto-erotism and narcissism. It follows that, in considering the preliminary phase of the scoptophilic instinct, when the subject's own body is the object of the scoptophilia, we must place it under the heading of narcissism; it is a narcissistic formation. From this phase the active scoptophilic instinct, which has left narcissism behind, is developed, while the passive scoptophilic instinct, on the contrary, holds fast to the narcissistic object. Similarly, the transformation from sadism to masochism betokens a reversion to the narcissistic object, while in both cases the narcissistic (active) subject is exchanged by identification for another, extraneous ego. Taking into consideration the preliminary narcissistic stage of sadism constructed by us, we approach the more general view that those vicissitudes which consist in the instinct being turned round upon the subject's own ego and undergoing reversal from activity to passivity are dependent upon the narcissistic organization of the ego and bear the stamp of that phase. Perhaps they represent attempts at defense which at higher stages of the development of the ego are effected by other means.

At this point we may remember that so far we have discussed only two paris of instincts and their opposites: sadism-masochism and scoptophilia-exhibitionism. These are the best-known sexual instincts which appear in ambivalent forms. The other components of the later sexual function are at present too inaccessible to analysis for us to be able to discuss them in a similar way. In general we can assert of them that their activities are auto-erotic, *i.e.* their object becomes negligible in comparison with the organ which is their source, and as a rule the two coincide. The object of the scoptophilic instinct, although it also in the first instance is a part of the subject's own body, nevertheless is not the eye itself; and with sadism the organic source, probably the musculature with its capacity for action, directly presupposes an object other than itself, even though that object be part of the subject's own body. In the auto-erotic instincts, the part played by the organic source is so decisive that, according to a plausible supposition of P. Federn and L. Jekels,[4] the form and function of the organ determine the activity or passivity of the instinct's aim.

The transformation of the "content" of an instinct into its opposite is observed in a single instance only — the changing of *love into hate*. It is particularly common to find both these directed simultaneously towards the same object, and this phenomenon of their co-existence furnishes the most important example of ambivalence of feeling.

The case of love and hate acquires a special interest from the circumstance that it resists classification in our scheme of the instincts. It is impossible to doubt the existence of a most intimate relation between these two contrary feelings and sexual life, but one is naturally unwilling to conceive of love as being a kind of special component-instinct of sexuality in the same way as are the others just discussed. One would prefer to regard loving rather as the expression of the whole sexual current of feeling, but this idea does not clear up our difficulties and we are at a loss how to conceive of an essential opposite to this striving.

Loving admits of not merely one, but of three antitheses. First there is the antithesis of loving/hating; secondly, there is loving/being loved; and, in addition to these, loving and hating together are the opposite of the condition of neutrality or indifference. The second of these two antitheses, loving/being loved, corresponds exactly to the transformation from active to passive and may be traced to a primal situation in the same way as the scoptophilic instinct. This situation is that of *loving oneself*, which for us is the charac-

[4] *Zeitschrift*, Bd. I., 1913.

teristic of narcissism. Then, according to whether the self as object or subject is exchanged for an extraneous one, there results the active aim of loving or the passive one of being loved, the latter remaining nearly related to narcissism.

Perhaps we shall come to a better understanding of the manifold opposites of loving if we reflect that our mental life as a whole is governed by *three polarities*, namely, the following antitheses: subject (ego)/object (external world), pleasure/pain, active/passive.

The antithesis of ego/non-ego (outer), *i.e.* subject/object, is, as we have already said, thrust upon the individual being at an early stage, by the experience that it can abolish external stimuli by means of muscular action but is defenceless against those stimuli that originate in instinct. This antithesis remains sovereign above all in our intellectual activity and provides research with a fundamental situation which no amount of effort can alter. The polarity of pleasure/pain depends upon a feeling-series, the significance of which in determining our actions (will) is paramount and has already been emphasized. The antithesis of active and passive must not be confounded with that of ego-subject/external object. The relation of the ego to the outer world is passive in so far as it receives stimuli from it, active when it reacts to these. Its instincts compel it to a quite special degree of activity towards the outside world, so that, if we wished to emphasize the essence of the matter, we might say that the ego-subject is passive in respect of external stimuli, active in virtue of its own instincts. The antithesis of active/passive coalesces later with that of masculine/feminine, which, until this has taken place, has no psychological significance. The fusion of activity with masculinity and passivity with femininity confronts us, indeed, as a biological fact, but it is by no means so invariably complete and exclusive as we are inclined to assume.

The three polarities within the mind are connected with one another in various highly significant ways. There is a certain primal psychic situation in which two of them coincide. Originally, at the very beginning of mental life, the ego's instincts are directed to itself and it is to some extent capable of deriving satisfaction for them on itself. This condition is known as narcissism and this potentiality for satisfaction is termed auto-erotic.[5] The outside world is at this time, generally speaking, not cathected with any interest and is indifferent for purposes of satisfaction. At this period, therefore, the ego-subject coincides with what is pleasurable and the outside world with what

[5] Some of the sexual instincts are, as we know, capable of this auto-erotic satisfaction and so are adapted to be the channel for that development under the sway of the pleasure-principle which we shall describe later. The sexual instincts which from the outset require an object and the needs of the ego-instincts, which are never capable of auto-erotic satisfaction, interfere, of course, with this condition and prepare the way for progress. More, the primal narcissistic condition would not have been able to attain such a development were it not that every individual goes through a period of helplessness and dependence on fostering care, during which his urgent needs are satisfied by agencies outside himself and thereby withheld from developing along their own line.

is indifferent (or even painful as being a source of stimulation): Let us for the moment define loving as the relation of the ego to its sources of pleasure: then the situation in which the ego loves itself only and is indifferent to the outside world illustrates the first of the polarities in which "loving" appeared.

In so far as it is auto-erotic, the ego has no need of the outside world, but, in consequence of experiences undergone by the instincts of self-preservation, it tends to find objects there and doubtless it cannot but for a time perceive inner instinctual stimuli as painful. Under the sway of the pleasure-principle there now takes place a further development. The objects presenting themselves, in so far as they are sources of pleasure, are absorbed by the ego into itself, "introjected" (according to an expression coined by Ferenczi); while, on the other hand, the ego thrusts forth upon the external world whatever within itself gives rise to pain (v. infra: the mechanism of projection).

Thus the original reality-ego, which distinguished outer and inner by means of a sound objective criterion, changes into a purified pleasure-ego, which prizes above all else the quality of pleasure. For this pleasure-ego the outside world is divided into a part that is pleasurable, which it has incorporated into itself, and a remainder that is alien to it. A part of itself it has separated off, and this it projects into the external world and regards as hostile. According to this new arrangement the congruence of the two polarities, ego-subject with pleasure, outside world with pain (or earlier with neutrality), is once more established.

When the stage of primary narcissism is invaded by the object, the second contrary attitude to that of love, namely, hate, attains to development.

As we have heard, the ego's objects are presented to it from the outside world in the first instance by the instincts of self-preservation, and it is undeniable also that hate originally betokens the relation of the ego to the alien external world with its afflux of stimuli. Neutrality may be classified as a special case of hate or rejection, after having made its appearance first as the forerunner of hate. Thus at the very beginning, the external world, objects and that which was hated were one and the same thing. When later on an object manifests itself as a source of pleasure, it becomes loved, but also incorporated into the ego, so that for the purified pleasure-ego the object once again coincides with what is extraneous and hated.

Now, however, we note that just as the antithesis love/indifference reflects the polarity ego/external world, so the second antithesis, love/hate, reproduces the polarity pleasure/pain, which is bound up with the former. When the purely narcissistic stage gives place to the object-stage, pleasure and pain denote the relations of the ego to the object. When the object becomes a source of pleasurable feelings, a motor tendency is set up which strives to bring the object near to and incorporate it into the ego; we then speak of the "attraction" exercised by the pleasure-giving object, and say that we "love" that object. Conversely, when the object is the source of painful feelings, there is a tendency which endeavours to increase the distance between object and ego and to repeat in relation to the former the primordial attempt at flight from the external world with its flow of stimuli. We feel a "repulsion" from the object, and hate it; this hate can then be intensified to the point of an aggressive tendency towards the object, with the intention of destroying it.

We might at a pinch say of an instinct that it "loves" the objects after which it strives for purposes of satisfaction, but to say that it "hates" an object strikes us as odd; so we become aware that the attitudes of love and hate cannot be said to characterize the relations of instincts to their objects, but are reserved for the relations of the ego as a whole to objects. But, if we consider a colloquial usage which is certainly full of meaning, we see that there is yet another limitation to the significance of love and hate. We do not say of those objects which serve the interests of self-preservation that we love them; rather we emphasize the fact that we need them, and perhaps add an element of a different kind in our relation to them by words which denote a much lesser degree of love — for example, to be fond of, to like, to find agreeable.

So the word "to love" becomes shifted ever further into the sphere of the pure pleasure-relation existing between the ego and its object and finally attaches itself to sexual objects in the narrower sense and to those which satisfy the needs of sublimated sexual instincts. The discrimination of the ego-instincts from the sexual, a discrimination which we have imposed upon our psychology, is seen, therefore, to be in conformity with the spirit of our speech. Since we do not customarily say that the single sexual component-instinct loves its object, but see the most appropriate case in which to apply the word "love" in the relation of the ego to its sexual object, we learn from this fact that the applicability of the word in this relation begins only with the synthesis of all the component-instincts under the primacy of the genitals and in the service of the function of reproduction.

It is noteworthy that in the use of the word "hate" no such intimate relation to sexual pleasure and the sexual function appears: on the contrary, the painful character of the relation seems to be the sole decisive feature. The ego hates, abhors and pursues with intent to destroy all objects which are for it a source of painful feelings, without taking into account whether they mean to it frustration of sexual satisfaction or of gratification of the needs of self-preservation. Indeed, it may be asserted that the true prototypes of the hate-relation are derived not from sexual life, but from the struggle of the ego for self-preservation and self-maintenance.

So we see that love and hate, which present themselves to us as essentially antithetical, stand in no simple relation to each other. They did not originate in a cleavage of any common primal element, but sprang from different sources and underwent each its own development before the influence of the pleasure-pain relation constituted them antitheses to each other. At this point we are confronted with the task of putting together what we know of the genesis of love and hate.

Love originates in the capacity of the ego to satisfy some of its instincts auto-erotically through the obtaining of "organ-pleasure." It is primarily narcissistic, is then transferred to those objects which have been incorporated in the ego, now much extended, and expresses the motor striving of the ego after these objects as sources of pleasure. It is intimately connected with the activity of the later sexual instincts and, when these have been completely synthetized, coincides with the sexual trend as a whole. The preliminary stages of love reveal themselves as temporary sexual aims, while the sexual instincts are passing through their complicated development. First amongst these we recognize the phase of incorporating or devouring, a type of love which is compatible with abolition of any separate existence on the part of the object, and which may therefore be designated ambivalent. At the higher stage of the pregenital sadistic-anal organization, the striving after the object appears in the form of an impulsion to mastery, in which injury or annihilation of the object is a matter of indifference. This form and preliminary stage of love is hardly to be distinguished from hate in its behaviour towards the object. Only when the genital organization is established does love become the antithesis of hate.

The relation of hate to objects is older than that of love. It is derived from the primal repudiation by the narcissistic ego of the external world whence flows the stream of stimuli. As an expression of the pain-reaction induced by objects, it remains in constant intimate relation with the instincts of self-preservation, so that sexual and ego-instincts readily develop an antithesis which repeats that of love and hate. When the sexual function is governed by the ego-instincts, as at the stage of the sadistic-anal organization, they impart the qualities of hate to the instinct's aim as well.

The history of the origin and relations of love makes us understand how it is that love so constantly manifests itself as "ambivalent," i.e. accompanied by feelings of hate against the same object. This admixture of hate in love is to be traced in part to those preliminary stages of love which have not been wholly outgrown, and in part is based upon reactions of aversion and repudiation on the part of the ego-instincts which, in the frequent conflicts between the interests of the ego and those of love, can claim to be supported by real and actual motives. In both cases, therefore, the admixture of hate may be traced to the source of the self-preservative instincts. When a love-relationship with a given object is broken off, it is not infrequently succeeded by hate, so that we receive the impression of a transformation of love into hate. This descriptive characterization is amplified by the view that, when this happens, the hate which is motivated by considerations of reality is reinforced by a regression of the love to the sadistic preliminary stage, so that the hate acquires an erotic character and the continuity of a love-relation is ensured.

The third antithesis of love, the transformation of loving into being loved, represents the operation of the ~~Imanity offensive~~ve and passive, and is to be judged in the same way as in scoptophilia and sadism. We may sum up by saying that the essential feature in the vicissitudes undergone by instincts is *their subjection to the influences of the three great polarities that govern mental life.* Of these three polarities we might describe that of activity/passivity as the *biological,* that of ego/external world as the *real,* and finally that of pleasure/pain as the *economic* respectively.

That possible vicissitude undergone by an instinct which we call *repression* will form the subject of a further inquiry.

SIGMUND FREUD

The Dissection of the Psychical Personality

Ladies and Gentlemen — I know you are aware in regard to your own relations, whether with people or things, of the importance of your starting point. This was also the case with psycho-analysis. It has not been a matter of indifference for the course of its development or for the reception it met with that it began its work on what is, of all the contents of the mind, most foreign to the ego — on symptoms. Symptoms are derived from the repressed, they are, as it were, its representatives before the ego; but the repressed is foreign territory to the ego — internal foreign territory — just as reality (if you will forgive the unusual expression) is external foreign territory. The path led from symptoms to the unconscious, to the life of the instincts, to sexuality; and it was then that psycho-analysis was met by the brilliant objection that human beings are not merely sexual creatures but have nobler and higher impulses as well. It might have been added that, exalted by their consciousness of these higher impulses, they often assume the right to think nonsense and to neglect facts.

You know better. From the very first we have said that human beings fall ill of a conflict between the claims of instinctual life and the resistance which arises within them against it; and not for a moment have we forgotten this resisting, repelling, repressing agency, which we thought of as equipped

Reprinted from *New Introductory Lectures on Psychoanalysis* by Sigmund Freud. Translated from the German and edited by James Strachey. By permission of W. W. Norton & Company, Inc. Copyright 1933 by Sigmund Freud. Copyright renewed 1961 by W. J. H. Sprott. Copyright © 1964, 1965 by James Strachey. First published as Chapter 3 of *Neue Folge der Vorlesungen zur Einführung in die Psychoanalyse,* Vienna, 1933.

with its special forces, the ego-instincts, and which coincides with the ego of popular psychology. The truth was merely that, in view of the laborious nature of the progress made by scientific work, even psycho-analysis was not able to study every field simultaneously and to express its views on every problem in a single breath. But at last the point was reached when it was possible for us to divert our attention from the repressed to the repressing forces, and we faced this ego, which had seemed so self-evident, with the secure expectation that here once again we should find things for which we could not have been prepared. It was not easy, however, to find a first approach; and that is what I intend to talk to you about to-day.

I must, however, let you know of my suspicion that this account of mine of ego-psychology will affect you differently from the introduction into the psychical underworld which preceded it. I cannot say with certainty why this should be so. I thought first that you would discover that whereas what I reported to you previously were, in the main, facts, however strange and peculiar, now you will be listening principally to opinions — that is, to specula- tions. But that does not meet the position. After further consideration I must maintain that the amount of intellectual working-over of the factual material in our ego-psychology is not much greater than it was in the psychology of the neuroses. I have been obliged to reject other explanations as well of the result I anticipate: I now believe that it is somehow a question of the nature of the material itself and of our being unaccustomed to dealing with it. In any case, I shall not be surprised if you show yourselves even more reserved and cautious in your judgement than hitherto.

The situation in which we find ourselves at the beginning of our enquiry may be expected itself to point the way for us. We wish to make the ego the matter of our enquiry, our very own ego. But is that possible? After all, the ego is in its very essence a subject; how can it be made into an object? Well, there is no doubt that it can be. The ego can take itself as an object, can treat itself like other objects, can observe itself, criticize itself, and do Heaven knows what with itself. In this, one part of the ego is setting itself over against the rest. So the ego can be split; it splits itself during a number of its functions — temporarily at least. Its parts can come together again after- wards. That is not exactly a novelty, though it may perhaps be putting an unusual emphasis on what is generally known. On the other hand, we are familiar with the notion that pathology, by making things larger and coarser, can draw our attention to normal conditions which would otherwise have escaped us. Where it points to a breach or a rent, there may normally be an articulation present. If we throw a crystal to the floor, it breaks; but not into haphazard pieces. It comes apart along its lines of cleavage into fragments whose boundaries, though they were invisible, were predetermined by the crystal's structure. Mental patients are split and broken structures of this same kind. Even we cannot withhold from them something of the reverential awe which peoples of the past felt for the insane. They have turned away from external reality, but for that very reason they know more about internal, psychical reality and can reveal a number of things to us that would otherwise be inaccessible to us.

We describe one group of these patients as suffering from delusions of being observed. They complain to us that perpetually, and down to their most intimate actions, they are being molested by the observation of unknown powers — presumably persons — and that in hallucinations they hear these persons reporting the outcome of their observation: "now he's going to say this, now he's dressing to go out" and so on. Observation of this sort is not yet the same thing as persecution, but it is not far from it; it presupposes that people distrust them, and expect to catch them carrying out forbidden actions for which they would be punished. How would it be if these insane people were right, if in each of us there is present in his ego an agency like this which observes and threatens to punish, and which in them has merely become sharply divided from their ego and mistakenly displaced into external reality?

I cannot tell whether the same thing will happen to you as to me. Ever since, under the powerful impression of this clinical picture, I formed the idea that the separation of the observing agency from the rest of the ego might be a regular feature of the ego's structure, that idea has never left me, and I was driven to investigate the further characteristics and connections of the agency which was thus separated off. The next step is quickly taken. The content of the delusions of being observed already suggests that the observing is only a preparation for judging and punishing, and we accordingly guess that another function of this agency must be what we call our conscience. There is scarcely anything else in us that we so regularly separate from our ego and so easily set over against it as precisely our conscience. I feel an inclination to do something that I think will give me pleasure, but I abandon it on the ground that my conscience does not allow it. Or I have let myself be persuaded by too great an expectation of pleasure into doing something to which the voice of conscience has objected and after the deed my conscience punishes me with distressing reproaches and causes me to feel remorse for the deed. I might simply say that the special agency which I am beginning to distinguish in the ego is conscience. But it is more prudent to keep the agency as something independent and to suppose that conscience is one of its functions and that self-observation, which is an essential preliminary to the judging activity of conscience, is another of them. And since when we recognize that something has a separate existence we give it a name of its own, from this time forward I will describe this agency in the ego as the "super-ego."

I am now prepared to hear you ask me scornfully whether our ego-psychology comes down to nothing more than taking commonly used abstractions literally and in a crude sense, and transforming them from concepts into things — by which not much would be gained. To this I would reply that in ego-psychology it will be difficult to escape what is universally known; it will rather be a question of new ways of looking at things and new ways of arranging them than of new discoveries. So hold to your contemptuous criticism for the time being and await further explanations. The facts of pathology give our esforts a background that you would look for in vain in popular psychology. So I will proceed.

Hardly have we familiarized ourselves with the idea of a super-ego like this which enjoys a certain degree of autonomy, follows its own intentions and is independent of the ego for its supply of energy, than a clinical picture forces itself on our notice which throws a striking light on the severity of this agency and indeed its cruelty, and on its changing relations to the ego. I am thinking of the condition of melancholia,[1] or, more precisely, of melancholic attacks, which you too will have heard plenty about, even if you are not psychiatrists. The most striking feature of this illness, of whose causation and mechanism we know much too little, is the way in which the super-ego — "conscience," you may call it, quietly — treats the ego. While a melancholic can, like other people, show a greater or lesser degree of severity to himself in his healthy periods, during a melancholic attack his super-ego becomes over-severe, abuses the poor ego, humiliates it and ill-treats it, threatens it with the direst punishments, reproaches it for actions in the remotest past which had been taken lightly at the time — as though it had spent the whole interval in collecting accusations and had only been waiting for its present access of strength in order to bring them up and make a condemnatory judgement on their basis. The super-ego applies the strictest moral standard to the helpless ego which is at its mercy; in general it represents the claims of morality, and we realize all at once that our moral sense of guilt is the expression of the tension between the ego and the super-ego. It is a most remarkable experience to see morality, which is supposed to have been given us by God and thus deeply implanted in us, functioning [in these patients] as a periodic phenomenon. For after a certain number of months the whole moral fuss is over, the criticism of the super-ego is silent, the ego is rehabilitated and again enjoys all the rights of man till the next attack. In some forms of the disease, indeed, something of a contrary sort occurs in the intervals; the ego finds itself in a blissful state of intoxication, it celebrates a triumph, as though the super-ego had lost all its strength or had melted into the ego; and this liberated, manic ego permits itself a truly uninhibited satisfaction of all its appetites. Here are happenings rich in unsolved riddles!

No doubt you will expect me to give you more than a mere illustration when I inform you that we have found out all kinds of things about the formation of the super-ego — that is to say, about the origin of conscience. Following a well-known pronouncement of Kant's which couples the conscience within us with the starry Heavens, a pious man might well be tempted

[1] [Modern terminology would probably speak of "depression."]

to honour these two things as the masterpieces of creation. The stars are indeed magnificent, but as regards conscience God has done an uneven and careless piece of work, for a large majority of men have brought along with them only a modest amount of it or scarcely enough to be worth mentioning. We are far from overlooking the portion of psychological truth that is contained in the assertion that conscience is of divine origin; but the thesis needs interpretation. Even if conscience is something "within us," yet it is not so from the first. In this it is a real contrast to sexual life, which is in fact there from the beginning of life and not only a later addition. But, as is well known, young children are amoral and possess no internal inhibitions against their impulses striving for pleasure. The part which is later taken on by the super-ego is played to begin with by an external power, by parental authority. Parental influence governs the child by offering proofs of love and by threatening punishments which are signs to the child of loss of love and are bound to be feared on their own account. This realistic anxiety is the precursor of the later moral anxiety.[2] So long as it is dominant there is no need to talk of a super-ego and of a conscience. It is only subsequently that the secondary situation develops (which we are all too ready to regard as the normal one), where the external restraint is internalized and the super-ego takes the place of the parental agency and observes, directs and threatens the ego in exactly the same way as earlier the parents did with the child.

The super-ego, which thus takes over the power, function and even the methods of the parental agency, is however not merely its successor but actually the legitimate heir of its body. It proceeds directly out of it, we shall learn presently by what process. First, however, we must dwell upon a discrepancy between the two. The super-ego seems to have made a one-sided choice and to have picked out only the parents' strictness and severity, their prohibiting and punitive function, whereas their loving care seems not to have been taken over and maintained. If the parents have really enforced their authority with severity we can easily understand the child's in turn developing a severe super-ego. But, contrary to our expectation, experience shows that the super-ego can acquire the same characteristic of relentless severity even if the up-bringing had been mild and kindly and had so far as possible avoided threats and punishments. We shall come back later to this contradiction when we deal with the transformations of instinct during the formation of the super-ego.[3]

I cannot tell you as much as I should like about the metamorphosis of the parental relationship into the super-ego, partly because that process is so complicated that an account of it will not fit into the framework of an introductory course of lectures such as I am trying to give you, but partly also because we ourselves do not feel sure that we understand it completely. So you must be content with the sketch that follows.

[2] ["*Gewissensangst*," literally "conscience anxiety."]
[3] [See p. 109, *New Introductory Lectures on Psychoanalysis*.]

The basis of the process is what is called an "identification" — that is to say, the assimilation of one ego to another one,[4] as a result of which the first ego behaves like the second in certain respects, imitates it and in a sense takes it up into itself. Identification has been not unsuitably compared with the oral, cannibalistic incorporation of the other person. It is a very important form of attachment to someone else, probably the very first, and not the same thing as the choice of an object. The difference between the two can be expressed in some such way as this. If a boy identifies himself with his father, he wants to *be like* his father; if he makes him the object of his choice, he wants to *have* him, to possess him. In the first case his ego is altered on the model of his father; in the second case that is not necessary. Identification and object-choice are to a large extent independent of each other; it is however possible to identify oneself with someone whom, for instance, one has taken as a sexual object, and to alter one's ego on his model. It is said that the influencing of the ego by the sexual object occurs particularly often with women and is characteristic of femininity. I must already have spoken to you in my earlier lectures of what is by far the most instructive relation between identification and object-choice. It can be observed equally easily in children and adults, in normal as in sick people. If one has lost an object or has been obliged to give it up, one often compensates oneself by identifying oneself with it and by setting it up once more in one's ego, so that here object-choice regresses, as it were, to identification.[5]

I myself am far from satisfied with these remarks on identification; but it will be enough if you can grant me that the installation of the super-ego can be described as a successful instance of identification with the parental agency. The fact that speaks decisively for this view is that this new creation of a superior agency within the ego is most intimately linked with the destiny of the Oedipus complex, so that the super-ego appears as the heir of that emotional attachment which is of such importance for childhood. With his abandonment of the Oedipus complex a child must, as we can see, renounce the intense object-cathexes which he has deposited with his parents, and it is as a compensation for this loss of objects that there is such a strong intensification of the identifications with his parents which have probably long been present in his ego. Identifications of this kind as precipitates of object-cathexes that have been given up will be repeated often enough later in the child's life; but it is entirely in accordance with the emotional importance of this first instance of such a transformation that a special place in the ego should be found for its outcome. Close investigation has shown us, too, that the super-ego is stunted in its strength and growth if the surmounting of the Oedipus complex is only incompletely successful. In the course of develop-

---

[4] [I.e. one ego coming to resemble another one.]
[5] [The matter is in fact only very briefly alluded to in the *Introductory Lectures* (see the later part of Lecture XXVI). Identification was the subject of Chapter VII of *Group Psychology* (1921). The formation of the super-ego was discussed at length in Chapter III of *The Ego and the Id* (1923), (Norton, 1961).]

ment the super-ego also takes on the influences of those who have stepped into the place of parents — educators, teachers, people chosen as ideal models. Normally it departs more and more from the original parental figures; it becomes, so to say, more impersonal. Nor must it be forgotten that a child has a different estimate of its parents at different periods of its life. At the time at which the Oedipus complex gives place to the super-ego they are something quite magnificent; but later they lost much of this. Identifications then come about with these later parents as well, and indeed they regularly make important contributions to the formation of character; but in that case they only affect the ego, they no longer influence the super-ego, which has been determined by the earliest parental imagos.[6]

I hope you have already formed an impression that the hypothesis of the super-ego really describes a structural relation and is not merely a personification of some such abstraction as that of conscience. One more important function remains to be mentioned which we attribute to this super-ego. It is also the vehicle of the ego ideal by which the ego measures itself, which it emulates, and whose demand for ever greater perfection it strives to fulfil. There is no doubt that this ego ideal is the precipitate of the old picture of the parents, the expression of admiration for the perfection which the child then attributed to them.[7]

I am sure you have heard a great deal of the sense of inferiority which is supposed particularly to characterize neurotics. It especially haunts the pages of what are known as *belles lettres*. An author who uses the term "inferiority complex" thinks that by so doing he has fulfilled all the demands of psycho-analysis and has raised his composition to a higher psychological plane. In fact "inferiority complex" is a technical term that is scarcely used in psycho-analysis. For us it does not bear the meaning of anything simple, let alone elementary. To trace it back to the self-perception of possible organic defects, as the school of what are known as "Individual Psychologists"[8] likes

[6] [This point was discussed by Freud in a paper on "The Economic Problem of Masochism" (1924).]

[7] [There is some obscurity in this passage, and in particular over the phrase "*der Träger des Ichideals*," here translated "the vehicle of the ego ideal." When Freud first introduced the concept in his paper on narcissism (1914c), he distinguished between the ego ideal itself and "a special psychical agency which performs the task of seeing that narcissistic satisfaction from the ego ideal is ensured and which, with this end in view, constantly watches the actual ego and measures it by the ideal." Similarly, in Lecture XXVI of the *Introductory Lectures* (1916–17) he speaks of a person sensing "an agency holding sway in his ego which measures his actual ego and each of its activities by an ideal ego that he has created for himself in the course of his development." In some of Freud's later writings this distinction between the ideal and the agency enforcing it became blurred. It seems possible that it is revived here and that the super-ego is being identified with the enforcing agency. The use of the term "*Idealfunktion*" three paragraphs lower down (p. 66) raises the same question.]

[8] [Their views are discussed in Lecture XXXIV, p. 140.]

to do, seems to us a short-sighted error. The sense of inferiority has strong erotic roots. A child feels inferior if he notices that he is not loved, and so does an adult. The only bodily organ which is really regarded as inferior is the atrophied penis, a girl's clitoris.[9] But the major part of the sense of inferiority derives from the ego's relation to its super-ego; like the sense of guilt it is an expression of the tension between them. Altogether, it is hard to separate the sense of inferiority and the sense of guilt. It would perhaps be right to regard the former as the erotic complement to the moral sense of inferiority. Little attention has been given in psycho-analysis to the question of the delimitation of the two concepts. . . .

But let us return to the super-ego. We have allotted it the functions of self-observation, of conscience and of [maintaining] the ideal.[10] It follows from what we have said about its origin that it presupposes an immensely important biological fact and a fateful psychological one: namely, the human child's long dependence on its parents and the Oedipus complex, both of which, again, are intimately interconnected. The super-ego is the representative for us of every moral restriction, the advocate of a striving towards perfection — it is, in short, as much as we have been able to grasp psychologically of what is described as the higher side of human life. Since it itself goes back to the influence of parents, educators and so on, we learn still more of its significance if we turn to those who are its sources. As a rule parents and authorities analogous to them follow the precepts of their own super-egos in educating children. Whatever understanding their ego may have come to with their super-ego, they are severe and exacting in educating children. They have forgotten the difficulties of their own childhood and they are glad to be able now to identify themselves fully with their own parents who in the past laid such severe restrictions upon them. Thus a child's super-ego is in fact constructed on the model not of its parents but of its parents' super-ego; the contents which fill it are the same and it becomes the vehicle of tradition and of all the time-resisting judgements of value which have propagated themselves in this manner from generation to generation. You may easily guess what important assistance taking the super-ego into account will give us in our understanding of the social behaviour of mankind — in the problem of delinquency, for instance — and perhaps even what practical hints on education. It seems likely that what are known as materialistic views of history sin in under-estimating this factor. They brush it aside with the remark that human "ideologies" are nothing other than the product and superstructure of their contemporary economic conditions. That is true, but very probably not the whole truth. Mankind never lives entirely in the present. The past,

[9] [Cf. a footnote of Freud's to his paper on the anatomical distinction between the sexes (1925).]
[10] [*"Idealfunktion."* Cf. footnote 7 above.]

the tradition of the race and of the people, lives on in the ideologies of the super-ego, and yields only slowly to the influences of the present and to new changes; and so long as it operates through the super-ego it plays a powerful part in human life, independently of economic conditions. . . .

Now, however, another problem awaits us — at the opposite end of the ego, as we might put it. It is presented to us by an observation during the work of analysis, an observation which is actually a very old one. As not infrequently happens, it has taken a long time to come to the point of appreciating its importance. The whole theory of psycho-analysis is, as you know, in fact built up on the perception of the resistance offered to us by the patient when we attempt to make his unconscious conscious to him. The objective sign of this resistance is that his associations fail or depart widely from the topic that is being dealt with. He may also recognize the resistance *subjectively* by the fact that he has distressing feelings when he approaches the topic. But this last sign may also be absent. We then say to the patient that we infer from his behaviour that he is now in a state of resistance; and he replies that he knows nothing of that, and is only aware that his associations have become more difficult. It turns out that we were right; but in that case his resistance was unconscious too, just as unconscious as the repressed, at the lifting of which we were working. We should long ago have asked the question: from what part of his mind does an unconscious resistance like this arise? The beginner in psycho-analysis will be ready at once with the answer: it is, of course, the resistance of the unconscious. An ambiguous and unserviceable answer! If it means that the resistance arises from the repressed, we must rejoin: certainly not! We must rather attribute to the repressed a strong upward drive, an impulsion to break through into consciousness. The resistance can only be a manifestation of the ego, which originally put the repression into force and now wishes to maintain it. That, moreover, is the view we always took. Since we have come to assume a special agency in the ego, the super-ego, which represents demands of a restrictive and rejecting character, we may say that repression is the work of this super-ego and that it is carried out either by itself or by the ego in obedience to its orders. If then we are met by the case of the resistance in analysis not being conscious to the patient, this means either that in quite important situations the super-ego and the ego can operate unconsciously, or — and this would be still more important — that portions of both of them, the ego and the super-ego themselves, are unconscious. In both cases we have to reckon with the disagreeable discovery that on the one hand (super-) ego and conscious and on the other hand repressed and unconscious are far from coinciding. . . .

I return now to our topic. In face of the doubt whether the ego and super-ego are themselves unconscious or merely produce unconscious effects, we have, for good reasons, decided in favour of the former possibility. And it is indeed the case that large portions of the ego and super-ego can remain unconscious and are normally unconscious. That is to say, the individual knows nothing of their contents and it requires an expenditure of effort to make them conscious. It is a fact that ego and conscious, repressed and unconscious do not coincide. We feel a need to make a fundamental revision of our attitude to the problem of conscious–unconscious. At first we are inclined greatly to reduce the value of the criterion of being conscious since it has shown itself so untrustworthy. But we should be doing it an injustice. As may be said of our life, it is not worth much, but it is all we have. Without the illumination thrown by the quality of consciousness, we should be lost in the obscurity of depth-psychology; but we must attempt to find our bearings afresh.

There is no need to discuss what is to be called conscious: it is removed from all doubt. The oldest and best meaning of the word "unconscious" is the descriptive one; we call a psychical process unconscious whose existence we are obliged to assume — for some such reason as that we infer it from its effects — but of which we know nothing. In that case we have the same relation to it as we have to a psychical process in another person, except that it is in fact one of our own. If we want to be still more correct, we shall modify our assertion by saying that we call a process unconscious if we are obliged to assume that it is being activated *at the moment,* though *at the moment* we know nothing about it. This qualification makes us reflect that the majority of conscious processes are conscious only for a short time; very soon they become *latent,* but can easily become conscious again. We might also say that they had become unconscious, if it were at all certain that in the condition of latency they are still something psychical. So far we should have learnt nothing new; nor should we have acquired the right to introduce the concept of an unconscious into psychology. But then comes the new observation that we were already able to make in parapraxes. In order to explain a slip of the tongue, for instance, we find ourselves obliged to assume that the intention to make a particular remark was present in the subject. We infer it with certainty from the interference with his remark which has occurred; but the intention did not put itself through and was thus unconscious. If, when we subsequently put it before the speaker, he recognizes it as one familiar to him, then it was only temporarily unconscious to him; but if he repudiates it as something foreign to him, then it was permanently unconscious.[11] From this experience we retrospectively obtain the right also to pronounce as something unconscious what had been described as latent. A consideration of these dynamic relations permits us now to distinguish two kinds of unconscious — one which is easily, under frequently occurring circumstances, transformed into something conscious, and another with which this transformation is difficult and takes place only subject to a considerable

[11] [Cf. *Introductory Lectures,* IV.]

expenditure of effort or possibly never at all. In order to escape the ambiguity as to whether we mean the one or the other unconscious, whether we are using the word in the descriptive or in the dynamic sense, we make use of a permissible and simple way out. We call the unconscious which is only latent, and thus easily becomes conscious, the "preconscious" and retain the term "unconscious" for the other. We now have three terms, "conscious," "preconscious" and "unconscious," with which we can get along in our description of mental phenomena. Once again: the preconscious is also unconscious in the purely descriptive sense, but we do not give it that name, except in talking loosely or when we have to make a defence of the existence in mental life of unconscious processes in general.

You will admit, I hope, that so far that is not too bad and allows of convenient handling. Yes, but unluckily the work of psycho-analysis has found itself compelled to use the word "unconscious" in yet another, third, sense, and this may, to be sure, have led to confusion. Under the new and powerful impression of there being an extensive and important field of mental life which is normally withdrawn from the ego's knowledge so that the processes occurring in it have to be regarded as unconscious in the truly dynamic sense, we have come to understand the term "unconscious" in a topographical or systematic sense as well; we have come to speak of a "system" of the preconscious and a "system" of the unconscious, of a conflict between the ego and the system Ucs., and have used the word more and more to denote a mental province rather than a quality of what is mental. The discovery, actually an inconvenient one, that portions of the ego and super-ego as well are unconscious in the dynamic sense, operates at this point as a relief — it makes possible the removal of a complication. We perceive that we have no right to name the mental region that is foreign to the ego "the system Ucs.," since the characteristic of being unconscious is not restricted to it. Very well; we will no longer use the term "unconscious" in the systematic sense and we will give what we have hitherto so described a better name and one no longer open to misunderstanding. Following a verbal usage of Nietzsche's and taking up a suggestion by Georg Groddeck [1923],[12] we will in future call it the "id".[13] This impersonal pronoun seems particularly well suited for expressing the main characteristic of this province of the mind — the fact of its being alien to the ego. The super-ego, the ego and the id — these, then, are the three realms, regions, provinces, into which we divide an individual's mental apparatus, and with the mutual relations of which we shall be concerned in what follows.

But first a short interpolation. I suspect that you feel dissatisfied because the three qualities of the characteristic of consciousness and the three prov-

[12] [A German psysician by whose unconventional ideas Freud was much attracted.]
[13] [In German "Es," the ordinary word for "it."]

inces of the mental apparatus do not fall together into three peaceable couples, and you may regard this as in some sense obscuring our findings. I do not think, however, that we should regret it, and we should tell ourselves that we had no right to expect any such smooth arrangement. Let me give you an analogy; analogies, it is true, decide nothing, but they can make one feel more at home. I am imagining a country with a landscape of varying configuration — hill-country, plains, and chains of lakes — and with a mixed population: it is inhabited by Germans, Magyars and Slovaks, who carry on different activities. Now things might be partitioned in such a way that the Germans, who breed cattle, live in the hill-country, the Magyars, who grow cereals and wine, live in the plains, and the Slovaks, who catch fish and plait reeds, live by the lakes. If the partitioning could be neat and clear-cut like this, a Woodrow Wilson would be delighted by it;[14] it would also be convenient for a lecture in a geography lesson. The probability is, however, that you will find less orderliness and more mixing, if you travel through the region. Germans, Magyars and Slovaks live interspersed all over it; in the hill-country there is agricultural land as well, cattle are bred in the plains too. A few things are naturally as you expected, for fish cannot be caught in the mountains and wine does not grow in the water. Indeed, the picture of the region that you brought with you may on the whole fit the facts; but you will have to put up with deviations in the details.

You will not expect me to have much to tell you that is new about the id apart from its new name. It is the dark, inaccessible part of our personality; what little we know of it we have learnt from our study of the dream-work and of the construction of neurotic symptoms, and most of that is of a negative character and can be described only as a contrast to the ego. We approach the id with analogies: we call it a chaos, a cauldron full of seething excitations. We picture it as being open at its end to somatic influences, and as there taking up into itself instinctual needs which find their psychical expression in it,[15] but we cannot say in what substratum. It is filled with energy reaching it from the instincts, but it has no organization, produces no collective will, but only a striving to bring about the satisfaction of the instinctual needs subject to the observance of the pleasure principle. The logical laws of thought do not apply in the id, and this is true above all of the law of contradiction. Contrary impulses exist side by side, without cancelling each other out or diminishing each other: at the most they may converge to form compromises under the dominating economic pressure towards the discharge of energy.

[14] [It may be remarked that only a year or so before writing this Freud had finished his collaboration with W.C. Bullitt (then American Ambassador in Berlin) on a study of President Wilson, of whose political judgement he was highly critical. The work has not hitherto (1965) been published.]
[15] [Freud is here regarding instincts as something physical, of which mental processes are the representatives.]

There is nothing in the id that could be compared with negation; and we perceive with surprise an exception to the philosophical theorem that space and time are necessary forms of our mental acts.[16] There is nothing in the id that corresponds to the idea of time; there is no recognition of the passage of time, and — a thing that is most remarkable and awaits consideration in philosophical thought — no alteration in its mental processes is produced by the passage of time. Wishful impulses which have never passed beyond the id, but impressions, too, which have been sunk into the id by repression, are virtually immortal; after the passage of decades they behave as though they had just occurred. They can only be recognized as belonging to the past, can only lose their importance and be deprived of their cathexis of energy, when they have been made conscious by the work of analysis, and it is on this that the therapeutic effect of analytic treatment rests to no small extent.

Again and again I have had the impression that we have made too little theoretical use of this fact, established beyond any doubt, of the unalterability by time of the repressed. This seems to offer an approach to the most profound discoveries. Nor, unfortunately, have I myself made any progress here.

The id of course knows no judgements of value: no good and evil, no morality. The economic or, if you prefer, the quantitative factor, which is intimately linked to the pleasure principle, dominates all its processes. Instinctual cathexes seeking discharge — that, in our view, is all there is in the id. It even seems that the energy of these instinctual impulses is in a state different from that in the other regions of the mind, far more mobile and capable of discharge;[17] otherwise the displacements and condensations would not occur which are characteristic of the id and which so completely disregard the *quality* of what is cathected — what in the ego we should call an idea. We would give much to understand more about these things! You can see, incidentally, that we are in a position to attribute to the id characteristics other than that of its being unconscious, and you can recognize the possibility of portions of the ego and super-ego being unconscious without possessing the same primitive and irrational characteristics.[18]

We can best arrive at the characteristics of the actual ego, in so far as it can be distinguished from the id and from the super-ego, by examining its relation to the outermost superficial portion of the mental apparatus,

---

[16] [The reference is to Kant.]

[17] [This difference was referred to by Freud in many passages. See, in particular, Section V of the metapsychological paper on "The Unconscious" (1915), and Chapter IV of *Beyond the Pleasure Principle* (1920). In both these passages Freud attributes the distinction to Breuer, apparently having in mind a footnote to Section 2 (A) of Breuer's theoretical contribution to *Studies on Hysteria* (1895). In "The Unconscious" he remarks that in his opinion this distinction represents the deepest insight we have gained up to the present into the nature of nervous energy.]

[18] [This account of the id is in the main based on Section V of the paper on "The Unconscious".]

which we describe as the system *Pcpt.-Cs.*[19] This system is turned towards the external world, it is the medium for the perceptions arising thence, and during its functioning the phenomenon of consciousness arises in it. It is the sense-organ of the entire apparatus; moreover it is receptive not only to excitations from outside but also to those arising from the interior of the mind. We need scarcely look for a justification of the view that the ego is that portion of the id which was modified by the proximity and influence of the external world, which is adapted for the reception of stimuli and as a protective shield against stimuli, comparable to the cortical layer by which a small piece of living substance is surrounded. The relation to the external world has become the decisive factor for the ego; it has taken on the task of representing the external world to the id — fortunately for the id, which could not escape destruction if, in its blind efforts for the satisfaction of its instincts, it disregarded that supreme external power. In accomplishing this function, the ego must observe the external world, must lay down an accurate picture of it in the memory-traces of its perceptions, and by its exercise of the function of "reality-testing" must put aside whatever in this picture of the external world is an addition derived from internal sources of excitation. The ego controls the approaches to motility under the id's orders; but between a need and an action it has interposed a postponement in the form of the activity of thought,[20] during which it makes use of the mnemic residues of experience. In that way it has dethroned the pleasure principle which dominates the course of events in the id without any restriction and has replaced it by the reality principle, which promises more certainty and greater success.

The relation to time, which is so hard to describe, is also introduced into the ego by the perceptual system; it can scarcely be doubted that the mode of operation of that system is what provides the origin of the idea of time.[21] But what distinguishes the ego from the id quite especially is a tendency to synthesis in its contents, to a combination and unification in its mental processes which are totally lacking in the id. When presently we come to deal with the instincts in mental life we shall, I hope, succeed in tracing this essential characteristic of the ego back to its source.[22] It alone produces the

[19] [Perceptual-conscious.]

[20] [This is further discussed in Lecture XXXII, p. 89.]

[21] [Freud gave some indication of what he had in mind by this at the end of his paper on the "Mystic Writing-Pad" (1925).]

[22] [Freud does not seem, in fact, to have returned to the subject in these lectures. — He had discussed this characteristic of the ego at length in Chapter III of *Inhibitions, Symptoms and Anxiety* (1926). Though he had stressed the synthetic tendency of the ego particularly in his later writings (e.g. among many others in Chapter II of *The Questions of Lay Analysis* (1926), (Norton, 1950), the concept was implicit in his picture of the ego from the earliest times. See, for instance, the term he almost invariably used during the Breuer period for ideas that had to be repressed: "incompatible" — i.e. that could not be synthesized by the ego. So in Section II of the first paper on the neuro-psychoses of defence (1849).]

high degree of organization which the ego needs for its best achievements. The ego develops from perceiving the instincts to controlling them; but this last is only achieved by the [psychical] representative of the instinct[23] being allotted its proper place in a considerable assemblage, by its being taken up into a coherent context. To adopt a popular mode of speaking, we might say that the ego stands for reason and good sense while the id stands for the untamed passions.

So far we have allowed ourselves to be impressed by the merits and capabilities of the ego; it is now time to consider the other side as well. The ego is after all only a portion of the id, a portion that has been expediently modified by the proximity of the external world with its threat of danger. From a dynamic point of view it is weak, it has borrowed its energies from the id, and we are not entirely without insight into the methods − we might call them dodges − by which it extracts further amounts of energy from the id. One such method, for instance, is by identifying itself with actual or abandoned objects. The object-cathexes spring from the instinctual demands of the id. The ego has in the first instance to take note of them. But by identifying itself with the object it recommends itself to the id in place of the object and seeks to divert the id's libido on to itself. . . . In the course of its life the ego takes into itself a large number of precipitates like this of former object-cathexes. The ego must on the whole carry out the id's intentions, it fulfils its task by finding out the circumstances in which those intentions can best be achieved. The ego's relation to the id might be compared with that of a rider to his horse. The horse supplies the locomotive energy, while the rider has the privilege of deciding on the goal and of guiding the powerful animal's movement. But only too often there arises between the ego and the id the not precisely ideal situation of the rider being obliged to guide the horse along the path by which it itself wants to go.

There is one portion of the id from which the ego has separated itself by resistances due to repression. But the repression is not carried over into the id: the repressed merges into the remainder of the id.

We are warned by a proverb against serving two masters at the same time. The poor ego has things even worse: it serves three severe masters and does what it can to bring their claims and demands into harmony with one another. These claims are always divergent and often seem incompatible. No wonder that the ego so often fails in its task. Its three tyrannical masters are the external world, the super-ego and the id. When we follow the ego's efforts to satisfy them simultaneously − or rather, to obey them simultaneously − we cannot feel any regret at having personified this ego and having set it up as a separate organism. It feels hemmed in on three sides, threatened by three kinds of danger, to which, if it is hard pressed, it reacts by generating anxiety. Owing to its origin from the experiences of the perceptual system, it is earmarked for representing the demands of the external world, but it strives too

[23] [See footnote 15 above.]

to be a loyal servant of the id, to remain on good terms with it, to recommend itself to it as an object and to attract its libido to itself. In its attempts to mediate between the id and reality, it is often obliged to cloak the *Ucs.* commands of the id with its own *Pcs.* rationalizations, to conceal the id's conflicts with reality, to profess, with diplomatic disingenuousness, to be taking notice of reality even when the id has remained rigid and unyielding. On the other hand it is observed at every step it takes by the strict super-ego, which lays down definite standards for its conduct, without taking any account of its difficulties from the direction of the id and the external world, and which, if those standards are not obeyed, punishes it with tense feelings of inferiority and of guilt. Thus the ego, driven by the id, confined by the super-ego, repulsed by reality, struggles to master its economic task of bringing about harmony among the forces and influences working in and upon it; and we can understand how it is that so often we cannot suppress a cry: "Life is not easy!" If the ego is obliged to admit its weakness, it breaks out in anxiety — realistic anxiety regarding the external world, moral anxiety regarding the super-ego and neurotic anxiety regarding the strength of the passions in the id.

I should like to portray the structural relations of the mental personality, as I have described them to you, in the unassuming sketch which I now present you with:

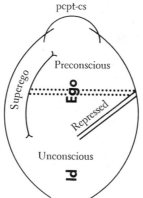

As you see here, the super-ego merges into the id; indeed, as heir to the Oedipus complex it has intimate relations with the id; it is more remote than the ego from the perceptual system.[24] The id has intercourse with the external

[24] [If this diagram is compared with the similar one in Chapter II of *The Ego and the Id* (1923), it will be seen that the earlier diagram differs principally from the present one in the fact that the super-ego is not indicated in it. Its absence is justified in a later passage in the same work. In the original edition of these lectures this picture was printed upright, like its predecessor in *The Ego and the Id*. For some reason, perhaps to economize space, it was turned over on to its side, though otherwise unchanged, in both G.S. and G.W.]

world only through the ego — at least, according to this diagram. It is certainly
hard to say to-day how far the drawing is correct. In one respect it is undoubtedly not. The space occupied by the unconscious id ought to have been
incomparably greater than that of the ego or the preconscious. I must ask
you to correct it in your thoughts.

And here is another warning, to conclude these remarks, which have certainly been exacting and not, perhaps, very illuminating. In thinking of this
division of the personality into an ego, a super-ego and an id, you will not,
of course, have pictured sharp frontiers like the artificial ones drawn in political geography. We cannot do justice to the characteristics of the mind by
linear outlines like those in a drawing or in primitive painting, but rather
by areas of colour melting into one another as they are presented by modern
artists. After making the separation we must allow what we have separated
to merge together once more. You must not judge too harshly a first attempt
at giving a pictorial representation of something so intangible as psychical
processes. It is highly probable that the development of these divisions is
subject to great variations in different individuals; it is possible that in the
course of actual functioning they may change and go through a temporary
phase of involution. Particularly in the case of what is phylogenetically the
last and most delicate of these divisions — the differentiation between the
ego and the super-ego — something of the sort seems to be true. There is no
question but that the same thing results from psychical illness. It is easy to
imagine, too, that certain mystical practices may succeed in upsetting the
normal relations between the different regions of the mind, so that, for instance, perception may be able to grasp happenings in the depths of the ego
and in the id which were otherwise inaccessible to it. It may safely be doubted,
however, whether this road will lead us to the ultimate truths from which
salvation is to be expected. Nevertheless it may be admitted that the therapeutic efforts of psycho-analysis have chosen a similar line of approach. Its
intention is, indeed, to strengthen the ego, to make it more independent
of the super-ego, to widen its field of perception and enlarge its organization,
so that it can appropriate fresh portions of the id.[25] Where id was, there ego
shall be. It is a work of culture — not unlike the draining of the Zuider Zee.

[25] [Freud had said something similar in the last chapter of *The Ego and the Id*.]

SIGMUND FREUD

Character and Anal Erotism

Among those whom one tries to help by means of psycho-analytic treatment, one very often meets with a type of character in which certain traits are strongly marked, while at the same time one's attention is arrested by the behaviour of these persons in regard to a certain bodily function and of the organ connected with it during their childhood. I can no longer say on what precise occasions I first received the impression that a systematic relationship exists between this type of character and the activities of this organ, but I can assure the reader that no theoretical anticipations of mine played any part in its production.

My belief in such a relationship has been so much strengthened by accumulated experience that I venture to make it the subject of a communication.

The persons whom I am about to describe are remarkable for a regular combination of the three following peculiarities: they are exceptionally *orderly, parsimonious,* and *obstinate.* Each of these words really covers a small group or series of traits which are related to one another. "Orderly" comprises both bodily cleanliness and reliability and conscientiousness in the performance of petty duties: the opposite of it would be "untidy" and "negligent." "Parsimony" may be exaggerated up to the point of avarice; and obstinacy may amount to defiance, with which irascibility and vindictiveness may easily be associated. The two latter qualities — parsimony and obstinacy — hang together more closely than the third, orderliness; they are, too, the more constant element in the whole complex. It seems to me, however, incontestable that all three in some way belong together.

From the history of the early childhood of these persons one easily learns that they took a long time to overcome the infantile *incontinentia alvi,* and that even in later childhood they had to complain of isolated accidents relating to this function. As infants they seem to have been among those who refuse to empty the bowel when placed on the chamber, because they derive an incidental pleasure from the act of defaecation[1]; for they assert that even

Chapter IV of Volume 2 of *The Collected Papers of Sigmund Freud,* edited by Ernest Jones, M.D., Basic Books, Inc., Publishers, New York, 1959. First published in the *Psychiatrisch-Neurologische Wochenschrift,* Bd. IX., 1908; reprinted in *Sammlung, Zweite Folge.* [Translated by R. C. McWatters.]

[1] Cf. Freud, *Drei Abhandlungen zur Sexualtheorie,* 1905.

in somewhat later years they have found a pleasure in holding back their stools, and they remember, though more readily of their brothers and sisters than of themselves, all sorts of unseemly performances with the stools when passed. From these indications we infer that the erotogenic significance of the anal zone is intensified in the innate sexual constitution of these persons; but since none of these weaknesses and peculiarities are to be found in them once childhood has been passed, we must conclude that the anal zone has lost its erotogenic significance in the course of their development, and that the constant appearance of this triad of peculiarities in their character may be brought into relation with the disappearance of their anal erotism.

I know that no one feels inclined to accept a proposition which appears unintelligible, and for which no explanation can be offered, but we can find the basis of such an explanation in the postulates I have formulated in my *Drei Abhandlungen zur Sexualtheorie*. I there attempt to show that the sexual instinct of man is very complex and is made up of contributions from numerous components and partial impulses. The peripheral stimulation of certain specialized parts (genitals, mouth, anus, urethra), which may be called erotogenic zones, furnishes important contributions to the production of sexual excitation, but the fate of the stimuli arising in these areas varies according to their source and according to the age of the person concerned. Generally speaking, only a part of them finds a place in the sexual life; another part is deflected from a sexual aim and is directed to other purposes, a process which may be called sublimation. During the period of life which may be distinguished as the "sexual latency period," *i.e.* from the end of the fourth year to the first manifestations of puberty at about eleven, reaction-formations, such as shame, disgust, and morality, are formed in the mental economy at the expense of the excitations proceeding from the erotogenic zones, and these reaction-formations erect themselves as barriers against the later activity of the sexual instinct. Now anal erotism is one of those components of the instinct which in the course of evolution and in accordance with our present civilizing education has become useless for sexual aims; it would therefore be no very surprising result if these traits of orderliness, parsimony, and obstinacy, which are so prominent in persons who were formerly anal erotics, turned out to be the first and most constant results of the sublimation of anal erotism.[2]

---

[2] Since it is just these remarks about the anal erotism of infants in my three contributions to the sexual theory that have most scandalized uncomprehending readers, I venture to insert here an observation which I owe to a very intelligent patient. "An acquaintance of mine who has read the *Drei Abhandlungen zur Sexualtheorie* was talking about the book and said he fully accepted it, but one passage — though naturally he also accepts and understands it — appeared to him so grotesque and comic that he sat down and laughed over it for a quarter of an hour. This passage runs: 'It is one of the best signs of later eccentricity or nervousness if an infant obstinately refuses to empty its bowel when placed on the chamber, that is, when the nurse wishes, but withholds this function at his own pleasure. Naturally it does not matter to the child

The inherent necessity of this relationship is naturally not clear even to myself, but I can make some suggestions which help towards an understanding of it. The cleanliness, orderliness, and reliability give exactly the impression of a reaction-formation against an interest in things that are unclean and intrusive and ought not to be on the body ("Dirt is matter in the wrong place"). To bring obstinacy into relation with interest in defaecation seems no easy task, but it should be remembered that infants can very early behave with great self-will about parting with their stools (see above), and that painful stimuli to the skin of the buttocks (which is connected with the anal erotogenic zone) are an instrument in the education of the child designed to break his self-will and make him submissive. As an expression of defiance or of defiant mockery, a challenge referring to a caress on this part of the body is used even at the present day, as in former times — that is, it represents a tender feeling which has undergone repression. An exposure of the buttocks corresponds to the reduction of this speech to a gesture; in Goethe's *Götz von Berlichingen* we find both speech and gesture introduced most appropriately as expression of defiance.

The connections which exist between the two complexes of interest in money and of defaecation, which seem so dissimilar, appear to be the most far-reaching. It is well known to every physician who has used psycho-analysis

---

if he soils his bed; his only concern is not to lose the pleasure incidental to the act of defecation.' The picture of this infant sitting on the chamber and deliberating whether he should allow such a limitation of his personal independence, and of his anxiety not to lose the pleasure of defecation, caused my friend the greatest merriment. Some twenty minutes later, as we were sitting at tea, my acquaintance suddenly remarked without any preliminary, 'Do you know, there just occurs to me as I see the cocoa in front of me, an idea that I always had as a child. I then always pretended to myself that I was the cocoa manufacturer Van Houten' (he pronounced it 'Van Hauten'), 'that I possessed a great secret for the preparation of this cocoa, and that all the world was trying to get this valuable secret from me, but that I carefully kept it to myself. Why it was Van Houten that I hit upon I do not know. Probably it was that his advertisements made the greatest impression on me.' Laughing, and without thinking much about the meaning of my words, I replied, '*Wann haut'n* (Van Houten) *die Mutter?*' [When do mothers smack?] It was only later that I realized that my pun really contained the key to the whole of his sudden recollection from childhood, which I now recognized as a striking example of a screen-phantasy, setting at rest the sense of guilt by means of a complete reversal of the value of its memory content, while it retained its reference to actual experience (the nutritional process) and was supported by a phonetic associaton: 'cocoa' — '*Wann haut'n*' (Van Houten). (Displacement from behind forwards; excrement becomes aliment; the shameful substance which has to be concealed turns into a secret which enriches the world.) It was interesting to me how in this case, after a defence-reaction, which to be sure took the comparatively mild form of a merely formal objection, the most striking evidence was supplied from the subject's own unconscious after a quarter of an hour without any effort on his part."

[Besides the pun on the word Van Houten, there is probably a further association between the German for cocoa (*Kakao*) and for the nursery term for feces in that language, *Kakis*. Compare also the English *caca* for feces. — Trans.]

that the most refractory and obdurate cases of so-called chronic constipation in neurotics can be cured by this means. This is less surprising if we remember that this function has shown itself equally amenable to hypnotic suggestion. But in psycho-analysis one only attains this result when one deals with the money complex of the persons concerned, and induces them to bring it into consciousness with all its connections. One might suppose that the neurosis is here only following a hint from common speech which calls a person who keeps too careful a hold on his money "dirty" or "filthy," but this would be far too superficial an explanation. In reality, wherever archaic modes of thought predominate or have persisted — in ancient civilizations, in myth, fairy-tale and superstition, in unconscious thoughts and dreams, and in the neuroses — money comes into the closest relation with excrement. We know how the money which the devil gives his paramours turns to excrement after his departure, and the devil is most certainly nothing more than a personifica-tion of the unconscious instinctual forces.[3] The superstition, too, which as-sociates the finding of treasure with defaecation is well known, and everyone is familiar with the figure of the "excretor of ducats" (*Dukatenscheisser*).[4] Even in the early Babylon cult gold is "the excrement of Hell," Mammon = ilu manman.[5] Thus in following common speech, the neurosis, here as elsewhere, takes the words in their original most significant sense, and wher-ever it appears to express a word figuratively it usually only reproduces its original meaning.

It is possible that the contrast between the most precious substance known to man and the most worthless, which he rejects as "something thrown out," has contributed to this identification of gold with faeces.

Yet another circumstance facilitates this equivalence in the mental processes involved in neurosis. The original erotic interest in defaecation is, as we know, destined to be extinguished in later years; it is in these years that the interest in money is making its appearance as something new which was unknown in childhood. This makes it easier for the earlier impulse, which is in process of relinquishing its aim, to be carried over to the new one.

If there is any reality in the relation described here between anal erotism and this triad of character-traits, one may expect to find but little of the "anal character" in persons who have retained the erotogenic quality of the anal zone into adult life, as for example certain homosexuals. Unless I am

---

[3] Compare hysterical possession and demoniac epidemics.

[4] [Unfamiliar to English readers, but compare "the goose which lays golden eggs." — Trans.]

[5] Jeremias, *Das Alte Testament im Lichte des alten Orients*, 1906, p. 216, and *Baby-lonisches im Neuen Testament*, 1906, p. 96. "Mammon is Babylonian 'Manman,' another name of Nergal, the god of the underworld. According to an Oriental myth which has passed over into sagas and folk-tales, gold is the excrement of hell; see *Monotheistische Strömungen innerhalb der babylonischen Religion*, S. 16, Anmk. i."

greatly mistaken experience on the whole is fully in accord with this anticipation.

One ought to consider whether other types of character do not also show
a connection with the excitability of particular erotogenic zones. As yet I am
aware only of the intense, "burning" ambition of those who formerly suffered
from enuresis. At any rate, one can give a formula for the formation of the
ultimate character from the constituent character-traits: the permanent
character-traits are either unchanged perpetuations of the original impulses,
sublimations of them, or reaction-formations against them.

SIGMUND FREUD

On the Transformation of Instincts

with Special Reference to Anal Erotism

Many years ago, observations made during psycho-analysis led me to surmise
that the constant co-existence in any person of the three character-traits of
orderliness, parsimony and *obstinacy* indicated an intensification of the anal-
erotic components in the sexual constitution of that person, and that these
were modes of reaction specially favoured by his ego which had been established during his development in the course of the absorption of his anal
erotism.[1]

In that publication my main object was to make known the fact of this
definite relation: I was little concerned about its theoretical significance. Since
then a general consensus of opinion has arisen that each one of the three
qualities, avarice, pedantry and stubbornness, springs from anal-erotic sources — or, to express it more cautiously and more completely — draws powerful
contributions from these sources. The cases in which these defects of character
were combined and which in consequence bore a special stamp (the "anal

Chapter XVI of Volume 2 of *The Collected Papers of Sigmund Freud*, edited by
Ernest Jones, M.D., Basic Books, Inc., Publishers, New York, 1959. Parts of footnotes
have been omitted. First published in *Zeitschrift*, Bd. IV., reprinted in *Sammlung*,
Vierte Folge. [Translated by Edward Glover.]
[1] "Character and Anal Eroticism," 1908. . . .

character") were merely extreme instances, which even to superficial observation afforded illustration of the particular connection which concerns us here.

As a result of numerous impressions, and in particular of one specially cogent analytical experience, I came to the conclusion a few years later that in the development of the libido in man the phase of genital primacy must be preceded by a "pregenital organization" in which sadism and anal erotism play the leading parts.[2]

From that moment we had to face the following question: what becomes of anal-erotic impulses subsequently when, after the establishment of complete genital primacy, they have lost their importance in sexual life? Do they preserve their original nature, but in a state of repression? Are they sublimated and absorbed by transformation into character-traits? Or do they find a place and function within the new organization of sexuality characterized by genital primacy? Or, to put the question more accurately, since none of these three possibilities is likely to be the exclusive fate of the anal erotism, to what extent and in what way does each of them share in deciding that fate? For the organic sources of anal erotism cannot be exhausted by the establishment of the genital organization.

One would think that there could be no lack of material from which to provide an answer, since the processes of instinctual transformation in question must have taken place in all persons undergoing analysis. Yet the material is so obscure, the abundance of ever-recurring impressions so confusing, that even now I am unable to solve the problem fully and can only contribute in part towards its solution. In this paper I shall also not neglect the opportunity to refer where connections arise to transformations of other impulses besides the anal-erotic. I need not emphasize the fact that the processes of development here described — just as the others found in psycho-analysis — have been inferred from the regressions into which they had been forced by neurotic processes.

To begin with, it would appear that in the products of the unconscious — spontaneous ideas, phantasies, symptoms — the conceptions *faeces* (money, gift), *child* and *penis* are seldom distinguished and are easily interchangeable. We realize, of course, that to express oneself in this way is incorrectly to apply to the sphere of the unconscious terms which belong properly to other regions of mental life; in fact, that we have been tempted by the advantages offered by an analogy. To put the matter in a form less open to objection, these elements in the unconscious are often treated as if they were equivalent and could replace one another.

The most evident connection is that between "child" and "penis." It cannot be without significance that in the symbolic language of dreams, as well as of everyday speech, both are replaced by a single symbol; both child and penis are called "little one" (*das Kleine*). It is a well-known fact that symbolic

[2] "The Predisposition to Obsessional Neurosis," 1913. . . .

speech often ignores the difference of sex. The "little one," which originally meant the male genital organ, may have achieved a secondary application to the female genitals.

If we penetrate deeply into the neuroses of women, we not infrequently meet with the repressed wish to possess a penis. We call this infantile wish "penis-envy" and include it within the castration complex. Chance mishaps in a woman's life, mishaps which are themselves frequently the result of a very masculine disposition, have re-activated this infantile wish and, through the backward flow of libido, made it the chief vehicle of the neurotic symptoms. In other women we find no evidence of the penis-wish; is is replaced by the wish for a child, the frustration of which in real life can lead to outbreak of a neurosis. It looks as if such women had understood (although this could not possibly have acted as a motive) that nature has given children to women as a substitute for the penis that has been denied them. From other women, again, we learn that both wishes co-existed in infancy, and that one had replaced the other. At first they had wanted a penis like a man; then at a later, though still infantile, stage there appeared instead the wish for a child. The impression is forced upon us that this variety is caused by accidental factors during childhood, *e.g.* the presence or absence of brothers, the birth of another child at some critical time of life, so that the penis-wish and the child-wish were fundamentally identical.

We can indicate the ultimate outcome of the infantile penis-wish in those persons in whom the conditions for a neurosis in later life are absent: it changes into the wish for a *man*, accepting the man as an appendage, as it were, of the penis. A tendency hostile to the female sexual function is thus transformed into one favourable to it. Such women are capable of a love based on the masculine type of object-love, which can exist alongside the feminine one proper, which is derived from narcissism. We have already seen that in other cases the child is the first link in the transition from narcissistic self-love to object-love. In this way also, then, a child can be represented by the penis.

I have occasionally had the opportunity of hearing some dreams of women occurring after the first act of intercourse. They revealed an unmistakable wish in the woman to keep for herself the penis with which she had come in contact. Apart from their libidinal origin these dreams indicated a temporary regression from the man to the penis as an object of desire. One would certainly be inclined to trace back the wish for a man in a purely rationalistic way to the wish for a child, since a woman is bound to understand sooner or later that there can be no child without the agency of a man. It is, however, more likely that the wish for a man arises independently of the wish for a child, and that when — from obvious motives derived exclusively from ego-psychology — it does arise an unconscious reinforcement of libido from the original penis-wish becomes attached to it.

The importance of the process described lies in the fact that a part of the young woman's narcissistic masculinity is thus changed into femininity, and so can no longer operate in a way harmful to the female sexual function. By yet another process a part of the erotism of the pregenital phase becomes available for use in the phase of genital primacy. The child is regarded as "lumf"[3] (*Lumpf*), *i.e.* as something which becomes detached from the body by passing through the bowel. A certain amount of libidinal cathexis which originally attached to the contents of the bowel can thus be extended to the child born through it. Linguistic evidence of this identity of child and faeces is contained in the expression "to *give* some one a child." For its faeces are the infant's first gift, a part of his body which he will give up only on persuasion by a loved person, to whom, indeed, he will make a spontaneous gift of it as a token of affection, since as a rule infants do not soil strangers. (There are similar if less intensive reactions with urine.) The process of defaecation affords the first occasion on which the child must decide between a narcissistic and an object-loving attitude. He either parts obediently with his faeces, "offers them up" to his love, or else retains them for purposes of auto-erotic gratification and later as a means of asserting his own will. The latter choice constitutes the development of defiance (obstinacy), a quality which springs, therefore, from a narcissistic clinging to the pleasure of anal erotism.

It is probable that the first significance which faecal interest develops is not "gold/money," but "gift." The child has no knowledge of money other than that received as a gift, no idea of money earned or belonging to it, inherited. Since its faeces constitute its first gift, the child easily transfers interest from this substance to the new one that meets it as the most valuable form of gift in life. Those who question this derivation of gifts should review their experience of psycho-analytic treatment, study the gifts they receive as doctors from their patients, and watch the storms of transference which a gift from them can rouse in their patients.

Thus the interest in faeces is carried on partly as interest in money, partly as a wish for a child, in which latter an anal-erotic and a genital impulse ("penis-envy") coincide. But the penis has another anal-erotic significance apart from its relation to the interest in a child. The relationship between the penis and the passage lined with mucous membrane which it fills and excites has already its prototype in the pregenital, anal-sadistic phase. The faecal mass, or as one patient called it, the faecal "stick," represents as it were the first penis, and the stimulated mucous membrane of the rectum represents that of the vagina. There are persons whose anal erotism remains vigorous and unmodified up to the age preceding puberty (ten to twelve years); we learn from them that already during the pregenital phase such persons had developed in phantasy and in perverse activity an organization analogous to the genital one, in which penis and vagina were represented by the faecal stick and the rectum. In other cases (obsessional neurotics) we can observe the result of a regressive deterioration of the genital organization:

---

[3] [A child's word for faeces.] . . .

all the phantasies originally conceived on the genital level are set back on to the anal level; the penis is replaced by the faecal mass, the vagina by the rectum.

Normally, when the interest in faeces recedes, the structural analogy we have described here effects a transference of the interest to the penis. Then if later inquiry yields the discovery that babies are born from the bowel, the greater part of the anal erotism becomes transferred to the baby, as chief heir, so to speak, of the anal erotism; the penis, however, has been its predecessor in this as well as in another sense.

I feel sure that by this time the manifold interrelations of the series, faeces, penis, child, have become utterly confused; so I will attempt to remedy this defect by presenting them diagramatically, and in considering the diagram we can review the same material in a different order. Unfortunately, this technical device is not sufficiently plastic for our purpose, or possibly we have not yet learned to use it with effect. In any case we ask the reader not to expect too much from it.

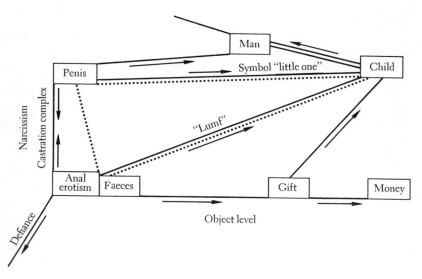

Defiance springs from anal erotism and serves narcissistic purposes, forming an important ego-reaction against demands made by others. Interest in faeces is carried over first to interest in gifts, then to interest in money. In girls, the discovery of the penis gives rise to penis-envy, which later changes into the wish for a man as the possessor of a penis. At an earlier stage the wish for a penis was changed into the wish for a child, or the latter replaced the former. An organic analogy between penis and child (dotted line) is expressed by the existence of a symbol ("little one") common to both. A rational wish (double line) leads from the wish for a child to the wish for a man: we have already appreciated the importance of this instinctual transformation.

A different series of relations can be observed much more distinctly in the male. It is formed when the boy's sexual curiosity leads him to discover the absence of a penis in women. He concludes that the penis must be a detachable part of the body, something analogous to faeces, the first bodily substance the child had to part with. Thus the original anal defiance enters into the composition of the castration complex. The structural analogy which enabled the intestinal contents to be the forerunner of the penis during the pregenital phase cannot come into account as a motive, but a substitute in the mind for it is provided by sexual investigation.

When a baby appears on the scene it is labelled "lumf," in accordance with the conclusions arrived at by sexual investigation, and becomes invested with powerful anal-erotic interest. When social experiences teach that a baby is to be regarded as a love-token, a gift, the wish for a child is reinforced from the same source. Faeces, penis and child are all three solid bodies: they all three, by forcible entry or expulsion, stimulate a membranous passage, *i.e.* the rectum and the vagina, the latter being as it were "rented" from the rectum, as Lou Andreas-Salome aptly remarks.[4] Infantile inquiry into sexual matters can only lead to the conclusion that the child comes down by the same route as the faecal mass: the function of the penis is not usually discovered by it. But it is interesting to note that after so many vicissitudes an organic correspondence re-appears in the mental sphere as an unconscious identity.

[4] Lou Andreas-Salome, *"Anal" und "Sexual."*

HENRY A. MURRAY
CLYDE KLUCKHOHN

A Conception of Personality

A Few Basic Definitions and Assumptions

PERSONS. The psychologist's objects of concern are individual human organisms, or persons, rather than groups (the sociologist's objects of concern).

PERSON IN AND OF ENVIRONMENTS. A person is an emergent entity *of* and *in* a certain physical, social, and cultural milieu. He cannot be properly represented in isolation from his locale, or from the culture of the group of which he is a member, or from his status (role) in the structure of that group. Basically, every person is a social person, an interdependent part of a system of human interactions.

SEAT OF THE PERSONALITY OF A PERSON. The superordinate governing institution of the human organism is the *personality*, or mind. Its main physiological and neurological basis lies in the head.

According to this view, the *establishments* and *processes* which constitute personality are out of sight, but their characteristics, relations, and operations can be defined and conceptualized on the basis of the subject's verbal reports (memories of events, introspective judgments, and avowals) and on the basis of the observations of his overt behaviors, physical and verbal. Thus the psychologist is directly concerned only with the manifestations of personality, *the facts*. The personality is something that must be inferred from the facts. Hence, in actual practice, the personality is an abstract formulation composed by the psychologist.

Much evidence goes to show that the brain is the locus of the integrations which are manifested in all co-ordinated and effective actions of the total organism. It is surely the locus of the feelings which evaluate situations as they appear and discriminate goals for action. It is the seat of consciousness, of streams of thought, of conflict, and of decision. It is also the repository of all *establishments* of personality: traces of past experiences, images, symbols, concepts, beliefs, attached emotions, ideologies, plans, commitments, resolutions, and expectations. Thus, both the enduring components and the

From *Personality in Nature, Society and Culture,* 2nd edition, by Clyde K. Kluckhohn and Henry A. Murray, editors. Copyright 1948, 1953 by Alfred A. Knopf, Inc. Reprinted by permission of the publisher.

ceaseless, kinetic processes of personality are — physically and concretely — located in the head.

The operations of personality are markedly affected by brain injuries and lesions, by the operations of lobotomy, lobectomy, and topectomy, by infections of the brain, by a narrowing of the cranial blood vessels, and by changes in the composition of the circulating blood (its internal physiological environment).

Personality may be greatly modified, temporarily or permanently, by happenings in other parts of the body. The glands of internal secretion, in fact, are so influential in determining energy level, temperament, emotion, and drive that these might well be included as outlying organs of the personality, contributing, say, to what psychoanalysts have termed the "id." But other considerations militate against this notion: the operations of personality are even more dependent upon atmospheric oxygen; they are modified by low oxygen tension just as they may be modified by drugs or by happenings in distant regions of the globe (e.g. death of a beloved person). It seems preferable, then, to regard the glands of internal secretion as important chemical or constitutional *determinants*, rather than anatomical centers, of personality.

The *establishments* of the personality, such as a person's knowledge, value-system, or vocational goal, and the *processes* of personality, such as a transient perception, emotion, or intention, have been located physically in the brain region because there is no other possible place for them — except as abstractions. Furthermore, the day may come when advances in neurophysiology and electronics will reveal some of the physical correlates of psychic processes. But it should be understood that according to our present conception no components of the personality are identified with any particular structures or processes of the brain as we know it, morphologically and physiologically, today. The physico-chemical brain is not the personality, but one of its constitutional determinants. For the present at least, most psychologists will be content to forget the brain and restrict themselves to the psychical-behavioral level of analysis and formulation. . . .

PERSONALITY IN PROCESS. The personality is participant in a long succession of activities from birth to death, regularly punctuated by periods of sleep. From one point of view the history of the personality *is* the personality. It cannot be properly represented as a fixed structure. Personality is an on-going manifold of structured processes.

PROCEEDINGS OF PERSONALITY, INTERNAL. The waking hours of a person's life may, for convenience, be divided into a sequence of temporal segments, or *proceedings*, some of which are mostly *internal*, some mostly *external*. An *internal proceeding* is a temporal segment during which the person, abstracted from his environment, is attending to his feelings, memories, evaluations, fantasies, artistic or theoretical creations, plans, or expectations of the future. Knowledge of a person cannot be restricted to the observation of his overt behaviors. Reported memories of internal proceedings as well as verbalizations of concurrent streams of thought are indispensable to the psychologist.

EXTERNAL PROCEEDINGS. An *external proceeding* is a stretch of time during which the person is overtly engaged in coping with some part of his immediate physical or social environment. Such a proceeding consists of the concrete chronological activities of a concrete chronological person in a concrete chronological situation. This is the psychologist's simplest *real entity*, the thing he should observe, analyze, try to reconstruct and represent, if possible, with a model, and thus explain; it is the thing he attempts to predict, and against which he tests the adequacy of his formulations and hypotheses. Real entities have duration: to perceive and interpret them the psychologist must be present and alert from start to finish. Furthermore, they are complex, occur rapidly, and are gone, never to be repeated exactly as before. Hence for detailed and precise studies, a moving picture film with sound track, which can be examined over and over again by any number of experts, is of the greatest utility.

SITUATIONS. Since the environmental situation from moment to moment is an integral part of every external proceeding (real entity), a description or symbolic representation of the more relevant portions of it is required. A person's behavior cannot be adequately characterized by a list of adjectives; it is necessary to record the nature of the successive situations, imposed or selected, in relation to which the person's activity has been oriented. According to this notion, then, a human life, as objectively viewed, consists of a chronology of distinguishable person-situation transactions.

INTERPERSONAL PROCEEDINGS. An interpersonal or dyadic proceeding (a discussion, say, between parent and child, two siblings, two enemies, two friends, or two lovers) is the psychologist's most significant type of real entity, or transaction. Here the object (alter, second person) constitutes the ever-changing situation for the subject (first person), and the subject constitutes the ever-changing situation for the object. Consequently, both sides of the equation must be given equal analytical consideration, that is to say, the psychologist's reconstruction of the episode should include as much formulation of object's status, sentiments, thought, and speech as of the subject's status, sentiments, thought, and speech. For, among the things a psychologist wants to know about a subject is how he behaves in the presence of this and that kind of person, say, a shy stranger of lower status, a boastful person of the opposite sex, a teacher who makes frequent dogmatic statements, etc.

FIELDS. The course or result of a proceeding, the total effect, say, of the subject's and the object's behavior, can be roughly indicated by representing the structure of the *field* (defined as the instantaneous total situation) at the beginning and at the end of the transaction. For a more exact understanding, however, it is necessary to conceive of a proceeding as a succession of instantaneous fields, each of which determines the action that ensues at that moment. According to Lewin's definition the *field* at an instant includes both the external situation (say, the smile of a certain acquaintance who wants to borrow money) and the internal situation (say, fatigue and a feeling of depression) and *both* are within the head of the subject, because for him external reality is what *he* perceives and apperceives out there, no more, no less. Since this formulation abolishes the important difference between normal verifiable perceptions and apperceptions, on the one hand, and illusions and delusions, on the other — not to speak of the many extravagant projections of normal people — it has seemed advisable to call the external situation as it actually exists (insofar as this can be determined by careful inquiry) the *alpha situation,* and to call the external situation as the subject apperceives it the *beta situation.* Although the subject's response to a given situation provides a fairly reliable clue to the nature of the beta situation, the latter should be ascertained, whenever possible, by direct inquiry.

UNIQUENESS OF PROCEEDINGS. Every proceeding leaves behind it some trace of its occurrence — a new fact, the germ of an idea, a re-evaluation of something, a more affectionate attachment to some person, a slight improvement of skill, a renewal of hope, another reason for despondency. Thus, slowly, by scarcely perceptible gradations — though sometimes suddenly by a leap forward or a slide backward — the person changes from day to day. Since his familiar associates also change, it can be said that every time he meets with one of them, both are different. In short, every proceeding is in some respects unique. As a rule, the psychologist looks for uniformities among events, but if he attends exclusively to these he will overlook those exceptional occasions which leave a person, let us say, with an incurable psychic injury, or start him off on a fresh path, perhaps a new vocation.

SERIALS. Many actions, though temporally discrete, are by no means functionally discrete; they are continuations of a shorter or longer series of preceding actions and are performed in the expectation of further actions of a similar sort in the future. Of this nature are skill-learning activities and behaviors which are oriented toward some distant goal, a goal which cannot be reached without months or years of effort. Also to be included here are the behaviors which form part of an enduring friendship or marriage. Such an intermittent series of proceedings, each of which is dynamically related to the last and yet separated from it by an interval of time for recuperation and the exercise of other functions, may be termed a *serial.*

Most people are in the midst of several on-going serials which occupy their minds whenever they are not forced by circumstance to attend to more pressing matters. Men who are intensely interested in constructing something — a house, a relationship, a political group, a scientific book — return eagerly every day to the next step or stage of their endeavor. Their behavior is so different from what is denoted by the old S–R formula — since there is no distinguishable stimulus which evokes a response — that it calls for a differentiating word. I will suggest, then, that the term *proaction* (in contrast to *reaction*) be used to designate an action that is not initiated by the confronting external situation, but spontaneously from within. An action of this sort is likely to be part of a serial program, one that is guided by some directional force, which, in turn, may be subsidiary to a more comprehensive aim. As a rule, a *proaction* is not merely homeostatic, in the sense that it serves to restore a previously experienced physical, social, or cultural condition. If successful, a proaction may be said to be *superstatic*, inasmuch as it results in the acquisition or in the production of something new, small though it may be, over and above the previous condition — a little physical growth, more strength, more property, a new instrument, a more cohesive friendship, the conception of an offspring, another chapter of a novel, or the statement of a proposition. The integrates of serials, of plans, strategies, and intended proactions directed toward distal goals constitute a large portion of the ego system, the establishment of personality which inhibits irrelevant impulses and renounces courses of action that interfere with progress along the elected paths of life.

Since a substantial part of means-end learning, skill learning, value learning, as well as what has been termed emotional development, occurs during the course of *serials*, representative samples of the major on-going serials should be carefully studied by the psychologist in order to determine the kinds and rates of transformations which are characteristic for a person. In predicting future behaviors, values, and achievements it is not enough to know a subject's more consistent current dispositions, habits, and abilities; in addition one must have evidences necessary to an estimation both of his capacity and his determination to develop further. . . .

FORMS OF ACTIVITY, PROCESS ACTIVITY. Aside from the simpler segmental reflexes, there appear to be three major types of activity: (1), *ungoverned, or process, activity*, and (2), *governed activity*, of which there are two forms: (a), *modal, or formal, activity*, and (b), *directional, or instrumental, activity*. The latter, *directional activity*, differs from the other two, insofar as it is oriented towards a supposedly satisfying end state, or goal. Both *process activity* and *modal activity* are enjoyed in their own right from start to finish, and hence are intrinsically, rather than extrinsically, satisfying. *Modal activity*, however, differs from mere *process activity*, insofar as it is governed by some effort to appreciate or to achieve a certain degree of sensuous, dramatic, humorous, or purely technical excellence for its own sake.

Process activity is both effortless and aimless. The personality is not an institution that remains inert unless excited by extracranial stimuli (as the S-R formula suggests). It is marked from first to last by a continuous flow of on-going activities. These unabatable processes are fundamental "givens," the most elementary characteristics of the mind — random perceptions, random sequences, and combinations of images, words, and sentences (symbols), random moods and feelings, random vocalizations (hummings) and verbalizations (babblings), random gestures and movements (manipulations and locomotions). When the energy level is high, such spontaneities are rapid, abundant, and, as a rule, highly pleasurable *per se* (process pleasure). They are sluggish during periods of exhaustion or staleness.

In their more elementary forms, as observed in infancy, these mental processes are so unco-ordinated, impersistent, and seemingly ineffective that they can hardly be called motivated in the ordinary sense, even though they do occasionally arrive (as if by accident) at something which gratifies a latent need.

Whenever some strong viscerogenic need, such as hunger, or a social need is activated, these self-same mental processes become the integrated instruments of its fulfillment. But, in the dependent and irresponsible days of childhood, these needful moments are periodic and relatively brief. Furthermore, they require, in the last analysis, hardly more than one instrumental act, that of crying. The mother does the rest. Thus, because of the protective parent's constant ministrations, the child's mind is not by necessity held down (as a young animal's mind is held down) to external realities and practical adjustments. For long periods the mind is free to exercise its own processes in its own way. What these mental processes do, naturally and without prompting, is to *transform* percepts into images and also, later, into words (symbols), and out of these images and words to *construct* dreams and fantasies. At one extreme these imaginations consist of elementary animistic conceptions of environmental events (world pictures), and, at the other, dramas in which invented selves play leading roles, tragic or triumphant.

MODAL ACTIVITY. The neglect of modal activity (which is more closely related to *being* than to *doing*) by American psychologists may perhaps be correlated with our addiction to competitive strivings and tangible rewards. The chief difference between modal activity and directional activity is this: in the former, satisfaction is normally concurrent with the activity, whereas in the latter satisfaction is linked with the ultimate effect of the activity. The activity itself may be tedious, boring, or even painful. The two types, of course, are often compounded: a person may enjoy the exercise of his functions as well as the results which they achieve. Furthermore, it is not at all unlikely that the satisfaction which has been so commonly associated with the attainment of a final state (reduction of tension, satiation) is, in fact, more closely correlated with the exciting modal activities (gustatory sensations in eating, and genital sensations in sexual intercourse) which precede the end point.

The most obvious illustrations of modal activity are expressions and receptions of sensuous, dramatic, or comic patterns: ballet dancing and witnessing a ballet, playing music and listening to music, acting in a drama and watching a drama, telling a funny story and laughing at it, exhibitionism and voyeurism. Whether other elements (such as vicarious identification with the hero in a play, or catharsis of aggression in certain types of humor) are present or not, the essence of the presentation lies in its form or style. For example, a joke that belittles a disliked person will not evoke laughter if it is ineptly told. Considering the number of hours that millions of Americans spend at the movies or before a television set, it is strange that neither this type of activity nor its complement, the activity of the actors, has been given a place in catalogues of behavior. Perhaps one reason for this omission is that we have been slow in realizing that the mind is not always bent on serving some somatic or social need, but has its own peculiar occupations and enjoyments (see MENTAL NEEDS).

DIRECTIONAL ACTIVITY. Most dynamic psychologists have assumed, explicitly or implicitly, that the most important thing to observe, to define, and to represent in formulating any single proceeding or any single serial in the career of a person is the superordinate, or major, *directionality* of its activity, whether this activity be chiefly physical, verbal, or mental. Instead of *directionality* one might say the *effect* of the activity, if it were not that we often wish to characterize the behavior of a person when no significant effect has been produced. Either (1) the man is "on his way" to some effect but has not had time to achieve it, or he has not achieved it (2) because of lack of relevant knowledge or ability, or (3) because it was a "competitive ect" and his efforts were surpassed by one or more rivals.

Since directional activities vary in respect to their intensity and duration, ?ir degree of co-ordination and focality (definiteness of aim), it has been lged necessary to conceptualize a directing superordinate "force" in the in region (merely analogous to a physical force). It has been variously ned — tendency, drive, need, propensity, instinct, urge, impulse, desire, h, purpose, motive, conation, resolution, intention, etc. The number of ⌐....erent, yet more or less synonymous, terms which have been used to designate this hypothetical force suggest confusion of thought and/or the absence in our language of the precisely definitive word. Anyhow, the conception is that of a vector (directional magnitude) which guides mental, verbal and/or physical processes along a certain course.

Conforming with Lewin and many others, we may use the term "need" or "need disposition" to refer to the roughly measurable "force" in the personality which is co-ordinating activities in the direction of a roughly definable goal; and we may use the term "aim" to refer to this need's *specific* goal (to be achieved perhaps in association with a *specific* object in a *specific* place at a *specific* time). For example, a man may be motivated by a general *need* for dominance (power, authority, leadership, a decision-making role, an administrative position, etc.), but his *aim* at a particular time may be to persuade residents of Bordeaux to elect him mayor of that city.

In a need of this class the satisfaction comes at the end with the attainment of the goal (effect pleasure), and perhaps also along the way from anticipations of the goal (anticipatory effect pleasure).

Thus, "directionality" means the *trend* of the activity and this can be defined only in terms of its *aim*, or *goal*, or *intended effect*. Since Freud we have not been troubled by the absence of a conscious aim in the actor's (subject's) mind. It is now scientifically respectable to speak of an *unconscious* aim, or goal, or intention if sufficient evidence for it is at hand. It is only necessary to exclude those cases where the effect was clearly a mistake, or accident.

In America it is customary for psychologists to take the hunger drive (food-seeking and eating behavior) and the sex drive (mate-seeking and copulating behavior) in animals (rats, monkeys) as basic illustrations of motivated activity. This practice has helped to clarify certain issues, but by restricting reflections to two kinds of relatively simple tendencies, it has served to discourage efforts to conceptualize other kinds of activities, especially "higher order" activities. These last will have to be investigated before much progress can be made towards a satisfactory classification of human tendencies.

MENTAL NEEDS. The infant's mind is not acting most of the time as the instrument of some urgent animal drive (as many psychologists assume), but is preoccupied with *gratifying itself*. Among these purely mental gratifications of early life is the need to dramatize everything, to invent another world that is more exciting and hence more "real" than the reality of sheer perception. This inner world of childhood provides the basic stuff out of which are shaped forms of play, myths and religious rituals, songs and dances, folk-tales and poetry, and even, at a later date, philosophies, scientific theories, and technical inventions. When the child is not fabricating its own stories, it is listening with rapt attention to stories told by others, or reading the comics, or watching television. In childhood, furthermore, these dreams are influential in determining what is perceived in the external world and how it is interpreted. Figures of the imagination are constantly projected into objects of the environment, into animals, into sun, moon, and stars, into trees and streams, the deeps of the sea, and the expanse of heaven.

All this sustains the proposition expounded years ago by Santayana: in the human being it is *not* perception that is fundamental, but imagination. It also conforms to the views advanced more recently by Suzanne Langer: the human mind is inherently a transforming, creating, and representing organ; its function is to make symbols for things, to combine and re-combine these symbols incessantly, and to communicate the most interesting of these combinations in a variety of languages, discursive (referential, scientific) and expressive (emotive, artistic).

In short, the mind lives in two worlds — the world of the imagination (religion, art, and science) and the world of perception and practical action. In some areas the two may coalesce; in other areas they may be poles apart. Of these two worlds, it is the first — the inner world of heaven and hell, of literature and music, of philosophies and scientific speculations (cultural productions) — which chiefly distinguishes human beings from the predominantly practical lower organisms. By satisfying the "higher" mental needs, the internal world may be more compelling than the external world in which the prepotent viscerogenic and socio-relational needs are gratified. The mental needs are a good deal more important in the lives of intellectuals — scientists, artists, philosophers, religionists — all of whom (positivists included) are more attached to their abstractions, theories, fables, poems, or mystical visions than they are to any facts.

Furthermore, the mind's imaginations — especially in their religious and artistic forms — not infrequently provide fantasied satisfactions of viscerogenic and socio-relational needs (in addition to the real satisfactions of mental needs).

In insanity a person does not "go out of his mind," but wholly "in his mind" (as Santayana said) and out of the external world. At the other end of the detachment-attachment continuum are the people who apply their imaginations to the solution of environmental problems. Creative mental needs are peculiar in having no clearly envisaged target or goal, the goal being something that has never existed (new machine or gadget, new social group, new political constitution, new dramatic epic, new scientific hypothesis or theory, new philosophy). The goal is something that must be constructed step by step. This might be compared to nest building in animals.

DIAGNOSIS OF NEEDS. Some critics have objected to the need theory on the grounds that one cannot immediately tell them which need is being exhibited by a given person at a given time. But if anything should be clear it is that needs are not discernible facts. A need is an intervening variable, hidden in the head, the operation of which can only be inferred on the basis of certain criteria. Hence, the task of identifying an active need is not that of labeling the kind of behavior that is observed, but of making a diagnosis. Sometimes the diagnosis is easy: the need is almost as obvious as the movements and the words. But, often, it is impossible to decide, even after hours of investigation, whether or not this or that disposition was operating during the observed event. . . .

SOCIAL COMMITMENTS, ROLE ACTIONS. As the sociologists have shown us, the concept of role is strategic to the integration of the two levels of theoretical analysis, psychological and sociological. To make this clear we might stretch this concept, for the moment, beyond its intended limits and say that every self-and-body, in order to develop, maintain, express, and reproduce itself, must perform a number of *individual* roles (functions) such as respiration, ingestion of food, construction of new tissue, excretion, defense against assault and disease, expression of emotions and sentiments, copulation, and so forth. Likewise, it can be said, that every group (social system), in order to develop, maintain, express, and reproduce itself, must perform a number of *social* roles, such as recruitment and training of new members, hierarchical organization of functions, elimination of incorrigible members, defense against attack by rival groups, expansion by reproduction (formation of similar groups in other parts of the world), and so forth. Also, both persons and social systems are devoted to the accomplishment of one or more further purposes, such as the manufacture and exchange of utilities, the acquisition and communication of knowledge, the creation and performance of plays (on the stage, through moving pictures), correction of delinquents, the subjugation of enemies, and so forth. Finally, both persons and social systems (each taken as a consensus of intentions) are desirous of improvement, of living up to their ideals, of deserving recognition and prestige. In the personality it is the governing ego system which assumes responsibility for the integration of *individual* roles and the actualization of plans. In the group it is the leader or government (system of legislators and administrators) that assumes responsibility for the structuring of *social* roles and the carrying out of policies (domestic and foreign). The id of the personality is somewhat comparable to the disaffected low status members of a social system, the "unwashed masses," including the "creative minority" (Toynbee), the radical reformers and fanatics, as well as the criminals and psychotics. Every structured ego "holds a lunatic in leash" (Santayana).

Thus, by extending the concept of role (social role) to include personal roles, a personality action system and a social action system can be represented as roughly homologous, at least in certain respects.

Furthermore, all social roles require the execution of one or more kinds of actions, that is, the habitual production of one or more kinds of effects, and these effects (goals) can be classified in the same manner as needs are classified. Indeed, the need-aim and the role-aim may exactly correspond. For example, a gifted actor with a need for artistic expression may be asked by a theater manager to play Hamlet (the very part which has long excited his ambition). Thus a man may *want* to do exactly what he is expected to do. But, so happy a congruence of "want" and "must" is, in the lives of most people, more of an ideal than an actual daily occurrence.

The chief reason for the frequent discrepancy between desire and obligation is the differentiation of society into sub-systems, and the differentiation of sub-systems into specialized and *temporally integrated* role functions, and, finally, the necessity of *committing* men to the scheduled performance of these functions. It is not so much that a man is obliged (expected) to do certain things, but that he is obliged (in order to intergrate his actions with others) to do them at a *fixed time.* Consequently, it may happen that a man eats when he is not hungry, converses when he feels unsociable, administers justice when he has a hangover, makes a speech when his head is bereft of enlivening ideas, goes to the theater when he wants to sleep. Thus, in many, many cases, a need is not the initiator of action, but the hands of the clock. Spontaneity is lost, and will-power (an unpermitted concept) must be constantly exerted to get through the days.

The point is that here every action is an instrumental one, not satisfying in itself. Instrumental to what? This varies from individual to individual: the need for sheer survival and hence the need for money, the need for upward mobility, or for fellowship, or for authority, or for prestige; but, more generally and more closely, the *need for roleship*, that is, the need to become and to remain an accepted and respected, differentiated and integrated, part of a congenial, functioning group, the collective purposes of which are congruent with the individual's ideals. So long as the individual feels this way about the group that he has joined, he will try to abide, as best he can, by its *schedule* of role functions.

GENERALITY AND SPECIFICITY: DIFFUSE AND FOCAL NEEDS. A need is a general disposition which commonly becomes associated (through "focalization," or "canalization," as Murphy would say) with a number of *specific* entities (e.g. a certain doll, or dog, or person, or group, or town, or theory, or work of art, or religion, etc.), and (through "generalization") with a number of *kinds* of (*semi-specific*) entities (e.g. French wines, or horses, or women, or music, or novels, or philosophies, etc.).

These focalizations (specificities and semi-specificities) rarely exhaust the possibilities of need activity. Unless the structure of the disposition has become rigid and fixated, it is always capable of becoming attached to a new object — new kind of food, new place, new acquaintance, new organization, new kind of art, new ideology. Indeed, the development of personality can be partially represented by listing, in chronological order, the attachments it has acquired and outgrown in the course of its career (e.g. a series of material objects, such as a rattle, toy truck, mechano set, bicycle, motorcycle, automobile, airplane; or a series of aesthetic forms, such as nursery tales, adventure stories, Dickens, Tolstoy, Sophocles). Attachments (sentiments, attitudes), then, may be more or less enduring.

A permanent attachment to a nurturant person (e.g. mother fixation) dating from infancy is regarded by psychoanalysts as a sign of emotional immaturity. Equally indicative of retardation is its apparent opposite: lack of enduring attachments, that is, the inability to remain loyally committed to anybody or anything. Here we might speak of a *diffuse* need which is sensitive to a large number or variety of objects (e.g. free-floating sociability, free-floating anxiety, free-floating irritability) in contrast to a *focal* need which is enduringly centered on one object (e.g. satisfying marriage, specific phobia, canalized revenge).

... An entity (material object, person, group, political policy, philosophy) to which one or more needs have become attached is said to have value, or *cathexis* (power to excite). A *liked* entity which attracts the subject is said to have *positive* cathexis whereas a *disliked* entity is said to have *negative* cathexis. An entity with negative cathexis (negatively cathected object) may evoke avoidant reactions, defensive reactions, or destructive reactions. Thus a goal object may be either a positively cathected (loved) person or a negatively cathected (hated) person whom the subject wants to subdue, injure, insult, or murder. Entities (places, animals, persons, topics of conversation) which the subject wishes to avoid (withdraw or flee from) may be called *noal* objects. The distribution in any personality of these different kinds of cathections (evaluations, sentiments, attitudes) is correlated with the relative potency of the three vectorial dispositions so well described by Horney: moving toward people (positive goal objects), moving against people (negative goal objects), and moving away from people (noal objects).

In a developing individual, positively cathected goals and goal objects (kinds of values) are of two classes: (1) satisfying goals which have been experienced more or less regularly week after week, and (2) goals which have not yet been attained, but which sway the imagination and orient the planning processes of the mind. In sanguine temperaments, visions of future goals (grass on the other side of the fence) are likely to be given higher *value* than goals which are attainable every day. This applies especially to the creative needs, the goals of which are always novel, never-yet-constructed entities.

We can affirm that goals of the above-defined first class are learned, but can we say this about the more greatly esteemed goals of the second class? Perhaps it can be said that these are learned by "trial and error" in the imagination. Many of them, we know, become established through identification with some exemplar, in conformity with cultural expectations, and are therefore to be subsumed under the heading of social imitation or mimesis. In any event, they are not innately given.

The fact that the word "learning" (when used by an American psychologist) refers almost always to the process of acquiring effective instrumental action patterns, might, I suppose, be cited as another illustration of how a prevailing ideology (e.g. the high valuation of technical skills, "How to Make Friends and Influence People," etc.) can influence the course of our supposedly chaste science.

More important than means-end learning, of course, is goal and goal-object learning, that is, the process whereby an individual comes to some conclusions as to the relative *values* of different possible goals and goal objects, or, looking at it from a developmental or educational standpoint, the process whereby he learns to enjoy (and so discovers for himself) the kinds of goals and goal-objects which are worth striving for.

ATTITUDES, INTERESTS, VALUES. Social psychologists looking in at themselves and looking out at others concluded some time back that a great deal of human thought and behavior is value-oriented. It seemed, for example, that the psychologist's own intellectual preoccupations, conversations, and activities could be largely explained by stating that he was *interested* in theories of personality and social behavior, *interested* in research, *interested* in educational procedures, *interested* in political policies, and so forth. These regions of thought and action were highly *valued*. He had a *positive attitude* towards them. More specifically, his attitude was positive towards *certain* concepts (e.g. traits), certain *kinds* of research (e.g. opinion polling), certain *kinds* of educational procedures (e.g. small research seminars), certain *kinds* of political policies (e.g. labor legislation), and so forth. "Attitude," as defined by Allport and others, became the social psychologist's key concept. A man's personality was conceived as a more or less integrated system of attitudes, each of which is a relatively permanent disposition to evaluate some entity negatively or positively, and, as a rule, to support this evaluation with reasons, or arguments. The general or specific entity (object of the attitude) *was* a *value*, positive or negative, or *had* value (power to attract or repel).

(Here it might be said parenthetically that "attitude" and "sentiment" are synonyms, both of them referring to a more or less lasting disposition in the personality; also that "value" in one sense is synonymous with "cathexis" and "valence," and, in the other sense, with "cathected entity" and "object with valence." There is always a representation (image) of the valued, or cathected, entity *in* the personality.)

In the judgment of most social psychologists there is a big difference or gap between attitudes (vaguely defined as dynamical forces) and needs (or drives), probably because the latter are fixedly associated in their minds with hunger and sex. They are willing to concede that there are such "pushes from the rear" as hunger and sex, but these are said to be "segmental" and "lower." Attitudes, on the contrary, are consciously and rationally selected "pulls from the front." The principle of functional autonomy is usually invoked to sever whatever associations might have existed in the subject's past between needs and attitudes.

Assuming that this greatly telescoped account of the concept of attitude conforms roughly to the conventional notion, we submit that two modifications are required before it can be assigned an importnat place in a theoretical system. First, its scope must be extended to include all affect-invoking entities from faeces to the Fallen Angel. There is no reason to limit the term to dispositions towards "higher" entities. We must be able to speak of attitudes towards the mother's breast, the mother herself, siblings, spinach, mechanical toys, play group, comics, fairy tales, and so forth. Second, the concept must be logically connected with directional activity, that is to say, with the concept of need. Knowledge that a certain person has, let us say, a positive attitude towards music does not tell us what he *does* about it, if anything. Perhaps he values music very highly (as checked on a questionnaire), but is too busy to listen to it. Or, to take the opposite extreme, he may be a composer of music. If we are not told, the man does not become alive. We cannot guess how he spends his day, or predict what he would do at a certain choice-point. Does he keep music alive in his head by humming it? Does he discuss music with other appreciators and defend the excellence of his favorite concertos? Does he play some instrument, privately for his own satisfaction, or publicly for the satisfaction of others? Is playing in an orchestra his professional role, his path to money and eminence? He may be a music critic, a writer of books on music, or a singing teacher. Or, is he merely an enjoyer of music as it comes over the radio? If a high evaluation of music is linked with one or more vectorial dispositions (such as reception, construction, expression), we can represent what a given appreciator *does* with music; we can picture many proceedings in his life. Otherwise, one has a dangling abstraction.

Now, having pointed to the beam in the eye of the attitude construct, it is time for us to acknowledge the mote in the conception of need: *not all needs have been defined as dispositions operating in the service of a certain kind of value.* Take, for example, anger and aggression (the goal of which is partial or complete destruction of some object). This is usually defined as a general drive or need which is likely to be provoked by frustration. In the discussion of a case, a psychologist will usually mention the object (e.g. mother, father, sibling, enemy) towards which the aggression is directed, but rarely, if ever, do we find any reference to the value in the service of which aggression has operated. Since observation and experience testify to the fact that aggression, as well as every other kind of action, has an effect (function) which can be best defined in terms of some valued entity (its construction, conservation, expression, or reproduction), the naming of the valued entity in conjunction with the named activity should contribute a good deal to our understanding of the dynamics of the behavior. Aggression, for example, may serve to defend the *body* from injury, to establish an *erotic relationship* (when obstructed by a rival), to acquire more *property*, to maintain *authority*, to increase one's area of *freedom*, to depreciate the over-all values of others in order to make way for the acceptance (reproduction) of one's own *ideology*, to revenge an insult in order to restore one's self-respect, or *prestige*, and so forth.

This means that both valued entities and action tendencies must be classified. Following Lewin and Erikson we are calling the action tendencies *vectors*, each of which is a physical or psychological *direction* of activity, such as (1) *rejection*, (2) *reception*, (3) *acquisition*, (4) *construction*, (5) *conservation*, (6) *expression*, (7) *transmission*, (8) *elimination*, (9) *destruction*, (10) *defendance*, and (11) *avoidance*. The classification of the valued entities presents more difficulties. Merely as an illustration the following might be listed: (A) Body (physical well-being), (B) Property (useful objects, wealth), (C) Authority (decision-making power), (D) Affiliation (interpersonal affection), (E) Knowledge (facts and theories, science, history), (F) Aesthetic Form (beauty, art), (G) Ideology (system of values, philosophy, religion). These are the six well-known Spranger values, with the addition of Body (which includes sex and reproduction as well as all the other viscerogenic needs). Others should be included, but this number is sufficient to indicate how each *kind of value* and each *kind of vector* can be combined to form a manageable number of *value-vectors*. For example, a man might serve his knowledge, E (valued entity), by (1) *rejecting* irrelevant or inaccurate observations, (2) passively *receiving* reliable information, (3) actively seeking and *acquiring* more facts, (4) *constructing* an adequate theory, (5) *conserving* (remembering, recording, and utilizing) the knowledge he has acquired, (6) *expressing* his thoughts, (7) *transmitting* (implanting) his theories into the minds of others, (8) *eliminating* (from his mind) fallacious notions, (9) *destroying* rival (erroneous) theories, (10) *defending* his conceptions, or (11) *avoiding* harmful criticism by concealing his ideas or by escaping from the field of discourse (changing the topic). According to this conception each value-vector is a need.

Such a scheme can be used to distinguish the action trend (*need-aim*) in the subject as well as the action trend (*press-aim*) in the object. The two in sequence might be said to constitute the *thema* of a proceeding. For example, the proaction of the subject could be that of expressing (6) an idea (E) and the reaction of the object might be that of rejecting (1) the idea (E): Thema: sE6 → oE1. For a more complete statement of the thema other variables (cathexis, status, conformity to role) must be added to each side of the formula.

This scheme is not yet ready to be applied to the topics which will be discussed next. It is still in process of construction, tentative and incomplete.

ID, EGO. Up to the time of Janet and Freud the human mind was almost wholly equated with consciousness, with rationality and voluntary action. Psychology was restricted to "ego psychology." But the discovery of dissociated subconscious complexes in patients with hysteria, and, then, of primitive unconscious establishments and processes in all people, normal as well as abnormal, called for a greatly expanded conception of the mind.

Freud's first distinction was between the conscious parts and the unconscious parts of the personality. Neuroses were products of conflict between the former and the latter. But this distinction was abandoned by Freud as soon as he concluded that the unconscious processes of repression and resistance operated in the service of the conscious parts of the personality. This led to a new distinction, that between the *ego* and the *id*, the latter consisting of a medley of unconscious pleasure-seeking processes that were unacceptable to the ego, and hence subject to repression. The ego was the conscious, objective, rational, and reality-oriented part of the personality. It was supported by a variety of unconscious "defense-mechanisms."

In due time it became apparent to other analysts, if not to Freud, that the concept of id could not be limited to unacceptable dispositions. In infancy, for example, when the ego system is non-existent or at best very rudimentary, the mind is a hive of involuntary spontaneities, emotions, and needs, many of which are not only acceptable to the child and its mother during these early years, but continue to be acceptable and, what is more, culturally encouraged throughout life. It would not be proper to say that respiration, ingestion of food, defecation, expressions of affection, endeavors to master the environment, and so forth, had their sources in the ego. Also, as Jung, Rivers, and others have pointed out, the id is evidently the breeding ground of love and worship, as well as of the novel imaginations which are eventually applauded, instituted, and cherished by society. For these and other reasons, it seems best to think of the id as consisting of all the basic energies, emotions, and needs (value-vectors) of the personality, some of which are wholly acceptable and some wholly unacceptable, but most of which are acceptable when expressed in a culturally approved form, towards a culturally approved object, in a culturally approved place, at a culturally approved time. Thus, the function of the ego is not so much to suppress instinctual needs as to govern them by moderating their intensities and determining the modes and times of their fulfillment.

Some of the criteria of ego structure, or ego strength, are the following:

A. Perception and apperception
   1. External objectivity: the ability to perceive human actions and events without distortion, to analyze and interpret them realistically, to predict the behavior of others.
   2. Internal objectivity: the capacity for self-detachment and self-analysis; insight into one's own motives, evaluations, and emotional reactions; also, the entertainment of a goal of personal development and accomplishment which is suited to one's own circumstances and capacities.
   3. Long apperceptive span: the habit of making causal connections between events that are not temporally contiguous in experience; the ability to foresee broad or distant consequences of one's actions (time-binding power or long time-perspective).

B. Intellection
   4. Concentration, directionality: the ability to apply one's mind to an assigned or selected topic, to direct one's thoughts along a chosen path, to persist when bored, to inhibit day-dreaming.
   5. Conjunctivity of thought and speech: the ability to think, speak, and write clearly, coherently, and logically, to inhibit irrelevant ideas.
   6. Referentiality of thought and speech: the habit of using concepts and words which refer to real things, events, and experiences; the absence of vague, undefined, and essentially meaningless terms and expressions.

C. Conation
   7. Will-power: the ability to do what one resolves to do and is capable of doing, to persist in the face of difficulties, to complete a prescribed or elected course of action; also, to re-strive after failure (counteraction).
   8. Conjunctivity of action: the ability to schedule and organize one's activities, to make a plan and follow it, to live an ordered life.
   9. Resolution of conflicts: the ability to choose between alternative courses of action. The absence of protracted periods of hesitation, indecision, vacillation, or perplexity.
   10. Selection of impulses: the power to repress temporarily, inhibit, or modify unacceptable emotions or tendencies, to resist "temptations"; also, the habit of selecting and expressing, without qualms or conflict, impulses which are intrinsically enjoyable or extrinsically rewarding; absence of disturbing worries or anxieties.
   11. Selection of social pressures and influences: the ability to choose among the demands, claims, enticements, and suggestions that are made by other people, to comply with those that are acceptable and reject those that are not; especially the power to resist intolerable coercions from society, but to submit if there is no way out; power "to will the obligatory."
   12. Initiative and self-sufficiency: the ability to decide for oneself and

act without waiting to be stimulated, urged, or encouraged. The habit of trusting one's own nature, of having reasonable confidence in one's own decision (self-reliance). Also, the ability to stand alone, to do and finish things alone, without help; to endure solitude and to tolerate misfortune without appealing for sympathy; absence of marked dependence on others.

13. Responsibility for collective action: the willingness and ability to take responsibility and effectively organize and direct the behaviors of others; the experience of feeling secure in a position of authority, rather than being threatened, worried, and on the defensive.

14. Adherence to resolutions and agreements: the disposition and ability to abide by long-term decisions and commitments, to keep a promise or pledge.

15. Absence of pathological symptoms: freedom from incapacitating neurotic or psychotic symptoms.

Since the ego system is the differentiated governing establishment of the personality, it is not possible to estimate its power (relative to other ego systems) without some knowledge of the strength of the id forces with which it has to cope. Some "egos" are sitting in the saddle of a docile Shetland pony, others are astride a wild bronco of the plains.

The chief criteria of id strength are these: (1) intense energy, zest, spontaneity, enthusiasm; (2) intense needs and appetites; (3) intense emotions; (4) abundant, vivid imaginations. As stated above, some of these needs, emotions, and imaginations are accepted, enjoyed, and cherished; others are unacceptable and, if possible, repressed. Of the latter, Freud has stressed the need for sex (deviant forms of it especially) and the need for aggression, that is, lust and wrath, two of the Catholic Church's seven Cardinal Sins. But equally important in American culture is the need for acquisition (greed) and the need for superiority or prestige, manifesting itself as ruthless competitiveness, vainglorious self-display, extravagant pride, boasting, and envy of the accomplishments or statuses of others. All of these tendencies must be inhibited, appropriately moderated, or modified.

A weak id is conducive to another of the seven sins, sloth or passivity. In extreme cases one speaks of neurasthenia or psychasthenia.

SUPEREGO, EGO IDEAL. According to Freud's conception, the *superego*, or conscience, is a part of the personality which interiorly represents and enforces the moral imperatives of the society insofar as these have been implanted by the parents and parent-surrogates during childhood. It is an establishment which is gradually constructed by the internalization of the system of rewards for "good" behavior and punishments for "bad" behavior that is practiced by each of the succession of respected authorities — parents, nurses, teachers, priests, etc. — who assume responsibility for the education of the child's character. If socialization has been completed, the superego will privately reward and punish the self in conformity with cultural standards and in this way replace the authorities who inculcated these standards. Thus, the concept of the superego provides the necessary link between the laws and customs of a society as a whole and the conforming behavior of its individual members. Each socialized person bears in his superego the value system of his society, and in terms of this system he is disposed to judge others and to discipline his children. This over-simplified account of the superego must, of course, be radically qualified and revised.

In the first place, the superego develops by stages, stratum upon stratum. In its most primitive form it consists of no more than projections of the child's own oral acquisitive and aggressive tendencies, represented, say, by a vampire, werewolf, or gigantic biting animal, such as Moby Dick himself, or, possibly, by a child-devouring witch or deity such as Cronos. In the child's imagination "totem" animal figures are gradually replaced, as they were in the evolution of religions, by human figures, first, perhaps, by an affrighting Jehovah image, and then usually by a more kindly symbol of moral authority. These are "father" figures, for the most part, but in some cultures, and in some personalities in our culture, the superego is more mother-oriented, represented sometimes by an androgynic figure. Here we are speaking largely of the lower layers of superego formation, marked by archaic, semi-human, and mostly punishing images. As socialization proceeds in Western cultures these strata, overlaid by others, become unconscious, and in later life are manifested only in dreams, artistic productions, and insane delusions.

Contemporaneous with the development of these imaginative, figurative, mythological, or religious aspects of the superego, one finds the gradual structuration of behavior according to certain abstract moral imperatives, transmitted by parental example, suggestion, persuasion, promises, rewards, threats, or punishments. At one extreme, these imperatives amount to scarcely more than a medley of arbitrary and inconsistent injunctions or aggregate of heterogeneous apothegms; at the other, they constitute a fairly rational ordering of ethical principles. But even if the system of rewards and punishments practiced by the parents is reasonably clear and coherent in the child's mind, there are bound to be serious conflicts *within* the superego as soon as the boy or girl goes to a school or becomes a member of a clique in which a somewhat different code of conduct is respected and enforced.

The reciprocative and co-operative interactions among members of a peer group constitute, as Piaget has pointed out, the second major source of superego constituents. No doubt there have always been antagonisms between parental standards and peer group standards, but in recent years there has been an almost world-wide exacerbation of the conflict, resulting in a step by step compliance, if not surrender, by each parental pair to the mass demands of the adolescent peer group for an earlier emancipation and a greater range of freedom, especially for young girls in the sphere of sex. Since in America the youth culture is unanimous only in its opposition to authority, lacks a unifying ideal, and is split in several ways by rivalries, the superegos of its members are, for the most part, in a state of flux, if not of *anomie*.

One more class of superego determinants should be mentioned — literature. An intelligent youth who reads widely will be exposed to a great variety of contrasting moral judgments: the Bible, Aristotle, Epicurus, Seneca, Montaigne, Spinoza, Hobbes, Rousseau, Jefferson, Nietzsche, Whitman, Tolstoy — each may contribute something to his maturing superego. Since the majority of mortals are incapable of making order out of such diversity, and since among Protestants and Jews there is no body of philosophers officially delegated to create and re-create such order, it is only in members of a totalitarian system — Catholic, Communist, Fascist — that one finds considerable agreement in respect to basic assumptions and rationalized derivations.

As a result of these several factors the disposition to adjust one's behavior to accord with the evaluations of one's peers, fitful as they may be, is gaining ground in America, whereas, the strength of the elevated superego with most of its manifestations — inwardness, moral aspiration, righteous indignation, guilt, remorse, penitence, reformation, and so forth — is in process of decline.

This recent weakening of conscience is all of a piece with Freud's conception of it as a chiefly prohibitive, repressive, life-denying agency. In short, the superego, or puritan conscience, of the Western world lost its "charm" (to use Toynbee's apt term) sometime ago and became an establishment of bearded threats, a purely negative Maginot Line which was destined to succumb in due course to the onslaughts of freedom-loving moral revolutionists.

The deterioration of the religious and ethical superego becomes apparent when it is compared to the intellectual or scientific superego. The latter is not only highly evaluated but it invites continuous creative efforts, attempts at re-definition, refinement, elaboration, and re-construction. In brief, instead of demanding more leniency from their superegos, scientists are generally vying with each other to see who can define and then conform to ever more exacting standards.

In childhood the principal conflicts are between insurgent id tendencies and parental standards. Later, if socialization advances, many conflicts are between id and superego (internalized standards). During these phases, the ego is hardly more than a battle ground, or possibly a puppet, dominated sometimes by the id and sometimes by the superego. Eventually, however, guided by an exemplar, or an envisaged ideal self (ego ideal), the ego becomes more differentiated and integrated, more self-conscious and self-reliant, until eventually it acquires enough power to arbitrate to some extent between emotional impulses from the id and superego imperatives.

At best, the superego is an inviting conception of an ideal future world, or at least a better world, to be constructed by stages, and its imperatives define those modes of behavior which are most conducive to that end. The ego ideal, on the other hand, is an inviting conception of an ideal future self, or at least a more able or better self, also to be attained by stages. If integrated with the superego, the ego ideal will portray an individual who is promoting in some small or large way the development of a better world. If not so integrated, the ego ideal may consist of images of the Master Criminal or of any other wholly egotistical "successful" person.

HENRY A. MURRAY

Proposals for a Theory of Personality

NEEDS, VISCEROGENIC AND PSYCHOGENIC

Needs may be conveniently divided into: (1) primary (viscerogenic) needs, and (2) secondary (psychogenic) needs. The former are engendered and stilled by characteristic periodic bodily events, whereas the latter have no subjectively localizable bodily origins; hence the term "psychogenic." They are occasioned by regnant tensions, with or without emotion, that are closely dependent upon certain external conditions or upon images depicting these conditions. Thus, speaking loosely, we may say that from a subjective standpoint the viscerogenic needs have to do with physical satisfactions and the psychogenic needs with mental or emotional satisfactions.

The viscerogenic needs are: (1) n Air, (2) n Water, (3) n Food, (4) n Sex, (5) n Lactation, (6) n Urination, (7) n Defecation, (8) n Harmavoidance, (9) n Noxavoidance, (10) n Heatavoidance, (11) n Coldavoidance, and (12) n Sentience. We also recognize a need for Passivity, which includes relaxation, rest and sleep, but this may be neglected for the present.[1]

It is hard to decide whether one should concoct new words as names for the needs or attempt to get along with old and ill-used terms. In the present endeavour sometimes one and sometimes the other of these two possibilities was adopted but without conviction. It was found that no system of nomenclature could be consistently maintained: appropriate words were not forthcoming.

From *Explorations in Personality: A Clinical and Experimental Study of Fifty Men of College Age,* edited by Henry A. Murray. Copyright 1938 by Oxford University Press, Inc., 1966 by Henry A. Murray. Reprinted by permission of Oxford University Press, Inc.

[1] It is heartening to discover, as P. T. Young's . . . book (*Motivation of Behavior,* New York, 1936) makes evident, that psychologists are reaching agreement in regard to the most convenient classification of viscerogenic drives.

The words used for most of the viscerogenic needs indicate in each case what effect is brought about by the need action. The n Noxavoidance refers to the tendency to avoid or rid oneself of noxious stimuli: to look or draw away from repulsive objects, to cough, spit or vomit up irritating or nauseating substances. The needs for Heatavoidance and Coldavoidance together refer to the tendency to maintain an equable temperature: to avoid extremes of heat and cold, to clothe the body or seek shelter when necessary. The n Harmavoidance refers to the tendency to avoid physical pain: to withdraw, flee or conceal oneself from injuring agents. It includes "startle" and "fear" reactions generally, to loud noises, loss of support, strangers. The n Sentience refers to the inclination for sensuous gratification, particularly from objects in contact with the body: taste sensations and tactile sensations (ex: thumb-sucking). The need moves in a direction opposite to that of the n Noxavoidance and the n Harmavoidance. But it may be associated with any one of the other needs: local sensations are an important part of sexual activity and they may accompany urination and defecation; moderate changes in temperature are sensuously agreeable and food may give rise to delicious olfactory and gustatory impressions.

The effect of the need action in each case can be represented by the B-E [Behavioral Event] form.

B. S. [Beginning of Stimulus]	E.S. [End of Stimulus]
Lack of food	Repletion
Genital tumescence	Detumescence
Fluid in the bladder	Evacuation
Pain	Absence of pain

A few remarks at this point may not be amiss:

1. Some of the needs here distinguished represent gross groupings of a number of more specific needs. The n Food, for instance, could be divided into separate needs for different kinds of food. Here they are combined for convenience because they all involve "feeding behaviour" and the objects are all nourishing.

(i) Certain animals go to salt licks — as certain tribes used to travel to salt mines — for the sole purpose of adding this necessary ingredient to their diet.
(ii) Diabetics have an appetite for sugar; sufferers from deficiency diseases "need" this or that vitamin, and so forth.

2. It will be noticed that the B.S. for most of the viscerogenic needs are afferent impulses from some region of the body.

3. The viscerogenic needs are of unequal importance as variables of personality. The personological significance of a need seems to depend upon whether there are marked differences between individuals in the frequency, intensity and duration of its activity, and upon whether the strength of any psychogenic needs are functions of such differences. A need, furthermore, does not usually become a dominant element of personality if there is no obstruc-

tion to its satisfaction. If its activity and gratification can be "taken for granted," it may be neglected. The n Air, for example, is perhaps the most essential of all the needs from a biological standpoint, since if the organism does not attain this need's E.S. in three or four minutes, it dies. And yet the n Air is rarely of any personological importance. Air is free and most human beings get enough of it. There is little competition for air. The n Sex, on the other hand, ordinarily depends upon the co-operation of another person, is commonly interfered with by rivals, is highly unstable, and is hemmed in by all kinds of social restrictions. This is enough to account for its importance.

The viscerogenic needs enumerated above may be grouped in a number of ways. One convenient grouping (which calls for the division of the n Air into inspiration and expiration) is the following.

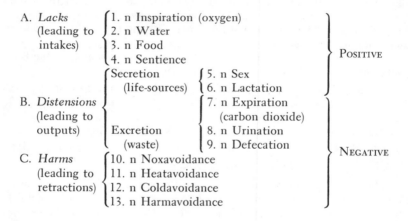

A. *Lacks*
   (leading to
   intakes)
   { 1. n Inspiration (oxygen)
     2. n Water
     3. n Food
     4. n Sentience

B. *Distensions*
   (leading to
   outputs)
   Secretion
   (life-sources)
   { 5. n Sex
     6. n Lactation
     7. n Expiration
        (carbon dioxide)
   Excretion
   (waste)
   { 8. n Urination
     9. n Defecation

} POSITIVE

} NEGATIVE

C. *Harms*
   (leading to
   retractions)
   { 10. n Noxavoidance
     11. n Heatavoidance
     12. n Coldavoidance
     13. n Harmavoidance

The first six needs may be called "positive" or "adient" needs because they force the organism in a positive way towards other objects: air, water, food, sensuous patterns, a sex object, a suckling. The last seven needs, on the other hand, may be called "negative" or "abient" needs because they force the organism to separate itself from objects: to eliminate waste matter or to avoid unpleasant or injuring agents. The positive needs are chiefly characterized subjectively by a desire to reach the E.S., whereas the negative needs are chiefly characterized by a desire to get away from the B.S. The division of needs into lacks with intakes, distensions with outputs, and harms with retractions may also be found useful.

The secondary or psychogenic needs, which are presumably dependent upon and derived from the primary needs, may be briefly listed. They stand for common reaction systems and wishes. It is not supposed that they are

fundamental, biological drives, though some may be innate. The first five
pertain chiefly to actions associated with inanimate objects.[2]

N ACQUISITION (ACQUISITIVE ATTITUDE). To gain possessions and property.
To grasp, snatch or steal things. To bargain or gamble. To work for money
or goods.

N CONSERVANCE (CONSERVING ATTUTUDE). To collect, repair, clean and
preserve things. To protect against damage.

N ORDER (ORDERLY ATTITUDE). To arrange, organize, put away objects. To
be tidy and clean. To be scrupulously precise.

N RETENTION (RETENTIVE ATTITUDE). To retain possession of things. To
refuse to give or lend. To hoard. To be frugal, economical and miserly.

N CONSTRUCTION (CONSTRUCTIVE ATTITUDE). To organize and build.

Actions which express what is commonly called ambition, will-to-power,
desire for accomplishment and prestige have been classified as follows:

N SUPERIORITY (AMBITIOUS ATTITUDE). This has been broken up into two
needs: the n Achievement (will to power over things, people and ideas) and
the n Recognition (efforts to gain approval and high social status).

N ACHIEVEMENT (ACHIEVANT ATTITUDE). To overcome obstacles, to exercise
power, to strive to do something difficult as well and as quickly as possible.
(This is an elementary Ego need which alone may prompt any action or be
fused with any other need.)

N RECOGNITION (SELF-FORWARDING ATTITUDE). To excite praise and com-
mendation. To demand respect. To boast and exhibit one's accomplishments.
To seek distinction, social prestige, honours or high office.

We have questioned whether the next need should be distinguished from
the Recognition drive. In the present study the two have been combined.

N EXHIBITION (EXHIBITIONISTIC ATTITUDE). To attract attention to one's
person. To excite, amuse, stir, shock, thrill others. Self-dramatization.

Complementary to Achievement and Recognition are the desires and actions which involve the defense of status or the avoidance of humiliation:

N INVIOLACY (INVIOLATE ATTITUDE). This includes desires and attempts
to prevent a depreciation of self-respect, to preserve one's "good name," to
be immune from criticism, to maintain psychological "distance." It is based
on pride and personal sensitiveness. It takes in the n Seclusion (isolation,
reticence, self-concealment) which in our study was considered to be the
opposite of n Exhibition and, for this reason, was not separately considered.
The n Inviolacy has been broken up into three needs: n Infavoidance (the
fear of and retraction from possible sources of humiliation), n Defendance

[2] To some extent the same tendencies are exhibited towards people (acquiring friends,
maintaining loyalties, possessiveness, organizing groups).

(the verbal defence of errors and misdemeanours), and n Counteraction (the attempt to redeem failures, to prove one's worth after frustration, to revenge an insult). Counteraction is not truly a separate need. It is n Achievement or n Aggression acting in the service of n Inviolacy.

N INFAVOIDANCE (INFAVOIDANT ATTITUDE). To avoid failure, shame, humiliation, ridicule. To refrain from attempting to do something that is beyond one's powers. To conceal a disfigurement.

N DEFENDANCE (DEFENSIVE ATTITUDE). To defend oneself against blame or belittlement. To justify one's actions. To offer extenuations, explanations and excuses. To resist "probing."

N COUNTERACTION (COUNTERACTIVE ATTITUDE). Proudly to overcome defeat by restriving and retaliating. To select the hardest tasks. To defend one's honour in action.

The next five needs have to do with human power exerted, resisted or yielded to. It is a question of whether an individual, to a relatively large extent, initiates independently his own behaviour and avoids influence, whether he copies and obeys, or whether he commands, leads and acts as an exemplar for others.

N DOMINANCE (DOMINATIVE ATTITUDE). To influence or control others. To persuade, prohibit, dictate. To lead and direct. To restrain. To organize the behaviour of a group.

N DEFERENCE (DEFERENT ATTITUDE). To admire and willingly follow a superior allied O. To co-operate with a leader. To serve gladly.

N SIMILANCE (SUGGESTIBLE ATTITUDE). To empathize. To imitate or emulate. To identify oneself with others. To agree and believe.

N AUTONOMY (AUTONOMOUS ATTITUDE). To resist influence or coercion. To defy an authority or seek freedom in a new place. To strive for independence.

N CONTRARIENCE (CONTRARIENT ATTITUDE). To act differently from others. To be unique. To take the opposite side. To hold unconventional views.

The next two needs constitute the familiar sado-masochistic dichotomy. Aggression seems to be either (1) the heightening of the will-to-power (Achievement, Dominance) when faced by stubborn opposition, (2) a common reaction (fused with n Autonomy) towards an O that opposes any need, or (3) the customary response to an assault or insult. In the latter case (revenge) it is Counteraction acting in the service of n Inviolacy. One questions whether n Abasement should be considered a drive in its own right. Except for the phenomenon of masochism, Abasement seems always to be an attitude serving some other end: the avoidance of further pain or anticipated punishment, or the desire for passivity, or the desire to show extreme deference.

N AGGRESSION (AGGRESSIVE ATTITUDE). To assault or injure an O. To murder. To belittle, harm, blame, accuse or maliciously ridicule a person. To punish severely. Sadism.

n ABASEMENT (ABASIVE ATTITUDE). To surrender. To comply and accept punishment. To apologize, confess, atone. Self-depreciation. Masochism.

The next need has been given a separate status because it involves a subjectively distinguishable form of behaviour, namely *inhibition*. Objectively, it is characterized by the absence of socially unacceptable conduct. The effect desired by the subject is the avoidance of parental or public disapprobation or punishment. The need rests on the supposition that there are in everybody primitive, asocial impulses, which must be restrained if the individual is to remain an accepted member of his culture.

n BLAMAVOIDANCE (BLAMAVOIDANCE ATTITUDE). To avoid blame, ostracism or punishment by inhibiting asocial or unconventional impulses. To be well-behaved and obey the law.

The next four needs have to do with affection between people; seeking it, exchanging it, giving it, or withholding it.

n AFFILIATION (AFFILIATIVE ATTITUDE). To form friendships and associations. To greet, join, and live with others. To co-operate and converse sociably with others. To love. To join groups.

n REJECTION (REJECTIVE ATTITUDE). To snub, ignore or exclude an O. To remain aloof and indifferent. To be discriminating.

n NURTURANCE (NURTURANT ATTITUDE). To nourish, aid or protect a helpless O. To express sympathy. To "mother" a child.

n SUCCORANCE (SUCCORANT ATTITUDE). To seek aid, protection or sympathy. To cry for help. To plead for mercy. To adhere to an affectionate, nurturant parent. To be dependent.

To these may be added with some hesitation:

n PLAY (PLAYFUL ATTITUDE). To relax, amuse oneself, seek diversion and entertainment. To "have fun," to play games. To laugh, joke and be merry. To avoid serious tension.

Finally, there are two complementary needs which occur with great frequency in social life, the need to ask and the need to tell.

n COGNIZANCE (INQUIRING ATTITUDE). To explore (moving and touching). To ask questions. To satisfy curiosity. To look, listen, inspect. To read and seek knowledge.

n EXPOSITION (EXPOSITIVE ATTITUDE). To point and demonstrate. To relate facts. To give information, explain, interpret, lecture.

On the basis of whether they lead a subject to *approach* or *separate* himself from an object, these derived needs may be divided into those which are *positive* and those which are *negative*, respectively. Positive needs may again be divided into *adient* needs: those which cause a subject to approach a *liked* object, in order to join, amuse, assist, heal, follow or co-operate with it; and *contrient* needs: those which cause a subject to approach a *disliked* object in order to dominate aggressively, abuse, injure, or destroy it. Negative needs, following Holt,[3] are *abient* needs.

This classification of needs is not very different from lists constructed by McDougall, Garnett, and a number of other writers. At first glance it is quite different from the scheme most commonly used in psycho-analysis. According to the latter there are two fundamental urges, or two classes of drives: ego instincts and sex instincts. Among the ego instincts is the hunger drive and the need for aggression. Hunger is rarely mentioned, but within recent years aggression has become one of the chief variables in the analyst's conceptual scheme. Aggression, the concomitant of hate, is considered to be the force which is operating when an individual attacks, injures and murders others. It may also be turned inward, in which case the subject may abuse, mutilate or even kill himself. Contrasting with aggression and other unnamed ego instincts are the sex instincts — the force underlying them all being termed "libido." Under sex has been subsumed:

1. The sex instinct proper, as biologists have described it, that is, the force which leads to the development of sexual characteristics and to intercourse between the sexes (n Sex).

2. All tendencies which seek and promote sensuous gratification (n Sentience), particularly the enjoyment of tactile sensations originating in certain sensitive regions of the body (the erogenous zones). Thus, analysts speak of oral, anal, urethral and genital erotism.

3. All desires and actions which are attended by genital excitement or by that characteristic emotional state — the palpitating, ecstatic-like feeling — which is the usual accompaniment of sexual activity. Here one speaks of the erotization of a need (fusions with n Sex).

4. All manifestations of love and humane feeling: the emotions of a lover, feelings of friendship, social inclinations (n Affiliation) and maternal tenderness (n Nurturance). Here the sex instinct takes the place of the biologist's herd instinct. It binds people together and leads to peace and concord.

5. Self-love, or Narcism, is also considered to be a manifestation of the sex instinct, but here it is the sex instinct turned inward upon the subject (Narcism, or Egophilia).

[3] Holt, F. B., *Animal Drive and the Learning Process*, New York, 1931.

DAVID RAPAPORT

The Theory of Ego Autonomy: A Generalization

My purpose is to bring up to date the summary of the theory of ego autonomy which I presented in 1950.[61] This attempt inevitably leads into theoretically little explored regions, where I can do no more than identify issues and point to possible solutions.

To open up the issues, I will contrast the Berkeleian view of man with the Cartesian. In the Berkeleian view, the outside world is the creation of man's imagination. In this solipsistic view, man is totally *independent* of the environment, and totally *dependent* on the forces and images residing within him: he cannot envisage an external world independent of these inner forces. In turn, he need not come to terms with the outside world: since that world is created by forces inherent in man, he is a priori in harmony with it. In the Cartesian world, on the other hand, man is born as a clean slate upon which experience writes. No forces or images exist in man except for those which arise from the impingements of the outside world. In this world, man is totally *dependent* on and in harmony with the outside world. In turn, he is totally *independent* from, *i.e.* autonomous from,. internal forces, which in this conception do not exist.*

Observation confirms neither of these views. It shows that while man's behavior *is* determined by drive forces which originate in him, it is not totally at their mercy since it has a certain independence from them. We refer to this independence as *the autonomy of the ego from the id.* † The most com-

Reprinted with permission from the *Bulletin of the Menninger Clinic*, Volume 22, pp. 13-35, copyright 1958 by The Menninger Foundation. Some of the footnotes have been omitted. Presented to the Topeka Psychoanalytic Institute, December 11, 1956. This article leans heavily on the concepts of primary and secondary autonomy introduced by Heinz Hartmann, on the psychosocial point of view introduced by Erik Erikson, and on Merton Gill's unpublished theoretical considerations about hypnosis. The specific references to these authors do not sufficiently reflect how much this article owes them.

* This sketch of Berkeley's and Descartes' views is oversimplified. Neither actually held such an extreme view. For instance, *internal forces* (passions) were conceived of in Descartes' system (see his *Passion de l'Ame*), particularly as interferences with the ordered working of the veridical association mechanism.

† This conception was formulated by Hartmann.[29-31] Its roots, however, go back to Freud's treatment of the *secondary process* in the seventh chapter of *The Interpretation of Dreams*,[15] in "Formulations Regarding the Two Principles in Mental Functioning,"[17] and to *The Problem of Anxiety*.[23]

mon observation which necessitated this conception was the responsiveness and relevance of behavior to external reality. But this dependence of behavior on the external world and on experience is not complete either. Man can interpose delay and thought not only between instinctual promptings and action, modifying and even indefinitely postponing drive discharge, he can likewise modify and postpone his reaction to external stimulation. This independence of behavior from external stimulation we will refer to as *the autonomy of the ego from external reality*.* Since the ego is never completely independent from the id nor from external reality, we always speak about *relative* autonomy.

I

My previous discussion of autonomy focused on the relative independence of behavior from internal drive forces. *The* great discovery of psychoanalysis was the existence of these unconscious forces. It took quite a while to realize that this discovery does not compel us to embrace a solipsistic theory in which a chimney is primarily a phallic symbol and only secondarily the means for letting smoke out of the house. It was some time before we began to take account of the chimney as a smokestack, because these realistic meanings were not the focus of our early interests.† However, after psychoanalysis extended its scope to the study of the ego, it became possible and indeed necessary to create conceptual tools to deal with these realistic meanings and their role in behavior. This led to the study of the ego's relative autonomy †† from the id, the guarantee of our relatively even and solid relationship to the outside world.

I tried to illuminate the autonomy of the ego from the id by an old Jewish story** in which Moses' portrait was brought to an Oriental king whose astrologers and phrenologists concluded from it that Moses was a cruel, greedy, craven, self-seeking man. The king, who had heard that Moses was a leader, kindly, generous, and bold, was puzzled, and went to visit Moses. On meeting him, he saw that the portrait was good, and said: "My phrenologists and

* While the psychoanalytic reactions to the theories of the culturalists (Horney, Sullivan, *etc.*) imply some idea of this sort, to date it has not been explicitly formulated. Note, however, Hartmann:[32] "Once the ego has accumulated a reservoir of neutralized energy of its own, it will — in interaction with the outer and the inner world — develop aims and functions whose cathexis can be derived from this reservoir, which means that they have not always to depend on *ad hoc* neutralizations. *This gives the ego a comparative independence from immediate outside or inside pressure, a fact that one is used to considering (though usually not in this terminology) as a general trend in human development*" [ital. mine, D.R.].

† But see Freud.[17]

†† For the concept of relative autonomy see Rapaport.[61]

** I erroneously attributed it to the Talmud. I learned from the late Dr. Maurice Finkelstein that this form of it stems from the 18th century. For a previous history see Ginzberg.[27]

astrologers were wrong." But Moses disagreed: "Your phrenologists and astrologers were right, they saw what I was made of; what they couldn't tell you was that I struggled against all that and so became what I am." In other words, the ego, which arises in the course of life's struggles, can become unlike the original impulses — can be relatively autonomous from them — and can control them.

Now I have another story[60] to illuminate the autonomy of the ego from external reality. "A king returned to his capital followed by his victorious army. The band played and his horse, the army, the people, all moved in step with the rhythm. The king, amazed, contemplated the power of music. Suddenly he noticed a man who walked out of step and slowly fell behind. The king, deeply impressed, sent for the man, and told him: 'I never saw a man as strong as you are. The music enthralled everybody except you. Where do you get the strength to resist it?' The man answered, 'I was pondering, and that gave me the strength.'"

In other words, it is possible for man to maintain relative autonomy, *i.e.* a degree of independence, from his environment. This relative autonomy of man from his environment is the subject of the following discussion.

Though the conception of the relative autonomy of the ego from the id readjusted the position of the id concept in psychoanalytic theory, it did not dispense with the theory of the id nor did it even alter it radically. Likewise, the theory of the ego's relative autonomy from the environment eliminates neither the theory of the ego's autonomy from the id, nor the theory of the id. In fact, far from being rendered superfluous, our theories of the id, of the ego in general, and of the autonomous ego in particular, may appear in a new light and some of the gaps in our knowledge of them may be bridged by developing the theory of the ego's *relative* autonomy from the environment.

There is actually nothing radically new in what follows. To the medical man, it is a commonplace that nonliving matter cannot escape the impact of its environment and its reactions are strictly (or statistically) predictable, but that organisms can escape such impacts, can avoid responding to them, and when they respond, they can do so in a variety of alternative (vicarious) ways. Man's simultaneous relative dependence on and independence from his environment is an issue well within the biological tradition. While psychoanalytic theory, in general, has had a biological cast from the beginning, this did not extend to its consideration of the environment's role in determining behavior.*

Our task is to seek the answers to two questions: What are the guarantees of the ego's autonomy from the environment? How is the autonomy of the ego from the environment related to the autonomy of the ego from the id?

---

* But see Hartmann[30] and Erikson.[10]

II

To approach the first question I will review the guarantees of the ego's relative autonomy from the id. That autonomy is guaranteed by ego apparatuses of primary and secondary autonomy.*

We no longer assume that the ego arises from the id, but rather that the ego and the id both arise by differentiation from a common undifferentiated matrix,[34] in which the apparatuses that differentiate into the ego's means of orientation, of reality-testing, and of action, are already present. These, termed *apparatuses of primary autonomy*, serve drive gratification and enter conflict as independent ego-factors. They are the memory apparatus, the motor apparatus, the perceptual apparatuses, and the threshold apparatuses (including the drive- and affect-discharge thresholds). They are evolutionary givens which, by virtue of their long history of selection and modification, have become the primary guarantees of the organism's "fitting in" with (adaptedness to) its environment.[30] In other words, the primary guarantees of the ego's autonomy from the id seem to be the very apparatuses which guarantee the organism's adaptedness to the environment.

The *apparatuses of secondary autonomy* arise either from instinctual modes and vicissitudes, as these become "estranged"[9] from their instinctual sources, or from defensive structures formed in the process of conflict-solution, as these undergo a "change of function"[30] and become apparatuses serving adaptation. In other words, the apparatuses of secondary autonomy are not "innate" but arise from "experience." Thus this second guarantee of ego autonomy also involves reality relations. While it is obvious that without relationships to a real external environment we would be solipsistic beings, a long detour was necessary before we could see clearly that the autonomy of the ego from the id — our safeguard against solipsism — is guaranteed by these innate and acquired apparatuses which keep us attuned to our environment.

Now to the guarantees of the ego's autonomy from the environment.

The empiricist *nurture* theories of psychology — association theories and simple Pavlovian conditioning theories — have sought no such guarantees. They shared the Cartesian-Humian world view, which, admitting no guarantees of man's autonomy from his environment, makes him virtually a slave to it. Huxley's *Brave New World* is a caricature of this sort of psychology. Academic psychology's recognition that man is not a passive perceiver and not a blank sheet on which experience can write without restriction implies an autonomy conception,[35, 64] but the lack of an explicit autonomy concept was and remains its major impediment. Only a Humian-Cartesian theory can do without a concept of autonomy from the environment, and the validity of such a theory is emphatically contradicted by psychoanalytic observations,

* These concepts were formulated by Hartmann.[29, 31]

which amply demonstrate the survival of pathological behavior forms in defiance of environmental conditions and requirements. In fact, psychoanalytic observations and theory indicate that the instinctual drives are the causal agents and *ultimate guarantees* of the survival of the (pathological and normal) behavior forms which are countermanded by the environment.* The evidence amassed by clinical psychoanalysis for this causal role of drives in the persistence of all symptoms and many character traits is overwhelming.

There seems to be equally good evidence that cognitive organizations, ego interests, values, ideals, ego identity and superego influences — all of which are relatively autonomous from the drives — also play a causal role in the persistence of many behavior forms. However, since the autonomy of these is secondary, they may be regarded as only *proximal guarantees* of the ego's autonomy from the environment. That the drives (*e.g.* sex, hunger), which at peak tension may cause enslavement to the environment should be the *ultimate guarantees* of the autonomy from the environment, is a paradox, which however — as I will attempt to show later on — can be resolved.

Man's constitutionally given drive equipment appears to be the *ultimate* (primary) *guarantee* of the ego's autonomy from the environment, that is, its safeguard against stimulus-response slavery. But this autonomy too has *proximal* (secondary) *guarantees:* namely, higher-order superego and ego structures as well as the motivations pertaining to them. Like the ego's autonomy from the id, its autonomy from the environment also is only relative.

Thus, while the *ultimate guarantees of the ego's autonomy from the id* are man's constitutionally given apparatuses of reality relatedness, the *ultimate guarantees of the ego's autonomy from the environment* are man's constitutionally given drives.

III

To approach the relationship between the two autonomies, let us examine the conditions which interfere with either or both.

Three examples will illustrate the conditions in which the ego's autonomy from the id is impaired. *First,* there are periods of development in which the drives are intensified and threaten this autonomy of the ego. In puberty, the intensified drives interfere with ego autonomy so extensively that the ego combats them with — among other defenses — intellectualization, which is perhaps the most powerful means of enlisting environmental reality and the apparatuses of memory and thought against the encroachments of the id.[14] The adolescent's subjectivity, his rebellion against his environment and his seclusiveness, as well as the converse of these — for instance his striving for

---

* Hartmann[33] wrote: "In his stages of rebelliousness the growing individual also rebels against the commonly accepted view of reality. His tendency toward objective knowledge may also muster the help of instinctual drives. However, after having become autonomous, it may reach a considerable amount of stability."

intellectual understanding and objectivity and the quest for all-embracing companionship – indicate the pubertal intensification of id forces and the consequent decrease of the ego's autonomy. The climacteric (both male and female) often involves a similar loss of ego autonomy.

Some recent experiments will serve as the *second* example. Hebb and his students[3, 36-38] put subjects into a sound-proof, blacked-out room, in which restraints minimized tactile and kinesthetic sensations. They made two important observations: (a) the subjects experienced autistic fantasies and a decrease of their ability to pursue ordered sequences of thought; (b) repetitive verbal information given to the subjects – against the background of the stimulus-void – attained such an impact on their minds that some of them came to experience it as "truth,"[62] that is, this experience approached delusional intensity and persevered for several weeks. Lilly[51, 52] carried out a similar experiment in a blacked-out, sound-proof water tank, in which the subject floated free of gravitational, tactile, and kinesthetic stimulation. His findings corroborated Hebb's. Thus stimulus deprivation too is a condition which may interfere with this autonomy.

Our third example is the hypnotic state.* A common technique of inducing hypnosis is to make the subject concentrate on something and thus in effect to reduce the intake of other external stimulation. The hypnotist further interferes with attention to external stimulation by pouring forth a steady patter. These measures pre-empt the attention cathexes available, and interfere not only with stimulus intake but also with organized, logical, reality-oriented thinking. Thus both the outside and inside sources of signals – which subserve reality orientation and support the ego's autonomy – are blocked. The result – in hypnotizable people – is a regressive state in which the countercathectic barriers differentiating ego and id processes become fluid; images, ideas, and fantasies representing id contents rise to consciousness, and the sense of voluntariness disappears. In the lack of other stimulation which could serve as a comparison, pivot, or means of reality-testing, the utterances of the hypnotist attain a great impact, just like the repetitive information droned at the subject in Hebb's room. The reduction of reality relationships to a single interpersonal relationship, in hypnosis, impairs the ego's autonomy from the id.

Disregarding for the moment the subject's increased susceptibility to the information given in Hebb's room and by the hypnotist, we will consider only the interferences with the ego's autonomy from the id in these three examples.

The generally held assumption that ego structures (controls, defenses, as well as the means used in reality-testing and action) are stable, and altered only by major disorders, is amply justified by the continuity of character and

* The starting point of this paper was Merton Gill's and Margaret Brenman's hypnotic work and their discussions of this work with me throughout the 1940's. Cf. also Kubie and Margolin.[46-48]

behavior, as well as by the great "resistance" these structures offer to therapeutic intervention. The very concept "structure" implies a slow rate of change in comparison to processes of drive-tension accumulation and discharge. Yet Hebb's and Lilly's experiments suggest that these structures depend upon stimulation for their stability, or to use Piaget's terms,[57] they require stimulation as nutriment for their maintenance. When such stimulus-nutriment is not available, the effectiveness of these structures in controlling id impulses may be impaired, and some of the ego's autonomy from the id may be surrendered.* The example of hypnotic induction seems to corroborate this inference, and the interference of intensified drives with ego autonomy may be considered as due to drive representations commanding attention and thus pre-empting the attention cathexes necessary for effective intake of stimulus-nutriment. . . . The interference of passionate love and deep mourning with the ego's autonomy and reality-testing are familiar phenomena, and the work of mourning appears to be the actual process of overcoming the state of absorption which militates against the intake of stimulus-nutriment.[20] Without assuming that ego structures (other than those of primary autonomy) need stimulus-nutriment for their autonomous effectiveness and even for their maintenance, the very process of therapy would be inconceivable (see Section V).

We have long known this dependence on nutriment of certain structures, *e.g.* those underlying the conscious superego. When a man pulls up stakes and moves far away where his past is not known, he is subject to temptations: in the course of his sea voyage, the mutt he left behind may grow into a Saint Bernard, or the painting by a local amateur which he owned may turn into a Rembrandt. The superego is a persistent structure, but its conscious parts seem to require stimulus-nutriment. In the lack of nutriment it becomes prone to compromise and corruption, and the greater their extent, the more mercilessly does the unconscious superego exact its pound of flesh: the unconscious sense of guilt.[22] The maintenance of conscience seems to require the continuous input of the nourishment readily provided by a stable, traditional environment in which the individual is born, grows up, and ends his life; that is, the stimulus of the presence, opinions, and memories of the "others" who have always known him and always will. We seem to choose the social bonds of marriage, friendship, *etc.*, to secure that familiar (paternal, maternal) pattern of stimulation which we need as nutriment for our various superego and ego structures (for example, those which underlie our values and ideologies).†

---

* L. Goldberger and R. R. Holt's isolation study indicates that stimulus deprivation results in differential impairments of various structures and in individual subjects. R. R. Holt (personal communication) raises the question whether these findings are compatible with the "nutriment" explanation given here. The explanation of such differences may lie in the "relativity of autonomy," the degree of which, naturally, varies from individual to individual and from structure to structure, or in the "internal nutriment."

† This is one of the implications of Erikson's psychosocial theory.[8, 11]

Now, some examples of interference with the ego's autonomy from the environment:

First, I will mention those catatonic conditions of echopraxia, echolalia and cerea flexibilitus, which are the prototypes of surrender of the autonomy from the environment. We view these little understood disorders as the results of massive blocking of libidinous and aggressive drives. If this be so, it stands to reason that when these ultimate guarantees of the ego's autonomy from the environment are rendered ineffective, the result is stimulus slavery. The literal and concrete thinking of schizophrenics* may be considered a milder form of this loss of autonomy.

For the *second* example, I take the procedures lumped together under the term "brain-washing." Instead of reviewing the literature, I will discuss Orwell's *Nineteen-Eighty-Four*,[55] in which the writer's intuition epitomizes the means used by most "brain-washing" procedures to bring the individual to the point where the ego's autonomy from the environment is surrendered. The aim of these procedures is not just to force a false *confession* of guilt, but rather to bring about a *profession* of, or a *conversion* to, a particular view and a *belief* in the "facts" pertaining to it.[49, 50]

In the world of *Nineteen-Eighty-Four*, the individual is robbed of his privacy, the environment invades it: whenever the individual is alone he is watched through "telescreens"; whenever he is not driven by his work, he is driven by the "telescreen," which constantly bombards him with information and with instructions which he *must* obey. The language is so simplified that it can convey only factual information and orders; it carries no implications, connotations, allusions, or individual expression. Memory is undermined: when the political alliances of the state change, the books and newspaper files are destroyed and replaced by a revised version which fits the new circumstances. Finally, the fear of unknown but horrible punishment is kept constant. The lack of unobserved privacy coupled with the steady shower of information and orders, the lack of personal expression, the changing records which attack even the continuity vouchsafed by memory, and the mortal fear of punishment, are the means by which the world of *Nineteen-Eighty-Four* robs the individual ego of its autonomy and turns the person into an automaton at the command of the environment. *Nineteen-Eighty-Four* is an overdrawn caricature of our own world and a good montage of "brain-washing" procedures. The individual rebellion which Orwell describes has its roots in a yearning for tenderness, love, and sex, which — as I suggested above — are *ultimate* guarantees of the ego's autonomy from the environment. *Nineteen-Eighty-Four* is fiction, but its implications are corroborated by the evidence available concerning "brain-washing," which indicates that the measures summarized above are potent means for impairing the ego's autonomy from the environment.[49, 50, 65]

* See Kasanin,[39] particularly Benjamin's and Goldstein's contributions.

The *third* example, Bettelheim's paper "Individual and Mass Behavior in Extreme Situations,"[1] (see also Bettelheim[2]) will stand here for all the litera-ture on concentration camps and on Nazi methods of mass psychology. Its study shows that in concentration camps two overlapping sets of conditions interfere with autonomy from the environment, both of which — though not discussed above — obtain to varying degrees in "brain-washing" situations also.

The first set of conditions includes extreme needfulness (hunger, cold, etc.) and danger, as well as an attack on the inmates' "identity" (see Erikson[11]). In extreme needfulness and danger, the drives — which are otherwise the *ultimate guarantees* of this autonomy — endow drive-satisfying objects with a power the effect of which amounts to slavery and surrender of autonomy. The attack on identity (operating through identification with the aggressor, dependence on arbitrary authority akin to the dependence of childhood, and absence of all encomia of status and other supports of identity) impairs the *proximal guarantees* of autonomy.

The second set of conditions includes curtailment of information and stimulation (though less stringent than in Hebb's room), and against the background of this stimulus-void, a steady stream of humiliating, degrading and guilt-arousing information (akin in its role to the repetitive information of the Hebb room and to the hypnotist's patter). The deprivation contributes to the surrender of autonomy both by enhancing needfulness and by providing the background for the steady and overwhelming impact of the environment.

Thus the outstanding conditions which impair the ego's autonomy from the environment are: (1) massive intrapsychic blocking of the instinctual drives which are the *ultimate guarantees* of this autonomy; (2) maximized needful-ness, danger, and fear which enlist the drives (usually the guarantees of this autonomy) to prompt surrender of autonomy; (3) lack of privacy, deprivation of stimulus-nutriment, memorial and verbal supports, all of which seem to be necessary for the maintenance of the structures (thought-structures, values, ideologies, identity) which are the *proximal guarantees* of this autonomy; (4) a steady stream of instructions and information which, in the lack of other stimulus-nutriment, attain such power that they have the ego completely at their mercy.*

Just as with the guarantees of autonomy from the id, neither the *ultimate* nor the *proximal* guarantees of autonomy from the environment are absolute. Both autonomies require external and/or drive stimulation of a specific in-tensity and quality for maintenance and effectiveness.

IV

We are now ready to examine the relations between the ego's two autonomies. In hypnotic states (as well as in Hebb's room) both autonomy from the id

---

* Cf. Gruenthal's explanation of the Korsakow thought disorder, in Buerger-Prinz and Kaila[5] (p. 659 ff., particularly the footnotes).

and from the environment are impaired. How are such impairments related to each other?

A consideration of certain aspects of compulsive and obsessional disorders may serve to clarify the relationships.[18] What follows is only an *ex parte* consideration of these conditions, a supplement to, not a substitute for, the knowledge we have of them. One of the concomitants of obsessive-compulsive conditions is an increased elaboration of the secondary process. This elaboration has two aspects: on the one hand, it provides means for the defenses of intellectualization and isolation; on the other hand it enables intensified observation and logical analysis to substitute for affective and ideational signals, those natural regulators of judgment and decision which are suppressed by obsessive-compulsive defenses.

Obsessive-compulsive defense thus maximizes the ego's autonomy from the id, but it does so at the cost of an ever-increasing impairment of the ego's autonomy from the environment: the suppression of affective and ideational cues of drive origin renders the ego's judgments and decisions increasingly dependent on external cues. Hence the infirmness of convictions and gullibility of certain obsessive people, but also — as a reaction-formation — the blind and rigid clinging to a view once it has been adopted. An extreme form of the obsessive's lack of internal steering is his paralyzing doubt, which may border on the stimulus-slavery of the catatonic conditions discussed above. But while the ego's autonomy from the environment is reduced, another development also takes place. The drives and their representations, whose access to motility and consciousness was so strenuously barred, invade "objective" reality by infiltrating the very thought processes and logic which were elaborated to curb them, and succeed in filling the person's perception and thought with magic and animism.

Thus maximizing the ego's autonomy from the id reduces the ego's autonomy from the environment and results in stimulus slavery. Conversely, the reduction of the ego's autonomy from the id (as by the intensification of drives) results in a loss of touch with reality, which amounts to a maximized autonomy from the environment. In turn, maximizing the ego's autonomy from the environment (as in stimulus deprivation) results in a reduction of the ego's autonomy from the id; and the reduction of the ego's autonomy from the environment may result in a maximized autonomy from the id. But can such maximized or minimized autonomy of the ego, either in relation to the id or in relation to the environment, still be considered autonomy in the proper sense of the word?

Let us examine, for instance, stimulus deprivation as maximized autonomy. It is not that the ego's autonomy from the environment reaches its maximum, but rather that the ego has to make do with an environment which provides insufficient stimulus-nutriment for its structures. Stimulus deprivation provides a test of the limits of the ego's autonomy from the environment.*

* This formulation was suggested by Dr. Stuart C. Miller.

Examination of the other instances of "maximized" or "minimized" autonomy leads to similar conclusions.

Yet these extreme instances provide good models for the relationships of the autonomies. They show that the ego's autonomy from the id may be impaired either when its necessary dependence on the environment is excessively increased, or when environmental support is excessively decreased. Likewise, the ego's autonomy from the environment may be impaired when either its necessary independence from or its necessary dependence on the id becomes excessive. Since these autonomies are always relative, their extremes are never reached. Hence, a further implication of the relativity of the autonomies is: only a relative autonomy of the ego from the id — that is, only autonomy within the optimal range — is compatible with a relative — that is, optimal — autonomy of the ego from the environment, and vice versa. This conclusion is consistent with the one reached in our discussion of the autonomy guarantees. Since reality relations guarantee autonomy from the id, excessive autonomy from the environment must impair the autonomy from the id; and since drives are the ultimate guarantees of the autonomy from the environment, an excessive autonomy from the id must impair the autonomy from the environment.

Whether the treatment of these issues in terms of autonomies and their relations is more useful than a treatment in terms of the dependence on (or distance from) id and environment, remains to be seen.

V

Do the concepts of ego autonomies and of their relationships have any immediate relevance for clinical psychoanalysis and psychotherapy?[24] They seem to be relevant, though it is hard to say whether they capture something new or merely translate something already known into a new language.

The technical conditions of psychoanalysis — the couch, the injunction against "acting out," the psychoanalyst as a blank screen, etc. — involve stimulus deprivation. Psychoanalytic technique explicitly recognizes that a reduction of contact with reality is necessary to permit id derivatives to rise to consciousness. Effective application of this technique brings about a shift in the autonomy balance, increasing autonomy from the environment and decreasing autonomy from the id. Once the theory of autonomy is consolidated, it may become a cornerstone of the theory of psychoanalytic *technique*: there has been a continuous increase in our knowledge of psychoanalytic technique, its applications, and its problems,[12, 13] but the *theory* of the technique, and particularly its metapsychology, has sadly lagged behind.

The autonomy conceptions also have immediate relevance for the psychotherapy of borderline cases.[40-42] The modifications of psychoanalytic technique for this purpose replaced the couch by the face-to-face situation, the relatively silent psychoanalyst by the participating and supporting psychotherapist, etc., and thus lessened the stimulus-deprivation.[7] However, it is still not clear when a borderline case, or a severe neurotic, should or should not be "taken off the couch." We still do not know when stimulus deprivation will tend to overshoot the therapeutically necessary "regression in the service of and under the control of the ego," and lead to pathological regression. But we do know that the relative and reversible reduction of the ego's autonomy from the id — which the technical rules are designed to foster — can get out of hand. How to achieve therapeutically effective insight, while guarding against further regressive, pathological reduction of the ego's autonomy from the id, and against further impairment of the patient's reality relationships, is one of the fundamental problems of the psychotherapy of borderline cases, and perhaps of all therapy.

Psychiatric hospitals for the psychotherapy of borderline and psychotic patients are faced with the problem of organizing the patient's everyday life so as to combat the tendency of hospitalization and of insight-seeking psychotherapy to foster regression.[58, 59] Hospitalization tends to reduce the environmental stimulus-nutriment necessary to those structures which guarantee the ego's autonomy from the id and from the environment. The self-absorption attendant on psychotherapy accentuates this effect of hospitalization. On the other hand, the removal of the patient from his usual surroundings to a hospital, and psychotherapy itself, tend to deprive those defensive structures which have become part and parcel of the patient's pathology of their stimulus-nutriment, and thereby undermine their effectiveness and persistence. (The effect of hospitalization and psychotherapy on the vicious circle of a sadomasochistic symbiosis is an obvious example of this.)

VI

The concept of nutriment is derived from Piaget.[57]* According to him, "structures of intelligence" arise by differentiation from constitutionally given sensorimotor coordinations, but require stimulus-nutriment to do so. So far no evidence exists to clarify the relationship between Piaget's structures and those structures which psychoanalytic theory has conceptualized. But since our considerations suggest that psychoanalytic "structures" require stimulus-nutriment for their *maintenance* and *effectiveness*, the question arises: does the *development* as well as the maintenance and effectiveness of psychoanalytic "structures" require stimulus-nutriment?

To explore this question, let us consider the differences between the stimuli withdrawn in the various situations discussed. The stimulus-deprivation experiments withdraw that stimulus-nutriment which, conveyed through the senses, is necessary for the maintenance and effectiveness of elementary reality orientation. This nutriment is never directly and massively removed in the psychoanalytic situation, which, though it fosters the voluntary and/or spon-

---

* Note particularly his distinction of this concept from learning theory's "reinforcement" and "practice."

taneous renunciation of such nutriment, is really aimed at the nutriment of those structures which underlie proprieties, logical orderliness, defenses, etc.[16] Nor do the concentration camp and brain-washing procedures bank primarily on the withdrawal of this elementary stimulus-nutriment, though they have used that too as an auxiliary technique. The concentration camp removes first of all the nutriment of the structures underlying dignity, self-respect, and identity.[1, 2] The aim of brain-washing is to remove the nutriment for the structures which underlie beliefs, political convictions, ideology, social and personal allegiances, and ultimately identity.[49, 50] These differences point to what psychoanalysis has already discovered about defenses, controls, etc., namely that psychological structures form a complex hierarchy within the psychic apparatus.[66] Moreover, these differences suggest that the structures on each hierarchic level may require a different nutriment, ranging from simple, minimally organized sensory stimulations, to those complex experiences which a society provides to maintain, in its individuals, ideological beliefs and identities compatible with that society.

Once the differences in the stimulus-nutriment required for the maintenance of various structures are observed, we begin to see what evidence there is that the structures psychoanalysis deals with require stimulus-nutriment for their *development*. The vicissitudes of instincts and the development of defenses and controls are codetermined by experience, and reconstructions in therapy show that the effectiveness of the experience in question always stems from an antecedent "complementary series" of experiences. Thus the dependence of such structure development upon stimulus-nutriment becomes probable, though our reconstructions of these complementary series usually do not carry us back to simple sensory stimulus-nutriments.

The dependence of such structure development upon stimulus-nutriment has, however, been stated in more specific terms by Erikson. He has shown that the development of the social modalities of behavior proceeds from the organ modes in general and from the modes of erogenous zones in particular, as these become "estranged," *i.e.* differentiated, from their zone. He has also demonstrated that the occurrence of this differentiation, and the quality of the behavior modality which is its product, are codetermined by the impact of traditions and institutions provided by the society in which the individual develops, and by the social "niches" available in it.[10, 8] * Thus Erikson's organ-modes and Piaget's sensory-motor coordinations seem to be analogous points of departure for structure development; likewise Erikson's institutions and Piaget's stimuli appear to be analogous nutriments for structure development. Thus, just like Piaget's "intelligence structures," the psychological structures Erikson studied (including such primitive behavior modalities as giving and taking, and as complex ones as value, role, ideology, and identity) appear to depend on stimulus-nutriment provided by the environment. Since these

* See especially chapters two, six and seven.

structures shade into those customarily discussed by psychoanalysis, the role of stimulus-nutriment in structure development may prove ubiquitous.* But it should be noted that the nutriment of the structures dealt with by psychoanalysis in general, and by Erikson in particular, is of a highly organized character in contrast to the nutriment of those structures discussed by Piaget.

Erikson has furthermore emphasized that the structure development — termed ego development — here discussed, even though codetermined by drives and environmental stimulus-nutriment, follows a lawful sequence of its own, *i.e.* it is autonomous. This facet of ego autonomy we have not discussed so far,† though it is crucial since if ego development were not autonomous, only *secondary* ego autonomy (derived either from drives or from environmental influences or from *ad hoc* combinations of the two) would be conceivable. Autonomous ego development (its sequence and regulative principles) is a primary guarantee of ego-autonomy: it links the apparatuses of secondary autonomy to those of primary autonomy and regulates both the environmental and drive contributions to ego structure formation.

Before leaving this subject, we must at least touch on the crucial observation that structures can persist and remain effective even when deprived of external stimulus-nutriment. What are the facts and how are they to be explained?

The already mentioned study by Goldberger and Holt shows that some structures (*e.g.* "style-structures") are relatively little affected by short-term stimulus deprivation and recover rapidly once such deprivation is terminated. Persistence in spite of deprivation is a hallmark of autonomy. Since autonomy is relative, long-range persistence despite deprivation needs further explanation. It is known that people have spent years in solitary confinement without suffering striking impairments of either of the ego-autonomies, and that people have maintained their ego-autonomy in spite of "brain-washing," though of these only a few have survived to tell the tale.[4, 69] There is the familiar figure of the Englishman who, totally isolated from the setting which would provide the natural nutriment for his proprieties, traditions, outlook and values, maintains these essentially unchanged in the solitude of the jungle or the desert. Last but not least, clinical and therapeutic observation shows that defenses (in the form of both character traits and symptoms) may survive without tangible environmental nourishment, or where the person has to "provoke" nourishment from the environment.††

---

* The literature on "wild" and "autistic" children is pertinent here.

† Autonomous ego development has been repeatedly discussed by Hartmann. See also R. Loewenstein.[53] But Erikson was the first to trace its course,[9] and to propose a scheme encompassing its phases.[8, 10]

†† "Provocative" and "demanding" behavior may well appear in a different light when treated as quests for stimulus-nutriment. A. Schmale's discussion (unpublished memoranda of the Conferences on Separation, Depression and Illness, of the Department

This survival of defense structures without external stimulus-nutriment is understood by psychoanalysis: these structures are maintained, ultimately, by internal (drive) stimulus-nutriment.[23] Clinical evidence shows that values, ideologies, and even more complex structures (like identity) too may be maintained by drive-nutriment, to the degree to which they are part of a defensive system. The explanation of the maintenance of such higher order ego structures in instances of solitary confinement seems at first glance equally obvious: the method of survival seems to be a deliberate application of physical and mental exercise to prevent weakening of ego autonomy and drifting into fearful or wishful daydreaming, or into mindless, empty surrender. This deliberate application has taken various forms: physical exercise, a chronological review of past life, mental arithmetic, solving all sorts of other problems, dictionary-making in several languages, or reviewing other kinds of knowledge.

But what, in these cases, is the intrapsychic source of this deliberate application, which is the *proximal provider* of stimulus-nutriment? We cannot seek this source in the ultimate drive nutriment because, as we have seen, in extreme deprivation situations, drive nutriment tends to abet surrender of the autonomy from the environment. Nor would it do to seek the source simply in *ego identity*:[11] though the major attack of such confinements is on ego identity, and stronger ego identities will persist better, to locate the source of stimulus-nutriment *solely* and without further analysis in ego identity would amount to a vicious circle.

The reports of the unscathed survivors of solitary confinement reveal little about the internal source of nutriment. More suggestive are the reports of people whose autonomy from either the id or the environment was on the brink of destruction, but was restored at the last moment by what might be described as a conversion experience.[6, 28, 54] While we are far from a full understanding of conversion experiences, what we do know about them, and what we can infer from these reports, points primarily to the superego, but also to ego interests and ego identity as the sources of voluntary application.

Tentatively, then, it may be assumed that in certain people strikingly, but probably in all people to some degree, external stimulus-nutriment may be replaced by internal nutriment. This nutriment may take the form of various deliberate activities, whose motivations (*i.e.*, the *ultimate* source of the nourishment) may be drives, superego, ego identity or ego interests, depending on the structure involved. Hartmann[29, 31] made it plausible that we have to assume the existence of intrasystematic conflicts within the ego; likewise it may become necessary to assume intrasystemic cooperation of forces by which one substructure of the ego would give rise to ego forces which, by initiating (motor or thought) activity, would provide stimulus-nutriment to other sub-

---

of Psychiatry, University of Rochester Medical School) of the "object" concept, in relation to the role "separation" plays in psychosomatic disorders, may be considered a step towards such a treatment.

structures, enabling them to function and to give rise to their own brand of ego interests, which in turn would initiate activity providing stimulus-nutriment for yet other ego substructures. Indeed it seems probable that closed circles of such mutually sustaining structures can persist — within those limits which show up ultimately as the relativity of autonomy. Since various structures require different external stimulus-nutriment, it is likely that each requires a different kind of internal nutriment also.

VII

This paper has underplayed the id aspects of the phenomena discussed, and has hardly mentioned points showing that this treatment of autonomy is phenomenological and thus incomplete. Yet the concept of autonomy is but one aspect of ego-psychology, which in turn — just like id-psychology — is only a part of psychoanalytic theory. Metapsychology has also been underplayed, and thus the impression may have arisen that these autonomy considerations are phenomenological in essence and lack a metapsychological foundation. But the concept of ego-autonomy is amenable to metapsychological analysis.[63, 68]

Classic metapsychology comprises the dynamic, economic and structural points of view. Gill and I[26] have attempted to demonstrate that this triad must be supplemented by the genetic point of view (which has always been explicit in psychoanalytic theory), and the adaptive point of view (the indispensability of which has become clear in the last two decades). Gill's discussion[25] of the metapsychology of regression in general and of hypnotic regression in particular has provided the framework for the metapsychological treatment of the autonomies, and we do have partial metapsychological treatments of the ego's autonomy from the id. My discussion of the hierarchy of derivative drives (motivations) is an implicit treatment of this autonomy from the dynamic and genetic points of view;[63, 66*] the use of the neutralization concept by Hartmann[29] and Kris[43, 44] has laid the foundation for the treatment of autonomy from the economic point of view. Hartmann's discussions of autonomy, "automatization" and "functional change,"[30] and Kris's discussions of "regression in the service of the ego"[45] are treatments of this autonomy from the structural point of view. Hartmann's conception of adaptation and reality,[33] and Erikson's conception of psychosocial ego-epigenesis,[10, 8†] treat it from the adaptive point of view.

But so far we have no comparable treatments of the ego's autonomy from the environment. This missing link must be provided before the autonomies and their relation to each other can be given a full-scale metapsychological treatment. In an attempt to fill part of this gap, I will review here a so-far unpublished paper[67] in which I proposed dual conceptual models for activity and passivity.

* See especially Part VII.
† See chapter seven.

The *first model of passivity* is the situation of helplessness which ensues when mounting drive tension meets a countercathectic barrier and tension discharge is prevented. The *second model of passivity:* the situation in which the discharge of accumulated drive tension occurs *without* a contribution by the ego. Since drive discharge always involves executive ego apparatuses, the latter situation never exists in reality, but it does exist as a psychological reality in fantasies of wish-fulfillment and in therapeutic reconstructions. The *first model of activity* is the discharge of drive tension by means of the ego's control and executive apparatuses. The *second model of activity* is the defensive and/or controlling prevention or postponement of the drive discharge by the ego.

Let us compare the first model of passivity with the second model of activity. The first model of passivity refers to a non-autonomous ego which does not regulate id-tension but rather is regulated by it, since the more the drive tension mounts the more unyielding the ego's discharge-barring function becomes. In contrast, the second model of activity refers to a relatively autonomous ego, which controls, postpones, or prevents drive discharge in keeping with the demands of its own organization, but also in veiw of the state of the whole organism and the reality circumstances. Likewise a comparison of the second model of passivity and the first model of activity shows that the former refers to a non-autonomous ego, that is, to a condition dominated and regulated by drive tension, while the latter refers to an autonomous ego which executes drive discharge in keeping with its controls, but also with regard to the economy of the whole psychic apparatus (or organism), and the reality circumstances.

Now, these models should be complemented by a parallel set representing the passive endurance of and the passive response to external stimulation as well as the active endurance of and the active response to it. It seems that as soon as the "stimulus barriers" and sensory thresholds become insufficient to scale down external stimulation to manageable intensities, psychological — that is, countercathectic — barriers come into play. These in turn seem to be naturally integrated with — and often identical to — the countercathectic barriers which control drive discharge. If these relationships can be conclusively demonstrated, the explanation of the interrelations between the autonomies as well as those between external stimuli and drives will be at hand. The paper referred to did not deal with these latter models of activity and passivity, and was thus incomplete.

If it is realized that the establishment of the "inner world"[30] and of representations (of drives as well as of external objects) is a turning of "passive" sensorimotor experience into activity (as Piaget has demonstrated[56, 57, 70]), if, furthermore, we keep in mind the clinical facts which show that the turning of passive experience into active performance is at the core of psychological structure development;[19, 21] and finally, if it is noted that the drive and/or stimulus versus structure balance expressed in these conceptions of activity and passivity is at the core of the problems of pathology, then the suggested relation of the ego's autonomies to the conditions of the ego's activity and passivity places the autonomy concepts in the very center of our clinical and metapsychological theory. Moreover, since a metapsychological analysis of activity and passivity appears possible, a way seems to be open to a full-fledged metapsychological treatment of the autonomies.

VIII

Summing up, the organism is endowed by evolution with apparatuses which prepare it for contact with its environment, but its behavior is not a slave of this environment since it is also endowed with drives which rise from its organization, and are the ultimate guarantees against stimulus slavery. In turn, the organism's behavior is not simply the expression of these internal forces, since the very apparatuses through which the organism is in contact with its environment are the ultimate guarantees against drive slavery. These autonomies have proximal guarantees also, in intrapsychic structures. The balance of these mutually controlling factors does not depend on the outcome of their chance interactions, but is controlled by the laws of the epigenetic sequence, termed autonomous ego-development.

Both kinds of protective intrapsychic structures are essential components of the ego's structure and organization and the behavior attributes, conceptualized as ego-autonomies, are characteristics of this ego structure and organization. These structures need nutriment for their development, maintenance and effectiveness, and their ultimate nutriments are drive stimuli on the one hand and external stimuli on the other. But such nutriment is also provided by other ego structures and by the motivations arising from them, and the more autonomous the ego, the more the nutriment is provided from these internal sources. But this "proportionality" obtains only within an optimal range, since ego-autonomy from the id and ego-autonomy from the environment mutually guarantee each other only within an optimal range. Maximization or minimization of either disrupts their balance. *Thus these autonomies are always relative.* In terms of the story with which I introduced our problem, the strength which makes a man independent from reality stimulation tends to lead him to build an impenetrable wall around himself.

The ego's autonomy may be defined in terms of ego activity, and impairment of autonomy in terms of ego passivity. The old adage, that freedom is the acceptance of the restraints of the law, returns to us here with renewed significance. The elementary phenomenology from which we started seems to have led us into the very center of metapsychological considerations.

BIBLIOGRAPHY

1. Bettelheim, Bruno. "Individual and Mass Behavior in Extreme Situations." *J. Abnorm. & Soc. Psychol.* 36:417–452, 1943.

2. _____. "The Dynamism of Anti-Semitism in Gentile and Jew." *J. Abnorm. & Soc. Psychol.* 42:153–168, 1947.

3. Bexton, W. H., Heron, Woodburn and Scott, T. H. "Effects of Decreased Variation in the Sensory Environment." *Canad. J. Psychol.* 8:70–76, 1954.

4. Bone, E. *Prisoner in Hungary.* London, Hamish Hamilton, 1957.

5. Buerger-Prinz, Hans and Kaila, Martti. "On the Structure of the Amnesic Syndrome." In *Organization and Pathology of Thought,* David Rapaport, ed. New York, Columbia University, 1951, pp. 650–686.

6. Burney, Christopher. *Solitary Confinement.* New York, Coward-McCann, 1953.

7. Eissler, K. R. "Ego-Psychological Implications of the Psychoanalytic Treatment of Delinquents." *Psa. Study of the Child* 5:97–121, 1950.

8. Erikson, E. H. *Childhood and Society.* New York, Norton, 1950.

9. _____. "Configurations in Play — Clinical Notes." *Psa. Quart.* 6:139–214, 1937.

10. _____. "Growth and Crisis of the 'Healthy Personality.' " In *Personality in Nature, Society and Culture,* 2nd ed., Clyde Kluckhohn and H. A. Murray, eds. New York, Knopf, 1953, pp. 185–225.

11. _____. "The Problem of Ego Identity." *J. Am. Psa. Assn.* 4:56–121, 1956.

12. Fenichel, Otto. "Concerning the Theory of Psychoanalytic Technique." *Collected Papers,* First Series. New York, Norton, 1953, pp. 332–348.

13. _____. *Problems of Psychoanalytic Technique.* Albany, New York, Psychoanalytic Quarterly, 1941.

14. Freud, Anna. *The Ego and the Mechanisms of Defence.* New York, International Universities, 1946.

15. Freud, Sigmund (1900). "The Interpretation of Dreams." In *The Basic Writings of Sigmund Freud,* A. A. Brill, ed. New York, Modern Library, 1938, pp. 179–549.

16. _____ (1910–1919). "Papers on Technique." *Collected Papers* 2:285–402, 1924.

17. _____ (1911). "Formulations Regarding the Two Principles in Mental Functioning." *Collected Papers.* 4:13–21, 1925.

18. _____ (1911). "Psychoanalytic Notes Upon an Autobiographical Account of a Case of Paranoia (Dementia Paranoides)." *Collected Papers* 3:387–470, 1925.

19. _____ (1915). "Instincts and Their Vicissitudes." *Collected Papers* 4:60–83, 1925.

20. _____ (1917). "Mourning and Melancholia." *Collected Papers* 4:152–170, 1925.

21. _____ (1920). *Beyond the Pleasure Principle.* London, Hogarth, 1942.

22. _____ (1923). *The Ego and the Id.* London, Hogarth, 1927.

23. _____ (1926). *The Problem of Anxiety.* New York, Psychoanalytic Quarterly and Norton, 1936.

24. Gill, Merton. "Psychoanalysis and Exploratory Psychotherapy." *J. Am. Psa. Assn.* 2:771–797, 1954.

25. _____ and Brenman, Margaret. *Hypnosis: A Research Report.* (In preparation.)

26. _____ and Rapaport, David. "A Reconsideration of Psychoanalytic Metapsychology." (Unpublished manuscript.)

27. Ginzberg, Louis. *Legends of the Jews,* Vol. 2. Philadelphia, Jewish Publication Society of America, 1946, p. 276.

28. Gollwitzer, Helmut and others, eds. *Dying We Live.* New York, Pantheon, 1956.

29. Hartmann, Heinz. "Comments on the Psychoanalytic Theory of the Ego." *Psa. Study of the Child* 5:74–96, 1950.

30. _____. "Ich-Psychologie und Anpassungsproblem." *Int. Z. Psa. Imago* 24:62–135, 1939; abridged translation, "Ego Psychology and the Problem of Adaptation" in

Organization and Pathology of Thought, David Rapaport, ed. New York, Columbia University, 1951, pp. 362–396.

31. _____. "The Mutual Influences in the Development of the Ego and Id." *Psa. Study of the Child* 7:9–30, 1952.
32. _____. "Notes on the Theory of Sublimation." *Psa. Study of the Child* 10:9–29, 1955.
33. _____. "Notes on the Reality Principle." *Psa Study of the Child* 11:31–53, 1956.
34. _____, Kris, Ernst and Loewenstein, R. M. "Comments on the Formation of Psychic Structure." *Psa. Study of the Child* 2:11–38, 1946.
35. Hebb, D. O. *The Organization of Behavior: A Neuropsychological Theory.* New York, Wiley, 1949.
36. Heron, Woodburn. "The Pathology of Boredom." *Sci. Am.* 196:52–56, 1957.
37. _____, Bexton, W. H. and Hebb, D. O. "Cognitive Effects of a Decreased Variation in the Sensory Environment." *Am. Psychol.* 8:366, 1953.
38. _____, Doane, B. K. and Scott, T. H. "Visual Disturbances after Prolonged Perceptual Isolation." *Canad. J. Psychol.* 10:13–18, 1956.
39. Kasanin, J. S., ed. *Language and Thought in Schizophrenia.* Berkeley, University of California, 1944.
40. Knight, R. P. "Borderline States." *Bull. Menninger Clin.* 17:1–12, 1953.
41. _____. "Management and Psychotherapy of the Borderline Schizophrenic Patient." *Bull. Menninger Clin.* 17:139–150, 1953.
42. _____ and Friedman, C. R., eds. *Psychoanalytic Psychiatry and Psychology, Clinical and Theoretical Papers,* Vol. 1. New York, International Universities, 1954.
43. Kris, Ernst. "On Preconscious Mental Processes." *Psa. Quart.* 19:540–560, 1950.
44. _____. "On Some Vicissitudes of Insight in Psychoanalysis." *Int. J. Psa.* 37:445–455, 1956.
45. _____. *Psychoanalytic Explorations in Art.* New York, International Universities, 1952.
46. Kubie, L. S. "The Use of Induced Hypnagogic Reveries in the Recovery of Repressed Amnesic Data." *Bull. Menninger Clin.* 7:172–182, 1943.
47. _____ and Margolin, Sydney. "A Physiological Method for the Induction of States of Partial Sleep, and Securing Free Association and Early Memories in Each State." *Trans. Am. Neurol. Assn.* 68:136–139, 1942.
48. _____ and Margolin, Sydney. "The Process of Hypnotism and the Nature of the Hypnotic State." *Am. J. Psychiat.* 100:611–622, 1943.
49. Lifton, R. J. "Thought Reform of Chinese Intellectuals: A Psychiatric Evaluation." *J. Asian Stud.* 16:75–88, 1956.
50. _____. " 'Thought Reform' of Western Civilians in Chinese Communist Prisons." *Psychiatry* 19:173–195, 1956.
51. Lilly, J. C. Discussion in *Illustrative Strategies for Research on Psychopathology in Mental Health,* Symposium No. 2, Group for the Advancement of Psychiatry, June, 1956, pp. 13–20.
52. _____. "Mental Effects of Reduction of Ordinary Levels of Physical Stimuli on Intact, Healthy Persons." *Psychiat. Res. Reports* 5:1–9, 1956.
53. Loewenstein, Rudolph M. "Some Remarks on Defenses, Autonomous Ego and Psychoanalytic Technique." *Int. J. Psa.* 35:188–193, 1954.
54. Moen, P. *Peter Moen's Diary.* London, Faber and Faber, n.d.
55. Orwell, George. *Nineteen-Eighty-Four.* New York, Harcourt, Brace, 1949.

56. Piaget, Jean. *The Construction of Reality in the Child.* New York, Basic Books, 1954.
57. ———. *The Origins of Intelligence in Children.* New York, International Universities, 1952.
58. Polansky, N. A., Miller, S. C. and White, R. B. "Determinants of the Role-Image of the Patient in a Psychiatric Hospital." In *The Patient and the Mental Hospital,* Milton Greenblatt, ed. Glencoe, Ill., Free Press, 1957, pp. 380–401.
59. ———. "Some Reservations Regarding Group Psychotherapy in Inpatient Psychiatric Treatment." *Group Psychother.* 8:254–262, 1955.
60. Popper-Lynkeus, J. "Zeichen der Macht." In *Die Phantasien eines Realisten.* Dresden, Reissner, 1922.
61. Rapaport, David. "The Autonomy of the Ego." *Bull. Menninger Clin.* 15:113–123, 1951.
62. ———. "Cognition, Cognitive Organizations, and Consciousness." Presented at the Symposium on Cognition, Boulder, Colorado, 1955. (In press.)
63. ———. "The Conceptual Model of Psychoanalysis." *J. Pers.* 20:56–81, 1951–52.
64. ———. "Discussion of C. Osgood's 'A Behavioristic Analysis of Perception and Meaning as Cognitive Phenomena.'" Presented at the Symposium on Cognition, Boulder, Colorado, 1955. (In press.)
65. ———. Discussion in *Mass Communications Seminar: Proceedings of an Interdisciplinary Seminar,* H. Powdermaker, ed. New York, Wenner-Gren Foundation, 1953, pp. 121–128.
66. ———, ed. *Organization and Pathology of Thought.* New York, Columbia University, 1951.
67. ———. "Some Metapsychological Considerations Concerning Activity and Passivity." Given at the Austen Riggs Center, 1953. (Unpublished manuscript.)
68. ———. "The Structure of Psychoanalytic Theory (A Systematizing Attempt)." In *Systematic Resources of Psychology,* S. Koch, ed. (In press.)
69. Weissberg, Alexander. *Conspiracy of Silence.* London, Hamish Hamilton, 1952.
70. Wolff, P. H. *Piaget and Psychoanalysis.* (In preparation.)

ERIK H. ERIKSON

Eight Ages of Man

Basic Trust Versus Basic Mistrust

The first demonstration of social trust in the baby is the ease of his feeding, the depth of his sleep, the relaxation of his bowels. The experience of a mutual regulation of his increasingly receptive capacities with the maternal techniques of provision gradually helps him to balance the discomfort caused by the immaturity of homeostasis with which he was born. In his gradually increasing waking hours he finds that more and more adventures of the senses arouse a feeling of familiarity, of having coincided with a feeling of inner goodness. Forms of comfort, and people associated with them, become as familiar as the gnawing discomfort of the bowels. The infant's first social achievement, then, is his willingness to let the mother out of sight without undue anxiety or rage, because she has become an inner certainty as well as an outer predictability. Such consistency, continuity, and sameness of experience provide a rudimentary sense of ego identity which depends, I think, on the recognition that there is an inner population of remembered and anticipated sensations and images which are firmly correlated with the outer population of familiar and predictable things and people.

What we here call trust coincides with what Therese Benedek has called confidence. If I prefer the word "trust," it is because there is more naïveté and more mutuality in it: an infant can be said to be trusting where it would go too far to say that he has confidence. The general state of trust, furthermore, implies not only that one has learned to rely on the sameness and continuity of the outer providers, but also that one may trust oneself and the capacity of one's own organs to cope with urges; and that one is able to consider oneself trustworthy enough so that the providers will not need to be on guard lest they be nipped.

The constant tasting and testing of the relationship between inside and outside meets its crucial test during the rages of the biting stage, when the teeth cause pain from within and when outer friends either prove of no avail or withdraw from the only action which promises relief: biting. Not that

Reprinted from *Childhood and Society*, Second Edition, Revised, by Erik H. Erikson. By permission of W. W. Norton & Company, Inc. Copyright 1950, © 1963 by W. W. Norton & Company, Inc.

teething itself seems to cause all the dire consequences sometimes ascribed to it. As outlined earlier, the infant now is driven to "grasp" more, but he is apt to find desired presences elusive: nipple and breast, and the mother's focused attention and care. Teething seems to have a prototypal significance and may well be the model for the masochistic tendency to assure cruel comfort by enjoying one's hurt whenever one is unable to prevent a significant loss.

In psychopathology the absence of basic trust can best be studied in infantile schizophrenia, while lifelong underlying weakness of such trust is apparent in adult personalities in whom withdrawal into schizoid and depressive states is habitual. The re-establishment of a state of trust has been found to be the basic requirement for therapy in these cases. For no matter what conditions may have caused a psychotic break, the bizarreness and withdrawal in the behavior of many very sick individuals hides an attempt to recover social mutuality by a testing of the borderlines between senses and physical reality, between words and social meanings.

Psychoanalysis assumes the early process of differentiation between inside and outside to be the origin of projection and introjection which remain some of our deepest and most dangerous defense mechanisms. In introjection we feel and act as if an outer goodness had become an inner certainty. In projection, we experience an inner harm as an outer one: we endow significant people with the evil which actually is in us. These two mechanisms, then, projection and introjection, are assumed to be modeled after whatever goes on in infants when they would like to externalize pain and internalize pleasure, an intent which must yield to the testimony of the maturing senses and ultimately of reason. These mechanisms are, more or less normally, reinstated in acute crises of love, trust, and faith in adulthood and can characterize irrational attitudes toward adversaries and enemies in masses of "mature" individuals.

The firm establishment of enduring patterns for the solution of the nuclear conflict of basic trust versus basic mistrust in mere existence is the first task of the ego, and thus first of all a task for maternal care. But let it be said here that the amount of trust derived from earliest infantile experience does not seem to depend on absolute quantities of food or demonstrations of love, but rather on the quality of the maternal relationship. Mothers create a sense of trust in their children by that kind of administration which in its quality combines sensitive care of the baby's individual needs and a firm sense of personal trustworthiness within the trusted framework of their culture's life style. This forms the basis in the child for a sense of identity which will later combine a sense of being "all right," of being oneself, and of becoming what other people trust one will become. There are, therefore (within certain limits previously defined as the "musts" of child care), few frustrations in either this or the following stages which the growing child cannot endure if the frustration leads to the ever-renewed experience of greater sameness and stronger continuity of development, toward a final integration of the individual life cycle with some meaningful wider belongingness. Parents must not only have certain ways of guiding by prohibition and permission; they must also be able to represent to the child a deep, an almost somatic conviction that there is a meaning to what they are doing. Ultimately, children become neurotic not from frustrations, but from the lack or loss of societal meaning in these frustrations.

But even under the most favorable circumstances, this stage seems to introduce into psychic life (and become prototypical for) a sense of inner division and universal nostalgia for a paradise forfeited. It is against this powerful combination of a sense of having been deprived, of having been divided, and of having been abandoned — that basic trust must maintain itself throughout life.

Each successive stage and crisis has a special relation to one of the basic elements of society, and this for the simple reason that the human life cycle and man's institutions have evolved together. In this chapter we can do little more than mention, after the description of each stage, what basic element of social organization is related to it. This relation is twofold: man brings to these institutions the remnants of his infantile mentality and his youthful fervor, and he receives from them — as long as they manage to maintain their actuality — a reinforcement of his infantile gains.

The parental faith which supports the trust emerging in the newborn, has throughout history sought its institutional safeguard (and, on occasion, found its greatest enemy) in organized religion. Trust born of care is, in fact, the touchstone of the *actuality* of a given religion. All religions have in common the periodical childlike surrender to a Provider or providers who dispense earthly fortune as well as spiritual health; some demonstration of man's smallness by way of reduced posture and humble gesture; the admission in prayer and song of misdeeds, of misthoughts, and of evil intentions; fervent appeal for inner unification by divine guidance; and finally, the insight that individual trust must become a common faith, individual mistrust a commonly formulated evil, while the individual's restoration must become part of the ritual practice of many, and must become a sign of trustworthiness in the community. [1] We have illustrated how tribes dealing with one segment of nature develop a collective magic which seems to treat the Supernatural Providers of food and fortune as if they were angry and must be appeased by prayer and self-torture. Primitive religions, the most primitive layer in all religions, and the religious layer in each individual, abound with efforts at atonement which try to make up for vague deeds against a maternal matrix and try to restore faith in the goodness of one's strivings and in the kindness of the powers of the universe.

[1] This is the communal and psychosocial side of religion. Its often paradoxical relation to the spirituality of the individual is a matter not to be treated briefly and in passing (see *Young Man Luther*). (E.H.E.)

Each society and each age must find the institutionalized form of reverence which derives vitality from its world-image — from predestination to indeterminacy. The clinician can only observe that many are proud to be without religion whose children cannot afford their being without it. On the other hand, there are many who seem to derive a vital faith from social action or scientific pursuit. And again, there are many who profess faith, yet in practice breathe mistrust both of life and man.

Autonomy Versus Shame And Doubt

In describing the growth and the crises of the human person as a series of alternative basic attitudes such as trust vs. mistrust, we take recourse to the term a "sense of," although, like a "sense of health," or a "sense of being unwell," such "senses" pervade surface and depth, consciousness and the unconscious. They are, then, at the same time, ways of *experiencing* accessible to introspection; ways of *behaving*, observable by others; and unconscious *inner states* determinable by test and analysis. It is important to keep these three dimensions in mind, as we proceed.

Muscular maturation sets the stage for experimentation with two simultaneous sets of social modalities: holding on and letting go. As is the case with all of these modalities, their basic conflicts can lead in the end to either hostile or benign expectations and attitudes. Thus, to hold can become a destructive and cruel retaining or restraining, and it can become a pattern of care: to have and to hold. To let go, too, can turn into an inimical letting loose of destructive forces, or it can become a relaxed "to let pass" and "to let be."

Outer control at this stage, therefore, must be firmly reassuring. The infant must come to feel that the basic faith in existence, which is the lasting treasure saved from the rages of the oral stage, will not be jeopardized by this about-face of his, this sudden violent wish to have a choice, to appropriate demandingly, and to eliminate stubbornly. Firmness must protect him against the potential anarchy of his as yet untrained sense of discrimination, his inability to hold on and to let go with discretion. As his environment encourages him to "stand on his own feet," it must protect him against meaningless and arbitrary experiences of shame and of early doubt.

The latter danger is the one best known to us. For if denied the gradual and well-guided experience of the autonomy of free choice (or if, indeed, weakened by an initial loss of trust) the child will turn against himself all his urge to discriminate and to manipulate. He will overmanipulate himself, he will develop a precocious conscience. Instead of taking possession of things in order to test them by purposeful repetition, he will become obsessed by his own repetitiveness. By such obsessiveness, of course, he then learns to repossess the environment and to gain power by stubborn and minute control, where he could not find large-scale mutual regulation. Such hollow victory is the infantile model for a compulsion neurosis. It is also the infantile source of later attempts in adult life to govern by the letter, rather than by the spirit.

Shame is an emotion insufficiently studied, because in our civilization it is so early and easily absorbed by guilt. Shame supposes that one is completely exposed and conscious of being looked at: in one word, self-conscious. One is visible and not ready to be visible; which is why we dream of shame as a situation in which we are stared at in a condition of incomplete dress, in night attire, "with one's pants down." Shame is early expressed in an impulse to bury one's face, or to sink, right then and there, into the ground. But this, I think, is essentially rage turned against the self. He who is ashamed would like to force the world not to look at him, not to notice his exposure. He would like to destroy the eyes of the world. Instead he must wish for his own invisibility. This potentiality is abundantly used in the educational method of "shaming" used so exclusively by some primitive peoples. Visual shame precedes auditory guilt, which is a sense of badness to be had all by oneself when nobody watches and when everything is quiet — except the voice of the superego. Such shaming exploits an increasing sense of being small, which can develop only as the child stands up and as his awareness permits him to note the relative measures of size and power.

Too much shaming does not lead to genuine propriety but to a secret determination to try to get away with things, unseen — if, indeed, it does not result in defiant shamelessness. There is an impressive American ballad in which a murderer to be hanged on the gallows before the eyes of the community, instead of feeling duly chastened, begins to berate the onlookers, ending every salvo of defiance with the words, "God damn your eyes." Many a small child, shamed beyond endurance, may be in a chronic mood (although not in possession of either the courage or the words) to express defiance in similar terms. What I mean by this sinister reference is that there is a limit to a child's and an adult's endurance in the face of demands to consider himself, his body, and his wishes as evil and dirty, and to his belief in the infallibility of those who pass such judgment. He may be apt to turn things around, and to consider as evil only the fact that they exist: his chance will come when they are gone, or when he will go from them.

Doubt is the brother of shame. Where shame is dependent on the consciousness of being upright and exposed, doubt, so clinical observation leads me to believe, has much to do with a consciousness of having a front and a back — and especially a "behind." For this reverse area of the body, with its aggressive and libidinal focus in the sphincters and in the buttocks, cannot be seen by the child, and yet it can be dominated by the will of others. The "behind" is the small being's dark continent, an area of the body which can be magically dominated and effectively invaded by those who would attack one's power of autonomy and who would designate as evil those products of the bowels which were felt to be all right when they were being passed. This basic sense of doubt in whatever one has left behind forms a substratum for later and more verbal forms of compulsive doubting; this finds its adult expression in paranoiac fears concerning hidden persecutors and secret persecutions threatening from behind (and from within the behind).

This stage, therefore, becomes decisive for the ratio of love and hate, cooperation and willfulness, freedom of self-expression and its suppression. From a sense of self-control without loss of self-esteem comes a lasting sense of good will and pride; from a sense of loss of self-control and of foreign overcontrol comes a lasting propensity for doubt and shame.

If, to some reader, the "negative" potentialities of our stages seem over-stated throughout, we must remind him that this is not only the result of a preoccupation with clinical data. Adults, and seemingly mature and un-neurotic ones, display a sensitivity concerning a possible shameful "loss of face" and fear of being attacked "from behind" which is not only highly irrational and in contrast to the knowledge available to them, but can be of fateful import if related sentiments influence, for example, interracial and international policies.

We have related basic trust to the institution of religion. The lasting need of the individual to have his will reaffirmed and delineated within an adult order of things which at the same time reaffirms and delineates the will of others has an institutional safeguard in the *principle of law and order*. In daily life as well as in the high courts of law — domestic and international — this principle apportions to each his privileges and his limitations, his obliga-tions and his rights. A sense of rightful dignity and lawful independence on the part of adults around him gives to the child of good will the confident expectation that the kind of autonomy fostered in childhood will not lead to undue doubt or shame in later life. Thus the sense of autonomy fostered in the child and modified as life progresses, serves (and is served by) the preservation in economic and political life of a sense of justice.

INITIATIVE VERSUS GUILT

There is in every child at every stage a new miracle of vigorous unfolding, which constitutes a new hope and a new responsibility for all. Such is the sense and the pervading quality of initiative. The criteria for all these senses and qualities are the same; a crisis, more or less beset with fumbling and fear, is resolved, in that the child suddenly seems to "grow together" both in his person and in his body. He appears "more himself," more loving, relaxed and brighter in his judgment, more activated and activating. He is in free posses-sion of a surplus of energy which permits him to forget failures quickly and to approach what seems desirable (even if it also seems uncertain and even dangerous) with undiminished and more accurate direction. Initiative adds to autonomy the quality of undertaking, planning and "attacking" a task for the sake of being active and on the move, where before self-will, more often than not, inspired acts of defiance or, at any rate, protested independence.

I know that the very word "initiative" to many, has an American, and industrial connotation. Yet, initiative is a necessary part of every act, and man needs a sense of initiative for whatever he learns and does, from fruit--gathering to a system of enterprise.

The ambulatory stage and that of infantile genitality add to the inventory of basic social modalities that of "making," first in the sense of "being on the make." There is no simpler, stronger word for it; it suggests pleasure in attack and conquest. In the boy, the emphasis remains on phallic-intrusive modes; in the girl it turns to modes of "catching" in more aggressive forms of snatching or in the milder form of making oneself attractive and endearing.

The danger of this stage is a sense of guilt over the goals contemplated and the acts initiated in one's exuberant enjoyment of new locomotor and mental power: acts of aggressive manipulation and coercion which soon go far beyond the executive capacity of organism and mind and therefore call for an energetic halt on one's contemplated initiative. While autonomy concentrates on keeping potential rivals out, and therefore can lead to jealous rage most often directed against encroachments by younger siblings, initiative brings with it anticipatory rivalry with those who have been there first and may, therefore, occupy with their superior equipment the field toward which one's initiative is directed. Infantile jealousy and rivalry, those often embittered and yet essentially futile attempts at demarcating a sphere of unquestioned privilege, now come to a climax in a final contest for a favored position with the mother; the usual failure leads to resignation, guilt, and anxiety. The child indulges in fantasies of being a giant and a tiger, but in his dreams he runs in terror for dear life. This, then, is the stage of the "castration complex," the intensified fear of finding the (now energetically erotized) genitals harmed as a punishment for the fantasies attached to their excitement.

Infantile sexuality and incest taboo, castration complex and superego all unite here to bring about that specifically human crisis during which the child must turn from an exclusive, pregenital attachment to his parents to the slow process of becoming a parent, a carrier of tradition. Here the most fateful split and transformation in the emotional powerhouse occurs, a split between potential human glory and potential total destruction. For here the child becomes forever divided in himself. The instinct fragments which before had enhanced the growth of his infantile body and mind now become divided into an infantile set which perpetuates the exuberance of growth potentials, and a parental set which supports and increases self-observation, self-guidance, and self-punishment.

The problem, again, is one of mutual regulation. Where the child, now so ready to overmanipulate himself, can gradually develop a sense of moral responsibility, where he can gain some insight into the institutions, functions, and roles which will permit his responsible participation, he will find pleasurable accomplishment in wielding tools and weapons, in manipulating meaningful toys — and in caring for younger children.

Naturally, the parental set is at first infantile in nature: the fact that human conscience remains partially infantile throughout life is the core of human tragedy. For the superego of the child can be primitive, cruel, and uncompromising, as may be observed in instances where children overcontrol and overconstrict themselves to the point of self-obliteration; where they develop an over-obedience more literal than the one the parent has wished to exact; or where they develop deep regressions and lasting resentments because the parents themselves do not seem to live up to the new conscience. One of the deepest conflicts in life is the hate for a parent who served as the model and the executor of the superego, but who (in some form) was found trying to get away with the very transgressions which the child can no longer tolerate in himself. The suspiciousness and evasiveness which is thus mixed in with the all-or-nothing quality of the superego, this organ of moral tradition, makes moral (in the sense of moralistic) man a great potential danger to his own ego — and to that of his fellow men.

In adult pathology, the residual conflict over initiative is expressed either in hysterical denial, which causes the repression of the wish or the abrogation of its executive organ by paralysis, inhibition, or impotence; or in overcompensatory showing off, in which the scared individual, so eager to "duck," instead "sticks his neck out." Then also a plunge into psychosomatic disease is now common. It is as if the culture had made a man over-advertise himself and so identify with his own advertisement that only disease can offer him escape.

But here, again, we must not think only of individual psycho-pathology, but of the inner powerhouse of rage which must be submerged at this stage, as some of the fondest hopes and the wildest fantasies are repressed and inhibited. The resulting self-righteousness — often the principal reward for goodness — can later be most intolerantly turned against others in the form of persistent moralistic surveillance, so that the prohibition rather than the guidance of initiative becomes the dominant endeavor. On the other hand, even moral man's initiative is apt to burst the boundaries of self-restriction, permitting him to do to others, in his or in other lands, what he would neither do nor tolerate being done in his own home.

In view of the dangerous potentials of man's long childhood, it is well to look back at the blueprint of the life-stages and to the possibilities of guiding the young of the race while they are young. And here we note that according to the wisdom of the ground plan the child is at no time more ready to learn quickly and avidly, to become bigger in the sense of sharing obligation and performance than during this period of his development. He is eager and able to make things cooperatively, to combine with other children for the purpose of constructing and planning, and he is willing to profit from teachers and to emulate ideal prototypes. He remains, of course, identified with the parent of the same sex, but for the present he looks for opportunities where work-identification seems to promise a field of initiative without too much infantile conflict or oedipal guilt and a more realistic identification based on a spirit of equality experienced in doing things together. At any rate, the "oedipal" stage results not only in the oppressive establishment of a moral sense restricting the horizon of the permissible; it also sets the direction toward the possible and the tangible which permits the dreams of early childhood to be attached to the goals of an active adult life. Social institutions, therefore, offer children of this age an *economic ethos*, in the form of ideal adults recognizable by their uniforms and their functions, and fascinating enough to replace, the heroes of picture book and fairy tale.

Industry Versus Inferiority

Thus the inner stage seems all set for "entrance into life," except that life must first be school life, whether school is field or jungle or classroom. The child must forget past hopes and wishes, while his exuberant imagination is tamed and harnessed to the laws of impersonal things — even the three R's. For before the child, psychologically already a rudimentary parent, can become a biological parent, he must begin to be a worker and potential provider. With the oncoming latency period, the normally advanced child forgets, or rather sublimates, the necessity to "make" people by direct attack or to become papa and mama in a hurry: he now learns to win recognition by producing things. He has mastered the ambulatory field and the organ modes. He has experienced a sense of finality regarding the fact that there is no workable future within the womb of his family, and thus becomes ready to apply himself to given skills and tasks, which go far beyond the mere playful expression of his organ modes or the pleasure in the function of his limbs. He develops a sense of industry — i.e., he adjusts himself to the inorganic laws of the tool world. He can become an eager and absorbed unit of a productive situation. To bring a productive situation to completion is an aim which gradually supersedes the whims and wishes of play. His ego boundaries include his tools and skills: the work principle (Ives Hendrick) teaches him the pleasure of work completion by steady attention and persevering diligence. In all cultures, at this stage, children receive some *systematic instruction*, although, . . . it is by no means always in the kind of school which literate people must organize around special teachers who have learned how to teach literacy. In preliterate people and in nonliterate pursuits much is learned from adults who become teachers by dint of gift and inclination rather than by appointment, and perhaps the greatest amount is learned from older children. Thus the *fundamentals of technology* are developed, as the child becomes ready to handle the utensils, the tools, and the weapons used by the big people. Literate people, with more specialized careers, must prepare the child by teaching him things which first of all make him literate, the widest possible basic education for the greatest number of possible careers. The more confusing specialization becomes, however, the more indistinct are the eventual goals of initiative; and the more complicated social reality, the vaguer are the father's and mother's role in it. School seems to be a culture all by itself, with its own goals and limits, its achievements and disappointment.

The child's danger, at this stage, lies in a sense of inadequacy and inferiority. If he despairs of his tools and skills or of his status among his tool partners, he may be discouraged from identification with them and with a section of the tool world. To lose the hope of such "industrial" association may pull him back to the more isolated, less tool-conscious familial rivalry of the oedipal time. The child despairs of his equipment in the tool world and in anatomy, and considers himself doomed to mediocrity or inadequacy. It is at this point that wider society becomes significant in its ways of admitting the child to an understanding of meaningful roles in its technology and economy. Many a child's development is disrupted when family life has failed to prepare him for school life, or when school life fails to sustain the promises of earlier stages.

Regarding the period of a developing sense of industry, I have referred to *outer and inner hindrances* in the use of new capacities but not to aggravations of new human drives, nor to submerged rages resulting from their frustration. This stage differs from the earlier ones in that it is not a swing from an inner upheaval to a new mastery. Freud calls it the latency stage because violent drives are normally dormant. But it is only a lull before the storm of puberty, when all the earlier drives remerge in a new combination, to be brought under the dominance of genitality.

On the other hand, this is socially a most decisive stage: since industry involves doing things beside and with others, a first sense of division of labor and of differential opportunity, that is, a sense of the *technological ethos* of a culture, develops at this time. We have pointed in the last section to the danger threatening individual and society where the schoolchild begins to feel that the color of his skin, the background of his parents, or the fashion of his clothes rather than his wish and his will to learn will decide his worth as an apprentice, and thus his sense of *identity* — to which we must now turn. But there is another more fundamental danger; namely man's restriction of himself and constriction of his horizons to include only his work to which, so the Book says, he has been sentenced after his expulsion from paradise. If he accepts work as his only obligation, and "what works" as his only criterion of worthwhileness, he may become the conformist and thoughtless slave of his technology and of those who are in a position to exploit it.

IDENTITY VERSUS ROLE CONFUSION

With the establishment of a good initial relationship to the world of skills and tools, and with the advent of puberty, childhood proper comes to an end. Youth begins. But in puberty and adolescence all samenesses and continuities relied on earlier are more or less questioned again, because of a rapidity of body growth which equals that of early childhood and because of the new addition of genital maturity. The growing and developing youths, faced with this physiological revolution within them, and with tangible adult tasks ahead of them are now primarily concerned with what they appear to be in the eyes of others as compared with what they feel they are, and with the question of how to connect the roles and skills cultivated earlier with the occupational prototypes of the day. In their search for a new sense of continuity and sameness, adolescents have to refight many of the battles of earlier years, even though to do so they must artificially appoint perfectly well-meaning people to play the roles of adversaries; and they are ever ready to install lasting idols and ideals as guardians of a final identity.

The integration now taking place in the form of ego identity is, as pointed out, more than the sum of the childhood identifications. It is the accrued experience of the ego's ability to integrate all identifications with the vicissitudes of the libido, with the aptitudes developed out of endowment, and with the opportunities offered in social roles. The sense of ego identity, then, is the accrued confidence that the inner sameness and continuity prepared in the past are matched by the sameness and continuity of one's meaning for other, as evidenced in the tangible promise of a "career."

The danger of this stage is role confusion.[2] Where this is based on a strong previous doubt as to one's sexual identity, delinquent and outright psychotic episodes are not uncommon. If diagnosed and treated correctly, these incidents do not have the same fatal significance which they have at other ages. In most instances, however, it is the inability to settle on an occupational identity which disturbs individual young people. To keep themselves together they temporarily overidentify, to the point of apparent complete loss of identity, with the heroes of cliques and crowds. This initiates the stage of "falling in love," which is by no means entirely, or even primarily, a sexual matter — except where the mores demand it. To a considerable extent adolescent love is an attempt to arrive at a definition of one's identity by projecting one's diffused ego image on another and by seeing it thus reflected and gradually clarified. This is why so much of young love is conversation.

Young people can also be remarkably clannish, and cruel in their exclusion of all those who are "different," in skin color or cultural background, in tastes and gifts, and often in such petty aspects of dress and gesture as have been temporarily selected as the signs of an in-grouper or out-grouper. It is important to understand (which does not mean condone or participate in) such intolerance as a defense against a sense of identity confusion. For adolescents not only help one another temporarily through much discomfort by forming cliques and by stereotyping themselves, their ideals, and their enemies; they also perversely test each other's capacity to pledge fidelity. The readiness for such testing also explains the appeal which simple and cruel totalitarian doctrines have on the minds of the youth of such countries and classes as have lost or are losing their group identities (feudal, agrarian, tribal, national) and face world-wide industrialization, emancipation, and wider communication.

The adolescent mind is essentially a mind of the *moratorium*, a psychosocial stage between childhood and adulthood, and between the morality learned by the child, and the ethics to be developed by the adult. It is an

[2] See "The Problem of Ego-Identity," *J. Amer. Psa. Assoc.*, 4:56–121.

ideological mind — and, indeed, it is the ideological outlook of a society that speaks most clearly to the adolescent who is eager to be affirmed by his peers, and is ready to be confirmed by rituals, creeds, and programs which at the same time define what is evil, uncanny, and inimical. In searching for the social values which guide identity, one therefore confronts the problems of *ideology* and *aristocracy*, both in their widest possible sense which connotes that within a defined world image and a predestined course of history, the best people will come to rule and rule develops the best in people. In order not to become cynically or apathetically lost, young people must somehow be able to convince themselves that those who succeed in their anticipated adult world thereby shoulder the obligation of being the best. We will discuss later the dangers which emanate from human ideals harnessed to the management of super-machines, be they guided by nationalistic or international, communist or capitalist ideologies. In the last part of [*Childhood and Society*] we shall discuss the way in which the revolutions of our day attempt to solve and also to exploit the deep need of youth to redefine its identity in an industrialized world.

INTIMACY VERSUS ISOLATION

The strength acquired at any stage is tested by the necessity to transcend it in such a way that the individual can take chances in the next stage with what was most vulnerably precious in the previous one. Thus, the young adult, emerging from the search for and the insistence on identity, is eager and willing to fuse his identity with that of others. He is ready for intimacy, that is, the capacity to commit himself to concrete affiliations and partnerships and to develop the ethical strength to abide by such commitments, even though they may call for significant sacrifices and compromises. Body and ego must now be masters of the organ modes and of the nuclear conflicts, in order to be able to face the fear of ego loss in situations which call for self-abandon: in the solidarity of close affiliations, in orgasms and sexual unions, in close friendships and in physical combat, in experiences of inspiration by teachers and of intuition from the recesses of the self. The avoidance of such experiences because of a fear of ego loss may lead to a deep sense of isolation and consequent self-absorption.

The counterpart of intimacy is distantiation: the readiness to isolate and, if necessary, to destroy those forces and people whose essence seems dangerous to one's own, and whose "territory" seems to encroach on the extent of one's intimate relations. Prejudices thus developed (and utilized and exploited in politics and in war) are a more mature outgrowth of the blinder repudiations which during the struggle for identity differentiate sharply and cruelly between the familiar and the foreign. The danger of this stage is that intimate, competitive, and combative relations are experienced with and against the selfsame people. But as the areas of adult duty are delineated, and as the competitive encounter, and the sexual embrace, are differentiated, they eventually become subject to that *ethical sense* which is the mark of the adult. Strictly speaking, it is only now that *true genitality* can fully develop; for much of the sex life preceding these commitments is of the identity-searching kind, or is dominated by phallic or vaginal strivings which make of sex-life a kind of genital combat. On the other hand, genitality is all too often described as a permanent state of reciprocal sexual bliss. This then, may be the place to complete our discussion of genitality.

For a basic orientation in the matter I shall quote what has come to me as Freud's shortest saying. It has often been claimed, and bad habits of conversation seem to sustain the claim, that psychoanalysis as a treatment attempts to convince the patient that before God and man he has only one obligation: to have good orgasms, with a fitting "object," and that regularly. This, of course, is not true. Freud was once asked what he thought a normal person should be able to do well. The questioner probably expected a complicated answer. But Freud, in the curt way of his old days, is reported to have said: "Lieben und arbeiten" (to love and to work). It pays to ponder on this simple formula; it gets deeper as you think about it. For when Freud said "love" he meant *genital* love, and genital *love;* when he said love *and* work, he meant a general work-productiveness which would not preoccupy the individual to the extent that he loses his right or capacity to be a genital and a loving being. Thus we may ponder, but we cannot improve on "the professor's" formula.

Genitality, then, consists in the unobstructed capacity to develop an orgastic potency so free of pregenital interferences that genital libido (not just the sex products discharged in Kinsey's "outlets") is expressed in heterosexual mutuality, with full sensitivity of both penis and vagina, and with a convulsion-like discharge of tension from the whole body. This is a rather concrete way of saying something about a process which we really do not understand. To put it more situationally: the total fact of finding, via the climactic turmoil of the orgasm, a supreme experience of the mutual regulation of two beings in some way takes the edge off the hostilities and potential rages caused by the oppositeness of male and female, of fact and fancy, of love and hate. Satisfactory sex relations thus make sex less obsessive, overcompensation less necessary, sadistic controls superfluous.

Preoccupied as it was with curative aspects, psychoanalysis often failed to formulate the matter of genitality in a way significant for the processes of society in all classes, nations, and levels of culture. The kind of mutuality in orgasm which psychoanalysis has in mind is apparently easily obtained in classes and cultures which happen to make a leisurely institution of it. In more complex societies this mutuality is interfered with by so many factors of health, of tradition, of opportunity, and of temperament, that the proper formulation of sexual health would be rather this: A human being should be potentially able to accomplish mutuality of genital orgasm, but he should also be so constituted without undue regression wherever emotional preference or considerations of duty and loyalty call for it.

While psychoanalysis has on occasion gone too far in its emphasis on genitality as a universal cure for society and has thus provided a new addiction and a new commodity for many who wished to so interpret its teachings, it has not always indicated all the goals that genitality actually should and must imply. In order to be of lasting social significance, the utopia of genitality should include:

1. mutuality of orgasm
2. with a loved partner
3. of the other sex
4. with whom one is able and willing to share a mutual trust
5. and with whom one is able and willing to regulate the cycles of
   a. work
   b. procreation
   c. recreation
6. so as to secure to the offspring, too, all the stages of a satisfactory development.

It is apparent that such utopian accomplishment on a large scale cannot be an individual or, indeed, a therapeutic task. Nor is it a purely sexual matter by any means. It is integral to a culture's style of sexual selection, cooperation, and competition.

The danger of this stage is isolation, that is the avoidance of contacts which commit to intimacy. In psychopathology, this disturbance can lead to severe "character-problems." On the other hand, there are partnerships which amount to an isolation à deux, protecting both partners from the necessity to face the next critical development — that of generativity.

Generativity Versus Stagnation

Generativity . . . encompasses the evolutionary development which has made man the teaching and instituting as well as the learning animal. The fashionable insistence on dramatizing the dependence of children on adults often blinds us to the dependence of the older generation on the younger one. Mature man needs to be needed, and maturity needs guidance as well as encouragement from what has been produced and must be taken care of.

Generativity, then, is primarily the concern in establishing and guiding the next generation, although there are individuals who, through misfortune or because of special and genuine gifts in other directions, do not apply this drive to their own offspring. And indeed, the concept generativity is meant to include such more popular synonyms as *productivity* and *creativity*, which, however, cannot replace it.

It has taken psychoanalysis some time to realize that the ability to lose oneself in the meeting of bodies and minds leads to a gradual expansion of ego-interests and to a libidinal investment in that which is being generated. Generativity thus is an essential stage on the psychosexual as well as on the psychosocial schedule. Where such enrichment fails altogether, regression to an obsessive need for pseudo-intimacy takes place, often with a pervading sense of stagnation and personal impoverishment. Individuals, then, often begin to indulge themselves as if they were their own — or one another's — one and only child; and where conditions favor it, early invalidism, physical or psychological, becomes the vehicle of self-concern. The mere fact of having or even wanting children, however, does not "achieve" generativity. In fact, some young parents suffer, it seems, from the retardation of the ability to develop this stage. The reasons are often to be found in early childhood impressions; in excessive self-love based on a too strenuously self-made personality; and finally (and here we return to the beginnings) in the lack of some faith, some "belief in the species," which would make a child appear to be a welcome trust of the community.

As to the institutions which safeguard and reinforce generativity, one can only say that all institutions codify the ethics of generative succession. Even where philosophical and spiritual tradition suggests the renunciation of the right to procreate or to produce, such early turn to "ultimate concerns," wherever instituted in monastic movements, strives to settle at the same time the matter of its relationship to the Care for the creatures of this world and to the Charity which is felt to transcend it.

If this were a book on adulthood, it would be indispensable and profitable at this point to compare economic and psychological theories (beginning with the strange convergencies and divergencies of Marx and Freud) and to proceed to a discussion of man's relationship to his production as well as to his progeny.

EGO INTEGRITY VERSUS DESPAIR

Only in him who in some way has taken care of things and people and has adapted himself to the triumphs and disappointments adherent to being, the originator of others or the generator of products and ideas — only in him may gradually ripen the fruit of these seven stages. I know no better word for it than ego integrity. Lacking a clear definition, I shall point to a few constituents of this state of mind. It is the ego's accrued assurance of its proclivity for order and meaning. It is a post-narcissistic love of the human ego — not of the self — as an experience which conveys some world order and spiritual sense, no matter how dearly paid for. It is the acceptance of one's one and only life cycle as something that had to be and that, by necessity, permitted of no substitutions: it thus means a new, a different love of one's parents. It is a comradeship with the ordering ways of distant times and different pursuits. Although aware of the relativity of all the various life styles which have given meaning to human striving, the possessor of integrity is ready to defend the dignity of his own life style against all physical and economic threats. For he knows that an individual life is the accidental coincidence of but one life cycle with but one segment of history; and that for him all human integrity stands or falls with the one style of integrity of which he partakes. The style of integrity developed by his culture or civilization thus becomes the "patrimony of his soul," the seal of his moral paternity of himself ("... pero el honor/Es patrimonio del alma": Calderón). In such final consolidation, death loses its sting.

The lack or loss of this accrued ego integration is signified by fear of death: the one and only life cycle is not accepted as the ultimate of life. Despair expresses the feeling that the time is now short, too short for the attempt to start another life and to try out alternate roads to integrity. Disgust hides despair, if often only in the form of "a thousand little disgusts" which do not add up to one big remorse: "mille petits dégôuts de soi, dont le total ne fait pas un remords, mais un gêne obscure." (Rostand)

Each individual, to become a mature adult, must to a sufficient degree develop all the ego qualities mentioned, so that a wise Indian, a true gentleman, and a mature peasant share and recognize in one another the final stage of integrity. But each cultural entity, to develop the particular style of integrity suggested by its historical place, utilizes a particular combination of these conflicts, along with specific provocations and prohibitions of infantile sexuality. Infantile conflicts become creative only if sustained by the firm support of cultural institutions and of the special leader classes representing them. In order to approach or experience integrity, the individual must know how to be a follower of image bearers in religion and in politics, in the economic order and in technology, in aristocratic living and in the arts and sciences. Ego integrity, therefore, implies an emotional integration which permits participation by followership as well as acceptance of the responsibility of leadership.

Webster's Dictionary is kind enough to help us complete this outline in a circular fashion. Trust (the first of our ego values) is here defined as "the assured reliance on another's integrity," the last of our values. I suspect that Webster had business in mind rather than babies, credit rather than faith. But the formulation stands. And it seems possible to further paraphase the relation of adult integrity and infantile trust by saying that healthy children will not fear life if their elders have integrity enough not to fear death.

An Epigenetic Chart

... The foregoing conception of the life cycle awaits systematic treatment. To prepare this, I shall conclude this chapter with a diagram. In this ... the diagonal represents the normative sequence of psychosocial gains made as at each stage one more nuclear conflict adds a new ego quality, a new criterion of accruing human strength. Below the diagonal there is space for the precursors of each of these solutions, all of which begin with the beginning; above the diagonal there is space for the designation of the derivatives of these gains and their transformations in the maturing and the mature personality.

The underlying assumptions for such charting are (1) that the human personality in principle develops according to steps predetermined in the growing person's readiness to be driven toward, to be aware of, and to interact with, a widening social radius; and (2) that society, in principle, tends to be so constituted as to meet and invite this succession of potentialities for interaction and attempts to safeguard and to encourage the proper rate and the proper sequence of their enfolding. This is the "maintenance of the human world."

But a chart is only a tool to think with, and cannot aspire to be a prescription to abide by, whether in the practice of child-training, in psychotherapy, or in the methodology of child study. In the presentation of the psychosocial stages in the form of an *epigenetic chart* . . . we have definite and delimited methodological steps in mind. It is one purpose of this work to facilitate the comparison of the stages first discerned by Freud as sexual to other schedules of development (physical, cognitive). But any one chart delimits one schedule only, and it must not be imputed that our outline of the psychosocial schedule is intended to imply obscure generalities concerning other aspects of development — or, indeed, of existence. If the chart, for example, lists a series of conflicts or crises, we do not consider all development a series of crises: we claim only that psychosocial development proceeds by critical steps — "critical" being a characteristic of turning points, of moments of decision between progress and regression, integration and retardation.

It may be useful at this point to spell out the methodological implications of an epigenetic matrix. The more heavily lined squares of the diagonal signify both a sequence of stages and a gradual development of component parts: in other words, the chart formalizes a progression through time of a differentiation of parts. This indicates (1) that each critical item of psychosocial strength discussed here is systematically related to all others, and that they all depend on the proper development in the proper sequence of each item; and (2) that each item exists in some form before its critical time normally arrives.

If I say, for example, that a favorable ratio of basic trust over basic mistrust is the first step in psychosocial adaptation, a favorable ratio of autonomous will over shame and doubt, the second, the corresponding diagrammatic statement expresses a number of fundamental relations that exist between the two steps, as well as some facts fundamental to each. Each comes to its ascendance, meets its crisis, and finds its lasting solution during the stage indicated. But they all must exist from the beginning in some form, for every act calls for an integration of all. Also, an infant may show something like "autonomy" from the beginning in the particular way in which he angrily tries to wriggle himself free when tightly held. However, under normal conditions, it is not until the second year that he begins to experience the whole *critical opposition of being an autonomous creature and being a dependent one;* and it is not until then that he is ready for a decisive encounter with his environment, an environment which, in turn, feels called upon to convey to him its particular ideas and concepts of autonomy and coercion in ways decisively contributing to the character and the health of his personality in his culture. It is this encounter, together with the resulting crisis, that we have tentatively described for each stage. As to the progression from one stage to the next, the diagonal indicates the sequence to be followed. However, it also makes room for variations in tempo and intensity. An individual, or a culture, may linger excessively over trust and proceed from I 1 over I 2 to II 2, or an accelerated progression may move from I 1 over II 1 to II 2. Each such acceleration or (relative) retardation, however, is assumed to have a modifying influence on all later stages.

	1	2	3
III Locomotor-Genital			Initiative vs. Guilt
II Muscular-Anal		Autonomy vs. Shame, Doubt	
I Oral-Sensory	Basic Trust vs. Mistrust		

FIGURE 1

An epigenetic diagram thus lists a system of stages dependent on each other; and while individual stages may have been explored more or less thoroughly or named more or less fittingly, the diagram suggests that their study be pursued always with the total configuration of stages in mind. The diagram invites, then, a thinking through of all its empty boxes: if we have entered Basic Trust in I 1 and Integrity in VIII 8, we leave the question open, as to what trust might have become in a stage dominated by the need for integrity even as we have left open what it may look like and, indeed,

	1	2	3	4	5	6	7	8
VIII Maturity								Ego Integrity vs. Despair
VII Adulthood							Generativity vs. Stagnation	
VI Young Adulthood						Intimacy vs. Isolation		
V Puberty and Adolescence					Identity vs. Role Confusion			
IV Latency				Industry vs. Inferiority				
III Locomotor-Genital			Initiative vs. Guilt					
II Muscular-Anal		Autonomy vs. Shame, Doubt						
I Oral-Sensory	Basic Trust vs. Mistrust							

FIGURE 2

be called in the stage dominated by a striving for autonomy (II 1). All we mean to emphasize is that trust must have developed in its own right, before it becomes something more in the critical encounter in which autonomy develops — and so on, up the vertical. If, in the last stage (VIII 1), we would expect trust to have developed into the most mature *faith* that an aging person can muster in his cultural setting and historical period, the chart permits the consideration not only of what old age can be, but also what its preparatory stages must have been. All of this should make it clear that a chart of epigenesis suggests a global form of thinking and rethinking which leaves details of methodology and terminology to further study.[3]

[3] To leave this matter truly open, certain misuses of the whole conception would have to be avoided. Among them is the assumption that the sense of trust (and all the other "positive" senses postulated) is an *achievement*, secured once and for all at a given state. In fact, some writers are so intent on making an *achievement scale* out of these stages that they blithely omit all the "negative" senses (basic mistrust, etc.) which are and remain the dynamic counterpart of the "positive" ones throughout life. The assumption that on each stage a goodness is achieved which is impervious to new inner conflicts and to changing conditions is, I believe, a projection on child development of that success ideology which can so dangerously pervade our private and public daydreams and can make us inept in a heightened struggle for a meaningful existence in a new, industrial era of history. The personality is engaged with the hazards of existence continuously, even as the body's metabolism copes with decay. As we come to diagnose a state of relative strength and the symptoms of an impaired one, we face only more clearly the paradoxes and tragic potentials of human life.

The stripping of the stages of everything but their "achievements" has its counterpart in attempts to describe or test them as "traits" or "aspirations" without first building a systematic bridge between the conception advanced throughout this book and the favorite concepts of other investigators. If the foregoing sounds somewhat plaintive, it is not intended to gloss over the fact that in giving to these strengths the very designations by which in the past they have acquired countless connotations of superficial goodness, affected niceness, and all too strenuous virtue, I invited misunderstandings and misuses. However, I believe, that there is an intrinsic relationship between ego and language and that despite passing vicissitudes certain basic words retain essential meanings.

I have since attempted to formulate for Julian Huxley's *Humanist Frame* (Allen and Unwin, 1961; Harper and Brothers, 1962) a blueprint of essential strengths which evolution has built both into the ground plan of the life stages and into that of man's institutions. While I cannot discuss here the methodological problems involved (and aggravated by my use of the term "basic virtues"), I should append the list of these strengths because they are really the lasting outcome of the "favorable ratios" mentioned at every step of the chapter on psychosocial stages. Here they are:

Basic Trust vs. Basic Mistrust: Drive and *Hope*
Autonomy vs. Shame and Doubt: Self-Control and *Willpower*
Initiative vs. Guilt: Direction and *Purpose*
Industry vs. Inferiority: Method and *Competence*
Identity vs. Role Confusion: Devotion and *Fidelity*
Intimacy vs. Isolation: Affiliation and *Love*
Generativity vs. Stagnation: Production and *Care*
Ego Integrity vs. Despair: Renunciation and *Wisdom*

The italicized words are called *basic* virtues because without them, and their re-emer-

HARRY S. SULLIVAN

Basic Conceptions

Human performances, the subject of our study, including revery processes and thought, are susceptible of a two-part classification which is based on the end states, the end conditions toward which these processes are obviously moving, or which our prevision has reached. In other words, now and then you set out to start for somewhere. You preview the steps which will be necessary to get there and we can foresee the whole process on the basis of your reaching that place.

The most general basis on which interpersonal phenomena, interpersonal acts, may be classified, is one which separates the sought end states into the group which we call satisfactions and those which we call security or the maintenance of security. Satisfactions in this specialized sense are all those end states which are rather closely connected with the bodily organization of man. Thus the desire for food and drink leads to certain performances which are in this category. The desire for sleep leads to such performances. The state of being which is marked by the presence of lust is in this group; and finally, as the most middling example, the state of being which we call loneliness. All these states lead to activity which is the pursuit of satisfaction.

On the other hand, the pursuit of security pertains rather more closely to man's cultural equipment than to his bodily organization. By "cultural" I mean what the anthropologist means — all that which is man-made, which survives as monument to preexistent man, that is the cultural. And as I say, all those movements, actions, speech, thoughts, reveries and so on which pertain more to the culture which has been imbedded in a particular individual than to the organization of his tissues and glands, is apt to belong in this classification of the pursuit of security.

Reprinted from *Conceptions of Modern Psychiatry* by Harry Stack Sullivan. By permission of W. W. Norton & Company, Inc. Copyright 1940, 1945, 1947, 1953 by the William Alanson White Psychiatic Foundation.

gence from generation to generation, all other and more changeable systems of human values lose their spirit and their relevance. Of this list, I have been able so far to give a more detailed account only for Fidelity (see *Youth, Change and Challenge*, E. H. Erikson, editor, Basic Books, 1963). But here again, the list represents a total conception within which there is much room for a discussion of terminology and methodology. (E.H.E.)

The thing which many people if they were quite honest with themselves would say that they were after when they are showing a process of this type is prestige, and one of my long-acquainted colleagues, Harold D. Lasswell, a political scientist, worked out a statement for this field in three terms: security, income, and deference. All these pertain to the culture, to the social institutions, traditions, customs, and the like, under which we live, to our social order rather than to the peculiar properties of our bodily or somatic organizations.

This second class, the pursuit of security, may be regarded as consisting of ubiquitous artifacts — again in the anthropological sense, man-made — evolved by the cultural conditioning or training; that is, education of the impulses or drives which underlie the first class. In other words, given our biological equipment — we are bound to need food and water and so on — certain conditioning influences can be brought to bear on the needs for satisfaction. And the cultural conditioning gives rise to the second group, the second great class of interpersonal phenomena, the pursuit of security.

To follow this line of thought profitably, however, one must look closely at this conception of conditioning, and one must consider especially the states characterized by the feeling of ability or power. This is ordinarily much more important in the human being than are the impulses resulting from a feeling of hunger, or thirst, and the fully developed feeling of lust comes so very late in biological maturation that it is scarcely a good source for conditioning.

We seem to be born, however, with something of this power motive in us. An oft-told story beautifully illustrates the early appearance of what I am discussing as the motive toward the manifestation of power or ability. The infant seeing for the first time the full moon, reaches for it. Nothing transpires. He utters a few goos and nothing transpires; then he starts to cry in rage, and the whole household is upset. But he does not get the moon, and the moon becomes "marked" unattainable.

This is an instance of the frustration of the manifestation of power; one has failed at something which you might say one expects oneself to be able to achieve — not that the infant does much thinking, but the course of events indicates the application of increasingly complex techniques in the effort to achieve the object.

The full development of personality along the lines of security is chiefly founded on the infant's discovery of his powerlessness to achieve certain desired end states with the tools, the instrumentalities, which are at his disposal. From the disappointments in the very early stages of life outside the womb — in which all things were given— comes the beginning of this vast development of actions, thoughts, foresights, and so on, which are calculated to protect one from a feeling of insecurity and helplessness in the situation which confronts one. This accultural evolution begins thus, and when it succeeds, when one evolves successfully along this line, then one respects oneself, and as one respects oneself so one can respect others. That is one of the peculiarities of human personality that can always be depended on. If there is a valid and real attitude toward the self, that attitude will manifest as valid and real toward others. It is not that as ye judge so shall ye be judged, but as you judge yourself so shall you judge others; strange but true so far as I know, and with no exception.

The infant has as perhaps his mightiest tool the cry. The cry is a performance of the oral apparatus, the lips, mouth, throat, cheeks, vocal cords, intercostal muscles, and diaphragm. From this cry is evolved a great collection of most powerful tools which man uses in the development of his security with his fellow man. I refer to language behavior, operations including words.

Originally the infant's magical tool for all sorts of purposes, all too many of us still use vocal behavior as our principal adaptive device; and while none of you, of course, would do this, you must all know some people who can do in words practically anything and who have a curious faith that having said the right thing, all else is forgiven them. In other words, they are a little more like the infant than we are; they figure that a series of articulate noises turns any trick. We have, of course, learned that many other acts, performances, and foresights are necessary for success in living. None the less, denied our language behavior and the implicit revery processes that reach their final formulations in words, we would be terribly reduced in our competence and materially diminished in our security in dealing with other people.

At this point, I wish to say that if this series of lectures is to be reasonably successful, it will finally have demonstrated that there is nothing unique in the phenomena of the gravest functional illness. The most peculiar behavior of the acutely schizophrenic patient, I hope to demonstrate, is made up of interpersonal processes with which each one of us is or historically has been familiar. Far the greater part of the performances, the interpersonal processes, of the psychotic patient are exactly of a piece with processes which we manifest some time every twenty-four hours. Some of the psychotic performances seem very peculiar indeed, and, as I surmised in 1924,[1] for the explanation and familiarization of these performances, we have to look to the interpersonal relations of the infant, to the first eighteen months or so of life after birth. In most general terms, we are all much more simply human than other-

---

[1] See discussion of "Primitive Mentality and the Racial Unconscious," *Amer. J. Psychiatry* (1925) 4:671. The matter in point is illustrated, for example, by Ribble, Margarethe A., "Clinical Studies of Instinctive Reactions in New Born Babies," *Amer. J. Psychiatry* (1938) 93:149-158. Note the stupor reaction following defeat of the infant's efforts at sucking — pp. 154-157. See then, Sullivan, Harry Stack, "The Oral Complex," *Psychoanalytic Rev.* (1925) 12:31-38 and, the same, "Erogenous Maturation," *Psychoanalytic Rev.* (1926) 13:1-15. Note also Hadley, Ernest E., "The Psychoanalytic Clarification of Personality Types," *Amer. J. Psychiatry* (1938) 94:1417-1430; in particular, pp. 1424-1425. Some observations in this connection were reported at the 1938 meeting of the Association for Research in Nervous and Mental Diseases; McGraw, Myrtle B., *Research Publications* 19:244-246.

wise, be we happy and successful, contented and detached, miserable and mentally disordered, or whatever.

To return to the epoch of infancy, first let me state that this is the period of maturation, of experimentation, of empathic "observation," and of autistic invention in the realm of power. Two of these terms may need some explanation.

From birth it is demonstrable that the infant shows a curious relationship or connection with the significant adult, ordinarily the mother. If the mother, for example, hated the pregnancy and deplores the child, it is a pediatric commonplace that there are feeding difficulties, unending feeding difficulties, with the child. If a mother, otherwise deeply attached to the infant, is seriously distrubed by some intercurrent event around nursing time, is frightened by something or worried about something around the time of nursing, then on that occasion there will be feeding difficulty or the infant has indigestion. All in all we know that there is an emotional linkage between the infant and the significant adult.

Empathy is the term that we use to refer to the peculiar emotional linkage that subtends the relationship of the infant with other significant people — the mother or the nurse. Long before there are signs of any understanding of emotional expression, there is evidence of this emotional contagion or communion. This feature of the infant-mother configuration is of great importance for an understanding of the acculturation or cultural conditioning to which I have referred.

We do not know much about the fate of empathy in the developmental history of people in general. There are indications that it endures throughout life, at least in some people. There are few unmistakable instances of its function in most of us, however, in our later years; I find it convenient to assume that the time of its great importance is later infancy and early childhood — perhaps age six to twenty-seven months. So much for empathy.

The other strange term in our statement about the epoch of infancy is *autistic*, an adjective by which we indicate a primary, unsocialized, unacculturated state of symbol activity, and later states pertaining more to this primary condition than to the conspicuously effective consensually validated symbol activities of more mature personality. The meaning of the autistic will become clearer in my discussion of language.

We see our infant, then, expanding as a personality through the exercise of ability or power. We see him using the magic tool for the cry. We now see him acquiring another tool, which in turn also becomes magical. I refer here to his expression of satisfaction. It is biological for the infant when nourished to show certain expressive movements which we call the satisfaction-response, and it is probably biological for the parent concerned to be delighted to see these things. Due to the empathic linkage, this, the reaction of the parent to the satisfaction-response of the infant, communicates good feeling to the infant and thus he learns that this response has power.

Actually, this may be taken to be the primitive root of human generosity, the satisfaction in giving satisfaction and pleasure: another thing learned by some people in infancy.

I shall pass infancy now, to return presently to one aspect of it. As soon as the infant has picked up a vocal trick, saying perhaps "ma" and getting a tremendous response from the significant adult, without any idea of precisely what has happened but catching on the second time it happens, as soon as the rudiments of language habits have appeared, we say that infancy as a state of personality development has ceased and that the young one has become a child.

Childhood includes a rapid acculturation, but not alone in the basic acquisition of language, which is itself an enormous cultural entity. By this I mean that in childhood the peculiar mindlessness of the infant which seems to be assumed by most parents passes off and they begin to regard the little one as in need of training, as being justifiably an object of education; and what they train the child in consists of select excerpts from the cultural heritage, from that surviving of past people, incorporated in the personality of the parent. This includes such things as habits of cleanliness — which are of extremely good repute in the Western culture — and a great many other things. And along with all this acculturation, toilet habits, eating habits, and so on and so forth, there proceeds the learning of the language as a tool for communication.

The ability to make articulate noises and the ability to pick phonemal stations in vocal sound — that is, the peculiar ones of a continuum of sounds which are used in the forming of words, which varies, incidentally, from language to language — the ability, as I say, to learn phonemes,[2] to connect them into syllables and words, is inborn. That is given in the human organism. The original usage of these phonemal stations, syllables, words, however, is magical, as witness the "ma" and as witness, for example, any of you who have a child who has been promised on a certain birthday a pony. As you listen to the child talk about the pony you realize perhaps sadly that twenty-five years from now when he talks about ponies, pony will not have a thousandth of the richness of personal meaning that pony has for him now. The word

[2] The *phoneme* is a particular zone or station in the continuum of audible vibrations around which the use of a particular language has established meaning for the identification of verbal intention. A phoneme is more than a particular number of cycles per second of vibration; it is a family of such particular c.p.s. plus overtones, etc. The K sounds in *can, cool, keep, come* are of one phoneme. The phoneme is the linguistic unit of the person's speech; the *diaphone* is the corresponding term for the approximate phonemal coincidences that make up intelligible speech. See Sapir, Edward, *Language, An Introduction to the Study of Speech*; New York, Harcourt, Brace, 1921, reprinted 1929 (vii and 258 pp.); Sound Patterns in Language. *Language* (1925) 1:37-51; Dialect. *Encyclopoedia of the Social Sciences*; New York, MacMillian (1931) 5:123-126; Language. *The same* (1933) 30:247-265. A selected bibliography of this great linguist and cultural anthropologist appears in PSYCHIATRY (1938) 1:154-157.

of the child is autistic, it has a highly individual meaning, and the process of learning language habits consists to a great extent, once one has got a vocabulary, in getting a meaning to each particular term which is useful in communication. None of us succeeds completely in this; some of us do not succeed noticeably.

Along with learning of language, the child is experiencing many restraints on the freedom which it had enjoyed up till now. Restraints have to be used in the teaching of some of the personal habits that the culture requires everyone should show, and from these restraints there comes the evolution of the self-system — an extremely important part of the personality — with a brand-new tool, a tool so important that I must give you its technical name, which unhappily coincides with a word of common speech which may mean to you anything. I refer to *anxiety*.

With the appearance of the self system or the self dynamism, the child picks up a new piece of equipment which we technically call anxiety. Of the very unpleasant experiences which the infant can have we may say that there are generically two, pain and fear. Now comes the third.

It is necessary in the modification of activity in the interest of power in interpersonal relations, including revery and elementary constructive revery — that is, thought — that one focus, as it were, one's interest into certain fields that work. It is in learning this process that the self is evolved and the instrumentality of anxiety comes into being.

As one proceeds into childhood, disapproval, dissatisfaction with one's performances becomes more and more the tool of the significant adult in educating the infant in the folk ways, the tradition, the culture in which he is expected to live. This disapproval is felt by the child through the same empathic linkage which has been so conspicuous in infancy. Gradually he comes to perceive disapproving expressions of the mother, let us say; gradually he comes to understand disapproving statements; but before this perception and understanding he has felt the disapproval which he was not able to comprehend through the ordinary sensory channels.

This process, coupled with the prohibitions and the privations that he must suffer in his education, sets off the experiences that he has in this education and gives them a peculiar coloring of discomfort, neither pain nor fear but discomfort of another kind. Along with these experiences there go in all well regulated homes and schools a group of rewards and approbations for successes. These, needless to say, are not accompanied by this particular type of discomfort, and when that discomfort is present and something is done which leads to approbation, then this peculiar discomfort is assuaged and disappears. The peculiar discomfort is the basis of what we ultimately refer to as anxiety.

The self dynamism is built up out of this experience of approbation and disapproval, of reward and punishment. The peculiarity of the self dynamism is that as it grows it functions, in accordance with its state of development, right from the start. As it develops, it becomes more and more related to a microscope in its function. Since the approbation of the important person is very valuable, since disapprobation denies satisfaction and gives anxiety, the self becomes extremely important. It permits a minute focus on those performances of the child which are the cause of approbation and disapprobation, but, very much like a microscope, it interferes with noticing the rest of the world. When you are staring through your microscope, you don't see much except what comes through that channel. So with the self dynamism. It has a tendency to focus attention on performances with the significant other person which get approbation or disfavor. And that peculiarity, closely connected with anxiety, persists thenceforth through life. It comes about that the self, that to which we refer when we say "I," is the only thing which has alertness, which notices what goes on, and, needless to say, notices what goes on in its own field. The rest of the personality gets along outside of awareness. Its impulses, its performances, are not noted.

Not only does the self become the custodian of awareness, but when anything spectacular happens that is not welcome to the self, not sympathetic to the self dynamism, anxiety appears, almost as if anxiety finally became the instrument by which the self maintained its isolation within the personality.

Needless to say, the self is extremely important in psychiatry and in everyday life. Not only does anxiety function to discipline attention, but it gradually restricts personal awareness. The facilitations and deprivations by the parents and significant others are the source of the material which is built into the self dynamism. Out of all that happens to the infant and child, only this "marked" experience is incorporated into the self, because through the control of personal awareness the self itself from the beginning facilitates and restricts its further growth. In other words, it is self-perpetuating, if you please, tends very strongly to maintain the direction and characteristics which it was given in infancy and childhood.

For the expression of all things in the personality other than those which were approved and disapproved by the parent and other significant persons, the self refuses awareness, so to speak. It does not accord awareness, it does not notice; and these impulses, desires, and needs come to exist disassociated from the self, or *dissociated*. When they are expressed, their expression is not noticed by the person.

Our awareness of our performances, and our awareness of the performances of others are permanently restricted to a part of all that goes on and the structure and character of that part is determined by our early training; its limitation is maintained year after year by our experiencing anxiety whenever we tend to overstep the margin.

Needless to say, limitations and peculiarities of the self may interfere with the pursuit of biologically necessary satisfactions. When this happens, the person is to that extent mentally ill. Similarly, they may interfere with security, and to that extent also the person is mentally ill.

The self may be said to be made up of reflected appraisals. If these were chiefly derogatory, as in the case of an unwanted child who was never loved, of a child who has fallen into the hands of foster parents who have no real interest in him as a child; as I say, if the self dynamism is made up of experience which is chiefly derogatory, then the self dynamism will itself be chiefly derogatory. It will facilitate hostile, disparaging appraisals of other people and it will entertain disparaging and hostile appraisals of itself.

As I have said, the peculiarity exists that one can find in others only that which is in the self. And so the unhappy child who grows up without love will have a self dynamism which shows great capacity for finding fault with others and, by the same token, with himself. That low opinions of oneself are seldom expressed with simple frankness can also be explained.

So difficult is the maintenance of a feeling of security among his fellows for anyone who has come to have a hostile-derogatory self, that the low self-appreciation must be excluded from direct communication. A person who shrewdly attacks the prestige of sundry other people can scarcely add to each such performance, a statement to the effect that he knows, because he has the same fault or defect. At the same time, we know that that which is in the self is not dissociated from the self; in other words, if it shows in the witting performances towards others, it is within the limits of personal awareness and not outside, resisted, so to say, by anxiety.

The relative silence about the low self-appraisal is achieved in part by the clamor of derogating others, in part by preoccupation with implicit revery processes that dramatize the opposite of one's defects, or protest one's rights, or otherwise manifest indirectly one's feeling of unworthiness and inferiority.

Let us rest this matter here for the time being, and review what has been said. We have seen something of the origin and organization of the self and of its marked tendency to stabilize the course of its development. We have seen that if, for example, it is a self which arose through derogatory experience, hostility toward the child, disapproval, dissatisfaction with the child, then this self more or less like a microscope tends to preclude one's learning anything better, to cause one's continuing to feel a sort of limitation in oneself, and while this can not be expressed clearly, while the child or the adult that came from the child does not express openly self-depreciatory trends, he does have a depreciatory attitude toward everyone else, and this really represents a depreciatory attitude toward the self.

The stabilizing influence of past experience is due to the fact that when it is incorporated in the organization of the self, the structure of the self dynamism, it precludes the experience of anything corrective, anything that would be strikingly different. The direction of growth in the self is maintained by the control exercised over personal awareness and by the circumscribing of experience by anxiety when anything quite different from one's prevailing attitude tends to be noticed.

We have seen how the self can be a derogatory and a hateful system, in which case the self will inhibit any experience of friendliness, of positive attitude toward other persons, and thus continue to go on derogatory, hostile, negative, in its attitude toward others.

This selective exclusion of experience which leads to one's being occupied with or noticing only the hostile unfriendly aspect of living not only is manifested in one's attitude toward others, but also is represented in the attitude toward the self. No matter how well the outward manifestations of self-contempt may be disguised, we may be assured that they are there. We see here the explanation of one of the greatest mysteries of human life, how some unfortunate people carry on in the face of apparently overwhelming difficulties, whereas other people are crushed by comparatively insignificant events, contemplate suicide, perhaps actually attempt it.

This is to be understood on the basis not of the particular "objective" events which bring about the circumstance of success under great hardship or self-destruction; it is to be understood on the basis of the experience which is the foundation of the self system, the organization of experience reflected to one from the significant people around one — which determines the personal characteristics of those events. In no other fashion can we explain the enormous discrepancy between people's reactions to comparable life situations.

Every one of you knows of circumstances in which people encounter things which you would regard as too much to be borne, yet they go on with a certain measure of cheerfulness and optimism; whereas other people who, so far as you can see, have every advantage, have much to look forward to, meet some, to you, rather trifling rebuff, become depressed, and may actually destroy themselves. . . .

HARRY S. SULLIVAN

Developmental Syndromes

We shall now consider the phase of personality development which is the last stage on the road to the fully human estate. Once successfully negotiated, the person comes forth with self-respect adequate to almost any situation, with the respect for others that this competent self-respect entails, with the dignity that befits the high achievement of competent personality, and with the freedom of personal initiative that represents a comfortable adaptation of one's personal situation to the circumstances that characterize the social order of which one is a part.

The epochs that lead up to adolescence are closely if obscurely related to somatic maturation. Adolescence begins with the most spectacular maturation of all, the puberty change, with its swift alteration of physiological processes to the completion of bodily development. I still find virtue in dividing the epoch of adolescence into three eras: early adolescence, from the first evidences of puberty to the completion of voice change; mid-adolescence, to the patterning of genital behavior; and late adolescence, to the establishment of durable situations of intimacy such that all the major integrating tendencies are freely manifested within awareness in the series of one's interpersonal relations.

The farther one moves from birth, the less relevant an absolute physiological chronology becomes. The epoch of adolescence is thus the least fixed by mere somatic duration. It varies from culture to culture, and its actual time of appearance in young people among us is very widely varied. Over the world, the puberty change would seem to occur from as early an age as eight to as late as the twenties. Among some 250 people whom I have studied more or less intensively, I have seen quite a few in whom the inception of adolescence was deferred to around the eighteenth year.

It is from the data of these patients that I have come to feel that environmental influences, cultural influences emanating from significant people, are the predominant factor in bringing about delays — and accelerations — in the later stages of personality development.

Reprinted from *Conceptions of Modern Psychiatry* by Harry Stack Sullivan. By permission of W. W. Norton & Company, Inc. Copyright 1940, 1945, 1947, 1953 by the William Alanson White Psychiatric Foundation.

The data of these patients, in so far as they have been of American and Western European stock, certainly emphasizes the significance of experience — remote and recent — connected with genital (sexual) behavior and the emotion of lust. I have to add a word of caution, here, for there are those among us psychiatrists who make of sex a nuclear explanatory concept of personality, or at least of personality disorder. This is an error from insufficiency of the data. The highly civilized Chinese of the pre-Christian era were not bowled over by sex. A number of the primitive peoples who have been studied by anthropologists are found to take sex rather in their stride. Even the American Negro crashes through adolescence with relative impunity — if he is of the lower classes.

The lurid twilight which invests sex in our culture is primarily a function of two factors. We still try to discourage premarital sexual performances; hold that abstinence is the moral course before marriage. And we discourage early marriage; in fact progressively widen the gap between the adolescent awakening of lust and the proper circumstances for marriage. These two factors work through many cultural conventions to make us the most sex-ridden people of whom I have any knowledge.

I think that it might be well at this point to indicate something of what this means by discussing an instance of maladjustment in adolescence. To do this, I must go a long way back from the problem as it presents itself, say, at age 15. To formulate any personal situation, one must almost certainly know a great deal about how it came into being. I shall then take a few minutes to sketch the picture of a boy to whom adolescence will be quite disastrous.

We will take him in the cradle, and here we will see him, after the fashion of all his predecessors, actively and pleasantly engaged in the exercise of such ability as he has discovered. He will perhaps not have kicked a slat out of the cradle, but he certainly will have poked all the slats of the cradle, he will have felt of nearly everything, including a great deal of himself, he may have put a good deal of himself in his mouth, or tried to, but in this business of exercising newly elaborated motor systems and gradually clarifying sensory feel, he will almost inevitably, since we make it a "him," have fallen upon a small protuberance in the groin, and in doing this he will have found it handy. It is suited to manipulation. It is astonishingly well located geometrically. A slight curve in the elbow puts it well within reach of the already nimble fingers.

So far nothing of any moment has occurred. But we will now have, let us say, the mother — fathers usually keep fairly far from the nursery — we will have the mother encounter this discovery of the infant, and we will make her a person who has been forced to organize the self on the basis of our more rigid puritanic tradition.

Under these circumstances, although in ordinary consciousness she is not wholly unaware of this anatomical peculiarity of the male, in her own infant she will feel that Satan is in the very near vicinity, that here is a manifestation of the bestial nature of man in the very act of erupting in her infant, and she will want to do something about it. She will wish to save this infant; Lord knows what awful visions unroll before her eyes as she witnesses this; but anyway the infant is badly upset by empathy, undergoes various somatic disturbances, and experiences what amounts to an acute and severe discomfort.

Infants are not afflicted by long, carefully formulated memories. To the infant whose discrimination of such things is nil, this discomfort does not attach to the manipulation of the little protuberance. Almost anything in the situation may be related to this feeling of discomfort so far as the infant is concerned. He has not learned.

This course of events is discovered again, perhaps the same day. The stress in the mother is terrific. The doctor is consulted, and we will say that the doctor is either very anxious to build up a good practice and surmises that this mother will bring him patients, or that he, too, knows no better; so he puts medical "intelligence" or rumor that has come to him, to work. And so the infant has a mitten put on the hand and tied around the wrist.

Thus begins the emphasis in the infant's mind that something about this hand is connected with the recurrent feelings of acute and severe discomfort — the *anlage* of insecurity and later of anxiety.

Well, infants, like people, are ingenious. And the immobilization of, let us say, the right hand, does not effect the immobilization of the left. As the genital is handy, and as it has a slightly different sensation from the thumb, the nose, and so on, the event recurs. Again there is the great discomfort in the presence of the mother. Presently both hands may be tied at the side, and by that time even an infant begins to realize that it has something to do with the genital.

All animals tend to react with rage to immobilization, or to any thwarting or restraint which amounts generically to immobilization. To leap over months of struggle between the mother, aided by her medical adviser, and the infant's natural impulse to explore all his abilities and the limits of himself and the rest of the world; after months of struggle there has been impressed upon this infant a type of interest, a mark, if you please — an emotional mark — about the groin area which is so significant that when I was younger and more reckless about language, I called that state "primary genital phobia," which, being translated, is primary fear, irrational fear, of the genitals.

One does not fear something of no interest to one. Anything invested with fear must by definition, by the inherent character of our contact with the universe, be of interest to us. And, therefore, because of this taboo — the child has interest, unusual interest, an utterly useless interest so far as the development of personality is concerned, attached to the penis.

As a child and as a juvenile he continues to have this interest. Why? Because this thing was precipitated in personality very early, very firmly. All the red flags of anxiety came to attach to it. Moreover, mamma is always watching. Where the devil has shown up once, you may confidently expect him to return — quite unlike lightning.

And so here we have a person who, long before the puberty changes, has come to have a considerable conflict of impulse pertaining to genital manipulation, a thing fully meaningful only years later; and a conscious center of interest in the genitals, but a negative one, in that they are to be left alone at any cost.

Of course, one is always waking up to discover that one has violated this regulation in one's sleep. Interest has some way or other gotten one to violate this taboo. One is horrified. One has the feeling, "Oh, the devil that is in me. Here I am, doing this worst of possible things in my sleep."

Such a person, having stumbled through preadolescence, let us say, carefully avoiding any physical intimacies with anybody, comes to adolescence. At adolescence the genital dynamism awakens. Experience begins to be colored by a new emotion, and one of singular emphasis, to which we apply the term, lust.[1] As hunger is generically a state of dissatisfaction which orients awareness towards the integration of nutritive — and related — situations chiefly affecting the oral zone of interaction, so lust is a state of dissatisfaction which orients awareness towards the tendency to integrate situations chiefly affecting the genital zone.

Even in our particular boy with the puritanical mother, lust swings his attention towards his penis as an instrument in social situations. Along with the coming of this impulse there appears a curiosity as to the stories about it which the social environment produces, and it gets to be frightfully troublesome. Being compelled to enter into interpersonal situations, and being subjected to powerful social pressure which makes it proper, right, respectable and decent for him to go with a girl, he now goes with a girl.

What, then, occurs? He comes presently to realize quite clearly that he is not acting as was expected. He may know what should be done, but cannot do it. He may have to inquire to discover what is the matter. The knowledge does not help him. Nor does his inability in any way relieve him of the driving lust. It does not resolve the activity of the genital dynamism. But it does put very serious kinks in his relations with a member of the other sex. He is doubly unsatisfied, and, in all likelihood more or less chronically anxious. The failure reflected to him from the companion also strikes at self-esteem and the feeling of personal competence and security. It is small wonder that things go from bad to worse with him.

[1] I can picture the commotion to which this statement may provoke the more conforming of the psychoanalysts by recollecting a conversation had some ten years ago with Ives Hendrick — *Facts and Theories of Psychoanalysis* [2 ed.]; New York, Knopf 1939 (xiv and 369 pp.) in the course of which I remarked that I could not accept the *phallic* phase of development, as formulated by Freud.

Let us say that this boy about whom we are talking has had anxiety a number of times when he awoke to discover that he was violating the taboo that had been written into his personality. We have said that the instrumentality of anxiety is ordinarily sufficient to maintain in dissociation impulses which are entirely contradictory to the self dynamism, impulses which are entirely unsuited to the type of life for which the self system has been organized.

What happens when the sexual impulses, the impulses to genital behavior, collide with the self system, as in our particular example? Under certain circumstances, the self is able to dissociate lust and the impulses to genital behavior. This can be achieved only by the development of new and elaborate "apparatus" in living. I make here but a crude and hurried touching on something which I will develop at greater length, presently. The point which I wish to emphasize now is that, late as it is in maturing, the genital lust dynamism is something that can be dissociated only at grave risk to effective living, and that in most people it cannot be dissociated at all. It will again and again, at whatever great expense to security, whatever suffering from anxiety, manifest itself.

When the genital drive is dissociated, what precisely do we observe? I shall use this rather uncommon situation to give new emphasis to the meaning of our interpersonal viewpoint. When we speak of drives, impulses, tendencies, we mean always tendencies to integrate situations that will be resolved in a particular significant fashion — often by activity chiefly pertaining to one of our zones of interaction with the environment, and activity chiefly that of one of our several dynamisms.

Without hoping to make clear in a small part of one lecture the greater than somatic character of these dynamisms, let me make a rather necessary digression to discuss the physiological substrate of the zones of interaction of the personality.

We say that the principal zones of interaction are as follows: the *oral*, the retinal, the auditory, the general tactile, the vestibulo-kinaesthetic, the *genital*, and the *anal*, or aboral.[2]

The zones of interaction are developed, elaborated, equipped for dealing with particular phases of the physico-chemical, biological, and interpersonal environment.

The oral zone is made up of a great deal of apparatus. It includes for practical purposes the respiratory apparatus and the food-taking apparatus, from which is evolved the speaking apparatus; so that this zone is very important indeed, and is utilized from the first moment of life to the last. It has special tactile equipment in the lips, in the mouth, and in the nasopharynx. It includes our two most purely chemical receptors, the gustatory sense, and the olfactory.

[2] By the italics, I wish to set off the three zones the dynamisms of which are greatly varied from person to person because of the special cultural influences that are included in their organization and functional activity.

As I say, this oral zone may be considered as a unit, and while it is always reckless to speak of any part of a person as a unit, still the oral zone is at least a describable part of the person, and the function of the oral zone, in common with all of these zones of interaction, is probably awarded a certain amount of the vital energy, whether it is needed there or not. Given, let us say, twenty units of vital energy from the chemical changes going on in us, two units, perhaps, will be partitioned to this oral zone and will tend very strongly to be used in oral activity, which as you can conceive may be very highly variegated in later life, but in the beginning consists largely of breathing, sucking, and crying.

The retinal area of interaction brings us our most incredibly expanded integration with things not immediately within reach — the retinal receptor is the distance receptor par excellence, and with the aid of optical apparatus permits us to see over distances of a great many light years. Besides this, it is peculiarly related to things *within* reach, for its evolution is closely connected with dexterity, with our prehensile and manipulative skills shown primarily in the functional activity of the hands.

The auditory apparatus dealing with air vibrations, vibrations in fluid media, is also a distance receptor, but one of very slight ability compared with the retinal. Regardless of this comparative weakness in overcoming distance, it is the exceedingly important channel for word-learning, and is closely connected with speech — thus being involved with the oral dynamism, of which it might be considered a part. This fusion is not helpful, however, excepting that it shows the interdependence of the parts in the whole.

The general tactile receptors, on the other hand, are for immediate contact.

The kinaesthetic apparatus is involved with the activities of the muscles and joints, and locating ourselves in regard to the relevant geometry of space. It includes the equilibrium equipment.

The genital zone combines highly specialized tactile receptors and apparatus which could be put in the kinaesthetic class except that it pertains to involuntary muscles rather than to striated muscles, equipment connected with corpus spongiosum, the prostatic urethra, the motor elements in the seminal vesicles, and the prostate itself.

At the other end of the alimentary tract again around a muco-cutaneous juncture there is a highly specialized tactile apparatus, similar to that around the lips — conceivably necessary for the maintenance of safety of these delicate areas, there being special nutritional problems wherever the mucous membrane joins the skin.[3]

The oral, genital, and anal zones of interaction with the environment are

---

[3] They are quite different types of tissue, the skin and mucous membrane, with different biochemical processes; the blood supply of the two is specifically different, and the junctures are unusually vulnerable because all this differentiated tissue is combined more or less along a line. Injuries of the muco-cutaneous junctures are troublesome, as all of you who have had cold sores or anal fissures must know.

greatly affected in the educational acculturation procedure. Many people have their olfactory abilities seriously reduced as a result of the distaste with which culture-carriers in authority treat interest in smells and acts of smelling on the part of the child.

The special tactile activity of the mouth is conditioned by peculiarities and restrictions about taking nourishment, sucking, and the like. The gustatory part is conditioned by prejudices about what is food and what is clean and proper to take into the mouth, and so on and so forth. We shall have more to say about this, presently.

The genital is so conditioned by the prejudices and beliefs of the parents that it is apt to be permanently impaired for its biological function, if not for all forms of interpersonal activity, and similarly, the anal zone is strongly conditioned by culture, in the teaching of our rather elaborate toilet habits.

The result of this strong invasion of culture into the physiology of the organism is very apt to be attended with phenomena of symbolic segregation of various parts of the body. If you are taught that you are a good boy when you do not put your thumb in your mouth, *not doing* so as a virtue begins to be mixed up with being a good boy; and when you are impressed with the cataclysmic character of manipulating your genital, the genital is apt to get invested with marks of danger to be avoided, and also mixed up in yourself, in the self dynamism; and tinkering around the lower end of one's alimentary tract is quite distracting to many parents, and one is apt to get to understand that that particular part of one's anatomy is to be treated only indirectly. You must have your hand wrapped in paper before you approach this part of the body, and that is apt to get itself invested with considerable interest in itself.

The oral zone is involved in such varied functions that it is perhaps the central trunk, the main stem for evolutions of the self. It is fortunate that the excrementary orifice does not get so much significance. Now and then, however, it gets rather remarkable significance. What with the parent's interest in cleanliness and the general American conviction that regularity of bowel action is vital — and the delicate organization of the infant, anyway, so that one can't ignore its bowel action completely — quite often this zone is used in interaction with the parents to express hostility and resentment which usually takes the form of extraordinary interferences with the excrementary function. Biologically things are so keyed that when the rectum is pretty well engorged, its emptying is automatic. That does not do at all among civilized people who wear clothes, and late in infancy or early in childhood quite often the parents have to cudgel their brains, and sometimes the child, a great deal to overcome his *excessive* control of the sphincters. In other words, he refuses to accommodate. Having had his excrementary function thoroughly acculturated, he simply improves on example, you might say, and outdoes this highly desirable learning, and that causes consternation in the environment — thus proving that it is an instrument of power.

The cry was originally the powerful tool of the infant. All too frequently the constipation becomes the powerful tool of the child. The parents have gotten used to listening to him talk and he does not get very much that way, but clamping down on the sphincters at the lower end of the alimentary tract gets action — lots of action, lots of attention, and, thereby, begins to take on significance in this important matter of power, which is so woven into the self dynamism as to be in one way the explanation of the self's existence. One of the great elements in the feeling of security is the conviction that one has power enough in an interpersonal situation: One can feel "in control" of the situation.

Let us now return to the question; what do we observe in our young man. He is free from awareness of lust, he does not wittingly enter any situation with the purpose of having something genital happen. What do we perceive? We perceive that this man is hounded by the accidents by which he finds himself involved with the wrong type of person. What does this mean? It means that the power of this integrating tendency is such that even though it works entirely outside of his awareness, it works, and works conspicuously, and while he believes that he has become interested in a young lady, has sought her company and has finally got himself noticed so that he can discuss calculus with her, the facts which determine that situation are very much more on the side of the genital lust motive than they are on the intellectual pursuit of calculus. But it is only of the latter that he can be aware, and so he is constantly having difficulties in his interpersonal relations.

The girl has regarded his "approach" as quite subtle — but he never arrives. She may give him a helping hand, but he somehow overlooks or misinterprets it. If she makes the best of a bad job and they actually discuss calculus problems; even then — as under any other circumstance — he leaves unsatisfied, with a feeling that things have not worked well. That night, he awakens wet with perspiration, from a dream in which he has been kissing and fondling this girl's breasts — and has just bitten one and swallowed the nipple!

And here we must digress again from our young man, and consider the psychiatrist's views of sleep and dreams. I have asserted that psychiatry is the study of interpersonal relations. What are the interpersonal relations of one who is asleep? It is true that most people have a relatively short period each night of what we call *deep* sleep, in which there are no evidences of anything personal at work. Most of the time that one is asleep, however, one is engaged in a peculiar kind of interpersonal activity. Now and then the sleeper is awakened by a dream. If you were to ask why he awoke, he might say that he had been frightened by the dream. He may have had a dream attended by terror, or horror, or a danger that grew so threatening that, almost as if by force, he suspended sleep. He woke up, he says, to reassure himself. Perhaps this was not too successful; when wide awake — according to his judgment — the shadows of the dream hung on. The familiar furnishings of the bedroom did not appear. The bureau persisted in being a menacing object. Perhaps he had to rise from bed and walk around before he was again quite at home in his bedroom, quite free from the threat of a resumption of the dream did he but fall asleep again.

Now these are phenomena of dreams, you say. And what are dreams? Dreams are interpersonal phenomena in which the other fellow is wholly illusory, wholly fantastic, a projection, if you please, of certain constructive impulses, or of certain destructiveness, or of certain genital motivations, or something of that kind.

Dreams, we have to assume, are for the purpose of maintaining sleep, and the fact that they fail now and then is not any reflection on the utility and efficacy of dreams, but is an index to the gravity of the situation with which the person is confronted. If one awakes from a terror dream, it is quite certain that one's life situation is treacherous. If one awakes with inexplicable anxiety, it is quite certain that one's life situation includes plenty of cause for anxiety. The fact that he knows nothing about what he dreamed is a suggestion, not an inevitable index, but a strong suggestion that the problem is in the field of something dissociated from the self system, or by the self system, as you will.

This tells us something about dreams. It is quite possible that minor integrating tendencies dissociated from the awareness often discharge themselves predominantly during sleep, and, therefore, the dream-work not only protects the incident of sleep but also helps to maintain adjustment and mental health despite dissociation.

Our boy, in whom the genital lust dynamism is involved in conflict — and some components of which are dissociated — has horrible disturbances of sleep. Either he commits sins in his sleep and awakens feeling ruined, all tired out, or he commits these sins and wakens feeling fine, which again is a sin. More often than that, however, he has no clear sexual dreams. He has dreams in which he commits atrocious crimes, like his dream of cannibalistic incorporation of the girl's nipple.

How does this come about? Clearly in sleep, in dreams, impulses which in waking life are dissociated make their appearance and play out dramas of interpersonal relations with more or less purely fictitious people. This suggests that in sleep the force which maintains the dissociation in waking life is enfeebled. We say that as the self system was evolved primarily for the maintenance of interpersonal security, since sleep is impossible unless some distinct measure of security exists, it is only natural that the self dynamism might be somewhat in abeyance, somewhat weaker in its manifestations, in sleep, when by definition we will have no contact with a real person — and you will remember that the self was derived from very real people.

Even though this is true, only rather strikingly healthy people have rather explicit, quite simply meaningful, perhaps quite simply constructive, dreams. Most people dream things which, as they recall them on awakening, are fantastic and meaningless.

Some of this is due to the transition from sleep to wakening. The transition from a state of being asleep with some remembered dreams to the state of being awake is a great change in consciousness. One can dream in the most illogical, perhaps, literally in a ruleless, way. When we are conscious, however, we are more or less completely under the sway of the processes of consensually valid communicative thinking that we have had to learn. Therefore, in the very act of changing from one stage of consciousness to another, where different frames of reference are applied, many details of the dream are just too intricate to be fitted into the waking consciousness and they disappear or they get themselves simplified. There is a real barrier in this very transition of consciousness that makes us somewhat obscure in our relation to that which went on when we were asleep.

Besides that, while the self is relatively dormant in sleep it does not disappear, it is a perduring aspect of personality and the dissociated impulses must, by fantastic means in many cases, follow a principle which is very strikingly manifested in the waking life in many of the mental disorders; the character of the interpersonal phenomena which are manifested in sleep is often regressive in the sense that it is of an earlier stage of development.

I have tried to suggest to you that the awareness of the infant is of a very diffuse and unspecified kind. We may, therefore, say that the maximum regression of prehending processes is to a sort of an amorphous universe in which one has one's being — doubtless, a fairly early infantile mental state. If there were necessity, one could revert in dreams to that sort of attack upon one's problems. Seemingly quite insignificant changes in this vague sort of center-of-the-universe picture might mean very great things at the adult day-consciousness level.

Regression is not usually anything like so deep. There is no necessity for such profound recessions. One can drop back from too disturbing a clarity as to what is going on to a time in one's past when any such disturbing clarity had not been comprehended, and actions could go on then which adultly, in our waking state, would mean the satisfaction of a tendency, but which, as we recall the dream, just seem to be sort of childish.

Also, much is made in dreams of a process familiar to the children of many a home. Take the case of the boy caught getting into the jam. And mother says, "Willie, I told you not to touch that jam," and Willie says, "I didn't touch the jam; my hand did."

Also, in dreams one may show some displacing of feeling, and that again is an ancient habit. For example, when one is angry at the teacher who has quite unjustly punished one for somebody else's act, one does not show it, if one is wise and well controlled, but on the way home one can raise hob with some other schoolboy. The affect, you might say, has been carried for a while and deposited on a less dangerous object. And so in dreams, feeling may be moved around so that it does not focus too keenly the alertness on what is actually the case.

These processes occur to enable one to avoid the disturbing anxiety or the feeling of insecurity which will suspend sleep. They usually become notable in the period of adolescence when the problems of adaptation to others become pressing. Let me now proceed to a consideration of adolescents and chronologically adult people as we encounter them.

When we seek to formulate the syndromes[4] of maladjustment or mental disorder we have to consider two fields of data, two somewhat remarkable separate universes of phenomenal completeness, the — to use old-fashioned words — world of the subjective, and the world of the objective.

What does this person, this patient if you please, notice, and what else is there to be noticed by the ideally unhampered observer? The subjective, that which the person himself notices, has always to be communicated to the observer. We have been ingenious in devising apparatus and in refining observational techniques which show that the subject person, the patient, is experiencing something. Thus, for example, we may put a person in the circuit of a very delicate galvanometer, notice the resistance that his skin interposes to the passage of an electric current, and find that when certain stimuli are presented there is an abrupt change in this electrical resistance. It falls rapidly, many thousands of ohms, and we know that this change in skin resistance is intimately, if not absolutely, associated with some change in the integration of the person. Or we may, with less refinement, have a way of counting the number of breaths which a person takes per minute, and we find that at a certain time this rate of breathing is markedly augmented. We know that at certain times a person stops breathing for a measurable interval. There is a brief inhibition of the impulses which make for breathing. We know that these phenomena mean that something has happened in our patient. And we know, if we have sufficiently refined our own instruments — in this case, our hearing — that there are times in which the tone of the voice loses its rich quality and becomes flat, monotonous as it were, and we know again that this, the moment that it occurs, represents the particular timing of some event in the configuration involving the person.

But all these ingenious instrumental expansions of our senses in interaction with people, and all the acuity which we can develop from long contact with people, tells us only that something has happened. When it comes to testing the validity of our notion as to what has happened our only recourse is to listen for a long time to the reports of the patient as to what seems to him to be going on.

When we do this, we find some very interesting correlations; of a thousand

---

[4] The term *syndrome*, literally a concourse or concurrence, means a pattern of phenomena — signs and symptoms — which is frequently encountered, and the abstracting of which from the flux of events is presumed to be based on a valid insight into human life. It is much to be preferred in psychiatry to the term, *disease*. *Mental disorder* may be used, if mental refers to those aspects of living that are manifested in behavior and thought.

people we find that 942, for example, report that when we said so and so, they experienced so and so. And the instruments in the meanwhile recorded a shift in the resistance of the skin and a change in the breath rhythm. But when it comes to discovering what that person experienced subjectively, what meaning the situation had for him, we have only the report, the attempt to communicate by the use of words and gestures to us, of something that is extraordinarily private.

The facts are that it is only by the skilful use of our most specialized tool of communication that we can seem to overcome the privacy of these so personal worlds. By responsive speech we are able to bridge the gap with inferences of high probability as to what is actually the case.

You may remember in the first hour that I suggested to you that our perceptions of the physical universe are always separated from that physical universe by the act of perceiving. I went on to say that in the realm of inter-personal relations, the mediation between the personal situation outside us; namely, our idea of that personal situation, is much more complex. We again recur here to this point and suggest that the best that speech — by far our most refined instrument of communication, a tool for relating ourselves meaningfully to another person — can bring about is an understanding of the other person which has high probability of correctness.

High probability of correctness is very different, indeed, from absolute certainty. The moment that one introduces the concept of probability one realizes that it may approach one hundred per cent as a limit, but that it never gets to that limit; that it may approach zero as a limit, but it is never quite that low. Probability is always uncertainty, but it is sometimes very little uncertainty and sometimes very great uncertainty, and to understand the other fellow in his most intimate relationship with us, the best we can achieve is a partial understanding of what is going on. If we are wise and clever, this may have high probability of being correct.

Now the syndromes which are most useful in the diagnosis of personal situations, come more and more clearly to appear to be statements of the past, the momentary present, and the future of the career of the person who is our subject. The career that we are discussing is made up of the events which have connected, now connect, and will presently connect him with the lives of other persons.[5]

---

[5] The term *diagnosis* — literally a discrimination, and medically a deciding as to the character of the situation before one — is in the study of personality inextricably involved with *prognosis* — literally a foreknowing — the formulation of the probable outcome. Kraepelin's famous classification of the functional psychoses had an all but absolute prognostic slant. Current internal medical diagnosis is more inclined to consider the multiplicity of events that *may* influence the outcome — thus tending to set diagnosis apart from prognosis. Personality problems involve an even greater number of unpredictable factors than do most problems of internal medicine. The use of statistical experience as a basis for prognostic formulations is, therefore, a very dubious performance. It is well-known among physicians that all persons suffering tuberculous meningitis

These useful syndromes are different from the category of mental and nervous diseases which are taught to the medical student even to this day. They are perhaps somewhat more like the statements about this and that one which are heard in the privacy of the home, among intimate friends. The point we make here is that the ancient preoccupation of psychiatrists was a diagnosis of mental disorder, which had every now and then to be revised. From this field, the interest has moved on to considerations of how people could be classified. All that is out of sympathy with the central view of this series of lectures, to the effect that the subject of psychiatry is the study of interpersonal relations. Dementia praecox, schizophrenia, neurasthenia — these things are the privilege of the person who has them, in blissful separation from any suggestion of the social communality. The symptoms are ordinarily discussed as if they are static characteristics of a thing, very different indeed from statements about "How does Mr. A. act with Mr. B.?" "What goes on in the situation integrated between Mr. A. and Mr. B.?"

As I say, as one shifts the emphasis in psychiatry from the study of alleged personalities with alleged disorders to that which beyond any doubt is scientifically accessible; namely, what goes on in the situation with this person, then this panoply of neurasthenia, dementia praecox, anxiety neuroses, and so on, fade out of the picture. The picture becomes somewhat simpler and at times much more complex.

It becomes somewhat simpler in that one is relieved of the necessity of maintaining a God-like objectivity as if literally from an ivory tower. It becomes much more complex because one really has to notice what is going on and to derive some inferences as to the past, the present and the future of the career-line from these participantly observed events.

If I say neurasthenia is a condition characterized by pain in the neck, great readiness for fatigue, and preoccupation with fancied disorders, often of the genitals, which cannot be explained on any organic basis, the medical man feels that he has been told something useful to him. If I say that as a student of personality I cannot find any virtue in the conception, neurasthenia, that is another matter, much less satisfying.

The person who has an acute belly-ache followed by a feeling of extreme sickness, great anxiety, fear of death, and so on, calls the family physician, who takes his temperature and a blood specimen, pokes him around, hits some very tender spots in the abdomen and says, "Johnny, you have appendicitis." Johnny is greatly relieved to hear this word "appendicitis." It is not entirely a matter of verbal magic, if you please. When the doctor says, "Oh, this is appendicitis," this indicates that the doctor knows what he is talking about.

---

die. A patient at the Sheppard and Enoch Pratt Hospital, so diagnosed by three outstanding internists — and confirmed by the laboratory — recovered. The internists became unhappy about their diagnosis. The patient has been doing well for ten years.

Even if the patient is very much worried, here is the doctor, representative of medical science, who regards the thing much as he regards the weather — it is clearly not anything to be much excited about.

The new viewpoint of psychiatry teaches us that we cannot parallel the performances implied in the medical diagnosis, and, however enthusiastic the patient or his relatives may be about having a scientific name for the trouble, we must discontinue the finalist performances by which, for example, we have been classifying large groups of our fellows who are chronic inhabitants of mental hospitals. They are there. Something is the matter with them, but we should no longer feel happy because we have applied a label to them.

The first group of our syndromes pertain to the relatively uninterrupted career-lines of people; the second group, to more or less clearly episodic changes in direction. The first group, therefore, appear to be diagnoses of personality; the second, of disorders of personality. Actually, the first group refer to degrees of development and the second to a blend of the developmental factors with the vicissitudes of the person in his communal existence with others.

We have seen how the culture in which we chance to live comes finally to have great prescriptive power over our thoughts and behavior, not only because other people, the carriers of the culture, thwart, humiliate, punish and reward us, and facilitate our securing satisfaction and maintaining a sense of personal security, but finally in preadolescence and adolescence, because some of these other people become highly significant to us.

Our first syndrome is made up of phenomena which appear at first sight to contradict these considerations. There are people among us whose integration of interpersonal situations is chiefly characterized by lack of duration. These people live through a great number of fugitive, fleeting, involvements with other people — and even with the more tangible of the institutions of the particular society in which they have their being. They are disappointing to everyone who is interested in them. They are themselves always disappointed in other people — but this does not make them bitter, nor does it excite them to inquiry as to what may be the matter. Without troubling to think it out, they exemplify the saying that all the world is queer, except. . . . They move through life giving many of the appearances of human beings; they just miss being human — and they do not lack fluency in verbal behavior. They almost always say the right thing. They often say it well. But it signifies very little.

The striking things about these people are their inability to profit from what we would consider to be their experience, and their disregard for the future. The intelligence factor is not involved. They experience life differently from others and their insight into reality is correspondingly different. Not only is it different, but it is far more imperfect than the average. Here and now may be grasped quite well. The past is vague and the future is of no real interest.

These are the non-integrative, the so-called *psychopathic*, personalities[6] who are superlative in social nuisance value and of great theoretical interest for psychiatry. This latter interest arises from their peculiarly qualified insight into their personal reality — and that of others — which implies an extraordinary peculiarity of their self dynamism. It is so difficult and disconcerting to deal with them that but little valuable data has been accumulated.[7] I believe that the first essential in a research in this field is the application of the techniques used in the study of anthropoids. This will give us useful clues towards the elucidation of language behavior in the psychopath, and thus we may come to unravel their relatively vestigial self.

Secondly, in these syndromes, we come upon the *self-absorbed*, or fantastic person. To those of you who are given to reading about psychoanalysis, this is the person whose relations with others and with the more objective institutions of society are shot through with "wishful thinking" — for me, a difficult concept.

The prototype of these people is to be sought in early childhood. To make this clear, I must say something as to the prehension[8] and perception of significant people, as we conceive them to develop in infancy. The nipple is probably first prehended as a part of one's vague cosmic entity. It gradually stands out as an attribute of the Good Mother. There gradually evolves another complexus of impressions which — because of the empathic linkage — is the Bad Mother. Objectively, to us, the person concerned is the mother; to the infant, these are two vaguely limited but entirely distinct people. The discrimination of the Good Mother pattern of events and the Bad Mother pattern of events constitutes a primary bifurcation of interpersonal experience evidences of which persist in most people, throughout life.

In later infancy there is a synthesis of experience which dulls this primary discrimination and gradually evolves an adequate perception of the mother as a person who is sometimes good — giving satisfactions and security — and

---

[6] Comment on two patients of the category appears in "Regression: . . ." *State Hospital Quart.* (1926) 11:208–217, 387–394, and 651–668. The (1925) view expressed in footnote 2, p. 119, is in part erroneous. An "unconsciously determined inability to profit from experience" is now seen to be equivalent to *biological* defeat. The factors of personality exterior to awareness do not arrange difficulties of this sort; the self dynamism is the "part" that interferes.

[7] Kraepelin classified psychopathic personalities under seven rubrics: the excitable; the unstable; the impulsive; the egocentric; the liars and swindlers; the antisocial; and the quarrelsome. Eugen Kahn — *Psychopathic Personalities* [tr. by H. F. Dunbar]; New Haven, Yale University Press, 1931 (521 pp.) — has a most elaborate classification, some of which doubtless pertains to the people whom I am discussing. See in particular, Partridge, George E., "Current Conception of Psychopathic Personality," *Amer. J. Psychiatry* (1930) 10[o.s. 87]:53–99. See also, Henderson, David K., *Psychopathic States*; New York, Norton, 1939 (178 pp.), and Partridge, George E., "A Study of 50 Cases of Psychopathic Personality," *Amer. J. Psychiatry* (1928) 7 [o.s.84]:953–973.

[8] To prehend is to have potential information or misinformation about something: to perceive is to have information or misinformation in or readily accessible to awareness.

sometimes bad. The fantasies of childhood show, however, that the earlier formulations have not disintegrated. For that matter, many of the puzzling excesses in the child's emotional reactions arise from the continuance of these dynamic factors. But for practical purposes, the child has learnt that mother is not as good as was the lost Good Mother, nor as bad as the other one. There is loss and gain.

The loss, being a privation, is more vivid than is the gain. I believe that we can safely read back into these early times, the usual ways of dealing with irreparable losses of this kind; and if so, we may feel sure that constructive fantasy appears only after mere representative fantasy has worn itself out. The child fogs the undesirable aspects of mother with recollections of the Good Mother; thus reinstating security and satisfaction enough to sleep in peace and to remedy slights and frustrations. This gradually fades from waking life, as better adaptations to the more real mother are invented. It probably persists in the preliminary stages of falling asleep.

In people who show our self-absorbed type of performances, however, the element of representative fantasy continues as a major ingredient of life. All sorts of interpersonal prehensions are fogged into what is called "wishful" distortions or misinformation about people. These people have no grey; every-thing tends to be black or white. Their friends are simply wonderful people. People whom they dislike are just simply impossible. Their "love" is melodra-matic to a degree that confounds its object — excepting the object be another self-absorbed person. Together, by a sustained miracle of accommodating — or ignoring — the individualistic misconceptions of each other, two of these folk can have quite a good time. With the rest of us, however, they are apt to be disappointed, wounded, misunderstood. And we, if we care to study the processes at work, cannot but marvel at the failure of learning which has left their capacity for fantastic, self-centered, illusion so utterly unaffected by a life-long series of educative events. These people integrate situations with foggy embodiments projected upon us from their fantasies about themselves.

Let us now look at a type of organization which represents less blandly a cosmic centering in the person concerned. We shall call this syndrome of characteristics that of the *incorrigible* person, choosing this none too satis-factory term for the reason that these people have actively evaded or resisted the educative influences that in more fortunate people lead to a more prac-tical organization of the self dynamism. I may suggest their characteristics by saying that they integrate more durable situations only with people whom they regard as their inferiors. Towards all others, their basic attitude is hostile, unfriendly, or morose and forbidding. It is clear that these people have a grave defect in the field of security; often inculcated by a parent who just would not be satisfied with the child.

The syndrome makes clear appearance in the juvenile development. These young folk cannot progress to the stage of give-and-take, of competition and self-satisfying compromise.

The incorrigible person does not attack the really strong. He has failed in the most significant of efforts to overcome dissatisfaction with him. The scar of this failure remains and he is forewarned from contests that might renew the pain. Authority — paradigmatic of the disapproving parent — is anathema to him, but to smooth-working, competent, authority he interposes no objection. To authority that is exercised with any uncertainty, any irrational contradictions, any "stupidity," the incorrigible person is intolerant and intolerable. If he is intelligent, he shows a genius for finding defects in the exercise of social controls, and for making trouble about it. He is a thorn in the side of teachers. From school, he proceeds into the larger world, to put "stuffed shirts" where they belong.

The fourth syndrome that I shall present you is the *negativistic* person. These are the people, to keep to our earlier figure, who have no black or white, but only grey. They are in many ways antithetic to the self-absorbed person; their selves are organized on the basis of appraisals that make them insignificant — until their constructive fantasy hit upon negation as a device for forcing notice if not approval. If mother says "It's time for little Willie to go to bed" and little Willie goes; that is one thing. It may be but one of unnumbered brushings of little Willie out of the way. If now, instead of going to bed, little Willie says "No" and reinforces his non-cooperation with all means at his disposal, his significance in his world may become at least briefly, very great.

I shall not digress to consider various reactions to the child's negation; the submersion in "sweetness and light," the submission to tantrums, and so on and so forth. I wish rather to indicate the typical negativistic syndrome which has its origin in the discovery that it is better to be a problem child than a mere necessary evil.

Insecurity in the negativistic is met with an assertion of refusal. If such a person feels any tendency towards minimizing him or taking him for granted, he resists a suggestion, or refutes a statement, or differs with an opinion, or in some other nugatory way accentuates his significance in the interpersonal situation. If he is keenly insecure, he may be simply uncooperative in everything, to such an extent that the other fellow can but go away.

The negativistic way of life is apt to be highly educative, and it thus comes about that many prevailingly negativistic people get to be quite expert in some field — even that of conciliation. Being highly competent, it is no longer necessary to feel insecure in situations in which they are recognized as the expert, and their long experience with divergent views comes in handy.

It was necessary for me to present the negativistic category before mentioning a syndrome of the interpersonal phenomena which is in many ways a super-incorrigibility, and in some ways a super-negativism. This, our fifth syndrome, I shall call that of *the stammerer*. These people make use of vocal behavior — or misbehavior — not for communication but for defiance and domination. They have discovered a magic of articulate sounds that really works. By demonstrating their inability to produce a word — and to desist from effort at producing it — they immobilize the other person and arrest the flow of process in the world. This is a power operation of no mean proportions. It represents a grave disorder of development at the time when sheerly magic operations were being abandoned and the consensual validation of verbal behavior was beginning. The disorder of speech is but one of several striking phenomena in this syndrome, about which, however, I shall say no more at this point.

It is to be noted that these first five of our syndromes are of early origin in the development of personality. They all come from the time of predominantly autistic verbal behavior. They are deviations of growth that are not chiefly a result of verbal communication between parent and child, teacher and pupil. They occur before the mediate acculturation of the juvenile era, which includes, among many other important accomplishments, the learning of things through the written and printed form of the language; and in particular, learning about legendary people who embody ideals, mores, and norms of the particular culture-complex.

One learns, for example, of Hans Brinker's feats. We learn of him through the mediation of speech, but he becomes an immediate ingredient of our thinking. We do not expect to meet him, as we did Uncle Herbert; but he is just as significant. He more or less adequately represents, perhaps by his very abstractness, his purely traditional existence, traits of character that are praiseworthy. As something greater and less than life, Hans Brinker becomes a denizen of the self.

The syndromes that present distortions of development after this spread of acculturation are of a greater complexity than are the first five. I shall present them in the order of complexity, which is naturally the order of developmental stage chiefly concerned in each.

The sixth syndrome may be called the *ambition-ridden* personality. These people have to use everyone with whom they are integrated. If you are no good for advancing his interest, the ambition-ridden person can find someone who is, with whom to enjoy whatever other satisfaction he had been having in your company. Some of them are scrupulous about some ideals, some of them are almost wholly unscrupulous. Some are clever at avoiding dangerous competition; some have to compete with everybody. Your personal experience will fill in this picture, for there is no dearth of these folk among us.

We come to a seventh syndrome, the *asocial*. Please note that the term is asocial, not antisocial. Antisocial is a nuisance-word which carries a penumbra of confusion: it is used indiscriminately to refer to the asocial, the incorrigible, and the psychopathic. The asocial are by no manner of means brigands, criminals, or people who are always rude without provocation. Many asocial people are among the more delightful folks I have known. They are the people whose integrations with others are assumed by them to be of no special moment *to* the other person, and to be of the duration of his convenience only.

Some of them show considerable error of judgment as to the other fellow's convenience, being as we say, so sensitive that they are put off by quite insignificant things and withdraw long before one would lose them. Some of them are quite obtuse and drift along with us long after we have been discouraged as to the possibility of intimacy with them.

They may be thought to be extraordinarily lacking in self-esteem, and in one way this is quite correct. They often esteem themselves, quite properly, quite highly — many of them are competent people. But they have not grasped the possibility that they themselves may be valued, cherished, by others. All that category of experience is missing from their self dynamism. The approvals which are incorporated are chiefly the products of mediate acculturation, and not of direct early experience. It is not strange, therefore, that these people often have highly formulated and rigidly held ideals of behavior. This does not exempt them from loneliness, and many of them have no difficulty in overlooking shortcomings in themselves and others with whom they have relations.

For an eighth syndrome, we may consider the *inadequate person*, including under this rubric all those people who integrate situations of dependency with others, and the people who derive their feeling of personal significance from identification with some extravagantly overvalued "cause." Some of these people have been obedient children of a dominating parent. They go on through life needing a strong person to make decisions for them. Some of them learned their helplessness and clinging-vine adaptation from a parental example. Some of them took over a justifying invalidism from a similar source.

A ninth syndrome may be named the *homosexual*, although this term has accumulated so great a freight of misunderstanding that I could wish for something less ambiguous. These are the people whose earlier experience has erected a barrier to integrations with persons of the other sex. The barrier may be relative or absolute. It may be highly specific in regard of the type of situation concerned, or it may be quite general — as in the "woman hater" who really dislikes the presence of any woman. We would say that his barrier was absolute and general in its effect. We encounter men who preferred to play with girls, in the juvenile era, and whose most enjoyable companionship is still with women but who cannot integrate sexual situations with them. We encounter men who have no use for women except for integrating sexual situations with them — and, believe me, these situations include nothing of love. I need not say that parallel deviations appear in women, though the cultural definitions of rôle add and subtract features from the phenomena that we encounter.

Some of these people, in preadolescence or later, learn to integrate sexual situations with persons of their own sex. Some of these are relations of love, and are stable and durable. Some are devoid of love and are very transient. Some are relations of hatred, durable or otherwise as the determining circumstances dictate.

Many of these people discharge their lustful impulses by self-manipulation, with or without explicit fantasy of another person. Some of them depend chiefly on processes that go on in sleep. A marginal group follows the heterosexual pattern of genital behavior with women of a particularly highly differentiated type, and some of these integrations are relationships of love, and wholly durable.

Our tenth syndrome, the last that I shall indicate, is really a congeries of syndromes, but it has enough of consistency to merit its title of the *chronically adolescent*. These are the people who never find the right love object. Some of them are driven by lust, and go on seeking the right person, always disappointed with anyone who has been available. Some of them become cynical and adopt lustful performances as an ideal indoor sport. Some of them are celibate, withdrawn from genital behavior, and — as I said earlier — in real danger as to personal stability. They all pursue the ideal and they find it not.

These are some of the more outstanding diagnostic syndromes which appear in the series of interpersonal relations through which one passes. They tell us of the past and permit shrewd guesses — predictions of high probability — as to the future integrations which the person will show. More significant for the clinical practice of psychiatry, they provide the meaning for otherwise mystifying episodes that occur in the lives of those who experience mental disorder. For the broader aspects of psychiatry, they are reference-frames for understanding what will and what will not work, in connection with a particular person.

III
Conflict Theory:
Intrapsychic Version

In the selections by Rank, Angyal, and Bakan one can perceive the nature of intrapsychic conflict positions. Both great forces are localized within the person from birth, and hence, the source of conflict is internal rather than arising from the incompatibility of man and society. But because the conflict is inherent, ideal personality is construed as a dynamic balance of the two internal forces.

Rank details his view of the core of personality: everyone is afraid to be an individual (life fear) and afraid to become indistinguishable from the masses (death fear). Life is conceptualized as a series of decision points from which one can strike out on a new path, and court life fear, or hold on to the old ways, and court death fear. At the peripheral level of personality, Rank discusses three personality types. The artist is the person who can minimize both life and death fears by trying to be an individual in a manner that will not alienate others. The average man is so overwhelmed by fear of life that he becomes a conformist without any true identity. And the neurotic has such strong fear of death that he develops a strident individualism which alienates him from others and society.

Angyal's short paper expresses a very similar position, though not in terms of fears. He assumes opposing tendencies toward autonomy and toward surrender. Once again, it is considered best to strike a working balance between these two tendencies; an overexpression of one at the expense of the other is considered unhealthy. Bakan also speaks that way, adopting the terms agency and communion to refer to the two opposing tendencies. He elaborates the misfortunes attendant upon too much expression of individuality and mastery. The disasters awaiting include not only psychological but also physical illness.

OTTO RANK

Life Fear and Death Fear

> Cowards die many times before their deaths;
> The valiant never taste of death but once.
> —SHAKESPEARE, *Julius Caesar*

We can now proceed from the indubitable psychological fact of the fear of death as it manifests itself in human consciousness. Regarding death fear in the actual meaning of the words, however, we can speak only in terms of the knowledge of death, that is, on a level of consciousness, which the infant at the time of the first development of fear certainly cannot yet have. On the other hand, we know that the child experiences his first feeling of fear in the act of birth, not fear of death however, but fear in the face of life. It seems, therefore, as if fear were bound up somehow with the purely biological life process and receives a certain content only with the knowledge of death. Whether this contentual tie up, which so frequently increases to a pathological fear of dying or being dead, represents the rationalization of another more fundamental fear we will discuss later in detail; at all events, this primary fear cannot be castration fear, for this also presupposes a certain development of consciousness which we could not assume for the infant. Moreover the point of view which I have maintained regarding the historical

From *Will Therapy and Truth and Reality*, by Otto Rank, trans. by Jessie Taft. Copyright 1936 and renewed 1964 by Alfred A. Knopf, Inc. Reprinted by permission of the publisher.

and genetic primacy of the birth fear as compared with castration fear, in spite of all the arguments of psychoanalysts to the contrary, seems undeniable. Since I was concerned first of all in the "Trauma of Birth" (1923) with an explanation of the fears of the infant I did not evaluate the death fear sufficiently, as it belonged to a later level, although it can appear astonishingly early in childhood; on the other hand I confess that at that time I had not advanced far enough beyond the birth symbolism, which here as elsewhere covered the death theme therapeutically. When for example, P. Schilder doubts the existence of a death instinct and asks "whether the impulse to death may not be a covering for erotic strivings, the wish for a rebirth"[1] it is certainly to the point in many cases, especially of neurosis or psychosis, but no argument against the death instinct, as little as are all the other erotic or masochistic disguises of it, which are covered by Freud's assumption of the pleasure principle as a special case of death instinct. This disguise, moreover, Schopenhauer has already seen clearly when he speaks in his "Metaphysics of Sex Love" of the pleasure primacy (Lustprämie) with which nature entices men to pay tribute in the sex act.

Responsibility for this erotic disguise of death seems to me to rest not only on the psychic tendency to denial of its terrors, but much more on the polar nature of the life process itself. For otherwise it would not be comprehensible why the death complex appears so much more clearly in religion, mythology and folklore than in the individual who apparently can bear the idea of death only collectively, just because this again promises therapeutic consolation. So it happened that I myself brought out the death symbolism first in the "Myth of the Birth of the Hero" (1909) and still more clearly in the related "Lohengrinsage" (1911); also in my further "Mythologischen Beiträgen" (1912–1914) which appeared collected in 1919. I finally undertook a decided advance in this direction with the investigation of the problem of the "double" in folklore (1914), which I then continued in my book "Seelenglaube und Psychologie" (1930) even to the theme of religious belief in immortality and its scientific presentation in the modern doctrine of the psychic. In terms of individual psychology I have never lost sight of the problem of fear since the "Trauma of Birth," although therapeutic interests forced me to build up my conception first in the direction of a constructive theory of will. This, however, had become clear to me, that we have before us in the individual neurotic, as it were, the opposite of collective belief in the soul and immortality ideology: that is, instead of the more or less naïvely expressed wish for eternal life, as it appears today in collective ideologies, we find an apparent desire to die, one might almost say a wish for eternal death. From the analysis of the role of the analyst in the therapeutic situation, there came to me finally a direct individual approach to the problem of death, and the idea that one could understand neurosis in general, including the

[1] Psychiatrie auf psychoanalytischer Grundlage 1925 S. 12.

therapy, only from this negative side of the soul life. In this sense the present presentation is the completion of my work on the belief in the soul, and as this finally leads to psychology, so the neurotic opposite of the belief in immortality, namely the death fear, leads to the need for therapy, as an individual doctrine of faith.

Freud has approached the problem of therapy from the forces of life (the libido) and has finally arrived at the death instinct, that is, at the death problem; for it hardly concerns an "instinct."[2] As I have already pointed out in the "Trauma of Birth," it seems to me essential for the understanding of the neurotic to go at the human problem from the side of fear, not from the side of instinct; that is to consider the individual not therapeutically as an instinctive animal but psychologically as a suffering being. It soon becomes evident that, approached from the instinct side, a whole series of problems will be viewed falsely, or will be located incorrectly, which from the death side, are approachable. Again we face the paradox of psychoanalysis, yes, of every ideology in general, which only happens to appear with peculiar clarity in the Freudian teaching today, namely, the therapeutic orientation in the broadest sense, which despite its scientific nature aims not at knowledge but at consolation, and always emphasizes in its facts just that side which affords help for human need. Freud's emphasis on the instinctual was therapeutic in this human sense, but he used it theoretically for a specific etiology of the neuroses which it was intended not only to heal but at the same time to explain. His pragmatic presupposition was, as is also the case with other practical sciences, that what helps must also be true. So his teaching from the beginning was directed toward consolation in the sense of a therapeutic ideology, and even when he finally stumbled upon the inescapable death problem, he sought to give a new meaning to that also in harmony with the wish, since he spoke of death instinct instead of death fear. The fear itself he had meantime disposed of elsewhere, where it was not so threatening, and was therapeutically more easily accessible. That the instinctual is repressed in the neurotic, certainly seems clear; equally that it is fear, from which the repression arises: since Freud however conceived of the instinct life sexually, he had the double therapeutic advantage on the one hand of having made the general fear into a special sexual fear (castration fear), and on the other of being able to cure this fear through the freeing of sexuality.

This therapeutic ideology rests on the presupposition that man is purely instinctual and that fear is brought in from the outside (hence the concept of castration fear). It has for a second presupposition the displacement of general fear to a partial field, a therapeutic release with which we shall occupy ourselves in the next chapter. The discovery that the freeing or satisfaction of sexuality does not necessarily do away with fear but often even increases

---

[2] Even analysts like Bernfeld and Westerman-Holstijn find the term "death instinct" inappropriate.

it, and the observation that the infant experiences fear at a time when there can be no question of outer threats of any kind, have made the theory of the sexual origin of fear, and its derivation from the outside, untenable. The individual comes to the world with fear and this inner fear exists independently of outside threats, whether of a sexual or other nature. It is only that it attaches itself easily to outer experiences of this kind but the individual makes use of them therapeutically since they objectify and make partial the general inner fear. Man suffers from a fundamental dualism, however one may formulate it, and not from a conflict created by forces in the environment which might be avoided by a "correct bringing up" or removed by later re-education (psychoanalysis).

The inner fear, which the child experiences in the birth process (or perhaps even brings with it?) has in it already both elements, fear of life and fear of death, since birth on the one hand means the end of life (former life) on the other carries also the fear of the new life. The stronger emphasis on the one or other of these two fear components in the birth act itself still seems to me to contain the empirical meaning of the birth trauma for the later fate of the individual. Beyond that, however, for me, the birth trauma was also a symbol of the original suffering nature of man which according to the psychoanalytic conception had been caused in the first place by some guilt of the individual or the environment and could be corrected, therapeutically or prophylactically (educationally). Here it is again evident that one very soon strikes the boundary of the metaphysical in the discussion of these basic human problems no matter whether one takes it religiously or philosophically. This involves no danger, as long as one does not succumb to the attempt to justify the one viewpoint at the cost of the other. I believe that one can never understand the human being purely empirically, as psychoanalysis strives to do; on the other hand the purely metaphysical conception of man seems to me unsatisfactory also, as soon as it aims at knowledge and fails to consider the purely human.[3]

Birth fear one can only designate as death fear metaphysically, since ideally one should separate it from the fear of empirical death, and find in it primarily that undifferentiated feeling of insecurity on the part of the individual, which might then better be called fear of life. The fact is just this, that there is in the individual a primal fear, which manifests itself now as fear of life, another time as fear of death. If birth fear, therefore, has nothing to do empirically with the fear of actual death, one must also test as to its empirical soundness the extreme metaphysical interpretation of Achelis. To call birth

---

[3] Such a dissatisfaction is presented in the profound book of Werner Achelis, . . . "Principia mundi, Versuch einer Auslegung des Wesens der Welt." The author who seeks to complete the empiricist Freud with the metaphysician Schopenhauer in a deeper sense, remains thereby as much guilty of empiricism as Freud of metaphysics, since he leaps far beyond the empirically comprehensible directly into the metaphysical, instead of letting himself be led to the boundaries of both spheres.

fear the first visible condensation of fear of death, that is, fear of the loss of individuality, seems to me open to attack on two grounds: first, the fear of loss of individuality seems to me to underlie fear of (empirical) death, second, I cannot see at all how birth can be viewed as loss or threat of loss of individuality, when it represents exactly the opposite; that would be possible only if one conceives of mother and child as one (which however Achelis does not mean) as I have done in the birth trauma theory, and then considers the loss of the mother in terms of an injury to the ego. In this case, however, fear is a reaction to the trauma of separation as which I have comprehended it factually as birth fear. Here lies also the connection made by the analysts, including Freud, between birth fear and castration fear, both of which in this sense appear as reaction to the loss of an important part of the ego. Birth fear remains always more universal, cosmic as it were, loss of connection with a greater whole, in the last analysis with the "all," while the castration fear is symbolic of the loss of an important part of the ego, which however is less than the whole, that is, is partial. The fear in birth, which we have designated as fear of life, seems to me actually the fear of having to live as an isolated individual, and not the reverse, the fear of the loss of individuality (death fear). That would mean, however, that primary fear corresponds to a fear of separation from the whole, therefore a fear of individuation, on account of which I should like to call it fear of life, although it may appear later as fear of the loss of this dearly bought individuality, as fear of death, of being dissolved again into the whole. Between these two fear possibilities, these poles of fear, the individual is thrown back and forth all his life, which accounts for the fact that we have not been able to trace fear back to a single root, or to overcome it therapeutically.

After this theoretical clarification of concepts I turn to clinical observation and should like first of all to establish the fact that the neurotic, to an even greater degree than the average, suffers from this double fear, yes, that the outbreak of the neurosis actually becomes explicable from the streaming together of these two sources of fear, which even in the "Trauma of Birth" I had designated as the fear both of going forward and of going backward. So there is already included in the fear problem itself a primary ambivalence which must be assumed, and not derived through the opposition of life and death instincts. We have almost come to the point of refusing to man as a suffering being positive life instinct, and of looking upon that which apparently manifests itself as such as a mere not-wishing-to-die.[4] The opposite of the positive life instinct would be not the death instinct, but fear, whether it be of having to die or of wanting to die. At all events the neurotic gives the impression of a negative instinctual being who continuously strives to delay dying and to ward off death, but who by these efforts only hastens and strengthens the process of destruction because he is not able to overcome

[4] The Chicago biologist, Professor Hayes, allows dying to begin with birth.

it creatively. On the other side the neurotic illness appears as a constant self-inhibiting of the life instinct, for any expression of which the individual seems to punish himself either before or afterwards. Both impressions are surely correct, corresponding to the ambivalent conflict of life fear and death fear; both, however, have been acquired relatively late.

Above all, it is strange that the punishment mechanism of the neurotic illness which seems so clear today had not drawn the attention of the analyst much earlier. However, as Freud had attacked the neuroses from the libido problem and not from the fear problem, it was natural first of all to emphasize the pleasure gain which the patient drew from his condition, the so-called reward of illness, and to consider the suffering bound up with it only as unavoidable evil. The therapy undertook, therefore, to bring him to the giving up of this pleasure gain through illness since it held out the prospect of a greater pleasure reward. Thus normal sexual satisfaction became avowedly or tacitly the goal of analytic therapy, a viewpoint which many analysts still hold as a standard. As Freud, however, learned to consider the punishment tendencies of the individual not only as hindrances to this goal, but also as the greatest resistances to the analytic process itself, he ascribed to them that genuine meaning, which found theoretical expression in the setting up of a death instinct. The works of Reik and Alexander which followed have pointed out a libidinal goal even in the self-punishment tendencies of the individual, and thus protected the Freudian theory of the neuroses from being stranded in the invincibility of the guilt feeling.

Before we take this leap into therapeutic ideology, however, we should keep in mind another type of experience which one cannot understand from the study of neurotics alone, but only if one approaches the problem from the development of the creative personality as I have attempted to do, especially in recent years. Thus I have recognized not only the constructive meaning of resistances in the analysis but also the creative side of guilt feeling, and have attempted simultaneously to utilize these negative manifestations therapeutically. What expresses itself in the individual on the one side as driving force, does not always have to be an certainly not exclusively "instinct," as little as resistances of different kinds must necessarily work only as hindrances. The self-punishment tendency which operates as inhibition (restraint) is not merely as Alexander has expressed it, a bribing of the super-ego in the interest of id satisfaction; on the contrary what manifests itself in this correct observation is a general life principle, on the basis of which no creating is possible without destruction, and no destroying without some kind of new creation.[5] When accordingly the neurotic must punish himself so much more severely and strikingly than the average man, this is not merely

---

[5] As far as I know, Dr. Sabina Spielrein first demonstrated these thoughts analytically and applied them to the explanation of the fear inherent in the sexual instinct. "Die Destruktion als Ursache des Werdens" Jahrbuch, f, psa Forschungen Bd. IV 1912 S. 465ff.

because he can only grant himself this or that pleasure satisfaction thus, but because he must bribe life itself, for which, according to Schopenhauer's deep insight, we all pay with death.

The neurotic then is a man whom extreme fear keeps from accepting this payment as a basis of life, and who accordingly seeks in his own way to buy himself free from his guilt. He does this through a constant restriction of life (restraint through fear); that is, he refuses the loan (life) in order thus to escape the payment of the debt (death). The more or less clear self-punishment tendency, which only represents one aspect of this picture, has not so much the intention of granting him life, as of escaping death, from which he seeks to buy himself free by daily partial self-destruction; applied to fear, guilt and inhibition symptomatology, this means that the neurotic gains from all the painful and tormenting self-punishments no positive pleasure, but the economic advantage of avoiding a still more painful punishment, namely fear of death.[6] In this way the lengthening of punishment (drawing out) is at the same time a drawing out of life, for as long as he punishes himself, feels pain as it were, he still lives. This neurotic attitude of the individual toward the problem of death, in the last analysis is comprehensible only from the will psychology, which shows that the human being seeks to subject death, this original symbol of the "must," to his will, and, as it were, at his own instigation transforms the death punishment which is placed upon life into a lifelong punishment which he imposes upon himself. On the other hand the ancient idea of the sacrifice plays a part in this, the idea that one could escape the hardest punishment by voluntary assumption of lighter self-punishment. These basic remarks are only to characterize the general point of view under which I learned to understand the self-punishment tendency in man. Applied to the neurotic type, it results not only in a deepened understanding of the symptomatology in particular cases, but also of neurosis as a whole, showing it to be an individual attempt at healing, against the arch enemy of mankind, the death fear, which can no longer be cured by the collective method of earlier ages.

It would be alluring to build up a theory of the neuroses on the basis of the death fear and to show how the particular symptoms and not merely the neurosis as a whole can be understood in one way or another as an expression of it, but since we are concerned with the neurotic as a type, as he is opposed to the therapist type, the therapeutic aspects of this concept lie nearer than the theoretical. From the therapeutic standpoint, however, one gets the impression that the overstrong fear of the neurotic is only the necessary defense against an overstrong instinctual basis and a correspondingly strong will, which is prevented by fear from full expression in living, which would be death. For, in spite of the predominance of the death fear in the neurotic,

---

[6] The ancient and universally distributed conception of death as punishment I have tried to explain in "Seelenglaube und Psychologie" from the human longing for immortality.

he still stands nearer to the creative type than to the average man, on account of which also he can be understood only as a miscarried artist, not as an incomplete or undeveloped normal type. In this sense the neurosis is a facing on the part of the individual of the metaphysical problems of human existence, only he faces them not in a constructive way as does the artist, philosopher or scientist but destructively. It is exactly on this account that the neurosis has taught us so much about the nature of man, because it represents the most inexorable form of self-knowledge and self-exposure than which nothing has less therapeutic value. With his therapeutic ideology the analyst protects not only the patient from the complete doubt as to the possibility of overcoming fear, but also himself from the destruction of his own illusions. Also the analyst like the artist can only overcome this fear creatively, as he is, in a certain sense, a new artist type, such as has not existed since the Greek period and has not been needed before since the Christian era. The type of artist who works in living human material, who seeks to create men not like the parents, physically, but spiritually, like God. How far this likeness to God corresponds to a creating of one's self in another, I have worked out elsewhere.[7]

In order to understand the creative and therewith also the neurotic expressions of this inhibiting, often destructive, life principle, we must first orient ourselves with regard to its normal forms of expression. The most important is sexuality, whose close relationship to the death principle is not only given biologically, but also holds psychologically. Not only in the act of birth but also in the sexual act itself the resemblance to death, yes, the nearness of death, is unmistakable. The sexual act has a different meaning certainly for the two sexes, a giving up (of an ego part), a surrender, yes, occasionally a complete loss of self; on the other hand it leads not only to new creation (in the child) but is at the same time perceived by the individual as the high point of the life principle, if the negative ego-destroying aspect does not win the upper hand. Viewed from the individual pleasure gratification which sex affords, it means biologically also a toll from life to death. Sexuality becomes thus the most current coin of this individual guilt to the race. This explains the attractive power which the so-called perversions exercise on the individual, but also why these sexual practices which lack biological market value or lessen it, are tied up with biological guilt feeling. On the other hand, we have learned to understand that often enough guilt feelings coming from other sources are paid in sexual coin, as many a physical surrender, and even masturbation, proves. Of the latter one could say paradoxically that its shamefulness, actual or acquired, comes just from the fact of its harmlessness to the individual; one has not really paid and accordingly one feels so guilty.[8]

Besides these biological connections between sexuality and death, there

[7] See chapter on "Love and Force" in O. Rank, *Will Therapy and Truth and Reality,* and also Genetische Psychologie II.

[8] The unavoidable nature of the masturbation conflict lies not in a false system of education, but corresponds as most conflicts do to a therapeutic attempt of the individual to overcome fear, which thereby is partially transformed into guilt (sin).

are psychological connections which are therapeutically more important. The retrieving of death fear through sexual fear represents an attempt to erotize the painful as it meets us grossly in masochism today. In this we have a use of sexuality characteristic of man alone, which is only comprehensible on the ground of will psychology. The individual will, as it were, seizes upon sexuality as a means to make suffering and pain, which in the last analysis are symbols of death, into a desired source of pleasure. It is the same ideology which creates from death fear a death instinct. At the basis of this apparently masochistic ideology there lies always the enormous strength of will of the personality, which is able by the erotization of pain to force the sexual instinct into the service of fear avoidance, and at the same time to strip the primal fear of its dangerous quality. Another means to the same end, which the individual employs in order to escape the fear of sexuality together with the compulsion to it, is love. We can only refer in this connection to one aspect of this perhaps most important of all human phenomena, the significance of which psychoanalysis missed in its identification of sexuality and love. There is just the contrast between love and sexuality that often enough causes love to resist sexuality or to fly before it, just as under certain conditions sexuality can be a flight from love. Naturally everything depends on how one defines or interprets love. In its erotic meaning, it includes at all events the concentration upon a single person, and represents therefore in this sense a turning away from the promiscuity natural to the sexual instinct, which is provided only for the maintenance of the species and not for the satisfaction of the individual. From this theoretical standpoint, which is also confirmed by practical observations, one can conceive of human love as a protection, so to speak, as an economic device, against the waste of the sexual instinct which could impoverish the individual, while he feels himself enriched by love. The much discussed promiscuity which may seem to the sexually repressed person like a symbol of freedom, proves from the viewpoint of the individual to be the greatest danger, which he seeks to escape ethically by a definite moral code, and practically through love. That thereby the individual only falls from the Scylla of sexual partial payment into the Charybdis of pledging his whole ego, is a problem which is to occupy us again elsewhere.

A further means for defending the ego against death fear, and one just as universal as love, is aggression. One does not need to assume an actual instinct of aggression as Freud does in order to justify this primary evil in man, by explaining it as a derivation of the death instinct, which only leads beyond this to speculations as to whether the original aggression turns toward the inside or the original death instinct to the outside. Here also a dynamic conception shows up a more immediate fact which one easily overlooks from the metapsychological point of view. The death fear of the ego is lessened by the killing, the sacrifice, of the other; through the death of the other, one buys oneself free from the penalty of dying, of being killed. One recognizes at once that this "criminal" solution represents the opposite of the neurotic, for in both cases we are dealing with anticipation of death punishment, of dying; with the neurotic in the form of self punishment, with criminals in the form of the punishment or killing of the other, which, however, is followed by the punishment of the ego through society (See my comment on the deeper meaning of the death punishment in Seelenglaube — S. 95). The neurotic is only a man who cannot allay his own death fear by killing the other, who, in other words, is not capable of aggressive protective behavior, although he experiences the impulse to it strongly enough. By this "killing" of the other for the protection of the self naturally I do not mean the legal concept of "self-defense" (legitimate), nor the biological concept of self-maintenance, but a purely psychic ideology, which rests upon the primitive feeling of the group (collectivity). According to this conception, which quite naturally values one life equally with the other without considering the individual as such, one death can also take the place of another. To the naïve consciousness of immortality, death must appear as punishment; later it became a self-merited punishment which for the most part followed sexual transgression or more correctly the transgressing of sexuality, because just this in the last analysis leads to death; finally the individual preferred self-punishment coming from the idea of sin, and again turning toward the outside, but as protection, not as aggression, will buy himself free from his own death through the death of another (sacrifice). The impulse to aggression therefore arises from within and has the tendency to transform one's own suffering into the pain of the other, from whom the suffering ostensibly comes. The guilt feeling ensues then not as a reaction to the aggression, but corresponds to the death fear, not done away with by the projection but only transformed, and thus moralized. Besides, the guilt feeling is an expression of the identification which is implied in the sacrifice of the other in the place of the own ego. In this sense, guilt feeling and self-punishment appear in the neurotic also as expression of love for the other, for whom one then takes sin and punishment upon oneself instead of blaming him; for somewhere the bad, the arch evil must be placated either in the other or in the own self; a distinction which explains the sadistic or masochistic attitude toward life, and also the close connection of the two.

In this briefly sketched development of the idea of sin, the killing of the other appears as a developmental phase, that is, the sacrifice of a life to death with the neglect of the individual difference. However, this primitive form of the sacrifice which we call murder has undergone a development and therewith a refinement. There are various forms of murder as there are various forms of self-destruction, as for example, in the neurotic symptoms. Ibsen speaks of "soul murder"[9] and means by that a making use of, or exploitation of the other. The killing does not need to be actual, it can occur symbolically

---

[9] This reminds one of Oscar Wilde's saying, "The coward kills with kisses, the brave man with the sword."

as for example in the withdrawal of love or in the desertion of a person; it can also ensue partially instead of totally, a slow murder, as it were, through constant tormenting. Always, however, it takes place as a self protection against the own death fear, and not as an expression of a primary death wish. The death wish against loved persons shows itself frequently as the expression of strong attachment, which can be resolved only through death and not otherwise. Accordingly also in the treatment of many "depressives" the appearance of death wishes against others is not to be interpreted as infantile regression, but as a sign of the inner unburdening and strengthening of the ego.

For the problem of the overcoming of ego phases through the killing of the other I refer the reader to an earlier work (Genetische Psychologie), and here turn to a broader means of defense against death fear, which still falls under normal psychology although it is more closely related to the neurosis. This is the borderline case, where the individual neither punishes himself, like the neurotic, nor the other, like the criminal, but lets himself be punished by the other with certain limits. This function of external punishment as a means for inner unburdening is as it were the "pedagogical" agent in the therapeutic situation. With the very decision to accept treatment the patient takes a powerful forward step beyond his neurosis, since he makes the therapist the active agent for self punishment, a role which the latter cannot avoid however much he may try to protect himself from it. When this punishing agent can also be loved, it represents a further step toward healing, for love presupposes the overcoming of fear. We will follow out these therapeutic meanings later and now turn again to normal punishment situations, which are only crystallized like a paradigm in the therapeutic situation. In every more intimate human relation, whether it be that between parents and child, teacher and pupils, master and subordinate, likewise in the relation of the sexes and particularly in marriage, the punishing element is set up in the other spontaneously and unavoidably, and this is what makes the relationship, as a rule, so hard to understand and often impossible to bear. Even in the child we deal always with a self-punishment displaced outward, which serves as a palliative for fear.

One might object that the conception of self-punishment as a reducer of fear is only another kind of interpretation of a fact which psychoanalysis interpreted libidinally, that is, as sanction for instinct satisfaction. Certainly this phenomenon also, like every other, has two aspects, but this is not only a question of theory, it means that every single individual can emphasize this or that aspect in his general attitude, that is, can interpret life positively or negatively. If one speaks of types, however, it seems to me certain that the neurotic is that type which aims primarily not at pleasure gain but at the reduction of fear, while the application of self-punishment in the service of instinct satisfaction, seems rather to correspond to the normal type (for example to work in order to be able to permit himself pleasure afterwards). That the reducing of fear then often leads to the expression of instinct is probably correct, but that must not be misunderstood to mean that punishment serves primarily for instinct freeing, for sanction, which always rests on the presupposition of an original repression of instinct from without. For besides the lightening of fear through punishment, the individual has yet another motive for instinct expression, which complicates still further a process already far from simple. In order to displace the punishing factor to the outside (to let himself be punished) the individual must feel himself guilty, and thus it comes to the paradoxical appearance of instinct expression with punishment as its goal, which analytically can be explained only from masochistic pleasure, which itself by no means represents an original phenomenon. The vicious circle is closed by the realization that the freeing of instinct from repressions causes fear because life and experience increase the fear of death; while on the other side, renunciation of instinct increases guilt not because it represents repressed aggression which turns against the own ego (Freud) but because instinct renunciation is a renunciation of life, and therefore the individual feels himself guilty. The paradox that the lightening of fear (through punishment and instinct freeing) leads to fear, is explained as was mentioned in the beginning, from the double function of fear, which at one time is life fear, at another, death fear. From the life fear, a direct path leads to consciousness of guilt, or better, to conscience fear, which can be understood always as regret for the possibility of life that has been neglected, but its full expression, on the other hand, creates death fear.

ANDRAS ANGYAL

A Theoretical Model for Personality Studies

In this paper I shall not discuss the question whether model building is fruitful or not in the study of personality; valid arguments in favor of such a procedure are adequately covered by other contributions to this symposium. Neither will I argue the comparative merits and disadvantages of the various types of model that have been or may be employed in this field. Instead I shall present a particular model which I have advocated previously for the formulation of a theory of personality (1), reformulating certain aspects of this theo-

Reprinted with permission from the *Journal of Personality*, 20 (1951), pp. 131–142.

retical orientation and illustrating my points with pertinent examples taken mainly from the field of psychotherapeutic theory and practice.

Personality may be described most adequately when looked upon as a unified dynamic organization — dynamic, because the most significant fact about a human being is not so much his static aspect as his constituting a specific *process*: the life of the individual. This process, the life of the person, is an organized, patterned process, a Gestalt, an organization. A true organization presupposes an organizing principle, a unifying pattern. All part processes obtain their specific meaning or specific function from this unifying over-all pattern. Therefore, it seems plausible that a tentative phrasing of the nature of this total pattern — the broad pattern of human life — may serve as an adequate model for the formulation of the problems pertaining to the study of personality.

The over-all pattern of personality function can be described from two different vantage points. Viewed from one of these vantage points, the human being seems to be striving basically to assert and to expand his self-determination. He is an autonomous being, a self-governing entity that asserts itself actively instead of reacting passively like a physical body to the impacts of the surrounding world. This fundamental tendency expresses itself in a striving of the person to consolidate and increase his self-government, in other words to exercise his freedom and to organize the relevant items of his world out of the autonomous center of government that is his self. This tendency — which I have termed "the trend toward increased autonomy" — expresses itself in spontaneity, self-assertiveness, striving for freedom and for mastery. In an objective fashion this tendency can be described as follows: the human being is an autonomous unit that, acting upon the surrounding world, molds and modifies it. His life is a resultant of self-determination on the one hand, and the impacts of the surrounding world, the situation, on the other. This basic tendency, the trend toward increased autonomy, expresses the person's striving from a state of lesser self-determination (and greater situational influence) to a state of greater self-determination (and lesser situational influence).

Seen from another vantage point, human life reveals a very different basic pattern from the one described above. From this point of view, the person appears to seek a place for himself in a larger unit of which he strives to become a part. In the first tendency we see him struggling for centrality in his world, trying to mold, to organize, the objects and the events of his world, to bring them under his own jurisdiction and government. In the second tendency he seems rather to strive to surrender himself willingly, to seek a home for himself in and *to become an organic part of something that he conceives as greater than himself.* The superindividual unit of which one feels oneself a part or wishes to become a part, may be variously formulated according to one's cultural background and personal understanding. The superordinate whole may be represented for a person by a social unit — family, clan, nation, by a cause, by an ideology, or by a meaningfully ordered universe.

In the realm of aesthetic, social, and moral attitudes this basic human tendency has a central significance. Its clearest manifestation, however, is in the religious attitude and religious experience.

I wish to state with emphasis that I am not speaking here about a tendency which is an exclusive prerogative of some people only, e.g., of those with a particular religious bent or aesthetic sensitivity, but of a tendency that I conceive as a universal and basic characteristic in all human beings.

These two tendencies of the human being, the tendency to increase his self-determination in his expanding personal world, and the tendency to surrender himself willingly to a superordinate whole, can be summed up by saying that the human being comports himself *as if he were a whole of an intermediate order.* By this I mean a "part-Gestalt," like, for example, the cardiovascular system, or the central nervous system, each of which is a *whole,* an organization of many parts, but at the same time a *part* with regard to its superordinate whole, the body. The human being is both a *unifier,* an organizer of his immediate personal world, and a *participant* in what he conceives as the superordinate whole to which he belongs.

The basic human attitude that makes man behave as a part of a larger whole reflects itself also in his "horizontal relationships," that is in his relationship to the other "parts," to other persons. Were man's behavior determined exclusively by his urge for mastery, his attitude toward others could be only as toward means to his ends. Experiencing others as co-participants in a larger whole brings, however, another facet of his nature into manifestation. To avoid the coining of some outlandish term, we call this basic relation "love." In common usage this word has been badly misused to denote not only cheap sentimentality, but even relationships that are actually founded on exploitation, possessiveness, helplessness, and similar destructive attitudes. The basic nature of love consists in a recognition of the *value* and acceptance of the *otherness* of the loved "object" while at the same time one experiences an essential *sameness* that exists between oneself and what one loves.

To recognize and to accept the otherness of a person means to respect him as a valuable being in his own right, in his independence. This attitude is incongruous with any idea of possessiveness or any tendency to use him as means to an end, be this in the form of exploitation, domination, possessiveness, or some other attitude. In other words, it is incongruous with the nature of love to try to reduce the loved person to "an item in one's personal world," or to try to make him comply with one's demands, or to try to exert power over him in whatever way. Love has to be recognized as a basic human attitude which is quite distinct from and irreducible to man's self-assertive tendencies.

The recognition and acceptance of the otherness of the person implies, furthermore, an *understanding* of him. There can be no real love without understanding of the other person, only some sort of deceptive feeling based on an illusion. One does not recognize the otherness of a person as a reality by projecting into him one's fantasies, however flattering they may be. And when one sees in a person one's mother or father or anyone else, one ignores the person as he really is. In the last analysis this is a fundamental disregard for and destructive attitude toward the other person. The understanding of the other person — as we are now using this expression — is not some sort of shrewd "practical psychology" which has a keen eye for the weakness of people, but a deep perception of the core, of the essential nature of the other person. In love this essential nature of the other person is experienced as a value, as something that is very dear to one. Love is not "blind" but visionary: it sees into the very heart of its object, and sees the "real self" behind and in the midst of the frailties and shortcomings of the person.

Love has a second basic component which is complementary to respect for the otherness of its object: the experience of a certain fundamental belongingness and *sameness* between lover and the loved. Experientially, this is not "identification," that is, an identity that is more or less artificially created, but an existing identity that is *acknowledged*. Man behaves in certain fundamental respects *as if* he were a part, a shareholder in some kind of superordinate unit, in some kind of commonwealth. When two persons love one another they clearly or dimly have the feeling that something greater is involved therein than their limited individualities, that they are one in something greater than themselves or, as the religious person says, they are "one in God."[1]

Without such an implicit orientation all interests of a person would be centered in himself alone as an individual. He as an isolated entity would be facing an alien world and his reaching beyond himself would be only to possess, master and govern the surrounding world. He would compete with other people or he would calculatingly co-operate with them, but he would not love them. In order to love it is essential that a man come out of his shell, that he transcend his individuality, that he "lose himself." Somehow this self-abandonment is the precondition to a broadened existence in loving. One rejoices in the characteristic ways, in the real being, beyond the surface of pretense, of the other; one suffers in the other's misfortunes and in his misdeeds: therein one gains a whole new life with its joys and sorrows. One is enriched through a vital participation in another life without wanting, however, to possess the other person. The significant truth is expressed in the paradox that the one "who loses his life [of isolation], will gain it [in a broadened existence]." The paradox is resolved by recognizing that man functions as a part of a large whole. He has a life as a part — and that is all he has, as long as he remains in his self-enclosure. But it is possible for

---

[1] This statement does not have to be understood in a theological sense. In this context it is not our concern, e.g., whether or not the "superordinate whole" is reality or not; we state only that man appears to function *as if* he were or would experience himself as a part of a superordinate whole.

him to have a greater life, the life of the whole, as it is manifested in himself, in the other "parts," and in the totality.

I have described the over-all pattern of personality functioning as a two-directional orientation: *self-determination* on the one hand and *self-surrender* on the other. The first is the adequate attitude toward the items within one's individual world, the second, toward the greater whole toward which one behaves as a part. A particularly important aspect of this second orientation is the "horizontal" relatedness of the parts to other parts within the whole. I spoke in some detail of love because I believe — largely in agreement with current clinical views — that this is the very crux of the entire problem of personality and of interpersonal relationships.

Actual samples of behavior, however, cannot be ascribed exclusively to one or the other orientation. It is only in the counterfeit, the unhealthy, behavior that one or the other of these basic orientations is partially obliterated; in a well-integrated person the behavioral items always manifest both orientations in varying degrees. Instead of conflicting, the two orientations complement each other. As in the tendency toward increased autonomy one strives to master and govern the environment, one discovers that one cannot do this effectively by direct application of force, by sheer violence, but can do it by obedience, understanding, and respect for the laws of the environment — attitudes that in some way are similar to those of loving relationships. Similarly: bringing one's best to a loving relationship requires not only capacity for self-surrender but also a degree of proficient mastery of one's world, resourcefulness and self-reliance, without which the relationship is in danger of deteriorating into helpless dependency, exploitation, possessiveness, etc.

The central point of the model which we suggest here for the study of personality is the assumption that the total function of the personality is patterned according to a double orientation of self-determination — self-surrender. In the study of personality, as in any other scientific field, model building has its sole justification in its practical applicability, that is in its suitability for interpretation of the pertinent phenomena and for the formulation of meaningful problems. I have chosen the problem of the neuroses as a testing ground and I hope to demonstrate that the suggested model is useful for clarification of pertinent problems. Needless to say, only a few outstanding aspects of this broad field can here be touched upon, but this consideration may suffice to give a first impression as to the usefulness of the suggested frame of reference.[2]

I suggest the following thesis: The backbone of neurosis consists in a disturbance of the two basic tendencies that we have assumed as forming the over-all pattern of personality functioning. The two cardinal disturbances on

---

[2] This nucleus of a model can be broadened and made more detailed. I have made efforts in this direction in the previously quoted book and also in (2).

which the neurosis rests consist, first, in the person's *loss of mastery* over his own fate, and second, what is rather generally accepted as a basic factor in the neuroses, namely *anxiety*. Loss of mastery is another expression for impairment of capacity for self-determination; anxiety, as we will try to show, is related to the impairment of the capacity for self-surrender and the capacity for love. These points may be best demonstrated by quickly surveying some of the crucial points in the development of a neurosis.

Although we have only vague and inferential knowledge of the infant's subjective experiences, there is sufficient evidence for assuming that his self and the world are not clearly distinguished, but rather blend into a single totality. This differentiation may be near zero in the prenatal life; it is small in the early days of infancy and usually is not quite complete even in adulthood — witness ubiquitous wishful thinking and other autistic phenomena. The gradual birth of individuality may be largely a matter of maturation, but it is also stimulated and precipitated by *painful* contacts with the surrounding world. The hurtfulness of some objects of the environment and their frustrating resistance and independence in regard to one's wishes, so to say their disobedience, are impelling experiences to the recognition of their otherness.

These pains and frustrations — even the pain of being born into an uncomfortable world — are possibly not traumatic in themselves. Their chief significance seems to lie in their hastening both the birth of individuality and the experience of an outside world that is distinct from oneself. And with the birth of individuality the stage is set, the *human situation* is created. Here for the first time the opportunity is given to the person to manifest and unfold his essential nature. The experience of separateness from the surrounding world, which is governed by forces outside oneself, supplies the impetus to strive for mastery over the environment. At the same time, the experience of oneself, as a separated, limited individual gives one the feeling of incompleteness and the urge to seek for a larger life to be part of and to participate lovingly in other lives. The experience of one's separateness represents both the necessity and the opportunity for the person to manifest his basic tendencies.

The real traumatising factors are those which prevent the person from expressing these basic tendencies. In the neurotic development there are always a number of unfortunate circumstances which instil in the child a self-derogatory feeling. This involves on the one hand a feeling of weakness which discourages him from the free expression of his wish for mastery, and on the other hand a feeling that there is something fundamentally wrong with him and that, therefore, he cannot be loved. The whole complicated structure of neurosis appears to be founded on this secret feeling of worthlessness, that is, on the belief that one is inadequate to master the situations that confront him and that he is undeserving of love.

The traumatising circumstances which condition this loss of self-confidence and of self-respect are many. They have been rather carefully explored by therapists who deal with neuroses. It will be sufficient here to call to mind some of the most common factors.

1. The *over-protective attitude* of an insecure, anxious parent tends to convey to the child a feeling that he lives in a world that is full of dangers, and with which he is inadequate to cope. When a parent does too much for the child, he is telling him by implication that he is incapable of doing things by himself.

2. When the parent is too eager for the child to do well and is *excessively critical* of him, he is likely to instil in the child the feeling "something must be very wrong with me; I can't do anything right."

3. When parents distort and exaggerate the child's achievement, when they cast him into a *superior role* and have great expectations of him, they plant the seed of self-derogation in still another way. Deep down the child knows that the parents' picture of him is untrue, and measuring himself by these excessive and often fantastic standards, he secretly begins to feel utterly worthless.

4. The too many "don'ts" which the child hears tend to create in him the feeling that those things which he *most wants* are the things that are forbidden and *evil*. This easily can give rise in him to a secret conviction that he is a fundamentally evil person.

5. The ways in which children are being treated without *understanding* and without *respect* are many, and these are likely to create in the child the feeling that he just doesn't matter in this adult world, that he is of no account, that he is worthless. Often one wonders why the child accepts the verdict that he is worthless, instead of blaming the parent for being so obviously lacking in understanding, so wrong and selfish. The answer suggests itself that the child needs so much to feel that he has "good parents" that he tenaciously adheres to this belief and would rather assume himself to be evil or worthless than give up the idea that he has good parents.

The whole complex of self-derogation can be roughly — and admittedly somewhat artificially — divided into a feeling of inadequacy and the feeling of being unloved. The first leads to an impairment of self-determination, the second to the impairment of the capacity to love.

One important way in which the self-determination of a person may be impaired is his trading the birthright of mastery over his own destiny for the mess of pottage of protection — and dependency. In addition to the assumption of his weakness, an overvaluation of the power of his parents and of the protection which they can give induces the child to make this fatal bargain. The terms of the bargain are set, at least by implication: "You are weak and helpless against the world which is full of dangers; if you are good, if you do what we want you to do, and don't follow your impulses, we will take care of you and protect you."

Another circumstance that may induce a child to give up or "escape" from his freedom is the exploitation by the adult of the child's loving nature. This is often done by holding up to the child the suffering his behavior may cause to others: "You may do it if you want to, but mother will be hurt"; or more directly: "What you do shortens my life"; "You put another nail in my coffin," etc. Particularly vicious and destructive is the influence of the "self-sacrificing mother," who holds up to the child the many sufferings, deprivations and unhappinesses which she has had to endure for the child, implying the tremendous ingratitude that a self-assertion of the child against her wishes would mean.

In response to these and similar emotional insults the child is gradually led to deny himself, to hide his spontaneous impulses — which he assumes to be evil — and to pretend to be or to try to be someone else, a more impressive and a more desirable person. This step is literally suicidal, and it is born out of an extreme despair. Indeed, only an extreme despair of any possibility to live in reality can induce a person to content himself with appearances, with the impression he makes. The exaggerated importance and value given to any external trappings with which a person may decorate himself is equivalent to declaring one's naked self worthless. If one basks in some sort of reflected glory, one declares one's real being to be ignominious.

All these various roads lead to loss of spontaneity, initiative, and genuineness. The child loses originality, which should not be the privilege of a few, but a rightful heritage of everyone. The neurotic person experiences himself as a straw in the wind who cannot act under his own power but has to *wait for things to happen*, who is a "victim of circumstances" and whose fate depends on good or bad "breaks."

The discussion of another basic disturbance, the impairment of the person's capacity to love, leads us into the problem of anxiety, which we should now briefly consider. It seems to me that the original word-meaning that suggests constriction, being narrowed in (*Beengung*), expresses best the essential nature of anxiety. A person who feels weak and unlovable and surrounded by a very alien and unfriendly world, will draw in his feelers and will surround himself with some protective shell. This shell, however, limits him and narrows him in to such an extent that he can barely move or breathe. We propose to define anxiety as this condition of the person. It seems preferable to use the term in this sense, as a "psycho-physically-neutral" term (William Stern), denoting a condition of the person which may or may not be consciously experienced. This usage would avoid the confusing issues of unconscious anxiety and such manifestations of anxiety that are conscious but not characterized by anxious feelings. Anxiety is not a mental phenomenon but a state of limitation of life. When we have sufficient information about a person's mode of living, we can determine whether his life is a narrowed one or not; that is, we can determine the presence and degree of the condition of anxiety, independently of the presence and degree of anxious feelings.

Anxiety is dynamically related to fears in a twofold manner: it is born out of fears and it leads to fears. It is fear that makes the person erect his defenses with the resultant state of constriction or anxiety. The person's impulses, however, rebel against the enclosure, against the limitation, and threaten to break through the wall of defenses. This threat from within is experienced in those nameless fears, fears without a conscious object, which one usually refers to as "anxiety."

This narrowed-in condition of anxiety paralyzes the effectiveness of the person in dealing with his environment. He does not really dare to venture into the outside world, but looks out upon it from behind his defenses with suspicion, fear, apprehension, envy, and hatred. The most destructive aspect of anxiety, of this self-enclosure, is, however, the loss of the capacity or rather the loss of the freedom to love. For love presupposes that instead of anxiously standing watch over one's safety, one dares to go out of oneself, to abandon oneself, to venture out in order to participate in the life of others and in a larger life of which he feels himself a part. It is the nature of the human being that he finds fulfilment only in a broadened existence, and that for him life confined to the limits of one's individuality in segregation from others is worthless. He can find happiness and peace only if he loves, that is, participates in life outside the confines of his individuality; and if he is loved, that is, received into and held fast and dear by another life.

Summing up this sketch of the origin of the neuroses, we have assumed that certain traumatising experiences create in the child a derogatory picture, a feeling of the worthlessness of his self. This feeling of worthlessness has two components: first, the feeling that one is inadequate, too weak to cope with the environment; and second, the feeling that one is unloved and unworthy of love. These then lead to an impairment of the person's self-determination on the one hand, and to anxiety with the loss of capacity to love, on the other. Neurosis represents a complicated interlocking system of maneuvers that are designed to maintain life in a human sense in spite of the fact that the person is wounded at the very core of his nature. This hypothesis of the origin of the neurosis I believe is more in agreement than at variance with many of the current views on the subject.

This view is also in good agreement with certain current theories of therapy. There are several psychotherapeutic factors to which, in general, a particularly important curative effect is ascribed. We shall mention only two such factors for further illustration of the main points of this paper: first, the patient's expression of anger in the therapeutic setting, and second, the positive relationship of the therapist to the patient.

The expression of angry feelings toward the therapist is assumed to have a beneficial therapeutic effect on the patient. This expression should be, however, more than just "blowing off steam," a catharsis. The patient's experience that he can express anger toward the therapist without being rejected or punished for it — important as it is — is not in itself the crucial therapeutic experience, but only preparatory to it. On the basis of a series of observations I am persuaded that not all forms of angry expressions are therapeutically valuable, but only certain kinds with well-defined differential characteristics. An outburst of anger, if it is not more than a blind expression of impotent rage, does not produce therapeutic effects, but is likely to leave the patient ashamed and guilty and worse off than before. The therapeutically effective anger is always a courageous expression and often clearly expresses the feeling that one would rather die than continue to live in fear and trepidation, tolerate injustice, etc. Such anger says emphatically: "I won't stand for it!" Daring to take this final aggressive stand makes one regain respect for oneself. And therein lies the therapeutic effect of this type of anger: it tends to abolish the feeling of inadequacy which is one component of self-derogation and which in turn is the foundation for the neurosis.

Even more fundamental is, however, the therapist's persistent attitude toward the patient, expressed in respect for him as a person of value, in understanding, in confidence that the patient can be saved, in sincere desire and devoted effort to help him to live a happier life. When the patient reaches the point of being able to trust the sincerity of the therapist's attitude, he will no longer be able to uphold completely the fiction of being unloved and unworthy, undeserving of love. And with this the other foundation of his neurosis begins to crumble.

The above examples, taken from the dynamics and therapy of the neuroses, may serve to illustrate the degree of usefulness and applicability of the model that was proposed here for the study of personality. It is not claimed that this brief exposition proves anything definitely, but perhaps it is sufficient to give a first impression of an avenue of approach which may be worth while to follow.

REFERENCES

1. Angyal, A. *Foundations for a Science of Personality.* New York: Commonwealth Fund, 1941.
2. _____. "The Holistic Approach in Psychiatry." *Amer. J. Psychiat.*, 1948, 105:178–182.

DAVID BAKAN

Unmitigated Agency and Freud's "Death Instinct"

I have adopted the terms "agency" and "communion" to characterize two fundamental modalities in the existence of living forms, agency for the existence of an organism as an individual, and communion for the participation of the individual in some larger organism of which the individual is a part. Agency manifests itself in self-protection, self-assertion, and self-expansion; communion manifests itself in the sense of being at one with other organisms. Agency manifests itself in the formation of separations; communion in the lack of separations. Agency manifests itself in isolation, alienation, and aloneness; communion in contact, openness, and union. Agency manifests itself in the urge to master; communion in noncontractual cooperation. Agency manifests itself in the repression of thought, feeling, and impulse; communion in the lack and removal of repression. One of the fundamental points which I attempt to make is that the very split of agency from communion, which is a separation, arises from the agency feature itself; and that it represses the communion from which it has separated itself. The meaning of these two terms requires a lengthier exposition than any simple dictionary definition, and the remainder of this book is an attempt to provide this exposition.

As will become evident in the course of this essay, I conceive of agency and communion at a rather high level of abstraction, as manifested in various ways and in various contexts. I have sought to avoid the idolatry associated with abstractions by continuously referring back to varieties of expressions of important human experience and to systematic studies of them. And I have sought to overcome the idolatry of concreteness by returning to the abstract. Thus, this is a discourse which goes in circles. And I hope thereby to somehow push back the fringe of the unmanifest. In the last analysis, of course, the validation of the various considerations which are set forth must be in human experience — in our *individual* experience and in our *collective* experience. . . .

INDICATIONS THAT FREUD'S WRITINGS ON THE DEATH INSTINCT PERTAIN TO CANCER

There are several reasons for suspecting that Freud's writings on the death instinct pertain to cancer.

From David Bakan, *The Duality of Human Existence*, © 1966 by Rand McNally and Company, Chicago, pp. 14-15, 160-196.

Freud, as we know from his other writings, was very much given to combining his own life with his scientific contributions. *The Interpretation of Dreams* is probably the best example of this, in which he created a theory of dreams largely out of a personal analysis of his own dreams. Thus, it would not be at all inconsistent that the considerations which he presented on the death instinct should pertain to the relevant aspects of his experiences at the time. We have already seen that Jones sensed that the ideas on the death instinct were "transmuted from some personal and profound source." If cancer has any psychological features associated with it, then we are in the unusual position of having available to us what we may interpret as the introspective work of the man who was perhaps the greatest psychologist and introspectionist of our age.

Dr. Roy R. Grinker has cited the possibility that a patient may be unconsciously aware of a malignancy before clinical diagnosis. "Our liaison psychiatrists have often found that the nature of a patient's depression and insomnia or the degree of his anxiety enables them to predict that he unconsciously is aware of the presence of a malignant or disintegrating disease often long before the internist is able to make a correct diagnosis." [1] Could we not then suppose that so great an introspectionist, indeed the one from whom these psychiatrists have learned much of their art, might equally have displayed such psychological signs, and futhermore have been somewhat more insightful than these patients? If cancer has any psychological involvement, then we might learn something from the close examination of Freud's writings during the period when we can presume that the factors associated with the development of cancer were operative; and perhaps take some further hints from him from the fact that he lived so long into a "ripe old age" with cancer.

Beyond the Pleasure Principle is an explicit attempt to bring the psychoanalytic orientation to bear on the cellular level. Freud wrote: "Accordingly, we might attempt to apply the libido theory which has been arrived at in psychoanalysis to the mutual relationship of cells." [2] He also explicitly referred to cancer as narcissism: "The *cells of the malignant neoplasms* which destory the organism should also perhaps be described as *narcissistic* in this same sense. . . . " [3]

In Freud's relationship to Georg Groddeck, we can find some grounds for suspecting that he may have been aware of and concerned with the relationship between psychological factors and cancer.

In Groddeck's *The Book of the It*, a psychological hypothesis with respect to cancer is clearly formulated:

It is the unknown It, not the conscious intelligence, which is responsible for various diseases . . . or do you find it impossible that a being which has pro-

---

[1] Roy R. Grinker, "Psychosomatic Aspects of the Cancer Problem," duplicated unpublished manuscript, p. 13.
[2] *Beyond the Pleasure Principle*, pp. 67–68.
[3] *Ibid.*, p. 68. Italics added.

duced from spermatozoon and egg a man with a man's brain and a man's heart can also bring forth cancer . . . ?[4]

I do not consider it unreasonable to suppose that it [the It] can even manufacture . . . cancer [p. 101].

Freud had certainly read Groddeck's book, having taken the notion of the *It* from it for *The Ego and the Id*, acknowledging his debt to Groddeck for contributions to his thought.[5] In a letter of June 5, 1917, he told Groddeck that he considered him "an analyst of the first order who has grasped the essence of the matter once for all."[6] Not only had Freud read Groddeck's work on organic diseases as psychologically determined, but he had even bickered a bit with him over priority with respect to the notion:

Whether he [Groddeck] gives the "UCS" the name of "Id" as well makes no difference. Let me show you that the notion of the UCS requires *no extension* to cover your experiences with organic diseases. In my essay on the UCS which you mention you will find an inconspicuous note: "An additional important prerogative of the UCS will be mentioned in another context." I will divulge to you what this note refers to: the assertion that the UCS exerts on somatic processes an influence of far greater plastic power than the conscious act ever can [p. 317].

He also wrote, "No doubt the UCS is the right mediator between the physical and mental, perhaps it is the long-sought-for 'missing link' " (p. 318). Groddeck's book was actually not published until 1923, but it is clear that it was available to Freud much earlier. In a letter of March 25, 1923, he congratulated Groddeck on the book being published "at last" and referred to the use to which he put it in *The Ego and the Id*, saying, "I like the little book very much" (p. 342).

I can find no reference in Freud to Groddeck's discussion of cancer specifically, but it is clear that Freud had read Groddeck and was favorable to his notions, even to the point of claiming that he had advanced the psychogenic notion of disease himself before Groddeck. I have already indicated that Freud was thinking about cancer and alluded to it in *Beyond the Pleasure Principle*. The extension I make is that in Freud's writings on the death instinct, it was the phenomenon of cancer which was largely involved in his theoretical speculations.

In *The Ego and the Id*, Freud wrote that the ego, in which the death instinct is located, is "first and foremost a body-ego."[7] In a late paper, he wrote that "for the psychical field, the biological field does in fact play the

---

[4] Georg Groddeck, *The Book of the It* (New York: The New American Library, 1961), p. 31.
[5] Sigmund Freud, *The Ego and the Id* (London: The Hogarth Press, Ltd., 1950), pp. 27–28.
[6] *Letters*, p. 316.
[7] Standard Edition, XIX, 27.

part of the underlying bedrock."[8] In much of Freud's writings, the biological is taken as such. In *Beyond the Pleasure Principle,* he dealt rather extensively with biological data and theory in connection with the cells, and, as I have indicated, specifically mentioned "malignant neoplasms." He located the death instinct in the ego in personality and within each individual cell. He indicated that he was "driven to conclude that the death instincts are by their nature mute"[9] and that "the death instincts seem to do their work unobtrusively,"[10] which might in some way be allusions to the mute and unobtrusive way in which cancer develops in the early stages. Of all diseases, cancer is most prominent in that it appears to be based on forces "immanent in the organism itself" (p. 51), as Freud referred to the death instinct.

Freud's Modification of the Libido Theory

Before writing *Beyond the Pleasure Principle,* Freud had already modified his original libido theory by making the distinction between the sexual instincts and the ego instincts.[11] In *Beyond the Pleasure Principle,* he took the next step of identifying the death instinct[12] with the latter. Yet he was still handicapped by his former libido theory, so that his use of the concept of libido is sometimes entangling and inhibiting of understanding. Thus, instead of abandoning the libido theory completely, he continued to drag it around. He almost literally was not quite sure where to put it. In his earlier treatment, he had considered the ego as the "great reservoir" of libido.[13] In *The Ego and the Id,* he wrote that, with the distinction of ego and id, "we must recognize the id as the great reservoir of libido."[14] The awkwardness of conceptualization was so great that he was forced to produce such a logical atrocity as a "desexualized Eros" (p. 63). The modification of the theory was not thoroughgoing. I believe that much of the unclarity associated with *Beyond the Pleasure Principle* and *The Ego and the Id* inheres in the fact that Freud was struggling to present something which appeared more valid to him, and yet trying to reconcile his newer notions with the older ones.

I have no difficulty in identifying the libido of Freud's earlier treatment with what I have been calling agency. Libido is associated with all of the sexual perversions,[15] with masturbation (pp. 588ff.), with sadism, independence, solitariness, and estrangement (p. 596). Libido is associated with cruelty and looking at the genitalia (p. 596). Libido is associated with acquisition.

[8] *Ibid.,* XXIII, 252.
[9] *Ibid.,* XIX. 46.
[10] *Beyond the Pleasure Principle,* p. 87.
[11] On Narcissism: An Introduction" (1914), in *Collected Papers* IV, 35.
[12] Freud sometimes used this in the singular and sometimes in the plural.
[13] Freud, *Three Contributions to the Theory of Sex,* p. 611.
[14] Standard Edition, XIX, 30.
[15] *Three Contributions to the Theory of Sex,* pp. 553ff. Cf. the discussion of the perversions.

Libido is associated with mastery (*Bemächtigungstrieb*) (p. 590). Its aim is to get rid of sexual substances, reducing tension (p. 608). It is associated with the musculature (pp. 598, 600, 662) and with the urgency of sexual desire (pp. 612–13). It is related to aggression (pp. 612–13). Furthermore, the libido theory which Freud developed appeared to pertain much more to males than to females, although he did try to work it in for females. He discussed the forepleasure of sexuality as a perversion (p. 607). We have seen that there are differences between the sexes in regard to the importance of the relationship as a precondition for sexual relations. He wrote quite candidly, "The male sexual development is more consistent and easier to understand . . ." (p. 604). I would suggest that the male is "easier to understand" *from the libido theory*; because of the greater agency in the male than in the female.

A rather interesting change is manifest in Freud's conception of libido. Whereas, in his earlier writing, love is conceived as secondary and in some way *derivative* from libido, in his later writing, after his formulations of *Beyond the Pleasure Principle*, he attempted to identify libido in some *original* sense with love, moving from a definition of libido as agentic to libido as communal. Thus, whereas earlier libido is defined as "a quantitative energy directed to an object" (p. 553), he subtly changed libido so that it is not defined as directed toward an object. Thus, he wrote, in *Group Psychology and the Analysis of the Ego*:

Libido is an expression taken from the theory of the emotions. We call by that name the energy, regarded as a quantitative magnitude . . . of those instincts which have to do with all that may be comprised under the word "love." The nucleus of what we mean by love naturally consists (and this is what is commonly called love, and what the poets sing of) in sexual love with sexual union as its aim. But we do not separate from this — what in any case has a share in the name "love" — on the one hand, self-love, and on the other, love for parents and children, friendship and love for humanity in general, and also devotion to concrete objects and to abstract ideas. Our justification lies in the fact that psycho-analytic research has taught us that all these tendencies are an expression of the same instinctual impulses; in relations between the sexes these impulses force their way towards sexual union, but in other circumstances they are diverted from this aim or are prevented from reaching it, though always preserving enough of their original nature to keep their identity recognizable (as in such features as the longing for proximity, and self-sacrifice).[16]

What is evident in this paragraph is a struggle. He had an original notion of libido which was largely agentic. Yet the communion feature of sexuality was pressing itself on his attention. He shifted the meaning of libido to love

---

[16] From *Group Psychology and the Analysis of the Ego* (1921), Volume XVIII of the Standard Edition of *The Complete Psychological Works of Sigmund Freud*, pp. 90–91, by permission of Liveright, Publishers, N.Y., Sigmund Freud Copyrights Ltd., Mr. James Strachey and The Hogarth Press Ltd.

that "the poets sing of," which is generally love in the communion sense. And then he added that libido is to be recognized in such things as longing for proximity and self-sacrifice, again the communion feature of sexuality. I might point out parenthetically that, whereas in his earlier thinking sadism and masochism were linked together as simply the expression of ambivalence with an underlying unity, he backed away from this position. Sadism, he wrote, may be regarded as "a pure culture of the death instinct."[17] Masochism he earlier saw as sadism turned around. He wrote that he had been led to believe "that masochism . . . must be regarded as sadism that has been turned round upon the subject's own ego."[18] But he was forced to change his view: "The account that was then given of masochism would need to be emended for being too sweeping: there *might* be such a thing as primary masochism − a possibility which I had contested at that time" (p. 75). What Freud is struggling with here can, I believe, be clarified by the distinction between agency and communion. Phenotypic masochism may indeed obscure two different forms of genotypic masochism. First, we may identify the masochism which emerges from the agency feature. These are "the mysterious masochistic trends of the ego" (p. 11), which Freud had in mind as he was expounding the nature of the death instinct. Second, there are the tendencies associated with identifying with others and exaggeratedly deferring to them, the type of masochism Deutsch has identified in female sexuality, which is much more closely related to the communion feature.[19] Indeed, the so-called masochistic trends in women, trends which appear to be related to the communion feature, may be masochistic only in a very special sense. Such genuine indications of masochism as alcoholism, suicide, and self-flagellation are much more frequent among males than among females. Freud has a footnote to his comment about "primary" masochism, alluding to the writing of a woman, saying "A considerable portion of these speculations have been anticipated by Sabina Spielrein . . . in an instructive and interesting paper which, however, is unfortunately not entirely clear to me."[20] I believe that the "primary" masochism to which Freud was alluding is the masochism which is associated with the communion feature. Indeed, he referred to it as a regression (p. 75), which is exactly the way in which he characterized female sexuality more generally.[21]

In this connection, too, it is interesting to note the way in which Freud dealt with the matter of the death instinct in women. In the psyche, he identified the death instinct as largely in the superego and traced it to the

---

[17] Standard Edition, XIX, 53.

[18] *Beyond the Pleasure Principle*, p. 74.

[19] *The Psychology of Women*. Feminine masochism, Deutsch says, "lacks the cruelty, destructive drive, suffering, and pain by which masochism manifests itself in perversions and neuroses" (I, 191).

[20] *Beyond the Pleasure Principle*, p. 75.

[21] *Three Contributions to the Theory of Sex*, p. 604.

Oedipus complex.[22] Yet, somehow, all of this is not so evident to him in women. In discussing the development of the superego, he commented, "It seems that the male sex has taken the lead in developing all of these moral acquistions; and that they have then been transmitted to women by cross-inheritance" (p. 50).

In a paper published in 1925, he wrote that in girls "the Oedipus complex . . . is . . . a secondary formation,"[23] and that he "cannot escape the notion (though I hesitate to give it expression) that for women the level of what is ethically normal is different from what it is in men" (p. 196). "Their superego is never so inexorable" (p. 196), and "they show less sense of justice than men" (p. 197). Freud was clearly dealing with the agentic. Guilt is hardly a feature associated with communion, for, as I have indicated, communion is much more important for female sexuality. It might be pointed out parenthetically that one of the major differences Ehrmann found in his study of sexuality is that whereas men often show a large discrepancy between their sexual code and their sexual behavior, women show a very close correspondence, which would suggest less guilt in the latter.[24]

THE DEATH INSTINCT AND "DEFUSION"

We are now in a position to understand somewhat better why Freud should have identified the death instinct as being in the ego. *He recognized the force toward death which was associated with the agentic,* which the data cited earlier tend to indicate, as evidenced in the greater propensity for death in males. Understanding that there were reasons for confusion in Freud's thought, let us attempt to extract what may be considered to be positive.

One of the major roles which Freud assigned to the death instinct is that of "defusion." He ascribed to the death instinct a variety of separations both biological and psychological and dealt with these various separations very syncretistically. He cited with favor the view of Plato that there was an original being who was cut in two to make the two sexes. "Shall we follow the hint given to us by the poet-philosopher, and venture upon the hypothesis that living substance at the time of its coming to life was torn apart into small particles, which have ever since endeavoured to reunite through the sexual instincts?" Out of the ego is differentiated the superego, which becomes a "pure culture of the death instinct." And in the same way that he showed that single-celled organisms are destroyed by their own products, the ego is destroyed: ". . . the ego is meeting with a fate like that of the protista which are destroyed by the products of decomposition that they themselves have created."[25] Ambivalence and sublimation are conceived of as instances

---

[22] *The Ego and the Id,* pp. 68ff.
[23] Standard Edition, XIX, 251.
[24] *Op. cit.*
[25] Freud, Standard Edition, XIX, 56–57.

of defusion (pp. 58, 80). There is the "gulf between the actual individual and the conception of the species" (p. 52). He was attracted by Weismann's distinction between the soma and the germ-plasm, the latter being immortal, providing an "unexpected analogy with our own view."[26] He saw the male orgasm as a separation of the semen in which Eros is located.

The ejection of sexual substances in the sexual act corresponds in a sense to the separation of soma and germ-plasm. This accounts for the likeness of the condition that follows complete sexual satisfaction to dying, and for the fact that death coincides with the act of copulation in some of the lower animals. These creatures die in the act of reproduction because, after Eros has been eliminated through the process of satisfaction the death instinct has a free hand for accomplishing its purposes.[27]

The aim of the death instinct is the

return to the quiescence of the inorganic world. We have all experienced how the greatest pleasure attainable by us, that of the sexual act, is associated with a momentary extinction of a highly intensified excitation.[28]

There are also normal purposes which are achieved by the death instinct. It is associated with self-preservation, even though it leads to death in its own time (p. 51). It is associated with self-assertion and mastery (p. 51). It provides the pleasure of tension reduction for the individual (pp. 3ff., 27ff.), and especially sexual gratification. In "the stage of genital primacy, it takes on, for the purposes of reproduction, the function of overpowering the sexual object to the extent necessary for carrying out the sexual act" (p. 74). It separates the organism from the outside world by creating a dead outer layer which, "By its death . . . has saved all the deeper ones from a similar fate" (p. 32), which outer layer, by the way, protects against stimulation in the identity of the cortex with the ego (p. 28). And, what is perhaps most important psychologically, it is associated with repression, the profound separation of that which is conscious from that which is unconscious.[29]

According to Freud, the death instinct is also associated with illness. Even before he had developed the notion of the death instinct, the communion feature was involved in psychoanalysis, in overcoming repression, transference, and even suspension of the use of the musculature, as when the patient lies on a couch. In his paper on narcissism, in which we can see the beginning of the thought associated with his later development of the death instinct, he wrote: "A strong egoism is a protection against falling ill, but in the last resort we must begin to love in order not to fall ill, and we are bound to fall ill if, in consequence of frustration, we are unable to love."[30] It is the separated

[26] *Beyond the Pleasure Principle*, pp. 60ff.
[27] Standard Edition, XIX, 47.
[28] *Beyond the Pleasure Principle*, p. 86.
[29] *The Ego and the Id*, 28.
[30] Standard Edition, XIV, 85.

unconscious superego, as a "pure culture of the death instinct," which works against the effectiveness of psychoanalysis. There are people who "get worse during the treatment instead of getting better. . . . There is no doubt that there is something in these people that sets itself against their recovery, and its approach is dreaded as though it were a danger."[31] And "there is often no counteracting force of similar strength which the treatment can put in motion against it" (p. 72).

"Specialization" of the Death Instinct

Freud envisaged the possibility that the death instinct can be subject to differentiation and specialization both on the psychological and biological levels. Psychologically, it is lodged in the ego, and more particularly in the superego. It is manifest in such psychological conditions as the repetition compulsion and sadism. When cells unite to form a multicellular organism under the influence of Eros, the death instinct can, so to speak, be concentrated in single organs and directed outward.

It appears that, as a result of the combination of unicellular organisms into multicellular forms of life, the death-instinct of the single cell can successfully be neutralized and *the destructive impulses be diverted towards the external world through the instrumentality of a special organ. This special organ would seem to be the musculature;* and the death-instinct would thus seem to express itself — though probably only in part — as an instinct of destruction directed against the external world and other living organisms [pp. 56–57. Italics added.].

The activity of the dangerous death-instincts within the individual organism is dealt with in various ways; in part they are rendered harmless by being fused with erotic components, in part they are diverted towards the external world in the form of aggression, while for the most part they undoubtedly continue their inner work unhindered [p. 79].

The relationship of the ego, the death instinct which it contains, and the musculature was indicated by Freud as the ego being in control of the musculature: "The functional importance of the ego is manifested in the fact that normally control over the approaches to motility devolves upon it" (p. 30). The relationship of the ego to the outside world is primarily visual, although it also wears "an auditory lobe . . . crooked, as one might say" (p. 29). Verbal images are much more important in internal perception. We might recall at this point the observations that auditory is more important than visual perception in female as contrasted with male sexuality, the greater communicative skill of females, the greater degree of "intuition" in women as described by Deutsch, and Freud's observation that the latent dream thoughts are not visual, as contrasted with the manifest dream. Thus, the

---

[31] Standard Edition, XIX, 49

ego has its place principally in connection with the "reality" of the visual world and the control of the musculature acting upon it.

Eros itself, to some degree, also tends to become differentiated and lodged in particular parts of the multicellular organism. But the organism can remain alive if it yields to the major function of Eros itself, the coalescence with other cells:

> the whole path of development to natural death is not trodden by *all* the elementary entities which compose the complicated body of one of the higher organisms. Some of them, the germ-cells, probably retain the original structure of living matter and, after a certain time . . . separate themselves from the organism as a whole. . . . These germ-cells therefore, work against the death of the living substance and succeed in winning for it what we can only regard as potential immortality. . . . We must regard as in the highest degree significant the fact that this function of the germ-cell is reinforced, or only made possible, if it coalesces with another cell similar to itself and yet differing from it.[32]

As long as the death instinct is thus aided by Eros in keeping aggression turned outward, there is some possibility of survival. However, when this diversion through the specialized functions of the ego and the musculature is not possible, the death instinct is turned against the ego itself:

> It is remarkable that the more a man checks his aggressive tendencies towards the exterior the more severe — that is aggressive — he becomes in his ego ideal. . . . The fact remains, however, as we have stated it: the more a man controls his aggressiveness, the more intense becomes his ideal's inclination to aggressiveness against his ego. It is like a displacement, a turning round upon his own ego.[33]

THE DEATH INSTINCT AND ASEXUAL REPRODUCTION

I have indicated earlier that the image of Satan is associated with asexual reproduction, as seen, for example, in Goethe's Homunculus. . . . It is thus interesting to note that Freud associated asexual reproduction with the death instinct. He discussed Weismann's view that unicellular organisms are immortal and that death is only present in multicellular organisms, and some experiments which demonstrated reproduction by fission alone for 3,029 generations by isolating the parts and putting them in fresh water.[34] These data would speak against a death instinct in the single-celled organism. For Freud, the death instinct was conceived of as having come into existence *prior* to the development of Eros and heterosexual reproduction. Thus, whether the data are cogent or not, he seemed to be taken by another series of experiments which demonstrated that single-celled organisms tend to grow weaker,

[32] *Beyond the Pleasure Principle*, pp. 52–53.
[33] Standard Edition, XIX, 54.
[34] *Beyond the Pleasure Principle*, pp. 62–63.

become smaller, lose part of their organization, and die unless they engage in conjugation, "no doubt the fore-runner of the sexual reproduction of higher creatures," which saves them from growing old and rejuvenates them (p. 64). Rather than accepting the view of the immortality of the single-celled organisms, which would seem to indicate that they had no death instinct, he tried to argue that there is a tendency toward death within them, at least insofar as they do not display a union with other cells. He backed away from data which would force a contrary position by writing,

> The primitive organization of these creatures may conceal from our eyes important conditions which, though in fact present in them too, only become *visible* in higher animals where they are able to find morphological expression. And if we abandon the morphological point of view and adopt the dynamic one, it becomes a matter of complete indifference to us whether natural death can be shown to occur in protozoa or not. The substance which is later recognized as being immortal has not yet become separated in them from the mortal one [p. 66].

What we see here is an effort by Freud to have the death instinct associated with asexual reproduction. He went to the empirical data, cited them at length, and then, when they did not quite bear out the point of view which he wished to express, spoke of them as being of "complete indifference."

I believe that had he been able to find full confirmation of a primary death instinct in the single-celled organism, he undoubtedly would have given it considerable weight, for he would have had a confirmation of a relationship between asexual reproduction and the death instinct. But not finding it, he shrugged it off and continued in the same line of thought.

My hypothesis is that what Freud was in some sense trying to point out is a relationship between that which he identified as the death instinct and cancer. For, in the latter, we have a rather clear instance of a kind of asexual reproduction. He handicapped himself with a notion of the death instinct as being more original than Eros — agency more original than communion — and some obligation to find what he was looking for in the single-celled organism. We can, indeed, see in this the same handicap dealt with earlier, the older libido theory which made love derivative from libido. There is no a priori reason for supposing agency to be prior to communion.

Yet the more particular point remains, if we add our interpretation to it. Freud was attempting to formulate the psychological condition which is associated with cancer: *that cancer is associated with the agentic feature*. His insistence on a cellular locus of the death instinct, although his presentation is perhaps superficially lacking in cogency, may become cogent if we consider it to be an allusion to the psychological condition which may be associated with the physical state in which certain cells begin to reproduce asexually within a multicellular organism independent of the organization of the organism as a whole, finally leading to the death of that organism. In addition, he appeared to be making the point that *there is a parallelism between what takes place between the organism and the environment, including other organisms, and what takes place within the organism on the cellular level.* Agency, in its normal functioning, actually serves to bring the total organism into sexual relations. When this normal functioning of the agency feature is broken down, however, it turns upon itself, with the result that there is a corresponding disintegration of the normal organizational structure of the single organism. The "specialization" of the agentic into the ego, and into the musculature, expressing itself as sexual aggressiveness which leads to orgasm, is one of the principal ways in which the death instinct is normally diverted outward. When this outlet is not possible for any reason, the death instinct works to disintegrate the organizational whole of the individual and expresses itself in the asexual reproduction of some of the cells. When the relationship of the organism to other organisms breaks down, the personality becomes narcissistic, and, correspondingly, "The cells of the malignant neoplasms which destroy the organism should also perhaps be described as narcissistic . . ." (p. 68).

EROS

As significant as the notion of the death instinct in Freud's modification of his libido theory is his introduction of the notion of Eros.

One of the major functions of Eros is that of having led to the creation of multicellular organisms. Freud conceived of an original condition of single-celled organisms that do not reproduce sexually, but only by fission. The binding of cells into a multicellular organism is conceived of as analogous to sexual relations between organisms. Thus, the yearning of the sexes for each other is the same as the bondage between the cells, expressions of the same instinct, Eros. Conjugation between single-celled organisms is the forerunner of both sexual intercourse *and* the establishment of multicellular organisms. Both are life-producing. Conjugation is rejuvenating to the organism, and sexual relations lead to a kind of immortality in the offspring. As the "coalescence of two germ-cells" (p. 58) is life-producing, so is the bondage of cells life-producing and enhancing. Eros is that which "seeks to force together and hold together the portions of living substance" (p. 84).

Freud wrote:

It is generally considered that the union of a number of cells into a vital association — the multicellular character of organisms — has become a means of prolonging their life. One cell helps to preserve the life of another, and the community of cells can survive even if individual cells have to die [p. 67].

The dynamics whereby this takes place are presumed to be as follows:

the life instincts or sexual instincts which are active in each cell take the other cells as their object, that they partly neutralize the death instincts (*i.e.* the processes set up by them) in those other cells and thus preserve their life; while the other cells do the same for *them*, and still others sacrifice themselves in the performance of this libidinal function [p. 68].

But the work of Eros does not stop with the individual organism, for Eros attempts "to combine organic substances into ever larger unities" (p. 57). The elaboration of the notion of Eros as that which makes for *social cohesion* was made by Freud in *Group Psychology and the Analysis of the Ego*. Thus, starting with his analysis of the psyche, he simultaneously moved in two directions, the cells and the social group, with Eros as the cohesive force on the three levels, the cellular, the psychological, and the social. He contrasted the social with the narcissistic and cited the organismic conception of the group of Le Bon and Trotter.[35] Le Bon stated:

> The psychological group is a provisional being formed of heterogeneous elements, which for a moment are combined, exactly as the cells which constitute a living body form by their reunion a new being which displays characteristics very different from those possessed by each of the cells singly [p. 7].

Of Trotter,[36] Freud wrote, ". . . we shall be reminded of a valuable remark of Trotter's, to the effect that the tendency toward the formation of groups is biologically a continuation of the multicellular character of all the higher organisms."[37]

Freud's consideration of group psychology at this time leads to a further observation in connection with my view that the growth of cancer may have been significant in his writings at this period. He viewed cancer as a "narcissism" of the cells. If there is a parallelism between the relationship of the cells to the total organism and the total organism to society, then a turn to society at large as the larger organism may have been felt by him as "therapeutic." I have already voiced the suspicion that there may have been a "therapeutic" role connected with Freud's writings. His interest in the transindividual work of Eros, expressed in his growing concern with society at large, may well have been his effort to find a more integrated role for his ego in the larger whole. It was perhaps possible for the death instinct to be "rendered harmless by being fused with erotic components"[38] — by a vigorous entry into the social.

My analysis of Freud's state of mind as he wrote about the death instinct and Eros also suggests an explanation of the meaning of the title *Beyond the Pleasure Principle*. In German this is *Jenseits des Lustprinzips*, which might be more literally translated as "the other side of the pleasure principle." "*Jenseits*" as a noun also means the other world or the life after death, and,

[35] *Group Psychology and the Analysis of the Ego*, p. 4.
[36] W. Trotter, *Instincts of the Herd in Peace and War* (London: T. F. Unwin, 1916).
[37] *Group Psychology and the Analysis of the Ego*, p. 25.
[38] Standard Edition, XIX, 54.

according to Jones, Freud jocularly referred to this book as "The Hereafter."[39] The pleasure principle was for Freud one of the essential principles associated with his *individual* psychology. *Jenseits* is the other side of the individual, the place of the individual in the larger whole. Freud was able to conceive of that larger whole as possibly immortal, with the part itself, except for the germ plasm, being mortal. For the relationship of the individual to the larger society, there was another instinct, Eros. I might suggest that the psychological Lamarckianism to which Freud clung was partly an expression of his struggle away from the individual to a transindividual conception.

EMPIRICAL LINES OF EVIDENCE WHICH INDICATE AN ASSOCIATION OF AGENCY AND CANCER

My analysis of the thought of Freud, together with my own considerations, suggests that the notions of agency and communion must be understood as being on a level of generality which transcends the biological, the psychological, and the social, yet manifested in each of them. Our common modes of thought tend to separate the latter three, because these modes are deeply based in two traditional dualisms, the mind-body and the mind-world. Allowing these dualisms, we then seek to find the *interactions*. Certain developments in modern thought, exemplified in the work of John Dewey and in the researches in psychosomatic medicine, have led us to recognize the conceptual mischievousness among these separations. Yet the state of affairs in our collective intellectual enterprises is such that, although we are pressed to drop these artificial distinctions, there is no single comprehensive conceptualization to replace it. Thus, we must blunder along without the aid of these dualisms and without anything else to reasonably enlighten us otherwise.

I have extracted a "Freudian" theory of cancer from his writings on the death instinct and Eros. The quotation marks around the word "Freudian" are, of course, important, since Freud's writings are certainly not explicit in this connection. But, using my term "agency" and the considerations which Freud has advanced, it would seem that unmitigated agency is *somehow* associated with cancer.

In the following pages, I review some empirical studies on cancer which have been conducted largely outside of Freudian contexts. Each of the studies, in one way or another, tends to point to the possibility of unmitigated agency being associated with cancer. This body of research is sparse. Each of the studies is subject to various criticisms, and none are completely definitive. Furthermore, each of the studies, taken by itself, easily allows alternative explanation of the data. Yet they have a collective impact, at least to me, which I cannot easily shake off, which suggests, albeit only in some global manner, that there may be some validity in what I call the "Freudian" theory of cancer.

One does not eagerly enter into a position of being classified among those who have advanced various quackeries to fill the vacuum of knowledge in

[39] *Op. cit.*, 41.

connection with cancer. But there is a danger of overmeticulousness as well as undermeticulousness in the effort to advance our understanding. This is that in our pursuit of rigor we may actually become rigid; that we may reject a *possibly* significant approach because it does not immediately submit fully to all of our scientific criteria. What the data I cite constitute is a hint, perhaps not much more. Yet, in something as vital as this, even a hint is valuable.

Attitudes toward a Psychosomatic View of Cancer

There is the beginning of the hint of a relationship between agency and cancer in the very attitudes people have toward the disease. There is a fantastically huge literature which seeks a "cause" of cancer. It is important, however, to qualify what I say here. I in no way wish to disparage the research on various aspects of the cancer problem. Certainly, the various discoveries of substances provocative of cancer growth, including the viruses, for example, and the varieties of medical measures associated with the treatment of cancer, are of great value. And yet, one cannot escape the observation that much of this research is premised upon a notion of "otherness" in connection with the "cause" of cancer, that is, the attribution of agency to an outside "agent." I cannot but see in this research, at least to some degree, the mechanism which I outlined in the discussion of the image of Satan, the mechanism of projection of the intrinsically agentic on an outside image.

Freud clearly saw the significance of what is psychologically represented in the image of the Devil, and the possibility that in modern times we would tend to somatize this psychological state. He dealt with this image in detail in a paper, published in the year that he reported the cancerous growth in his mouth, entitled "A Neurosis of Demoniacal Possession in the Seventeenth Century." In this paper he noted the projective quality associated with the Devil and saw how the "otherness" of the Devil becomes the "otherness" of disease.

> The demonological theory of those dark times has won in the end against all the somatic views of the period of "exact" science. The states of possession correspond to our neuroses, for the explanation of which we once more have recourse to psychical powers. In our eys, the demons are bad and reprehensible wishes, derivatives of instinctual impulses that have been repudiated and repressed. We merely eliminate the projection of these mental entities into the external world which the middle ages carried out; instead, we regard them as having arisen in the patient's internal life, where they have their abode.[40]

I might again cite the finding by McClelland and Greenberger, in the TAT responses of women with cancer, of the appearance of the illicit lover, Harlequin or the Devil, who takes them to their death.[41]

[40] Standard Edition, XIX, 72.
[41] "The Harlequin Complex," pp. 107ff.

I would suggest that cancer entails the agency feature in man so thoroughly that even those who have come to understand the nature of projection in the formation of physical disease must balk somewhat at this point. Dr. George L. Engel, in a presidential address before the American Psychosomatic Society, indicated that even among the members of that society, there was "unconscious resistance" to the study of "psychogenesis or psychological triggering mechanisms" with respect to cancer.[42] In a study of the attitudes of physicians to cancer, Dr. Donald Oken was brought to the conclusion that among physicians,

> There is a strong tendency to avoid looking at the subject of cancer and the facts related to it. There is an avoidance of research and teaching, opposition to potential research, resistance to personal experimentation and change, and the projection of strongly held rationalizations into the vacuum of knowledge. To some extent, we do not *want* to know about what we are doing or why, because the subject is so upsetting. Unfortunately, in our denial we go beyond the limits of usefulness. By blocking off access to new knowledge, we cut ourselves off from the acquisition of facts which could be of real help.[43]

It is evident that there is something about cancer, as contrasted with many other diseases, even fatal ones, which creates aversion to beholding it. I suggest that this is because it is a disease which in some very deep sense entails the agentic.

Data collected by Ruth D. Abrams and Jacob E. Finesinger in comprehensive interviews with cancer patients and their relatives also suggest that there is some unconscious association of cancer with the agentic among them. The investigators report that "the most significant and characteristic concept held by our patients was that cancer was a disease of unclean origin. . . . The idea that cancer is 'a dirty disease,' 'unclean,' 'repellent,' was repeated over and over again."[44] They frequently heard that cancer was associated with venereal disease. Sexual demands made by spouses were frequently suggested as the cause of cancer by relatives. In 56 out of 60 patients, the onset of cancer was regarded as someone's *fault*, either of the patient or of someone associated with the patient. I would suspect also that within the complex attitudes toward cancer patients on the part of physicians, which Oken pointed to, there may be some deference to the agentic of the patient which is unconsciously recognized by the physician.

In spite of this, however, there has been some work in connection with the relationship between personality and cancer, although the resources

---

[42] George L. Engel, "Selection of Clinical Material in Psychosomatic Medicine: The Need for a New Physiology," *Psychosomatic Medicine*, XVI, No. 5 (1954), 369.

[43] Donald Oken, "What to Tell Cancer Patients: A Study of Medical Attitudes," *Journal of the American Medical Association*, CLXXV (1961), 1127.

[44] Ruth D. Abrams, and Jacob E. Finesinger, "Guilt Reactions in Patients with Cancer," *Cancer*, VI (1953), 478.

directed to this are minor in comparison with those which have sought the cause of cancer in outside agency. The work which has been conducted has warranted two reviews of this literature.[45]

Sexual Maladjustment in Cancer Patients

There is accumulating evidence to indicate that people who develop cancer are also people who are deficient in achieving normal heterosexual relationships. A. Beatrix Cobb observed that in men with cancer of the prostate, there was an unusual "sexual preoccupation leading to multiple marriages."[46] Milton Tarlau and Irwin Smalheiser, studying women with cancer of the breast and cancer of the cervix, concluded that there was "a general disturbance in sexual functioning" in both groups, their attitudes toward sexuality entailing rejection of the feminine role and "uniformly negative feelings toward heterosexual relations."[47] It was found that these women characteristically had mothers who had warned them to stay away from men, and that their reaction to the onset of menstruation "was uniformly one of rejection, ranging from feelings of fear, shame, and disgust to strong hysterical outbursts" (p. 118). The Tarlau and Smalheiser study, which was the first to make this observation, suffered methodologically, especially in the lack of a control group for comparison. The study was replicated by John I. Wheeler and Bettye McD. Caldwell, with the addition of a control group. They confirmed the conclusions of Tarlau and Smalheiser, finding in both breast and cervical cancer patients "greater negative feelings toward sexual relations."[48] Catherine L. Bacon, Richard Renneker, and Max Cutler, in a detailed study of the personalities and personal histories of 40 women with breast cancer, similarly concluded that "sexual inhibition and frustration" were considerably higher than even what "we normally observe in our clinical investigations of neurotic women."[49]

This group has followed up the observation reported in this study with the comprehensive psychoanalysis of five cases of breast cancer. Adding to what they had already reported, they indicate that women with cancer of the breast tend to accept lovers or husbands who are extremely unsatisfactory.

[45] Lawrence L. LeShan, "Psychological States as Factors in the Development of Malignant Disease: A Critical Review," *Journal of the National Cancer Institute*, XXII (1959), 1–18; George M. Perrin and Irene R. Pierce, "Psychosomatic Aspects of Cancer: A Review," *Psychosomatic Medicine*, XXI (1959), 397–421.

[46] A. Beatrix Cobb, "A Social Psychological Study of the Cancer Patient," unpublished doctoral dissertation. University of Texas, 1953, p. 52.

[47] Milton Tarlau and Irwin Smalheiser, "Personality Patterns in Patients with Malignant Tumors of the Breast and Cervix: An Exploratory Study," *Psychosomatic Medicine*, XIII, No. 2 (1951), 118.

[48] John I. Wheeler, Jr., and Bettye McDonald Caldwell, "Psychological Evaluation of Women with Cancer of the Breast and of the Cervix," *Psychosomatic Medicine*, XVII, No. 4 (1955), 264.

[49] Catherine L. Bacon, Richard Renneker, and Max Cutler, "A Psychosomatic Survey of Cancer of the Breast," *Psychosomatic Medicine*, XIV, No. 6 (1952), 455.

These women experience

frustration of feminine needs through the choice of an inadequate type of lover or husband. The mates of our patients were outstandingly unsatisfying in any of several ways: they were cold, sadistic, alcoholic, seclusive, impotent, uninterested, opposed to having children, or monumentally narcissistic.[50]

They also observed that in some of the patients, after a disruption of their relations, there is a tendency to "act out," to engage in promiscuous sexual relations, a type of behavior which, on the basis of our earlier discussion of sexuality, can be interpreted as an expression of the agentic feature.

Reznikoff compared a group of women with cancer of the breast with women who had benign tumors and with women who were free of breast pathology, using a questionnaire, the TAT test, and the Sentence Completion Test. The women with cancer of the breast tended to be older when they married. In comparison with the normal and benign tumor subjects, the cancer group tended to describe masculine figures in the TAT cards as "rejecting and unresponsive to women's entreaties for love and attention. Fewer stories expressed basic contentment with interpersonal contacts in this area. . . ,"[51] and "In addition to viewing men as not gratifying their needs for affection and less frequently displaying contentment with their relations in this sphere, the cancer subjects, compared with the normal women, on fewer occasions conceived of men as protective or sympathetic" (p. 102). He also found that cancer patients much more frequently indicated that their marriages were not happy (p. 102). The Reznikoff data are of further interest because, although the cancer group exceeds both the normal group and the benign group on this dimension, the data suggest that the benign group is also alienated from men, although not to the same degree as the cancer group. This would suggest a correlation between the sense of alienation from men on the one hand and a no-growth, benign-growth, malignant-growth dimension on the other. However, "stronger" data would be necessary before this could be maintained.

Outside of the study by Cobb, all of the studies I have been able to find which indicate sexual maladjustment in cancer patients are of women. There is a definite need for information concerning sexual adjustment in male cancer patients. Cancer of the sexual sites occurs in about 44 per cent of female cancer patients and in only about 14 per cent of male cancer patients.[52] A

[50] Richard E. Renneker, et al., "Psychoanalytical Explorations of Emotional Correlates of Cancer of the Breast," Psychosomatic Medicine, XXV (1963), 119.

[51] Marvin Reznikoff, "Psychological Factors in Breast Cancer: A Preliminary Study of Some Personality Trends in Patients with Cancer of the Breast," Psychosomatic Medicine, XVII, No. 2 (1955), 100.

[52] Based on data presented in Herbert L. Lombard, "Statistical Studies in Cancer," in Freddy Homburger (ed.), The Physiopathology of Cancer (2nd ed.; New York: Paul B. Hoeber, 1959), p. 998.

subsidiary hypothesis, which would require much closer investigation, is that those organs which are most intimately involved in communion are more likely to be targets for cancer than organs associated with agency. To put it metaphorically, the parts of the body which are the most prominent objects for the agency of the male in heterosexuality become the targets of agency in the development of cancer in the female. It is also interesting to point out that cancer of the musculature, which Freud called the organ of the death instinct, is either rare or nonexistent. If, as I have pointed out, the communion feature is a much more important part of female than male sexuality, and if it should turn out that the sexual maladjustment of the male cancer patient is not as dramatic as that of the female, it would suggest that the inhibition of their sexuality is largely an inhibition of the communion feature, the inhibition of Eros in their personality which would normally have the effect of "neutralizing the death instinct," in the Freudian terminology.

Inhibition of Maternality

Not only is there an inhibition of sexuality in female cancer patients, but also an inhibition of their maternality. Bacon, Renneker, and Cutler report that only one of their 40 cases indicated a desire for children. Renneker and his associates write:

> Most of our patients displayed disturbances of the maternal drive. Children were not cathected through identification. . . . Conflict over the caring for children disturbed several of our patients. . . . One wonders whether a sustained, conflictful, psychopathological drive toward pregnancy frustrated by infertility may be part of the hormonal disturbance in developing cancer of the breast. A psychogenical factor could conceivably be the block against pregnancy which frustrates the life-restitutive urge. . . . We would postulate that this powerful conflictual intrapsychic constellation may constitute a force which would upset the normal hormonal balance. This, too, is a subject for further research.[53]

Reznikoff found that "the cancer subjects were more ambivalent toward accepting responsibilities associated with raising children and distinctly more fearful and threatened by pregnancy and the birth process."[54]

Lack of Social Involvement

Cobb, on the basis of her study of 100 male cancer patients, concludes the following about their social adjustment:

> As a group they seem to have had some difficulty in making their way into a world of adequate social relationships . . . they often regard emotional involvements as dangerous . . . they tend to avoid emotional involvements.[55]

[53] *Op. cit.*, p. 121.
[54] *Op. cit.*, p. 101.
[55] *Op. cit.*, pp. 254, 257.

Reznikoff found that female cancer patients "apparently . . . had developed few interests or diversions outside their homes,"[56] and that "their husbands tended to spend less available leisure time with them than did the mates of the normal women" (p. 102).

Inhibition of Aggression

The relationship of aggression to agency has been discussed earlier. Freud, in his discussion of the death instinct, conceived of Eros as neutralizing the death instinct of the cells and of the death instinct as being directed outward in the form of aggression. It is thus extremely telling that one should find cancer patients to be people who are remarkably unable to express aggression.

The observation has been made that males with cancer of the prostate are superficially very "nice," in the sense of not expressing aggression and being very compliant and superficially cooperative.[57] In 25 out of their 40 cases of breast cancer, Bacon, Renneker, and Cutler observed that there was

> excessive pleasantness . . . under all conditions and a common inability to deal appropriately with anger. Thirty had no technique for discharging anger directly or in a sublimated fashion. Most of these even denied having ever been angry. These were the ones who maintained a cheerful, pleasant facade through all adversities. Friends were prone to describe them as "the nicest woman we know," "she wouldn't hurt a fly," or "always thinking of others."[58]

This group indicates that in cancer patients "the pattern of caring for the needs of others rather than their own gradually assumed a coloring of superficial cheerfulness and pleasantness."[59] LeShan and Worthington found that 64 per cent of cancer patients compared with 32 per cent of a normal group showed "inhibition of hostility" as inferred from a paper-and-pencil questionnaire.[60]

Not only does the tendency to express aggression outward seem to distinguish persons without cancer from persons with cancer, but there is also some evidence that it is related to the *rate* of growth of cancer among cancer patients. Dr. Philip M. West and his co-workers had casually observed that patients in whom the cancer grew slowly were "too mean to die" and that patients in whom the cancer grew rapidly were "too good to live." "Or . . . when contrasting two similar cases of early rectal carcinoma; — one a 'worth-

[56] *Op. cit.*, p. 100.
[57] Cobb, *op. cit.*, p. 39.
[58] *Op. cit.*, p. 456.
[59] Renneker, *et al.*, *op. cit.*, p. 119.
[60] Lawrence L. LeShan and Richard E. Worthington, "Some Recurrent Life History Patterns Observed in Patients with Malignant Disease," *Journal of Nervous and Mental Disease*, CXXIV (1956), 461.

less rascal' was apparently cured, the other, 'a prince of a fellow' was dead of generalized metastases in a few months."[61] This group indicates that they

were impressed by the polite, apologetic, almost painful acquiescence of the patients with rapidly progressing disease, as contrasted with the more expressive and sometimes bizarre personalities of those who responded brilliantly to therapy with long remissions and long survival.[62]

There is the suggestion in the literature that psychotherapeutic measures, especially those entailing aid in ventilating aggression, may have some effect on the course of the development of the disease. Needless to say, such an approach must be evaluated by research conducted in the most meticulous fashion. One study which opens up this possibility is that by LeShan and Gassman, in which patients with cancer were undergoing psychotherapy. The investigators cite, for example, the following case:

> A 34-year-old female, with a markedly anaplastic carcinoma of the breast, had visible metastatic growths in the right shoulder region. These had slowly and steadily increased in size over a three-month period. This woman had never accepted her hostility toward her husband and children, and had guilt feelings over the fact that she sometimes wished she were free of them. After approximately 45 hours of psychotherapy, she was able to accept and ventilate some of her hostility toward her children, and to accept the reassurance of the therapist that these were normal and valid emotions, and that they would not cause her to hurt or desert her family. In the following three days, there was a temporary but definite shrinkage of the visible tumor growths.[63]

Loss of a Significant Person as a Precipitant of Cancer

The data cited thus far would tend to confirm that part of the "Freudian" theory which suggests that health of the individual is associated with his relationship to the larger social "organism." They have largely pointed to features which are within the personality which prevent the individual from relating to others. The data also indicate that when such a separation takes place as a result of external factors, the probability of developing cancer also increases.

[61] Philip M. West, "Origin and Development of the Psychological Approach to the Cancer Problem," in Joseph A. Gengerelli and Frank J. Kirkner, *The Psychological Variables in Human Cancer: A Symposium* (Berkeley: University of California Press, 1954), p. 24.

[62] Eugene M. Blumberg, Philip M. West, and Frank W. Ellis, "A Possible Relationship Between Psychological Factors and Human Cancer," *Psychosomatic Medicine*, XVI, No. 4 (1954), 277.

[63] Lawrence L. LeShan and Martha L. Gassmann, "Some Observations on Psychotherapy with Patients Suffering from Neoplastic Disease," *American Journal of Psychotherapy*, XII (1958), 730.

Although one needs to be extremely cautious in attempting to draw inferences from lower animals to humans, there is one study on C3H mice which might be indicated parenthetically. C3H mice develop spontaneous mammary tumors and have been used extensively in laboratory research bearing on cancer. It was found that mice raised singly in cages developed mammary tumors significantly earlier than mice raised with cagemates.[64] One of the arguments which has sometimes been made against psychosomatic factors in cancer is that lower animals get cancer. This item might perhaps indicate that there may be psychological factors associated with cancer even in lower animals.

There are no doubt relationships between extrinsic and intrinsic alienation. In this section I cite some evidence of data which indicate that a loss of a significant person through death or other reasons is related to cancer. It should be pointed out that there is evidence that such a loss plays its role in other psychosomatic diseases as well.[65]

This observation is perhaps one of the oldest in connection with cancer. Kowal, in reviewing the literature of the eighteenth and nineteenth centuries, has shown that in numerous instances physicians have noted that a condition of despair, generally resulting from the loss of a husband or child, was the precursor of the cancerous condition.[66] One nineteenth-century physician commented, "The influence of grief appears to me to be, in a general way, the most common cause of cancer."[67] A statistical analysis of cases in the late nineteenth century in the London Cancer Hospital had demonstrated that in a large proportion of the cases "there had been immediately antecedent trouble, often in very poignant form, as the loss of a near relative" (p. 4). An observer in a report in 1931 said that there was reason to believe that "sad emotions" are associated with the precipitation of cancerous growth:

How many times have I heard . . . the litany: "Since the death of my child, doctor, I am not the same. I do not recognize myself. I cannot find my equilibrium, and that is certainly the beginning of my illness because before, nothing like this had come to my attention" [p. 6].

An early psychoanalyst, having studied 100 cases of cancer, concluded that "the downfall of the objective attachment" to another person was a precipi-

[64] Howard B. Andervont, "Influence of Environment on Mammary Cancer in Mice," *Journal of the National Cancer Institute*, IV (1944), 579–81. One of my students, Mr. Barry Dworkin, with the help of Dr. Eric Simmons, has been replicating this investigation. At the time of this writing the mice are about 470 days old. At this point 67 per cent of the mice caged alone have displayed tumors. In the group of mice caged together with other C3H mice, only 34 per cent have displayed tumors. This difference is significant at the 2.5 per cent level of confidence.
[65] Hyman L. Muslin and William J. Pieper, "Separation Experience and Cancer of the Breast," *Psychosomatics*, III (1962), 230.
[66] Samuel J. Kowal, "Emotions as a Cause of Cancer: 18th and 19th Century Contributions," *Psychoanalytic Review*, XLII (1955), 217–227.
[67] LeShan, "Psychological States . . .," p.3.

tant of cancer.[68] The loss of a person close to one in the relatively recent history of cancer patients has been confirmed by Bacon, Renneker, and Cutler, Greene, Greene and Miller, Muslin and Pieper, and Neumann.[69] LeShan and Worthington found "tension over the loss of a vital relationship" in 75 per cent of cancer patients compared with 14 per cent of a noncancer control group.[70]

In one comprehensive statistical analysis of cancer in women, the data very clearly indicate that the loss of a husband through death is associated with the occurrence of cancer. The author of this study concludes that the higher rate of cancer among widows, controlling for other variables, "should be traced . . . to the reactions of the body incident to the loss of the *pater familias*."[71] LeShan and Worthington administered questionnaires to 250 cancer patients, interviewed 71 patients for an average of 2.2 hours and 9 patients for an average of 119.3 hours, and used a control group of 150 cases without cancer. They reconstruct the following pattern, which, they say, would characterize 62 per cent of the cancer cases, but only 10 per cent of the noncancer cases. This is a composite "ideal type" of cancer patient in terms of personality and life experience.

Sometime in the first seven years of life, there was a trauma to the child's developing ability to relate to others. This trauma may have come from a variety of causes — the physical or psychological loss of a parent, the death of a sibling, or others. This trauma was related by the child to one or both of the parents, and a great deal of hostility resulted. However, the hostility could not be consciously accepted by the child for obvious reasons, and it was repressed. A large part of it was turned inward as self-hate and guilt feelings. *In addition, the ability to express emotion in relating to others was severely damaged, and the child experienced unusual difficulty in establishing strong cathexes of either a positive or negative nature.*

The ability to express positive emotions was weakened by the pain of withdrawing love from the parental figure. Negative feelings were hard to

[68] Elida Evans, *A Psychological Study of Cancer* (New York: Dodd, Mead and Company, 1926).

[69] Bacon, Renneker, and Cutler, *op. cit.*; William A. Greene, "Psychological Factors and Reticuloendothelial Disease: I. Preliminary Observations on a Group of Males with Lymphomas and Leukemias," *Psychosomatic Medicine* XVI, No. 3 (1954), 220–30; William A. Greene and Gerald Miller, "Psychological Factors and Reticuloendothelial Disease: IV. Observations on a Group of Children and Adolescents with Leukemia: An Interpretation of Disease Development in Terms of the Mother-Child Unit," *Psychosomatic Medicine*, XX (1958), 124–44; Muslin and Pieper, *op. cit.*; C. Neumann, "Psychische Besonderheiten bei Krebspatientinnen," *Zeitschrift für psychosomatische Medizin*, V (1959), 91–101.

[70] *Op. cit.*; p. 461.

[71] Sigismund Peller, "Cancer and Its Relations to Pregnancy, . . . Delivery, . . . to Marital and Social Status: I. Cancer of the Breast and Genital Organs," *Surgery, Gynecology, and Obstetrics*, LXXI (1940), 1–8; "II. Cancer of Organs Other than Reproductive: Total Cancer Mortality," *loc. cit.*, p. 186.

express due to the strong, unacceptable hostility also directed in this direction. Guilt feelings over the relationship with the parents tended to produce feelings of unworthiness.

The trauma producing these results was not of an intensity or timing likely to produce obvious neurotic problems or to prepare the person for a psychotic breakdown in the event of later stress. Although it made his later relationships generally superficial and invested in only cautiously, from a surface viewpoint, he managed to adjust to his social environment.

The personality development before the trauma was such that the individual had a need for warm relationships. As he developed and continued to have this need for, but inability to attain easily, warm cathexes, sooner or later a situation arose which offered him an opportunity to relate to others and which provided time for slow and cautious experimentation. This experimentation indicated that this was a "safe" relationship, one that would give him the warmth he needed, and would not mobilize the repressed hostile feelings.

The cathexis was accepted, and the person poured into it all the relationship needs that he had carried over the years since the original trauma. This tie became the focus of his life and all other relationships were essentially peripheral to it. The self-hatred was largely dissipated as the energy that once fed it was now rechanneled. Life-long patterns and basic guilt feelings, however, frequently still made it difficult for the person to express hostile feelings when his own needs were frustrated.

Eventually this cathexis was lost. This may have been due to any one of a number of events. The examples we have most frequently seen include the death of a spouse, or an event which markedly changed the marital roles, such as the chronic illness of a spouse; children growing up and attaining independence, thereby making parental roles obsolete; and job retirement. The self-hate was now rearoused as the blocked relationship energy turned inward through the old channels and was again expressed against the self. The loss of this all-important cathexis made it very difficult for the individual to relate again to others. He unconsciously saw what was happening as a "double desertion." The unconscious belief that to relate meaningfully to anyone brings the pain of desertion was reinforced by the second loss. The child's belief that he was responsible for the rejection was again accepted, and guilt and self-hate were again strongly felt.[72]

The Relative Success of Anti-Androgenic Measures in the Treatment of Cancer

Our earlier discussions indicated that the androgens were related rather closely to the agentic feature in personality, associated with aggression, the development of the musculature, and the agentic feature of sexuality. In this chapter, I have attempted to indicate that cancer is a disease which is associated with agency. It is thus telling that one of the most significant of the medical

---

[72] *Op. cit.*, pp. 462–63. Italics added.

measures in connection with cancer should be the so-called anti-androgenic forms of treatment.

There have been varieties of experiments on the treatment of cancer through the use of hormones. Among these has been the actual administration of androgens. However, as one reviewer has put it, "it may be concluded that androgen therapy does not prolong life."[73]

The data do indicate that anti-androgenic treatment is more effective. Huggins and his co-workers at the University of Chicago observed that orchiectomy (surgical removal of the testicles) and the administration of estrogens in dogs resulted in the arrest of the growth of neoplasms of the prostate gland.

> These findings in the dog proved to be pertinent to the human. Translated to man with prostatic carcinoma, they turned out to be directly applicable *en bloc* and permitted the introduction of anti-androgenic therapy in clinical practice. . . . Both orchiectomy and phenolic estrogens . . . were effective in controlling cancer of the prostate in certain cases, while, conversely, the administration of testosterone intensified the growth of the neoplasm.[74]

Androgens are found in both males and females. They are produced by the testes, the ovaries, and the adrenal glands, and possibly by other organs in the body.[75] There is evidence that the administration of estrogens can control growth of mammary cancers.[76] In women with cancer of the breast, the removal of the ovaries and the adrenal glands produces a significant drop in sexual desire, sexual activity, and sexual responsiveness to intercourse *simultaneously with* an increase in subjective well-being and arrest of metastatic activity as indicated by roentgenological evidence and clinical criteria.[77]

The nature of the detailed mechanisms of the interaction of hormones and personality and the great problems of "cause and effect" in psychosomatic conditions are beyond the scope of this essay. Yet I cannot but be impressed with the fact that "castration" should have been developed as a relatively effective way of controlling cancerous growth. It would appear that certain

[73] Alfred Gellhorn, "Clinical Cancer Chemotherapy," in Homburger, *op. cit.*, p. 1047.
[74] Charles Huggins, "Control of Cancers of Man by Endocrinologic Methods: A Review," *Cancer Research*, XVI (1956), 826.
[75] See Kinsey, A., *et al.*, *Sexual Behavior of the Human Female*. Philadelphia: W. B. Saunders Co., 1953.
[76] Huggins, *op. cit.*, p. 828.
[77] Sheldon E. Waxenberg, Marvin G. Drellich, and Arthur M. Sutherland, "The Role of Hormones in Human Behavior: I. Changes in Female Sexuality after Adrenalectomy," *Journal of Clinical Endocrinology*, XIX (1959), 193–202; Sheldon E. Waxenberg, John A. Finkbeiner, Marvin G. Drellich, and Arthur M. Sutherland, "The Role of Hormones in Human Behavior: II. Changes in Sexual Behavior in Relation to Vaginal Smears of Breast Cancer Patients after Oophorectomy and Adrenalectomy," *Psychosomatic Medicine*, XXII (1960), 435–42.

of the organs of the body are particularly associated with the agentic in human personality and that perhaps the removal of these organs has the effect of reducing the agentic and reducing what may be one of the manifestations of unmitigated agency, the growth of cancerous tissue.

I might comment, parenthetically, on what might be the deeper meaning entailed in Freud's frequent use of the notion of "castration" in his writings. Some of the critics have dealt with this as but another instance of Freud's great tendency to overconcretize what he was saying: that the notion of castration is simply a metaphorical concretization of something else. But such things as the fear of castration, castration complex, and penis envy can now be understood in terms of the way in which the individual manages the agentic feature of his personality. Penis envy, for example, may in part be the actual envy of the penis, but is better interpreted as the envy of the greater agency associated with the male, who has more specialized organs for the expression of the agentic; and the fear of castration is the fear of the removal of the specialized organs for the expression of the agentic.

In closing this chapter, I need to emphasize that it is not being suggested that what these data seem to point to, that internal and external barriers to social and sexual integration are in some way related to the onset of cancer, constitute the only factors associated with it. Such a position would be much too foolish and dogmatic. Yet it would seem, on the basis of these data which I have summarized, that the degree of social and sexual integration of the individual, which we have attempted to comprehend in terms of the notions of agency and communion, are certainly relevant, suggesting that further investigation along these lines may be fruitful.

IV Fulfillment Theory:
Actualization Version

The contrast between fulfillment and conflict theories is great, as shown by the selections from Rogers and Maslow. These fulfillment theorists assume only one great force, which can be best understood as a genetic blueprint determining each individual's inherent potentialities. When society does not interfere with the natural expression of these potentialities, a healthy personality results. Conflict, defensiveness, and maladjustment occur only when society attempts to shackle or change the person.

In "A Theory of Personality," Rogers sets forth in precise and comprehensive, if somewhat ponderous, fashion the important concepts of his theory of personality and their relationships. The theory bears the stamp of having evolved out of a theory of psychotherapy. At the core level, an actualizing tendency is assumed, which, in humans, has as a component a self-actualizing tendency. The actualizing tendency works toward an ever greater expression of the inherent potentialities, while the self-actualizing tendency works toward making the sense of self a reality. The major peripheral level statement, which is well documented in "A Therapist's View of the Good Life: The Fully Functioning Person," follows from the assumption that whereas the genetic blueprint is set by inheritance, the self-concept can be influenced by the reactions the person receives from the significant others in his life. If the self-concept is congruent with the genetic blueprint, then you have the ideal personality type, called the fully functioning person. But if the self-concept is incongruent, representing what others want one to be rather than what one is inherently equipped to become, then you have the non-ideal personality type, called the maladjusted person. Although the readings do not detail this type extensively, you can understand it for yourself by recognizing that it is the exact opposite of the fully functioning person.

The general emphasis of Maslow's theorizing is the same as that of Rogers. Maslow assumes a self-actualizing tendency and considers the best personality to be that which most fully expresses this tendency. In addition, in "Some Basic Propositions of a Growth and Self-Actualization Psychology," he goes further than Rogers in attempting to offer some bench marks whereby we may know the characteristics of genetic blueprints. But, in slight contrast to Rogers, Maslow also assumes a core tencency that presses toward physical survival. This tendency, called "deficiency motivation" in "Deficiency Motivation and Growth Motivation," refers to attempts to gratify biological and social security needs. Growth motivation, or self-actualization, aims at enhancing rather than merely preserving life. Once again, as in Rogers, we find that the personality type will express growth motivation if society has not had an inhibiting effect and deficiency motivation if it has.

CARL R. ROGERS

A Theory of Personality

In endeavoring to order our perceptions of the individual as he appears in therapy, a theory of the development of personality, and of the dynamics of behavior, has been constructed. It may be well to . . . note that the initial propositions of this theory are those which are furthest from the matrix of our experience and hence are most suspect. As one reads on, the propositions become steadily closer to the experience of therapy. . . . The defined terms and constructs are italicized. . . .

A. POSTULATED CHARACTERISTICS OF THE HUMAN INFANT

It is postulated that the individual, during the period of infancy, has at least these attributes.

1. He perceives his *experience* as reality. His *experience* is his reality.
    a. As a consequence he has greater potential *awareness* of what reality is for him than does anyone else, since no one else can completely assume his *internal frame of reference*.
2. He has an inherent tendency toward *actualizing* his organism.
3. He interacts with his reality in terms of his basic *actualizing* tendency. Thus his behavior is the goal-directed attempt of the organism to satisfy the experienced needs for *actualization* in the reality as *perceived*.
4. In this interaction he behaves as an organized whole, as a gestalt.
5. He engages in an *organismic valuing process*, valuing *experience* with reference to the *actualizing tendency* as a criterion. *Experiences* which are *perceived* as maintaining or enhancing the organism are valued positively. Those which are *perceived* as negating such maintenance or enhancement are valued negatively.
6. He behaves with adience toward positively valued *experiences* and with avoidance toward those negatively valued.

Comment

In this view as formally stated, the human infant is seen as having an inherent motivational system (which he shares in common with all living things) and

From *Psychology: A Study of a Science*, Volume 3 by S. Koch, ed. Copyright © 1959 by McGraw-Hill, Inc. Used by permission of McGraw-Hill Book Company.

a regulatory system (the valuing process) which by its "feedback" keeps the organism "on the beam" of satisfying his motivational needs. He lives in an environment which for theoretical purposes may be said to exist only in him, or to be of his own creation. This last point seems difficult for some people to comprehend. It is the perception of the environment which constitutes the environment, regardless as to how this relates to some "real" reality which we may philosophically postulate. The infant may be picked up by a friendly, affectionate person. If his perception of the situation is that this is a strange and frightening experience, it is this perception, not the "reality" or the "stimulus" which will regulate his behavior. To be sure, the relationship with the environment is a transactional one, and if his continuing experience contradicts his initial perception, then in time his perception will change. But the effective reality which influences behavior is at all times the perceived reality. We can operate theoretically from this base without having to resolve the difficult question of what "really" constitutes reality.

Another comment which may be in order is that no attempt has been made to supply a complete catalogue of the equipment with which the infant faces the world. Whether he possesses instincts, or an innate sucking reflex, or an innate need for affection, are interesting questions to pursue, but the answers seem peripheral rather than essential to a theory of personality.

B. The Development of the Self

1. In line with the tendency toward differentiation which is a part of the *actualizing tendency*, a portion of the individual's *experience* becomes differentiated and *symbolized* in an *awareness* of being, *awareness* of functioning. Such awareness may be described as *self-experience*.

2. *This representation in awareness* of being and functioning, becomes elaborated, through interaction with the environment, particularly the environment composed of significant others, into a *concept of self*, a perceptual object in his *experiential field*.

Comment

These are the logical first steps in the development of the self. It is by no means the way the construct developed in our own thinking, as has been indicated in the section of definitions. . . .

C. The Need for Positive Regard

1. As the awareness of self emerges, the individual develops a *need for positive regard*. This need is universal in human beings, and in the individual, is pervasive and persistent. Whether it is an inherent or learned need is irrelevant to the theory. Standal . . . who formulated the concept, regards it as the latter.

a. The satisfaction of this need is necessarily based upon inferences regarding the experiential field of another.

(1) Consequently it is often ambiguous.

b. It is associated with a very wide range of the individual's *experiences.*

c. It is reciprocal, in that when an individual discriminates himself as satisfying another's need for *positive regard,* he necessarily experiences satisfaction of his own need for *positive regard.*

(1) Hence it is rewarding both to satisfy this need in another, and to experience the satisfaction of one's own need by another.

d. It is potent, in that the *positive regard* of any social other is communicated to the total *regard complex* which the individual associates with that social other.

(1) Consequently the expression of positive regard by a significant social other can become more compelling than the *organismic valuing process,* and the individual becomes more adient to the *positive regard* of such others than toward *experiences* which are of positive value in *actualizing* the organism.

D. Development of the Need for Self-regard

1. The positive regard satisfactions or frustrations associated with any particular *self-experience* or group of *self-experiences* come to be *experienced* by the individual independently of *positive regard* transactions with social others. *Positive regard experienced* in this fashion is termed *self-regard.*

2. A *need for self-regard* develops as a learned need developing out of the association of *self-experiences* with the satisfaction or frustration of the *need for positive regard.*

3. The individual thus comes to *experience positive regard* or loss of *positive regard* independently of transactions with any social other. He becomes in a sense his own significant social other.

4. Like *positive regard, self-regard* which is *experienced* in relation to any particular *self-experience* or group of *self-experiences,* is communicated to the total *self-regard complex.*

E. The Development of Conditions of Worth

1. When *self-experiences* of the individual are discriminated by significant others as being more or less worthy of *positive regard,* then *self-regard* becomes similarly selective.

2. When a *self-experience* is avoided (or sought) solely because it is less (or more) worthy of *self-regard,* the individual is said to have acquired a *condition of worth.*

3. If an individual should *experience* only *unconditional positive regard,*

then no *conditions of worth* would develop, *self-regard* would be unconditional, the needs for *positive regard* and *self-regard* would never be at variance
with *organismic evaluation,* and the individual would continue to be *psychologically adjusted,* and would be fully functioning. This chain of events is
hypothetically possible, and hence important theoretically, though it does not
appear to occur in actuality.

Comment

This is an important sequence in personality development, stated more fully
by Standal. . . . It may help to restate the sequence in informal, illustrative,
and much less exact terms.

The infant learns to need love. Love is very satisfying, but to know whether
he is receiving it or not he must observe his mother's face, gestures, and other
ambiguous signs. He develops a total gestalt as to the way he is regarded
by his mother and each new experience of love or rejection tends to alter
the whole gestalt. Consequently each behavior on his mother's part such as
a specific disapproval of a specific behavior tends to be experienced as disapproval in general. So important is this to the infant that he comes to be guided
in his behavior not by the degree to which an experience maintains or enhances the organism, but by the likelihood of receiving maternal love.

Soon he learns to view himself in much the same way, liking or disliking
himself as a total configuration. He tends, quite independently of his mother
or others, to view himself and his behavior in the same way they have. This
means that some behaviors are regarded positively which are not actually
experienced organismically as satisfying. Other behaviors are regarded negatively which are not actually experienced as unsatisfying. It is when he behaves
in accordance with these introjected values that he may be said to have acquired conditions of worth. He cannot regard himself positively, as having
worth, unless he lives in terms of these conditions. He now reacts with adience
or avoidance toward certain behaviors solely because of these introjected
conditions of self-regard, quite without reference to the organismic consequences of these behaviors. This is what is meant by living in terms of introjected values (the phrase formerly used) or conditions of worth.

It is not theoretically necessary that such a sequence develop. If the infant
always felt prized, if his own feelings were always accepted even though some
behaviors were inhibited, then no conditions of worth would develop. This
could at least theoretically be achieved if the parental attitude was genuinely
of this sort: "I can understand how satisfying it feels to you to hit your baby
brother (or to defecate when and where you please, or to destroy things) and
I love you and am quite willing for you to have those feelings. But I am
quite willing for me to have my feelings, too, and I feel very distressed when
your brother is hurt, (or annoyed or sad at other behaviors) and so I do not
let you hit him. Both your feelings and my feelings are important, and each
of us can freely have his own." If the child were thus able to retain his own

organismic evaluation of each experience, then his life would become a balancing of these satisfactions. Schematically he might feel, "I enjoy hitting baby brother. It feels good. I do not enjoy mother's distress. That feels dissatisfying to me. I enjoy pleasing her." Thus his behavior would sometimes involve the satisfaction of hitting his brother, sometimes the satisfaction of pleasing mother. But he would never have to disown the feelings of satisfaction or dissatisfaction which he experienced in this differential way.

F. THE DEVELOPMENT OF INCONGRUENCE BETWEEN SELF AND EXPERIENCE

1. Because of the need for *self-regard*, the individual *perceives* his *experience* selectively, in terms of the *conditions of worth* which have come to exist in him.

    a. Experiences which are in accord with his *conditions of worth* are *perceived* and *symbolized* accurately in *awareness*.

    b. Experiences which run contrary to the *conditions of worth* are *perceived* selectively and distortedly as if in accord with the *conditions of worth*, or are in part or whole, *denied to awareness*.

2. Consequently some experiences now occur in the organism which are not recognized as *self-experiences*, are not accurately *symbolized*, and are not organized into the *self-structure* in *accurately symbolized* form.

3. Thus from the time of the first selective *perception* in terms of *conditions of worth*, the states of *incongruence between self and experience*, of *psychological maladjustment* and of *vulnerability*, exist to some degree.

Comment

It is thus because of the distorted perceptions arising from the conditions of worth that the individual departs from the integration which characterizes his infant state. From this point on his concept of self includes distorted perceptions which do not accurately represent his experience, and his experience includes elements which are not included in the picture he has of himself. Thus he can no longer live as a unified whole person, but various part functions now become characteristic. Certain experiences tend to threaten the self. To maintain the self-structure defensive reactions are necessary. Behavior is regulated at times by the self and at times by those aspects of the organism's experience which are not included in the self. The personality is henceforth divided, with the tensions and inadequate functioning which accompany such lack of unity.

This, as we see it, is the basic estrangement in man. He has not been true to himself, to his own natural organismic valuing of experience, but for the sake of preserving the positive regard of others has now come to falsify some of the values he experiences and to perceive them only in terms based upon their value to others. Yet this has not been a conscious choice, but a natural — and tragic — development in infancy. The path of development toward psychological maturity, the path of therapy, is the undoing of this estrangement in man's functioning, the dissolving of conditions of worth, the achievement of a self which is congruent with experience, and the restoration of a unified organismic valuing process as the regulator of behavior.

G. The Development of Discrepancies in Behavior

1. As a consequence of the incongruence between self and experience described in F, a similar incongruence arises in the behavior of the individual.
   a. Some behaviors are consistent with the *self-concept* and maintain and actualize and enhance it.
      (1) Such behaviors are *accurately symbolized* in *awareness*.
   b. Some behaviors maintain, enhance, and actualize those aspects of the experience of the organism which are not assimilated into the *self-structure*.
      (1) These behaviors are either unrecognized as *self-experiences* or *perceived* in distorted or selective fashion in such a way as to be *congruent* with the *self*.

H. The Experience of Threat and the Process of Defense

1. As the organism continues to *experience*, an *experience* which is incongruent with the self-structure (and its incorporated *conditions of worth*) is *subceived* as *threatening*.
2. The essential nature of the *threat* is that if the *experience* were *accurately symbolized* in *awareness*, the *self-concept* would no longer be a consistent gestalt, the *conditions of worth* would be violated, and the *need for self-regard* would be frustrated. A state of *anxiety* would exist.
3. The process of *defense* is the reaction which prevents these events from occurring.
   a. This process consists of the selective *perception* or *distortion* of the *experience* and/or the *denial to awareness* of the *experience* or some portion thereof, thus keeping the total *perception* of the *experience* consistent with the individual's *self-structure*, and consistent with his *conditions of worth*.
   b. Some behaviors maintain, enchance, and actualize those aspects of the experience of the organism which are not assimilated into the *self-structure*.
4. The general consequences of the process of *defense*, aside from its preservation of the above consistencies, are a rigidity of *perception*, due to the necessity of distorting *perceptions*, an inaccurate *perception* of reality, due to distortion and omission of data, and *intensionality*.

Comment

Section G describes the psychological basis for what are usually thought of as neurotic behaviors, and Section H describes the mechanisms of these behaviors. From our point of view it appears more fundamental to think of defensive behaviors (described in these two sections) and disorganized behaviors (described below). Thus the defensive behaviors include not only the behaviors customarily regarded as neurotic — rationalization, compensation, fantasy, projection, compulsions, phobias, and the like — but also some of the behaviors customarily regarded as psychotic, notably paranoid behaviors and perhaps catatonic states. The disorganized category includes many of the "irrational" and "acute" psychotic behaviors, as will be explained below. This seems to be a more fundamental classification than those usually employed, and perhaps more fruitful in considering treatment. It also avoids any concept of neurosis and psychosis as entities in themselves, which we believe has been an unfortunate and misleading conception.

Let us consider for a moment the general range of the defensive behaviors from the simplest variety, common to all of us, to the more extreme and crippling varieties. Take first of all, rationalization. ("I didn't really make that mistake. It was this way....") Such excuses involve a perception of behavior distorted in such a way as to make it congruent with our concept of self (as a person who doesn't make mistakes). Fantasy is another example. ("I am a beautiful princess, and all the men adore me.") Because the actual experience is threatening to the concept of self (as an adequate person, in this example), this experience is denied, and a new symbolic world is created which enhances the self, but completely avoids any recognition of the actual experience. Where the incongruent experience is a strong need, the organism actualizes itself by finding a way of expressing this need, but it is perceived in a way which is consistent with the self. Thus an individual whose self-concept involves no "bad" sexual thoughts may feel or express the thought "I am pure, but you are trying to make me think filthy thoughts." This would be thought of as projection or as a paranoid idea. It involves the expression of the organism's need for sexual satisfactions, but it is expressed in such a fashion that this need may be denied to awareness and the behavior perceived as consistent with the self. Such examples could be continued, but perhaps the point is clear that the incongruence between self and experience is handled by the distorted perception of experience or behavior, or by the denial of experience in awareness (behavior is rarely denied, though this is possible), or by some combination of distortion and denial.

I. The Process of Breakdown and Disorganization

Up to this point the theory of personality which has been formulated applies to every individual in a lesser or greater degree. In this and the following section certain processes are described which occur only when certain specified conditions are present.

1. If the individual has a large or significant degree of *incongruence between self and experience* and if a significant experience demonstrating this *incongruence* occurs suddenly, or with a high degree of obviousness, then the organism's process of *defense* is unable to operate successfully.

2. As a result *anxiety* is *experienced* as the *incongruence* is subceived. The degree of *anxiety* is dependent upon the extent of the *self-structure* which is *threatened*.

3. The process of *defense* being unsuccessful, the *experience* is *accurately symbolized* in *awareness*, and the gestalt of the *self-structure* is broken by this *experience* of the *incongruence* in *awareness*. A state of disorganization results.

4. In such a state of disorganization the organism behaves at times in ways which are openly consistent with experiences which have hitherto been distorted or denied to awareness. At other times the self may temporarily regain regnancy, and the organism may behave in ways consistent with it. Thus in such a state of disorganization, the tension between the concept of self (with its included distorted perceptions) and the experiences which are not accurately symbolized or included in the concept of self, is expressed in a confused regnancy, first one and then the other supplying the "feedback" by which the organism regulates behavior.

Comment

This section, as will be evident from its less exact formulation, is new, tentative, and needs much more consideration. Its meaning can be illuminated by various examples.

Statements 1 and 2 above may be illustrated by anxiety-producing experiences in therapy, or by acute psychotic breakdowns. In the freedom of therapy, as the individual expresses more and more of himself, he finds himself on the verge of voicing a feeling which is obviously and undeniably true, but which is flatly contradictory to the conception of himself which he has held. . . . Anxiety results, and if the situation is appropriate (as described under J) this anxiety is moderate, and the result is constructive. But if, through overzealous and effective interpretation by the therapist, or through some other means, the individual is brought face to face with more of his denied experiences than he can handle, disorganization ensues and a psychotic break occurs, as described in statement 3. We have known this to happen when an individual has sought "therapy" from several different sources simultaneously. It has also been illustrated by some of the early experience with sodium pentathol therapy. Under the drug the individual revealed many of the experiences which hitherto he had denied to himself, and which accounted for the incomprehensible elements in his behavior. Unwisely faced with the material in his normal state he could not deny its authenticity, his defensive processes could not deny or distort the experience, and hence the self-structure was broken, and a psychotic break occurred.

Acute psychotic behaviors appear often to be describable as behaviors which are consistent with the denied aspects of experience rather than consistent with the self. Thus the person who has kept sexual impulses rigidly under control, denying them as an aspect of self, may now make open sexual overtures to those with whom he is in contact. Many of the so-called irrational behaviors of psychosis are of this order.

Once the acute psychotic behaviors have been exhibited, a process of defense again sets in to protect the organism against the exceedingly painful awareness of incongruence. Here I would voice my opinion very tentatively as to this process of defense. In some instances perhaps the denied experiences are now regnant, and the organism defends itself against the awareness of the self. In other instances the self is again regnant, and behavior is consistent with it, but the self has been greatly altered. It is now a self concept which includes the important theme, "I am a crazy, inadequate, unreliable person who contains impulses and forces beyond my control." Thus it is a self in which little or no confidence is felt.

It is hoped that this portion of the theory may be further elaborated and refined and made more testable in the future.

J. The Process of Reintegration

In the situations described under sections G and H, (and probably in situations of breakdown as described under I, though there is less evidence on this) a process of reintegration is possible, a process which moves in the direction of increasing the *congruence* between *self* and *experience*. This may be described as follows:

1. In order for the process of *defense* to be reversed — for a customarily *threatening experience* to be *accurately symbolized* in *awareness* and assimilated into the *self-structure*, certain conditions must exist.
   a. There must be a decrease in the *conditions of worth*.
   b. There must be an increase in *unconditional self-regard*.
2. The communicated *unconditional positive regard* of a significant other is one way of achieving these conditions.
   a. In order for the *unconditional positive regard* to be communicated, it must exist in a context of *emphatic* understanding.
   b. When the individual *perceives* such *unconditional positive regard*, existing *conditions of worth* are weakened or dissolved.
   c. Another consequence is the increase in his own *unconditional positive self-regard*.
   d. Conditions 2a and 2b above thus being met, *threat* is reduced, the process of *defense is reversed*, and *experiences* customarily *threatening* are *accurately symbolized* and integrated into the *self concept*.

3. The consequences of 1 and 2 above are that the individual is less likely to encounter *threatening experiences;* the process of *defense* is less frequent and its consequences reduced; *self* and *experience* are more *congruent; self-regard* is increased; *positive regard* for others is increased; *psychological adjustment* is increased; the *organismic valuing process* becomes increasingly the basis of regulating behavior; the individual becomes nearly fully functioning.

Comment

This section is simply the theory of therapy which we presented earlier, now stated in a slightly more general form. It is intended to emphasize the fact that the reintegration or restoration of personality occurs always and only (at least so we are hypothesizing) in the presence of certain definable conditions. These are essentially the same whether we are speaking of formal psychotherapy continued over a considerable period, in which rather drastic personality changes may occur, or whether we are speaking of the minor constructive changes which may be brought about by contact with an understanding friend or family member.

One other brief comment may be made about item 2*a*, above. Empathic understanding is always necessary if unconditional positive regard is to be fully communicated. If I know little or nothing of you, and experience an unconditional positive regard for you, this means little because further knowledge of you may reveal aspects which I cannot so regard. But if I know you thoroughly, knowing and empathically understanding a wide variety of your feelings and behaviors, and still experience an unconditional positive regard, this is very meaningful. It comes close to being fully known and fully accepted.

SPECIFICATION OF FUNCTIONAL RELATIONSHIPS IN THE THEORY OF PERSONALITY

In a fully developed theory it would be possible to specify, with mathematical accuracy, the functional relationships between the several variables. It is a measure of the immaturity of personality theory that only the most general description can be given of these functional relationships. We are not yet in a position to write any equations. Some of the relationships . . . may be specified as follows:

The more actualizing the experience, the more adient the behavior (A5, 6).

The more numerous or extensive the conditions of worth, the greater the proportion of experience which is potentially threatening (F1, 2).

The more numerous or extensive the conditions of worth, the greater the degree of vulnerability and psychological maladjustment (F3).

The greater the proportion of experience which is potentially threatening, the greater the probability of behaviors which maintain and enhance the organism without being recognized as self-experiences (G1*a, b*).

The more congruence between self and experience, the more accurate will be the symbolizations in awareness (G1a, and H1, 2, 3).

The more numerous or extensive the conditions of worth, the more marked will be the rigidity and inaccuracies of perception, and the greater the degree of intensionality (H4).

The greater the degree of incongruence experienced in awareness, the greater the likelihood and degree of disorganization (I3).

The greater the degree of experienced unconditional positive regard from another, based upon empathic understanding, the more marked will be the dissolution of conditions of worth, and the greater the proportion of incongruence which will be eliminated (J2, 3).

In other respects the relationships in section J have already been specified in the theory of therapy.

Evidence

The first sections of this theory are largely made up of logical constructs, and propositions which are only partly open to empirical proof or disproof.

Because it is a closely reasoned and significant experimental testing of certain of the hypotheses and functional relationships specified in this portion of the theory, Chodorkoff's study . . . will be described briefly. His definitions were taken directly from the theory. Defensiveness, for example, is defined as the process by which accurate symbolizations of threatening experiences are prevented from reaching awareness.

He concentrated on three hypotheses which may be stated in theoretical terms as follows:

1. The greater the congruence between self and experience, the less will be the degree of perceptual defensiveness exhibited.

2. The greater the congruence between self and experience, the more adequate will be the personality adjustment of the individual, as this phrase is commonly understood.

3. The more adequate the personality adjustment of the individual (as commonly understood), the less will be the degree of perceptual defensiveness exhibited.

Thus it will be seen that he was testing one of the definitions of the theory (Congruence equals psychological adjustment) against clinical and common-sense reality. He was also testing one of the relationships specified by the theory (Degree of congruence is inversely related to degree of defensiveness). For good measure he also completes the triangle by testing the proposition that adjustment as commonly understood is inversely related to degree of defensiveness.

He gave the following operational meanings to the essential terms:

1. Self is defined as a Q sort of self-referent items sorted by the individual to represent himself as of now.

2. Experience. An exact matching of the theoretical meaning with given operations is of course difficult. Chodorkoff avoids the term "experience," but operationally defines it by an "objective description" which is a Q sort by a clinician of the same self-referent items, this sorting being based on a thorough clinical knowledge of the individual, gained through several projective tests. Thus the total experiencing of the individual, as distinct from the self-concept he possesses in awareness, is given a crude operational definition by this means.

3. Perceptual defensiveness is defined as the difference in recognition time between a group of neutral words tachistoscopically presented to the individual, and a group of personally threatening words similarly presented. (The selection of the words and the technique of presentation were very carefully worked out, but details would be too lengthy here.)

4. Personal adjustment as commonly understood was defined as a combined rating of the individual by four competent judges, the rating being based on biographical material, projective tests, and other information.

These definitions provide an operational basis for four measures entirely independent of one another.

Chodorkoff translates his hypotheses into operational predictions as follows:

1. The higher the correlation between the individual's self-sort and the clinician's sorting for his total personality, the less will be the difference in his recognition threshold between neutral and threatening words.

2. The higher the correlation between the self-sort and the clinician's sorting for the total personality the higher will be the rating of personal adjustment by the four judges.

3. The higher the adjustment rating by the four judges, the lower will be the difference in recognition threshold between neutral and threatening words.

All three of these predictions were empirically upheld at levels of statistical significance, thus confirming certain portions of the theory.

This study illustrates the way in which several of the theoretical constructs have been given a partial operational definition. It also shows how propositions taken or deduced from the theory may be empirically tested. It suggests, too, the complex and remote behavioral predictions which may be made from the theory.

CARL R. ROGERS

A Therapist's View of the Good Life:

The Fully Functioning Person

My views regarding the meaning of the good life are largely based upon my experience in working with people in the very close and intimate relationship which is called psychotherapy. These views thus have an empirical or experiential foundation, as contrasted perhaps with a scholarly or philosophical foundation. I have learned what the good life seems to be by observing and participating in the struggle of disturbed and troubled people to achieve that life.

I should make it clear from the outset that this experience I have gained comes from the vantage point of a particular orientation to psychotherapy which has developed over the years. Quite possibly all psychotherapy is basically similar, but since I am less sure of that than I once was, I wish to make it clear that my therapeutic experience has been along the lines that seem to me most effective, the type of therapy termed "client-centered."

Let me attempt to give a very brief description of what this therapy would be like if it were in every respect optimal, since I feel I have learned most about the good life from therapeutic experiences in which a great deal of movement occurred. If the therapy were optimal, intensive as well as extensive, then it would mean that the therapist has been able to enter into an intensely personal and subjective relationship with the client — relating not as a scientist to an object of study, not as a physician expecting to diagnose and cure, but as a person to a person. It would mean that the therapist feels this client to be a person of unconditional self-worth: of value no matter what his condition, his behavior, or his feelings. It would mean that the therapist is genuine, hiding behind no defensive façade, but meeting the client with the feelings which organically he is experiencing. It would mean that the therapist is able to let himself go in understanding this client; that no inner barriers keep him from sensing what it feels like to be the client at each moment of the relationship; and that he can convey something of his empathic understanding to the client. It means that the therapist has been comfortable in entering this relationship fully, without knowing cognitively where

From *On Becoming a Person*. Copyright © 1961 by Carl R. Rogers. Reprinted by permission of the publisher, Houghton Mifflin Company.

it will lead, satisfied with providing a climate which will permit the client the utmost freedom to become himself.

For the client, this optimal therapy would mean an exploration of increasingly strange and unknown and dangerous feelings in himself, the exploration proving possible only because he is gradually realizing that he is accepted unconditionally. Thus he becomes acquainted with elements of his experience which have in the past been denied to awareness as too threatening, too damaging to the structure of the self. He finds himself experiencing these feelings fully, completely, in the relationship, so that for the moment he *is* his fear, or his anger, or his tenderness, or his strength. And as he lives these widely varied feelings, in all their degrees of intensity, he discovers that he has experienced *himself*, that he *is* all these feelings. He finds his behavior changing in constructive fashion in accordance with his newly experienced self. He approaches the realization that he no longer needs to fear what experience may hold, but can welcome it freely as a part of his changing and developing self.

This is a thumbnail sketch of what client-centered therapy comes close to, when it is at its optimum. I give it here simply as a brief picture of the context in which I have formed my views of the good life.

A Negative Observation

As I have tried to live understandingly in the experiences of my clients, I have gradually come to one negative conclusion about the good life. It seems to me that the good life is not any fixed state. It is not, in my estimation, a state of virtue, or contentment, or nirvana, or happiness. It is not a condition in which the individual is adjusted, or fulfilled, or actualized. To use psychological terms, it is not a state of drive-reduction, or tension-reduction, or homeostasis.

I believe that all of these terms have been used in ways which imply that if one or several of these states is achieved, then the goal of life has been achieved. Certainly, for many people happiness, or adjustment, are seen as states of being which are synonymous with the good life. And social scientists have frequently spoken of the reduction of tension, or the achievement of homeostasis or equilibrium as if these states constituted the goal of the process of living.

So it is with a certain amount of surprise and concern that I realize that my experience supports none of these definitions. If I focus on the experience of those individuals who seem to have evidenced the greatest degree of movement during the therapeutic relationship, and who, in the years following this relationship, appear to have made and to be making real progress toward the good life, then it seems to me that they are not adequately described at all by any of these terms which refer to fixed states of being. I believe they would consider themselves insulted if they were described as "adjusted," and they would regard it as false if they were described as "happy" or "contented," or even "actualized." As I have known them I would regard it as most inaccurate to say that all their drive tensions have been reduced, or that they are in a state of homeostasis. So I am forced to ask myself whether there is any way in which I can generalize about their situation, any definition which I can give of the good life which would seem to fit the facts as I have observed them. I find this not at all easy, and what follows is stated very tentatively.

A Positive Observation

If I attempt to capture in a few words what seems to me to be true of these people, I believe it will come out something like this:

The good life is a *process*, not a state of being.

It is a direction, not a destination.

The direction which constitutes the good life is that which is selected by the total organism, when there is psychological freedom to move in *any* direction.

This organismically selected direction seems to have certain discernible general qualities which appear to be the same in a wide variety of unique individuals.

So I can integrate these statements into a definition which can at least serve as a basis for consideration and discussion. The good life, from the point of view of my experience, is the process of movement in a direction which the human organism selects when it is inwardly free to move in any direction, and the general qualities of this selected direction appear to have a certain universality.

THE CHARACTERISTICS OF THE PROCESS

Let me now try to specify what appear to be the characteristic qualities of this process of movement, as they crop up in person after person in therapy.

An Increasing Openness to Experience

In the first place, the process seems to involve an increasing openness to experience. This phrase has come to have more and more meaning for me. It is the polar opposite of defensiveness. Defensiveness I have described in the past as being the organism's response to experiences which are perceived or anticipated as threatening, as incongruent with the individual's existing picture of himself, or of himself in relationship to the world. These threatening experiences are temporarily rendered harmless by being distorted in awareness, or being denied to awareness. I quite literally cannot see, with accuracy, those experiences, feelings, reactions in myself which are significantly at variance with the picture of myself which I already possess. A large part of the process of therapy is the continuing discovery by the client that he is experiencing feelings and attitudes which heretofore he has not been able to be aware of, which he has not been able to "own" as being a part of himself.

If a person could be fully open to his experience, however, every stimulus — whether originating within the organism or in the environment — would be freely relayed through the nervous system without being distorted by any defensive mechanism. There would be no need of the mechanism of "subception" whereby the organism is forewarned of any experience threatening to the self. On the contrary, whether the stimulus was the impact of a configuration of form, color, or sound in the environment on the sensory nerves, or a memory trace from the past, or a visceral sensation of fear or pleasure or disgust, the person would be "living" it, would have it completely available to awareness.

Thus, one aspect of this process which I am naming "the good life" appears to be a movement away from the pole of defensiveness toward the pole of openness to experience. The individual is becoming more able to listen to himself, to experience what is going on within himself. He is more open to his feelings of fear and discouragement and pain. He is also more open to his feelings of courage, and tenderness, and awe. He is free to live his feelings subjectively, as they exist in him, and also free to be aware of these feelings. He is more able fully to live the experiences of his organism rather than shutting them out of awareness.

Increasingly Existential Living

A second characteristic of the process which for me is the good life, is that it involves an increasing tendency to live fully in each moment. This is a thought which can easily be misunderstood, and which is perhaps somewhat vague in my own thinking. Let me try to explain what I mean.

I believe it would be evident that for the person who was fully open to his new experience, completely without defensiveness, each moment would be new. The complex configuration of inner and outer stimuli which exists in this moment has never existed before in just this fashion. Consequently such a person would realize that "What I will be in the next moment, and what I will do, grows out of that moment, and cannot be predicted in advance either by me or by others." Not infrequently we find clients expressing exactly this sort of feeling.

One way of expressing the fluidity which is present in such existential living is to say that the self and personality emerge *from* experience, rather than experience being translated or twisted to fit preconceived self-structure. It means that one becomes a participant in and an observer of the ongoing process of organismic experience, rather than being in control of it.

Such living in the moment means an absence of rigidity, of tight organization, of the imposition of structure on experience. It means instead a maximum of adaptability, a discovery of structure *in* experience, a flowing, changing organization of self and personality.

It is this tendency toward existential living which appears to me very evident in people who are involved in the process of the good life. One might almost say that it is the most essential quality of it. It involves discovering the structure of experience in the process of living the experience. Most of us, on the other hand, bring a preformed structure and evaluation to our experience and never relinquish it, but cram and twist the experience to fit our preconceptions, annoyed at the fluid qualities which make it so unruly in fitting our carefully constructed pigeonholes. To open one's spirit to what is going on *now*, and to discover in that present process whatever structure it appears to have — this to me is one of the qualities of the good life, the mature life, as I see clients approach it.

An Increasing Trust in His Organism

Still another characteristic of the person who is living the process of the good life appears to be an increasing trust in his organism as a means of arriving at the most satisfying behavior in each existential situation. Again let me try to explain what I mean.

In choosing what course of action to take in any situation, many people rely upon guiding principles, upon a code of action laid down by some group or institution, upon the judgment of others (from wife and friends to Emily Post), or upon the way they have behaved in some similar past situation. Yet as I observe the clients whose experiences in living have taught me so much, I find that increasingly such individuals are able to trust their total organismic reaction to a new situation because they discover to an ever-increasing degree that if they are open to their experience, doing what "feels right" proves to be a competent and trustworthy guide to behavior which is truly satisfying.

As I try to understand the reason for this, I find myself following this line of thought. The person who is fully open to his experience would have access to all of the available data in the situation, on which to base his behavior; the social demands, his own complex and possibly conflicting needs, his memories of similar situations, his perception of the uniqueness of this situation, etc., etc. The data would be very complex indeed. But he could permit his total organism, his consciousness participating, to consider each stimulus, need, and demand, its relative intensity and importance, and out of this complex weighing and balancing, discover that course of action which would come closest to satisfying all his needs in the situation. An analogy which might come close to a description would be to compare this person to a giant electronic computing machine. Since he is open to his experience, all of the data from his sense impressions, from his memory, from previous learning, from his visceral and internal states, is fed into the machine. The machine takes all of these multitudinous pulls and forces which are fed in as data, and quickly computes the course of action which would be the most economical vector of need satisfaction in this existential situation. This is the behavior of our hypothetical person.

The defects which in most of us make this process untrustworthy are the inclusion of information which does *not* belong to this present situation, or the exclusion of information which *does*. It is when memories and previous learnings are fed into the computations as if they were *this* reality, and not memories and learnings, that erroneous behavioral answers arise. Or when certain threatening experiences are inhibited from awareness, and hence are withheld from the computation or fed into it in distorted form, this too produces error. But our hypothetical person would find his organism thoroughly trustworthy, because all of the available data would be used, and it would be present in accurate rather than distorted form. Hence his behavior would come as close as possible to satisfying all his needs — for enhancement, for affiliation with others, and the like.

In this weighing, balancing, and computation, his organism would not by any means be infallible. It would always give the best possible answer for the available data, but sometimes data would be missing. Because of the element of openness to experience, however, any errors, any following of behavior which was not satisfying, would be quickly corrected. The computations, as it were, would always be in process of being corrected, because they would be continually checked in behavior.

Perhaps you will not like my analogy of an electronic computing machine. Let me return to the clients I know. As they become more open to all of their experiences, they find it increasingly possible to trust their reactions. If they "feel like" expressing anger they do so and find that this comes out satisfactorily, because they are equally alive to all of their other desires for affection, affiliation, and relationship. They are surprised at their own intuitive skill in finding behavioral solutions to complex and troubling human relationships. It is only afterward that they realize how surprisingly trustworthy their inner reactions have been in bringing about satisfactory behavior.

The Process of Functioning More Fully

I should like to draw together these three threads describing the process of the good life into a more coherent picture. It appears that the person who is psychologically free moves in the direction of becoming a more fully functioning person. He is more able to live fully in and with each and all of his feelings and reactions. He makes increasing use of all his organic equipment to sense, as accurately as possible, the existential situation within and without. He makes use of all of the information his nervous system can thus supply, using it in awareness, but recognizing that his total organism may be, and often is, wiser than his awareness. He is more able to permit his total organism to function freely in all its complexity in selecting, from the multitude of possibilities, that behavior which in this moment of time will be most generally and genuinely satisfying. He is able to put more trust in his organism in this functioning, not because it is infallible, but because he can be fully open to the consequences of each of his actions and correct them if they prove to be less than satisfying.

He is more able to experience all of his feelings, and is less afraid of any of his feelings; he is his own sifter of evidence, and is more open to evidence from all sources; he is completely engaged in the process of being and becoming himself, and thus discovers that he is soundly and realistically social; he lives more completely in this moment, but learns that this is the soundest living for all time. He is becoming a more fully functioning organism, and because of the awareness of himself which flows freely in and through his experience, he is becoming a more fully functioning person.

SOME IMPLICATIONS

Any view of what constitutes the good life carries with it many implications, and the view I have presented is no exception. I hope that these implications may be food for thought. There are two or three of these about which I would like to comment.

A New Perspective on Freedom versus Determinism

The first of these implications may not immediately be evident. It has to do with the age-old issue of "free will." Let me endeavor to spell out the way in which this issue now appears to me in a new light.

For some time I have been perplexed over the living paradox which exists in psychotherapy between freedom and determinism. In the therapeutic relationship some of the most compelling subjective experiences are those in which the client feels within himself the power of naked choice. He is *free* — to become himself or to hide behind a façade; to move forward or to retrogress; to behave in ways which are destructive of self and others, or in ways which are enhancing; quite literally free to live or die, in both the physiological and psychological meaning of those terms. Yet as we enter this field of psychotherapy with objective research methods, we are, like any other scientist, committed to a complete determinism. From this point of view every thought, feeling, and action of the client is determined by what preceded it. There can be no such thing as freedom. The dilemma I am trying to describe is no different than that found in other fields — it is simply brought to sharper focus, and appears more insoluble.

This dilemma can be seen in a fresh perspective, however, when we consider it in terms of the definition I have given of the fully functioning person. We could say that in the optimum of therapy the person rightfully experiences the most complete and absolute freedom. He wills or chooses to follow the course of action which is the most economical vector in relationship to all the internal and external stimuli, because it is that behavior which will be most deeply satisfying. But this is the same course of action which from another vantage point may be said to be determined by all the factors in the existential situation. Let us contrast this with the picture of the person who is defensively organized. He wills or chooses to follow a given course of action, but finds that he *cannot* behave in the fashion that he chooses. He is determined by the factors in the existential situation, but these factors include his defensiveness, his denial or distortion of some of the relevant data. Hence it is certain that his behavior will be less than fully satisfying. His behavior is determined, but he is not free to make an effective choice. The fully functioning person, on the other hand, not only experiences, but utilizes, the most absolute freedom when he spontaneously, freely, and voluntarily chooses and wills that which is also absolutely determined.

I am not so naive as to suppose that this fully resolves the issue between subjective and objective, between freedom and necessity. Nevertheless it has meaning for me that the more the person is living the good life, the more he will experience a freedom of choice, and the more his choices will be effectively implemented in his behavior.

Creativity as an Element of the Good Life

I believe it will be clear that a person who is involved in the directional process which I have termed "the good life" is a creative person. With his sensitive openness to his world, his trust of his own ability to form new relationships with his environment, he would be the type of person from whom creative products and creative living emerge. He would not necessarily be "adjusted" to his culture, and he would almost certainly not be a conformist. But at any time and in any culture he would live constructively, in as much harmony with his culture as a balanced satisfaction of needs demanded. In some cultural situations he might in some ways be very unhappy, but he would continue to move toward becoming himself, and to behave in such a way as to provide the maximum satisfaction of his deepest needs.

Such a person would, I believe, be recognized by the student of evolution as the type most likely to adapt and survive under changing environmental conditions. He would be able creatively to make sound adjustments to new as well as old conditions. He would be a fit vanguard of human evolution.

Basic Trustworthiness of Human Nature

It will be evident that another implication of the view I have been presenting is that the basic nature of the human being, when functioning freely, is constructive and trustworthy. For me this is an inescapable conclusion from a quarter-century of experience in psychotherapy. When we are able to free the individual from defensiveness, so that he is open to the wide range of his own needs, as well as the wide range of environmental and social demands, his reactions may be trusted to be positive, forward-moving, constructive. We do not need to ask who will socialize him, for one of his own deepest needs is for affiliation and communication with others. As he becomes more fully himself, he will become more realistically socialized. We do not need to ask who will control his aggressive impulses; for as he becomes more open to all of his impulses, his need to be liked by others and his tendency to give affection will be as strong as his impulses to strike out or to seize for himself. He will be aggressive in situations in which aggression is realistically appropriate, but there will be no runaway need for aggression. His total behavior, in these and other areas, as he moves toward being open to all his experience, will be more balanced and realistic, behavior which is appropriate to the survival and enhancement of a highly social animal.

I have little sympathy with the rather prevalent concept that man is basically irrational, and that his impulses, if not controlled, will lead to destruction of others and self. Man's behavior is exquisitely rational, moving with subtle and ordered complexity toward the goals his organism is endeavoring to achieve. The tragedy for most of us is that our defenses keep us from being aware of this rationality, so that consciously we are moving in one direction, while organismically we are moving in another. But in our person who is living the process of the good life, there would be a decreasing number of such barriers, and he would be increasingly a participant in the rationality of his organism. The only control of impulses which would exist, or which would prove necessary, is the natural and internal balancing of one need against another, and the discovery of behaviors which follow the vector most closely approximating the satisfaction of all needs. The experience of extreme satisfaction of one need (for aggression, or sex, etc.) in such a way as to do violence to the satisfaction of other needs (for companionship, tender relationship, etc.) — an experience very common in the defensively organized person — would be greatly decreased. He would participate in the vastly complex self-regulatory activities of his organism — the psychological as well as physiological thermostatic controls — in such a fashion as to live in increasing harmony with himself and with others.

The Greater Richness of Life

One last implication I should like to mention is that this process of living in the good life involves a wider range, a greater richness, than the constricted living in which most of us find ourselves. To be a part of this process means that one is involved in the frequently frightening and frequently satisfying experience of a more sensitive living, with greater range, greater variety, greater richness. It seems to me that clients who have moved significantly in therapy live more intimately with their feelings of pain, but also more vividly with their feelings of ecstasy; that anger is more clearly felt, but so also is love; that fear is an experience they know more deeply, but so is courage. And the reason they can thus live fully in a wider range is that they have this underlying confidence in themselves as trustworthy instruments for encountering life.

I believe it will have become evident why, for me, adjectives such as happy, contented, blissful, enjoyable, do not seem quite appropriate to any general description of this process I have called the good life, even though the person in this process would experience each one of these feelings at appropriate times. But the adjectives which seem more generally fitting are adjectives such as enriching, exciting, rewarding, challenging, meaningful. This process of the good life is not, I am convinced, a life for the faint-hearted. It involves the stretching and growing of becoming more and more of one's potentialities. It involves the courage to be. It means launching oneself fully into the stream of life. Yet the deeply exciting thing about human beings is that when the individual is inwardly free, he chooses as the good life this process of becoming.

ABRAHAM H. MASLOW

Some Basic Propositions of

a Growth and Self-Actualization Psychology

When the philosophy of man (his nature, his goals, his potentialities, his fulfillment) changes, then everything changes. Not only the philosophy of politics, of economics, of ethics and values, of interpersonal relations and of history itself change, but also the philosophy of education, the theory of how to help men become what they can and deeply need to become.

We are now in the middle of such a change in the conception of man's capacities, potentialities and goals. A new vision is emerging of the possibilities of man and of his destiny, and its implications are many not only for our conceptions of education, but also for science, politics, literature, economics, religion, and even our conceptions of the non-human world.

I think it is finally possible to begin to delineate this view of human nature as a total, single, comprehensive system of psychology even though much of it has arisen as a reaction *against* the limitations (as philosophies of human nature) of the two most comprehensive psychologies now available, behaviorism, or associationism and classical, Freudian psychoanalysis. Finding a single label for it is still a difficult task, perhaps a premature one. I have called it the "holistic-dynamic" psychology to express my conviction about its major roots. Some have called it "organismic," following Goldstein. Sutich

From *Perceiving, Behaving, Becoming: A New Focus for Education.* Reprinted with permission of the Association for Supervision and Curriculum Development and A. H. Maslow. Copyright © 1962 by the Association for Supervision and Curriculum Development.

and others are calling it the "self-psychology." We shall see. My own guess is that, in a few decades, if it remains suitably eclectic and comprehensive, it will be called simply "psychology."

I think I can be of most service by writing primarily for myself and out of my own work rather than from that of other thinkers, even though I am sure that the areas of agreement among them are very large. A selection of works of this "third force" is listed in the references. Because of space limitation, I will present only some of the major propositions of this point of view, especially those of importance to the educator. In general, I should warn the reader that at many points I am out ahead of the data, sometimes *way* out.

1. We have, each one of us, an essential inner nature which is intrinsic, given, "natural" and, usually, very resistant to change.

It makes sense to speak here of the hereditary, constitutional and very early acquired roots of the *individual* self, even though this biological determination of self is only partial, and far too complex to describe simply. In any case, this is "raw material" rather than finished product, to be reacted to by the person, by his significant others, by his environment, etc.

I include in this essential inner nature instinctoid needs, capacities, talents, anatomical equipment, physiological balances, prenatal and natal injuries, and traumata to the neonatus. Whether defense and coping mechanisms, "style of life," and other characterological traits, all shaped in the first few years of life, should be included, is still a matter for discussion. I would say "yes" and proceed on the assumption that this raw material very quickly starts growing into a self as it meets the world outside and begins to have transactions with it.

2. Each person's inner nature has some characteristics which all other selves have (species-wide) and some which are unique to the person (idiosyncratic). The need for love characterizes every human being that is born (although it can disappear later under certain circumstances). Musical genius, however, is given to very few and these differ markedly from each other in style, e.g., Mozart and Debussy.

3. It is possible to study this inner nature scientifically and objectively (that is, with the right kind of "science") and to discover what it is like (*discover* — not invent or construct). It is also possible to do this subjectively, by inner search and by psychotherapy, and the two enterprises supplement and support each other.

4. Even though weak, this inner nature rarely disappears or dies, in the usual person, in the United States (such disappearance or dying is possible, however). It persists underground, unconsciously, even though denied and repressed. Like the voice of the intellect, it speaks softly, but it *will* be heard, even if in a distorted form. That is, it has a dynamic force of its own, pressing always for open, uninhibited expression. Effort must be used in its suppression or repression, from which fatigue can result. This force is one main aspect of the "will to health," the urge to grow, the pressure to self-actualization,

the quest for one's identity. It is this that makes psychotherapy, education and self-improvement possible in principle.

5. However, this inner core, or self, grows into adulthood only partly by (objective or subjective) discovery, uncovering and acceptance of what is "there" beforehand. Partly it is also a creation of the person himself. Life is a continual series of choices for the individual in which a main determinant of choice is the person as he already is (including his goals for himself, his courage or fear, his feeling of responsibility, his ego-strength or "will power," etc.). We can no longer think of the person as "fully determined" where this phrase implies "determined only by forces external to the person." The person, insofar as he *is* a real person, is his own main determinant. Every person is, in part, "his own project," and makes himself.

6. No psychological health is possible unless this essential core of the person is fundamentally accepted, loved and respected by others and by himself (the converse is not necessarily true, i.e., that if the core is respected, etc., then psychological health must result, since other prerequisite conditions must also be satisfied).

The psychological health of the chronologically immature is called healthy growth. The psychological health of the adult is called variously, self-fulfill-ment, emotional maturity, individuation, productiveness, self-actualization, etc.

Healthy growth is conceptually subordinate, for it is usually defined now as "growth toward self-actualization," etc. Some psychologists speak simply in terms of one overarching goal or end, or tendency of human development, considering all immature growth phenomena to be only steps along the path of self-actualization (5, 11).

Self-actualization is defined in various ways, but a solid core of agreement is perceptible. All definitions accept or imply: (a) Acceptance and expression of the inner core or self, i.e., actualization of these latent capacities and potentialities, "full functioning," availability of the human and personal es-sence, and (b) minimal presence of ill health, neurosis, psychosis, of loss or diminution of the basic human and personal capacities.

7. If this essential core (inner nature) of the person is frustrated, denied or suppressed, sickness results, sometimes in obvious forms, sometimes in subtle and devious forms, sometimes immediately, sometimes later. These psychological illnesses include many more than those listed by the American Psychiatric Association. For instance, the character disorders and disturbances are now seen as far more important for the fate of the world than the classical neuroses or even the psychoses. From this new point of view, new kinds of illness are most dangerous, e.g., "the diminished or stunted person," i.e., the loss of any of the defining characteristics of humanness, or personhood, the failure to grow to one's potential; valuelessness (see proposition 19); etc.

That is, general illness of the personality is seen as any falling short of growth, or of self-actualization. And the main source of illness (although not

the only one) is seen as frustration of the basic needs, of idiosyncratic potentials, of expression of the self, and of the tendency of the person to grow
in his own style, especialy in the early years of life.

8. This inner nature, as much as we know of it so far, is definitely not
"evil," but is either what we adults in our culture call "good" or else it is
neutral. The most accurate way to express this is to say it is "prior to good
and evil." There is little question about this if we speak of the inner nature
of the infant and child. The statement is much more complex if we speak
of the "infant" as he still exists in the adult.

This conclusion is supported by all the truth-revealing and uncovering
techniques that have anything to do with human nature: psychotherapy,
objective science, subjective science, education and art. For instance, uncovering therapy lessens hostility, fear, greed, etc., and increases love, courage,
creativeness, kindness, altruism, etc., leading us to the conclusion that the
latter are "deeper," more natural, and more basic than the former, i.e., that
what we call "bad" behavior is lessened or removed by uncovering, while what
we call "good" behavior is strengthened and fostered by uncovering.

9. "Evil" behavior has mostly referred to unwarranted hostility, cruelty,
destructiveness, aggressiveness. This we do not know enough about. To the
degree that this quality of hostility is instinctoid, mankind has one kind of
future. To the degree that it is reactive (a response to bad treatment), mankind has a very different kind of future. My opinion is that the weight of
the evidence so far indicates that *destructive* hostility is reactive, because
uncovering therapy reduces it and changes its quality into "healthy" self-affirmation, forcefulness, righteous indignation, etc. In any case, the *ability* to
be aggressive and angry is found in all self-actualizing people, who are able
to let it flow forth freely when the external situation "calls for" it.

The situation in children is far more complex. At the very least, we know
that the healthy child is also able to be justifiably angry, self-protecting and
self-affirming, i.e., reactive aggression. Presumably, then, a child should learn
not only how to control his anger, but also how and when to express it.

10. This inner core, even though it is biologically based and "instinctoid,"
is weak rather than strong. It is easily overcome, suppressed or repressed. It
may even be killed off permanently. Humans no longer have instincts in the
animal sense, powerful, unmistakable inner voices which tell them unequivocally what to do, when, where, how and with whom. All that we have left
are instinct-remnants. And furthermore, these are weak, subtle and delicate,
very easily drowned out by learning, by cultural expectations, by fear, by
disapproval, etc. They are *hard* to know, rather than easy. Authentic selfhood
can be defined in part as being able to hear these impulse-voices within oneself, i.e., to know what one really wants or does not want, what one is fit
for and what one is *not* fit for, etc.

11. For all these reasons, it is at this time best to bring out and encourage,
or, at the very least, to recognize this inner nature, rather than to suppress

or repress it. Pure spontaneity consists of free, uninhibited, uncontrolled, trusting, unpremeditated expression of the self, i.e., of the psychic forces, with minimal interference by consciousness. Control, will, caution, self-criticism, measure, deliberateness are the brakes upon this expression made intrinsically necessary by the laws of the social and natural worlds outside this psychic world, and, secondarily, made necessary by fear of the psyche itself. Speaking in a very broad way, controls upon the psyche which come from *fear of the psyche*, are largely neurotic or *psychotic*, or not intrinsically or theoretically necessary. (The healthy psyche is not terrible or horrible and therefore does not have to be feared, as it has been for thousands of years. Of course, the *unhealthy* psyche is another story). This kind of control is usually lessened by psychological health, by deep psychotherapy, or by any *deeper* self-knowledge and self-acceptance. There are also, however, controls upon the psyche which do not come out of fear, but out of the necessities for keeping it integrated, organized and unified. And there are also "controls," probably in another sense, which are necessary as capacities are actualized, and as higher forms of expression are sought for, e.g., acquisition of skills by the artist, the intellectual, the athlete. But these controls are eventually transcended and become aspects of spontaneity, as they become self.

The balance between spontaneity and control varies, then, as the health of the psyche and the health of the world vary. Pure spontaneity is not long possible because we live in a world which runs by its own, nonpsychic laws. It *is* possible in dreams, fantasies, love, imagination, the first stages of creativity, artistic work, intellectual play, free association, etc. Pure control is not permanently possible, for then the psyche dies. Education must be directed then *both* toward cultivation of controls and cultivation of spontaneity and expression. In our culture and at this point in history, it is necessary to redress the balance in favor of spontaneity, the ability to be expressive, passive, un-willed, trusting in processes other than will and control, unpremeditated, creative, etc. But it must be recognized that there have been and will be other cultures and other eras in which the balance was or will be in the other direction.

12. Coordinate with this "acceptance" of the self, of fate, of one's call, is the conclusion that the main path to health and self-fulfillment is via basic need gratification rather than via frustration. This contrasts with the suppressive regime, the mistrust, the control, the policing that is necessarily implied by basic evil in the human depths. Intrauterine life is completely gratifying and nonfrustrating and it is now generally accepted that the first year or so of life had better also be primarily gratifying and nonfrustrating. Asceticism, self-denial, deliberate rejection of the demands of the organism, at least in the West, tend to produce a diminished, stunted or crippled organism, and even in the East, bring self-actualization to very few, exceptionally strong individuals.

13. In the normal development of the normal child, it is now known that

most of the time, if he is given a really free choice, he will choose what is good for his growth. This he does because it tastes good, feels good, gives pleasure or *delight*. This implies that *he* "knows" better than anyone else what is good for him. A permissive regime means not that adults gratify his needs directly, but make it possible for *him* to gratify his needs and to make his own choices, i.e., let him *be*. It is necessary, in order for children to grow well, that adults have enough trust in them and in the natural processes of growth, i.e., not interfere too much, not *make* them grow, or force them into predetermined designs, but rather *let* them grow and *help* them grow in a Taoistic rather than an authoritarian way.

14. But we know also that the *complete absence* of frustration is dangerous. To be strong, a person must acquire frustration-tolerance, the ability to perceive physical reality as essentially indifferent to human wishes, the ability to love others and to enjoy their need-gratification as well as one's own (not to use other people only as means). The child with a good basis of safety, love and respect-need-gratification is able to profit from nicely graded frustrations and become stronger thereby. If they are more than he can bear, if they overwhelm him, we call them traumatic, and consider them dangerous rather than profitable.

It is via the frustrating unyieldingness of physical reality and of animals and of other people that we learn about *their* nature, and thereby learn to differentiate wishes from facts (which things wishing makes come true, and which things proceed in complete disregard of our wishes), and are thereby enabled to live in the world and adapt to it as necessary.

We learn also about our own strengths and limits by overcoming difficulties, by straining ourselves to the utmost, by meeting challenge, even by failing. There can be great enjoyment in a great struggle, and this can displace fear.

15. To make growth and self-actualization possible, it is necessary to understand that capacities, organs and organ systems press to function and express themselves and to be used and exercised, and that such use is satisfying and disuse irritating. The muscular person likes to use his muscles, indeed *has* to use them in order to "feel good" and to achieve the subjective feeling of harmonious, successful, uninhibited functioning (spontaneity) which is so important an aspect of good growth and psychological health. So also for intelligence, for the uterus, the eyes, the capacity to love. Capacities clamor to be used, and cease their clamor only when they *are* well used. That is, capacities are also needs. Not only is it fun to use our capacities, but it is also necessary. The unused capacity or organ can become a disease center or else atrophy, thus diminishing the person.

16. The psychologist proceeds on the assumption that for his purposes there are two kinds of worlds, two kinds of reality, the natural world and the psychic world, the world of unyielding facts and the world of wishes, hopes, fears, emotions, the world which runs by nonpsychic rules and the world which

runs by psychic laws. This differentiation is not very clear except at its extremes, where there is no doubt that delusions, dreams and free associations are lawful and yet utterly different from the lawfulness of logic and from the lawfulness of the world which would remain if the human species died out. This assumption does not deny that these worlds are related and may even fuse.

I may say that this assumption is acted upon by *many* or *most* psychologists, even though they are perfectly willing to admit that it is an insoluble philosophical problem. Any therapist must assume it or give up his functioning. This is typical of the way in which psychologists bypass philosophical difficulties and act "as if" certain assumptions were true even though unprovable, e.g., the universal assumption of "responsibility," "will power," etc.

17. Immaturity can be contrasted with maturity from the motivational point of view, as the process of gratifying the deficiency-needs in their proper order. Maturity, or self-actualization, from this point of view, means to transcend the deficiency-needs. This state can be described then as meta-motivated, or unmotivated (if deficiencies are seen as the only motivations). It can also be described as self-actualizing, Being, expressing, rather than coping. This state of Being, rather than of striving, is suspected to be synonymous with selfhood, with being "authentic," with being a person, with being fully human. The process of growth is the process of *becoming* a person. *Being* a person is different.

18. Immaturity can also be differentiated from maturity in terms of the cognitive capacities (and also in terms of the emotional capacities). Immature and mature cognition have been best described by Werner and Piaget. I wish to add another differentiation, that between D-cognition and B- cognition (D = Deficiency; B = Being). D-cognition can be defined as the cognitions which are organized from the point of view of basic needs or deficiency-needs and their gratification and frustration. That is, D-cognition could be called selfish cognition, in which the world is organized into gratifiers and frustrators of our own needs, with other characteristics being ignored or slurred. The cognition of the object, in its own right and its own Being, without reference to its need-gratifying or need-frustrating qualities, that is, without primary reference to its value for the observer or its effects upon him, can be called B-cognition (or self-transcending, or unselfish, or objective cognition). The parallel with maturity is by no means perfect (children can also cognize in a selfless way), but in general, it is mostly true that with increasing selfhood or firmness of personal identity (or acceptance of one's own inner nature) B-cognition becomes easier and more frequent. (This is true even though D-cognition remains for *all* human beings, including the mature ones, the main tool for living-in-the-world.)

To the extent that perception is desire-less and fear-less, to that extent is it more veridical, in the sense of perceiving the true, or essential or intrinsic whole nature of the object (without splitting it up by abstraction). Thus the goal of objective and true description of any reality is fostered by psychological health. Neurosis, psychosis, stunting of growth, all are, from this point of view, cognitive diseases as well, contaminating perception, learning, remembering, attending and thinking.

19. A by-product of this aspect of cognition is a better understanding of the higher and lower levels of love. D-love can be differentiated from B-love on approximately the same basis as D-cognition and B-cognition, or D-motivation and B-motivation. No ideally good relation to another human being, especially a child, is possible without B-love. Especially is it necessary for teaching, along with the Taoistic, trusting attitude that it implies. This is also true for our relations with the natural world, i.e., we can treat it in its own right or we can treat it as if it were there only for our purposes.

20. Though, in principle, growth toward self-actualization is easy, in practice it rarely happens (by my criteria, certainly in less than one percent of the adult population). For this, there are many, many reasons at various levels of discourse, including all the determinants of psychopathology that we now know. We have already mentioned one main cultural reason, i.e., the conviction that man's intrinsic nature is evil or dangerous, and one biological determinant for the difficulty of achieving a mature self, namely that humans no longer have strong instincts.

There is a subtle but extremely important difference between regarding psychopathology as blocking or evasion or fear of growth toward self-actualization and thinking of it in a medical fashion, as akin to invasion from without by tumors, poisons or bacteria, which have no relationship to the personality being invaded.

21. Growth has not only rewards and pleasures but also many intrinsic pains, and always will have. Each step forward is a step into the unfamiliar and is possibly dangerous. It also means giving up something familiar and good and satisfying. It frequently means a parting and a separation, with consequent nostalgia, loneliness and mourning. It also often means giving up a simpler and easier and less effortful life, in exchange for a more demanding, more difficult life. Growth forward *is in spite of* these losses and therefore requires courage and strength in the individual, as well as protection, permission and encouragement from the environment, especially for the child.

22. It is therefore useful to think of growth or lack of it as the resultant of a dialectic between growth-fostering forces and growth-discouraging forces (regression, fear, pains of growth, ignorance, etc.). Growth has both advantages and disadvantages. Non-growing has not only disadvantages, but also advantages. The future pulls, but so also does the past. There is not only courage but also fear. The total ideal way of growing healthily, is, in principle, to enhance all the advantages of forward growth and all the disadvantages of not-growing, and to diminish all the disadvantages of growth forward and all the advantages of not-growing.

Homeostatic tendencies, "need-reduction" tendencies, and Freudian defense mechanisms are not growth-tendencies but defensive, pain-reducing postures of the organism. But they are quite necessary and normal (not pathological, necessarily) and are generally prepotent over growth-tendencies.

23. All this implies a naturalistic system of values, a by-product of the empirical description of the deepest tendencies of the human species and of specific individuals (8). The study of the human being by science or by self-search can discover where he is heading, what is his purpose in life, what is good for him and what is bad for him, what will make him feel virtuous and what will make him feel guilty, why choosing the good is often difficult for him, what the attractions of evil are. (Observe that the word "ought" need not be used. Also such knowledge of man is relative to man only and does not purport to be "absolute".)

24. The state of being without a system of values is psychopathogenic, we are learning. The human being needs a framework of values, a philosophy of life, a religion or religion-surrogate to live by and understand by, in about the same sense that he needs sunlight, calcium or love. This I have called the "cognitive need to understand." The value-illnesses which result from valuelessness are called variously anhedonia, anomie, apathy, amorality, hopelessness, cynicism, etc., and can become somatic illness as well. Historically, we are in a value interregnum in which all externally given value systems have proven to be failures (political, economic, religious, etc.), e.g., nothing is worth dying for. What man needs but does not have, he seeks for unceasingly, and he becomes dangerously ready to jump at *any* hope, good or bad. The cure for this disease is obvious. We need a validated, usable system of human values that we can believe in and devote ourselves to (be willing to die for), because they are true rather than because we are exhorted to "believe and have faith." Such an empirically based *Weltanschauung* seems now to be a real possibility, at least in theoretical outline.

Much disturbance in children and adolescents can be understood as a consequence of the uncertainty of adults about their values. As a consequence, many youngsters in the United States live not by adult values by by adolescent values, which of course are immature, ignorant and heavily determined by confused adolescent needs. An excellent projection of these adolescent values is the cowboy, or "Western," movie.

25. At the level of self-actualizing, many dichotomies become resolved, opposites are seen to be unities and the whole dichotomous way of thinking is recognized to be immature. For self-actualizing people, there is a strong tendency for selfishness and unselfishness to fuse into a higher, superordinate unity. Work tends to be the same as play; vocation and avocation become the same thing. When duty is pleasant and pleasure is fulfillment of duty, then they lose their separateness and oppositeness. The highest maturity is discovered to include a childlike quality, and we discover healthy children to have some of the qualities of mature self-actualization. The inner-outer split, between self and all else, gets fuzzy and much less sharp, and they are

seen to be permeable to each other at the highest levels of personality development.

26. One especially important finding in self-actualizing people is that they tend to integrate the Freudian dichotomies and trichotomies, i.e., the conscious, preconscious and the unconscious (as well as id, ego, superego). The Freudian "instincts" and the defenses are less sharply set off against each other. The impulses are more expressed and less controlled; the controls are less rigid, inflexible, anxiety-determined. The superego is less harsh and punishing and less set off against the ego. The primary and secondary cognitive processes are more equally available and more equally valued (instead of the primary processes being stigmatized as pathological). Indeed in the "peak-experience" the walls between them tend to fall altogether.

This is in sharp contrast with the classical Freudian position in which these various forces were sharply dichotomized as (a) mutually exclusive, (b) with antagonistic interests, i.e., as antagonistic forces rather than as complimentary or collaborating ones.

27. Healthy people are more integrated in another way. In them the conative, the cognitive, the affective and the motor are less separated from each other, and are more synergic, i.e., working collaboratively without conflict to the same ends. The conclusions of rational, careful thinking are apt to come to the same conclusions as those of the blind appetites. What such a person wants and enjoys is apt to be just what is good for him. His spontaneous reactions are as capable, efficient and right as if they had been thought out in advance. His sensory and motor reactions are more closely correlated. His sensory modalities are more connected with each other (physiognomical perception). Furthermore, we have learned the difficulties and dangers of those age-old rationalistic systems in which the capacities were thought to be arranged hierarchically, with rationality at the top.

28. This development toward the concept of a healthy unconscious, and of a healthy irrationality, sharpens our awareness of the limitations of purely abstract thinking, of verbal thinking and of analytic thinking. If our hope is to describe the world fully, a place is necessary for preverbal, ineffable, metaphorical, primary process, concrete-experience, intuitive and esthetic types of cognition, for there are certain aspects of reality which can be cognized in no other way. Even in science this is true, now that we know (a) that creativity has its roots in the nonrational, (b) that language is and must always be inadequate to describe total reality, (c) that any abstract concept leaves out much of reality, and (d) that what we call "knowledge" (which is usually highly abstract and verbal and sharply defined) often serves to blind us to those portions of reality not covered by the abstraction. That is, it makes us more able to see some things, but *less* able to see other things. Abstract knowledge has its dangers as well as its uses.

Science and education, being too exclusively abstract, verbal and bookish, do not have enough place for raw, concrete, esthetic experience, especially of the subjective happenings inside oneself. For instance, organismic psychologists would certainly agree on the desirability of more creative education in perceiving and creating art, in dancing in (Greek style) athletics and in phenomenological observation.

The ultimate of abstract, analytical thinking is the greatest simplification possible, i.e., the formula, the diagram, the map, the blueprint, certain types of abstract paintings. Our mastery of the world is enhanced thereby, but its richness may be lost as a forfeit, *unless* we learn to value B-cognition, perception-with-love-and-care, free floating attention — all of which enrich the experience instead of impoverishing it.

29. This ability of healthier people to dip into the unconscious and preconscious, to use and value their primary processes instead of fearing them, to accept their impulses instead of always controlling them, to be able to regress voluntarily without fear, turns out to be one of the main conditions of creativity. We can then understand why psychological health is so closely tied up with certain universal forms of creativeness (aside from special talent) as to lead some writers to make them almost synonymous.

This same tie between health and integration of rational and irrational forces (conscious and unconscious, primary and secondary processes) also permits us to understand why psychologically healthy people are more able to enjoy, to love, to laugh, to have fun, to be humorous, to be silly, to be whimsical and fantastic, to be pleasantly "crazy," and in general to permit and value and enjoy emotional experiences in general and peak experiences in particular and to have them more often. And it leads us to the strong suspicion that learning *ad hoc* to be able to do all these things may help the child move toward health.

30. Esthetic perceiving and creating and esthetic peak experiences are seen to be a central aspect of human life and of psychology and education rather than a peripheral one. This is true for several reasons: (a) All the peak experiences are (among other characteristics) integrative of the splits within the person, between persons, within the world, and between the person and the world. Since one aspect of health is integration, the peak experiences are moves toward health and are themselves momentary healths. (b) These experiences are life-validating, i.e., they make life worthwhile. These are certainly an important part of the answer to the question, "Why don't we all commit suicide?"

31. Self-actualization does not mean a transcendance of all human problems. Conflict, anxiety, frustration, sadness, hurt, and guilt can all be found in healthy human beings. In general, the movement, with increasing maturity, is from neurotic pseudo-problems to the real, unavoidable, existential problems inherent in the nature of man (even at his best) living in a particular kind of world. Even though he is not neurotic he may be troubled by real, desirable, and necessary guilt rather than neurotic guilt (which is not desirable or necessary), by an intrinsic conscience (rather than the Freudian superego).

Even though he has transcended the problems of Becoming, there remain the problems of Being. To be untroubled when one *should* be troubled can be a sign of sickness. Sometimes, smug people have to be scared "*into* their wits."

32. Self-actualization is not altogether general. It takes place via femaleness *or* maleness, which are prepotent to general humanness. That is, one must first be a healthy, femaleness-fulfilled woman before general-human self-actualization becomes possible.

There is also a little evidence that different constitutional types actualize themselves in somewhat different ways (because they have different inner selves to actualize).

33. Another crucial aspect of healthy growth to selfhood is dropping away the techniques used by the child, in his weakness and smallness for adapting himself to the strong, large, all-powerful, omniscient, godlike adults. He must replace these with the techniques of being strong and independent and of being a parent himself. This involves especially giving up the child's desperate wish for the exclusive, total love of his parents while learning to love others. He must learn to gratify his own needs and wishes, rather than the needs of his parents, and he must learn to gratify them himself, rather than depending upon the parents to do this for him. He must give up being good out of fear and in order to keep their love, and must be good because *he* wishes to be. He must discover his own conscience and give up his internalized parents as a sole ethical guide. All these techniques by which weakness adapts itself to strength are necessary for the child, but immature and stunting in the adult.

34. From this point of view, a society or a culture can be either growth-fostering or growth-inhibiting. The sources of growth and of humanness are essentially within the human person and are not created or invented by society, which can only help or hinder the development of humanness, just as a gardener can help or hinder the growth of a rosebush, but cannot determine that it shall be an oak tree. This is true even though we know that a culture is a *sine qua non* for the actualization of humanness itself, e.g., language, abstract thought, ability to love; but these exist as potentialities in human germ plasm prior to culture.

This makes theoretically possible a comparative sociology, transcending and including cultural relativity. The "better" culture gratifies all basic human needs and permits self-actualization. The "poorer" cultures do not. The same is true for education. To the extent that it fosters growth toward self-actualization, it is "good" education.

As soon as we speak of "good" or "bad" cultures, and take them as means rather than as ends, the concept of "adjustment" comes into question. We must ask, "What kind of culture or subculture is the 'well adjusted' person well adjusted *to*?" Adjustment is, very definitely, *not* necessarily synonymous with psychological health.

35. The achievement of self-actualization (in the sense of autonomy) parodoxically makes *more* possible the transcendence of self, and of self-consciousness and of selfishness. It makes it *easier* for the person to be homonomous, i.e., to merge himself as a part in a larger whole than himself. The condition of the fullest homonomy is full autonomy, and, to some extent, vice versa, one can attain to autonomy only via successful homonomous experiences (child dependence, B-love, care for others, etc.). It is necessary to speak of levels of homonomy (more and more mature), and to differentiate a "low homonomy" (of fear, weakness and regression) from a "high homonomy" (of courage and full, self-confident autonomy).

36. An important existential problem is posed by the fact that self-actualized persons (and *all* people in their peak experiences) occasionally live out-of-time and out-of-the-world, (atemporal and aspatial) even though mostly they *must* live in the outer world. Living in the inner psychic world (which is ruled by psychic laws and not by the laws of outer-reality), i.e., the world of experience, of emotion, of wishes and fears and hopes, of love, of poetry, art and fantasy, is different from living in and adapting to the nonpsychic reality which runs by laws the person never made and which are not essential to his nature even though he has to live by them. The person who is not afraid of this inner, psychic world can enjoy it to such an extent that it may be called "heaven" by contrast with the more effortful, fatiguing, externally responsible, world of "reality," of striving and coping, of right and wrong, of truth and falsehood. This is true even though the healthier person can adapt more easily and enjoyably to the "real" world, and has better "reality testing," i.e., does not confuse it with his inner, psychic world.

It seems quite clear now that confusing these inner and outer realities, or having either closed off from experience, is highly pathological. The healthy person is able to integrate them both into his life and therefore has to give up neither, being able to go back and forth voluntarily. The difference is the same as the one between the person who can *visit* the slums and the one who is forced to live there always. (*Either* world is a slum if one can not leave it.) Then paradoxically that which was sick and pathological and the "lowest" becomes part of the healthiest and "highest" aspect of human nature. Slipping into "craziness" is frightening only for those who are not fully confident of their sanity. Education must help the person to live in both worlds.

37. The foregoing propositions generate a different understanding of the role of action in psychology. Goal-directed, motivated, coping, striving, purposeful action is an aspect or by-product of the necessary transactions between a psyche and a nonpsychic world.

a. The D-need gratifications come from the world outside the person, not from within. Therefore adaptation to this world is made necessary, e.g., reality-testing, knowing the nature of this world, learning to differentiate this world from the inner world, learning the nature of people and of society, learning to delay gratification, learning to conceal what would be dangerous, learning which portions of the world are gratifying and which dangerous or useless for need-gratification, learning and the approval and permitted cultural paths to gratification and techniques of gratification. b. The world is in itself interesting, beautiful and fascinating. Exploring it, manipulating it, playing with it, contemplating it, enjoying it are all motivated kinds of action (cognitive, motor and esthetic needs). But there is also action which has little or nothing to do with the world, at any rate at first. Sheer expression of the nature or state or powers (*Funktionslust*) of the organism is an expression of Being rather than of striving. And the contemplation and enjoyment of the inner life not only is a kind of "action" in itself but is also antithetical to action in the world, i.e., it produces stillness and cessation of muscular activity. The ability to wait is is a special case of being able to suspend action.

38. From Freud we learned that the past exists *now* in the person. Now we must learn, from growth theory and self-actualization theory that the future also *now* exists in the person in the form of ideals, hopes, goals, unrealized potentials, mission, fate, destiny, etc. One for whom no future exists is reduced to the concrete, to hopelessness, to emptiness. For him, time must be endlessly "filled." Striving, the usual organizer of most activity, when lost, leaves the person unorganized and unintegrated.

Of course, being in a state of Being needs no future, because it is already *there*. Then Becoming ceases for the moment and its promissory notes are cashed in the form of the ultimate rewards, i.e., the peak experiences, in which time disappears.

REFERENCES

1. Gordon W. Allport. *Becoming: Basic Considerations for a Psychology of Personality.* New Haven, Conn.: Yale University Press, 1955. 106 p.
2. Andras Angyal. *Foundations for a Science of Personality.* New York: Commonwealth Fund, 1941. 398 p.
3. C. Bühler. *Values in Psychotherapy.* Glencoe, Ill.: Free Press, 1962.
4. Erich Fromm. *Man for Himself; An Inquiry into the Psychology of Ethics.* New York: Holt, Rinehart, and Winston, 1947. 254 p.
5. Kurt Goldstein. *Organism: A Holistic Approach to Biology Derived from Pathological Data in Man.* New York: American Book Co., 1939. 533 p.
6. Karen Horney. *Neurosis and Human Growth; The Struggle Toward Self-Realization.* New York: W. W. Norton & Co., 1950. 391 p.
7. Abraham H. Maslow. *Motivation and Personality.* New York: Harper & Brothers, 1954. 411 p.
8. _____, editor. *New Knowledge in Human Values.* New York: Harper & Brothers, 1959. 268 p.
9. Rollo May and others, editors. *Existence; A New Dimension in Psychiatry and Psychology.* New York: Basic Books, 1958. 445 p.
10. Clark Moustakas, editor. *The Self; Explorations in Personal Growth.* New York: Harper & Brothers, 1956. 284 p.
11. Carl R. Rogers and Rosalind F. Dymond. *Psychotherapy and Personality Change.* Chicago: University of Chicago Press, 1954.

ABRAHAM H. MASLOW

Deficiency Motivation and Growth Motivation

The concept "basic need" can be defined in terms of the questions which it answers and the operations which uncovered it. My original question was about psychopathogenesis. "What makes people neurotic?" My answer (a modification of and I think an improvement upon the analytic one) was, in brief, that neurosis seemed at its core, and in its beginning, to be a deficiency disease; that it was born out of being deprived of certain satisfactions which I called needs in the same sense that water and amino acids and calcium are needs, namely that their absence produces illness. Most neuroses involved, along with other complex determinants, ungratified wishes for safety, for belongingness and identification, for close love relationships and for respect and prestige. My "data" were gathered through twelve years of psychotherapeutic work and research and twenty years of personality study. One obvious control research (done at the same time and in the same operation) was on the effect of replacement therapy which showed, with many complexities, that when these deficiencies were eliminated, sicknesses tended to disappear. Still another necessary long-time control research was on the family backgrounds of both neurotic and healthy people establishing, as many others have since done, that people who are later healthy are not deprived of these essential basic-need-satisfactions, i.e., the prophylactic control.

These conclusions, which are now in effect shared by most clinicians, therapists, and child psychologists (many of them would not phrase it as I have) make it more possible year by year to define need, in a natural, easy spontaneous way, as a generalization of actual experiential data (rather than by fiat, arbitrarily and prematurely; *prior* to the accumulation of knowledge rather than subsequent to it (22) simply for the sake of greater objectivity).

The long-run deficiency characteristics are then the following. It is a basic or instinctoid need if:

1. its absence breeds illness,
2. its presence prevents illness,

From A. H. Maslow, "Deficiency Motivation and Growth Motivation." In M. R. Jones, ed., *Nebraska Symposium on Motivation*. Lincoln, Neb.: University of Nebraska Press, 1955, pp. 3–30.

3. its restoration cures illness,

4. under certain (very complex) free choice situations, it is preferred by the deprived person over other satisfactions,

5. it is found to be inactive, at a low ebb, or functionally absent in the healthy person.

Two additional characteristics are subjective ones, namely, conscious or unconscious yearning and desire, and feeling of lack or deficiency, as of something missing on the one hand, and, on the other, palatability ("It tastes good").

One last word on definition. Many of the problems that have plagued . . . writers . . . as they attempted to define and delimit motivation are a consequence of the exclusive demand for behavioral, externally observable criteria. The original criterion of motivation and the one that is still used by all human beings except behavioral psychologists is the subjective one. I am motivated when I feel desire or want or yearning or wish or lack. No objectively observable state has yet been found that correlates decently with these subjective reports, i.e., no good behavioral definition of motivation has yet been found.

Now of course we ought to keep on seeking for objective correlates of subjective states. On the day when we discover such a public and external indicator of pleasure or of anxiety or of desire, psychology will have jumped forward by a century. But *until* we find it we ought not make believe that we have. Nor ought we neglect the subjective data that we do have. It is unfortunate that we cannot ask a rat to give subjective reports. Fortunately, however, we *can* ask the human being, and I see no reason in the world why we should refrain from doing so until we have a better source of data. If the "objective" psychologists trying to define motivation sometimes seem to be staggering about in the dark, perhaps it is because they have voluntarily blindfolded themselves.

It is these needs which are essentially deficits in the organism, empty holes, so to speak, which must be filled up for health's sake, and furthermore must be filled from without by human beings *other* than the subject that I shall call deficits or deficiency needs for purposes of this exposition and to set them in contrast to another and very different kind of motivation.

There is not a person in this room to whom it would occur to question the statement that we "need" iodine or vitamin C. I remind you that the evidence that we "need" love is of exactly the same type.

In recent years more and more psychologists have found themselves compelled to postulate some tendency to growth or self-perfection to supplement the concepts of equilibrium, homeostasis, tension-reduction, defense and other conserving motivations. This was so for various reasons.

1. PSYCHOTHERAPY. The pressure toward health makes therapy possible. It is an absolute *sine qua non*. If there were no such trend, therapy would

be inexplicable to the extent that it goes beyond the building of defenses against pain and anxiety. (Rogers [23], Angyal [2], et cetera.)

2. BRAIN-INJURED SOLDIERS. Goldstein's work (13) is well known to all. He found it necessary to invent the concept of self-actualization to explain the reorganization of the person's capacities after injury.

3. PSYCHOANALYSIS. Some analysts, notably Fromm (12), and Horney (15), have found it impossible to understand even neuroses unless one postulates an impulse toward growth, toward perfection of development, toward the fulfillment of the person's possibilities.

4. CREATIVENESS. Much light is being thrown on the general subject of creativeness by the study of healthy growing and grown people, especially when contrasted with sick people. Especially does the theory of art and art education call for a concept of growth and spontaneity (28).

5. CHILD PSYCHOLOGY. Observation of children shows more and more clearly that healthy children *enjoy* growing and moving forward, gaining new skills, capacities and powers. This is a flat contradiction to that version of Freudian theory which conceives of every child as hanging on desperately to each adjustment that it achieves and to each state of rest or equilibrium. According to this theory, the reluctant and conservative child has continually to be kicked upstairs, out of its comfortable, preferred state of rest *into* a new frightening situation.

While this Freudian conception is continually confirmed by clinicians as largely true for insecure and frightened children, and while it is a little bit true for all human beings, in the main it is *untrue* for healthy, happy, secure children. In these children we see clearly an eagerness to grow up, to mature, to drop the old adjustment as outworn, like an old pair of shoes. We see in them with special clarity not only the eagerness for the new skill but also the most obvious delight in repeatedly enjoying it, the so-called *Funktionslust* of Karl Buhler (8).

For the writers in these various groups, notably Fromm (12), Horney (15), Jung (16), C. Buhler (7), Angyal (2), Rogers (23), and G. Allport (1), and recently some Catholic psychologists (3, 21), growth, individuation, autonomy, self-actualization, self-development, productiveness, self-realization, are all crudely synonymous, designating a vaguely perceived area rather than a sharply defined concept. In my opinion, it is *not* possible to define this area sharply at the present time. Nor is this desirable either, since a definition which does not emerge easily and naturally from well-known facts is apt to be inhibiting and distorting rather than helpful, since it is quite likely to be wrong or mistaken if made by an act of the will on *a priori* grounds. We just don't know enough about growth yet to be able to define it well.

Its meaning can be *indicated* rather than defined, partly by positive pointing, partly by negative contrast, i.e., what it is *not*. For example, it is not equilibrium, homeostasis, tension-reduction, need-reduction, et cetera.

Its necessity has presented itself to its proponents partly because of dissatisfaction (certain newly noticed phenomena simply were not covered by extant theories); partly by positive needs for theories and concepts which would better serve the new humanistic value systems emerging from the breakdown of the older value systems.

This paper however derives mostly from a direct study of psychologically healthy individuals. This was undertaken not only for reasons of intrinsic and personal interest but also to supply a firmer foundation for the theory of therapy, of pathology and therefore of values. The true goals of education, of family training, of psychotherapy, of self-development, it seems to me, can be discovered only by such a direct attack. The end product of growth teaches us much about the processes of growth. In a recent book (19), I have described what was learned from this study and in addition theorized very freely about various possible consequences for general psychology of this kind of direct study of good rather than bad human beings, of healthy rather than sick people, of the positive as well as the negative. I must warn you that the data cannot be considered reliable until someone else repeats the study. The possibilities of projection are very real in such a study and of course are unlikely to be detected by the investigator himself. Today I should like to crystallize a little more some of the differences that I have observed to exist between the motivational lives of healthy people and of others, i.e., people motivated by growth needs contrasted with those motivated by the basic needs.

So far as motivational status is concerned, healthy people have sufficiently gratified their basic needs for safety, belongingness, love, respect and self-esteem so that they are motivated primarily by trends to self-actualization (defined as ongoing actualization of potential capacities and talents, as fulfillment of mission or call or fate or vocation, as a fuller knowledge of, and acceptance of, the person's own intrinsic nature, as an unceasing trend toward unity, integration or synergy within the person).

Much to be preferred to this generalized definition would be a descriptive and operational one which I have already published (19). These people are there defined by describing their clinically observed characteristics. These are:

1. Superior perception of reality.
2. Increased acceptance of self, of others and of nature.
3. Increased spontaneity.
4. Increase in problem-centering.
5. Increased detachment and desire for privacy.
6. Increased autonomy, and resistance to enculturation.
7. Greater freshness of appreciation, and richness of emotional reaction.
8. Higher frequency of mystic experiences.
9. Increased identification with the human species.
10. Changed (the clinician would say, improved) interpersonal relations.
11. More democratic character structure.
12. Greatly increased creativeness.
13. Certain changes in the value system.

Furthermore, in this book are described also the limitations imposed upon the definition by unavoidable shortcomings in sampling and in availability of data.

One major difficulty with this conception as so far presented is its somewhat static character.[1] Self-actualization, since I have found it only in older people, tends to be seen as an ultimate or final state of affairs, a far goal, rather than a dynamic process, active throughout life, Being rather than Becoming.

If we define growth as the various processes which bring the person toward ultimate self-actualization, then this conforms better with the observed fact that it is going on *all* the time in the life history. It discourages also the stepwise, *all* or none, saltatory conception of motivational progression toward self-actualization in which the basic needs are completely gratified, one by one, before the next higher one emerges into consciousness. Growth is seen then not only as progressive gratification of basic needs to the point where they disappear, but also in the form of specific growth motivations over and above these basic needs, e.g., talents, capacities, creative tendencies, constitutional potentialities. We are thereby helped also to realize that basic needs and self-actualization do not contradict each other any more than do childhood and maturity. One passes into the other and is a necessary prerequisite for it.

The differentiation between these growth-needs and basic needs which we shall explore in this paper is a consequence of the clinical perception of qualitative differences between the motivational lives of self-actualizers and of other people. These differences, listed below, are fairly well though not perfectly described by the names deficiency-needs and growth-needs. For instance, not all physiological needs are deficits, e.g., sex, elimination, sleep, rest.

At a higher level, needs for safety, belongingness, love and for respect are all clearly deficits. But the need for self-respect is a doubtful case. While the cognitive needs for curiosity-satisfaction and for a system of explanation can easily be considered deficits to be satisfied, as can also the hypothetical need for beauty, the need to create is another matter, as is also the need to express. Apparently not all basic needs are deficits but the needs whose frustration is pathogenic are deficits.

In any case, the psychological life of the person, in very many of its aspects, is lived out differently when he is deficiency-need-gratification-bent and when he is growth-dominated or "metamotivated" or growth-motivated or self-actualizing. The following differences make this clear.

---

[1] I was made aware of this mostly by Frances Wilson's work with art education and Gordon Allport's new book on "The Course of Becoming," which I was privileged to read in manuscript. I profited also from discussions with my students in a graduate seminar in motivation theory.

1. ATTITUDE TOWARD IMPULSE: IMPULSE-REJECTION AND IMPULSE-ACCEPTANCE. Practically all historical and contemporary theories of motivation unite in regarding needs, drives and motivating states in general as annoying, irritating, unpleasant, undesirable, as something to get rid of. Motivated behavior, goal seeking, consummatory responses are all techniques for reducing these discomforts. This attitude is very explicitly assumed in such widely used descriptions of motivation as need reduction, tension reduction, drive reduction, and anxiety reduction.

This approach is understandable in animal psychology and in the behaviorism which is so heavily based upon work with animals. It may be that animals have *only* deficiency needs. Whether or not this turns out to be so, in any case we have treated animals *as if* this were so for the sake of objectivity. A goal object has to be something outside the animal organism so that we can measure the effort put out by the animal in achieving this goal.

It is also understandable that the Freudian psychology should be built upon the same attitude toward motivation that impulses are dangerous and to be fought. After all this whole psychology is based upon experience with sick people, people who in fact suffer from bad experiences with their needs and with their gratifications and frustrations. It is no wonder that such people should fear or even loathe their impulses which have made so much trouble for them and which they handle so badly, and that a usual way of handling them is repression.

This derogation of desire and need has, of course, been a constant theme throughout the history of philosophy, theology and psychology. The Stoics, most hedonists, practically all theologians, many political philosophers and most economic theorists have united in affirming the fact that good or happiness or pleasure is essentially the consequence of amelioration of this unpleasant state of affairs, of wanting, of desiring, of needing.

To put it as succinctly as possible, these people all find desire or impulse to be a nuisance or even a threat and therefore will try generally to get rid of it, to deny it or to avoid it.

This contention is sometimes an accurate report of what is the case. The physiological needs, the needs for safety, for love, for respect, for information are in fact often nuisances for many people, psychic trouble-makers, and problem-creators, especially for those who have had unsuccessful experiences at gratifying them and for those who cannot now count on gratification.

Even with these deficiencies, however, the case is very badly overdrawn: one can accept and enjoy one's needs and welcome them to consciousness if (a) past experience with them has been rewarding, and (b) if present and future gratification can be counted on. For example, if one has in general enjoyed food and if good food is now available, the emergence of appetite into consciousness is welcomed instead of dreaded. ("The trouble with eating is that it kills my appetite.") Something like this is true for thirst, for sleepiness, for sex, for dependency needs and for love needs. However, a far more powerful refutation of the "need-is-a-nuisance" theory is found in the recently emerging awareness of, and concern with, growth (self-actualization) motivation.

The multitude of idiosyncratic motives which come under the head of "self-actualization" can hardly be listed since each person has different talents, capacities, potentialities. But some characteristics are general to all of them. And one is that these impulses are desired and welcomed, are enjoyable and pleasant, that the person wants more of them rather than less, and that if they constitute tensions, they are *pleasurable* tensions. The creator welcomes his creative impulses, the talented person enjoys using and expanding his talents.

It is simply inaccurate to speak in such instances of tension-reduction, implying thereby the getting rid of an annoying state. For these states are not annoying.

2. DIFFERENTIAL EFFECTS OF GRATIFICATION. Almost always associated with negative attitudes toward the need is the conception that the primary aim of the organism is to get rid of the annoying need and thereby to achieve a cessation of tension, an equilibrium, a homeostasis, a quiescence, a state of rest, a lack of pain.

The drive or need presses toward its own elimination. Its only striving is toward cessation, toward getting rid of itself, toward a state of not wanting. Pushed to its logical extreme, we wind up with Freud's Death-instinct.

Angyal, Goldstein, G. Allport, C. Buhler and others have effectively criticized this essentially circular position. If the motivational life consists essentially of a defensive removal of irritating tensions, and if the only end product of tension-reduction is a state of passive waiting for more unwelcome irritations to arise and in their turn, to be dispelled, then how does change, or development or movement or direction come about? Why do people improve? Get wiser? What does zest in living mean?

Charlotte Buhler (7) has pointed out that the theory of homeostasis is different from the theory of rest. The latter theory speaks simply of removing tension which implies that zero tension is best. Homostasis means coming not to a zero but to an optimum level. This means sometimes reducing tension, sometimes increasing it, e.g., blood pressure may be too low as well as too high.

In either case the lack of constant direction through a lifespan is obvious. In both cases, growth of the personality, increase in wisdom, self-actualization, strengthening of the character, and the planning of one's life are not and cannot be accounted for. Some long-time vector, or directional tendency, must be invoked to make any sense of development through the lifetime (7).

This theory must be put down as an inadequate description even of deficiency motivation. What is lacking here is awareness of the dynamic principle which ties together and interrelates all these separate motivational episodes. The different basic needs are related to each other in a hierarchical order such that gratification of one need and its consequent removal from the center of the stage brings about not a state of rest or Stoic apathy, but rather the emergence into consciousness of another "higher" need; wanting and desiring continues but at a "higher" level. Thus the coming-to-rest theory isn't adequate even for deficiency motivation.

However, when we examine people who are predominantly growth-motivated, the coming-to-rest conception of motivation becomes completely useless. In such people gratification breeds increased rather than decreased motivation, heightened rather than lessened excitement. The appetites become intensified and heightened. They grow upon themselves and instead of wanting less and less, such a person wants more and more of, for instance, education. The person rather than coming to rest becomes more active. The appetite for growth is whetted rather than allayed by gratification. Growth is, *in itself*, a rewarding and exciting process, e.g., the fulfilling of yearnings and ambitions, like that of being a good doctor; the acquisition of admired skills, like playing the violin or being a good carpenter; the steady increase of understanding about people or about the universe, or about oneself; the development of creativeness in whatever field, or, most important, simply the ambition to be a good human being.

Wertheimer (27) long ago stressed another aspect of this same differentiation by claiming, in a seeming paradox, that true goal-seeking activity took up less than 10% of his time. Activity can be enjoyed either intrinsically, for its own sake, or else have worth and value only because it is instrumental in bringing about a desired gratification. In the latter case it loses its value and is no longer pleasurable when it is no longer successful or efficient. More frequently, it is simply *not enjoyed at all*, but only the goal is enjoyed. This is similar to that attitude toward life which values it less for its own sake than because one goes to Heaven at the end of it. The observation upon which this generalization is based is that self-actualizing people enjoy life in general and in practically all its aspects, while most other people enjoy only stray moments of triumph, of achievement or of climax.

Partly this intrinsic validity of living comes from the pleasurableness inherent in growing and in being grown. But it also comes from the ability of healthy people to transform means-activity into end-experience, so that even instrumental activity is enjoyed as if it were end activity (19). Growth motivation may be long-term in character. Most of a lifetime may be involved in becoming a good psychologist or a good artist. All equilibrium or homeostasis or rest theories deal only with short-term episodes, each of which have nothing to do with each other. Allport particularly has stressed this point. Plan-fulness and looking into the future, he points out, are of the central stuff or healthy human nature. He agrees (1) that "Deficit motives do, in fact, call for the reduction of tension and restoration of equilibrium. Growth motives, on the other hand, maintain tension in the interest of distant and often unattainable goals. As such they distinguish human from animal becoming, and adult from infant becoming."

3. CLINICAL EFFECTS OF GRATIFICATION. Deficit-need gratifications and growth-need gratifications have differential subjective and objective effects upon the personality. If I may phrase what I am groping for here in a very generalized way, it is this: Satisfying deficiencies avoid illness; growth satisfactions produce positive health. I must grant that this will be difficult to pin down for research purposes at this time. And yet there is a real clinical difference between fending off threat or attack and positive triumph and achievement, between protecting, defending and preserving oneself and reaching out for fulfillment, for excitement and for enlargement. I have tried to express this as a contrast between living fully and *preparing* to live fully, between growing up and being grown.

4. DIFFERENT KINDS OF PLEASURE. Erich Fromm (12, p. 186) has made an interesting and important effort to distinguish higher from lower pleasures, as have so many others before him. This is a crucial necessity for breaking through subjective ethical relativity and is a prerequisite for a scientific value theory.

He distinguishes scarcity-pleasure from abundance-pleasure, the "lower" pleasure of satiation of a need from the "higher" pleasure of production, creation and growth of insight. The glut, the relaxation, and the loss of tension that follows deficiency-satiation can at best be called "relief" by contrast with the *Funktionslust*, the ecstasy, the serenity that one experiences when functioning easily, perfectly and at the peak of one's powers — in overdrive, so to speak.

"Relief," depending so strongly on something that disappears, is itself more likely to disappear. It must be less stable, less enduring, less constant than the pleasure accompanying growth, which can go on forever.

5. ATTAINABLE AND UNATTAINABLE GOAL-STATES. Deficiency-need gratification tends to be episodic and climactic. The most frequent schema here begins with an instigating, motivating state which sets off motivated behavior designed to achieve a goal-state, which, mounting gradually and steadily in desire and excitement, finally reaches a peak in a moment of success and consummation. From this peak curve of desire, excitement and pleasure fall rapidly to a plateau of quiet tension-release, and lack of motivation.

This schema, though not universally applicable, in any case contrasts very sharply with the situation in growth-motivation, for here characteristically there is no climax or consummation, no orgasmic moment, no end-state, even no goal if this be defined climactically. Growth is instead a continued, more or less steady upward or forward development. The more one gets, the more one wants so that this kind of wanting is endless and can never be attained or satisfied.

It is for this reason that the usual separation between instigation, goal-seeking behavior, the goal object and the accompanying affect breaks down completely. The behaving is itself the goal, and to differentiate the goal of growth from the instigation to growth is impossible. They too are the same.

6. SPECIES-WIDE GOALS AND IDIOSYNCRATIC GOALS. The deficit-needs are shared by all members of the human species and to some extent by other species as well. Self-actualization is idiosyncratic since every person is different. The deficits, i.e., the species requirements, must ordinarily be fairly well satisfied before real individuality can develop fully.

Just as all trees need sun, water, and foods from the environment, so do all people need safety, love and status from *their* environment. However, in both cases this is just where real development of individuality can begin, for once satiated with these elementary, species-wide necessities, each tree and each person proceeds to develop in his own style, uniquely, using these necessities for his own private purposes. In a very tangible sense, development then becomes more determined from within rather than from without.

7. DEPENDENCE AND INDEPENDENCE OF THE ENVIRONMENT. The needs for safety, belongingness, love relations and for respect can be satisfied only by other people, i.e., only from outside the person. This means considerable dependence on the environment. A person in this dependent position cannot really be said to be governing himself, or in control of his own fate. He *must* be beholden to the sources of supply of needed gratifications. Their wishes, their whims, their rules and laws govern him and must be appeased lest he jeopardize his sources of supply. He *must* be to an extent "other-directed" and *must* be sensitive to other people's approval, affection and good will. This is the same as saying that he must adapt and adjust by being flexible and responsive and by changing himself to fit the external situation. He is the dependent variable; the environment is the fixed, independent variable.

Because of this, the deficiency-motivated man must be more afraid of the environment, since there is always the possibility that it may fail or disappoint him. We now know that this kind of anxious dependence breeds hostility as well. All of which adds up to a lack of freedom, more or less, depending on the good fortune or bad fortune of the individual.

In contrast, the self-actualizing individual, by definition gratified in his basic needs, is far less dependent, far less beholden, far more autonomous and self-directed. Far from needing other people, growth-motivated people may actually be hampered by them. I have already reported their special liking for privacy, for detachment and for meditativeness.

Such people become far more self-sufficient and self-contained. The determinants which govern them are now primarily inner ones, rather than social or environmental. They are the laws of their own inner nature, their potentialities and capacities, their talents, their latent resources, their creative impulses, their needs to know themselves and to become more and more integrated and unified, more and more aware of what they really are, of what they really want, of what their call or vocation or fate is to be.

Since they depend less on other people, they are less ambivalent about them, less anxious and also less hostile, less needful of their praise and their affection. They are less anxious for honors, prestige and rewards.

Autonomy or relative independence of environment means also relative independence of adverse external circumstances, such as ill fortune, hard knocks, tragedy, stress, deprivation. As Allport has stressed, the notion of the human being as essentially reactive, the S-R man we might call him, who is set into motion by external stimuli, becomes completely ridiculous and untenable for self-actualizing people. The sources of *their* actions are internal rather than external. This relative independence of the outside world and its wishes and pressures, does not mean of course lack of intercourse with it. It means only that in these contacts, the self-actualizer's wishes and plans are the primary determiners, and that the environment becomes more and more a means to his ends. This I have called psychological freedom, contrasting it with geographical freedom.

Allport's very expressive contrast (1) between "opportunistic" and "propriate" determination of behavior parallels very closely our outer-determined, inter-determined opposition. It reminds us also of the uniform agreement among biological theorists in considering increasing autonomy and independence of environmental stimuli as *the* defining characteristics of full individuality, of true freedom, of the whole evolutionary process (29).

8. INTERESTED AND DISINTERESTED INTERPERSONAL RELATIONS. In essence, the deficit-motivated man is far more dependent upon other people than is the man who is predominantly growth-motivated. He is more "interested," more needful, more attached, more desirous.

This dependency colors and limits interpersonal relations. To see people primarily as need-gratifiers or as sources of supply is an abstractive act. They are seen not as wholes, as complicated, unique individuals, but rather from the point of view of usefulness. What in them is not related to the perceiver's needs is either overlooked altogether, or else bores, irritates, or threatens. This parallels our relations with cows, horses and sheep, as well as with waiters, taxicab drivers, porters, policemen or others whom we *use*.

Fully disinterested, desireless, objective and holistic perception of another human being becomes possible only when nothing is needed from him, only when *he* is not needed. Idiographic, aesthetic perception of the whole person is far more possible for self-actualizing people, and furthermore approval, admiration, and love are based less upon gratitude for usefulness and more upon the objective, intrinsic qualities of the perceived person. He is admired for objectively admirable qualities rather than because he flatters or praises. He is loved because he is love-worthy rather than because he gives out love. This is what will be discussed below as unneeded love.

One characteristic of "interested" and need-gratifying relations to other people is that to a very large extent these need-gratifying persons are interchangeable. Since, for instance, the adolescent girl needs admiration per se, it therefore makes little difference who supplies this admiration; one admiration-supplier is about as good as another. So also for the love-supplier or the safety-supplier.

Disinterested, unrewarded, useless, desireless perception of the other as unique, as independent, as end-in-himself, in other words as a person rather than as a tool is the more difficult, the more hungry the perceiver is for deficit satisfaction. A "high-ceiling" interpersonal psychology, i.e., an understanding of the highest possible development of human relationships, cannot base itself on deficit theory of motivation.

9. EGO-CENTERING AND EGO-TRANSCENDENCE. We are confronted with a difficult paradox when we attempt to describe the complex attitude toward the self or ego of the growth-oriented, self-actualized person. It is just this person, in whom ego-strength is at its height, who most easily forgets or transcends the ego, who can be most problem-centered, most self-forgetful, most spontaneous in his activities, most homonomous, to use Angyal's term (2). In such people, absorption in perceiving, in doing, in enjoying, in creating can be very complete, very integrated and very pure.

This ability to center upon the world rather than to be self-conscious, egocentric and gratification-oriented becomes the more difficult the more need-deficits the person has. The more growth-motivated the person is the more problem-centered can he be, and the more he can leave self-consciousness behind him as he deals with the objective world.

10. INTERPERSONAL PSYCHOTHERAPY AND INTRAPERSONAL PSYCHOGOGY. A major characteristic of people who seek psychotherapy is a former and/or present deficiency of basic-need gratification. To a larger extent than the Freudians are yet willing to admit, neurosis is a deficiency-disease. Because this is so, a basic necessity for cure is supplying what has been lacking or making it possible for the patient to do this himself. Since these supplies come from other people, ordinary therapy *must* be interpersonal.

But this fact has been very badly over-generalized. It is true that people whose deficiency needs have been gratified and who are primarily growth-motivated are by no means exempt from conflict, unhappiness, anxiety, and confusion. In such moments they too are apt to seek help and may very well turn to interpersonal therapy. And yet it is unwise to forget that *more* frequently the problems and the conflicts of the growth-motivated person are customarily solved by himself by turning inward in a mediatative way, i.e., self-searching rather than seeking for help from someone. Even in principle, many of the tasks of self-actualization are largely intrapersonal, such as the making of plans, the discovery of self, the selection of potentialities to develop, the construction of a life-outlook.

In the theory of personality improvement, a place must be reserved for self-improvement and self-searching contemplation and meditation. In the later stages of growth the person is essentially alone and can rely only upon himself. This improvement of an already well person Oswald Schwarz has called psychogogy. If psychotherapy makes sick people not-sick and removes symptoms, then psychogogy takes up where therapy leaves off and tries to make not-sick people healthy. I was interested to notice in Rogers' recent book (23) that successful therapy raised the patients' average score in The Willoughby Maturity Scale from the twenty-fifth to the fiftieth percentile. Who shall then lift him to the seventy-fifth percentile? Or the one hundredth? And are we not likely to need new principles and techniques to do this with?

11. INSTRUMENTAL LEARNING AND PERSONALITY CHANGE. So-called learning theory in this country has based itself almost entirely on deficit-motivation with goal objects usually external to the organism, i.e., learning the best way to satisfy a need. For this reason, among others, our psychology of learning is a very limited body of knowledge, useful only in small areas of life and of real interest only to other "learning theorists."

This is of very little help in solving the problems of growth and self-actualization. Here the techniques of repeatedly acquiring from the outside world satisfactions of motivational deficiencies are much less needed. Associative learning and canalizations give way more to perceptual learning (20), to the increase of insight and understanding, to knowledge of self and to the steady growth of personality, i.e., increased synergy, integration and inner consistency. Change becomes much less an acquisition of habits or associations one by one, and much more a total change of the total person, i.e., a new person rather than the same person with some habits added like new external possessions.

This kind of character-change-learning means changing a very complex, highly integrated, holistic organism, which in turn means that many impacts will make no change at all because more and more such impacts will be rejected as the person becomes more stable and more autonomous.

The most important learning experiences reported to me by my subjects were very frequently single life experiences such as tragedies, deaths, traumata, conversions, sudden insights, which forced change in the life-outlook of the person and consequently in everything that he did. (Of course the so-called "working through" of the tragedy or of the insight took place over a longer period of time but this too was not a matter of associative learning.)

To the extent that growth consists in peeling away inhibition and constraints and then permitting the person to "be himself," to emit behavior — "radioactively," as it were — rather than to repeat it, to allow his inner nature to express itself, to this extent the behavior of self-actualizers is unlearned, created and released rather than acquired, expressive rather than coping. (19, p. 180.)

12. DEFICIENCY-MOTIVATED AND GROWTH-MOTIVATED PERCEPTION. What may turn out to be the most important difference of all is the greater closeness of deficit-satisfied people to the realm of Being (26). Psychologists have never yet been able to claim this vague jurisdiction of the philosophers, this area

dimly seen but nevertheless having undoubted basis in reality. But it may now become feasible through the study of self-fulfilling individuals to have our eyes opened to all sorts of basic insights, old to the philosophers but new to us.

For instance, I think that our understanding of perception and therefore of the perceived world will be very much changed and enlarged if we study carefully the distinction between need-interested and need-disinterested or desireless perception. Because the latter is so much more concrete and less abstracted and selective, it is possible for such a person to see more easily the intrinsic nature of the percept. He can perceive simultaneously the opposites, the dichotomies, the polarities, the contradictions and the incompatibles (19, pp. 232–4). It is as if less developed people lived in an Aristotelian world in which classes and concepts have sharp boundaries and are mutually exclusive and incompatible, e.g., male-female, selfish-unselfish, adult-child, angel-devil, kind-cruel, good-bad. A is A and everything else is not A in the Aristotelian logic, and never the twain shall meet. But seen by self-actualizing people is the fact that A and not-A interpenetrate and are one, that any person is simultaneously good *and* bad, male *and* female, adult *and* child. One can not place a whole person on a continuum, only an abstracted aspect of a person.

We may not be aware when *we* perceive in a need-determined way. But we certainly are aware of it when *we* ourselves are perceived in this way, e.g., simply as a money-giver, a food-supplier, a safety-giver, someone to depend on, or as a waiter or other anonymous servant or means-object. When this happens we don't like it at all. We want to be taken for ourselves, as complete and whole individuals. We dislike being perceived as useful objects or as tools. We dislike being "used."

Because self-actualizing people ordinarily do not have to abstract need-gratifying qualities nor see the person as a tool, it is much more possible for them to take a non-valuing, non-judging, non-interfering, non-condemning attitude towards others, a desirelessness, a "choiceless awareness" (17). This permits much clearer and more insightful perception and understanding of what is there. This is the kind of untangled, uninvolved, detached perception that surgeons and therapists are supposed to try for and which self-actualizing people attain *without* trying for.

Especially when the structure of the person or object seen is difficult, subtle and not obvious is this difference in style of perception most important. Especially then must the perceiver have respect for the nature of the object. Perception must then be gentle, delicate, unintruding, undemanding, able to fit itself passively to the nature of things as water gently soaks into crevices. It must *not* be the need-motivated kind of perception which *shapes* things in a blustering, overriding, exploiting, purposeful fashion, in the manner of a butcher chopping apart a carcass.

The most efficient way to perceive the intrinsic nature of the world is to be more passive than active, determined as much as possible by the intrinsic organization of that which is perceived and as little as possible by the nature of the perceiver. This kind of detached, Taoist, passive, non-interfering awareness of all the simultaneously existing aspects of the concrete, has much in common with some descriptions of the aesthetic experience and of the mystic experience. The stress is the same. Do we see the real, concrete world or do we see our own system of rubrics, motives, expectations and abstractions which we have projected onto the real world? Or, to put it very bluntly, do we see or are we blind?

Needed Love and Unneeded Love

The love need as ordinarily studied, for instance by Bowlby (5), Spitz (24), and Levy (18), is a deficit need. It is a hole which has to be filled, an emptiness into which love is poured. If this healing necessity is not available, severe pathology results (5, 18); if it *is* available at the right time, in the right quantities and with proper style, then pathology is averted. Intermediate states of pathology and health follow upon intermediate states of thwarting or satiation. If the pathology is not too severe and if it is caught early enough, replacement therapy can cure. That is to say, the sickness, "love-hunger," can be cured in certain cases by making up the pathological deficiency. Love hunger is a deficiency disease exactly as is salt hunger or the avitaminoses.

The healthy person, not having this deficiency, does not need to give or to receive love except in steady, small maintenance doses and he may even do without these for periods of time. But if motivation is entirely a matter of satisfying deficits and thus getting rid of needs, then a crucial paradox results. Satisfaction of the need should cause it to disappear, which is to say that people who have stood in satisfying love relationships are precisely the people who should be *less* likely to give and to receive love! But clinical study of very healthy people, who have been love-need-satiated, shows that they are far more — not less — loving people than others.

This finding in itself exposes very clearly the inadequacy of ordinary (deficiency-need-centered) motivation theory and indicates how inescapable is the necessity for "metamotivation theory" (or growth-motivation, or self-actualization theory).

I have already described in a preliminary fashion (19) the contrasting dynamics of B-love (love for the Being of another person, unneeded love, unselfish love) and D-love (deficiency-love, love need, selfish love). . . . At this point, I wish only to use these two contrasting groups of people to exemplify and illustrate some of the generalizations made in this paper.

1. B-Love is welcomed into consciousness, and is completely enjoyed. Since it is non-possessive, and is admiring rather than needing, it makes no trouble and is practically always gratifiable.

2. It can never be sated; it may be enjoyed without end. It usually grows greater rather than disappearing. It is intrinsically enjoyable. It is end rather than means.

3. The B-love experience is often described as being the same as and having the same effects as the aesthetic experience or the mystic experience.

4. The therapeutic and psychogogic effects of experiencing B-love are very profound and widespread. Similar are the characterological effects of the relatively pure love of a healthy mother for her baby, or the perfect love of their God that some mystics have described. The details are too complex for description here.

5. B-love is, beyond the shadow of a doubt, a richer, "higher," more valuable subjective experience than D-love (which all B-lovers have also previously experienced). This preference is also reported by my other older, more average subjects, many of whom experience both kinds of love simultaneously in varying combinations.

6. D-love *can* be gratified. The concept "gratification" hardly applies at all to admiration-love for another person's admiration-worthiness and love-worthiness.

7. In B-love there is a minimum of anxiety-hostility. For all practical human purposes, it may even be considered to be absent. There *can*, of course, be anxiety-for-the-other. In D-love one must always expect some degree of anxiety-hostility.

8. B-lovers are more independent of each other, more autonomous, less jealous or threatened, less needful, more individual, more disinterested, but also simultaneously more eager to help the other toward self-actualization, more proud of his triumphs, more altruistic, generous and fostering.

9. The truest, most penetrating perception of the other is made possible by B-love. It is as much a cognitive as an emotional-conative reaction, as I have already emphasized (19, pp. 257, 260). So impressive is this, and so often validated by other people's later experience, that, far from accepting the common platitude that love makes people blind, I become more and more inclined to think of the *opposite* as true, namely that non-love makes us blind.

10. Finally I may say that B-love, in a profound but testable sense, creates the partner. It gives him a self-image, it gives him self-acceptance, a feeling of love-worthiness and respect-worthiness, all of which permit him to grow. It is a real question whether the full development of the human being is possible without it.

REFERENCES

1. Allport, G., *The Course of Becoming*. New Haven: Yale University Press, 1955.
2. Angyal, A., *Foundations for a Science of Personality*. New York: Commonwealth Fund, 1941.
3. Arnold, M., and Gasson, J., *The Human Person*. New York: Ronald Press, 1954.
4. Banham, K. M., "The Development of Affectionate Behavior in Infancy," *J. gen. Psychol.*, 1950, 76: 283–289.
5. Bowlby, J., *Maternal Care and Mental Health*. Geneva: World Health Organization, 1952.
6. Buber, M., *I and Thou*. Edinburgh: T. & T. Clark, 1937.

7. Buhler, C., "Motivation and Personality," *Dialectica*, 1951, 5: 312–361.
8. Buhler, K., *Die geistige Entwicklung des Kindes*, 4th ed. Jena: Fischer, 1924.
9. Cannon, W. B., *Wisdom of the Body*. New York: W. W. Norton, 1932.
10. Freud, S., *An Outline of Psychoanalysis*, New York: W. W. Norton, 1949.
11. Freud, S., *Beyond the Pleasure Principle*. International Psychoanalytic Press, 1922.
12. Fromm, E., *Man For Himself*. New York: Rinehart, 1947.
13. Goldstein, K., *Human Nature from the Point of View of Psychopathology*. Cambridge: Harvard University Press, 1940.
14. Goldstein, K., *The Organism*. New York: American Book Co., 1939.
15. Horney, K., *Neurosis and Human Growth*. New York: W. W. Norton, 1950.
16. Jung, C. G., *Psychological Reflections*. (Jacobi, J., editor), New York: Pantheon Books, 1953.
17. Krishnamurti, J., *The First and Last Freedom*. New York: Harper, 1954.
18. Levy, D., *Maternal Overprotection*. New York: Columbia University Press, 1943.
19. Maslow, A. H., *Motivation and Personality*, New York: Harper, 1954.
20. Murphy, G., and Hochberg, J., "Perceptual Development: Some Tentative Hypotheses," *Psychol. Rev.*, 1951, 58: 332–349.
21. Nuttin, J., *Psychoanalysis and Personality*. New York: Sheed and Ward, 1953.
22. Ritchie, B. F., "Comments on Professor Farber's Paper." In Marshall R. Jones ed., *Nebraska Symposium on Motivation*, 1954, 46–50.
23. Rogers, C., *Psychotherapy and Personality Change*. Chicago: University of Chicago Press, 1954.
24. Spitz, R., "Anaclitic Depression," *Psychoanal. Study of the Child*. 1946, 2: 313–342.
25. Suttie, I., *Origins of Love and Hate*. London: Kegan Paul, 1935.
26. Tillich, P., *The Courage To Be*. New Haven: Yale University Press, 1952.
27. Wertheimer, M., Unpublished lectures at the New School for Social Research, 1935–6.
28. Wilson, F., Unpublished papers on art education and psychology, 1954.
29. Woodger, J., *Biological Principles*. New York: Harcourt, Brace, 1929.

V

Fulfillment Theory: Perfection Version

In the perfection version of the fulfillment model, the great force acting upon persons entails ideals of what is good, fine, and excellent, rather than the specifics of their particular genetic blueprint. If the perfection theorists are right, persons will try to overcome weaknesses and endure suffering if doing so brings them closer to perfection. To use an analogy from the game of bridge, the actualization theorist sees man as playing his long suit, whereas the perfection theorist sees him as playing his short suits as capably as if they were long. True to the fulfillment model, perfection theorists do not see man as necessarily in conflict, and blame such conflict, when it occurs, on the arbitrary restrictions imposed by society.

Adler's theory virtually defines the perfection fulfillment category, emphasizing compensations for felt inferiorities. The outlines of this core statement are briefly but clearly presented here. Perhaps the clearest statement of the Adlerian position on the periphery of personality is to be found in the selection by Dreikurs, which traces the effects of family atmosphere and constellation on the developing person, with adult implications for constructive versus destructive and active versus passive personality types.

White establishes himself in the perfection fulfillment camp by emphasizing the importance of being and feeling competent, regardless of one's genetic beginnings. Although his position does not really include peripheral statements, there is some exciting criticism of the psychoanalytic position, because of its narrow reliance on the psychosocial conflict form of personality theorizing.

Allport elaborates a slightly different form of perfection fulfillment theorizing in "The Concept of Self." In essence, his position on the core of personality is that man attempts to enact his concept of self, which concept heavily includes an ideal view of life. But in contrast to Rogers, who seems to be saying something similar, Allport does not regard the self as heavily influenced by the reactions of significant others. The person is considered much more autonomous than that, unless he be such a rudimentary soul that Allport is not even very interested in talking about him. On emphasis, Allport is in the perfection camp, though he clearly shares the fulfillment model with Rogers. Allport takes an extreme position concerning peripheral personality in "Personal Dispositions." He will not offer typologies or even lists of common traits, believing such theorizing to violate the true individuality of persons. People are so unlike each other that one must steep onself in each individual life in order to recognize the personal dispositions guiding it. One man's personal dispositions will not be at all like those of his neighbor.

Fromm presents in his selection a rather complete theory of personality; it includes core, peripheral, and developmental statements, and even explores the sociocultural antecedents influencing parental actions toward their children. His work is a model for personality theorizing, though some of the parts of the theory could well be elaborated further. Although Fromm calls himself a humanist, I have classed him as a perfection theorist, with all the attendant implications of idealism. What he means by humanism is that he is explicating the fine and excellent things that all men can become. He does not really concern himself with the particular abilities of Harry or John. He even advocates that practice makes perfect. All these emphases incline me to the belief that he is best classified as a perfection fulfillment theorist.

ALFRED ADLER

Individual Psychology

The point of departure upon this line of research seems to me to be given in a work entitled "Der Aggressionstrieb im Leben und in der Neurose," published in 1906 in a collective volume, *Heilen und Bilden* (1). Even at that time I was engaged in a lively controversy with the Freudian school, and in opposition to them, I devoted my attention in that paper to the *relation* of the child and the adult to the demands of the external world. I tried to present, howbeit in a very inadequate fashion, the multifarious forms of attack and defense, of modification of the self and of the environment, effected by the human mind, and launched on the momentous departure of repudiating the sexual aetiology of mental phenomena as fallacious. In a vague way I saw even then that the impulsive life of man suffers variations and contortions, curtailments and exaggerations, *relative to the kind and degree of its aggressive power*. In accordance with the present outlook of individual psychology, I should rather say: relative to the way the power of cooperation has developed in childhood. The Freudian school, which at that time was purely sexual psychology, has accepted this primitive-impulse theory without any reservations, as some of its adherents readily admit.

I myself was too deeply interested in the problem of what determined the various forms of attack upon the outer world. From my own observations, and supported by those of older authors, also perhaps guided by the concept of a *locus minoris resistentiae*, I arrived at the notion that inferior organs might be responsible for the feeling of psychic inferiority, and in the year 1907 recorded my studies concerning this subject in a volume entitled *Studie über Minderwertigkeit der Organe und die seelische Kompensation* (2). The purpose of the work was to show that children born with hereditary organic weaknesses exhibit not only a physical necessity to compensate for the defect, and tend to overcompensate, but that the entire nervous system, too, may take part in this compensation; especially the mind, as a factor of life, may suffer a striking exaggeration in the direction of the defective function (breathing, eating, seeing, hearing, talking, moving, feeling, or even thinking), so that this overemphasized function may become the mainspring of life, in so far as a *"successful* compensation" occurs. This compensatory increase,

From Carl Murchison, ed., *Psychologies of 1930.* Worcester, Mass.: Clark University Press, 1930. Copyright by Clark University.

which, as I showed in the above-mentioned book, has originated and continued the development of a human race blessed with inferior organs, may in favorable cases affect also the endocrine glands, as I have pointed out, and is regularly reflected in the condition of the sexual glands, their inferiority and their compensation — a fact which seemed to me to suggest some connection between individual traits and physical heredity. The link between organic inferiority and psychic effects, which to this day cannot be explained in any other way, but merely assumed, was evident to me in the mind's experience of the inferior organ, by which the former is plunged into a *constant feeling of inferiority*. Thus I could introduce the body and its degree of excellence as a factor in mental development.

Experts will certainly not fail to see that the whole of our psychiatry has tended in this direction, both in part before that time and quite definitely thereafter. The works of Kretschmer, Jaensch, and many others rest upon the same basis. But they are content to regard the psychic minus quantities as congenital epiphenomena of the physical organic inferiority, without taking account of the fact that it is the *immediate* experience of physical disability which is the key to the failures of performance, as soon as the demands of the outer world and the creative power of the child lead in into "wrong" alleys and force upon it a one-sided interest. What I treated there as failure appeared to me later as a premature curtailment of the cooperative faculty, the social impulse, and a greatly heightened interest for the self.

This work also furnished a test for organic inferiority. As proofs of inferiority it mentions insufficient development of physical form, of reflexes, of functions, or retardation of the latter. Defective development of the nerves in connection with the organ and of the brain-centers involved was also considered. But the sort of compensation which would under favorable circumstances occur in any one of these parts was always insisted upon as a decisive factor. A valuable by-product of this study, and one which has not yet been sufficiently appreciated, was the discovery of the significance of the birthmark for the fact that the embryonic development at that point or in that segment had not been quite successful. Schmidt, Eppinger, and others have found this insight correct in many respects. I feel confident that in the study of cancer, too, as I suggested in this connection, the segmental naevus will someday furnish a clue to the aetiology of carcinoma.

In trying thus to bridge the chasm between physical and mental developments by a theory that vindicated in some measure the doctrine of heredity, I did not fail to remark explicitly somewhere that the stresses engendered by the relation between the congenitally inferior organ and the demands of the external world, though, of course, they were greater than those which related to approximately normal organs, were none the less mitigated, to some degree, by the variability of the world's demands; so that one really had to regard them as merely relative. I repudiated the notion of the hereditary character of psychological traits, in that I referred their origin to the various intensities of organic functions in each individual. Afterwards I added to this the fact that children, in cases of abnormal development, are without any guidance, so that their activity (aggression) may develop in unaccountable ways. The inferior organs offer a temptation but by no means a necessity for neuroses or other mental miscarriages. Herewith I established the problem of the education of such children, with prophylaxis as its aim, on a perfectly sound footing. Thus the family history, all its plus and minus factors, became an index to the serious difficulties which might be expected and combatted in early childhood. As I said at that time, a hostile attitude toward the world might be the result of excessive stresses which must express themselves somehow in specific characteristics.

In this way I was confronted with the problem of character. There had been a good deal of nebulous speculations on this subject. Character was almost universally regarded as a congenital entity. My conviction that the doctrine of congenital mental traits was erroneous helped me considerably. I came to realize that characters were guiding threads, *ready attitudes* for the solution of the problems of life. The idea of an "arrangement" of all psychical activities became more and more convincing. Therewith I had reached the ground which to this day has been the foundation of individual psychology, the belief that *all psychical phenomena originate in the particular creative force of the individual, and are expressions of his personality.*

But who is this driving force behind the personality? And why do we find mostly individuals whose psychological upbuilding was not successful? Might it be that, after all, certain congenitally defective impulses, i.e., congenital weaknesses, decided the fate of our mental development, as almost all psychiatrists supposed? Is it due to a divine origin that an individual, that the human race may progress at all?

But I had realized the fact that children who were born with defective organs or afflicted by injuries early in life go wrong in the misery of their existence, constantly deprecate themselves, and, usually, to make good this deficiency, behave differently all their lives from what might be expected of normal people. I took another step, and discovered that children may be artificially placed in the same straits as if their organs were defective. If we make their work in very early life so hard that even their relatively normal organs are not equal to it, then they are in the same distress as those with defective physique, and from the same unbearable condition of stress they will give wrong answers as soon as life puts their preparation to any test. Thus I found two further categories of children who are apt to develop an abnormal sense of inferiority — *pampered children and hated children.*

To this period of my complete defection from Freud's point of view, and absolute independence of thought, date such works as *Die seelische Wirzel der Trigeminusneuralgie* (3), in which I attempted to show how, besides cases of organic origin, there were also certain ones in which excessive partial increase of blood-pressure, caused by emotions such as rage, may under the influence of severe inferiority feelings give rise to physical changes. This was followed by a study, decisive for the development of individual psychology, entitled *Das Problem der Distanz*, wherein I demonstrated that every individual, by reason of his degree of inferiority feeling, hesitated before the solution of one of the three great problems of life, stops or circumvents, and preserves his attitude in a state of exaggerated tension through psychological symptoms. As the three great problems of life, to which everyone must somehow answer by his attitude, I named: (a) society, (b) vocation, (c) love. Next came a work on *Das Unbewusste*, wherein I tried to prove that upon deeper inspection there appears no contrast between the conscious and the unconscious, that both cooperate for a higher purpose, that our thoughts and feelings become conscious as soon as we are faced with a difficulty, and unconscious as soon as our personality-value requires it. At the same time I tried to set forth the fact that that which other authors had used for their explanations under the name of *conflict, sense of guilt,* or *ambivalence* was to be regarded as symptomatic of a *hesitant attitude,* for the purpose of evading the solution of one of the problems of life. Ambivalence and polarity of emotional or moral traits present themselves as an attempt at a multiple solution or rejection of a problem.

This and some other works dating from the time of the self-emancipation of individual psychology have been published in a volume bearing the title *Praxis und Theorie der Individual-psychologie* (6). This was also the time when our great Stanley Hall turned away from Freud and ranged himself with the supporters of individual psychology, together with many other American scholars who popularized the "inferiority and superiority complexes" throughout their whole country.

I have never failed to call attention to the fact that the whole human race is blessed with deficient organs, deficient for coping with nature; that consequently the whole race is constrained ever to seek the way which will bring it into some sort of harmony with the exigencies of life; and that we make mistakes along the way, very much like those we can observe in pampered or neglected children. I have quoted one case especially, where the errors of our civilization may influence the development of an individual, and that is the case of the underestimation of women in our society. From the sense of female inferiority, which most people, men and women alike, possess, both sexes have derived an overstrained desire for masculinity, a superiority complex which is often extremely harmful, a will to conquer all difficulties of life in the masculine fashion, which I have called the *masculine protest.*

Now I began to see clearly in every psychical phenomenon the *striving for superiority.* It runs parallel to physical growth. It is an intrinsic necessity of life itself. It lies at the root of all solutions of life's problems, and is manifested in the way in which we meet these problems. All our functions follow its direction; rightly or wrongly they strive for conquest, surety, increase. The impetus from minus to plus is never-ending. The urge from "below" to "above" never ceases. Whatever premises all our philosophers and psychologists dream of — self-preservation, pleasure principle, equalization — all these are but vague representations, attempts to express the great upward drive. The history of the human race points in the same direction. Willing, thinking, talking, seeking after rest, after pleasure, learning, understanding, work and love, betoken the essence of this eternal melody. Whether one thinks or acts more wisely or less, one always moves along the lines of that upward tendency. In our right and wrong conceptions of life and its problems, in the successful or the unsuccessful solution of any question, this striving for perfection is uninterruptedly at work. And even where foolishness and imbecility, inexperience, seem to belie the fact of any striving to conquer some defect, or tend to depreciate it, yet the will to conquer is really operative. From this net-work which in the last analysis is simply given with the relationship "man-cosmos," no one may hope to escape. For even if anyone wanted to escape, yet, even if he *could* escape, he would still find himself in the general system, striving "upward," from "below." This does not only fix a fundamental category of thought, the structure of our reason, but what is more, it yields *the fundamental fact of our life.*

The origin of humanity and the ever repeated beginning of infant life rubs it in with every psychic act: "Achieve! Arise! Conquer!" This feeling is never absent, this longing for the abrogation of every imperfection. In the search for relief, in Faustian wrestling against the forces of nature, rings always the basis chord: "I relinquish thee not, thou bless me withal." The unreluctant search for truth, the ever unsatisfied longing for solution of the problems of life, belongs to this hankering after perfection of some sort.

This, now, appeared to me as the fundamental law of all spiritual expression: that the total melody is to be found again in every one of its parts, as a greatest common measure — in every individual craving for power, for victory over the difficulties of life.

And therewith I recognized a further premise of my scientific proceeding, one which agreed with the formulations of older philosophers, but conflicted with the standpoint of modern psychology: *the unity of the personality.* This, however, was not merely a premise, but could to a certain extent be demonstrated. As Kant has said, we can never understand a person if we do not presuppose his unity. Individual psychology can now add to that: this unity, which we must presuppose, is the work of the individual, which must always continue in the way it once found toward victory.

These were the considerations which led me to the conviction that early in life, in the first four or five years, a *goal* is set for the need and drive of psychical development, a goal toward which all its currents flow. Such a goal has not only the function of determining a direction, of promising security, power, perfection, but it is also of its essence and of the essence of the mind that his portentous goal should awaken feelings and emotions through that which it promises them. Thus the individual mitigates its sense of weakness in the anticipation of its redemption.

Here again we see the meaninglessness of congenital psychic traits. Not that we could deny them. We have no possible way of getting at them. Whoever would draw conclusions from the results is making matters too simple. He overlooks the thousand and one influences after birth, and fails to see the power that lies in the necessity of acquiring a goal.

The staking of a goal compels the unity of the personality in that it draws the stream of all spiritual activity into its definite direction. Itself a product of the common, fundamental sense of inferiority — a sense derived from genuine weakness, not from any comparison with others — the goal of victory in turn forces the direction of all powers and possibilities toward itself. Thus every phase of psychical activity can be seen within one frame, as though it were the end of some earlier phase and the beginning of a succeeding one. This was a further contribution of individual psychology to modern psychology in general — that it insisted absolutely on the indispensability of *finalism* for the understanding of all psychological phenomena. No longer could causes, powers, instincts, impulses, and the like serve as explanatory principles, but the final goal alone. Experiences, traumata, sexual-development mechanisms could not yield us an explanation, but the perspective in which these had been regarded, the individual way of seeing them, which subordinates all life to the ultimate goal.

This final aim, abstract in its purpose of assuring superiority, fictitious in its task of conquering all the difficulties of life, must now appear in concrete form in order to meet its task in actuality. Deity in its widest sense, it is apperceived by the childish imagination, and under the exigencies of hard reality, as victory over men, over difficult enterprises, over social or natural limitations. It appears in one's attitude toward others, toward one's vocation, toward the opposite sex. Thus we find concrete single purposes, such as: to operate as a member of the community or to dominate it, to attain security and triumph in one's chosen career, to approach the other sex or to avoid it. We may always trace in these special purposes *what sort of meaning the individual has found in his existence,* and how he proposes to realize that meaning.

If, then, the final goal established in early childhood exerts such an influence for better or worse upon the development of the given psychical forces, our next question must be: What are the sources of the individuality which we find in final aims? Could we not quite properly introduce another causal factor here? What brings about the differences of individual attitudes, if one and the same aim of superiority actuates everyone?

Speaking of this last question, let me point out that our human language is incapable of rendering all the qualities within a superiority goal and of expressing its innumerable differences. Certainty, power, perfection, deification, superiority, victory, etc., are but poor attempts to illumine its endless variants. Only after we have comprehended the partial expressions which the final goal effects, are we in any position to determine specific differences.

If there is any casual factor in the psychical mechanism, it is the common and often excessive sense of inferiority. But this continuous mood is only activating, a drive, and does not reveal the way to compensation and overcompensation. Under the pressure of the first years of life there is no kind of philosophical reflection. There are only impressions, feelings, and a desire to renew the pleasurable ones and exclude those which are painful. For this purpose all energies are mustered, until motion of some sort results. Here, however, training or motion of any sort forces the establishment of an end. There is no motion without an end. And so, in this way, a final goal becomes fixed which promises satisfaction. Perhaps, if one wanted to produce hypotheses, one might add: Just as the body approximates to an ideal form which is posited with the germ-plasm, so does the mind, as a part of the total life. Certainly it is perfectly obvious that the soul (mind — *das seelische Organ*) exhibits some systematic definite tendency.

From the time of these formulations of individual psychology dates my book, *Ueber den nervösen Charakter* (7), which introduced *finalism* into psychology with especial emphasis. At the same time I continued to trace the connection between organic inferiority and its psychological consequences, in trying to show how in such cases the goal of life is to be found in the type of overcompensation and consequent errors. As one of these errors I mentioned particularly the *masculine protest*, developed under the pressure of a civilization which has not yet freed itself from its overestimation of the masculine principle nor from an abuse of antithetic points of view. The imperfection of childish modes of realizing the fictitious ideal was also mentioned here as the chief cause for the differences in style of living — the unpredictable character of childish expression, which always moves in the uncontrollable *realm of error*.

By this time, the system of individual psychology was well enough established to be applied to certain special problems. *Zum Problem der Homosexualität* (8) exhibited that perversion as a neurotic construct erroneously made out of early childhood impressions, and recorded researches and findings which are published at greater length in the *Handbuch der normalen und pathologischen Physiologie* (9). Uncertainty in the sexual rôle, over-estimation of the opposite sex, fear of the latter, and a craving for easy, irresponsible successes proved to be the inclining but by no means constraining factors. Uncertainty in the solution of the erotic problem and fear of failure in this direction lead to wrong or abnormal functioning.

More and more clearly I now beheld the way in which the varieties of failure could be understood. In all human failure, in the waywardness of children, in neurosis and neuropsychosis, in crime, suicide, alcoholism, morphinism, cocainism, in sexual perversion, in fact in all nervous symptoms, we may read lack of the proper degree of *social feeling*. In all my former work

I had employed the idea of the individual's attitude toward society as the main consideration. The demands of society, not as of a stable institution but as of a living, striving, victory-seeking mass, were always present in my thoughts. The total accord of this striving and the influence it must exert on each individual had always been one of my main themes. Now I attained somewhat more clarity in the matter. However we may judge people, whatever we try to understand about them, what we aim at when we educate, heal, improve, condemn — we base it always on the same principle: social feeling! cooperation! Anything that we estimate as valuable, good, right, and normal, we estimate simple in so far as it is "virtue" from the point of view of an ideal society. The individual, ranged in a community which can preserve itself only through cooperation as a human society, becomes a part of this great whole through socially enforced division of labor, through association with a member of the opposite sex, and finds his task prescribed by this society. And not only his task, but also his preparation and ability to perform it.

The unequivocally given fact of our organic inferiority on the face of this earth necessitates social solidarity. The need of protection of women during pregnancy and confinement, the prolonged helplessness of childhood, gains the aid of others. The preparation of the child for a complicated, but protective and therefore necessary civilization and labor requires the cooperation of society. The need of security in our personal existence leads automatically to a cultural modification of our impulses and emotions and of our individual attitude of friendship, social intercourse, and love. The social life of man emanates inevitably from the man-cosmos relation, and makes every person a creature and a creator of society.

It is a gratuitous burden to science to ask whether the social instinct is congenital or acquired, as gratuitous as the question of congenital instincts of any sort. We can see only the results of an evolution. And if we are to be permitted a question at all concerning the beginnings of that evolution, it is only this — whether anything can be evolved at all for which no possibilities are in any way given before birth. This possibility exists, as we may see through the results of development, in the case of human beings. The fact that our sense-organs behave the way they do, that through them we may acquire *impressions* of the outer world, may combine these physically and mentally in ourselves, shows our connection with the cosmos. That trait we have in common with all living creatures. What distinguishes man from other organisms, however, is the fact that he must conceive his superiority goal in the social sense as a part of a total achievement. The reasons for this certainly lie in the greater need of the human individual and in the consequent greater mobility of his body and mind, which forces him to find a firm vantage-point in the chaos of life.

But because of this enforced sociability, our life presents only such problems which require *ability to cooperate* for their solution. To hear, see, or speak "correctly," means to lose one's self completely in another or in a situation, to become *identified* with him or with it. The capacity for identification, which alone makes us capable of friendship, humane love, pity, vocation, and love, is the basis of the social sense and can be practiced and exercised only in conjunction with others. In this intended assimilation of another person or of a situation not immediately given, lies the whole meaning of comprehension. And in the course of this identification we are able to conjure up all sorts of feelings, emotions, and affects, such as we experience not only in dreams but also in waking life, in neurosis and psychosis. It is always the fixed style of life, the ultimate ideals, that dominates and selects. The style of life is what makes our experiences reasons for our attitude, that calls up these feelings and determines conclusions in accordance with its own purposes. Our very identification with the ultimate ideal makes us optimistic, pessimistic, hesitant, bold, selfish, or altruistic.

The tasks which are presented to an individual, as well as the means of their performance, are conceived and formulated within the framework of society. No one, unless he is deprived of his mental capacities, can escape from this frame. *Only within this framework is psychology possible at all.* Even if we add for our own time the aids of civilization and the socially determined pattern of our examples, we still find ourselves confronted with the same unescapable conditions.

From this point of vantage we may look back. As far as we can reasonably determine, it appears that after the fourth or fifth year of life the style of life has been fashioned as a prototype, with its particular way of seizing upon life, its strategy for conquering it, its degree of ability to cooperate. These foundations of every individual development do not alter, unless perchance some harmful errors of construction are recognized by the subject and corrected. Whoever has not acquired in childhood the necessary degree of social sense, will not have it later in life, except under the above-mentioned special conditions. No amount of bitter experience can change his style of life, *as long as he has not gained understanding.* The whole work of education, cure, and human progress can be furthered only along lines of better comprehension.

There remains only one question: What influences are harmful and what beneficial in determining differences in the style of life, i.e., in the capacity for cooperation?

Here, in short, we touch upon the matter of preparation for cooperation. It is evident, of course, that deficiencies of the latter become most clearly visible when the individual's capacity to cooperate is put to the test. As I have shown above, life does not spare us these tests and preliminary trials. We are always on trial, in the development of our sense-organs, in our attitude toward others, our understanding of others, in our morals, our philosophy of life, our political position, our attitude toward the welfare of others, toward love and marriage, in our aesthetic judgments, in our whole behavior. As long as one is not put to any test, as long as one is without any trials or problems, one may doubt one's own status as a fellow of the community. But as soon as a person is beset by any problem of existence, which, as I have demon-

ALFRED ADLER

strated, always involves cooperative ability, then it will unfailingly become apparent — as in a geographical examination — how far his preparation for cooperation extends.

The first social situation that confronts a child is its relation to its mother, from the very first day. By her educational skill the child's interest in another person is first awakened. If she understands how to train this interest in the direction of cooperation, all the congenital and acquired capacities of the child will converge in the direction of social sense. If she binds the child to herself exclusively, life will bear for it the meaning that all other persons are to be excluded as much as possible. Its position in the world is thereby rendered difficult, as difficult as that of defective or neglected children. All these grow up in a hostile world and develop a low degree of cooperative sense. Often in such cases there results utter failure to adjust to the father, brothers and sisters, or more distant persons. If the father fails to penetrate the circle of the child's interest, or if by reason of exaggerated rivalry the brothers and sisters are excluded, or if because of some social short-coming or prejudice the remoter environment is ruled out of its sphere, then the child will encounter serious trouble in acquiring a healthy social sense. In all cases of failure later in life it will be quite observable that they are rooted in this early period of infancy. The question of responsibility will naturally have to be waived there, since the debtor is unable to pay what is required of him.

Our findings in regard to these errors and erroneous deductions of early childhood, which have been gathered from a contemplation of this relation complex which individual psychology reveals, are exceedingly full. They are recorded in many articles in the *Internationalen Zeitschrift für Individualpsychologie*, in my *Understanding Human Nature* (10), in *Individualpsychologie in der Schule* (11), and in *Science of Living* (12). These works deal with problems of waywardness, neurosis and psychosis, criminality, suicide, drunkenness, and sexual perversion. Problems of society, vocation, and love have been included in the scope of these studies. In *Die Technik der Individualpsychologie* (13) I have published a detailed account of a case of fear and compulsion neurosis.

Individual psychology considers the essence of therapy to lie in making the patient aware of his lack of cooperative power, and to convince him of the origin of this lack in early childhood maladjustments. What passes during this process is no small matter; his power of cooperation is enhanced by collaboration with the doctor. His "inferiority complex" is revealed as erroneous. Courage and optimism are awakened. And the "meaning of life" dawns upon him as the fact that proper meaning must be given to life.

This sort of treatment may be begun at any point in the spiritual life. The following three points of departure have recommended themselves to me, among others: (a) to infer some of the patient's situation from his place in the order of births, since each successive child usually has a somewhat different position from the others; (b) to infer from his earliest childhood recollections some dominant interest of the individual, since the creative tendency of the imagination always produces fragments of the life ideal (*Lebensstyl*); (c) to apply the individualistic interpretation to the dream-life of the patient, through which one may discover in what particular way the patient, guided by the style-of-life ideal, conjures up emotions and sensations contrary to common sense, in order to be able to carry out his style of life more successfully.

If one seems to have discovered the guiding thread of the patient's life, it remains to test this discovery through a great number of expressive gestures on his part. Only a perfect coincidence of the whole and all the parts gives one the right to say: I understand. And then the examiner himself will always have the feeling that, if he had grown up under the same misapprehensions, if he had harbored the same ideal, had the same notions concerning the meaning of life, if he had acquired an equally low degree of social sense, he would have acted and lived in an "almost" similar manner.

REFERENCES

1. Adler, A. "Der aggressionstrieb im Leben und in der Neurose." In *Heilen und Bilden*. (3rd ed.) Munich: Bergmann, 1906.

2. _____. *Studie über Minderwertigkeit der Organe und die seelische Kompensation*. (2nd ed.) Munich: Bergmann, 1907. Pp. vii + 92.

3. _____. *Die seelische Wirzel der Trigeminusneuralgie*.

4. _____. *Das Problem der Distanz*.

5. _____. *Das Unbewusste*.

6. _____. *Praxis und Theorie der Individualpsychologie*. (2nd ed.) Munich: Bergmann, 1924. Pp. v + 527.
    The Practice and Theory of Individual Psychology. New York: Harcourt, Brace, 1924.

7. _____. *Ueber den nervösen Charakter: Grundzüge einer vergleichenden Individualpsychologie und Psychotherapie*. Wiesbaden: Bergmann, 1912, Pp. vii + 196.
    The Neurotic Constitution: Outlines of a Comparative Individualistic Psychology and Psychotherapy. (Trans. by B. Glueck & J. E. Lind.) New York: Moffat, Yard, 1917. Pp xxiii + 456.

8. _____. *Zum Problem der Homosexualität*. Munich: Reinhardt, 1917. (Out of print.)

9. _____. *Handbuch der normalen und pathologischen Physiologie*. Berlin: Springer.

10. _____. *Menschenkenntnis*. (2nd ed.) Leipzig: Hirzel, 1928. Pp. vii + 230.
    Understanding Human Nature. (Trans. by W. B. Wolfe.) New York: Greenberg, 1927. Pp. xiii + 286.

11. _____. *Individualpsychologie in der Schule*. Leipzig: Hirzel.

12. _____. *Science of Living*. New York: Greenberg, 1929.

13. _____. *Die Technik der Individualpsychologie. I. Die Kuntz, eine Lebens- und Krankengeschichte zu lesen*. Munich: Bergmann, 1928. Pp. iv + 146.
    The case of Miss R. New York: Greenberg, 1929.

14. _____. *Problems of Neurosis*. London: Kegan Paul, 1929.

RUDOLF DREIKURS

Individual Psychology:

The Adlerian Point of View

To understand the interpretation which a person gives to his immediate situation, we must know his general outlook on life and the basic assumptions on which he operates. These may give to each actual situation a meaning completely different than someone else would attach to it. Each personality is based on definite assumptions and concepts, integrated in one basic pattern which Adler called the "Life Style." Each of us has his own Life Style, resulting from our understanding of life and what we strive for in our attempt to find a place for ourselves.

These long range goals of the Life Style have been called fictitious. They constitute an idea of security which does not exist in life, an assumption of validity which is not universal, an abstraction and overgeneralization of partially correct approaches (Ansbacher and Ansbacher, 1956: Way, 1950). They result from misunderstandings in observing the world during the formative years and childhood, when we form our personal convictions. Once such a conviction is formed, one acts "as if" it were the absolute truth and the only possible choice (Vaihinger, 1925). To the extent to which our ideas of life are correct, we can function well in given situations. If we fail or misbehave, then we are acting under the impact of mistaken ideas about ourselves and about life, and particularly about the means by which we can find a place in life. These mistakes have to be recognized if we wish to help, correct, improve and treat people who are deficient or maladjusted.

While our theoretical orientation explains psychopathology, in contrast to other orientations it also permits — perhaps for the first time — a definition of normality. Adler's model of man permits a clear distinction of what is normal and what is not. Such a differentiation is almost absent in contemporary social science. Contrary to prevalent beliefs, social science is still in a prescientific stage, despite the fact that it uses the scientific method of exploration. Nevertheless, it has not established any global laws and, there-

Reprinted from Joseph M. Wepman and Ralph W. Heine, eds., *Concepts of Personality* (Chicago: Adline Publishing Company, 1963): copyright © 1963 by Aldine Publishing Company.

fore, finds itself in the same state in which physics was before basic physical laws were discovered. Isolated phenomena were studied empirically, but their integration into one body of knowledge was impossible because the underlying basic laws were unknown.

The lack of such global laws in the social sciences is probably due to the fact that present scientific tools are inadequate to deal with the complexities that are found in the social and behavioral sciences. Since social research concerns itself with individual communities or societies, it is not surprising that each society or group is considered qualified to determine what is normal and what is abnormal behavior. Most social scientists are inclined to assume that normality depends entirely on the judgment of society. However, it is obvious that not all human societies function in a way compatible with our own idea of correct behavior. Does this mean merely a difference between social systems, in which each one has the right to establish its own norms? Are there any social and ethical values possible outside those established in a given society? Many believe in a Divine Law which supersedes temporal laws; some look for a transcendental basis for ethical standards. The quest for absolute social value is pursued constantly, but our social theorists have found no universal answer, and meanwhile various contradictory theories and beliefs complete for ascendancy. Only when we know the basic laws that regulate the realtionship between individuals and between groups can we have a reliable yardstick by which not only individual behavior but societies can be judged. Only then can the contradictory laws advanced by different societies be examined and ranked in terms of the degree to which they distort the meaning of social living, as do individuals in their neuroses, psychoses and all the other manifold forms of maladjustment.

Adler provided just such a yardstick to measure the normality of an individual and of a society with its norms and regulations. "Norm" is not merely the absence of abnormality, nor the average. We feel justified in stating that it may be normal today to be abnormal — and this certainly holds true for our children. But by what standard can a norm be established? Where does abnormality begin? It begins where the Social Interest ends. In other words, adjustment and normality imply the ability to function adequately in any conceivable situation, and this ability depends on a fully developed Social Interest. One does not have to have symptoms or to be overtly sick and deficient to be abnormal in this sense. An inability to function may not become obvious, the diminished Social Interest constitutes vulnerability, regardless whether it is tested or not. Only when it is tested does a deficiency in functioning become evident. In other words, the normal person is one with an optimally developed Social Interest, who feels belonging, is willing and able to participate and to contribute, is concerned with the needs of his situation and the welfare of those of whom he feels belonging (Adler, 1929a). Any limitation or restriction of Social Interest implies pathology and abnormality.

whether small and insignificant or full blown. If the full development of Social Interest is really the prerequisite for mental and social adjustment and health, then it is obvious that we in our society are far from normal.

If this is true, then one may well assume that our society is not normal either. But how can that be measured? Adler attempted to establish a basic law of social cooperation, in speaking of the "iron clad logic of social living" (Ansbacher & Ansbacher, 1956). There is a logic, a fundamental law in social living, and any society and any individual violating it will run into trouble. On the other hand, anyone who senses and accepts this intrinsic knowledge of social living will be able to function adequately and successfully. Adler considered equality as the basic requirement for harmonious social relationships, and he believed that only among equals can social harmony exist. Wherever one individual or group sets itself up as superior to any other, the relationship is disturbed. It becomes unstable, since the one in the dominant position must constantly fear loss of status, and the subordinate individual, the one in an inferior position, will always try to free himself from this predicament. Nobody wants to be less than another.

While the concept of equality is difficult to comprehend, it is all-important for both social and political progress as well as for education, counseling and psychotherapy (Dreikurs, 1961). Psychopathology, neurosis, deficiency, and maladjustment are the result of one's doubt of one's worth, of one's status and ability (Adler, 1929). Only people who feel equal to those around them can be sure of their place. If they doubt their equality, if they feel inferior or inadequate, then they must regard their fellow men as their enemies, against whom they have to defend themselves. Out of this defensiveness comes psychopathology. It is equally disturbing for cooperation if one tries to elevate himself over others or gives up in discouragement, resigning himself to an inferior position. Even those who succeed in compensating or overcompensating for a sense of deficiency and inferiority can never find peace of mind or a feeling of security. Inevitably they must feel vulnerable for they can never be sure of remaining superior by being sufficiently ahead of others.

A sense of security is only possible if one is sure of his place, sure of his ability to cope with whatever may come, and sure of his worth and value. Anyone who believes he must energetically seek his place will never find it. He does not know that by his mere presence he already does belong and has a place. If one has to be more than he is in order to be somebody, he will never be anybody. If one does not realize that he is good enough as he is, he will never have any reason to assume that he is good enough, regardless of how much money, power, superiority, and academic distinction he may amass. It is obvious that in our society few people believe they are good enough as they are, and can therefore be sure of their esteemed place. Everyone tries to be more, to be better, to reach higher, and as a consequence, we are all neurotic, in a neurotic society which pays a premium to the overambitious search for prestige and striving for superiority. This search inspires a desire for self-elevation and personal glory, thereby restricting our ability for cooperation and our sense of human fellowship. Yet underneath we are all frightened people, not sure of ourselves, of our worth, or of our place. It is this doubt of oneself, expressed in a feeling of inadequacy and inferiority, which restricts our Social Interest and which is at the root of all maladjustment and psychopathology (Adler, 1929b).

In contrast to the motivation for self-elevation, which at great human expense can produce useful contributions, movement is possible on the horizontal plane, where we might desire to contribute, to share, to participate and to grow, out of a feeling of belonging, of enthusiasm, of expansion and of exploration. This motivation finds little stimulation in our society, either in our homes or our schools. According to the value system in our society, parents and teachers and fellow men instill in each one of us considerable doubt of our own strength and value. Only those who resist this constant threat to their self-confidence receive support and reassurance. The less self-confidence a person has, the less encouragement he receives and the more his low opinion of himself finds confirmation. Our methods of raising children constitute a series of discouraging experiences (Dreikurs, 1958). We raise children in the constant fear that they are not measuring up, that they are not good enough as they are. We are afraid that being satisfied with themselves would stop them from growing and developing. We think that only a drive toward self-elevation and glory can stimulate, and that only fear of losing status can prompt conformity and effort. We are living in a neurotic culture where no one is sure of his place, although everyone has one.

This paradox can be demonstrated in a simple situation. If a student enters a new class, meeting others he has never known before, he may look around and ask himself how he will fit in. He may see himself as a nonentity and the others as all-important and dangerous. Rarely does he realize that for everyone else, he, even as a newcomer, is part of the class, threatening to the others' status and position. We stand in awe of life and all the magnificence of a thunder-storm, of a snow-capped mountain, of a huge waterfall, but we do not realize that *we* are life as well. We feel: *there* is life and *here* am I. We have no realization that the same power of nature is within ourselves, at our disposal. In dealing with a deficient individual, we can trace the evolution of erroneous ideas about himself and his failure to recognize his strength, the only attribute on which he can rely to give him security (Wolfe, 1934). We can trace the development of his fictitious ideals of power, of beauty, of education, or of possessions which would guarantee him a social place (Way, 1950). They are all fictitious ideas of security, for nothing that one can get from the outside can provide it, since one can never be sure that he has enough, or that he may not lose what he has. Psychotherapy actally consists of a planned effort to extricate the individual from the faulty social values of our society and to restore the self-confidence which he has lost in his past struggles with people who actually or in his interpretation deprive him of a feeling of worth (Dreikurs, 1957). All corrective efforts attempt to counteract these impressions and their detrimental consequences for the person's ability to function.

Let us now examine the factors which contribute to the development of the personality, which form the field of experience that is perceived and interpreted by each individual in his own way. These interpretations are the basis of his attitudes and concepts of his Life Style.

There are, first, two opposing sets of experiences, presented by heredity and environment. Our prevalent mechanistic orientation leads to the general assumption that the individual is the result of hereditary endowment and environmental influences. In this scheme of thought, the individual is just a passive background on which hereditary traits encounter environmental stimulations and inhibitions. These forces are viewed as being engaged in a furious struggle, in the course of which the hapless individual is molded (Ansbacher & Ansbacher, 1956). The relative significance which a person attributes to heredity or environment seems to depend on his political outlook. The more conservative or reactionary he is, the more importance does he place on hereditary endowment; the more liberal, the greater the influence he attributes to environmental stimulations. (The pre-Hitler German psychiatrist Lange emphasized heredity in contrast to the American Watson's and the Russian Bechterev's belief in the primacy of environmental forces.) Adler felt that such mechanistic views eliminated the most important factor, namely, the individual himself. In his study of organ inferiority he observed that two individuals born with the same physical handicap or weakness may respond in an entirely different and opposite way to the same kind of deficiency which they experience in their body — their "Inner environment," as we call it. They may either stop functioning in the area where they feel deficient and thereby develop a full and lasting deficiency, or they may try to overcome their deficiency and in this way develop special skills in the very area in which they had encountered a difficulty of function. Therefore, what one is born with is less important than what one does with it afterwards (Ansbacher & Ansbacher, 1956).

This asserts the child's ability to decide what to do with an obstacle he encounters, although such a decision does not take place on the conscious level, for the child may not have developed more than a rudimentary verbal capacity when such a decision is required. Adler's contention of such freedom of choice was — and still is — incomprehensible to most students of psychology. They want to know what induces one child to give up, another to compensate, and still another to over-compensate. They cannot believe there is nothing that "makes" a child do it; that it is his own conclusion, his own response, his own evaluation of the situation which is influential. It is a creative act, which in itself is a phenomenon that our deterministically oriented contemporaries find difficult to comprehend.

We have to re-evaluate our concepts about infants. Their ability to size up situations and to act in accordance with their own evaluation of them transcends any notion we have about early childhood (Dreikurs, 1958). Normal infants, born to deaf mute parents, will cry with tears running down their cheeks, with face distorted and body shaking — but without a sound. They won't waste any sound on parents who do not respond to it. Even an infant a few months old can dominate a whole family of intelligent and powerful adults, who are no match for his determination and resourcefulness. To underestimate the power and ability of children is characteristic of our time. We consider them victims while they are becoming our masters. Neither the hereditary endowment nor the pressure of the environment can make a child behave in a given way. It is the child who interprets his experiences and situations, draws his conclusions about them, and acts in accordance with his perceptions and decisions.

Research into the laws of probability may eventually contribute to an understanding of the way a child develops his personality. Although he may start off with random choices, as soon as he makes one choice, this limits the number of next choices that are possible. By choosing his responses to the stimulations to which he is exposed, he tries to discover what is effective, what gives him desired results. He develops his own ideas about what is desirable to him and how he can obtain it. In establishing such a pattern, he eventually evolves a system of opinions and movements which, around the age of four and five, are pretty firmly entrenched. At that time the child has developed definite ideas of how to cope with people around him, how to meet difficulties and how to respond to frustrations.

The child, with his own concepts about life, people and himself, is well equipped to influence his parents so that they respond to him in line with his expectations, while they are usually at a loss as to how to make the child comply with their demands. As a whole society, we fail to realize the extent to which children in a democratic setting can influence adults, their parents and teachers alike, while we cling to the outdated notion that children are the result of what their parents, particularly their mothers, do to them. A mother who is accused of rejecting a child in most cases behaves in such a way that this accusation seems justified; however, the child, who for one reason or another comes to the conclusion that he is not properly loved, behaves in such a way that she constantly has to scold him. This in turn proves to him that his assumption of not being loved was correct.

In our culture, the average parent tries to do more for his children and is more concerned with their welfare than ever before in history. Most parents would sacrifice anything for the welfare of their child. And yet, there were probably never as many children who are sure that they are not loved. How is this possible? Because children are excellent observers and poor interpreters. A child who has experienced the constant attention and concern of his parents may think that being loved means getting constant attention, service, gifts, affection and whatever else he wants. Therefore, he concludes that he is no longer loved if he does not remain the center of attention, as occurs when a brother or sister is born. He really believes that his mother does not love him any more when she spends less time with him. Or some children act on the assumption that being loved means having the right to do as they please. "If you oppose me in any way, you don't care for me. If you loved me, you would let me do what I want." Children may often voice such convictions, while others may only act in accordance with them, without being fully aware of the reason that they feel insufficiently loved. But again, once they have this conviction, they proceed to prove its correctness, and untrained parents and teachers are victimized and thereby reconfirm the child's mistaken assumptions.

Unfortunately, not only unsophisticated parents and insufficiently trained teachers accept the child's mistaken evaluation of his situation. Many a disturbed child is seen by a child psychiatrist or counselor who spends hours, weeks and months with the child, listening to what he has to say and how he feels, and then comes to the conclusion that the child *is* rejected. This he then proceeds to tell the child's mother. In our over-protectiveness of children, we fail to see how they provoke, to a large extent, the treatment they receive, particularly when they are not our own children. We blame parents, teachers and society instead of helping the victims of a whole segment of our society who have found their freedom without accepting full responsibility for what they are doing. Unfortunately, in our democratic setting, a reversal to punitive retaliation and suppression has no chance to succeed either. It can only prompt more determined defiance and rebellion on the part of the children who, as a whole generation, are at war with adults — sometimes only in certain aspects of their daily living, sometimes completely and openly.

It is obvious that Adlerians see the child in a different light than is the custom today. His behavior has to be seen in the total field of his operation, and he has to be considered as an active participant from the beginning, and not as a passive recipient of what others do to him. He injects himself very early into the transactions of his family. It is his way of dealing with them and moving in the given family situation that develops his personality. He encounters his environment with all the problems it involves and takes a stand, not only for or against certain demands, but by making his own demands. If he wants to be picked up, he knows how to achieve that. If his parents are reluctant and try to convince him he shouldn't be picked up, he may cry until the parents weaken — which they usually do even after a temporary demonstration of power and assertion. It is obvious to anyone who observes the total field that children manage their parents pretty successfully and make them submit to their demands.

What are their demands? Usually parents — and teachers as well — are utterly unaware of what the children want, for it is not what the child says he wants. The overt contest between the child's conduct and the adult's objections or requests has little to do with the "issues" involved. The child, in any conflict between him and adults, uses whatever issue is convenient to pursue one of four goals (Dreikurs, 1957). These I have described as "the four goals of disturbing behavior in children." As long as the child cooperates and conforms, his goal is participation and contribution, fulfilling the implicit requirements of the given situation. When he misbehaves, he has other goals, all of which are related to his ideas of finding a place. They are, therefore, erroneous means of social participation.

The first goal is a bid for *attention* and *service*. It is found in most young children who cannot perceive their ability to find their place through what they do; therefore, they think that their place depends on what others do for them. If the struggle to stop the child's demand for undue attention becomes more intense, then the child tries to demonstrate his *power*, which is the second goal. He will refuse to do what he is told, and insist on doing what is forbidden. Should this fight become more intense and vicious, then the child cannot conceive of any other means of proving his existence than through hurting others. Thus the third goal is *revenge*. And then there are children who want to be left alone, because they are so discouraged that any demand to do something would only demonstrate their deficiency more painfully. Flaunting a real or assumed deficiency *in order to be left alone* is the fourth goal. The child is not aware of the reasons for his actions, but if properly confronted with his intentions, he quickly recognizes the situation and responds with a "Recognition Reflex." Unfortunately, neither parents nor teachers are trained to recognize the child's goals and to counteract them. As a consequence, in most cases, they do exactly what the child expects them to do. Instead of improving the situation, most corrective efforts actually enhance the child's mistaken goals and strengthen his objectionable goal-directed behavior.

These are principles applying to the behavior of children in general. They permit a psychological understanding of children and their problems without any investigation of their individual personalities. For this reason, our theory about personality development and the dynamics of behavior provides important psychological tools for those who work with people professionally and yet are not always able to explore the individual background development of each person. However, a clear perception of a person as a distinct individual requires information about certain circumstances during his formative years. From our holistic point of view, the developing pattern of the personality is linked to certain environmental patterns which are of fundamental importance and constitute significant aspects of social experiences to which the child is exposed. Hence, we do not consider *all* isolated experiences and stimulation as having a distinct influence on personality development, nor seek to unravel the almost endless series of isolated stimulations. Rather, we look for specific patterns in which all stimulations are imbedded and through which they derive their significance.

The first of these is *the family atmosphere*. The child has no direct access to society; he encounters society through his parents, who establish the characteristic pattern of each family. Through them he experiences the social values of his time — the economic, racial, national, and social conditions that affect his particular family. These conditions pertain to all children of the family alike. The parents communicate their concepts to their children, and exemplify them in their behavior, which is not random but displays a definite, recurrent pattern of relationships. One can say, by and large, that what children have in common is due to this family atmosphere, which creates a basis for values, for patterns of human relationship and for modes of behavior. The parents, by their relationship, demonstrate not only the functions of each sex, but a pattern of interactions that is usually followed by the children.

However, it is evident that the children of any one family are far from being alike, at least in our competitive society with its emphasis on superiority and inferiority. The dissimilarity of children within the same family is understandable through an examination of the specific *family constellation.* The first and second child of almost every family are fundamentally different, in character, interest and abilities. This has so far escaped the attention of most experts in psychology and psychiatry (Adler, 1928). It cannot be explained by current concepts of behavior. It defies the laws of heredity, which do not provide any rationale for the difference that is always observed between the first and second child. Nor could past stimulations or the psychosexual development of each child account for the regularity of the difference.

The Adlerian interpretation of behavior provides a more satisfactory explanation than any advanced thus far. The difference in personalities of the first and second child becomes understandable if we regard character traits as modes of behavior and behavior itself as purposive, as directed toward a specific goal. In our democratic, competitive society, no child wants to be inferior to another. Therefore, if children are competitive, then each will move in the direction where the other fails or encounters difficulties, and in turn will shun activities where the other excels. Experience shows that the strongest competition is between the first and second child. The first born wants to stay ahead, and the second does not want to remain behind. Thus, each watches for the other's areas of failure and success and acts accordingly. If the first is excellent in school, the second — in a competitive family — may not be interested in school but in other activities where the first may show a lack of interest or ability. However, if the first encounters a teacher who discourages him and consequently falls back, then the second may move in and become a good student. In this way, the children influence each other more than the parents influence them. The parents usually have no idea of what is going on, and what they are doing is apt to fortify and intensify competition and to re-affirm their childrens' assumptions of success or failure. The sibling who is most different is the one who exerts the greatest influence on personality development; each tries to find a different way to have his place as each becomes discouraged by the success of the other.

Here is a typical example: A young woman, a literary agent, came to me for therapy. She had no friends, no dates, and her life consisted mainly of work. She wanted to get married, but could neither attract men nor come close to anyone. In her formative years she was impressed with the success of her older sister as a beautiful child. As they grew older, her sister became exceedingly popular with boys. Her parents forced her to take her younger sister along when she went out, and our patient felt like the fifth wheel on a wagon. She was sure that nobody except her parents liked her, and that she just had no chance to be socially, and in particular, sexually attractive. She was neither as pretty as her sister nor could she impress others the way her sister did. In the course of treatment, her mistaken ideas about her "inability" to make friends and to attract men were corrected and she made a good adjustment, giving up her high standards and her doubts as well. (This is, of course, an over-simplified account of all her problems and their meaning, but it emphasizes the crucial role her sister played in her life.)

One day she reported that her sister had come into town and wanted to talk with me. She had lived in Europe, become involved in a scandal with a man, and had come back home. As she walked into my office it became immediately apparent that she put all her eggs into one basket — her femininity. She was not only attractive but highly seductive, in the way she walked, carried and expressed herself. When she spoke about her difficulties, it was only about her relationship with men. She always tried to conquer and wanted and received constant approval as a woman. She had been married and divorced and had had numerous affairs, which ended either with her losing interest or through a scandal. Discussing with her the reason for her limitations in seeking success only in the sexual area, she immediately pointed to her sister who, because she was "good" and did well in school, was favored by the parents. "I had no chance to compete with her except by having my own way, and a lot of boy friends." It was obvious that each of the sisters blamed the other for her discouragement; each regarded the other as a "real success" and considered her own achievements to be meaningless. I told the two girls to get together and to decide who was superior to whom. This had a dramatic effect on both girls, when they realized that each had motivated her parents to draw invidious comparisons between them. The parents had actually followed the lead of each girl, impressing the older with the goodness and scholastic success of the younger, and telling the younger to be outgoing and have friends like her sister, thereby reinforcing each one's sense of inadequacy.

In a similar way, children confirm each other's erroneous ideas about themselves. The family constellation provides each with a unique position and lets each develop his own approaches, in contrast or in line with those of others. The children who compete with each other develop in opposite directions, while those who are allied with each other become more alike. The lines of demarcation depend first of all on the sequence of birth. This gives each a special place, as the first, second, middle or youngest child. But this position does not "determine" each one's development; it merely provides him with special opportunities which he utilizes in the equilibrium he establishes with the other members of his family. Each is affected by each other member of the family, as he in turn affects them. Various other factors provide a child with special opportunities, either by being an only boy or an only girl, by being sickly or being outstanding through any other accidental circumstance.

This interaction within the family during the formative years is the basis for the personality development of each child. Whatever concepts he develops then are maintained throughout life and constitute the basis for his style of life. This is not the result of forces converging on him, of stimulations which he has received, or of incidental occurrences. These constitute merely opportunities. Under the same circumstances he could have developed differently had he responded differently to the situation which he encountered. With each adult patient we can determine his life style, his present *modus operandi*, by exploring the family constellation during his formative years. Then we can show him the movements he has chosen, how he has affected others and been affected by them, children and adults alike. Because of the transaction in which they were all involved, one cannot say that one affected the other. It was a constant relationship in which each developed with each other.

After we know the movements of the patient in his childhood and later through life, we have another highly effective diagnostic tool, which Adler provided: the early recollections (ECR — Early Childhood Recollections) (Adler, 1929b; Adler, 1959c; Mosak, 1958). It has been found that out of all the millions of experiences in our childhood, we remember only those incidents that fit in our outlook on life. If we know what a person remembers from his early childhood, then we know the concepts on the basis of which he operates and his mistaken concepts about himself and life. This projective technique is indispensable if we really want to know the basic structure of a given personality. It was tragic that the verdict of one man, namely Freud, could deprive psychiatry and psychology for almost fifty years of the use of such an important diagnostic tool, used only by Adlerians. Freud, in his *Psychopathology of Everyday Life* (Freud, 1951), declared childhood recollections to be irrelevant; to him they were merely screen memories to cover up really important but repressed traumatic events. Only in the last few years has the significance of early recollections found general recognition (Mosak, 1958). However, many use them in different ways, if they are still preoccupied with instinctual and emotional processes. We concern ourselves primarily with cognitive processes, with the private logic of each person. This becomes clearly visible in early recollections, so that we can understand how a person looks at life and help him to recognize it. This leads to a reorientation which is the final goal of psychotherapy.

All the basic mistakes we make in childhood and continue throughout life are the consequence of doubts in ourself and others and reflect an underestimation of our strength. The mistaken movements we make in life are the consequences. Therefore, an effective reorientation is only possible when we help the patient to restore his self-confidence, free him from his prejudice against himself, from the doubts with which he grew up and the unnecessary limitations which he accepts for himself. Once he can believe in himself and his strength, he can gain this inner freedom, where he no longer questions his place in society but feels able to cope with it, because he is no longer confronted with the danger of his inferiority nor with the compulsion to be superior. He is not preoccupied alone with success or failure, but rather with the task at hand (Dreikurs, 1957).

In this sense, then, Adlerian psychology represents a social rehabilitation therapy, *a behavioral therapy*, as Eysenck (1959) calls it. Psychotherapy is not a medical treatment but an educational process. The person learns to understand himself and his life. Psychotherapy implies a change of concepts, a change in the modes of finding one's place, an increase in the feeling of belonging through the diminution of self-doubt and of inferiority feelings. This is the basis for all correctional efforts: to overcome doubts about value and ability, and to develop a sufficient Social Interest to cope successfully with life and people.

REFERENCES

Adler, A. *Study of Organ Inferiority and Its Psychical Compensation*. New York: Nerv. Ment. Dis. Publ. Co., 1917.
———. "Characteristics of the First, Second and Third Child," *Children*, 1928, 3: 14-52.
———. *Problems of Neurosis*. London: Kegan Paul, Trench, Trubner, 1929. (a)
———. *The Science of Living*. New York: Greenberg, 1929. (b)
———. *The Case of Miss R*. New York: Greenberg, 1929. (c)
———. *The Education of Children*. London: Allen & Unwia, 1930.
———. *Social Interest*. London: Faber & Faber, 1938.
———. *The Practice and Theory of Individual Psychology*. Paterson, N. J.: Littlefield, Adams, 1959. (a)
———. *Understanding Human Nature*. New York: Premier Books, 1959. (b)
———. *What Life Should Mean to You*. New York: Capricorn Books, 1959. (c)
Ansbacher, H. L., and Ansbacher, Rowena. *The Individual Psychology of Alfred Adler*. New York: Basic Books, 1956.
Dreikurs, R. "Psychotherapy as Correction of Faulty Social Values," *J. indiv. Psychol.*, 1957, 2: 150-158.
———. *The Challenge of Parenthood*. New York: Duell, Sloan and Pearce, 1958.
———. *Equality: The Challenge of Our Times*. Chicago: Author, 1961.
Eysenck, H., ed. *Behaviour Therapy and the Neuroses*. London: Pergamon, 1959.
Freud, S. *Psychopathology of Everyday Life*. New York: New Amer. Libr., 1951.
Mosak, H. H. "Early Recollections as a Projective Technique," *J. proj. Tech.*, 1958, 22: 303-31.
———. "The Getting Type, a Parsimonious Social Interpretation of the Oral Character," *J. indiv. Psychol.*, 1959, 15: 193-196.

Shulman, B. H. "The Family Constellation in Personality Diagnosis," *J. indiv. Psychol.*, 1962, 18:35–47.

Vaihinger, H. *The Philosophy of "As If."* New York: Harcourt, Brace. 1925.

Way, L. *Adler's Place in Psychology.* London: Allen and Unwin, 1950.

Wolfe, W. B. *How to Be Happy though Human.* London: Routledge and Kegan Paul, 1932.

———. *Nervous Breakdown: Its Cause and Cure.* London: Routledge and Kegan Paul, 1934.

ROBERT W. WHITE

Competence and the Psychosexual Stages

of Development

The purpose of this paper is to reconsider a part of psychoanalytic theory, the part that deals with stages of emotional development. It will be necessary first, however, to show why I think it important to look again at a theory that has survived nearly half a century of critical onslaught and that enjoys enduring high esteem among clinicians. This will require a short exposition of the concept of competence and of certain related concepts which I have discussed at length elsewhere (1959). As you will see, my use of these concepts puts me at variance with theories that make drive the necessary condition for activity and learning; at variance, therefore, with Freud's theory of instincts. The concept of competence, moreover, leads to an idea of the ego that is different from the one we usually find in discussions of psychosexual stages. Freud's theory of these stages undoubtedly occupies a secure historical position. It will stand in the history of thought as an astonishing first approximation to a theory of growth in its dynamic aspects. Nevertheless, I believe that the time has come when its continued use will only block further insights. The theory that illuminated us all as a first approximation may only hinder us in reaching those closer approximations that always mark the forward steps in a scientific pilgrimage.

In M. R. Jones ed., *Nebraska Symposium on Motivation*, Lincoln, Neb.: University of Nebraska Press, 1960, pp. 97–140.

In broadest outline, Freud's theory is that the most important features of childhood development, the ones that are fateful for emotional well-being and for the shape of personality, have their motive power in sexual energy or libido. Conceiving sexuality broadly to include the obtaining of pleasure from various zones of the body, he postulated a maturational sequence whereby first the mouth, then the anal zone, finally the genitals become the dominant source of libidinal gratification. Aggressive impulses, fused with libidinal ones, enter importantly during the anal stage and from then on, but the movement from one stage to another is determined biologically by the sequence of libidinal changes. The latency period and the final genital stage likewise come into existence through developments strictly in the sphere of sexual energy. Thus it is possible to speak of psychosexual stages, and Freud intended the double adjective to be taken quite literally. It is libido, he said, that makes demands upon the mind, that calls forth psychic activity, that constitutes the motivating force behind the development of the mental apparatus (Freud, 1905, 1908, 1913, 1923).

The great virtue of this theory lies, of course, in its gathering and ordering of the confusingly diverse facts of development. For the first three and the last stages it provides us with a model or prototype of behavior: the infant at the breast, the child on the toilet, the phallic child concerned about genital impulses toward family members, the physically mature adult in the heterosexual relation. It tells us, moreover, that these prototypes are truly basic, that events in these situations are really the most important things that happen, so that if we know just these aspects of a person's history we know all that counts. Each prototype involves not only libidinal and aggressive energies but also frustrations, anxieties, defenses, ego developments, and relations with other people. But all these other things are brought to pass by the instincts, and we are thus permitted to place them in a subordinate relation to the central libidinal events. The theory thus achieves a heroic simplification. Right or wrong, it rescued us historically from a tangled mass of facts and made it possible for the first time to think coherently about emotional development.

Freud's ideas on this subject were completed nearly forty years ago. His ideas concerning the libido itself, a highly mobile and general source of energy, look anything but plausible in the light of recent research on motivation. Many psychoanalysts, however, retain the libido model as a working tool, finding that it greatly helps them to understand their patients' problems. Other workers have proposed more or less extensive revisions in the theory of development. In the writings of Horney (1939), Thompson (1950), and Fromm (1947), for instance, emphasis is shifted sharply from instinctual roots to human relations, especially those between child and parents. These neo-Freudians treat motivation in an offhand, pluralistic way, with perhaps special accent on security and anxiety. Development really turns, they believe, on a series of crises in parent-child relations, crises which arise because the parents, acting both for themselves and for the culture, make successive demands upon the infant that put the relation under strain. The libido model is thus displaced in favor of an interpersonal model.

One might suppose that this change of model would sweep away the prototypes provided by psychosexual theory. But the fact is that only Sullivan (1953) has seriously attempted to revise the scheme of crises in strictly interpersonal terms. With most of the revisionists the oral, anal, phallic, and genital prototypes live on, either quite literally or in such guises as "neurotic trends" and "character orientations." The familiar stages, no longer libidinal, are still considered to be crucial. This situation is most clearly recognized by Silverberg (1952), who translates Freud's stages into *"areas of experience* ... presented to the children of western civilization by parents performing the task of acculturating their offspring." Each area has its typical problem: deprivation in the oral area; obedience, conformity, and rebelliousness in the anal; rivalry and genitality in the phallic area. It is thus contended that the prototypes originally provided by libido theory are adequate models for the crucial events in the child's interpersonal development. Feeding, toilet training, and the Oedipal triangle are still the fateful battlefields of growth.

The thesis of this paper can be set forth at this point in the form of two propositions. I shall contend, first, that *the child's emotional development cannot be adequately conceptualized by an exclusive libido model*, no matter how liberally we interpret this concept. Second, I shall try to show that *when the prototypes derived from libido theory are translated into interpersonal terms they still do not constitute adequate models for development.* The best of these prototypes is undoubtedly the feeding child of the oral stage, who cuts a prominent figure even in Sullivan's revision, but from then on the models simply miss part of the significant problems of growth. In particular they fail to embody the development of competence, and they tend to direct attention away from certain crisis in the growth of the child's sense of competence. This weakness is attested most eloquently by the lack of a clear-cut model for the latency period, when competence is a central theme. What is needed, I shall argue, is a clearly conceived *competence model* that can be used throughout the stages. Sexual and interpersonal models will be needed too, but we can never do justice to emotional development until we work up a competence model to put beside them.

COMPETENCE AND SENSE OF COMPETENCE

By presenting my theme in this way I have placed a great burden on the word "competence," and I must now give this concept a fuller introduction. Let me say at the outset that it is not something I have invented. It has been distilled from the writings of a great many workers in animal psychology, child development, research on personality, and psychopathology — workers whose only common quality is a certain disenchantment with prevailing concepts of drive. It is a way of saying what I believe many voices have been saying, especially during the last twenty years. Among those who have moved in this direction, it seems to me, are Erikson, Hartmann, and other workers who are trying to carry psychoanalytic ego psychology forward from the point at which Freud left it. I am therefore not trying to promote a novel idea, but rather to find suitable expression for a concept which, suppressed for a time by the immensely popular drive theories, has lately begun to throw out restless derivatives in every direction.

Competence means fitness or ability. The competence of an organism means its fitness or ability to carry on those transactions with the environment which result in its maintaining itself, growing, and flourishing. Some parts of the environment must if possible be fought off, but other parts can safely be enjoyed, and still others can be ingested and transformed into materials for self-maintenance and growth. Some organisms are born more or less fully equipped with patterns of behavior that produce effective interactions with favorable surroundings. This is not the case with the higher animals, least of all with man, who has to learn almost everything that is useful in dealing with his world, yet who immeasurably surpasses all other living creatures in his ultimate ability to subdue and transform the environment to his own use. Man's prowess as a learner has long been an object of wonder. How does he do it, and when does he get it all done?

Theories in which drive is the central motivational concept deal quite simply with this problem. Drives arise from lacks and deficits. They are powerful and persistent internal stimuli which arouse the organism from homeostatic bliss and promote activities that ultimately eliminate the deficit, thus reducing the drive. Reduction of drive supplies the selective principle whereby patterns of behavior are retained or discarded. Our knowledge of the world and our competence in dealing with it are thus acquired in the course of satisfying our constantly recurring needs. We learn what helps us to reduce drives.

There have recently been some startling departures from this orthodoxy — not, as one might suppose, among soft-headed students of personality, but in the very heartland of hard-headedness, the animal laboratory. In a series of experiments Sheffield and others (1950, 1951, 1954) have shown that instrumental learning can take place without drive reduction, indeed under circumstances where one can suppose only that drive level is being increased. Olds and Milner (1954) have found a connection between reinforcement and the electrical stimulation of certain areas of the brain. A whole series of workers, including Harlow (1953), Butler (1958), Montgomery (1954), Berlyne (1950), and Meyers and Miller (1954), have pointed out that animals show persistent tendencies toward activity, exploration, and manipulation even when all known primary drives have been satiated. Clearly the original drive model, based on hunger and other internal deficits, stands in need of extensive revision.

One way of accomplishing this revision is to postulate new drives not hitherto included in the list. In addition to hunger, sex, and the avoidance of pain we must attribute an exploratory drive and perhaps an activity drive to the higher animals, even a manipulative drive to those forms that have free use of the forelimbs. These new drives are like the older ones, it is argued, in that they provoke activity and lead to the reinforcement of instrumental learning. I find myself unable to climb aboard this drive bandwagon because I am so impressed by the differences between the old and new drives. Exploration and manipulation have nothing to do with deficits, they appear to arise in the nervous system without visceral stimulation, and they produce instrumental learning without any signs of consummatory response or drive reduction. Call them drives if you are fixated on that term, but remember that in doing so you have destroyed the original conception of drive, including Freud's conception of the instincts. Remember that you are separating drives from visceral deficits and somatic cravings, so that hunger and sex must be treated as special cases rather than as prototypes for the whole idea. But if you do remember these things, what good are you getting out of the concept of drive? I prefer to leave the word in its excellent original meaning so that we can look with a fresh eye at the adaptive significance of activity, manipulation, and exploration.

The theory that we learn what helps us to reduce our viscerogenic drives will not stand up if we stop to consider the whole range of what a child must learn in order to deal effectively with his surroundings. He has much to learn about visual forms, about grasping and letting go, about the coordination of hand and eye. He must work out the difficult problem of the constancy of objects. He must put together an increasingly varied repertory of skilled acts such as locomotion and the use of words. He must learn many facts about his world, building up a cognitive map that will afford guidance and structure for his behavior. It is not hard to see the biological advantage of an arrangement whereby these many learnings can get under way before they are needed as instruments for drive reduction or for safety. An animal that has thoroughly explored its environment stands a better chance of escaping from a sudden enemy or satisfying a gnawing hunger than one that merely dozes in the sun when its homeostatic crises are past. Seen in this light, the many hours that infants and children spend in play are by no means wasted or merely recuperative in nature. Play may be fun, but it is also a serious business in childhood. During these hours the child steadily builds up his competence in dealing with the environment.

Careful study of exploratory play, even in the first year of life, shows it to have the characteristics of directedness, selectivity, and persistence. Piaget's observations (1952) make it plain that the child seeks opportunities to investigate his surroundings and will go to no little trouble to find them. My proposal is that activity, manipulation, and exploration, which are all pretty much of a piece in the infant, be considered together as aspects of competence, and that for the present we assume that one general motivational principle lies behind them. The word I have suggested for this motive is *effectance* because its most characteristic feature is seen in the production of effects upon the environment. At first these effects may consist of any changes in sensory input that follow upon activity or exertion, but before long the child becomes able to intend particular changes and to be content only with these. The experience that goes with producing such changes I have designated as the *feeling of efficacy*. Effectance is to be conceived as a neurogenic motive, in contrast to a viscerogenic one. It can be informally described as what the sensori-neuro-muscular system wants to do when it is not occupied with homeostatic business. Its adaptive significance lies in its promotion of spare-time behavior that leads to an extensive growth of competence, well beyond what could be learned in connection with drive reduction.

This, then, is the new motivational base from which I want to reconsider the stages of psychosexual development. But I must make it clear that my procedure will not consist merely of introducing a neglected motive and fighting for its recognition against the claims of sexuality and aggression. If the problem could be so easily solved, it would have been solved long ago. The difficulty is that effectance does not pursue a separate life. It does not typically come into sharp, decisive conflict with drives. It can be mobilized alone, as in the child's play or in the adult's fascination with puzzles, but it is often mobilized in close connection with other needs. The feeling of efficacy can be experienced alone, but it is often merged with other satisfactions, as when, for example, a campus Don Juan reduces his sexual drive while also congratulating himself on the success of his technique of seduction. Because of this high tendency toward fusion it is not profitable to carry on the analysis of later development in terms of effectance and feelings of efficacy. Competence is built up out of all kinds of interactions with the environment, including those due to effectance alone and those due to much more complex patterns of motives. Our interest from here on will be in *competence* and its very important subjective aspect, which I am calling *sense of competence*. And we shall not find it profitable to look for the sense of competence as if it were a separate thing in personality; rather, we must become aware of the *aspect of competence in a wide variety of actions and experiences*.

Sense of competence can be seen as the cumulative product of one's history of efficacies and inefficacies. It comes to operate in new behavior as a kind of set: we judge whether or not we can jump over a brook or carry out a proposed task. It also comes to be much cherished, so that we feel truly elated at new proofs of our ability and deeply humiliated when we cannot do something we supposed was within our power. The sense of competence thus has strong motivational backing, doubtless from a variety of sources. Its importance in personality will be more readily apparent if we bear in mind that it applies to interactions with people as well as to dealings with the inanimate environment. Just as the child explores his physical surroundings, finding out what he can do with objects and what they will do to him, so he investigates his human environment, learning what he can make people do and what he can expect of them. Sense of social competence may well be the more important of the two, though I think we should beware of the current fashion of discussing personality as if it grew in a physical vacuum where tumbles and bumps, victories of locomotion, and struggles with refractory objects are held to exist only insofar as they elicit social responses. We do not live exclusively in a social environment, but we live there importantly, and it is often harder to develop a stable sense of one's social competence than to know what one can accomplish with material objects.

COMPETENCE AND EGO PSYCHOLOGY

I should like now to indicate the relation between these ideas and some of the recent advances in psychoanalytic ego psychology. As you will see, there is a great deal of similarity when we talk on the level of general concepts. There are also many common implications for the psychosexual stages, though only Erikson has tried to reconsider these stages in a systematic way.

We start with Hartmann, whose important essay, *Ego Psychology and the Problem of Adaptation*, came out in the year of Freud's death and is considered by many workers to be, somewhat paradoxically, both a turning point in psychoanalytic theory and a direct sequel to Freud's own work on the ego (Hartmann, 1958). In this essay Hartmann questioned the adequacy of instincts, at least in the human case, to bring about adaptive behavior. He did not believe that the mere collision between instinctual urge and frustrating circumstance could ever generate the reality principle. The pressures of the environment can be met only with the aid of an innate ego apparatus which has its own laws of development through maturation and learning. To indicate the autonomous nature of this development he spoke of it as taking place in good part in a "conflict-free sphere." Functions like locomotion or the mastery of language ripen in the course of time without necessarily being caught up in anxious conflicts over erotic and aggressive satisfactions. Following a suggestion of Freud's, Hartmann concluded that the energy behind ego development is intrinsic, independent of the instincts, and that growth in this sphere yields a pleasure of its own. He further proposed that events in the conflict-free sphere might have important consequences for the handling of conflicts: adaptive capacities learned in this sphere can be transferred to libidinal and aggressive battlegrounds.

The agreement between this theory and the one I have already described seems thus far sufficient to make me a follower of Hartmann. You will notice that in language which is only slightly different he says that drive reduction cannot account for the range and variety of our adaptive accomplishments, that an independent source of motivation must be assumed for the growth of competence, and that effectiveness or ego strength cannot be understood apart from this growth. But now something happens that prevents me from following in Hartmann's footsteps. Suddenly I run into him, stopped in his tracks. As I see it, he makes practically no further effort to develop the concept of an autonomous ego factor. Instead, in later writings (Hartmann, Kris, & Loewenstein, 1949) he turns back to a notion apparently more favored by Freud, that of the neutralization of drive energies. According to this notion, ego development makes use of the energies of erotic and aggressive instincts, which energies, however, have become transformed or neutralized so that they no longer impel toward erotic or aggressive goals. This doctrine has its comforts, among them the removal of incentive to reconsider the psychosexual stages, for the instincts are neatly restored to their place of energic supremacy. But it seems to me a rather unfortunate attempt to hold the line at all costs for Freud's instinct theory, and I anticipate greater gains by pursuing the theme of autonomous ego development.

Other workers in psychoanalytic ego psychology have gone somewhat further with this theme. Hendrick (1942), for example, argued the case for an additional instinct, the *instinct to master*, and he produced in evidence a great many of the facts I have drawn together under the heading of competence. Calling mastery an instinct is open to the same objection as calling exploration or manipulation a drive; everyone jumped on Hendrick for using the concept in such a radically altered sense. Apart from this dubious bit of conceptual strategy, however, his ideas are in close accord with those I am advancing here. Let a single quotation suffice to indicate the similarity: "Primary pleasure is sought by the efficient use of the central nervous system for the performance of well-integrated ego functions which enable the individual to control and alter his environment" (Hendrick, 1943).

A somewhat different conceptualization, yet one much in the same direction, is Mittelmann's (1954) proposal of a *motility urge*. Mittelmann emphasizes the driven, persistent, time-consuming quality of motor activity. He points out its relation to reality testing, its service to ego development, and its vital role in the economy of self-esteem. During the second and third years of life, the traditional anal stage, the motility urge is the dominant one in behavior, and Mittelmann accordingly suggests calling this period "the motor level of ego and libido development." Although he treats motility as an urge in its own right, he refers to it as a "partial instinct," likens it to oral, excretory, and genital urges, and does not propose further changes in the psychosexual stages.

It is in the work of Erikson (1950, 1959) that one finds the most far-reaching attempt to extend the range of ego psychology. Erikson's eight stages in the development of the ego constitute, it seems to me, a major advance in psychoanalytic theory. For the first time the latency period is given a significance of its own. Likewise for the first time the problems of growth are seen as continuing beyond young adulthood when haply the goal of genital primacy has been achieved. But the most important step is the systematic relating of the child's unfolding capacities to his encounters with the social environment. Erikson sees early development as a process of mutual regulation between child and parents. The child's changing capacities and the parents' changing demands lead to a series of decisive encounters, the outcomes of which are fateful for future growth. Later on, these encounters involve the social environment more broadly conceived; in this way, Erikson achieves the social relatedness that is the virtue of neo-Freudian theories without falling into their vice of losing touch with the biological roots of behavior.

Erikson's description of development is remarkably inclusive. In his concept of zones he retains the essence of libido theory, though with a somewhat altered meaning. With the concept of mutual regulation he draws in the best features of the interpersonal model. With his idea of modes he introduces competence, describing at each stage the motor and cognitive capacities that determine the character of the crisis. Erikson's account therefore seems to have everything the heart could desire. But it has one thing I wish it did not have, namely, an implied close connection between zones and modes which I think can lead only to confusion.

In recasting libido theory Erikson undertakes to avoid the scientific crudeness of Freud's formulation by a generous broadening of the biological base. Zonal sensitivities are but part of the picture; the progression from oral to anal to phallic stages is determined by a general ripening of sensory-motor capacity as a whole. The concept of mode captures these broader possibilities. Thus the oral stage, called "oral-sensory," is dominated by the incorporative mode, which means that everything the infant does, even his visual and tactile exploration, has the character of a taking in of experience. The anal stage, renamed "muscular-anal," represents more advanced prowess in motor and manipulative control. It is dominated by the retentive and eliminative modes, which show themselves alike in bowel functions and in the familiar manipulative sequence characterized by grasping and a little later by letting go and throwing away. Likewise the "locomotor-genital" stage brings to full flower the intrusive mode, which includes "the intrusion into other bodies by physical attack; the intrusion into other people's ears and minds by aggressive talking; the intrusion into space by vigorous locomotion; the intrusion into the unknown by consuming curiosity" (Erikson, 1950, p. 83). Erogenous zones and neuro-muscular competence are thus seen as strictly isomorphic, set in the same patterns of interaction with the environment.

My discontent with this idea comes from my belief that in trying to put the stages of development on a broader base Erikson has not sufficiently disengaged himself from the old libidinal prototypes. He wants to assign significance to the growth of competence, but he describes this growth in generalizations carried over directly from the original theory. Incorporation, retention, elimination, and intrusion precisely describe the zonal impulses demanded by straight libido theory. Erikson then asks us to believe that these modes successively characterize virtually all the important things a young child does in the course of growth. This seems to me rather dubious, and I prefer a different strategy for finding out about it. It seems to me safer to treat visual exploration, manipulation, locomotion, and the many other aspects of competence as functions developing in their own right, more or less autonomously, without any presumed relation to zonal pleasures or presumed similarity to zonal impulses. By using the competence model in this way we can protect ourselves from unwarranted generalizations while yet leaving the facts free to tumble back into the old psychosexual stages if that is how they really look.

Let us proceed to re-examine the stages in the light of what I have said about effectance, feeling of efficacy, competence, and sense of competence, and let us see what happens.

The Oral Stage

The oral stage occupies approximately the first year of life. Following Abraham (1927), it is customarily divided into an early phase, in which pleasurable sucking is the predominant activity, and a later phase, often called "oral-sadistic," introduced by the eruption of teeth and the appearance of a strong urge to bite. According to psychoanalytic theory the oral zone during this stage is the chief seat of libidinal excitability. This means that it is the infant's main source of satisfaction and at the same time his principal point of contact with the environment. Ego development is therefore described in terms of the feeding model. The breast and then the mother become the first objects to be clearly discriminated. The infant's relation to the world, his basic trust or mistrust (as Erikson expresses it), is forever colored by his experience with these first objects. The consequences of oral experience for later development and for a possible psychotic outcome are well known to all students of Freud, and concepts such as oral-dependence, oral-receptivity, and oral-aggression have become commonplace tools in clinical diagnosis.

The psychoanalytic theory of development is not confined to the dimensions of love and hate, but there is a strong tendency to relate all other trends to the feeding model. The infant's cognitive outlook, his knowledge of reality, and his discrimination between self and outer world are all described as taking place almost exclusively in relation to the food-providing mother. The defense mechanisms attributed to the first year, especially introjection and projection, are easily cast in feeding terms. Such accomplishments as visual fixation and manual grasping are made analogous to feeding in Erikson's concept of the incorporative mode. It is even held that the infant's interest in the inanimate environment is somehow mediated by the mother. Spitz (1946) has argued that the child understands objects by analogy with food, so that his attitude toward toys can be considered a by-product of his attitude toward the mother and her more central gift.

It is of course a cardinal point in more orthodox psychoanalytic theory that the satisfactions involved in sucking and feeding are primarily libidinal satisfactions. On the basis of different assumptions about basic drives one could suppose that feeding involved primary satisfaction of the hunger drive and some undetermined amount of additional pleasure from stimulation of the sensitive oral zones. Sullivan (1953), who devoted many pages to the child at the breast, used the feeding model without any implication that its gratifications were libidinal. This issue, however, need not concern us here. Our problem is to try out the very different concept of competence.

Looking again at the familiar scene of the first year of life, we can see on the surface much that bespeaks the importance of feeding. Gesell's (1943) description of the feeding of the 16-week-old infant agrees closely with the picture painted by psychoanalytic writers. This genial observer does full justice to the tremendous eagerness and overt signs of satisfaction during and after feeding, and he does not overlook the evidences of an independent urge to suck. The eagerness stays at high pitch up to eight months. It is apt to be expressed vocally when the breast, the bottle, or even the spoon comes in sight, and the infant may become highly impatient if he has to watch the preparation of a meal.

So far there is nothing to violate Freud's conception of the oral stage, but we must not forget that the feeding pattern undergoes a considerable change before the end of the first year. In part the change can still be captured in the psychosexual formula: libido theory has its explanation for the marked decline of the sucking need, shown in the fact that a year-old infant may want but one bottle a day, and may toss it off in three or four minutes instead of the half hour that would have been required earlier. In part, however, the changes seem to me to imply that something else, some other need, is beginning to encroach upon pure oral gratification. For one thing, there are clear signs that additional entertainment is desired during a meal. The utensils are investigated, the behavior of spilled food is explored, toys are played with throughout the feeding. Gesell suggests that at one year of age a toy in each hand is the only guarantee that a meal will be completed without housekeeping disaster. A similar situation prevails during the bath, when water toys are needed and when the germ of scientific interest may express itself by "dabbling water onto the floor from the washcloth." More important, however, is the infant's growing enthusiasm for the doctrine of "do it yourself." He assists in his own nourishment by holding the bottle and by active finger feeding. Around one year there is likely to occur what Levy (1955) calls "the battle of the spoon," the moment "when the baby grabs the spoon from the mother's hand and tries to feed itself." From Gesell's painstaking description of the spoon's "hazardous journey" from dish to mouth we can be sure that the child is not motivated at this point by increased oral gratification. He gets more food by letting mother do it, but by doing it himself he gets more of another kind of satisfaction — a feeling of efficacy, and perhaps already a growth of the sense of competence.

Development in the sphere of competence can be observed more decisively if we turn to behavior that is not connected with feeding. Somehow the image has gotten into our minds that the infant's time is divided between eating and sleep. Peter Wolff (1959) is now showing that this is not true even for newborn infants, who show distinct forerunners of what will later become playful exploratory activity. Gesell notes that at four weeks there is apt to be a waking time in the late afternoon during which visual experience begins to be accumulated. At 16 weeks this period may last for half an hour, and the times increase steadily up to one year, when Gesell's typical "behavior day" shows an hour of play before breakfast, two hours before lunch, an hour's carriage ride and another hour of social play during the afternoon, and perhaps still another hour after being put to bed. At the age of 12 months the child is already putting in a six-hour day of play, not to mention the overtime that occurs during meals and the bath.

What goes on during these increasingly long intervals of play? At first visual exploration is the most concentrated form of activity, though babbling and gross motor movements are also present. Halfway through the year comes what Gesell calls the "heyday of manipulation," when grasping is an "eager and intent business." Here is his description of play with a clothespin at 28 weeks:

> The child wants to finger the clothespin, to get the feel of it. He puts it in his mouth, pulls it out, looks at it, rotates it with a twist of the wrist, puts it back into his mouth, pulls it out, gives it another twist, brings up his free hand, transfers the clothespin from hand to hand, bangs it on the high chair tray, drops it, recovers it, retransfers it from hand to hand, drops it out of reach, leans over to retrieve it, fails, fusses a moment, then bangs the tray with his empty hand. . . . He is never idle because he is under such a compelling urge to use his hands for manipulation and exploitation (Gesell & Ilg, 1943, pp. 108–109).

Later in the year the child will become a creeper and may even rise for his first step or two by the first birthday. The creeper can be something of an adventurer; things might be easier for his mother if he did not expose himself to so much of his environment. In the cognitive sphere we can consult Piaget (1952) for an account of what the infant does with his spare time. Five of the six stages in the development of "sensori-motor intelligence" were transversed by the three Piaget children, possibly a skewed sample, by the end of the first year. Active exploration of the environment, even to the extent of experimenting with the fall of objects from different positions, could be seen going on during the eleventh month, and quite early in the second year the children appeared to have mastered through experience the important concept of permanent substantial objects. Mind you, we are talking about the oral stage of development. The model of the feeding child does scant justice to Piaget's son, a youthful Galileo lying in his crib and dropping his celluloid swan from various positions overhead to see where it will fall.

If we look with similar attention at the realm of social competence we shall see once again that the infant's interest is not entirely confined to oral satisfaction. It is true that in exploring the properties of his mother, in finding out how to maximize gratifications and minimize neglect or punishment, he will be strongly influenced by her position as chief source of oral and affectionate supplies. Here the aspect of competence may be pretty well obscured by such powerful affects as love, anger, and anxiety. But there are other moments of social interaction that do not seem to be so mingled with basic drives. If we watch the child happily passing objects back and forth with another person, playing peek-a-boo, hiding behind chairs, or engaging in the hilarious pastime of being chased while creeping, it looks as if there were a good many quite different ways of having fun. I should not like to depreciate the affection that infants feel for those around them, but I am inclined to agree with Woodworth (1958) that part of the fun in social play comes simply from "the opportunity to do something interesting in the environment." Young chimpanzees, according to observations made by Welker (1956), prefer to play with objects that are brightly colored, that light up, or that make sounds; objects, in other words, that provide a rich return of stimulation in response to effort expended. Similarly, young children like to play with those objects which, because they are animated, give them the most for their money.

In summary concerning the oral stage, let me say that if one is determined to use a single model for everything that happens during the first year, the model of the feeding child is clearly the proper choice. The delights of feeding, the pleasures of sucking, and the central position of the mother in emotional development are attested equally by direct superficial observation and by deep psychoanalytic interpretation. But are we obliged to use only one model? Does this result in the best possible conceptualization? I am proposing that we use at least two models for this period of development: the oral model, typified by the infant at the breast, and a competence model, represented by the child's exploratory play — the active interaction with his surroundings that starts as fun but that contributes steadily to the attainment of adult competence. The addition of the competence model I believe to be necessary here, and much more so at the later stages, if we are to do justice to the child's adaptive prowess and to the manner in which natural growth takes place from year to year. We need it if we are to have an effective ego psychology to go with instinct psychology.

The psychoanalytic hypothesis of oral libido requires us, first, to merge nutritional satisfaction with erotic satisfaction; second, to find the motivation of all the competence sequences in oral eroticism. Competence sequences such as manipulation or exploration can be considered erotic through association with feeding, through secondary reinforcement by feeding, through symbolism, or through the kind of developmental analogy that is implied in Erikson's incorporative mode. Connections of this kind assuredly exist. I have no intention to dispute what Erikson (1950), among others, has shown about symbolism in children's play and about the erotic and aggressive preoccupations that lead to play disruption. But we lose rather than gain, in my opinion, if we consider the child's *undisrupted* play, six hours a day, to be a continuous expression of libidinal energy, a continuous preoccupation with the family drama, as if there could be no intrinsic interest in the properties of the external world and the means of coming to terms with it. We lose rather than gain if we look only for an incorporative element in the infant's cognitive and motor behavior, remembering, for instance, that he puts the clothespin in his mouth but forgetting that he uses it to bang on the chair. We lose rather than gain if we try to force upon the mother an exclusive part in interesting the child in his surroundings. The psychosexual theory of the oral stage involves us in a regrettable overgeneralization from a very sound core. It can be corrected only by a new discrimination such as the one I am proposing here.

I believe that this correction makes important differences. One brief example must suffice. Weaning appears both in psychoanalytic theory and in learning (reinforcement) theory as an unmitigated evil and a potential trauma. It involves the replacement of a more gratifying method by a temporarily less gratifying method of securing nourishment. It can be endured only if the mother draws upon her accumulated capital of dependent affection and rewards the child for his sacrifices by expressions of love and approval. In the absence of such capital the results are bound to be unfortunate. If at this point we add the competence model, we see at once that the process of weaning is very much assisted by the motive of effectance. It is aided by the infant's inherent satisfaction in mastering the cup and spoon, in the bringing these parts of the environment under the governance of his own effort and initiative. He does not have to do it wholly for mother; as an active living being he has his own stake in growing up.

THE ANAL STAGE

The second main stage in psychosexual development, to which we now turn, comes when the libidinal excitability of the oral zone yields its primacy to the anal region. According to libido theory, the anal zone becomes increasingly erotized or libidinized during the second and third years, with the result that the child's emotional development turns more and more on events connected with excretion. The model for this stage may be expressed as the child on the toilet, but this phrase should imply that the child is being trained to use the toilet in scheduled adult fashion. Freud's conception is as always firmly instinctual. Libidinal pleasure is involved in the passing and retaining of bowel movements. Frustration and crisis lurk in the fact that the child is required to sacrifice some of this pleasure, or at least to subordinate it to cultural regulations imposed by the parents. Neo-Freudian revisionists generally reject the libido postulate but retain the idea of a struggle with discipline, and often enough they continue to use toilet training as the central model for this crisis in growth (Thompson, 1950; Silverberg, 1952).

As with the oral stage, Abraham (1927) divided the "anal-sadistic stage," as he called it, into an early and late phase, characterized by predominant pleasure respectively in excretion and in retention. Erikson (1950) points out that the anal zone "lends itself more than any other to the display of stubborn adherence to contradictory impulses because it is the modal zone of two conflicting modes of approach, which must become alternating, namely *retention* and *elimination.*" The preoccupations of toilet training are held to radiate widely and to determine the course of emotional growth. Freud first postulated the anal stage when studying the ambivalences of adult compulsion neurotics, and he traced to it the famous "anal character" with its qualities of stubbornness, neatness, and parsimony. Fenichel (1945) asserted that the pinching off of feces was perceived as a sadistic act and that, later on, "persons are treated as the feces previously were treated." By such extensions, the model of the child on the toilet is made equal to every aspect of growth during the second and third years.

Erikson (1959), in his still strictly parallel stages of ego development, describes the crisis of this period as a "battle for autonomy," the outcome of which is "decisive for the ratio between love and hate, for that between co-operation and willfulness, and for that between the freedom of self-expression and its suppression." If the child can weather the struggle and achieve "self-control without loss of self-esteem," he will emerge with "a lasting sense of autonomy and pride." If he is less fortunate, his legacy will be one of doubt and shame, his later character will probably be compulsive, and at the worst he may fall into the cruel grip of obsessional neurosis.

Clearly we are dealing with important problems of development, but is it correct to place the decisive struggle in the bathroom? Does the child in toilet training provide an adequate model; a sufficient interpretative nucleus, for all that is going on? Let us introduce again the competence model and see whether or not it can help us with the problems of this stage. It is worth noticing at the outset that direct observation does not give the libido theory the kind of support it provided in the oral stage. To be sure, there is plenty of evidence, even in the pages of the clean-minded Gesell, that children are interested in anal functions, that they play with feces, and that they experience frustration and conflict over the process of training. But direct observation would never suggest that these happenings were the central preoccupations of the second and third years, nor would introspection convince us that retaining and eliminating could have anything like the intensity of oral pleasures. The evidence for a stage of predominant anal libido thus rests heavily upon the reconstructions that occur in psychoanalytic treatment. On the other hand direct observation has long recognized a sharp and significant crisis in human relations, usually called two-year-old negativism. This could be, of course, a displacement from bowel training, but the competence model suggests another possibility. We may be dealing here with a profound *intrinsic* crisis in the growth of social competence.

Let us ask what the child accomplishes during the second and third years in the way of competent interactions with his environment. As regards locomotion he starts as an awkward toddler, but by the middle of the second year he becomes a restless runabout who not only gets into everything but also clearly experiments with his prowess by such stunts as walking backwards or pushing his own carriage. His first upright steps may have been wildly applauded, but his locomotor accomplishments soon become cause for parental despair and seem to continue without benefit of social reward. By the third birthday he may display his astonishing gains in coordination by starting to ride a tricycle. Parallel growth in manipulation is shown in those long stretches of time when he is quite happy to play by himself. One observes a constant activity of carrying objects about, filling and emptying containers, tearing things apart and fitting them together, lining up blocks and eventually building with them, digging and constructing in the sandbox. Such play may look idle to an adult, but it brings about a tremendous increase in the child's ability to deal with the physical world.

It is this picture of persistent, driven motor activity that led Mittelmann (1954) to postulate a *motility urge*. The second and third year, he points out, show the most rapid growth of motility; he even asserts that at this stage the motor urge "dominates all other urges." Motility is seen by him as "one of the most important avenues for exercising such functions as mastery, integration, reality-testing, and control of impulses — usually referred to in analysis as ego functions." During the third year the child shows a desire to do things himself and may resent help. "There is an increasing emphasis now on motor accomplishment leading to self-esteem. Thus the evolution of self-assertiveness and self-esteem is intimately connected with motor development." In such fashion Mittelmann uses the idea that I am referring to as *sense of competence*.

Development in the sphere of motility seems important in its own right, and it helps us to understand the social crisis of negativism. The child busily tests his own growing capacities; he explores the properties of physical objects; he finds out the ways in which he can influence the environment and have effects upon it. In parallel fashion he begins new tests of his competence in the social sphere. Two developments introduce the crisis that has been so often described. In the first place, the span of consecutive action and intention reaches a point where interference before the end can be frustrating and successful completion can be rewarding. In the second place, the use of language advances to a point where commands can be attempted and where the consequences of the word "no," as uttered by oneself, begin to invite investigation. Behind these developments lies something a bit more inferential, described by Stern (1930) in these words: "The child deports and realizes himself as a living entity, a one complete center of power"; thus for the first time "he wishes to affirm himself, his existence, his importance — and to increase it." Earlier, his effectance behavior has seemed more like a series of discrete stabs resulting in discrete feelings of efficacy. Now he begins to act more like a self, with a more organized sense of competence.

At some point, then, the child begins quite directly to try out his social competence. The sharp-eyed Sully (1896) pointed out a "sudden emergence of self-will" around the age of two. Stern chose "wilfulness" as the proper term to characterize this phase of development. Words such as "obstinacy" and "defiance" are also common in the literature. Gesell, who sees these tendencies as reaching their peak at two and a half, feels certain that parents would vote this time "the most exasperating age in the preschool period," and he observes with disapproval that "the spanking curve comes to a peak at about this time." As an example of defiance and obstinacy, Stern, like Piaget an assiduous observer of his own children, chose a mealtime episode in which his little daughter Eva gave the command: "Father, pick up the spoon." A clash of wills followed because she had not said, and would not say, "please"; her obstinate refusal resulted in her having no dinner. Today we may be inclined to applaud Eva for her fight against excessive middle-class decencies, but in any event she illustrates the testing of social competence both by giving a command and by refusing to obey one.

The meaning of this early self-assertion and negativism has been examined carefully in a recent paper by Levy (1955). He uses the term "oppositional behavior" for this and certain similar phenomena both earlier and later in life, including the infant's refusal to suck when awakened too quickly and the generalized negativism found in catatonic schizophrenia. Although he calls such forms of behavior "oppositional," Levy makes it clear that they do not start as expressions of aggression. Their true adaptive significance is that of resisting external influence. If behavior were allowed to be governed wholly from outside, there would be no scope for inner needs and no way to develop inner controls. "The oppositional behavior of the second year of life," Levy writes, "is a general movement towards the autonomy of the whole person . . . the first flowering of self-determination, of which the budding had long been in evidence." The two forms, "I do it myself," and "No, no," are aspects of the same trend toward autonomy; indeed, there is evidence (Hetzer, 1929) that children who have a marked stubborn period are more independent later on. While Levy does not use the word "competence" he is certainly employing a similar idea.

During the second and third years, then, the child, because of practiced maturing of general coordination and of verbal capacity, reaches a critical juncture in his ability to interact with his social environment. His attempts to exploit the new possibilities and to increase his sense of social competence are at first somewhat crude and uncompromising. In his inexperience he challenges rather forcefully his parents' sense of competence. These tests are exacting for the parents. The temptation to prevail at all costs will be powerful not only for parents who like to exercise authority but also for apostles of permissiveness who are startled to find such tyranny emerging in their young. How much sense of social competence can the child preserve in these crises?

The outcome of his first concerted attempts to measure his efficacy against that of other people may leave quite a lasting mark upon his confidence.

You will notice that the competence model does not create any quarrel with Erikson's concept of a crisis in autonomy. There is agreement as to what constitutes the central problem in ego development at this stage. But the competence model, I maintain, is far better able to conceptualize this development than the model derived from libido theory. I do not want to make light of the child's excretory interests or to minimize his problems over bowel training. The analysis of children with psychosomatic complaints of the digestive tract attests the value of such concepts. My argument is that bowel training is not a correct prototype for the problem of autonomy. It is not the right model for those tryings and testings of the sense of competence that would have to go on anyway, even if bowel training were of no consequence at all.

The bowel training model is wrong, I think, in two ways. First, it concerns a function that is governed by the autonomic nervous system, that never comes under direct voluntary control, and that does not carry the experience of initiative that goes with voluntary action. The child may be proud when he can meet parental expectations, but it will be pride in meeting a somewhat mysterious demand by a somewhat mysterious process of habit formation, not the pride of mastering things directly by trial and by effort expended, as when one learns to throw or to bat a ball. Second, it is a situation in which cultural requirements inevitably prevail. Every child is bowel trained. This is a far greater victory for authority than generally prevails elsewhere; in other matters the child preserves more freedom to resist, plead, cajole, and force compromises on his surrounding adults. In short, the bowel training model all but eliminates the initiative and versatility on the child's part that is an essential aspect of any true autonomy. The best outcome of the bowel training problem is that the child will come to will the inevitable. The best outcome of the struggle for social competence is that he will face the world with self-respect and a measure of confidence in his own strength.

As with the oral stage, I shall take but one example to show how the proposed competence model makes a real difference. I think it throws new light on the anal-erotic character. There can be no doubt that Freud hit upon a very real pattern when he formulated this idea, but there has always been something peculiar about its interpretation in anal-libidinal terms. Of the triad of traits, parsimony and stubbornness go well enough together, and it is possible to see them as two forms of opposition to the demand for timely performance on the toilet. The third trait, orderliness, does not seem to belong in the same picture. It is said to be a reaction-formation against disorderly desires, a surrender to cultural pressure. Why does the anal problem give rise so frequently to this pattern of two oppositional traits and one reaction-formation, when other combinations seem equally possible?

The competence model helps us out of this dilemma by shedding new light on orderliness. You have probably noticed that orderliness is a suspect trait these days. It is taken to signify neuroticism, compulsiveness, rigidity, and failure to appreciate what is important in life. I remember the trouble that ensued when one of my course assistants, happily liberated from obsessional symptoms such as bookkeeping, handed back to the students a set of graded examination papers and kept no record of the grades he had assigned. This incident may help to convince you of the point I now want to make, which is that orderliness has an adaptive function, that it is within certain limits a competent way of dealing with one's surroundings. Neatness is not just something the culture forces upon us. If we look closely at the development of competence in the child, we can see that tendencies toward orderliness emerge spontaneously during the second year and that they have a function in dealing with the environment. This function proves to be not at all incongruous with stubbornness and parsimony.

The function of orderliness was pointed out by Goldstein (1940) in his account of brain-injured patients. Some of these patients were vehemently insistent that their belongings be always in the same place, so that when needed they could be found without difficult mental acts of remembering. The theme reappears in Kanner's (1951) work on autistic children, who demand a ritualistic sameness in the physical environment. In Gesell's pages we notice the emergence of similar tendencies during the second year: an interest in putting things away, in where things belong, and in the possibility of calling some things "mine." All these trends can be understood as attempts to establish control over things so that they can be readily found and kept. At the same time the child shows tendencies toward ritual, making demands, for instance, for certain foods at certain times, served in certain ways. Here again the rigidities serve the cause of controlling the environment, including the people in it, and assuring oneself that accustomed satisfactions can be made to reappear. Orderliness serves to increase competence, and it is very definitely imposed upon adults at times as a means of making their behavior more predictable and controllable.

In these terms, then, stubbornness, parsimony, and orderliness are completely of a piece. They are ways of preventing oneself from being pushed around by the environment. They emerge when they do because they depend upon certain other developmental achievements: the constancy of objects, and a continuity of play interests from day to day. The fixation of the triad of traits happens when there is a relative feeling of incompetence in relation to the environment, especially the human one: when toys are arbitrarily taken away by parents or other children, when gratifications seem to come whimsically, when demands are made without relation to inner inclinations – the demand for bowel regularity being one instance. A human environment that is not in good intuitive contact with the child's inclinations, one that is also fairly active with its demands, would seem most likely to evoke such a pattern.

The "anal character" is a person who somewhat mistrusts his environment. His traits coherently express how he adapted to this mistrust during the second year. Reaction formation need not be assumed for any of them. There is another kind of orderliness, however, which depends directly upon reaction formation. This kind of orderliness represents a docile response to parental requirements. In such children we would expect orderliness to appear without stubbornness or stinginess; it would be associated instead with other evidences of being a good, compliant child more or less on the side of parental values. Such children might have residual messy fantasies, but they would represent lost pleasures rather than a fighting issue. It would be a serious misdiagnosis to class them with "anal-erotic" characters in the other sense.

The Phallic Stage

According to Freud's theory of the libido, the third stage of psychosexual development comes about through a process of maturation whereby the genital organs become the chief seat of erotic excitability, overthrowing the primacy of the anal zone. As a consequence there is a marked increase of autoerotic activity, of erotic exploration and play, and of curiosity about the facts of reproductive life. There is also, Freud inferred, the beginning of a sexual feeling somewhat analogous to that of adults, sufficiently so to produce possessive love and jealousy and thus to give rise to that early cornerstone of psychoanalytic theory, the Oedipus complex. The ensuing emotional crisis he believed to be nuclear for neurosis and for development in general. The chances for a fearless outflow of libido after puberty, and for happiness in love and marriage, were very likely to be influenced by the outcome of this crucial first encounter. When later Freud conceived the idea of the superego, he related this agency directly to the Oedipus complex, which thereby assumed a central place in the processes of socialization and internal control. He believed that once the child had made his passage through this time of supreme trial the main outlines of his character were set for life.

Interpretation of the phallic stage according to an interpersonal model is made easy by the fact that Freud's own model included such specific interpersonal consequences. Though belittling the analogy between phallic and genital sexuality, the revisionists have been well satisfied to retain the Sophoclean prototype as a model for the interpersonal crisis of the period. But the issues are seen in somewhat different lights. Horney (1939) believed that most of the attachments of a child to a parent at this time were of a clinging, dependent nature, mobilized by a compelling need for security. Fromm (1944) emphasizes quite another aspect, the child's battle with irrational authority as represented by the parents and their prohibitions. Rivalry, jealousy, hostility are certainly all to be detected in these complex events. Erikson (1950), viewing the activities of the phallic stage as many-sided expressions of the intrusive mode, conceives the ego's crisis to be one of maintaining a sense of initiative. If fortunate, the child will continue to feel that his exuberant powers have a chance of asserting themselves. The danger of the stage is that guilt and anxiety will supervene so strongly that passive resignation or illness will become the only possible ways of life.

Erikson's formulation is actually very much in terms of our competence model. The child is brought nearer to his crisis, he says, by developments in three spheres of competence: locomotion, language, and imagination. Locomotion reaches the point of being a serviceable tool rather than a difficult stunt. The child can walk and run freely, covering a lot of territory, and he can use his tricycle to get about still more widely. He likes to race up and down stairs and perform spectacularly on the stair rail or jungle gym. Furthermore, he becomes able to saw and cut, to throw overhand, and to dress himself without any assistance. The emergence of these seemingly adult motor patterns makes it possible for him to compare himself with grown-ups, yet to wonder about the differences in size. This is the time when dressing up in adult clothes and imitating grown-up behavior becomes popular. It is also the time when children pretend to be engineers and truck-drivers, relishing the roles that imply remarkable power over the environment.

Language likewise reaches a stage of development at which it can support wider understanding and social exchange. Verbal humor and playing with rhymes attest and produce a growing mastery of speech, and the child begins to understand such subtleties as "might" and "could." The imperious "I" and "you" of the previous stage give place to "we," especially with family members. The important thing is that linguistic competence now opens ready channels for finding out about the world. Questions can be asked, as no parent will forget who has tried to bear up in the onrushing stream of four-year-old interrogation. Unfortunately for exhausted parents, these sieges must be regarded as highly important to the child's growth. Besides extending his knowledge about the world, he is securing needed practice in expressing himself and in listening with comprehension to what others have to say.

Imagination is the third sphere of competence in which a marked development takes place during the fourth and fifth years. This is the time when the child can first maintain the fantasy of an imaginary companion. It is the time when he can begin to dramatize himself in different adult roles, when he can clothe plain objects like blocks with all the attributes of airplanes, vehicles, animals, and people, when he begins to have frightening dreams involving injury and pursuit by wolves. For, as Erikson expresses it, "both language and locomotion permit him to expand his imagination over so many things that he cannot avoid frightening himself with what he himself has dreamed and thought up" (1959, p. 75).

If we consider the bearing of these developments on social competence, it is clear that the child has reached a point of understanding where for the first time he can contemplate his place in the family and his relation to other people in general. To some extent he continues to experiment with crude social power, especially with other children whom he may boss, hit, and threaten in various ways. But he is also beginning to grasp the nature of roles. It is at this time that he learns his culture's definition of sex roles, and he experiments with a variety of adult roles. For the first time he is intellectually capable of asking those questions, so portentous in libido theory, about marrying the parent of the opposite sex. Up to a point, the culture encourages his ripening capacity to act in grown-up fashion. At about four he probably has graduated to an adult-sized bed and may be taking some of his meals at the family table. But he is not yet an adult, so his aspirations are bound to be frustrated in many ways, including his proposals of matrimony.

It is interesting that Erikson, at that point in his account of the "locomotor-genital" stage at which he wants to assign centrality to the Oedipus complex, continues to write in terms of the competence model. "The increased locomotor mastery," he says, "and the pride in being big now and *almost* as good as father and mother receives its severest setback in the clear fact that in the genital sphere one is vastly inferior; furthermore, it receives an additional setback in the fact that not even in the distant future is one ever going to be father in sexual relationship to mother, or mother in sexual relationship to father" (1959, p. 77). But here I cannot help feeling that Erikson has mixed his models. From the point of view of competence, of pride in being big, genital inferiority is by no means greater than many other inferiorities such as stature, strength, speed of running, distance one can throw a ball. Father can start the power lawn mower and control it; he can drive the car; for the modern child these must be obvious and hopeless tokens of his superiority. If the genital comparison is to be made nuclear, it can hardly be in terms of the competence model. One must already have assumed that whatever is sexual is necessarily central.

I should make it clear at this point that I do not believe in using the competence model exclusively. Even if one hesitates a bit over the psychoanalytic evidence based on adult recollections of the phallic stage, it would be impossible to deny the direct evidence presented, for instance, by Susan Isaacs (1933) from her nursery school or by Anna Freud and Dorothy Burlingham (1944) from their wartime nurseries, not to mention what any observant person can notice in children of this age, that there is a clearly sexual flavor to some of the child's activities and interests. This must not be neglected, but neither should it be taken, I believe, as a matter so profound that the whole of emotional development hangs upon it. The growth of competence leads to intrinsic emotional and interpersonal crises. Perhaps the best way to make this clear is to imagine for the moment a child in the phallic stage who is normal in every way except that no increase in genital sensitivity takes place. This child would still make locomotor, linguistic, and imaginative progress, would become interested in being like adults, would make comparisons as to size, would be competitive and subject to defeats and humiliations, would be curious, ask endless questions and encounter rebuffs, would have bad dreams and guilt feelings over imagined assertive or aggressive actions, would learn about sex roles, would struggle to understand his relation to other family members, and might very well ask about marrying one of the parents. All of these things arise inescapably from progress in the growth of competence. They all have important emotional consequences. In all these situations there is a chance to maintain and strengthen a sense of initiative; in all there is also a chance that the environment will act so as to impose a burden of guilt.

If we now restore to our hypothetical child his genital sensitivity, his life may become yet more complicated, but it will still revolve around initiative and guilt. Oedipal wishes add an emotional dimension, but they do not completely change the nature of the interpersonal crisis. And it seems to me that the Oedipal prototype falls short as a general model for the phallic stage in just the way toilet training failed for the anal stage. Once again Freud selected as his central image a hopeless situation, one where defeat for the child is inevitable. The child must learn to renounce the whole Oedipal wish, just as he must learn to renounce any thought of not being bowel trained. I submit the idea that if these were the true and determinative models it would be quite a problem to explain the survival of any sense of initiative. These models help us to understand why we have shame and guilt, but they do not give us much reason to suppose that we could emerge with autonomy and initiative. The competence model is not so harsh, though it certainly is not intended to gloss over the tragic features of childhood. By its help we can more easily see where the child fights less unequal battles, where he sometimes achieves compromise and sometimes prevails, where he is free to increase the scope of his activities and build up his sense of competence. We can discover, in short, some of the places where initiative is likely to be strengthened, thus making the inevitable renunciations less bitter and overwhelming.

As before, I shall mention but one specific problem that might benefit by introducing the competence model. I believe that we can now make a consistent systematic distinction between shame and guilt. These two words have become so confused in the psychological literature that they are often used interchangeably. They are confused in experience, too; very few people can distinguish sharply between being ashamed and feeling guilty. It has been proposed that there are wide cultural differences in the use of these two deterrents, so that one can properly speak of shame-cultures and guilt-cultures, but this suggestion has by no means won the applause of anthropologists as a whole. The neo-Freudians have made the confusion systematic by their emphasis on rejection and abandonment as the true basic anxiety that guides our lives. Shame and guilt alike are painful because they signify desertion, so there is no point in trying for a sharp distinction.

A determined attempt to rescue and separate the two concepts has been made in a recent monograph by Piers and Singer (1953). Structurally, they say, shame arises from tension between ego and ego-ideal; guilt from tension between ego and superego. This means that shame occurs when there is short-coming or failure to reach a goal through lack of ability, whereas guilt implies touching or transgressing a moral boundary. In my own words I should say that shame is always connected with incompetence. It occurs when we cannot do something that either we or an audience thinks we should be able to do: when we cannot lift the weight, when we cannot hit the ball, when we offer to knock someone down and get knocked down ourselves. It means belittlement and loss of respect. In contrast, guilt does not imply that one is unable to do something; it signifies that one has done, or is thinking of doing, something within one's powers that is forbidden.

The distinction can be illustrated straight from the classical Oedipus situation. The father or the mother can discourage the little boy's erotic pretensions in either of two ways. They may tell him that his advances are wrong and bad, indicating that they don't like badness and will punish him, but making no suggestion that he could not carry out his intentions. Or they may tell him that he is too young, that his penis is too small to please his mother, thus belittling him but not implying that the impossible act would be morally wrong. It is doubtless more common to combine these implications, thus strengthening the subjective confusion between shame and guilt. But in principle the distinction seems to me to be clear.

It is unfortunate, I think, that Piers and Singer try to connect shame with fear of abandonment. Belittlement means to the child, they claim, that the parent will walk away in disgust and leave his offspring in the grip of separation anxiety. This is completely at odds with Erikson's conception of shame, which emphasizes a sense of exposure on the child's part and a desire to hide. Indeed the experience of shame seems always to involve an impulse to run away, hide, or sink through the floor. If the basic fear were desertion, the basic response should be clinging, but in fact we want to get away from those who belittle us.

Shame, then, is a response to incompetence, not to moral violation. Its pain comes from a diminished sense of competence, from a lowering of respect and of self-respect. I must not digress from my theme at this point, but I can hardly say how important I think it is for dynamic psychology, which has operated so long with love, hate, and anxiety as its chief tools, to bring back into its ways of thinking the variable of respect. For this, the concept of competence is indispensable.

The Latency Period

We come now to a stage of life during which, according to libido theory, there is a relative quiescence in the erotic sphere. Believing that sexual energies actually declined between the phallic stage and puberty, Freud seems to have found the period something of a bore. Psychoanalysis, which was prepared to shock the world with the Oedipus complex and with its reanimation at puberty, had no startling disclosures to make about the intervening years when the problem was so well controlled that the ego could busy itself with the real world. It was perhaps on this account that the unfortunate word "latent" came to be applied, with its all-too-effective suggestion that nothing of importance could happen until Nature enlivened things again by dramatically strengthening the sexual impulses at puberty. Freud provided no picturesque model or prototype for the stage. It can be described, however, in terms of his later structural concepts. The superego, more or less introjected as an outcome of the Oedipal conflict, is now for the first time available to assist the ego in controlling the id. The ego thus finds itself possessed of surplus energies for problems of adaptation.

Freud's handling of the latency period was not one of his happier ventures. In the first place, his assumption about the quiescence of sexual energies seems to be simply wrong. Anthropological evidence and better observation in our own society have combined to cast grave doubt on the hypothesis of a biologically determined sexual latency. For once we can almost say that Freud underestimated the importance of sex. The mistake has serious consequences. By leading us to assume that there is less to control, it falsifies our understanding of the problems of control that are so vital during these years. In the second place, Freud's gathering of six to eight years of the child's life under a single somewhat negative heading, in striking contrast to the fine discriminations upon which he insisted for the first five years, must be rated as one of those conceptualizations that tend to stifle research. Freud's attitude toward the latency period almost seems to imply that it is not worth investigating. Happily even his loyal followers have not always taken the hint, and the period has lately begun to receive a more searching scrutiny.

It is becoming clear that the latency period is not all of one piece. Hartmann, Kris, and Loewenstein (1947) describe the evolution of the superego, which at the start is harsh, rigid, yet erratic, in the manner of a person unfamiliar with newly found authority. In time, and with intellectual growth, this primitiveness gives place to a greater flexibility, so that what Murray (1938) calls the integration of ego and superego begins to take place. Bornstein (1951) takes this development as a basis for distinguishing two phases of the latency period, with a division point at eight years. Even direct observations with no pretension of depth, such as those made by Gesell and Ilg (1946), show marked changes in emotional outlook at six, seven, and eight which are consistent with the idea that the Oedipus problem is not resolved, nor the superego formed in a short time. Staying entirely within the framework of Freud's theories, one must still allow for important dynamic progressions during the latency stage.

The interpersonal model has been applied to this period in illuminating fashion by Sullivan (1953). His description of the "juvenile era," the time from six to twelve, is heavily based on the behavior of children with their contemporaries. Sullivan considered that the chief problems were *competition* and *compromise,* a pair of concepts that puts the emphasis on social competence rather than on affective gratifications. At school and on the playground the child finds himself in a competitive, unaffectionate society, with which it is possible to come to terms only by practicing new roles and learning new arts of participation, protection, and compromise. Sullivan's description of the "crudeness of interpersonal relations" at the beginning of the juvenile era matches the picture of the crude superego drawn by more orthodox workers. In terms of competence it is not surprising that crudeness should be characteristic of several kinds of complex behavior. School work from six to eight undoubtedly merits the same description.

Erikson's account of the latency period adheres quite strictly to the competence model. The child reaches a point where he is no longer satisfied with just play and make-believe. In line with his interest in becoming an adult, he needs to feel useful and to be able to make things and deal with things that have significance in the adult world. He needs, in other words, a *sense of industry*, and he is now capable of the "steady attention and persevering diligence" that foster this sense. His efforts may be enhanced by "positive identification with those who *know* things and know how to *do* things." The dangers lie in the possibility that success will prove to be elusive and social encouragement too weak, in which case the legacy of the stage may be a lasting sense of inadequacy and inferiority.

I hope you will have observed how well the case for competence has been made for me without my speaking a word in its behalf. Erikson makes it central for dealings with the humanly significant objective world; Sullivan made it central for the social world. Once we open up the problems of emotional development in these terms, we can begin to make connections with the findings of workers outside the psychoanalytic tradition who have observed the upbuilding of competence in great detail. One thing that is certainly not latent is the growth of capacities in the realms of both action and of understanding. Think of the differences between a child of six and a child of eleven — between first-graders and sixth-graders. What the child wants, what he dreads, where he runs into emotional crises, will be very much influenced by the level of his understanding and by the growth of sheer capacity for social interaction.

Let us take this last point to illustrate the benefits that come from using the competence model. Gesell tells us that at the age of nine the children in his sample begin to move in spontaneous groups or gangs that can be orderly and harmonious without adult supervision. Charlotte Bühler (1931) reports that first-grade classes cannot act as a whole, that positions of leadership are highly transient, and that the children cannot put their classmates in a rank order of importance. In contrast, fifth-grade classes readily act as units under class leaders, and the children find it a simple task to rank the membership. These observations suggest that a marked growth in social action and understanding takes place somewhere around nine. The nature of this growth has been approached from another angle in Piaget's studies of rules and moral ideas.

Piaget (1932) demonstrates that children of seven and eight are only just emerging from a conception of rules as something absolute and unchangeable, a finding which suggests that the early crudeness of the superego comes partly from immaturity of understanding. By the age of nine the Geneva children had a good idea of reciprocity, realizing, for instance, that it is fair to change the rules provided everyone agrees and the new rules apply to all. But one must wait two or three years more for the emergence of a steady sense of equity, in which fairness is achieved by giving special concessions to handicapped players. This implies that the child has grasped the possibility that another child's need and outlook may be different from his own. He has transcended egocentrism, or, as Lerner (1937) conceived it, he has attained the power to shift perspectives, a power manifested in Lerner's own experiment only at eleven or twelve. And it is between nine and twelve that Sullivan (1953) locates the first emergence of true chumship in which the other child's feelings and interests become as important as one's own.

These facts suggest that there is a definite pattern in the growth of social competence. Between six and nine the child has to find out how to get along with others in the sense of competing, compromising, protecting himself from hurt, and learning the rules of the game. He does this partly because he has to, being thrown with others at school, and partly because, as Woodworth (1958) expresses it, other children "afford him the opportunity to do something interesting in the environment." During this time, however, dependent needs, security, and affection must still find their satisfaction almost entirely in the family circle. Only the most assertive members of juvenile society are likely to achieve a sense of security in their new world. At home, therefore, a good many of the problems that start in the phallic stage continue through several more years. Jealousy, desire for a favored place, guilt, and demands for affection still characterize the child's emotional life at home.

At about nine, however, social competence and understanding advance to the point that the world of contemporaries begins to compete with the family circle. Membership in a gang or on a team starts to have the emotional yield known as "we-feeling," and friendships may begin to supply some of the affective response hitherto obtainable only under one's own rooftree. As Helene Deutsch (1944) has shown, these alliances serve the purpose of creating an alternative to the family world, thus opening the way for a new growth of independence.

Obviously there are crises along the route of these developments. The sense of competence is challenged on many fronts. The mastery of schoolwork and other adult tasks can build firm self-esteem and social approval, but it can also produce frustration and a deep sense of inferiority. The outcomes of competitive activity on the playground can yield superb self-confidence or painful feelings of inadequacy. Attempts to participate in groups, gangs, and team activities can confer the rewards of membership or the punishments of rejection and ridicule. The seeking of friendships can open avenues for warm and cherishing feelings, or it can lead to rebuffs and withdrawal into self. Are these crises of any lasting importance for the development of personality? Freud seems to have assigned little weight to any crisis that occurred after the age of six. Sullivan took the opposite view. The juvenile era, he said, was "the first developmental stage in which the limitations and peculiarities of the home as a socializing influence begin to be open to remedy." Even more influential, in his opinion, were preadolescent friendships, which under fortunate circumstances might rescue young people otherwise destined for emotional trouble and mental breakdown.

Does the competence model help us to deal with this problem on which the libidinal expert and the interpersonal expert so spectacularly disagree? I think it does, because it leads us to look for the aspect of competence in behavior and for the vicissitudes of the sense of competence. In thinking about characteristics of adult behavior it leads us to consider what part is played by competence, and this makes us more likely to detect the effects of the latency stage, when the sense of competence faces some of its most significant crises. So I take sides with Sullivan and propose the hypothesis that the effects of the first five years can be substantially changed by developments during later childhood. Mildly unfortunate residues of infancy can become increased to neurotic proportions because competence fares badly, so that the child dares not chip away at his old anxieties or branch out into new regions of satisfaction. Contrariwise, a badly troubled first five years can lead to a relatively healthy outcome when latency encourages a rich growth for the sense of competence in many directions.

One example must suffice here to make clear my meaning. And to be strictly classical, though something else would probably be more convincing, let this example again be the Oedipus complex. When insufficiently renounced, the Oedipus complex becomes a hazard in adolescence by charging heterosexual interests with all the urgencies and inhibitions acquired during the phallic stage. The young man, for instance, is drawn to girls who in some significant way resemble his mother, and from the start the relation is ill-starred. The search for intimacy founders because of childlike demandingness and jealousy, and sexual fulfillment is under a cloud of anxiety. We can attribute this to a fixation that has lain unchanged during latency, but the competence model suggests a more refined analysis. The young man of our instance is also exhibiting passivity and lack of initiative: he does nothing to find interesting companionship with girls and waits until his hand is forced, so to speak, by an irresistible unconscious attraction, at which point he proceeds with the unpracticed skill of a five-year-old. The inability to be interested in girls other than mother-surrogates is a distinctive feature of many such cases.

Suppose, however, that the latency period has encouraged initiative and a firm sense of competence. Suppose that events have conferred self-confidence in juvenile society, brought prominence in school life, included some fortunate chumships, and begotten a self-assured friendliness with girls. It may be that this young man will have one or more love affairs which will still be spoiled by Oedipal residues, but he will not be without alternative resources. No timid novice in social relations, he may be able to see and modify his demandingness and jealousy; or, if this fails, he will not find it impossible to explore the contentment that may be found with girls who are not like his mother. The young man, in other words, has acquired during latency a number of characteristics which are now available to give him a wide range of confident activity and keep him from being bound to the single type of relation that always ends in frustration. If this happens, the young man will not appear as a patient. It is conceivable, however, that he might appear as a candidate for training in psychoanalysis, and the study of training analyses, especially by analysts who see possible merit in the competence model, may prove to be a very good way to shed light on these problems.

The pictures I have drawn can be expressed in psychoanalytic terms. The two young men differ with respect to ego strength. But this is not saying much unless we have ideas about how ego strength develops. The competence model, as I have shown, can give us ideas on just this point.

The Final Genital Stage

We come now to the last stage in psychosexual development, the stage at which newly strengthened sexual impulses bring about the possibility of genital primacy. In view of the great length of this paper you will be happy to hear that I shall have few words to say about the final stage. The plot is already clear. A prolonged fifth act would add little to whatever impact it may already have made. Obviously I would have words of praise for the more orthodox description of adolescence as given, for instance, by Anna Freud (1937, 1958), Bernfeld (1938), and Helene Deutsch (1944). Obviously there is great illumination in the treatment of this period as a time of increased instinctual drive and threat to established patterns of ego control. Certainly it is fruitful to look upon some aspects of adolescent behavior as a struggle to maintain and expand one's defenses. You would expect me also to mention some merit in the interpersonal model as developed, for instance, by Sullivan (1953), who described the task of late adolescence as that of establishing "a fully human or mature repertory of interpersonal relations." But then you would predict complaints on my part about the neglect of competence and the failure of the two models to capture whole ranges of behavior that are essential for full understanding. To spell out what you can so easily anticipate would be a bad anticlimax, and it would be a pity to lend an air of anticlimax to anything as dramatic as adolescence and genital primacy.

Perhaps the one thing I should do is to indicate the kinds of behavior in adolescence that I consider important, well handled by a competence model, and neglected by libido and interpersonal models. Since the adolescent is reaching adult size, strength, and mental development, the behavior in question lies in the realm of serious accomplishment — serious in the terms either of the youth culture or of adult society. I am referring to the adolescent equivalent of what Erikson calls a *sense of industry* in the latency period, and I see this problem as continuing rather more strongly after puberty than seems to be implied in Erikson's account. No doubt I bring to this judgment an occupational bias different from that of a therapist. My professional life is spent among late adolescents whose sexual problems and social relations have for the most part not overwhelmed them. We talk together about their plans for study, their abilities and limitations, their struggles with materials to be learned and skills to be attained, their occupational leanings, career plans, and concerns about modern society as the scene of their future endeavors. We talk, in other words, mostly about their competence, and I do not believe that understanding is fostered by interpreting these concerns too much as displacements of instinctual drives, defense mechanisms, or interpersonal relations. They are real.

Adolescents today learn how to drive cars. Some of them learn to compete against adult records in sports, occasionally breaking them. Some of them become part of the football, band, and cheerleader complex that plays such an important part in community entertainment. Some of them try their hands at building workable radio sets, at scientific exploration, at editing newspapers, at writing stories and verse, at musical and dramatic performances, at political activity. Some of them with fewer opportunities or talents put their maturing bodies to heavy work or their maturing minds to white-collar office jobs. All this belongs in the sphere of work, and work, as Schilder (1942) so cogently argued, is importantly a phenomenon of competence. These happenings create many crises, many defeats, many victories for the sense of competence. Once again there are large spheres in which the adolescent can be suffering losses or making gains in ego strength. In theorizing about the subject we must not foreclose the possibility that these developments significantly affect what happens in the erotic and interpersonal realms.

I shall say no more about this stage of development except to launch my last complaint against the models bequeathed us by psychosexual theory. The model proffered by libido theory is that of heterosexual relations, and their ideal form is embodied in the concept of genital primacy. It is not argued, of course, that we all successfully become genital primates, but the ideal type serves to indicate the problems of the period. The sexual act itself plays a prominent part in genital primacy, reminding us that Freud's oft-mentioned broadened conception of sex sometimes touched base again in what no one has ever denied to be sexual. In libidinal terms, the regular discharge of genital tensions serves also to drain some of the energy from pregenital tensions, thus making the control and sublimation of the latter an easy problem for the ego. Erikson (1950) prefers "to put it more situationally: the total fact of finding, via the climactic turmoil of the orgasm, a supreme experience of the mutual regulation of two beings in some way breaks the point off the hostilities and potential rages caused by the oppositeness of male and female, of fact and fancy, of love and hate. Satisfactory sex relations thus make sex less obsessive, overcompensation less necessary, sadistic controls superfluous." Erikson's further account of what "the utopia of genitality" should include — mutual trust and a willingness to share lives in the interest of securing a happy development for the childeren — is something I commend to you all as an uncommonly beautiful statement of what we should aspire to in family life. It is an interpersonal statement as well as a libidinal one. I like it so well that I am sorry to point out that it has only the slightest relation to competence and to that other sphere of human concern — work.

Unfortunately the climactic turmoil of the orgasm is completely the wrong model for work. This is not to say that good sexual relations may not sometimes free a person from gnawing hates and doubts that have interfered with his capacity to work. But the emphasis of the idea of orgastic potency and mutuality is on an essential loss of ego, a drowning of all other considerations in the immense involuntary experience of the sexual relation. He who takes the ego to bed with him will never get a gold star for genital primacy. The orgastic model has virtue for certain human activities requiring a temporary submergence of self, such as inspiration, creative imagination, and thoroughly relaxed play. But it will never do for the serious, stable, lasting concerns of human life, the realm that I am trying to designate as work. This is the sphere in which the ego must always keep a firm hand on the helm.

Work requires a certain constancy of effort. There must be sustained endeavor with control of wayward impulses that distract from the requirements of external reality and social roles. There must be a capacity for persistent return to tasks, sometimes dull in themselves, that form part of the job requirement or that belong in a long-range plan to achieve remote goals. There must be a quality of reliability, so that one keeps promises and lives up to the obligations one has assumed. Even the fashion for being spontaneous and natural, even the bright vision of self-fulfilling work in Fromm's (1955) sane society, even Marcuse's (1955) fantasy of a nonrepressive civilization in which all work becomes libidinal pleasure cannot exorcize the true and somewhat stern nature of reality. And even Ernst Kris (1952), no enemy of psychoanalytic theory, reminded us that artistic creation required, in addition to a phase of inspiration, a second phase characterized by "the experience of purposeful organization and the intent to solve a problem." When we call an artist "merely competent" it is a weak form of praise, but if he were "merely inspired," without a certain rather high minimum of competence, we would never even see or hear his products.

I should like to close with a short coda on the words "merely competent." I particularly do not want to be misunderstood concerning the part to be assigned to competence and the sense of competence in human development. As a simple and sovereign concept it will never do. A person developed wholly along lines of competence, with no dimensions of passion, love, or friendliness, would never qualify for maturity. Competence is not intended to describe such experiences as enjoying food, immersing oneself in a sexual relation, loving children, cherishing friends, being moved by natural beauty or great works of art; nor is it designed to swallow up the problems created by aggression and anxiety. This is what I meant by saying that the competence model must always be used in conjunction with other models that do full justice to such things as hunger, sexuality, and aggression. It may hurt one's desire for logical simplicity to suppose that several models are needed to understand a problem. Yet I think no one can claim a probability that human nature was designed in the interests of logic.

It is my conviction, in short, that Freud's discoveries were of epoch-making importance, that psychoanalytic ego psychology has taken effective steps to fill out some of the undeveloped parts of Freud's theories, and that Erikson in particular has accomplished a synthesis that promises good things for future understanding of the growth of personality. But I also believe that our understanding cannot be rounded out by stretching Freud's concepts in a vain attempt to cover everything, or by calling everything interpersonal as if body and material world did not exist. We should add to the picture a meticulous consideration, at every level, of the growth of the child's capacity both for action and for understanding. We should try to be as shrewd in detecting the vicissitudes of the sense of competence as Freud was with sexuality, aggression, and defense. It is to encourage such a development that I have had so much to say about the concept of competence.

Summary

Even an idea as monumental as Freud's theory of the psychosexual stages of development can come to have an adverse effect upon scientific progress if it is believed too literally too long. Libido theory provided a series of models for critical phases in emotional growth: feeding, toilet training, the Oedipus situation, latency, and the adult heterosexual relation. These models are largely preserved in revisions of Freud, though changed to interpersonal terms, and they continue to dominate the thinking of workers in psychoanalytic ego psychology. In this paper it is maintained that the models are in certain respect inadequate and misleading. In particular, they encourage us to neglect a range of facts which is ordered here under the concept of competence. If these facts are slighted, it is held, there can be little hope of further progress in psychoanalytic ego psychology or in closing the gap between this and other theories of development.

The concept of competence subsumes the whole realm of learned behavior whereby the child comes to deal effectively with his environment. It includes manipulation, locomotion, language, the building of cognitive maps and skilled actions, and the growth of effective behavior in relation to other people. These acquisitions are made by young animals and children partly through exploratory and manipulative play when drives such as hunger and sex are in abeyance. The directed persistence of such behavior warrants the assumption of a motivation independent of drives, here called effectance motivation, which has its immediate satisfaction in a feeling of efficacy and its adaptive significance in the growth of competence. Effectance motivation can be likened to independent ego energies in the psychoanalytic scheme. The child's actual competence and his sense of competence are built up from his history of efficacies and inefficacies, and sense of competence is held to be a crucial element in any psychology of the ego.

It is proposed that libidinal and interpersonal models for critical points in development be supplemented by a competence model. For the oral stage this means taking serious account of the growth of manipulative prowess and experimentation as seen both in the child's many hours of play and in his zeal for self-help in feeding. For the anal stage it means attributing importance to negativism in the sphere of giving and receiving commands, an early crisis in social competence, and to the enormous growth of motility with its constant influence upon self-esteem. Neither development is adequately implied in the anal-erotic model. For the phallic stage it means detecting the consequences of growth in locomotion, linguistic understanding, and imagination; it also means noticing the child's waxing ability to comprehend and try out various social roles, in many of which he receives encouragement. The Oedipus model, with its foreordained inexplicable defeat, cannot be considered typical for the period. During latency the chief developments are in the sphere of competence; this is clear in Erikson's account of the sense of industry and Sullivan's of competition and compromise. For the final genital stage the competence model invites us to take seriously the adolescent's continuing concern with sense of industry and with social competence, problems that confront him with new crises in their own right. The heterosexual relation does not provide an adequate model for all the serious concerns of this stage of life, nor can they be fully conceptualized in terms of instinctual drive and defense.

In short, the competence model is held to supplement in significant ways the models of development derived from psychoanalysis. By directing attention to action and its consequences and to the vicissitudes of the sense of competence, it should help to speed the construction of an adequate ego psychology.

REFERENCES

Abraham, K. *Selected Papers on Psychoanalysis.* London: Hogarth, 1927.
Berlyne, D. E. "Novelty and Curiosity as Determinants of Exploratory Behavior." *Brit. J. Psychol.*, 1950, 41:68–80.
Bernfeld, S. "Types of Adolescence." *Psychoanal. Quart.*, 1938, 7:243–253.
Butler, R. A. "Exploratory and Related Behavior: A New Trend in Animal Research." *J. indiv. Psychol.*, 1958, 14:111–120.
Bornstein, B. "On Latency." *Psychoanal. Stud. Child*, 1951, 6:279–285.

Bühler, C. "The Social Behavior of the Child." In C. Murchison, ed., *A Handbook of Child Psychology*. Worcester, Mass.: Clark Univer. Press, 1931, 392–431.

Deutsch, Helene. *The Psychology of Women*, Vol. I. New York: Grune & Stratton, 1944.

Erikson, E. H. *Childhood and Society*. New York: Norton, 1950.

————. "Identity and the Life Cycle: Selected Papers." *Psychol. Issues*, 1959, Monograph 1.

Fenichel, O. *The Psychoanalytic Theory of Neurosis*. New York: Norton, 1945.

Freud, Anna. *The Ego and the Mechanisms of Defence*. (Trans. by C. Baines.) London: Hogarth, 1937.

————. "Adolescence." *Psychoanal. Stud. Child*, 1958, 13:255–278.

————, & Burlingham, D. T. *Infants without Families*. New York: International Univer. Press, 1944.

Freud, S. *Three Contributions to the Theory of Sex* (1905). (Trans. by A. A. Brill.) New York and Washington: Nerv. and Ment. Dis. Pub. Co., 1930.

————. "Character and Anal Erotism" (1908). *Collected Papers*. (Trans. under supervision of J. Riviere.) New York: Basic Books, 1959. Vol. II, 45–50.

————. "The Predisposition to Obsessional Neurosis" (1913). *Collected Papers*. (Trans. under supervision of J. Riviere.) New York: Basic Books, 1959. Vol. II, 122–131.

————. "The Infantile Genital Organization of the Libido" (1923). *Collected Papers*. (Trans. under supervision of J. Riviere.) New York: Basic Books. Vol. II, 244–249.

Fromm, E. "Individual and Social Origins of Neurosis." *Amer. Sociol. Rev.*, 1944, 9:380–384.

————. *Man for Himself*. New York: Rinehart, 1947.

————. *The Sane Society*. New York: Rinehart, 1955.

Gesell, A., and Ilg, Frances L. *Infant and Child in the Culture of Today*. New York: Harper, 1943.

————. *The Child from Five to Ten*. New York: Harper, 1946.

Goldstein, K. *Human Nature in the Light of Psychopathology*. Cambridge, Mass.: Harvard Univer. Press, 1940.

Harlow, H. F. "Mice, Monkeys, Men, and Motives." *Psychol. Rev.*, 1953, 60:23–32.

Hartmann, H. *Ego Psychology and the Problem of Adaptation*. (Trans. by D. Rapaport.) New York: International Univer. Press, 1958.

————, Kris, E., & Loewenstein, R. "Notes on the Theory of Aggression." *Psychoanal. Stud. Child*, 1949, 3/4:9–36.

Hendrick, I. "Instinct and the Ego during Infancy." *Psychoanal. Quart.*, 1942, 11:33–58.

————. "Work and the Pleasure Principle." *Psychoanal. Quart.*, 1943, 12:311–329.

Hetzer, H. "Entwicklungsbedingte Erziehungsschwierigkeiten." *Ztschr. pädagog. Psychol.*, 1929, 30:77–85.

Horney, Karen. *New Ways in Psychoanalysis*. New York: Norton, 1939.

Isaacs, Susan. *Social Development in Young Children*. London: Routledge, 1933.

Kanner, L. "The Conception of Wholes and Parts in Early Infantile Autism." *Amer. J. Psychiat.*, 1951, 108:23–26.

Kris, E. *Psychoanalytic Explorations in Art*. New York: International Univer. Press, 1952.

Lerner, E. "The Problem of Perspective in Moral Reasoning." *Amer. J. Sociol.*, 1937, 43:249–269.

Levy, D. M. "Oppositional Syndromes and Oppositional Behavior." In P. H. Hoch

& J. Zubin eds., *Psychopathology of Childhood*. New York: Grune & Stratton, 1955, 204–226.

Marcuse, H. *Eros and Civilization*. Boston: Beacon Press, 1955.

Mittelmann, B. "Motility in Infants, Children, and Adults." *Psychoanal. Stud. Child*, 1954, 9:142–177.

Montgomery, K. C. "The Role of the Exploratory Drive in Learning." *J. comp. physiol. Psychol.*, 1954, 47:60–64.

Murray, H. A. *Explorations in Personality*. New York: Oxford Univer. Press, 1938.

Myers, A. K., and Miller, N. E. "Failure to Find a Learned Drive Based on Hunger; Evidence for Learning Motivated by 'Exploration.'" *J. comp. physiol. Psychol.*, 1954, 47:428–436.

Olds, J., & Milner, P. "Positive Reinforcement Produced by Electrical Stimulation of Septal Area and Other Regions of Rat Brain." *J. comp. physiol. Psychol.*, 1954, 47:419–427.

Piaget, J. *The Moral Judgment of the Child*. (Trans. by M. Gabain.) New York: Harcourt, Brace, 1932.

———. *The Origins of Intelligence in Children*. (Trans. by M. Cook.) New York: International Univer. Press, 1952.

Piers, G., & Singer, M. B. *Shame and Guilt*. Springfield, Ill.: Charles C. Thomas, 1953.

Schilder, P. *Goals and Desires of Men*. New York: Columbia Univer. Press, 1942.

Sheffield, F. D., and Roby, T. B. "Reward Value of a Non-Nutritive Sweet Taste." *J. comp. physiol. Psychol.*, 1950, 43:471–481.

———, ———, & Campbell, B. A. "Drive Reduction vs. Consummatory Behavior as Determinants of Reinforcement." *J. comp. physiol. Psychol.*, 1954, 47:349–354.

———, Wulff, J. J., & Backer, R. "Reward Value of Copulation without Sex Drive Reduction." *J. comp. physiol. Psychol.*, 1951, 44:3–8.

Silverberg, W. V. *Childhood Experience and Personal Destiny*. New York: Springer, 1952.

Spitz, R. A. "Anaclitic Depression." *Psychoanal. Stud. Child*, 1946, 2:313–342.

Stern, W. *Psychology of Early Childhood*. (Trans. by A. Barwell.) (2nd ed.) New York: Holt, 1930.

Sullivan, H. S. *The Interpersonal Theory of Psychiatry*. New York: Norton, 1953.

Sully, J. *Studies of Childhood*. London & New York: Appleton, 1896.

Thompson, C. *Psychoanalysis: Evolution and Development*. New York: Hermitage, 1950.

GORDON W. ALLPORT

The Concept of Self

IS THE CONCEPT OF SELF NECESSARY?

We come now to a question that is pivotal for the psychology of growth: Is the concept of *self* necessary? While there is a vast literature in philosophy devoted to this issue from the points of view of ontology, epistemology, and axiology, let us for the time being by-pass such discussions. For it is entirely conceivable that a concept useful to philosophy or theology may turn out to be merely an impediment in the path of psychological progress.

Since the time of Wundt, the central objection of psychology to *self*, and also to *soul*, has been that the concept seems question-begging. It is temptingly easy to assign functions that are not fully understood to a mysterious central agency, and then to declare that "it" performs in such a way as to unify the personality and maintain its integrity. Wundt, aware of this peril, declared boldly for "a psychology without a soul." It was not that he necessarily denied philosophical or theological postulates, but that he felt psychology as science would be handicapped by the *petitio principii* implied in the concept. For half a century few psychologists other than Thomists have resisted Wundt's reasoning or his example.[1] Indeed we may say that for two generations psychologists have tried every conceivable way of accounting for the integration, organization, and striving of the human person without having recourse to the postulate of a self.

In very recent years the tide has turned. Perhaps without being fully aware of the historical situation, many psychologists have commenced to embrace what two decades ago would have been considered a heresy. They have reintroduced self and ego unashamedly and, as if to make up for lost time, have employed ancillary concepts such as *self-image, self-actualization, self-affirmation, phenomenal ego, ego-involvement, ego-striving,* and many other hy-

From G. W. Allport, *Becoming.* New Haven: Yale University Press, 1955, pp. 36–56. Copyright © 1955 by Yale University Press.
[1] Until about 1890 certain American writers, including Dewey, Royce, James, continued to regard self as a necessary concept. They felt that the analytical concepts of the New Psychology lost the manifest unity of mental functioning. But for the ensuing fifty years very few American psychologists made use of it, Mary Whiton Calkins being a distinguished exception; and none employed "soul." See G. W. Allport, "The Ego in Contemporary Psychology," *Psychological Review, 50* (1943):451–78; reprinted in *The Nature of Personality: Selected Papers* (Cambridge, Addison-Wesley, 1959).

phenated elaborations which to experimental positivism still have a slight
flavor of scientific obscenity.

We should note in passing that Freud played a leading, if unintentional
role, in preserving the concept of ego from total obliteration throughout two
generations of strenuous positivism. His own use of the term, to be sure,
shifted. At first he spoke of assertive and aggressive ego-instincts (in a Nietzs-
chean sense); later for Freud the ego became a rational, though passive,
agency, whose duty it was to reconcile as best it could through planning or
defense the conflicting pressures of the instincts, of conscience, and of the
outer environment. With the core concept thus preserved, even with strin-
gently limited meanings, it was easier for dynamically inclined psychologists,
including the neo-Freudians, to enlarge the properties of the ego, making it
a far more active and important agent than it was in the hands of Freud.

There still remains, however, the danger that Wundt wished to avoid,
namely that the ego may be regarded as a *deus ex machina*, invoked to reas-
semble the dismembered parts of the throbbing psychic machine after positivism has failed to do so. The situation today seems to be that many psychologists who first fit personality to an external set of co-ordinates are dissatisfied
with the result. They therefore re-invent the ego because they find no coherence among the measures yielded by positivistic analysis. But unfortunately
positivism and ego-theory do not go well together. Bergson has criticized the
use of "ego" in this face-saving way by likening the process to the dilemma
of an artist. An artist, he says, may wish to represent Paris — just as a psychologist may wish to represent personality. But all he can do with the limitations
of his medium is to draw this and then that angle of the whole. To each
sketch he applies the label "Paris," hoping somehow that the sections he has
ablated will magically reconstitute the whole.[2] Similarly in psychology we have
a state of affairs where empiricists, finding that they have gone as far as
possible with analytic tools and being dissatisfied with the product, resort
as did their predecessors to some concept of self in order to represent, however
inadequately, the coherence, unity, and purposiveness they know they have
lost in their fragmentary representations.

I greatly fear that the lazy tendency to employ self or ego as a factotum
to repair the ravages of positivism may do more harm than good. It is, of
course, significant that so many contemporary psychologists feel forced to
take this step, even though for the most part their work represents no theoretical gain over nineteenth-century usage. Positivism will continue to resent the
intrusion, and will, with some justification, accuse today's resurgent self-
psychologists of obscurantism.

The problem then becomes how to approach the phenomena that have

[2] H. Bergson, *Introduction to Metaphysics* (New York: G. Putnam's Sons, 1912),
p. 30.

led to a revival of the self-concept in a manner that will advance rather than retard scientific progress.

A possible clue to the solution, so far as psychology is concerned, lies in a statement made by Alfred Adler. "What is frequently labeled 'the ego,' " he writes, "is nothing more than the style of the individual."[3] Life-style to Adler had a deep and important meaning. He is saying that if psychology could give us a full and complete account of life-style it would automatically include all phenomena now referred somewhat vaguely to a self or an ego. In other words, a wholly adequate psychology of growth would discover all of the activities and all of the interrelations in life, which are now either neglected or consigned to an ego that looks suspiciously like a homunculus.

The first thing an adequate psychology of growth should do is to draw a distinction between what are matters of *importance* to the individual and what are, as Whitehead would say, merely matters of *fact* to him; that is, between what he feels to be vital and central in becoming and what belongs to the periphery of his being.

Many facets of our life-style are not ordinarily felt to have strong personal relevance. Each of us, for example, has innumerable tribal habits that mark our life-style but are nothing more than opportunistic modes of adjusting. The same holds true for many of our physiological habits. We keep to the right in traffic, obey the rules of etiquette, and make countless unconscious or semiconscious adjustments, all of which characterize our life-style but are not *propriate*, i.e., not really central to our sense of existence. Consider, for example, the English language habits that envelop our thinking and communication. Nothing could be of more pervasive influence in our lives than the store of concepts available to us in our ancestral tongue and the frames of discourse under which our social contacts proceed. And yet the use of English is ordinarily felt to be quite peripheral to the core of our existence. It would not be so if some foreign invader should forbid us to use our native language. At such a time our vocabulary and accent and our freedom to employ them would become very precious and involved with our sense of self. So it is with the myriad of social and physiological habits we have developed that are never, unless interfered with, regarded as essential to our existence as a separate being.

Personality includes these habits and skills, frames of reference, matters of fact and cultural values, that seldom or never seem warm and important. But personality includes what is warm and important also — all the regions of our life that we regard as peculiarly ours, and which for the time being I suggest we call the *proprium*. The proprium includes all aspects of personality that make for inward unity.

[3] A. Adler, "The Fundamental Views of Individual Psychology," *International Journal of Individual Psychology*, I (1935): 5–8.

Psychologists who allow for the proprium use both the term "self" and "ego" — often interchangeably; and both terms are defined with varying degrees of narrowness or of comprehensiveness. Whatever name we use for it, this sense of what is "peculiarly ours" merits close scrutiny. The principal functions and properties of the proprium need to be distinguished.

To this end William James over sixty years ago proposed a simple taxonomic scheme.[4] There are, he maintained, two possible orders of self: an empirical self (the Me) and a knowing self (the I). Three subsidiary types comprise the empirical Me: the material self, the social self, and the spiritual self. Within this simple framework he fits his famous and subtle description of the various states of mind that are "peculiarly ours." His scheme, however, viewed in the perspective of modern psychoanalytic and experimental research, seems scarcely adequate. In particular it lacks the full psychodynamic flavor of modern thinking. With some trepidation, therefore, I offer what I hope is an improved outline for analyzing the propriate aspects of personality. Later we shall return to the question, Is the concept of *self* necessary?

THE PROPRIUM

Bodily Sense

The first aspect we encounter is the bodily *me*. It seems to be composed of streams of sensations that arise within the organism — from viscera, muscles, tendons, joints, vestibular canals, and other regions of the body. The technical name for the bodily sense is *coenesthesis*. Usually this sensory stream is experienced dimly; often we are totally unaware of it. At times, however, it is well configurated in consciousness in the exhilaration that accompanies physical exercise, or in moments of sensory delight or pain. The infant, apparently, does not know that such experiences are "his." But they surely form a necessary foundation for his emerging sense of self. The baby who at first cries from unlocalized discomfort will, in the course of growth, show progressive ability to identify the distress as his own.

The bodily sense remains a lifelong anchor for our self-awareness, though it never alone accounts for the entire sense of self, probably not even in the young child who has his memories, social cues, and strivings to help in the definition. Psychologists have paid a great deal of attention, however, to this particular component of self-awareness, rather more than to other equally important ingredients. One special line of investigation has been surprisingly popular: the attempt to locate self in relation to specific bodily sensations. When asked, some people will say that they *feel* the self in their right hands, or in the viscera. Most, however, seem to agree with Claparède that a center midway between the eyes, slightly behind them within the head, is the focus. It is from this cyclopean eye that we estimate what lies before and behind

---

[4] *Principles of Psychology* (New York: Henry Holt, 1890), *I*, ch. 10.

ourselves, to the right or left, and above and below. Here phenomenologically speaking, is the locus of the ego.[5] Interesting as this type of work may be, it represents little more than the discovery that various sensory elements in the coenesthetic stream or various inferences drawn from sensory experience may for certain people at certain times be especially prominent.

How very intimate (propriate) the bodily sense is can be seen by performing a little experiment in your imagination. Think first of swallowing the saliva in your mouth, or do so. Then imagine expectorating it into a tumbler and drinking it! What seemed natural and "mine" suddenly becomes disgusting and alien. Or picture yourself sucking blood from a prick in your finger; then imagine sucking blood from a bandage around your finger! What I perceive as belonging intimately to my body is warm and welcome; what I perceive as separate from my body becomes, in the twinkling of an eye, cold and foreign.

Certainly organic sensations, their localization and recognition, composing as they do the bodily *me*, are a core of becoming. But it would be a serious mistake to think, as some writers do, that they alone account for our sense of what is "peculiarly ours."

Self-identity

Today I remember some of my thoughts of yesterday; and tomorrow I shall remember some of my thoughts of both yesterday and today; and I am subjectively certain that they are the thoughts of the same person. In this situation, no doubt, the organic continuity of the neuromuscular system is the leading factor. Yet the process involves more than reminiscence made possible by our retentive nerves. The young infant has retentive capacity during the first months of life but in all probability no sense of self-identity. This sense seems to grow gradually, partly as a result of being clothed and named, and otherwise marked off from the surrounding environment. Social interaction is an important factor. It is the actions of the other to which he differentially adjusts that force upon a child the realization that he is not the other, but a being in his own right. The difficulty of developing self-identity in childhood is shown by the ease with which a child depersonalizes himself in play and in speech.[6] Until the age of four or five we have good reason to believe that as perceived by the child personal identity is unstable. Beginning at about

[5] E. Claparède, "Note sur la localisation du mor," *Archives de psychologie, 19* (1924):172–82.

Another school of thought has placed considerable stress upon the total body-image, Its variations are said to mark changes in the course of development. Schilder, for example, points out that in experience of hate the body-image itself contracts; in experience of love it expands, and even seems phenomenally to include other beings. See P. Schilder, *The Image and Appearance of the Human Body,* Psyche Monograph (London, K. Paul, Trench, Trubner Co., 1935), p. 353.

[6] Cf. G. W. Allport, *Personality. A Psychological Interpretation* (New York: Henry Holt, 1937), pp. 159–65.

this age, however, it becomes the surest attest a human being has of his own existence.

Ego-enhancement

We come now to the most notorious property of the proprium, to its unabashed self-seeking.[7] Scores of writers have featured this clamorous trait in human personality. It is tied to the need for survival, for it is easy to see that we are endowed by nature with the impulses of self-assertion and with the emotions of self-satisfaction and pride. Our language is laden with evidence. The commonest compound of self is *selfish*, and of ego *egoism*. Pride, humiliation, self-esteem, narcissism are such prominent factors that when we speak of ego or self we often have in mind only this aspect of personality. And yet, self-love may be prominent in our natures without necessarily being sovereign. The proprium, as we shall see, has other facets and functions.

Ego-extension

The three facets we have discussed — coenesthesis, self-identiy, ego-enhancement — are relatively early developments in personality, characterizing the whole of the child's proprium. Their solicitations have a heavily biological quality and seem to be contained within the organism itself. But soon the process of learning brings with it a high regard for possessions, for loved objects, and later, for ideal causes and loyalties. We are speaking here of whatever objects a person calls "mine." They must at the same time be objects of *importance*, for sometimes our sense of "having" has no affective tone and hence no place in the proprium. A child, however, who identifies with his parent is definitely extending his sense of self, as he does likewise through his love for pets, dolls, or other possessions, animate or inanimate.

As we grow older we identify with groups, neighborhood, and nation as well as with possessions, clothes, home. They become matters of importance to us in a sense that other people's families, nations, or possessions are not. Later in life the process of extension may go to great lengths, through the development of loyalties and of interests focused on abstractions and on moral and religious values. Indeed, a mark of maturity seems to be the range and extent of one's feeling of self-involvement in abstract ideals.

Rational agent

The ego, according to Freud, has the task of keeping the organism as a whole in touch with reality, of intermediating between unconscious impulses and the outer world. Often the rational ego can do little else than invent and

---

[7] The term "proprium" was a favorite of Emanuel Swedenborg. He used it, however, in the narrow sense of selfishness and pride, a meaning that corresponds here fairly closely to "ego-enhancement." See his *Proprium*, with an introduction by John Bigelow (New York, New Church Board of Publication, 1907). I am grateful to Professor Howard D. Spoerl for his clarification of this matter.

employ defenses to forestall or diminish anxiety. These protective devices shape the development of personality to an extent unrealized sixty years ago. It is thanks to Freud that we understand the strategies of denial, repression, displacement, reaction formation, rationalization, and the like better than did our ancestors.

We have become so convinced of the validity of these defense mechanisms, and so impressed with their frequency of operation, that we are inclined to forget that the rational functioning of the proprium is capable also of yielding true solutions, appropriate adjustments, accurate planning, and a relatively faultless solving of the equations of life.

Many philosophers, dating as far back as Boethius in the sixth century, have seen the rational nature of personality as its most distinctive property. (*Persona est substantia individua rationalis naturae.*) It may seem odd to credit Freud, the supreme irrationalist of our age, with helping the Thomists preserve for psychology the emphasis upon the ego as the rational agent in personality, but such is the case. For whether the ego reasons or merely rationalizes, it has the property of synthesizing inner needs and outer reality. Freud and the Thomists have not let us forget this fact, and have thus made it easier for modern cognitive theories to deal with this central function of the proprium.

Self-image

A propriate function of special interest today is the self-image, or as some writers call it, the phenomenal self. Present-day therapy is chiefly devoted to leading the patient to examine, correct, or expand this self-image. The image has two aspects: the way the patient regards his present abilities, status, and roles; and what he would like to become, his *aspirations* for himself. The latter aspect, which Karen Horney calls the "idealized self-image,"[8] is of especial importance in therapy. On the one hand it may be compulsive, compensatory, and unrealistic, blinding its possessor to his true situation in life. On the other hand, it may be an insightful cognitive map, closely geared to reality and defining a wholesome ambition. The ideal self-image is the imaginative aspect of the proprium, and whether accurate or distorted, attainable or unattainable, it plots a course by which much propriate movement is guided and therapeutic progress achieved.

There are, of course, many forms of becoming that require no self-image, including automatic cultural learning and our whole repertoire of opportunistic adjustments to our environment. Yet there is also much growth that takes place only with the aid of, and because of, a self-image. This image helps us bring our view of the present into line with our view of the future. Fortu-

[8] Karen Horney, *Neurosis and Human Growth: The Struggle toward Self-realization* (New York: Norton, 1950).

nately the dynamic importance of the self-image is more widely recognized in psychology today than formerly.

Propriate Striving

We come now to the nature of motivation. Unfortunately we often fail to distinguish between propriate and peripheral motives. The reason is that at the rudimentary levels of becoming, which up to now have been the chief levels investigated, it *is* the impulses and drives, the immediate satisfaction and tension reduction, that are the determinants of conduct. Hence a psychology of opportunistic adjustment seems basic and adequate, especially to psychologists accustomed to working with animals. At low levels of behavior the familiar formula of drives and their conditioning appears to suffice. But as soon as the personality enters the stage of ego-extension, and develops a self-image with visions of self-perfection, we are, I think, forced to postulate motives of a different order, motives that reflect propriate striving. Within experimental psychology itself there is now plenty of evidence that conduct that is "ego involved" (propriate) differs markedly from behavior that is not.[9]

Many psychologists disregard this evidence. They wish to maintain a single theory of motivation consistent with their presuppositions. Their preferred formula is in terms of drive and conditioned drive. Drive is viewed as a peripherally instigated activity. The resultant response is simply reactive, persisting only until the instigator is removed and the tension, created by the drive, lessened. Seeking always a parsimony of assumptions, this view therefore holds that motivation entails one and only one inherent property of the organism: a disposition to act, by instinct or by learning, in such a way that the organism will as efficiently as possible reduce the discomfort of tension. Motivation is regarded as a state of tenseness that leads us to seek equilibrium, rest, adjustment, satisfaction, or homeostasis. From this point of view personality is nothing more than our habitual modes of reducing tension. This formulation, of course, is wholly consistent with empiricism's initial presupposition that man is by nature a passive being, capable only of receiving impressions from, and responding to, external goads.

The contrary view holds that this formula, while applicable to segmental and opportunistic adjustments, falls short of representing the nature of propriate striving. It points out that the characteristic feature of such striving is its resistance to equilibrium: tension is maintained rather than reduced.

In his autobiography Roald Amundsen tells how from the age of fifteen he had one dominant passion — to become a polar explorer. The obstacles seemed insurmountable, and all through his life the temptations to reduce the tensions engendered were great. But the propriate striving persisted. While he welcomed each success, it acted to raise his level of aspiration, to

---

[9] Cf. G. W. Allport, "The Ego in Contemporary Psychology," *Psychological Review*, 50 (1943):451–78.

maintain an over-all commitment. Having sailed the Northwest Passage, he embarked upon the painful project that led to the discovery of the South Pole. Having discovered the South Pole, he planned for years, against extreme discouragement, to fly over the North Pole, a task he finally accomplished. But his commitment never wavered until at the end he lost his life in attempting to rescue a less gifted explorer, Nobile, from death in the Arctic. Not only did he maintain one style of life, without ceasing, but this central commitment enabled him to withstand the temptation to reduce the segmental tensions continually engendered by fatigue, hunger, ridicule, and danger.[10]

Here we see the issue squarely. A psychology that regards motivation exclusively in terms of drives and conditioned drives is likely to stammer and grow vague when confronted by those aspects of personality — of every personality — that resemble Amundsen's propriate striving. While most of us are less distinguished than he in our achievements, we too have insatiable interests. Only in a very superficial way can these interests be dealt with in terms of tension reduction. Many writers past and present have recognized this fact and have postulated some principles of an exactly opposite order. One thinks in this connection of Spinoza's concept of conatus, or the tendency of an individual to persist, against obstacles, in his own style of being. One thinks of Goldstein's doctrine of *self-actualization,* used also by Maslow and others, or McDougall's *self-regarding* sentiment. And one thinks too of those modern Freudians who feel the need for endowing the ego not only with a rational and rationalizing ability but with a tendency to maintain its own system of productive interests, in spite of the passing solicitations of impulse and environmental instigation. Indeed the fortified ego, as described by neo-Freudians, is able to act contrary to the usual course of opportunistic, tension-reducing, adaptation.

Propriate striving distinguishes itself from other forms of motivation in that, however beset by conflicts, it makes for unification of personality. There is evidence that the lives of mental patients are marked by the proliferation of unrelated subsystems, and by the loss of more homogeneous systems of motivation.[11] When the individual is dominated by segmental drives, by compulsions, or by the winds of circumstance, he has lost the integrity that comes only from maintaining major directions of striving. The possession of long-range goals, regarded as central to one's personal existence, distinguishes the human being from the animal, the adult from the child, and in many cases the healthy personality from the sick.

Striving, it is apparent, always has a future reference. As a matter of fact, a great many states of mind are adequately described only in terms of their

[10] Roald Amundsen, *My Life as an Explorer* (Garden City, N.Y.: Doubleday, Doran, 1928).

[11] Cf. L. McQuitty, "A Measure of Personality Integration in Relation to the Concept of the Self," *Journal of Personality,* 18 (1950):461–82.

futurity. Along with *striving*, we may mention *interest, tendency, disposition, expectation, planning, problem solving*, and *intention*. While not all future-directedness is phenomenally propriate, it all requires a type of psychology that transcends the prevalent tendency to explain mental states exclusively in terms of past occurrences. People, it seems, are busy leading their lives into the future, whereas psychology, for the most part, is busy tracing them into the past.

The Knower

Now that we have isolated these various propriate functions — all of which we regard as peculiarly ours — the question arises whether we are yet at an end. Do we not have in addition a cognizing self — a knower, that transcends all other functions of the proprium and holds them in view? In a famous passage, William James wrestles with this question, and concludes that we have not. There is, he thinks, no such thing as a substantive self distinguishable from the sum total, or stream, of experiences. Each moment of consciousness, he says, appropriates each previous moment, and the knower is thus somehow embedded in what is known. "The thoughts themselves are the thinker."[12]

Opponents of James argue that no mere series of experiences can possibly turn themselves into an awareness of that series as a unit. Nor can "passing thoughts" possibly regard themselves as important or interesting. To whom is the series important or interesting if not to *me?* I am the ultimate monitor. The self as *knower* emerges as a final and inescapable postulate.

It is interesting to ask why James balked at admitting a knowing self after he had so lavishly admitted to psychology with his full approval material, social, and spiritual selves. The reason may well have been (and the reason would be valid today) that one who laboriously strives to depict the nature of propriate functions on an empirical level, hoping thereby to enrich the science of psychology with a discriminating analysis of self, is not anxious to risk a return to the homunculus theory by introducing a synthesizer, or a self of selves.

To be sure, the danger that abuse might follow the admission of a substantive knower into the science of psychology is no reason to avoid this step if it is logically required. Some philosophers, including Kant, insist that the pure or transcendental ego is separable from the empirical ego (i.e., from any of the propriate states thus far mentioned).[13] Those who hold that the know-

---

[12] *Principles of Psychology, I*, ch. 10.

[13] Kant's position on this matter is summarized in the following pronouncement: "One may therefore say of the thinking I (the soul), which represents itself as substance, simple, numerically identical in all time, and as the correlative of all existence, from which in fact all other existence must be concluded, that it *does not know itself through the categories*, but knows the *categories* only, and through them all objects, in the absolute unity of apperception, *that is through itself.*" *Critique of Pure Reason*, trans. by M. Muller (London, Macmillan, 1881), p. 347.

ing itself is not (as James argued) merely an aspect of the self as known, but is "pure" and "transcendental," argue, as Kant does, that the texture of knowledge is quite different in the two cases. Our cognition of our knowing self is always indirect, of the order of a presupposition. On the other hand, all features of the *empirical self* are known directly, through acquaintance, as any object is known which falls into time and space categories.[14]

While their metaphysical positions are directly opposed, both Kant and James agree with their illustrious predecessor, Descartes, that the knowing function is a vital attribute of the self however defined. For our present purpose this is the point to bear in mind.

We not only know *things*, but we know (i.e., are acquainted with) the empirical features of our own proprium. It is I who have bodily sensations, I who recognize my self-identity from day to day; I who note and reflect upon my self-assertion, self-extension, my own rationalizations, as well as upon my interests and strivings. When I thus think about my own propriate functions I am likely to perceive their essential togetherness, and feel them intimately bound in some way to the knowing function itself.

Since such knowing is, beyond any shadow of doubt, a state that is peculiarly ours, we admit it as the eighth clear function of the proprium. (In other words, as an eighth valid meaning of "self" or "ego.") But it is surely one of nature's perversities that so central a function should be so little understood by science, and should remain a perpetual bone of contention among philosophers. Many, like Kant, set this function (the "pure ego") aside as something qualitatively apart from other propriate functions (the latter being assigned to the "empirical me"). Others, like James, say that the ego *qua* knower is somehow contained within the ego *qua* known. Still others, personalistically inclined, find it necessary to postulate a single self as knower, thinker, feeler, and doer — all in one blended unit of a sort that guarantees the continuance of all becoming.[15]

We return now to our unanswered question: Is the concept of self necessary in the psychology of personality? Our answer cannot be categorical since all depends upon the particular usage of "self" that is proposed. Certainly all legitimate phenomena that have been, and can be ascribed, to the self or ego must be admitted as data indispensable to a psychology of personal becoming. All eight functions of the "proprium" (our temporary neutral term for central interlocking operations of personality) must be admitted and included. In particular the unifying act of perceiving and knowing (of comprehending propriate states as belonging together and belonging to me) must be fully admitted.

At the same time, the danger we have several times warned against is very

[14] For a fuller discussion of this matter see F. R. Tennant, *Philosophical Theology* (Cambridge: University Press, 1928), I, ch. 5.

[15] P. A. Bertocci, "The Psychological Self, the Ego, and Personality," *Psychological Review*, 52 (1945):91–9.

real: that a homunculus may creep into our discussions of personality, and be expected to solve all our problems without in reality solving any. Thus, if we ask "What determines our moral conduct?" the answer may be "The self does it." Or, if we pose the problem of choice, we say "The self chooses." Such question-begging would immeasurably weaken the scientific study of personality by providing an illegitimate regressus. There are, to be sure, ultimate problems of philosophy and of theology that psychology cannot even attempt to solve, and for the solution of such problems "self" in some restricted and technical meaning may be a necessity.

But so far as psychology is concerned our position, in brief, is this: all psychological functions commonly ascribed to a self or ego must be admitted as data in the scientific study of personality. These functions are not, however, coextensive with personality as a whole. They are rather the special aspects of personality that have to do with warmth, with unity, with a sense of personal importance. In this exposition I have called them "propriate" functions. If the reader prefers, he may call them self-functions, and in this sense self may be said to be a necessary psychological concept. What is unnecessary and inadmissible is a self (or soul) that is said to perform acts, to solve problems, to steer conduct, in a transpsychological manner, inaccessible to psychological analysis.

Once again we refer to Adler's contention that an adequate psychology of life-style would in effect dispense with the need for a separate psychology of the ego. I believe Adler's position, though unelaborated, is essentially the same as the one here advocated. An adequate psychology would in effect *be* a psychology of the ego. It would deal fully and fairly with propriate functions. Indeed, everyone would assume that psychology was talking about self-functions, unless it was expressly stated that peripheral, opportunistic, or actuarial events were under discussion. But as matters stand today, with so much of psychology preoccupied (as was Hume) with bits and pieces of experience, or else with generalized mathematical equations, it becomes necessary for the few psychologists who are concerned with propriate functions to specify in their discourse that they are dealing with them. If the horizons of psychology were more spacious than they are I venture to suggest that theories of personality would not need the concept of self or of ego except in certain compound forms, such as *self-knowledge, self-image, ego-enhancement, ego-extension.*

GORDON W. ALLPORT

Personal Dispositions

... [Some trait-names] are derived from individual historical or fictional characters: *quixotic, narcistic* (originally Narcissusistic, then narcissistic, now narcistic), *chauvinistic, sadistic, puckish,* a *quisling.* Some are spelled with capital letters, *Boswellian, Lesbian, Chesterfieldian, Rabelaisian, Pickwickian, Emersonian, Falstaffian, Homeric, Faustian.* We say a person is *Christlike,* a *Don Juan,* a *Beau Brummell,* a *Xantippe.* In all these cases, and many more like them, we note that some particular outstanding characteristic of a single person gave us a new label to apply occasionally (not often) to other people.

In such instances we are not dealing with a common trait. It would be absurd to try to compare all people — or any large number of them — on a scale designed to measure the peculiar *fastidious exhibitionism* of a Beau Brummell or the *sexual cruelty* of a Marquis de Sade. Yet the very fact that we now name the characteristic shows that we have abstracted it from the individual life with the intention of applying it to other lives to which it may fit. Words are general. Even if we say "this boy," we are using two abstract words to point to a particular. Only a proper name, such as Franklin Roosevelt, comes near to designating one unique personal event in nature.

The Uniqueness of
Personal Dispositions

We come again to the proposition that seems so shocking to science. Franklin Roosevelt was a unique historical event in nature, and the fabulously complex organization of his mental processes and nervous system was likewise unique. It could not be otherwise considering the individuality of his inheritance, the individuality of his life experience. ... Even the subsystems of his personality were ultimately unique. When confronted with this unassailable logic, one outraged psychologist exclaimed, "I think it is nonsense to say that no two men ever have the same trait. I mean, of course it is true, but it is one of those truths that can't be accepted." We reply: Unfortunately, this is one truth that the study of personality *must* accept, however great the difficulties it creates.

From Chapter 15, from *Pattern and Growth in Personality* by Gordon W. Allport. Copyright 1937, ©1961 by Holt, Rinehart and Winston, Inc. Copyright ©1965 by Gordon W. Allport. Reprinted by permission of Holt, Rinehart and Winston, Inc.

In order to keep the problem distinct from that of common traits, we shall adopt a different terminology. We could with propriety speak of *individual* (or of *personal*) traits as distinct from *common* traits, for there is similarity between the two conceptions (both, for example, refer to a complex level of organization). Yet for purposes of clarity we shall designate the individual unit not as a trait, but as a *personal disposition* (and shall occasionally use the abbreviation *p.d.*).[1]

Much that we have said concerning common traits applies also to personal dispositions. Both are broad (generalized) determining tendencies; both differ in the same way from habits, attitudes, and types; both refer to the level of analysis most suitable to the study of personality; the existence of both is inferred by the occurrence of activities having "functional equivalence."

But there are differences. It makes no sense to speak of the "normal distribution" of p.d.'s, since each is unique to one person. Trait-names fit common traits better than they fit p.d.'s. (Generally several words are needed to designate a disposition, as when we say, "Little Susan has a peculiar anxious helpfulness all her own"; or, "He will do anything for you if it doesn't cost him any effort.")

Our contention is that, if correctly diagnosed, p.d.'s reflect the personality structure accurately, whereas common traits are categories into which the individual is forced.

For example, by common trait methods, we find that Peter stands high in *esthetic interest* and *anxiety,* but low in *leadership* and *need-achievement.* The truth is that all these common traits have a special coloring in his life, and — still more important — they interact with one another. Thus it might

---

[1] Another possible label for the unit I have in mind is *morphogenic trait.* This term properly suggests a unit that carries the "form" of the personality structure, and helps to maintain this form over considerable periods of time.

Morphogenesis is a branch of biology that tries to account for the patterned properties of a whole organism. It is a relatively neglected area of biology, where major effort is expended on finding the ultimate elements that are common to all life. Molecular biology has demonstrated that these ultimate units, in terms of nucleic acids, proteins, genetic principles, are remarkably alike in all organisms whatever their form. This discovery, of course, makes it more imperative (not less imperative) that the forces accounting for the patterned integrity of individual organisms be sought. The parallel with psychology is almost perfect. With analytical zeal we have sought uniform units of all personalities (common traits, needs, factors, and so on), but have lost sight of internal morphogenic patterning along the way.

Still another helpful suggestion comes from F. H. Allport's conception of *trend.* This unit is a highly energized system or meaning-cycle characteristic of the individual personality. "It represents, in familiar terms, what the individual is 'characteristically trying to do,' that is, what meaning he is always trying to achieve. . . ." Trend structures are "interstructured into larger systems (unity of personality)." F. H. Allport, *Theories of Perception and the Concept of Structure* (New York: Wiley, 1955), p. 656.

Although these suggestions reinforce the argument of the present chapter, it seems best for our present purposes to employ the simpler descriptive label, *personal disposition.*

be more accurate to say that his personal disposition is a kind of *artistic and self-sufficient solitude*. His separate scores on common traits do not fully reflect this pattern.

But, one asks, is it not "more scientific" to work with common traits? We shall answer this question gradually. For the moment we merely insist that common traits are at best approximations. Often they fail to reflect the structure of a given personality.

An illustration of the point comes from Conrad's study of ratings. Three teachers rated a number of children of preschool age upon 231 common traits, thus being forced to make the assumption that all the children did possess exactly these self-same qualities in some degree. Proceeding on this precarious assumption there was only a low agreement among the teachers, with a median correlation of +.48. Many of the children, it seems, were rated by guesswork, simply because the investigation *required* that each child receive a rating on every quality. But in the course of the same study, the teachers were asked to *star* their ratings on such qualities as they considered to be of "central or dominating importance in the child's personality." On this part of their task the teachers agreed almost perfectly, their ratings correlating approximately +.95. This result shows that low reliability of rating may often be due to the fact that the subjects are forced into a common trait comparison where they do not belong. In a few cases (the starred qualities) the common trait concept seemed to correspond fairly well to some striking individual p.d., but in most cases the common dimensions fell wide of the mark.[2]

Let the reader bear in mind that we are not condemning the common trait-approach. Far from it. When we wish to compare people with one another, it is the only approach possible. Furthermore, the resulting scores, and profiles, are up to a point illuminating. We are simply saying that there is a second, more accurate way, of viewing personality: namely, the internal patterning (the morphogenesis) of the life considered as a unique product of nature and society.

We view personality — in the only way it can be intelligibly viewed — as a network of organization, composed of systems within systems, some systems of small magnitude and somewhat peripheral to the central or propriate structure, other systems of wider scope at the core of the total edifice; some easy to set into action, others more dormant; some so culturally conforming that they can readily be viewed as "common"; others definitely idiosyncratic. But in the last analysis this network — employing billions and billions of nerve cells fashioned by a one-time heredity and by environmental experiences never duplicated — is ultimately unique.

The diehard nomothetic scientist replies, "Well, everything in the world is unique — every stone in the meadow, every old shoe, every mouse, but they

---

[2] H. S. Conrad, "The Validity of Personality Ratings of Preschool Children," *J. educ. Psychol.*, 1932, 23: 671–680.

are all composed of the same elements. Uniqueness appears when common elements appear in different proportions. Organic chemistry is chiefly concerned with the various combinations of six or seven elements, and it has been estimated that about three million combinations of these few elements are possible. Allowing for still more elements (including common traits) we can ultimately account for the final uniqueness of every person."

My answer is this: Personality exists only at a postelementary state; it exists only when the common features of human nature have already interacted with one another and produced unique, self-continuing, and evolving systems. This is not to say that the search for common elements or common human functions is undesirable. For the most part the science of psychology does this and nothing else. I insist only that if we are interested in *personality*, we must go beyond the elementaristic and reach into the morphogenic realm.[3]

The Interdependence of Dispositions

With this picture before us let us ask whether it is reasonable to think of an individual personality as composed of separate dispositions. Is not the organization so interlocked that we cannot dismember the individual into p.d. components?

It is certainly true that we can never see one p.d. at a time. The continuous flow of behavior employs simultaneously all manner of determining tendencies. Consider the act of writing a letter: it requires the convergence of mental sets, motives of the moment, skills, stylistic habits, as well as deep personal convictions and values. Behavior always demands the effective convergence of many determining influences. Generalizing the illustration, we can say that no single performance is ever a univocal product of any one single trait or p.d.

At the same time, since adaptive acts distributed over a period of time show repeatedly the same purposes and the same expressive quality, it becomes necessary to assume some stable and continuous influences at work. A *talkative* person, who starts his stream of speech at the slightest provocation, must have some neuropsychic tendency that channels his conduct in this direction. His loquacity, provoked so easily (by an equivalence of stimuli), leads to fluent speech wherein all manner of ideas and words may be employed (equivalence of response). Though it is not easy to conceive in neurological terms, there must be some neural system with a low threshold of arousal capable of engendering this consistent behavior. At any one time, to be sure, the form the loquacity takes is determined also by other operative factors — by his ideas and attitudes toward the topic of the discourse and toward the interlocutor, by the availability of a listener, as well as by other p.d.'s in his nature.

[3] A morphogenic point of view is reflected in E. W. Sinnott, *The Biology of the Spirit* (New York: Viking, 1955). This author holds that the configuration of human personality is maintained chiefly by goal-directed motives (not by drives).

The expression *foci of organization* represents what we mean by personal dispositions. The average individual will have certain sets of interests and values, certain modes and manners of expression, and perhaps a magnificent obsession or two. These focalized dispositions can be aroused by a wide range of stimuli and lead to a wide range of equivalent responses. . . . But the boundaries between these systems are not rigid. Even so-called "logic-tight compartments" are not entirely separate; their boundaries are at least semipermeable.

A p.d., then, is identifiable not by sharp contours or boundaries, but by a nuclear quality. The nuclear quality will be some important goal or meaning, or sometimes a style of expression. All these betray the individual's effort at survival and mastery, and give shape or form to his personality.

The Consistency of Dispositions

Since the primary principle of behavior is its convergent flow, we cannot expect dispositions to be totally consistent and predictable. Yet our test for a p.d. (as for a common trait) lies in the demonstrable recurrence of "functionally equivalent" behavior. A New York executive, almost always decisive, orderly, and prompt, may be reduced to virtual paralysis when confronted in a restaurant with a tray of French pastry. Why? Perhaps it is just fatigue at the end of the day; perhaps it is a buried complex traceable to punishment in boyhood for stealing tarts. Dispositions are never wholly consistent. What a bore it would be if they were — and what chaos if they were not at all consistent.

We have already discussed inconsistency due to situation. Some authors, as we saw, go so far as to declare that personality has no inner consistency at all, but owes its uniformity to the likeness of situations recurrently faced. We have argued against this position. Even a person who is at one time ascendant and another time yielding, at one time gruff and another time sugary, must have these contrary tendencies *within himself.* Sometimes a person may harbor p.d.'s that are exactly opposite. Conquering and yielding, extraverted and introverted, saintly and sinful, dispositions may reside within one breast. Goethe creates Faust from such paradoxical trends. Jung's system of psychology rests heavily on the concept of contraries. A masculine person, for example, will have in his nature an unconscious *femina.*

One situation calls forth one p.d.; another calls forth another. We cannot deny this fact. But we should point out that what appears to be contradictory behavior is often not contradictory at all. The apparent contradiction comes from the fact that we have made a superficial diagnosis.

Take the case of Dr. D, always neat about his person and desk, punctilious about lecture notes, outlines, and files; his personal possessions are not only in order but carefully kept under lock and key. Dr. D is also in charge of the departmental library. In this duty he is careless; he leaves the library door unlocked, and books are lost; it does not bother him that dust accumulates.

Does this contradiction in behavior mean that D lacks personal dispositions? Not at all. He has two opposed stylistic dispositions, one of orderliness and one of disorderliness. Different situations arouse different dispositions. Pursuing the case further, the duality is at least partly explained by the fact that D has *one* cardinal (motivational) disposition from which these contrasting styles proceed. The outstanding fact about his personality is that he is a self-centered egotist who never acts for other people's interests, but always for his own. This cardinal self-centeredness (for which there is abundant evidence) demands orderliness for himself, but not for others.

We conclude, then, that the consistency of a disposition is a matter of degree. There must be some demonstrable relationship between separate acts before its existence can be inferred. Yet the occurrence of dissociated, specific, and even contradictory acts is not necessarily fatal to the inference. And we usually find that contradiction diminishes if we spot correctly the deepest (most propriate) disposition that is operating.

Genotypical, Phenotypical, and Pseudo Dispositions

This last point brings us to a helpful distinction proposed by Lewin. Descriptions in terms of "here and now" are *phenotypical*. Explanatory accounts, seeking deeper dispositions, are *genotypical*. In the case of D, he has both orderly and negligent ways of behaving (phenotypical), but these opposed readinesses (each covering a range of equivalent situations and responses) are anchored in a more fundamental (genotypical) p.d. that we identified as *self-centeredness*.

It would not be correct to say that phenotypical dispositions are not true dispositions. They are "true" in much the same sense that common traits are true. In other words, although they may not reflect the core-dynamics and central structure of the individual personality, they at least show some consistency in a person's behavior.

Psychoanalytic theory holds that the quality of *miserliness*, for example, is a reflection of an anal-erotic character syndrome. *If* this be the case, then miserliness is a phenotypical disposition. Only the anal-erotic character would be properly considered genotypical. But some misers may not have this particular underlying genotype. Perhaps their hoarding started out of dire necessity and became functionally autonomous. They simply like the feel of gold (or its equivalent). In this case the miserliness is conceivably a true genotype (that is to say, it is as fundamental a p.d. as one is likely to find in their personalities). This example shows that *only by studying exhaustively the single life can we hope to distinguish genotype from phenotype with reasonable success.*

Sometimes our inference can be wholly erroneous. We may, for example, think that a person who gives gifts is a *generous* person. But perhaps he is merely trying to buy favor. In this case we are not dealing even with a phenotypical disposition, for the person has no bent at all for generosity. The phenotypical disposition is bribery (not generosity), and the underlying geno-type, for all we know, may be a kind of core feeling of insecurity in life. *Pseudo traits*, then, are errors of inference, misjudgments that come from fixing at-tention solely upon appearances. Here again we see that only the soundest methods and the utmost of critical skill will lead to a proper diagnosis. It is chiefly by its ability to separate true dispositions from pseudo dispositions that psychology makes an advance over common sense.

Cardinal, Central, and Secondary Dispositions

In every personality there are p.d.'s of major significance and p.d.'s of minor significance. Occasionally some p.d. is so pervasive and so outstanding in a life that it deserves to be called a *cardinal* disposition. Almost every act seems traceable to its influence. The list of terms on page 319 derived from the proper names of historical and fictional characters (even allowing for exagger-ation and oversimplification) suggests what is meant by cardinal dispositions. No such disposition can remain hidden, an individual is known by it, and may become famous for it. Such a master quality has sometimes been called the *eminent trait*, the *ruling passion*, the *master-sentiment*, the *unity-thema*, or the *radix* of a life.

It is an unusual personality that possesses one and only one cardinal dispo-sition. Ordinarily the foci of a life seem to lie in a handful of distinguishable central p.d.'s. How many is the question we shall ask presently. Central dispo-sitions are likely to be those that we mention in writing a careful letter of recommendation. Conrad's study cited on page 321 also deals with the central (starred) dispositions in the personalities of preschool children (where, of course, we should not expect to find structures as firm as later in life).

On a still less important level we may speak of secondary p.d.'s — less conspicuous, less generalized, less consistent, and less often called into play than central dispositions. Secondary p.d.'s are likely to be more peripheral and less propriate than central p.d.'s.

It goes without saying that these three gradations are arbitrary and are phrased mainly for convenience of discourse. In reality there are all possible degrees of organization, from the most circumscribed and unstable to the most pervasive and firmly structured. It is helpful, however, to have these distinctions at hand when we wish to speak roughly of the relative prominence and intensity of various dispositions in a given personality.[4]

---

[4] A word should be said about "intensity." In one sense if a p.d. is regarded as unique, it cannot exist in "degree" because there is no outside standard to compare it with. Yet if we take the individual as our reference point we may — as we have here — estimate the intensity of one p.d. in relation to others, and thus arrive at our rough scale: cardinal central secondary. If, however, we try to compare some p.d. with similar p.d.'s in other people, then, of course, we have transformed p.d. into *common trait*.

How Many Dispositions Has a Person?

How many dispositions has a person is a most audacious question, and can be answered in only a preliminary and speculative way. For many reasons the question is audacious: Behavior is in continuous flow; dispositions never express themselves singly; people manifest contradictory dispositions in contradictory situations; furthermore, diagnostic methods are too ill developed to enable us to discover the answer.

Still, a few guesses can be made on the basis of partial evidence, provided we confine ourselves to the level of cardinal or central p.d.'s. We shall not even venture a guess concerning secondary dispositions.

We turn first to the realm of biography. In his definitive life of William James, Ralph Barton Perry writes that in order to understand this fascinating figure it is necessary to deal with eight leading "traits" or "ingredients." He first lists four "morbid" dispositions — tendencies which, taken by themselves, would prove to be severe handicaps: (1) hypochondria, (2) preoccupation with exceptional mental states, (3) marked oscillations of mood, and (4) repugnance to the processes of exact thought. Blended with these morbid p.d.'s, and redeeming them, are four "benign" dispositions: (5) sensibility, (6) vivacity, (7) humanity, (8) sociability. The labels Perry uses are, of course, common trait names; but he defines them in such a way that the peculiar Jamesian flavor of each is brought out. What is important for our purposes is the fact that, even after a most exhaustive study of a complex personality, Perry feels that a limited number of major dispositions (in this case eight) adequately covers the major structure of the life.

Let us consider a bit of experimental evidence. We asked 93 students "to think of some one individual of your own sex whom you know well"; and then "to describe him or her by writing words, phrases, or sentences that express fairly well what seem to you to be the essential characteristics of this person." The phrase *essential characteristic* was defined as "any trait, quality, tendency, interest, etc., that you regard as of major importance to a description of the person you select."

The average number listed by the students was 7.2. Only 10 percent of the writers felt that they needed more than 10 items to describe their friend's "essential characteristics."[5]

These are only suggestive bits of evidence, but they open a momentous possibility. *When psychology develops adequate diagnostic methods for discovering the major lines along which a particular personality is organized (personal dispositions), it may turn out that the number of such foci will*

---

[5] See G. W. Allport, "What Units Shall We Employ?" In G. Lindzey (Ed.), *Assessment of Human Motives* (New York: Holt, Rinehart and Winston, 1958), Chap. 9. The biographical evidence is found in R. B. Perry, *The Thought and Character of William James* (2 vols: Boston: Little, Brown, 1936), Vol. II, Chaps. 90–91.

normally vary between five and ten. We state this proposition as a hypothesis subject to eventual scientific testing.

How to Study Personal Dispositions?

Since psychology has so rarely fixed its attention on individuality, we have fewer methods for determining personal dispositions in single individuals than we should like. In most quarters the cliché prevails: "Psychology, as a science, deals with universals, not with particulars." For every study of individual traits we find a hundred, perhaps a thousand, studies of common traits. Yet methods — or suggestions of methods — are available, and we shall tell enough about them to show that our challenge to science is justified — namely, that it *can* do more than it does in exploring morphogenic organization.

Particularizing Common Traits

A first and fairly obvious method is to scrutinize the standing of individuals on universal testing instruments or rating scales. Significantly high or low scores on common variables may draw our attention to areas where, if we look more carefully, important personal dispositions will be found. For example, we refer again to Conrad's rating study (page 321), where the method of "starred" ratings among over 200 common traits showed which variables seemed to point to important dispositions in individual children. It will be recalled that teachers agreed particularly well on these starred items. Having thus identified probable p.d.'s, we could then proceed to discover the coloring of each as it exists in a given life.

Case Studies

The most obvious of all methods is the study of biography, life-history, or single cases. Offhand this would seem to be the method of literature and common sense, but . . . it can, through the use of safeguards and analytic tools, become an important scientific method.

Testing for Hypothesized p.d.'s

Suppose, like any sensible scientist, we first take a common-sense look at the object we are studying. We then hypothesize that the object — in this case a particular personality — will be found to consist of certain major dispositions. We then, like any scientist, try empirically to verify our hypothesis and, if need be, correct it. This method has been proposed by F. H. Allport in the following case.[6]

A certain boy at school showed exemplary conduct; he was orderly, industrious, and attentive. But at home he was noisy, unruly, and a bully toward the younger children. Phenotypically he showed contrary dispositions.

[6] F. H. Allport, "Teleonomic Description in the Study of Personality," *Charact. & Pers.*, 1937, 6:202–214.

Now the psychologist might make the hypothesis: This boy's central disposition is a craving for attention. He finds that he gains his end best at school by conforming to the rules; at home, by disobeying them.

Having made this hypothesis, the psychologist could then actually count the boy's acts during the day (being checked by some independent observer) to see how many of them were "functionally equivalent," i.e., manifested a clear bid for attention. If the proportion is high, we can regard the hypothesis as confirmed, and the p.d. as established.

A wider use of this hypothesis method would lead us to a wholesome focusing on individual lives.

Empirical Analysis of One Person's Acts

If we have a large array of acts of a single person available for study, we can in various ways make a revealing "content analysis" of them. For example, the letters or the diary of a person contains recurrent groupings of thoughts. How to make scientific use of such data is shown by the work of Baldwin, who calls his method "personal structure analysis."[7]

This investigator analyzed over one hundred letters written by Jenny between her fifty-ninth and seventieth year. He asked the question, If Jenny mentions one subject, what else does she mention at the same time (in the same thought sequence)? By this method he determined that Jenny displayed only a few unmistakable central dispositions in her life. She was highly jealous of her son; she was paranoid concerning her relations with women; she had a strong esthetic interest; and she was scrupulous in matters of money.

Although these letters, of course, may not have revealed the whole structure of Jenny's personality, the method nonetheless shows that careful quantitative work can be conducted in the area of unique personal dispositions. Psychology *can* be concerned with the single case.

The Clinical Approach

Since counselors, consultants, or therapists deal with individuals, they unavoidably make judgments concerning personal dispositions. For the duration of the consultation they are absorbed by the client's own structure. They will, of course, think of general laws that may apply to the person's conduct or problem, but their attention is riveted upon the present personal pattern.

Unfortunately, up to now clinical psychologists, psychoanalysts, and other counselors have let their interest in general laws and actuarial (average) predictions take precedence in their theorizing. Sometimes they even disparage the value of studying the morphogenic formations in the individual life.

It is, however, clear that the clinical approach in principle offers an envi-

---

[7] A. L. Baldwin, "Personal Structure Analysis: A Statistical Method for Investigating the Single Personality," *J. abnorm. soc. Psychol.*, 1942, 37:163–183.

able opportunity for investigating morphogenic dispositions. In the future we may hope for enlightening research from this source.

Enough has been said to establish our point: Science can and should deal with individual personality directly, and not merely compare persons in the customary common-trait manner.

ERICH FROMM

Human Nature and Character

THE HUMAN SITUATION

One individual represents the human race. He is one specific example of the human species. He is "he" and he is "all"; he is an individual with his peculiarities and in this sense unique, and at the same time he is representative of all characteristics of the human race. His individual personality is determined by the peculiarities of human existence common to all men. Hence the discussion of the human situation must precede that of personality.

Man's Biological Weakness

The first element which differentiates human from animal existence is a negative one: the relative absence in man of instinctive regulation in the process of adaptation to the surrounding world. The mode of adaptation of the animal to its world remains the same throughout; if its instinctual equipment is no longer fit to cope successfully with a changing environment the species will die out. The animal can adapt itself to changing conditions by changing itself — autoplastically; not by changing its environment — alloplastically. In this fashion it lives harmoniously, not in the sense of absence of struggle but in the sense that its inherited equipment makes it a fixed and unchanging part of its world; it either fits in or dies out.

The less complete and fixed the instinctual equipment of animals, the more developed is the brain and therefore the ability to learn. The emergence of man can be defined as occurring at the point in the process of evolution

From *Man for Himself* by Erich Fromm. Copyright 1947 by Erich Fromm. Reprinted by permission of Holt, Rinehart and Winston, Inc. Some footnotes have been omitted.

where instinctive adaptation has reached its minimum. But he emerges with new qualities which differentiate him from the animal: his awareness of himself as a separate entity, his ability to remember the past, to visualize the future, and to denote objects and acts by symbols; his reason to conceive and understand the world; and his imagination through which he reaches far beyond the range of his senses. Man is the most helpless of all animals, but this very biological weakness is the basis for his strength, the prime cause for the development of his specifically human qualities.

PERSONALITY

Men are alike, for they share the human situation and its inherent existential dichotomies; they are unique in the specific way they solve their human problem. The infinite diversity of personalities is in itself characteristic of human existence.

By personality I understand the totality of inherited and acquired psychic qualities which are characteristic of one individual and which make the individual unique. The difference between inherited and acquired qualities is on the whole synonymous with the difference between temperament, gifts, and all constitutionally given psychic qualities on the one hand and character on the other. While differences in temperament have no ethical significance, differences in character constitute the real problem of ethics; they are expressive of the degree to which an individual has succeeded in the art of living. . . .

Character

THE DYNAMIC CONCEPT OF CHARACTER. Character traits were and are considered by behavioristically orientated psychologists to be synonymous with behavior traits. From this standpoint character is defined as "the pattern of behavior characteristic for a given individual," [1] while other authors like William McDougall, R. G. Gordon, and Kretschmer have emphasized the conative and dynamic element of character traits.

Freud developed not only the first but also the most consistent and penetrating theory of character as a system of strivings which underlie, but are not identical with, behavior. In order to appreciate Freud's dynamic concept of character, a comparison between behavior traits and character traits will be helpful. Behavior traits are described in terms of actions which are observable by a third person. Thus, for instance, the behavior trait "being courageous" would be defined as behavior which is directed toward reaching a certain goal without being deterred by risks to one's comfort, freedom, or life. Or parsimony as a behavior trait would be defined as behavior which aims at saving money or other material things. However, if we inquire into the motivation and particularly into the unconscious motiva-

---

[1] Leland E. Hinsie and Jacob Shatzky, *Psychiatric Dictionary.* (New York: Oxford University Press, 1940.)

tion of such behavior traits we find that the behavior trait covers numerous and entirely different character traits. Courageous behavior may be motivated by ambition so that a person will risk his life in certain situations in order to satisfy his craving for being admired; it may be motivated by suicidal impulses which drive a person to seek danger because, consciously or unconsciously, he does not value his life and wants to destroy himself; it may be motivated by sheer lack of imagination so that a person acts courageously because he is not aware of the danger awaiting him; finally, it may be determined by genuine devotion to the idea or aim for which a person acts, a motivation which is conventionally assumed to be the basis of courage. Superficially the behavior in all these instances is the same in spite of the different motivations. I say "superficially" because if one can observe such behavior minutely one finds that the difference in motivation results also in subtle differences in behavior. An officer in battle, for instance, will behave quite differently in different situations if his courage is motivated by devotion to an idea rather than by ambition. In the first case he would not attack in certain situations if the risks are in no proportion to the tactical ends to be gained. If, on the other hand, he is driven by vanity, this passion may make him blind to the dangers threatening him and his soldiers. His behavior trait "courage" in the latter case is obviously a very ambiguous asset. Another illustration is parsimony. A person may be economical because his economic circumstances make it necessary; or he may be parsimonious because he has a stingy character, which makes saving an aim for its own sake regardless of the realistic necessity. Here, too, the motivation would make some difference with regard to behavior itself. In the first case, the person would be very well able to discern a situation where it is wise to save from one in which it is wiser to spend money. In the latter case he will save regardless of the objective need for it. Another factor which is determined by the difference in motivation refers to the prediction of behavior. In the case of a "courageous" soldier motivated by ambition we may predict that he will behave courageously only if his courage can be rewarded. In the case of the soldier who is courageous because of devotion to his cause we can predict that the question of whether or not his courage will find recognition will have little influence on his behavior.

Closely related to Freud's concept of unconscious motivation is his theory of the conative nature of character traits. He recognized something that the great novelists and dramatists had always known: that, as Balzac put it, the study of character deals with "the forces by which man is motivated"; that the way a person acts, feels, and thinks is to a large extent determined by the specificity of his character and is not merely the result of rational responses to realistic situations; that "man's fate is his character." Freud recognized the dynamic quality of character traits and that the character structure of a person represents a particular form in which energy is canalized in the process of living.

Freud tried to account for this dynamic nature of character traits by combining his characterology with his libido theory. In accordance with the type of materialistic thinking prevalent in the natural sciences of the late nineteenth century, which assumed the energy in natural and psychical phenomena to be a substantial not a relational entity, Freud believed that the sexual drive was the source of energy of the character. By a number of complicated and brilliant assumptions he explained different character traits as "sublimations" of, or "reaction formations" against, the various forms of the sexual drive. He interpreted the *dynamic nature* of character traits as an expression of their *libidinous source*.

The progress of psychoanalytic theory led, in line with the progress of the natural and social sciences, to a new concept which was based, not on the idea of a primarily isolated individual, but on the *relationship* of man to others, to nature, and to himself. It was assumed that this very relationship governs and regulates the energy manifest in the passionate strivings of man. H. S. Sullivan, one of the pioneers of this new view, has accordingly defined psychoanalysis as a "study of interpersonal relations."

The theory presented in the following pages follows Freud's characterology in essential points: in the assumption that character traits underlie behavior and must be inferred from it; that they constitute forces which, though powerful, the person may be entirely unconscious of. It follows Freud also in the assumption that the fundamental entity in character is not the single character trait but the total character organization from which a number of single character traits follow. These character traits are to be understood as a syndrome which results from a particular organization or, as I shall call it, orientation of character. I shall deal only with a very limited number of character traits which follow immediately from the underlying orientation. A number of other character traits could be dealt with similarly, and it could be shown that they are also direct outcomes of basic orientations or mixtures of such primary traits of character with those of temperament. However, a great number of others conventionally listed as character traits would be found to be not character traits in our sense but pure temperament or mere behavior traits.

The main difference in the theory of character proposed here from that of Freud is that the fundamental basis of character is not seen in various types of libido organization but in specific kinds of a person's relatedness to the world. In the process of living, man relates himself to the world (1) by acquiring and assimilating things, and (2) by relating himself to people (and himself). The former I shall call the process of assimilation; the latter, that of socialization. Both forms of relatedness are "open" and not, as with the animal, instinctively determined. Man can acquire things by receiving or taking them from an outside source or by producing them through his own effort. But he must acquire and assimilate them in some fashion in order to satisfy his needs. Also, man cannot live alone and unrelated to others. He has to associate with others for defense, for work, for sexual satisfaction, for play, for the upbringing of the young, for the transmission of knowledge and material possessions. But beyond that, it is necessary for him to be related to others, one with them, part of a group. Complete isolation is unbearable and incompatible with sanity. Again man can relate himself to others in various ways: he can love or hate, he can compete or cooperate; he can build a social system based on equality or authority, liberty or oppression; but he must be related in some fashion and the particular form of relatedness is expressive of his character.

These orientations, by which the individual relates himself to the world, constitute the core of his character; character can be defined as the *(relatively permanent) form in which human energy is canalized in the process of assimilation and socialization.* This canalization of psychic energy has a very significant biological function. Since man's actions are not determined by innate instinctual patterns, life would be precarious, indeed, if he had to make a deliberate decision each time he acted, each time he took a step. On the contrary, many actions must be performed far more quickly than conscious deliberation allows. Furthermore, if all behavior followed from deliberate decision, many more inconsistencies in action would occur than are compatible with proper functioning. According to behavioristic thinking, man learns to react in a semiautomatic fashion by developing habits of action and thought which can be understood in terms of conditioned reflexes. While this view is correct to a certain extent, it ignores the fact that the most deeply rooted habits and opinions which are characteristic of a person and resistant to change grow from his character structure: they are expressive of the particular form in which energy has been canalized in the character structure. The character system can be considered the human substitute for the instinctive apparatus of the animal. Once energy is canalized in a certain way, action takes place "true to character." A particular character may be undesirable ethically, but at least it permits a person to act fairly consistently and to be relieved of the burden of having to make a new and deliberate decision every time. He can arrange his life in a way which is geared to his character and thus create a certain degree of compatibility between the inner and the outer situation. Moreover, character has also a selective function with regard to a person's ideas and values. Since to most people ideas seem to be independent of their emotions and wishes and the result of logical deduction, they feel that their attitude toward the world is confirmed by their ideas and judgments when actually these are as much a result of their character as their actions are. This confirmation in turn tends to stabilize their character structure since it makes the latter appear right and sensible.

Not only has character the function of permitting the individual to act consistently and "reasonably"; it is also the basis for his adjustment to society. The character of the child is molded by the character of its parents in response to whom it develops. The parents and their methods of child training in turn are determined by the social structure of their culture. The average family is the "psychic agency" of society, and by adjusting himself to his family the child acquires the character which later makes him adjusted to the tasks he has to perform in social life. He acquires that character which makes him want to do what he has to do and the core of which he shares with most members of the same social class or culture. The fact that most members of a social class or culture share significant elements of character and that one can speak of a "social character" representing the core of a character structure common to most people of a given culture shows the degree to which character is formed by social and cultural patterns. But from the social character we must differentiate the individual character in which one person differs from another within the same culture. These differences are partly due to the differences of the personalities of the parents and to the differences, psychic and material, of the specific social environment in which the child grows up. But they are also due to the constitutional differences of each individual, particularly those of temperament. Genetically, the formation of individual character is determined by the impact of its life experiences, the individual ones and those which follow from the culture, on temperament and physical constitution. Environment is never the same for two people, for the difference in constitution makes them experience the same environment in a more or less different way. Mere habits of action and thought which develop as the result of an individual's conforming with the cultural pattern and which are not rooted in the character of a person are easily changed under the influence of new social patterns. If, on the other hand, a person's behavior is rooted in his character, it is charged with energy and changeable only if a fundamental change in a person's character takes place.

In the following analysis *nonproductive orientations* are differentiated from the *productive orientation.* It must be noted that these concepts are "ideal-types," not descriptions of the character of a given individual. Furthermore, while, for didactic purposes, they are treated here separately, the character of any given person is usually a blend of all or some of these orientations in which one, however, is dominant. Finally, I want to state here that in the description of the nonproductive orientations only their negative aspects are presented. . . .[2]

TYPES OF CHARACTER: THE NONPRODUCTIVE ORIENTATIONS. *The receptive orientation.* In the receptive orientation a persons feels "the source of all good" to be outside, and he believes that the only way to get what he wants — be it something material, be it affection, love, knowledge, pleasure — is to receive it from that outside source. In this orientation the problem of love is

---

[2] . . . The following description of the non-productive orientations, except that of the marketing, follows the clinical picture of the pregenital character given by Freud and others. The theoretical difference becomes apparent in the discussion of the hoarding character.

almost exclusively that of "being loved" and not that of loving. Such people tend to be indiscriminate in the choice of their love objects, because being loved by anybody is such an overwhelming experience for them that they "fall for" anybody who gives them love or what looks like love. They are exceedingly sensitive to any withdrawal or rebuff they experience on the part of the loved person. Their orientation is the same in the sphere of thinking: if intelligent, they make the best listeners, since their orientation is one of receiving, not of producing, ideas; left to themselves, they feel paralyzed. It is characteristic of these people that their first thought is to find somebody else to give them needed information rather than to make even the smallest effort of their own. If religious, these persons have a concept of God in which they expect everything from God and nothing from their own activity. If not religious, their relationship to persons or institutions is very much the same; they are always in search of a "magic helper." They show a particular kind of loyalty, at the bottom of which is the gratitude for the hand that feeds them and the fear of ever losing it. Since they need many hands to feel secure, they have to be loyal to numerous people. It is difficult for them to say "no," and they are easily caught between conflicting loyalties and promises. Since they cannot say "no," they love to say "yes" to everything and everybody, and the resulting paralysis of their critical abilities makes them increasingly dependent on others.

They are dependent not only on authorities for knowledge and help but on people in general for any kind of support. They feel lost when alone because they feel that they cannot do anything without help. This helplessness is especially important with regard to those acts which by their very nature can only be done alone — making decisions and taking responsibility. In personal relationships, for instance, they ask advice from the very person with regard to whom they have to make a decision.

This receptive type has great fondness for food and drink. These persons tend to overcome anxiety and depression by eating or drinking. The mouth is an especially prominent feature, often the most expressive one; the lips tend to be open, as if in a state of continuous expectation of being fed. In their dreams, being fed is a frequent symbol of being loved; being starved, an expression of frustration or disappointment.

By and large, the outlook of people of this receptive orientation is optimistic and friendly; they have a certain confidence in life and its gifts, but they become anxious and distraught when their "source of supply" is threatened. They often have a genuine warmth and a wish to help others, but doing things for others also assumes the function of securing their favor.

The exploitative orientation. The exploitative orientation, like the receptive, has as its basic premise the feeling that the source of all good is outside, that whatever one wants to get must be sought there, and that one cannot produce anything oneself. The difference between the two, however, is that the exploitative type does not expect to receive things from others as gifts, but to take them away from others by force or cunning. This orientation extends to all spheres of activity.

In the realm of love and affection these people tend to grab and steal. They feel attracted only to people whom they can take away from somebody else. Attractiveness to them is conditioned by a person's attachment to somebody else; they tend not to fall in love with an unattached person.

We find the same attitude with regard to thinking and intellectual pursuits. Such people will tend not to produce ideas but to steal them. This may be done directly in the form of plagiarism or more subtly by repeating in different phraseology the ideas voiced by others and insisting they are new and their own. It is a striking fact that frequently people with great intelligence proceed in this way, although if they relied on their own gifts they might well be able to have ideas of their own. The lack of original ideas or independent production in otherwise gifted people often has its explanation in this character orientation, rather than in any innate lack of originality. The same statement holds true with regard to their orientation to material things. Things which they can take away from others always seem better to them than anything they can produce themselves. They use and exploit anybody and anything from whom or from which they can squeeze something. Their motto is: "Stolen fruits are sweetest." Because they want to use and exploit people, they "love" those who, explicitly or implicitly, are promising objects of exploitation, and get "fed up" with persons whom they have squeezed out. An extreme example is the kleptomaniac who enjoys things only if he can steal them, although he has the money to buy them.

This orientation seems to be symbolized by the biting mouth which is often a prominent feature in such people. It is not a play upon words to point out that they often make "biting" remarks about others. Their attitude is colored by a mixture of hostility and manipulation. Everyone is an object of exploitation and is judged according to his usefulness. Instead of the confidence and optimism which characterizes the receptive type, one finds here suspicion and cynicism, envy and jealousy. Since they are satisfied only with things they can take away from others, they tend to overrate what others have and underrate what is theirs.

The hoarding orientation. While the receptive and exploitative types are similar inasmuch as both expect to get things from the outside world, the hoarding orientation is essentially different. This orientation makes people have little faith in anything new they might get from the outside world; their security is based upon hoarding and saving, while spending is felt to be a threat. They have surrounded themselves, as it were, by a protective wall, and their main aim is to bring as much as possible into this fortified position and to let as little as possible out of it. Their miserliness refers to money and material things as well as to feelings and thoughts. Love is essentially a possession; they do not give love but try to get it by possessing the "beloved." The hoarding person often shows a particular kind of faithfulness toward people and even toward memories. Their sentimentality makes the past appear as golden; they hold on to it and indulge in the memories of bygone feelings and experiences. They know everything but are sterile and incapable of productive thinking.

One can recognize these people too by facial expressions and gestures. Theirs is the tight-lipped mouth; their gestures are characteristic of their withdrawn attitude. While those of the receptive type are inviting and round, as it were, and the gestures of the exploitative type are aggressive and pointed, those of the hoarding type are angular, as if they wanted to emphasize the frontiers between themselves and the outside world. Another characteristic element in this attitude is pedantic orderliness. The hoarder will be orderly with things, thoughts, or feelings, but again, as with memory, his orderliness is sterile and rigid. He cannot endure things out of place and will automatically rearrange them. To him the outside world threatens to break into his fortified position; orderliness signifies mastering the world outside by putting it, and keeping it, in its proper place in order to avoid the danger of intrusion. His compulsive cleanliness is another expression of his need to undo contact with the outside world. Things beyond his own frontiers are felt to be dangerous and "unclean"; he annuls the menacing contact by compulsive washing, similar to a religious washing ritual prescribed after contact with unclean things or people. Things have to be put not only in their proper place but also into their proper time; obsessive punctuality is characteristic of the hoarding type; it is another form of mastering the outside world. If the outside world is experienced as a threat to one's fortified position, obstinacy is a logical reaction. A constant "no" is the almost automatic defense against intrusion; sitting tight, the answer to the danger of being pushed. These people tend to feel that they possess only a fixed quantity of strength, energy, or mental capacity, and that this stock is diminished or exhausted by use and can never be replenished. They cannot understand the self-replenishing function of all living substance and that activity and the use of one's powers increase strength while stagnation paralyzes; to them, death and destruction have more reality than life and growth. The act of creation is a miracle of which they hear but in which they do not believe. Their highest values are order and security; their motto: "There is nothing new under the sun." In their relationship to others intimacy is a threat; either remoteness or possession of a person means security. The hoarder tends to be suspicious and to have a particular sense of justice which in effect says: "Mine is mine and yours is yours."

The marketing orientation. The marketing orientation developed as a dominant one only in the modern era. In order to understand its nature one must consider the economic function of the market in modern society as being not only analogous to this character orientation but as the basis and the main condition for its development in modern man.

Barter is one of the oldest economic mechanisms. The traditional local market, however, is essentially different from the market as it has developed in modern capitalism. Bartering on a local market offered an opportunity to meet for the purpose of exchanging commodities. Producers and customers became acquainted; they were relatively small groups; the demand was more or less known, so that the producer could produce for this specific demand.

The modern market[3] is no longer a meeting place but a mechanism characterized by abstract and impersonal demand. One produces for this market, not for a known circle of customers; its verdict is based on laws of supply and demand; and it determines whether the commodity can be sold and at what price. No matter what the *use value* of a pair of shoes may be, for instance, if the supply is greater than the demand, some shoes will be sentenced to economic death; they might as well not have been produced at all. The market day is the "day of judgment" as far as the *exchange value* of commodities is concerned.

The reader may object that this description of the market is oversimplified. The producer does try to judge the demand in advance, and under monopoly conditions even obtains a certain degree of control over it. Nevertheless, the regulatory function of the market has been, and still is, predominant enough to have a profound influence on the character formation of the urban middle class and, through the latter's social and cultural influence, on the whole population. The market concept of value, the emphasis on exchange value rather than on use value, has led to a similar concept of value with regard to people and particularly to oneself. The character orientation which is rooted in the experience of oneself as a commodity and of one's value as exchange value I call the marketing orientation.

In our time the marketing orientation has been growing rapidly, together with the development of a new market that is a phenomenon of the last decades — the "personality market." Clerks and salesmen, business executives and doctors, lawyers and artists all appear on this market. It is true that their legal status and economic positions are different: some are independent, charging for their services; others are employed, receiving salaries. But all are dependent for their material success on a personal acceptance by those who need their services or who employ them.

The principle of evaluation is the same on both the personality and the commodity market: on the one, personalities are offered for sale; on the other, commodities. Value in both cases is their exchange value, for which use value is a necessary but not a sufficient condition. It is true, our economic system could not function if people were not skilled in the particular work they have to perform and were gifted only with a pleasant personality. Even the best bedside manner and the most beautifully equipped office on Park Avenue would not make a New York doctor successful if he did not have a minimum

---

[3] Cf., for the study of history and function of the modern market, K. Polanyi's *The Great Transformation* (New York: Rinehart & Company, 1944).

of medical knowledge and skill. Even the most winning personality would not prevent a secretary from losing her job unless she could type reasonably fast. However, if we ask what the respective weight of skill and personality as a condition for success is, we find that only in exceptional cases is success predominantly the result of skill and of certain other human qualities like honesty, decency, and integrity. Although the proportion between skill and human qualities on the one hand and "personality" on the other hand as prerequisites for success varies, the "personality factor" always plays a decisive role. Success depends largely on how well a person sells himself on the market, how well he gets his personality across, how nice a "package" he is; whether he is "cheerful," "sound," "aggressive," "reliable," "ambitious"; furthermore what his family background is, what clubs he belongs to, and whether he knows the right people. The type of personality required depends to some degree on the special field in which a person works. A stockbroker, a salesman, a secretary, a railroad executive, a college professor, or a hotel manager must each offer different kinds of personality that, regardless of their differences, must fulfill one condition: to be in demand.

The fact that in order to have success it is not sufficient to have the skill and equipment for performing a given task but that one must be able to "put across" one's personality in competition with many others shapes the attitude toward oneself. If it were enough for the purpose of making a living to rely on what one knows and what one can do, one's self-esteem would be in proportion to one's capacities, that is, to one's use value; but since success depends largely on how one sells one's personality, one experiences oneself as a commodity to be sold. A person is not concerned with his life and happiness, but with becoming salable. This feeling might be compared to that of a commodity, of handbags on a counter, for instance, could they feel and think. Each handbag would try to make itself as "attractive" as possible in order to attract customers and to look as expensive as possible in order to obtain a higher price than its rivals. The handbag sold for the highest price would feel elated, since that would mean it was the most "valuable" one; the one which was not sold would feel sad and convinced of its own worthlessness. This fate might befall a bag which, though excellent in appearance and usefulness, had the bad luck to be out of date because of a change in fashion.

Like the handbag, one has to be in fashion on the personality market, and in order to be in fashion one has to know what kind of personality is most in demand. This knowledge is transmitted in a general way throughout the whole process of education, from kindergarten to college, and implemented by the family. The knowledge acquired at this early stage is not sufficient, however; it emphasizes only certain general qualities like adaptability, ambition, and sensitivity to the changing expectations of other people. The more specific picture of the models for success one gets elsewhere. The pictorial magazines, newspapers, and newsreels show the pictures and life stories of the successful in many variations. Pictorial advertising has a similar function. The successful executive who is pictured in a tailor's advertisement is the image of how one should look and be, if one is to draw down the "big money" on the contemporary personality market.

The most important means of transmitting the desired personality pattern to the average man is the motion picture. The young girl tries to emulate the facial expression, coiffure, gestures of a high-priced star as the most promising way to success. The young man tries to look and be like the model he sees on the screen. While the average citizen has little contact with the life of the most successful people, his relationship with the motion-picture stars is different. It is true that he has no real contact with them either, but he can see them on the screen again and again, can write them and receive their autographed pictures. In contrast to the time when the actor was socially despised but was nevertheless the transmitter of the works of great poets to his audience, our motion-picture stars have no great works or ideas to transmit, but their function is to serve as the link an average person has with the world of the "great." Even if he can not hope to become as successful as they are, he can try to emulate them; they are his saints and because of their success they embody the norms of living.

Since modern man experiences himself both as the seller and as the commodity to be sold on the market, his self-esteem depends on conditions beyond his control. If he is "successful," he is valuable; if he is not, he is worthless. The degree of insecurity which results from this orientation can hardly be overestimated. If one feels that one's own value is not constituted primarily by the human qualities one possesses, but by one's success on a competitive market with ever-changing conditions, one's self-esteem is bound to be shaky and in constant need of confirmation by others. Hence one is driven to strive relentlessly for success, and any setback is a severe threat to one's self-esteem; helplessness, insecurity, and inferiority feelings are the result. If the vicissitudes of the market are the judges of one's value, the sense of dignity and pride is destroyed.

But the problem is not only that of self-evaluation and self-esteem but of one's experience of oneself as an independent entity, of one's *identity with oneself*. As we shall see later, the mature and productive individual derives his feeling of identity from the experience of himself as the agent who is one with his powers; this feeling of self can be briefly expressed as meaning "*I am what I do*." In the marketing orientation man encounters his own powers as commodities alienated from him. He is not one with them but they are masked from him because what matters is not his self-realization in the process of using them but his success in the process of selling them. Both his powers and what they create become estranged, something different from himself, something for others to judge and to use; thus his feeling of identity becomes as shaky as his self-esteem; it is constituted by the sum total of roles one can play: "*I am as you desire me.*"

Ibsen has expressed this state of selfhood in Peer Gynt: Peer Gynt tries to discover his self and he finds that he is like an onion — one layer after the other can be peeled off and there is no core to be found. Since man cannot live doubting his identity, he must, in the marketing orientation, find the conviction of identity not in reference to himself and his powers but in the opinion of others about him. His prestige, status, success, the fact that he is known to others as being a certain person are a substitute for the genuine feeling of identity. This situation makes him utterly dependent on the way others look at him and forces him to keep up the role in which he once had become successful. If I and my powers are separated from each other then, indeed, is my self constituted by the price I fetch.

The way one experiences others is not different from the way one experiences oneself. Others are experienced as commodities like oneself; they too do not present *themselves* but their salable part. The difference between people is reduced to a merely quantitative difference of being *more or less* successful, attractive, hence valuable. This process is not different from what happens to commodities on the market. A painting and a pair of shoes can both be expressed in, and reduced to, their exchange value, their price; so many pairs of shoes are "equal" to one painting. In the same way the difference between people is reduced to a common element, their price on the market. Their individuality, that which is peculiar and unique in them, is valueless and, in fact, a ballast. The meaning which the word *peculiar* has assumed is quite expressive of this attitude. Instead of denoting the greatest achievement of man — that of having developed his individuality — it has become almost synonymous with *queer*. The word *equality* has also changed its meaning. The idea that all men are created equal implied that all men have the same fundamental right to be considered as ends in themselves and not as means. Today, equality has become equivalent to *interchangeability*, and is the very negation of individuality. Equality, instead of being the condition for the development of each man's peculiarity, means the extinction of individuality, the "selflessness" characteristic of the marketing orientation. Equality was conjunctive with difference, but it has become synonymous with "in-difference" and, indeed, indifference is what characterizes modern man's relationship to himself and to others.

These conditions necessarily color all human relationships. When the individual self is neglected, the relationships between people must of necessity become superficial, because not they themselves but interchangeable commodities are related. People are not able and cannot afford to be concerned with that which is unique and "peculiar" in each other. However, the market creates a kind of comradeship of its own. Everybody is involved in the same battle of competition, shares the same striving for success; all meet under the same conditions of the market (or at least believe they do). Everyone knows how the others feel because each is in the same boat: alone, afraid to fail, eager to please; no quarter is given or expected in this battle.

The superficial character of human relationships leads many to hope that they can find depth and intensity of feeling in individual love. But love for one person and love for one's neighbor are indivisible; in any given culture, love relationships are only a more intense expression of the relatedness to man prevalent in that culture. Hence it is an illusion to expect that the loneliness of man rooted in the marketing orientation can be cured by individual love.

Thinking as well as feeling is determined by the marketing orientation. Thinking assumes the function of grasping things quickly so as to be able to manipulate them successfully. Furthered by widespread and efficient education, this leads to a high degree of intelligence, but not of reason. For manipulative purposes, all that is necessary to know is the surface features of things, the superficial. The truth, to be uncovered by penetrating to the essence of phenomena, becomes an obsolete concept — truth not only in the prescientific sense of "absolute" truth, dogmatically maintained without reference to empirical data, but also in the sense of truth attained by man's reason applied to his observations and open to revisions. Most intelligence tests are attuned to this kind of thinking; they measure not so much the capacity for reason and understanding as the capacity for quick mental adaptation to a given situation; "mental adjustment tests" would be the adequate name for them.[4] For this kind of thinking the application of the categories of comparison and of quantitative measurement — rather than a thorough analysis of a given phenomenon and its quality — is essential. All problems are equally "interesting" and there is little sense of the respective differences in their importance. Knowledge itself becomes a commodity. Here, too, man is alienated from his own power; thinking and knowing are experienced as a tool to produce results. Knowledge of man himself, psychology, which in the great tradition of Western thought was held to be the condition for virtue, for right living, for happiness, has degenerated into an instrument to be used for better manipulation of others and oneself, in market research, in political propaganda, in advertising, and so on.

Evidently this type of thinking has a profound effect on our educational system. From grade school to graduate school, the aim of learning is to gather as much information as possible that is mainly useful for the purposes of the market. Students ae supposed to learn so many things that they have hardly time and energy left to *think*. Not the interest in the subjects taught or in knowledge and insight as such, but the enhanced exchange value knowledge gives is the main incentive for wanting more and better education. We find today a tremendous enthusiasm for knowledge and education, but at the same time a skeptical or contemptuous attitude toward the allegedly impractical

---

[4] Cf. Ernest Schachtel, "Zum Begriff und zur Diagnosis der Persönlichkeit in 'Personality Tests' [On the Concept and Diagnosis of Personality Tests]," *Zeitschrift für Sozialforschung* (Jahrgang 6, 1937), 597–624.

and useless thinking which is concerned "only" with the truth and which has no exchange value on the market.

Although I have presented the marketing orientation as one of the nonproductive orientations, it is in many ways so different that it belongs in a category of its own. The receptive, exploitative, and hoarding orientations have one thing in common: each is one form of human relatedness which, if dominant in a person, is specific of him and characterizes him. . . . The marketing orientation, however, does not develop something which is potentially in the person (unless we make the absurd assertion that "nothing" is also part of the human equipment); its very nature is that no specific and permanent kind of relatedness is developed, but that the very changeability of attitudes is the only permanent quality of such orientation. In this orientation, those qualities are developed which can best be sold. Not one particular attitude is predominant, but the emptiness which can be filled most quickly with the desired quality. This quality, however, ceases to be one in the proper sense of the word; it is only a role, the pretense of a quality, to be readily exchanged if another one is more desirable. Thus, for instance, respectability is sometimes desirable. The salesmen in certain branches of business ought to impress the public with those qualities of reliability, soberness, and respectability which were genuine in many a businessman of the nineteenth century. Now one looks for a man who instills confidence because he *looks* as if he had these qualities; what this man sells on the personality market is his ability to look the part; what kind of person is behind that role does not matter and is nobody's concern. He himself is not interested in his honesty, but in what it gets for him on the market. The premise of the marketing orientation is emptiness, the lack of any specific quality which could not be subject to change, since any persistent trait of character might conflict some day with the requirements of the market. Some roles would not fit in with the peculiarities of the person; therefore we must do away with them — not with the roles but with the peculiarities. The marketing personality must be free, free of all individuality.

The character orientations which have been described so far are by no means as separate from one another as it may appear from this sketch. The receptive orientation, for instance, may be dominant in a person but it is usually blended with any or all of the other orientations. . . . I want to stress at this point that all orientations are part of the human equipment, and the dominance of any specific orientation depends to a large extent on the peculiarity of the culture in which the individual lives. Although a more detailed analysis of the relationship between the various orientations and social patterns must be reserved for a study which deals primarily with problems of social psychology, I should like to suggest here a tentative hypothesis as to the social conditions making for the dominance of any of the four nonproductive types. It should be noted that the significance of the study of the correlation between character orientation and social structure lies not only in the fact that it helps us understand some of the most significant causes for the formation of character, but also in the fact that specific orientations — inasmuch as they are common to most members of a culture or social class — represent powerful emotional forces the operation of which we must know in order to understand the functioning of society. In view of the current emphasis on the impact of culture on personality, I should like to state that the relationship between society and the individual is not to be understood simply in the sense that cultural patterns and social institutions "influence" the individual. The interaction goes much deeper; the whole personality of the average individual is molded by the way people relate to each other, and it is determined by the socioeconomic and political structure of society to such an extent that, in principle, one can infer from the analysis of one individual the totality of the social structure in which he lives.

The receptive orientation is often to be found in societies in which the right of one group to exploit another is firmly established. Since the exploited group has no power to change, or any idea of changing, its situation, it will tend to look up to its masters as to its providers, as to those from whom one receives everything life can give. No matter how little the slave receives, he feels that by his own effort he could have acquired even less, since the structure of his society impresses him with the fact that he is unable to organize it and to rely on his own activity and reason. As far as contemporary American culture is concerned, it seems at first glance that the receptive attitude is entirely absent. Our whole culture, its ideas, and its practice discourage the receptive orientation and emphasize that each one has to look out, and be responsible, for himself and that he has to use his own initiative if he wants to "get anywhere." However, while the receptive orientation is discouraged, it is by no means absent. The need to conform and to please, which has been discussed in the foregoing pages, leads to the feeling of helplessness, which is the root of subtle receptiveness in modern man. It appears particularly in the attitude toward the "expert" and public opinion. People expect that in every field there is an expert who can tell them how things are and how they ought to be done, and that all they ought to do is listen to him and swallow his ideas. There are experts for science, experts for happiness, and writers become experts in the art of living by the very fact that they are authors of best sellers. This subtle but rather general receptiveness assumes somewhat grotesque forms in modern "folklore," fostered particularly by advertising. While everyone knows that realistically the "get-rich-quick" schemes do not work, there is a widespread daydream of the effortless life. It is partly expressed in connection with the use of gadgets; the car which needs no shifting, the fountain pen which saves the trouble of removing the cap are only random examples of this phantasy. It is particularly prevalent in those schemes which deal with happiness. A very characteristic quotation is the following: "This book," the author says, "tells you how to be twice the man or woman you ever were before — happy, well, brimming with energy, confident, capable and free of care. You are required to follow no laborious mental or physical program; it is much simpler than that. . . . As laid down here the route to the promised profit may appear strange, for few of us can imagine *getting without striving*. . . . Yet that is so, as you will see."[5]

The exploitative character, with its motto "I take what I need," goes back to piratical and feudal ancestors and goes forward from there to the robber barons of the nineteenth century who exploited the natural resources of the continent. The "pariah" and "adventure" capitalists, to use Max Weber's terms, roaming the earth for profit, are men of this stamp, men whose aim was to buy cheap and sell dear and who ruthlessly pursued power and wealth. The free market as it operated in the eighteenth and nineteenth centuries under competitive conditions nurtured this type. Our own age has seen a revival of naked exploitativeness in the authoritarian systems which attempted to exploit the natural and human resources, not so much of their own country but of any other country there were powerful enough to invade. They proclaimed the right of might and rationalized it by pointing to the law of nature which makes the stronger survive; love and decency were signs of weakness; thinking was the occupation of cowards and degenerates.

The hoarding orientation existed side by side with the exploitative orientation in the eighteenth and nineteenth centuries. The hoarding type was conservative, less interested in ruthless acquisition than in methodical economic pursuits, based on sound principles and on the preservation of what had been acquired. To him property was a symbol of his self and its protection a supreme value. This orientation gave him a great deal of security; his possession of property and family, protected as they were by the relatively stable conditions of the nineteenth century, constituted a safe and manageable world. Puritan ethics, with the emphasis on work and success as evidence of goodness, supported the feeling of security and tended to give life meaning and a religious sense of fulfillment. This combination of a stable world, stable possessions, and a stable ethic gave the members of the middle class a feeling of belonging, self-confidence, and pride.

The marketing orientation does not come out of the eighteenth or nineteenth centuries; it is definitely a modern product. It is only recently that the package, the label, the brand name have become important, in people as well as in commodities. The gospel of working loses weight and the gospel of selling becomes paramount. In feudal times, social mobility was exceedingly limited and one could not use one's personality to get ahead. In the days of the competitive market, social mobility was relatively great, especially in the United States; if one "delivered the goods" one could get ahead. Today, the opportunities for the lone individual who can make a fortune all by himself are, in comparison with the previous period, greatly diminished. He

[5] Hal Falvey, *Ten Seconds That Will Change Your Life* (Chicago: Wilcox & Follett, 1946).

who wants to get ahead has to fit into large organizations, and his ability to play the expected role is one of his main assets.

The depersonalization, the emptiness, the meaninglessness of life, the automatization of the individual result in a growing dissatisfaction and in a need to search for a more adequate way of living and for norms which could guide man to this end. The productive orientation which I am going to discuss now points to the type of character in whom growth and the development of all his potentialities is the aim to which all other activities are subordinated.

THE PRODUCTIVE ORIENTATION. *General characteristics.* From the time of classic and medieval literature up to the end of the nineteenth century a great deal of effort was expended in describing the vision of what the good man and the good society ought to be. Such ideas were expressed partly in the form of philosophical or theological treatises, partly in the form of utopias. The twentieth century is conspicuous for the absence of such visions. The emphasis is on critical analysis of man and society, in which positive visions of what man ought to be are only implied. While there is no doubt that this criticism is of utmost significance and a condition for any improvement of society, the absence of visions projecting a "better" man and a "better" society has had the effect of paralyzing man's faith in himself and his future (and is at the same time the result of such a paralysis).

Contemporary psychology and particularly psychoanalysis are no exception in this respect. Freud and his followers have given a splendid analysis of the neurotic character. Their clinical description of the nonproductive character (in Freud's terms, the pregenital character) is exhaustive and accurate — quite regardless of the fact that the theoretical concepts they used are in need of revision. But the character of the normal, mature, healthy personality has found scarcely any consideration. This character, called the genital character by Freud, has remained a rather vague and abstract concept. It is defined by him as the character structure of a person in whom the oral and anal libido has lost its dominant position and functions under the supremacy of genital sexuality, the aim of which is sexual union with a member of the opposite sex. The description of the genital character does not go far beyond the statement that it is the character structure of an individual who is capable of functioning well sexually and socially.

In discussing the *productive character* I venture beyond critical analysis and inquire into the nature of the fully developed character that is the aim of human development and simultaneously the ideal of humanistic ethics. It may serve as a preliminary approach to the concept of productive orientation to state its connection with Freud's genital character. Indeed, if we do not use Freud's term literally in the context of his libido theory but *symbolically*, it denotes quite accurately the meaning of productiveness. For the stage of sexual maturity is that in which man has the capacity of natural production; by the union of the sperm and the egg new life is produced. While this type of production is common to man and to animals, the capacity for material production is specific for man. Man is not only a rational and social animal. He can also be defined as a producing animal, capable of transforming the materials which he finds at hand, using his reason and imagination. Not only *can* he produce, he *must* produce in order to live. Material production, however, is but the most frequent symbol for productiveness as an aspect of character. The "productive orientation"[6] of personality refers to a fundamental attitude, *a mode of relatedness* in all realms of human experience. It covers mental, emotional, and sensory responses to others, to oneself, and to things. Productiveness is man's ability to use his powers and to realize the potentialities inherent in him. If we say *he* must use *his* powers we imply that he must be free and not dependent on someone who controls his powers. We imply, furthermore, that he is guided by reason, since he can make use of his powers only if he knows what they are, how to use them, and what to use them for. Productiveness means that he experiences himself as the embodiment of his powers and as the "actor"; that he feels himself one with his powers and at the same time that they are not masked and alienated from him.

In order to avoid the misunderstandings to which the term "productiveness" lends itself, it seems appropriate to discuss briefly what is not meant by productiveness.

Generally the word "productiveness" is associated with creativeness, particularly artistic creativeness. The real artist, indeed, is the most convincing representative of productiveness. But not all artists are productive; a conventional painting, e.g., may exhibit nothing more than the technical skill to reproduce the likeness of a person in photographic fashion on a canvas. But a person can experience, see, feel, and think productively without having the gift to create something visible or communicable. *Productiveness is an attitude which every human being is capable of, unless he is mentally and emotionally crippled.*

The term "productive" is also apt to be confused with "active," and "productiveness" with "activity." While the two terms can be synonymous (for instance, in Aristotle's concept of activity), activity in modern usage frequently indicates the very opposite of productiveness. Activity is usually defined as behavior which brings about a change in an existing situation by an expenditure of energy. In contrast, a person is described as passive if he is unable to change or overtly influence an existing situation and is influenced or moved by forces outside himself. This current concept of activity takes into account only the actual expenditure of energy and the change brought about by it. It does not distinguish between the underlying psychic conditions governing the activities.

[8] Productiveness as used [here] is meant as an expansion of the concept of spontaneity described in *Escape from Freedom*.

An example, though an extreme one, of nonproductive activity is the activity of a person under hypnosis. The person in a deep hypnotic trance may have his eyes open, may walk, talk, and do things; he "acts." The general definition of activity would apply to him, since energy is spent and some change brought about. But if we consider the particular character and quality of this activity, we find that it is not really the hypnotized person who is the actor, but the hypnotist who, by means of his suggestions, acts through him. While the hypnotic trance is an artificial state, it is an extreme but characteristic example of a situation in which a person can be active and yet not be the true actor, his activity resulting from compelling forces over which he has no control.

A common type of nonproductive activity is the reaction to anxiety, whether acute or chronic, conscious or unconscious, which is frequently at the root of the frantic preoccupations of men today. Different from anxiety-motivated activity, though often blended with it, is the type of activity based on submission to or dependence on an authority. The authority may be feared, admired, or "loved" — usually all three are mixed — but the cause of the activity is the command of the authority, both in a formal way and with regard to its contents. The person is active because the authority wants him to be, and he does what the authority wants him to do. This kind of activity is found in the authoritarian character. To him activity means to act in the name of something higher than his own self. He can act in the name of God, the past, or duty, but not in the name of himself. The authoritarian character receives the impulse to act from a superior power which is neither assailable nor changeable, and is consequently unable to heed spontaneous impulses from within himself.[7]

Resembling submissive activity is automaton activity. Here we do not find dependence on overt authority, but rather on anonymous authority as it is represented by public opinion, culture patterns, common sense, or "science." The person feels or does what he is supposed to feel or do; his activity lacks spontaneity in the sense that it does not originate from his own mental or emotional experience but from an outside source.

Among the most powerful sources of activity are irrational passions. The person who is driven by stinginess, masochism, envy, jealousy, and all other forms of greed is compelled to act; yet his actions are neither free nor rational but in opposition to reason and to his interests as a human being. A person so obsessed repeats himself, becoming more and more inflexible, more and more stereotyped. He is active, but he is not productive.

Although the source of these activities is irrational and the acting persons

---

[7] But the authoritarian character does not only tend to submit but also wishes to dominate others. In fact, both the sadistic and the masochistic sides are always present, and they differ only in degree of their strength and their repression respectively. (See the discussion of the authoritarian character in *Escape from Freedom*, pp. 141ff.)

are neither free nor rational, there can be important practical results, often leading to material success. In the concept of productiveness we are not concerned with activity *necessarily* leading to practical results but with an attitude, with a mode of reaction and orientation toward the world and oneself in the process of living. We are concerned with *man's character, not with his success.*[8]

Productiveness is man's realization of the potentialities characteristic of him, the use of his *powers*. But what is "power"? It is rather ironical that this word denotes two contradictory concepts: *power of* = capacity and *power over* = domination. This contradiction, however, is of a particular kind. Power = domination results from the paralysis of power = capacity. *"Power over" is the perversion of "power to."* The ability of man to make productive use of his powers is his potency; the inability is his impotence. With his power of reason he can penetrate the surface of pehnomena and understand their essence. With his power of love he can break through the wall which separates one person from another. With his power of imagination he can visualize things not yet existing; he can plan and thus begin to create. Where potency is lacking, man's relatedness to the world is perverted into a desire to dominate, to exert power over others as though they were things. Domination is coupled with death, potency with life. Domination springs from impotence and in turn reinforces it, for it an individual can force somebody else to serve him, his own need to be productive is increasingly paralyzed.

How is man related to the world when he uses his powers productively?

The world outside oneself can be experienced in two ways: *reproductively* by perceiving actuality in the same fashion as a film makes a literal record of things photographed (although even mere reproductive perception requires the active participation of the mind); and *generatively* by conceiving it, by enlivening and re-creating this new material through the spontaneous activity of one's own mental and emotional powers. While to a certain extent everyone does react in both ways, the respective weight of each kind of experience differs widely. Sometimes either one of the two is atrophied, and the study of these extreme cases in which the reproductive or the generative mode is almost absent offers the best approach to the understanding of each of these phenomena.

The relative atrophy of the generative capacity is very frequent in our culture. A person may be able to recognize things as they are (or as his culture maintains them to be), but he is unable to enliven his perception from within.

[8] An interesting although incomplete attempt to analyze productive thinking is Max Wertheimer's posthumously published work, *Productive Thinking* (New York: Harper & Brothers, 1945). Some of the aspects of productiveness are dealt with by Munsterberg, Natorp, Bergson, and James; in Brentano's and Husserl's analysis of the psychic "act"; in Dilthey's analysis of artistic production and in O. Schwarz, *Medizinische Anthropologie* (Leipzig: Hirzel, 1929), pp. iii ff. In all these works, however, the problem is not treated in relation to character.

Such a person is the perfect "realist," who sees all there is to be seen of the surface features of phenomena but who is quite incapable of penetrating below the surface to the essential, and of visualizing what is not yet apparent. He sees the details but not the whole, the trees but not the forest. Reality to him is only the sum total of what has already materialized. This person is not lacking in imagination, but his is a calculating imagination, combining factors all of which are known and in existence, and inferring their future operation.

On the other hand, the person who has lost the capacity to perceive actuality is insane. The psychotic person builds up an inner world of reality in which he seems to have full confidence; he lives in his own world, and the common factors of reality as perceived by all men are unreal to him. When a person sees objects which do not exist in reality but are entirely the product of his imagination, he has hallucinations; he interprets events in terms of his own feelings, without reference to, or at least without proper acknowledgment of, what goes on in reality. A paranoid person may believe that he is being persecuted, and a chance remark may indicate a plan to humiliate and ruin him. He is convinced that the lack of any more obvious and explicit manifestation of such intention does not prove anything; that, although the remark may appear harmless on the surface, its real meaning becomes clear if one looks "deeper." For the psychotic person actual reality is wiped out and an inner reality has taken its place.

The "realist" sees only the surface features of things; he sees the manifest world, he can reproduce it photographically in his mind, and he can act by manipulating things and people as they appear in this picture. The insane person is incapable of seeing reality as it is; he perceives reality only as a symbol and a reflection of his inner world. Both are sick. The sickness of the psychotic who has lost contact with reality is such that he cannot function socially. The sickness of the "realist" impoverishes him as a human being. While he is not incapacitated in his social functioning, his view of reality is so distorted because of its lack of depth and perspective that he is apt to err when more than manipulation of immediately given data and short-range aims are involved. *"Realism" seems to be the very opposite of insanity and yet it is only its complement.*

The true opposite of both "realism" and insanity is productiveness. The normal human being is capable of relating himself to the world simultaneously by perceiving it as it is and by conceiving it enlivened and enriched by his own powers. If one of the two capacities is atrophied, man is sick; but the normal person has both capacities even though their respective weights differ. The presence of both reproductive and generative capacities is a precondition for productiveness; they are opposite poles whose interaction is the dynamic source of productiveness. With the last statement I want to emphasize that productiveness is not the sum or combination of both capacities but that it is something new which springs from this interaction.

We have described productiveness as a particular mode of relatedness to the world. The question arises whether there is anything which the productive person produces and if so, what? While it is true that man's productiveness can create material things, works of art, and systems of thought, *by far the most important object of productiveness is man himself.*

Birth is only one particular step in a continuum which begins with conception and ends with death. All that is between these two poles is a process of giving birth to one's potentialities, of bringing to life all that is potentially given in the two cells. But while physical growth proceeds by itself, if only the proper conditions are given, the process of birth on the mental plane, in contrast, does not occur automatically. It requires productive activity to give life to the emotional and intellectual potentialities of man, to give birth to his self. It is part of the tragedy of the human situation that the development of the self is never completed; even under the best conditions only part of man's potentialities is realized. Man always dies before he is fully born.

Although I do not intend to present a history of the concept of productiveness, I want to give some outstanding illustrations which may help to clarify the concept further. Productiveness is one of the key concepts in Aristotle's system of ethics. One can determine virtue, he says, by ascertaining the function of man. Just as in the case of a flute player, a sculptor, or any artist, the good is thought to reside in the specific function which distinguishes these men from others and makes them what they are, the good of man also resides in the specific function which distinguishes him from other species and makes him what he is. Such a function is an *"activity* of the soul which follows or implies a rational principle."[9] "But it makes perhaps no small difference," he says, "whether we place the chief good in possession or in use, in state of mind or activity. For the state of mind may exist without producing any good result, as in a man who is asleep or in some other way quite inactive, but the activity can not; for one who has the activity will of necessity be acting, and acting well."[10] The good man for Aristotle is the man who by his activity, under the guidance of his reason, brings to life the potentialities specific of man.

"By virtue and power," Spinoza says, "I understand the same thing."[11] Freedom and blessedness consist in man's understanding of himself and in his effort to become that which he potentially is, to approach "nearer and nearer to the model of human nature."[12] Virtue to Spinoza is identical with the use of man's powers and vice is his failure to use his power; the essence of evil for Spinoza is impotence.[13]

---

[9] *Nicomachean Ethics*, 1098[a], 8.
[10] *Ibid.*, 1098[b], 32.
[11] Spinoza, *Ethics*, IV, Def. 8.
[12] *Ibid.*, IV, Preface.
[13] *Ibid.*, IV, Def. 20.

VI Consistency Theory: Cognitive Dissonance Version

Consistency theorizing views personality as determined by the match or mismatch between internal expectations and external events. Kelly states a pure form of this position: man is considered as primarily concerned with predicting and controlling his world. Man construes events, and with the concepts thus developed, formulates hypotheses about subsequent experience and tests these hypotheses. Whenever hypotheses do not match occurrences, anxiety results, and the constructs underlying hypotheses are changed in some fashion. The constructs a person has, organized into a construction system, constitute his personality, according to Kelly. To have much of a position on the periphery of personality, Kelly would have to detail the various kinds of constructs and construction systems that commonly occur. As you will see, however, he does none of this; like Allport, Kelly takes an extreme position by emphasizing individuality.

McClelland expresses a variant on the cognitive dissonance model, in that only large discrepancies between expectations and occurrences are considered unpleasant and to be avoided. In contrast, small discrepancies are considered pleasant and actually sought in order to protect against the boredom of complete accuracy of prediction. This core level modification enables McClelland to postulate, at the peripheral level, that there are approach and avoidance versions of each motive. The avoidance version of a need is learned when the relevant content area has been fraught with large discrepancies between expectation and occurrence, whereas the approach version is learned when small discrepancies have been predominant. The intricacies of this position are detailed both in terms of core considerations and periphery considerations.

GEORGE A. KELLY

Basic Theory

[First] we lay down the Fundamental Postulate of our psychology of personal constructs. The theory is then elaborated by means of eleven corollaries.

FUNDAMENTAL POSTULATE

Fundamental Postulate: A person's processes are psychologically channelized by the ways in which he anticipates events.

Let us try to lay down a postulate. . . . In doing so we shall have to recognize certain limitations in our theory-building efforts. The postulate we formulate will not necessarily provide a statement from which everyone will make the same deductions. The system built upon the postulate will therefore not be completely logic-tight. Rather, we shall strive to make our theoretical position provocative, and hence fertile, rather than legalistic.

The initial statement, *a person's processes are psychologically channelized by the ways in which he anticipates events,* seems to meet our specifications. Before we go on to examine the explicit meanings and the ensuing implications of this rather simple declarative sentence, let us have a brief look at what we mean by a fundamental postulate in a scientific theory. A postulate

Reprinted from *The Psychology of Personal Constructs,* Vol. One by George A. Kelly, Ph.D. By permission of W. W. Norton & Company, Inc. Copyright 1955 by George A. Kelly.

is, of course, an assumption. But it is an assumption so basic in nature that it antecedes everything which is said in the logical system which it supports.

Now, a person may question the truth of a statement which is proposed as a fundamental postulate; indeed, we are always free, as scientists, to question the truth of anything. But we should bear in mind that the moment we do question the truth of a statement proposed as a postulate, that statement is no longer a postulate in our subsequent discourse. A statement, therefore, is a postulate only if we accord it that status. If we bring the statement into dispute, as well we may in some instances, we must recognize that we are then arguing from other postulates either explicitly stated or, more likely, implicitly believed. Thus, in scientific reasoning nothing antecedes the postulate, as long as it is a postulate, and the truth of a statement is never questioned as long as that statement is in use as a postulate.

What we have really said, then, is: let us suppose, for the sake of the discussion which is to follow, that a person's processes are psychologically channelized by the ways in which he anticipates events. Let it be clearly understood that we are not proposing this postulate as an ultimate statement of truth. In modern scientific thought it is always customary to accept even one's postulates as tentative or ad interim statements of truth and then to see what follows.

Terms

Let us look at the words we have carefully chosen for this Fundamental Postulate.

PERSON. This term is used to indicate the substance with which we are primarily concerned. Our first consideration is the individual person rather than any part of the person, any group of persons, or any particular process manifested in the person's behavior.

PROCESSES. Instead of postulating an inert substance, a step which would inevitably lead to the necessity for establishing, as a corollary, the existence of some sort of mental energy, the subject of psychology is assumed at the outset to be a process. This is akin to saying that the organism is basically a behaving organism, a statement which has been emphasized by certain psychologists for some time now. But our emphasis, if anything, is even more strongly upon the kinetic nature of the substance with which we are dealing. For our purposes, the person is not an object which is temporarily in a moving state but is himself a form of motion.

PSYCHOLOGICALLY. Here we indicate the type of realm with which we intend to deal. Our theory lies within a limited realm, which is not necessarily overlapped by physiology on the one hand or by sociology on the other. Some of the phenomena which physiological systems seek to explain or which sociological systems seek to explain are admittedly outside our present field of interest and we feel no obligation to account for them within this particular theoretical structure.

As we have indicated before, we do not conceive the substance of psychology to be itself psychological — or physiological, or sociological, or to be preempted by any system. A person's processes are what they are; and psychology, physiology, or what have you, are simply systems concocted for trying to anticipate them. Thus, when we use the term *psychologically*, we mean that we are conceptualizing processes in a psychological manner, not that the processes are psychological rather than something else.

Psychology refers to a group of systems for explaining behavior, all of which seem to offer similar coverage. Thus, when we identify our system as psychological, we are loosely identifying it with certain other systems because it has a similar realm and range of convenience.

In theorizing, some people think that one ought to start out by defining the boundaries of the field of psychology. But we see no point in trying to stake out property claims for psychology's realm. The kinds of realms we are talking about are not preemptive at all — what belongs to one can still belong to another. The thing for one to do is simply erect his system and then set out to explore its range of convenience, whether that be large or small.

CHANNELIZED. We conceive a person's processes as operating through a network of pathways rather than as fluttering about in a vast emptiness. The network is flexible and is frequently modified, but it is structured and it both facilitates and restricts a person's range of action.

WAYS. The channels are established as means to ends. They are laid down by the devices which a person invents in order to achieve a purpose. A person's processes, psychologically speaking, slip into the grooves which are cut out by the mechanisms he adopts for realizing his objectives.

HE. Our emphasis is upon the way in which the individual man chooses to operate, rather than upon the way in which the operation might ideally be carried out. Each person may erect and utilize different ways, and it is the way he chooses which channelizes his processes.

ANTICIPATES. Here is where we build into our theory its predictive and motivational features. Like the prototype of the scientist that he is, man seeks prediction. His structured network of pathways leads toward the future so that he may anticipate it. This is the function it serves. Anticipation is both the push and pull of the psychology of personal constructs.

EVENTS. Man ultimately seeks to anticipate real events. This is where we see psychological processes as tied down to reality. Anticipation is not merely carried on for its own sake; it is carried on so that future reality may be better represented. It is the future which tantalizes man, not the past. Always he reaches out to the future through the window of the present.

We now have a statement of a fundamental postulate for which we have high hopes. Perhaps there can spring from it a theory of personality with movement as the phenomenon rather than the epiphenomenon, with the psychological processes of the layman making the same sense as those of the scientist, a dynamic psychology without the trappings of animism, a perceptual psychology without passivity, a behaviorism in which the behaving person is credited with having some sense, a learning theory in which learning is considered so universal that it appears in the postulate rather than as a special class of phenomena, a motivational theory in which man is neither pricked into action by the sharp points of stimuli nor dyed with the deep tones of hedonism, and a view of personality which permits psychotherapy to appear both lawful and plausible. Let us call this theory *the psychology of personal constructs.*

CONSTRUCTION COROLLARY

> *Construction Corollary: A person anticipates events by construing their replications.*

In building the system which we call *the psychology of personal constructs* we have chosen to rely upon one basic postulate and to amplify the system by stating certain propositions which, in part, follow from the postulate and, in part, elaborate it in greater detail. These propositions are termed *corollaries,* although, logically, they involve somewhat more than what is minimally implied by the exact wording of the postulate. Our corollary introduces the notions of construing and replication.

Terms

CONSTRUING. By construing we mean "placing an interpretation": a person places an interpretation upon what is construed. He erects a structure, within the framework of which the substance takes shape or assumes meaning. The substance which he construes does not produce the structure; the person does.

The structure which is erected by construing is essentially abstractive, though the person may be so limited in the abstraction that his construing may, in effect, be relatively concretistic. In this connection we shall need to say much more later about the forms of construing. For the present, however, since we are sketching the psychology of personal constructs in preliminary outline only, we shall not go into great detail.

In construing, the person notes features in a series of elements which characterize some of the elements and are particularly uncharacteristic of others. Thus he erects constructs of similarity and contrast. Both the similarity and the contrast are inherent in the same construct. A construct which implied similarity without contrast would represent just as much of a chaotic undifferentiated homogeneity as a construct which implied contrast without similarity would represent a chaotic particularized heterogeneity. The former would leave the person engulfed in a sea with no landmarks to relieve the monotony; the latter would confront him with an interminable series of kaleidoscopic changes in which nothing would ever appear familiar.

Construing is not to be confounded with verbal formulation. A person's behavior may be based upon many interlocking equivalence-difference patterns which are never communicated in symbolic speech. Many of these preverbal or nonverbal governing constructs are embraced in the realm of physiology. That is to say, they deal with elements which fall within the ranges of convenience of physiological construction systems. Thus they may have to do with such matters as digestion, glandular secretion, and so on, which do not normally fall within the ranges of convenience of psychological systems.

If a person is asked how he proposes to digest his dinner, he will be hard put to answer the question. It is likely that he will say that such matters are beyond his control. They seem to him to be beyond his control because he cannot anticipate them within the same system which he must use for communication. Yet digestion is an individually structured process, and what one anticipates has a great deal to do with the course it takes.

What we are saying is that the notion of construing has a wide range of convenience, if we choose to use it that way. It may even be used within borderland areas of the realm of physiology. To be sure, it operates somewhat less conveniently there, but the overlapping functions of psychological and physiological systems in this regard help to make it clear that psychology and physiology ought not to try to draw preemptive boundaries between themselves. We recognize that the psychological notion of construing has a wide range of convenience, which is by no means limited to those experiences which people can talk about or those which they can think about privately.

Construing also transcends disciplinary boundaries in another manner. A person develops a physiological construct system. We say it is a physiological construct system because it is designed around the same foci of convenience as other "physiological" systems. We are perfectly willing, therefore, to call it a "physiological" system. But that does not prevent us from examining the person's private system from a psychological point of view. Why, psychologically, did he find it convenient to look at matters this way rather than that? When we examine the personal thinking which takes the form of a physiological construction system, we may find it useful to appraise it from a psychological point of view. Thus, we may subsume a person's physiological construction system within our own psychological system.

The physiologist may turn around and do the same thing to the psychologist. He may, if he wishes, try to subsume a person's psychological system within his own professional physiological system. He may interpret ideas of grandeur in terms of physiological constructs of circulation, cortical topography, and so on. One person may subsume the constructs of A and B under the construct of C. Another may subsume B and C under A. In fact, this kind of upsetting of the hierarchical apple cart characterizes much of our day-to-day thinking, as we shall see later.

REPLICATIONS. The substance that a person construes is itself a process — just as the living person is a process. It presents itself from the beginning as an unending and undifferentiated process. Only when man attunes his ear to recurrent themes in the monotonous flow does his universe begin to make sense to him. Like a musician, he must phrase his experience in order to make sense out of it. The phrases are distinguished events. The separation of events is what man produces for himself when he decides to chop up time into manageable lengths. Within these limited segments, which are based on recurrent themes, man begins to discover the bases for likenesses and differences.

Consider a day. Concretely, today is not yesterday, nor is tomorrow today. Time does not double back on itself. But after a succession of time man is able to detect a recurrent theme in its ever flowing process. It is possible to abstract the recurrent theme in terms of the rising and the setting of the sun. Moreover, the same theme does not recur when time is segmented in other ways. Thus, the concept of a day is erected along the incessant stream of time — a day which is, in its own way, like other days and yet clearly distinguishable from the moments and the years.

Once events have been given their beginnings and endings, and their similarities and contrasts construed, it becomes feasible to try to predict them, just as one predicts that a tomorrow will follow today. What is predicted is not that tomorrow will be a duplicate of today but that there are replicative aspects of tomorrow's event which may be safely predicted. Thus man anticipates events by construing their replications.

Mathematical Implications of the Construction Corollary

The statistics of probability are based upon the concept of replicated events. And, of course, they are also contrived to measure the predictability of further replications of the events. The two factors from which predictions are made are the number of replications already observed and the amount of similarity which can be abstracted among the replications. The latter factor involves some complicated logical problems — for example, representative sampling — and, in practice, it is the one which usually makes predictions go awry. Since the abstractive judgment of what it is that has been replicated is the basis for measuring the amount of similarity, we find that the concept-formation task which precedes the statistical manipulation of data is basic to any conclusions one reaches by mathematical logic.

The old arithmetic adage that "you can't add cows and horses" holds here. An event is replicative of another only if one is willing to accept the abstracted similarity of the two. Thus a person who owns one *cow* and one *horse* may say that he owns two *animals* — if he is willing to accept the *animal-like* abstraction of the two of them.

At a more complicated level one may average the results of two test performances of the same person, provided, again, he is willing to accept the abstraction of the similarity in both of them. For example, one test may be a *performance* type of test and the other a *verbal* type of test. If one averages the results, what he gets is an expression of the underlying feature in both of them. If he uses a weighted average, what he gets is an expression which is a more concrete representation of the more heavily weighted test score.

We may think of it this way. All mathematical expressions, when applied to real events, are, at best, approximations. One can always question the appropriateness of the use of a statistical measure such as chi-square, regardless of the context. The events to which this nonparametric statistic is applied must be assumed to be replications of each other. We can enter the cells of a chi-square table with cows and horses, but when we do so the cow-ness must be dropped from the cows, the horse-ness must be dropped from the horses, and only the animal-ness in both of them allowed to remain. Thus, whenever one uses the chi-square statistic, he must be aware of the abstractive implications in his data. What one could conclude from a chi-square computation from a table in which both cows and horses had been entered is that, *in the sense that cows and horses are replicated events, such and such is true of them.*

We have been talking about the mathematical expression of chi-square. What we have said might have been said about simple enumeration. We point to each of a series of things and count: *one, two, three. . . .* The counting makes sense if the things are distinguishable from each other, and it makes sense only in the respect that they are alike. Before we can count them we must construe their concrete difference from each other, their abstract likeness to each other, and their abstract difference from other things which are not to be counted. We must be able to construe where one thing leaves off and another begins, which one is similar enough to the others to be counted, and what is extraneous. What we count depends on what we abstract to be counted; thus, any mathematical expression relies upon the concept-formation task which has preceded it. Mathematical manipulation does not reify data, though it often provides a handy way of testing the adequacy of our conceptualizations.

What we are saying is that when a person anticipates events by construing their replications, he lays the ground for mathematical reasoning. All mathematical reasoning is utterly dependent upon the premathematical construing process which gives it something to enumerate. We think this is important.

INDIVIDUALITY COROLLARY

> *Individuality Corollary: Persons differ from each other in their construction of events.*

Since our Fundamental Postulate throws our emphasis upon the ways in which a person anticipates events, it provides grounds for a psychology of individual differences. People can be seen as differing from each other, not only because there may have been differences in the events which they have sought to anticipate, but also because there are different approaches to the anticipation of the same events.

Persons anticipate both public events and private events. Some writers have considered it advisable to try to distinguish between "external" events and "internal" events. In our system there is no particular need for making this kind of distinction. Nor do we have to distinguish so sharply between stimulus and response, between the organism and his environment, or between the self and the not-self.

No two people can play precisely the same role in the same event, no matter how closely they are associated. For one thing, in such an event, each experiences the other as an external figure. For another, each experiences a different person as the central figure (namely, himself). Finally, the chances are that, in the course of events, each will get caught up in a different stream and hence be confronted with different navigational problems.

But does this mean that there can be no sharing of experience? Not at all; for each may construe the likenesses and differences between the events in which he himself is involved, together with those in which he sees that the other person is involved. Thus, while there are individual differences in the construction of events, persons can find common ground through construing the experiences of their neighbors along with their own. It is not inevitable that they should come upon such common ground; indeed, where the cultural identifications are different or where one person has given up seeking common ground with his neighbors, individuals can be found living out their existence next door to each other but in altogether different subjective worlds.

ORGANIZATION COROLLARY

> *Organization Corollary: Each person characteristically evolves, for his convenience in anticipating events, a construction system embracing ordinal relationships between constructs.*

Different constructs sometimes lead to incompatible predictions, as everyone who has experienced personal conflict is painfully aware. Man, therefore, finds it necessary to develop ways of anticipating events which transcend contradictions. Not only do men differ in their constructions of events, but they also differ in the ways they organize their constructions of events. One man may resolve the conflicts between his anticipations by means of an ethical system. Another may resolve them in terms of self-preservation. The same man may resolve in one way at one time and in the other way at another. It all depends upon how he backs off to get perspective.

Terms

CHARACTERISTICALLY. Again we emphasize the personalistic nature of the process: here in the case of the system. Not only are the constructs personal, but the hierarchical system into which they are arranged is personal too. It is this systematic arrangement which characterizes the personality, even more than do the differences between individual constructs.

EVOLVES. The construction system does not stand still, although it is relatively more stable than the individual constructs of which it is composed. It is continually taking new shape. This is a way of saying that the personality is continually taking new shape. Deep psychotherapy may help a person with this evolvement and thus possibly accomplish important readjustments in a person's style of life.

CONSTRUCTION SYSTEM. A system implies a grouping of elements in which incompatibilities and inconsistencies have been minimized. They do not disappear altogether, of course. The systematization helps the person to avoid making contradictory predictions.

ORDINAL RELATIONSHIPS BETWEEN CONSTRUCTS. One construct may subsume another as one of its elements. It may do this in either of two ways; it may extend the cleavage intended by the other or it may abstract across the other's cleavage line. For example, the construct *good vs. bad* may subsume, respectively, among other things, the two ends of the intelligent-stupid dimension. In this sense, "good" would include all "intelligent" things plus some things which fall outside the range of convenience of the *intelligent vs. stupid* construct. "Bad" would include all the "stupid" things plus some others which are neither "intelligent" nor "stupid." This is what we mean by extending the cleavage intended by the construct *intelligent vs. stupid*.

An example of abstracting across the *intelligent vs. stupid* cleavage line would be the construct of *evaluative vs. descriptive*. In this case the *intelligent vs. stupid* construct would be subsumed as a dimension. The construct would itself be identified as an "evaluative" type of construct and would be contrasted with other constructs such as *light vs. dark*, which might be considered "descriptive" only. Both *good vs. bad* and *evaluative vs. descriptive* may thus be used as superordinating constructs, the former in what some writers would call an "absolutistic" sense and the latter in what they would call a "relativistic" sense.

Within a construction system there may be many levels of ordinal relationships, with some constructs subsuming others and those, in turn, subsuming still others. When one construct subsumes another its ordinal relationship may be termed *superordinal* and the ordinal relationship of the other becomes *subordinal*. Moreover, the ordinal relationship between the constructs may reverse itself from time to time. For example, "intelligent" may embrace all things "good" together with all things "evaluative," and "stupid" would be the term for "bad" and "descriptive" things; or, if the other kind of subsuming is involved, "intelligent" might embrace the construct *evaluative vs. descriptive* while "stupid" would be the term for the *good vs. bad* dichotomy. Thus man systematizes his constructs by concretely arranging them in hierarchies and by abstracting them further. But whether he pyramids his ideas or penetrates them with insights, he builds a system embracing ordinal relationships between constructs for his personal convenience in anticipating events.

Implications of the Organization Corollary

. . . It may be helpful to offer some passing hints as to the practical implications of our corollaries. The Organization Corollary is basic to our understanding of that most common of all clinic commodities, anxiety. It also sets the stage for the way we shall look upon the clinic client's mirrored image of himself.

Thus far we have said that the person is bent on anticipating events. His psychological processes are channelized with this in mind. Each person attunes his ear to the replicative themes he hears and each attunes his ear in a somewhat different way. But it is not mere certainty that man seeks; if that were so, he might take great delight in the repetitive ticking of the clock. More and more he seeks to anticipate all impending events of whatsoever nature. This means that he must develop a system in which the most unusual future can be anticipated in terms of a replicated aspect of the familiar past.

Now it so happens that a person must occasionally decide what to do about remodeling his system. He may find the job long overdue. How much can he tear down and still have a roof over his head? How disruptive will a new set of ideas be? Dare he jeopardize the system in order to replace some of its constituent parts? Here is the point at which he must choose between preserving the integrity of the system and replacing one of its obviously faulty parts. Sometimes his anticipation of events will be more effective if he chooses to conserve the system. It is precisely at this point that the psychotherapist may fail to understand why his client is so resistive. It is also at this point that he may do his client harm.

Lecky has emphasized a person's need for self-consistency. In doing so he has thrown particular emphasis upon the preservation of those aspects of one's system which have to do with the self. Certain essential features of what Lecky says are, in effect, reiterated here, and we are indebted to him. However, our view is that it is not consistency for consistency's sake nor even self-consistency that gives man his place in the world of events. Rather, it is his seeking to anticipate the whole world of events and thus relate himself to them that best explains his psychological processes. If he acts to preserve the system, it is because the system is an essential chart for his personal adventures, not because it is a self-contained island of meaning in an ocean of inconsequentialities.

Dichotomy Corollary

> *Dichotomy Corollary: A person's construction system is composed of a finite number of dichotomous constructs.*

We have already said that a person anticipates events by noting their replicative aspects. Having chosen an aspect with respect to which two events are replications of each other, we find that, by the same token, another event is definitely not a replication of the first two. The person's choice of an aspect determines both what shall be considered similar and what shall be considered contrasting. The same aspect, or the same abstraction, determines both. If we choose an aspect in which A and B are similar, but in contrast to C, it is important to note that it is the same aspect of all three, A, B, *and* C, that forms the basis of the construct. It is not that there is one aspect of A and B that makes them similar to each other and another aspect that makes them contrasting to C. What we mean is that there is an aspect of A, B, and C which we may call z. With respect to this aspect, A and B are similar and C stands in contrast to them. This is an important notion, for on it is built much of the technical procedure that characterizes the psychology of personal constructs.

Let us pursue our model further. Let us suppose that there is an element O in which one is unable to construe the aspect of z. O then falls outside the range of convenience of the construct based on z. The aspect of z is irrelevant in that part of the realm occupied by O. Not so C, however. The aspect of z is quite relevant to C. It is z that enables us to differentiate between C and the two similar elements, A and B. The aspect of z performs no such service in helping us discriminate between O and the two similar elements, A and B.

Suppose, for example, A and B are men, C is a woman, and O is the time of day. We abstract an aspect of A, B, and C which we may call *sex*. Sex, then, is our z. Sex is not applicable to O, the time of day; at least most of us would not so abstract it. The time of day, O, does not fall within the range of convenience of the construct of sex, z. Now, with respect to sex, z, the two men, A and B, are alike and in contrast to the woman, C. Moreover, the construct is no less applicable to the woman, C, than it is to the two men, A and B.

But suppose we say that the construct is not sex, z, but masculinity, y. Then is not the woman, C, just as unmasculine as the time of day, O? Our answer is no. She is much more relevantly unmasculine than is the time of day. The notion of masculinity is predicated upon a companion notion of femininity, and it is the two of them together which constitute the basis of the construct. Masculinity would mean nothing if it were not for femininity. There would be no point in using the term *man* in the masculine sense if it were not for the notion of sex.

What we propose to do is to assume that all constructs follow this basic dichotomous form. Inside its particular range of convenience a construct denotes an aspect of all the elements lying therein. Outside this range of convenience the aspect is not recognizable. Moreover, the aspect, once noted, is meaningful only because it forms the basis of similarity and contrast between the elements in which it is noted. In laying down this assumption we are departing from the position of classical logic. But we suspect that this comes nearer representing the way people actually think. In any case, we propose to pursue the implications of this assumption and see where we are led.

Terms

COMPOSED. By this we mean that the system is composed entirely of constructs. It consists of nothing but constructs. Its organizational structure is based upon constructs of constructs, concretistically pyramided or abstractly cross-referenced in a system of ordinal relationships.

DICHOTOMOUS CONSTRUCTS. The construct denotes an aspect of the elements lying within its range of convenience, on the basis of which some of the elements are similar to others and some are in contrast. In its minimum context a construct is a way in which at least two elements are similar and contrast with a third. There must therefore be at least three elements in the context. There may, of course, be many more.

FINITE NUMBER. Man's thinking is not completely fluid; it is channelized. If he wants to think about something he must follow the network of channels he has laid down for himself, and only by recombining old channels can he create new ones. These channels structure his thinking and limit his access to the ideas of others. We see these channels existing in the form of constructs.

Implications of the Dichotomy Corollary

But do people really think in terms of dichotomies? Do they always abstract on the basis of both similarity and contrast? These are questions which are bound to be asked. Since they challenge a part of our assumptive structure, we would have to step outside our system in order to try to answer them. We can, however, clarify the assumption somewhat further and thus perhaps make it more acceptable for the time being.

Not long ago a client said, in effect, to her therapist, "I believe that everything in the world is good. There is nothing bad. All people are good. All inanimate things are good. All thoughts are good." These statements, faintly suggestive of Voltaire's *Candide*, alerted the clinician to a probable underlying hostility. Obviously the client's statement was intended to mean something; the therapist's task was to find the implied contrast which she was unable to put into words.

The client could have meant several things. She could have meant that everything is now good whereas formerly it was bad. She could have been denying the good-bad dimension as a meaningful dimension and have chosen to do so by asserting the universality of one end of the dimension. She could have meant that everything other than herself was good. Or she could have meant that she was one who saw good in everything whereas others were seers of the bad. As matters turned out, she was expressing her construct in the latter two senses. She meant, "I suspect that I am bad and I suspect that you see me as bad, even though I have the compensating virtue of myself being willing to see everyone as good." There is a suggestion of what the clinicians call "an idea of reference" here, and the way the client expressed it suggests what some clinicians call "acting out."

Perhaps this illustration will suffice, for the time being, to indicate how the Dichotomy Corollary affects the clinician in dealing with his client. Instead of seeing his client as the victim of a submerged conflict between opposing instinctual forces, he see the dichotomy as an essential feature of thinking itself. As he seeks to understand what his client means, he looks for the elements in the construct context. As long as he approaches man's thinking from the standpoint of formal logic, it is impossible for him to comprehend any thinking which man is unable to verbalize. But as we approach man's thinking psychologically, using both the clinical and the more fragmentary methods of investigation, we can see the operational dichotomization of his constructs into similarities and contrasts.

Much of our language, as well as of our everyday thinking, implies contrast which it does not explicitly state. Our speech would be meaningless otherwise. If we proceed on this assumption, we may be able to gain insights into the psychological processes which have long been concealed by a formal logic which was altogether too much shackled by words.

How does our notion of dichotomous constructs apply to such "class concepts" as *red*? Is *red* a statement of contrast as well as of similarity? We might point out that, according to one of the prevalent color theories, red is the complement of green. Among the hues it stands in sharpest contrast to green. But *red* is used in other ways also. When we say that a person has red hair we are distinguishing it from the nonredness of white, yellow, brown, or black. Our language gives no special word for this nonredness, but we have little difficulty in knowing what the contrast to red hair actually is.

Similarly other constructs, such as *table*, express, within their ranges of convenience, both likenesses and differences. The differences are just as relevant as the likenesses; they are applicable within the constructs' ranges of convenience. Unlike classical logic, we do not lump together the contrasting and the irrelevant. We consider the contrasting end of a construct to be both relevant and necessary to the meaning of the construct. It falls within the range of convenience of the construct, not outside. Thus the construct of *table* has meaning, not merely because a series of objects, called *tables*, are similar to each other in this respect, but also because certain other objects of furniture stand in contrast in this same respect. For example, it makes sense to point to a chair and say, "That is not a table." It makes no sense to point to a sunset and say, "That is not a table."

The Dichotomy Corollary assumes a structure of psychological processes which lends itself to binary mathematical analysis. The concepts of modern physics, particularly electron theory, and the devices, such as the vacuum tube, which have been developed as the implements of those concepts, are having a far-reaching influence these days. The practical task of reducing information to a form which can be handled by electronic computing machines has forced scientists to reconsider the mathematical structure of knowledge itself. Psychology, for a half century an initiator of mathematical inventions relating to human behavior, is now itself caught up in the new nonparametric mathematics. Personal-construct theory, with its emphasis upon the dichotomous nature of the personal constructs which channelize psychological processes, is in full accord with this modern trend in scientific thinking. But personal-construct theory would not lose sight of premathematical construct formation. A sorting machine, no matter how complex, is not a thinking machine as long as we have to select data to feed into it.

CHOICE COROLLARY

> *Choice Corollary: A person chooses for himself that alternative in a dichotomized construct through which he anticipates the greater possibility for extension and definition of his system.*

If a person's processes are psychologically channelized by the ways in which he anticipates events, and those ways present themselves in dichotomous form, it follows that he must choose between the poles of his dichotomies in a manner which is predicted by his anticipations. We assume, therefore, that whenever a person is confronted with the opportunity for making a choice, he will tend to make that choice in favor of the alternative which seems to provide the best basis for anticipating the ensuing events.

Here is where inner turmoil so frequently manifests itself. Which shall a man choose, security or adventure? Shall he choose that which leads to immediate certainty or shall he choose that which may eventually give him a wider understanding? For the man of constricted outlook whose world begins to crumble, death may appear to provide the only immediate certainty which he can lay hands on. And yet, in the words of Shakespeare's Hamlet,

> But that the dread of something after death —
> The undiscover'd country, from whose bourn
> No traveler returns — puzzles the will;
> And makes us rather bear those ills we have
> Than fly to others that we know not of?

Whatever the breadth of his viewpoint, it is our assumption that man makes his choice in such a fashion as to enhance his anticipations. If he constricts his field of vision, he can turn his attention toward the clear definition of his system of constructs. If he is willing to tolerate some day-by-day uncertainties, he may broaden his field of vision and thus hope to extend the predictive range of the system. Whichever his choice may be — for constricted certainty or for broadened understanding — his decision is essentially elaborative. He makes what we shall call hereinafter *the elaborative choice*.

Terms

CHOOSES. Not only is a person's construction system composed of dichotomous constructs but, within the system of dichotomies, the person builds his life upon one or the other of the alternatives represented in each of the dichotomies. This is to say that he places relative values upon the ends of his dichotomies. Some of the values are quite transient and represent merely the convenience of the moment. Others are quite stable and represent guiding principles. Even the stable ones are not necessarily highly intellectualized — they may appear, rather, as appetitive preferences.

FOR HIMSELF. When one makes a choice he involves himself in the selection. Even if the choice is no more than a temporary hypothesis explored in the course of solving a mathematical problem or in looking for a lost screwdriver, he must perceive himself as being modified through the chain of ensuing events. Some of his choices will seem to be major turning points in his life; others may appear to be no more than a passing impulse — a decision to glance to the left rather than to the right.

ALTERNATIVE. If a person sets up the construct of *black vs. white*, an object cannot, for him, be both black and white. The construct tends to force upon him either one or the other of the two alternatives. If it were not so, the construct would have no meaning.

What about shades of gray? While the construct of *black vs. white* is composed of mutually exclusive alternatives, this does not preclude the use of the construct in a relativistic manner. Relativism is not the same as ambiguity, although some persons try to construe it that way. Of two objects, one may be blacker than the other; but it cannot be blacker than the other and at the same time the other be blacker than it is. As we shall see later, dichotomous constructs can be built into scales, the scales representing superordinate constructs which are further abstractions of the separate scalar values. Thus, *more grayness vs. less grayness* is a further abstraction of the construct *black vs. white*.

THROUGH. We must keep in mind that constructs have to do with processes and not merely with the spatial arrangement of static objects. The use of the constructs is itself a process also. Thus the use of constructs is a matter of choosing vestibules *through* which one passes during the course of his day.

ANTICIPATES. Since we have postulated that all human movement is based on anticipations, the choice of an alternative through which to move is itself a matter of what one anticipates.

GREATER POSSIBILITY. Not only is one's choice based upon the anticipation of some particular thing, but it may also be based upon one's anticipation of things in general. A person does not have to know specifically what it is that he expects in order to make his elaborative choice. He can go fishing, choosing only a well-stocked stream.

EXTENSION. Instead of saying that one makes his choice in favor of the alternative that seems to offer the greater possibility for extension and definition, we might have said that he makes his choice in favor of the greater possibility for further elaboration of the system. But we wish to make it clear that elaboration of one's construct system can be in the direction either of extension or of definition, or of both. The extension of the system includes making it more comprehensive, increasing its range of convenience, making more and more of life's experiences meaningful.

DEFINITION. The principle of the elaborative choice also includes a person's tendency to move toward that which appears to make his system more explicit and clear-cut. As we have already indicated, this may, in some instances, appear to call for constriction of one's field — even to the point of ultimate constriction, suicide. Internal conflict, as in the case of Hamlet, is often a matter of trying to balance off the secure definiteness of a narrowly encompassed world against the uncertain possibilities of life's adventure. One may anticipate events by trying to become more and more certain about fewer and fewer things or by trying to become vaguely aware of more and more things on the misty horizon.

HIS SYSTEM. Here we emphasize the assumption that, while it is events that one seeks to anticipate, he makes his elaborative choice in order to define or extend the system which he has found useful in anticipating those events. We might call this "a seeking of self-protection," or "acting in defense of the self," or "the preservation of one's integrity." But it seems more meaningful to keep clearly in mind what the self is, what it is designed to do, and what integral function is served. Thus we hope it is clear that what we assume is that the person makes his choice in favor of elaborating a system which is functionally integral with respect to the anticipation of events. To us it seems meaningless to mention a system qua system. It must be a system *for something*. From our point of view a person's construction system is for the anticipation of events. If it were for something else, it would probably shape up into something quite different.

Implications of the Choice Corollary

The Choice Corollary lays down the grounds upon which we can make some predictions regarding how people will act after they have construed the issues with which they are faced. Frequently the therapist finds it difficult to understand why his client, in spite of insights which would appear to make it clear how he should behave, continues to make the "wrong" choices. The therapist, seeing only the single issue which he has helped the client to define, often fails to realize that, within the system of personal constructs which the client has erected, the decision for action is not necessarily based on that issue alone but on a complex of issues.

For example, no matter how obvious it may be that a person would be better off if he avoided a fight or spoke pleasantly to his boss, it may so happen that such a course of action would seem to him personally to limit the definition and extension of his system as a whole. He may, therefore, in spite of the neatest psychotherapeutic interpretations, continue to quarrel with his neighbors and to snub anyone who seems to be invested with authority. The Choice Corollary, therefore, suggests ways in which a therapeutic program can go beyond mere intellectual insight and how it might enable the client to enter the experimental phases of the program.

Under the Choice Corollary we are able to reconstrue some of the issues for which hedonism and motivational theory provide awkward answers. Stimulus-response theory requires some sorts of assumptions to explain why certain responses become linked to certain stimuli. In certain theoretical structures this is managed by some supplementary theorizing about the nature of motives or need satisfactions. But in our assumptive structure we do not specify, nor do we imply, that a person seeks "pleasure," that he has special "needs," that there are "rewards," or even that there are "satisfactions." In this sense, ours is not a commercial theory. To our way of thinking, there is a continuing movement toward the anticipation of events, rather than a series of barters for temporal satisfactions, and this movement is the essence of human life itself.

RANGE COROLLARY

Range Corollary: A construct is convenient for the anticipation of a finite range of events only.

Just as a system or a theory has its focus and range of convenience, so a personal construct has a focus and range of convenience. There are few if any personal constructs which one can say are relevant to everything. Even such a construct as *good vs. bad*, in its personalized form, is not likely to be considered by the user to be applicable throughout the range of his perceptual field. Of course, some persons use the construct more comprehensively than others; but, even so, they are inclined to erect boundaries of convenience beyond which elements are neither good nor bad. A construct of *tall vs. short* is much easier to see as having a limited range of convenience. One may construe tall houses versus short houses, tall people versus short people, tall trees versus short trees. But one does not find it convenient to construe tall weather versus short weather, tall light versus short light, or tall fear versus short fear. Weather, light, and fear are, for most of us at least, clearly outside the range of convenience of *tall vs. short*.

Sometimes one is surprised to learn how narrowly a certain person applies some of his constructs. For example, one person may use the construct of *respect vs. contempt* to apply broadly to many different kinds of interpersonal relationships. Another person may use it to apply only to a very narrow range of events, perhaps only to the choice of words in a formally structured situation, such as a court proceeding.

As we have indicated before, in our discussion of the Dichotomy Corollary, our position here is somewhat different from that of classical logic. We see relevant similarity and contrast as essential and complementary features of the same construct and both of them as existing within the range of convenience of the construct. That which is outside the range of convenience of the construct is not considered part of the contrasting field but simply an area of irrelevancy.

While we have not said so before, it is probably apparent by now that we use the term *construct* in a manner which is somewhat parallel to the common usage of "concept." However, if one attempts to translate our *construct* into the more familiar term, "concept," he may find some confusion. We have included, as indeed some recent users of the term "concept" have done, the more concretistic concepts which nineteenth-century psychologists would have insisted upon calling "percepts." The notion of a "percept" has always carried the idea of its being a personal act — in that sense, our *construct* is in the tradition of "percepts," but we also see our *construct* as involving abstraction — in that sense our *construct* bears a resemblance to the traditional usage of "concept." And finally, we prefer the use of the term *construct* because, as a term, it has emerged more within the context of experimental psychology than within the context of mentalistic psychology or of formal logic.

Now when we assume that the construct is basically dichotomous, that it includes percepts, and that it is a better term for our purposes than the term "concept," we are not quarreling with those who would use it otherwise. Within some systems of logic the notion of contrast as something distinct from irrelevancy is not part of the assumptive structure. We, on the other hand, are simply assuming that this is the way people do, in fact, think. . . . We do not insist that people ought to think in this way, nor are we greatly concerned if others believe that people ought to think in the classical way. Ours is simply a psychological theory, and the nature of personal constructs is built into the assumptive structure.

Implications of the Range Corollary

The Range Corollary, together with the Dichotomy Corollary, provides a somewhat new approach to the analysis of human thought processes. Consider a given person's use of the construct of *respect vs. contempt*. Under conventional logic one would consider these as two separate concepts. If we wished to understand the person's use of the term "respect," we might seek to find out how broadly he applied the term — how he "generalized the concept." We would want to know what acts he considered to be characterized by "respect" and what acts he did not consider "respectful." Thus we might be able to discover by the method of varying concomitants just what abstraction among the acts he had been able to make.

But when we approach the thinking of a person, say a clinic client, in this way, we miss a great deal. We miss it because we are tacitly assuming that everything which he does not construe as "respect" is irrelevant. Yet his use of the construct may be particularly meaningful because of what he excludes rather than because of what he includes. When we approach his thinking from the standpoint of the psychology of personal constructs, we do not lump together what he excludes as irrelevant with what he excludes as contrasting. We see the construct as composed essentially of a *similarity-contrast* dimension which he strikes through a part of his field of experience. We need to look at both ends of it if we want to know what it means to him. We cannot understand him well if we look only at the similarity — "respect" — end of the dimension. We cannot understand what he means by "respect" unless we know what he sees as relevantly opposed to "respect."

The psychologist who employs the approach of the psychology of personal constructs is led always to look for the contrasting elements of his client's constructs as well as the similar elements. Until he has some notion of the contrast, he does not presume to understand the similarity. He would therefore seek to understand what his client construed as the opposite of respect and what the range of convenience of the whole construct covered. As his client continues to talk about the construct of "respect," the psychologist may discover just what it is that the client is condemning, by implication, as contemptuous or contemptible.

Freud found that he needed to understand what his clients meant by what they *did not say*. He used the notions of "repression" and "reaction formation" to explain what he observed. These he saw as perverse tendencies, somewhat characteristic of all men but particularly of certain disturbed persons. Our position is that contrast is an essential feature of all personal constructs, a feature upon which their very meaning depends. We would agree with Freud that there are instances in which the person is so self-involved with a construct that he avoids expressing its contrasting aspect lest he misidentify himself.

In practice, then, one looks not only for the similarities but also for the contrasts in understanding a client's construct. Moreover, he looks to see how extensive is the range of convenience of the construct, both for the similar elements and for the contrast elements. Until he understands how extensively the contrast is construed, he cannot realize the full import of the client's thinking.

EXPERIENCE COROLLARY

> *Experience Corollary: A person's construction system varies as he successively construes the replications of events.*

Since our Fundamental Postulate establishes the anticipation of events as the objective of psychological processes, it follows that the successive revelation of events invites the person to place new constructions upon them whenever something unexpected happens. Otherwise one's anticipations would become less and less realistic. The succession of events in the course of time continually subjects a person's construction system to a validation process. The constructions one places upon events are working hypotheses, which are about to be put to the test of experience. As one's anticipations or hypotheses are successively revised in the light of the unfolding sequence of events, the construction system undergoes a progressive evolution. The person reconstrues. This is experience. The reconstruction of one's life is based upon just this kind of experience. We have tried to express this implication of our Fundamental Postulate in the Experience Corollary.

Terms

SYSTEM. We have already indicated that a system implies a grouping of elements in which incompatibilities and inconsistencies have been minimized. We have also indicated that a person's construction system involves ordinal relationships between constructs. Construction is systematic in that it falls into a pattern having features of regularity. Since construing is a kind of refinement process involving abstraction and generalization, it is a way of looking at events as having a kind of identity with each other and as not being wholly unique. These features of identity and regularity are given shape through construction, which itself has been shaped up as a system.

VARIES. The changes in the construction system are not always "for the good" nor do they necessarily always tend to stabilize. They do vary, however. The variation may disrupt the system and lead to further and more rapid variation. It may precipitate a major shake-up in the system. Contrariwise, the variation may stabilize the system and make its basic features resistant to further modification.

SUCCESSIVELY. Construing, like all processes, may be chopped up into segments having beginnings and endings. Construing may itself be considered a sequence of events. Segmented in this manner it is proper to speak of construing as taking place successively. Like other features of life, its principal dimension is time, and it is itself a process, a phenomenon. The events of one's construing march single file along the path of time.

REPLICATIONS OF EVENTS. As new events are added to the record of those which have passed, the person has an opportunity to reconsider the replicative aspects which link the recent with the remote. What is it which has been repeated? What now constitutes the recurrent theme? Concretely, the new events are unique; it is only by abstracting them that the person finds that which is replicated.

Experience, Orderliness, and Time

By calling this corollary the Experience Corollary we indicate what we assume to be the essential nature of experience. Experience is made up of the successive construing of events. It is not constituted merely by the succession of events themselves. A person can be be a witness to a tremendous parade of episodes and yet, if he fails to keep making something out of them, or if he waits until they have all occurred before he attempts to reconstrue them, he gains little in the way of experience from having been around when they happened. It is not what happens around him that makes a man experienced; it is the successive construing and reconstruing of what happens, as it happens, that enriches the experience of his life.

Our corollary also throws emphasis upon construing the replicative features of experience. The person who merely stands agog at each emerging event may experience a series of interesting surprises, but if he makes no attempt to discover the recurrent themes, his experience does not amount to much. It is when man begins to see the orderliness in a sequence of events that he begins to experience them.

The notion of an organized and potentially lawful universe has not been easy for men to accept. How can one accept lawfulness unless he can state the law? Must not one resort to anthropomorphism whenever his predictions go awry? Should we not attribute all such unexpected events to "manlike" caprice? There are actually some scientists who see great orderliness within their physical frames of reference but who throw up their hands and say, "There must be a psychological factor," whenever they fail to find orderliness. This might be all right if what they meant was that it was time to apply some psychological constructs. But what they usually mean is that the phenomena are disorderly.

Sometimes the notion of the world as an orderly development of events seems downright threatening to a person. Particularly is this likely to be true when he deals with psychological events. If he sees orderliness in the behavior of a friend or in his own behavior, it seems to preclude the possiblity of seeing the actions of either as being free. This is a personal problem that the psychotherapist must frequently face in trying to help his client. If the client perceives himself as an orderly succession of events, he feels trapped by his own structure or by the events of his biography. Yet, if he sees himself as deciding each moment what he shall do next, it may seem as though one little false step will destroy his integrity.

In spite of the personal hazards and the difficulties of construing the succession of events which make up his universe, man has gradually extended his constructs of orderliness through the centuries. Perhaps he first perceived orderliness in the stately procession that marched across the night sky. Perhaps he first saw replication in the rolling of a stone along the ground and, from its rapid succession of events, was able to construct the notion of cycles and epicycles. Perhaps it came much earlier, as he detected the beating of his own pulse. But wherever it started, man's widening awareness of the universe as an orderly unfolding of events gave him increased capacity to predict and made his world more and more manageable. Even rare cataclysms assumed the familiarity of *déja vu*. Man gradually discovered that he could lay a sight on the future through the experience of the past.

The essential referent dimension along which all orderliness and organization must be construed is that of time. Except as there is a seasonable replication of events or aspects of events, no organization whatsoever can be ascribed to the universe and there is no such thing as experience. The discovery of replicative themes is not only the key to experience, it is the key to natural law.

Experience and Learning

The Experience Corollary has profound implications for our thinking about the topic of learning. When we accept the assumption that a person's construction system varies as he successively construes the replications of events, together with the antecedent assumption that the course of all psychological processes is plotted by one's construction of events, we have pretty well bracketed the topic of learning. What has been commonly called "learning" has been covered at the very outset. Learning is assumed to take place. It has been built into the assumptive structure of the system. The question of whether or not it takes place, or what is learned and what is not learned, is no longer a topic for debate within the system we have proposed. Of course, if we wish to step outside the system and argue within the framework of some other system, we can take sides on these topics.

The burden of our assumption is that learning is not a special class of psychological processes; it is synonymous with any and all psychological processes. It is not something that happens to a person on occasion; it is what makes him a person in the first place.

The net effect of incorporating learning into the assumptive structure of a psychological theory is to remove the whole topic from the realm of subsequent discourse. Some readers may be dismayed at this turn of events. Psychology now has a considerable investment of research effort in the topic. But psychology's investment is not altogether depreciated by the new set of assumptions, even though much of the research is ambiguous when viewed in the new light. If it is any comfort to do so, one may say that learning has been given a preeminent position in the psychology of personal constructs, even though it has been taken out of circulation as a special topic. In the language of administrators, it has been "kicked upstairs."

Now what happens to the venerable laws of learning and to the family of notions which have more recently grown up in the household of learning? Much! Let us take a look again at what we mean by "construing" and "system." Construing is a way of seeing events that makes them look regular. By construing events it becomes possible to anticipate them. To be effective, the construction system itself must have some regularity. The palpable feature of regularity is repetition, not mere repetition of identical events, of course — in a strict sense that would deny the idea of time its rightful place in the scheme of things — but repetition of some characteristic which can be abstracted from each event and carried intact across the bridge of time and space. To construe is to hear the whisper of the recurrent themes in the events that reverberate around us.

The subject in a learning experiment is no exception to our psychological rule. He too directs his psychological processes by seeking the recurrent theme in the experiment. If he segments the experience into separate "trials" and then further separates the "trials" into "reinforced trials" and "unreinforced trials," he may hear the same repetitive theme which the experimenter hears. On the other hand, he may not be so conventional. He may listen for other kinds of themes he has heard before. He may not even segment his experience into the kinds of trials or events the experimenter expects. In the language of music, he may employ another way of phrasing. Viewed in this manner, the problem of learning is not merely one of determining how *many* or what kinds of reinforcements fix a response, or how *many* nonreinforcements extinguish it, but rather, how does the subject phrase the experience, what recurrent themes does he hear, what movements does he define, and what validations of his predictions does he reap? When a subject fails to meet the experimenter's expectations, it may be inappropriate to say that "he has not learned"; rather, one might say that what the subject learned was not what the experimenter expected him to learn. If we are to have a productive science of psychology, let us put the burden of discovery on the experimenter rather than on the subject. Let the experimenter find out what the subject is thinking about, rather than asking the subject to find out what the experimenter is thinking about.

A more adequate discussion of the role of learning in personal-construct theory is reserved for another section on experience presented at a later point in our exposition of the psychology of personal constructs. The present remarks may suffice to suggest the possible extent of the implications of our basic assumptions.

MODULATION COROLLARY

Modulation Corollary: The variation in a person's construction system is limited by the permeability of the constructs within whose range of convenience the variants lie.

If we are to see a person's psychological processes operating lawfully within a system which he constructs, we need also to account for the evolution of the system itself in a similarly lawful manner. Our Experience Corollary states that a person's construction system varies as he successively construes the replications of events. Next, we must note that the progressive variation must, itself, take place within a system. If it were not so, we would be in the position of claiming that little everyday processes are systematically governed but that the system-forming processes are not subordinate to any larger, more comprehensive system. We cannot insist upon the personal lawfulness of the *elements* of human behavior and at the same time concede that the *patterns* of human behavior are unlawful. Nor can we insist that the elements follow a personal system but that the patterns can evolve only within a suprapersonal system.

The problem is a special case of the problem of determinism and free will, which we discussed in an earlier section. There we indicated that we assumed that determination and freedom are two complementary aspects of structure. They cannot exist without each other any more than *up* can exist without *down* or *right* without *left*. Neither freedom nor determination are absolutes. A thing is free *with respect to something;* it is determined *with respect to something else.*

The solution proposed for the problem of determinism and free will provides us with the pattern for understanding how persons can vary and still be considered as lawful phenomena of nature. A person's construction system is composed of complementary superordinate and subordinate relationships. The subordinate systems are determined by the superordinate systems into whose jurisdiction they are placed. The superordinate systems, in turn, are free to invoke new arrangements among the systems which are subordinate to them.

This is precisely what provides for freedom and determination in one's personal construct system. The changes that take place, as one moves toward creating a more suitable system for anticipating events, can be seen as falling under the control of that person's superordinating system. In his role identifying him with his superordinating system, the person is free with respect to subordinate changes he attempts to make. In his role as the follower of his own fundamental principles, he finds his life determined by them. Just as in governmental circles instructions can be changed only within the framework of fixed directives, and directives can be changed only within the framework of fixed statutes, and statutes can be changed only within the framework of fixed constitutions, so can one's personal constructs be changed only within subsystems of constructs and subsystems changed only within more comprehensive systems.

Our position is that even the changes which a person attempts within himself must be construed by him. The new outlook which a person gains from experience is itself an event; and, being an event in his life, it needs to be construed by him if he is to make any sense out of it. Indeed, he cannot even attain the new outlook in the first place unless there is some comprehensive overview within which it can be construed. Another way of expressing the same thing is to say that one does not learn certain things merely from the nature of the stimuli which play upon him; he learns only what his framework is designed to permit him to see in the stimuli.

Terms

PERMEABILITY. Here we introduce a special construction within the psychology of personal constructs which we shall have occasion to use quite frequently in later sections. Particularly in the sections dealing with psychotherapy and the ways of helping persons reconstrue their lives, we shall expect to invoke the notion of *permeability of superordinate constructs.*

A construct is permeable if it will admit to its range of convenience new elements which are not yet construed within its framework. An utterly concrete construct, if there were such a thing, would not be permeable at all, for it would be made up of certain specified elements — those and no others. Such a construct would have to be impermeable.

There are, of course, relative degrees of permeability and impermeability. One person's construct of *good* vs. *bad* might be sufficiently permeable to permit him to see many new ideas and new acquaintances as good or bad. Another person's construct of *good* vs. *bad* might include many things but not be open to the inclusion of many new things; most of the good things and most of the bad things have already been labeled — and he has almost run out of labels.

The notion of permeability as a feature of conceptualization stems from the painstaking research of L. S. McGaughran, who approached the problems of conceptualization empirically and inductively. As a result of his investigation he was able to show that certain highly abstracted characteristics of a person's verbal behavior were predictive of his nonverbal behavior when dealing with palpable objects. While he does not use the term in his writings, in a conversation he once did propose the word *permeability* as a symbol for one of the aspects of conceptualization which he had abstracted. For his purposes, he found *permeability* to be a more useful dimension on which to plot conceptualization than the classical *abstract-concrete* dimension.

In our own usage a permeable construct is not necessarily loose, inconsistent, comprehensive, or tenuous. It may be quite definite; it may have little tendency to vary; it may embrace elements which are similar in other ways; and it may be persistently held. When we say that a construct is permeable we refer only to the particular kind of plasticity we have described — the capacity to embrace new elements.

It must be admitted that when new elements are added to the context of a construct there is a tendency for the construct itself to change somewhat. The abstraction of A and B versus C is likely to change when D is taken into consideration. For this reason permeable constructs may show a tendency to shift slightly from time to time. But the shift may be minimal, and shifting is not what we have in mind when we speak of permeability.

In earlier formulations of the theory of personal constructs we used the term "stable aspects" instead of "permeability." Permeable constructs, because they possess resiliency under the impact of new experience, do tend to be stable, but "permeability" is a more precise and operationally useful mark of identification for the kinds of constructs we have in mind than is "stability."

We do not necessarily refer to stability in the sense of longevity or lasting qualities, although a certain permeability in one's constructs gives them durability. Nor do we refer necessarily to a construct's intransigent rigidity in the face of its repeated systematic failures to anticipate events adequately. We refer rather, to those aspects of the system which can span a greater variety of new subordinate variations, which are less shaken by the impact of unexpected minor daily events.

A construct, or an aspect of one's construction system, can be called permeable if it is so constituted that new experience and new events can be discriminatively added to those which it already embraces. A construct which "takes life in its stride" is a permeable one. It is under the regnancy of such constructs that the more subordinate aspects of one's construction system can be systematically varied without making his whole psychological house fall down on him. Sometimes, of course, the house does fall down. Frequently, on a clinical basis, we can see the so-called "decompensation" taking place in a client in the space of a few days or weeks. We are able also to see how the brittleness and impermeability of his construction system failed to support the alterations which he was finding it necessary to make. But more about this later!

The kind of construct which is permeable has more of the qualities of a theoretical formulation, as contrasted with a hypothetical formulation, in science. A hypothesis is deliberately constructed so as to be relatively impermeable and brittle, so that there can be no question about what it embraces and no doubt about its being wholly shattered or left intact at the end of an experiment. A theory is not so inflexibly constructed. It is stated in relatively permeable terms so that it may, in the future, embrace many things which we have not yet thought of. It is stated in an open-ended form. A theory, then, both provokes and accepts a wide variety of experimental ventures, some of which may even be antithetical to each other.

Just as a scientific experimenter's formulations of successive experiments may undergo progressive changes in a manner which is always subordinate to the more theoretical aspects of his system, so any person, scientist or not, may vary his construction system in a manner which is subordinate to certain more permeable aspects of his system. The way the scientist uses his theory to accomplish this is a special case. We have tried, in this corollary, to state the more general case.

VARIANTS. The constructs which replace each other may be considered to be the variants. Suppose a person starts out with a construct of *fear vs. domination* and shifts it to a construct of *respect vs. contempt*. Whereas once he divided his acquaintances between those he was afraid of and those whom he could dominate, he may, as he grows more mature, divide his acquaintances between those whom he respects and those whom he holds in contempt. But, in order for him to make this shift, he needs another construct, within whose range of convenience the *fear vs. domination* construct lies and which is sufficiently permeable to admit the new idea of *respect vs. contempt*. The two constructs, the old and the new, are the variants.

The permeable construct within whose range of convenience the variants lie may be such a notion as that of *maturity vs. childishness*. The attitude of *fear vs. domination* may be construed as a "childish" notion and the attitude of *respect vs. contempt* may be considered to be a relatively "mature" idea. Or it may be that both old and new constructs are seen as similar with respect to maturity vs. childishness. In the former case the person will see his new attitude as contrasting with the old in this respect; in the latter case he will see the new attitude as essentially similar to the old in this respect.

The psychotherapist who is concerned with his clients' psychological reconstruction of their lives runs across both types of transition in the course of his practice. The essential feature, from the standpoint of the assumptive structure of this theory, is that any transition needs to be subsumed by some overriding construction which is permeable enough to admit the new construct to its context. It is extremely difficult in practice to accomplish extensive psychotherapeutic results in a client whose superordinate structures are impermeable and most of whose basic conceptualizations are rooted exclusively in the past.

The client whose overriding structures are all permeable also presents certain therapeutic problems. Some of the structures which might better have their contexts closed out so that they will not be used to deal with new ideas may cause difficulty for the client as he construes the changes which are taking place in himself. But we are getting ahead of ourselves in this exposition of the psychology of personal constructs! The technical problems in the psychological reconstruction of life are reserved for a later discussion.

FRAGMENTATION COROLLARY

> *Fragmentation Corollary: A person may successively employ a variety of construction subsystems which are inferentially incompatible with each other.*

A person's construction system is continually in a state of flux. Yet, even though it is fluctuating within a superordinate system, his successive formulations may not be derivable from each other. It is possible that what Willie thinks today may not be inferred directly from what he was thinking yesterday. His shift, nevertheless, in the light of our Modulation Corollary, is consistent with the more stable aspects of his system. What we are being careful to say now is that new constructs are not necessarily direct derivatives of, or special cases within, one's old constructs. We can be sure only that the changes that take place from old to new constructs do so within a larger system.

Now those larger systems may have been altered (within a still greater system, of course) by the impact of the old construct. In that case and in that sense the old construct is a legitimate precursor of the new construct. The relationship is still a collateral one, however, rather than a lineal one. The old and the new constructs may, in themselves, be inferentially incompatible with each other.

This is an important corollary. It should make even clearer the assumed necessity for seeking out the regnant construct system in order to explain the behavior of men, rather than seeking merely to explain each bit of behavior as a derivative of its immediately antecedent behavior. If one is to understand the course of the stream of consciousness, he must do more than chart its headwaters; he must know the terrain through which it runs and the volume of the flood which may cut out new channels or erode old ones.

This is the point where statistical sampling theory may lead us astray if we are not careful to use it discriminatingly. If we are making an idiographic study by analyzing a sample of the population of previous behaviors, we may make the mistake of assuming that a sample of future behaviors would be drawn from a universe having exactly the same parameters. From this kind of inference we would be led to believe that a four-year-old child who sucks his thumb fifteen hours a day would grow up to be a man who most likely would suck his thumb about fifteen hours a day. If we turn to sampling theory in a nomothetic framework, we may make another kind of mistake. We may assume that since most men do not suck their thumbs at all, this child will also grow up to be a man who will have no unusual habit of this type.

We are less likely to make a mistake if we are careful to look at the problem in the manner which was suggested in the preceding chapter. If we study the sample of past behaviors and extract our abstraction generalization, not in terms of a quantitative prediction of behaviors of the same order, but rather in terms of an abstraction or regnant construct of those behaviors, we may be able to solve our problem. We may come up with some such answer as the following: a sample of this particular child's behavior appears to be drawn from a population of behavior whose average is fifteen hours of thumb sucking a day. Up to this point we shall have used sampling theory within the idiographic frame. Now let us form a concept. Sampling theory will not help us do that; indeed, there is no reason to expect it to. Let us look at the child's other behaviors in a manner which will enable us to construe them, to form a construct, or, better still, to discover the child's own construction, verbalized or unverbalized, under which these different behaviors emerge. We look at the other behaviors. We sample them also idiographically. Since a construct is a way of seeing some things as being alike and, by the same token, as being different from other things, we shall seek the way in which some of the child's behaviors are alike and at the same time different from other behaviors. To use the common notion of "abstraction," we shall *abstract* his behavior and, possibly, come up with such a construct as "oral behavior," or "ingestive behavior," or "comfort behavior," or "narcissistic behavior." At this second stage in our reasoning process we shall have used concept formation, not sampling theory.

As a third step, let us move over into the nomothetic frame and try out our newly formed construct. Let us see whether it fits other children, whether their behavior can be similarly construed as having elements some of which consistently fall into the category of our construct of oral behavior and others of which clearly do not. Again, this is concept-formation or sorting procedure, not statistical sampling in the ordinary sense.

The fourth step is to see whether the construct fits adult behaviors. Again the framework is nomothetic.

The fifth step is statistical sampling in the nomothetic frame. We see whether or not a sample of childhood behaviors, of the abstract type we have construed, is correlated with a sample of adult behaviors of the same construct type. Presumably we will want to study the same people — as children, then as adults — although, under certain assumptions, we may study the correlation by some indirect method, such as by matching children with adults on some relevant variables which are already known to remain fairly constant throughout life.

Let us note that sampling and concept formation are not wholly different processes, though, for the purposes of the preceding discussion, it was convenient to label them so. In sampling, one makes certain hypotheses (an experimental and a null) as to the way in which two samples are similar, and then tests them.

The Problem of Consistency

One of the difficulties which arise in propounding a system like the psychology of personal constructs is that the reader is likely to expect any true construct system to be logic-tight and wholly internally consistent. Yet a candid inspection of our own behavior and our own thinking makes it difficult to see how such an ideal system could exist in reality. Consistency is not an easy concept to handle in a meaningful fashion. What is consistent with what? Is thumb sucking in childhood consistent with thumb sucking in adulthood? Is it consistent with pipe smoking in adulthood? Is it consistent with the accumulation of property? Is it consistent with financial success? Is there anything that it is not consistent with? Is anything inconsistent with anything else?

If everything can be reconciled and made to appear consistent with everything else, the notion of consistency fails to meet our standards for a construct — a way in which at least two things are alike and at the same time different from at least one other thing. If it is not a construct, it cannot help us anticipate events. If it cannot help us anticipate events, it is of no service to science whose goal is prediction. Unless we accord to the notion of consistency a special meaning that gives it the status of a construct, either in the eyes of the person who seeks to reconcile his own behaviors or in the eyes of the observer who seeks to understand those behaviors, the term might better not be relied upon.

Before discussing a particular way of understanding consistency, let us take time to mention the theme of self-consistency that underlies some of the neophenomenological systems of today: Rainey's self-concept theory, Lecky's self-consistency theory, Rogers' client-centered approach, and Snygg and Combs's phenomenal field approach. All of these contemporary theories have enough similarity to personal-construct theory to make it important, from time to time in this discussion, to distinguish their differences as well as their similarities.

Lecky's self-consistency theory treated consistency as if it were a property of the ideas one has. He said that one method of dealing with inconsistency is to try to injure or destroy the objects or persons in connection with which the alien idea arose. Another method is "to reinterpret the disturbing incident in such a manner that it can be assimilated." Another is "to alter the opinion one holds of himself." This all seems reasonable enough, but one soon finds himself wondering what constitutes consistency or inconsistency.

Part of the answer, probably anticipated by Lecky, although he did not express it in so many words, is that consistency and inconsistency are personal labels. What one person sees as inconsistent another may see as consistent. While Lecky was concerned primarily with the problem of consistency and inconsistency of new ideas with the underlying self-idea, his view of consistency per se was that it was a property attributed to experience by the person who has the experience. In our own terms, his "consistency" is a construct, and it is a personal one.

But to say the *consistency-inconsistency* construct is a personal one is not enough to make it applicable. When we hold to two views which are consistent with each other we expect to choose similar, or at least compatible, courses of action under them. The two views are inconsistent if they require us to perform the impossible feat of riding off in opposite directions at the same time. They are inconsistent if they lead us to anticipate two incompatible events. The key to the proper labeling of consistency lies in our Fundamental Postulate: a person's processes are psychologically channelized by the way in which he anticipates events. The operational definition of consistency can be written in terms of the way events are anticipated. Do the wagers one lays on the outcome of life cancel each other out or do they add up?

Our Fragmentation Corollary avers that a person may *successively* employ a variety of construction subsystems which are inferentially incompatible with each other. This means that his subsequent bets on the turn of minor events may not always add up with his earlier bets. Does this mean that his personality is structured only with respect to his minor anticipations? No!

The Fragmentation Corollary is, in part, a derivative of the Modulation Corollary. We said in the latter corollary that the variation in a person's construction system is limited by the permeability of the constructs within whose ranges of convenience the variants lie. We did not assume that variation in a person's constructions is subordinate to all antecedent (in time) aspects of his system. Our assumption is simply that it is in the context of the more permeable aspects of one's system that consistency is the law.

Now that we have suggested a more operational definition of consistency, the intent of the Modulation Corollary should be more clearly communicated. The Fragmentation Corollary follows as an explicit statement of the kind of inconsistency which the Modulation Corollary implicitly tolerates. The Modulation Corollary tolerates inconsistency between subsystems. More specifically, it tolerates the successive use of subsystems which do not, in themselves, add up.

A few sentences back, when we stated that a person's bets on the turn of minor events may not add up with his earlier bets, we asked if this meant that his personality is structured only with respect to his minor anticipations. We gave an emphatic no. Looking at the Fragmentation Corollary in the context of the Modulation Corollary one can give a more comprehensive answer. Now we can say that while a person's bets on the turn of minor events may not appear to add up, his wagers on the outcome of life do tend to add up. He may not win each time, but his wagers, in the larger contexts, do not altogether cancel themselves out. The superordinate permeable features of his system may not be verbalized, they may be more "vegetative" than "spiritual," or they may be seen as what Adler would have called a "style of life"; but they are part of a *system* and, therefore, may be considered from the viewpoint of their lawful as well as from the viewpoint of their free aspects.

As in the case of the idiographic-nomothetic issue, and as in the case of the determinism-free will issue, it is by considering the relative levels of abstraction and generality involved, or the permeability-impermeability levels with which we are dealing, or, in brief, by considering our problem in terms of the individual's personal construct system and the person's attempts to anticipate events, that we are able to come to a satisfactory answer to the important psychological question of how the human organism can be organized and still appear to behave in a disorganized fashion.

Further Implications of the Fragmentation Corollary

Since the variation in a person's construction system is subordinate to certain more permeable aspects of his system, each time his behaviors or his ideas undergo a change he must invoke, in some way or other, the permeable construct which provides the thread of consistency in his behaviors. If that permeable construct is not too clearly patterned, or if it is not too permeable, he may have to abandon its use and seek frantically for new ways of making sense out of life. These frantic attempts at new large concept formation may yield some weirdly new constructs, as he attempts to find the respects in which the events of life have definite likenesses and differences.

There is no clearer example of the limitation of one's ability to adjust to the vicissitudes of life, due to the impermeability of his superordinate constructs, than the case of a compulsion-neurosis client who is undergoing a marked decompensation process. The construct system of such a client is characteristically impermeable; he needs a separate pigeonhole for each new experience and he calculates his anticipations of events with minute pseudomathematical schemes. He has long been accustomed to subsume his principles. The variety of construction subsystems which are inferentially incompatible with each other may, in the train of rapidly moving events, become so vast that he is hard put to it to find ready-made superordinate constructs which are sufficiently permeable or open-ended to maintain over-all consistency. He starts making new ones. While he has very little successful experience with concept formation at the permeable level, these are the kinds of concepts he tries to develop. They may turn out to be generalized suspicions of the motives of other people. They may have to do with reevaluations of life and death. They may lead him to anticipate reality in very bizarre ways.

A person's tolerance of incompatibility in his daily construction of events is also limited by the definition of the regnant constructs upon whose permeability he depends to give life its over-all meaning. If those constructs are so loosely defined that he has trouble getting organized, as in an emotional state, we may see him shifting his behavior pattern back and forth, or reducing it to a childlike pattern which, though not very applicable to the present situation, does appear to provide optimal anticipations at the moment. In this case, too, we see what happens when the permeability and definition of one's superordinate constructs ceases to provide consistency, and the person is thrown back upon a more primitive and less effectual system, albeit a more permeable one.

COMMONALITY COROLLARY

Commonality Corollary: To the extent that one person employs a construction of experience which is similar to that employed by another, his psychological processes are similar to those of the other person.

We come now to a discussion of the implications of our Fundamental Postulate in the field of interpersonal relations. As we have already indicated, it is possible for two people to be involved in the same real events but, because they construe them differently, they will anticipate them differently and will behave differently as a consequence of their anticipations. That there should be such differences seems to be a logical outcome of our Fundamental Postulate, and we have stated that fact in the Individuality Corollary. But if we have an Individuality Corollary, we must also have a Commonality Corollary.

As with the other corollaries the Commonality Corollary is little more than a clarification of what seems to be implicit in our Fundamental Postulate. If a person's processes are psychologically channelized by the ways in which he anticipates events, and if he anticipates events by construing their replications, it may seem obvious that we are assuming that, if two persons employed the same construction of experience, their psychological processes would have to duplicate each other. This seems like an innocent statement. But as we examine this corollary closely, we find it has some implications which are not generally accepted among psychologists.

It is important to make clear that we have not said that if one person has experienced the same events as another he will duplicate the other's psychological processes. This is the assumption of stimulus-response psychology and, in its way, a perfectly respectable assumption; but it is not our assumption, and because we have not chosen to make it, we are free to develop our theoretical position in ways in which the stimulus-response psychologist is not. We could say, with systematic consistency, that two persons with identical experience would have identical psychological processes. But such a statement might be misleading unless the reader kept clearly in mind just what we mean by *experience*. He might have to keep turning back to our discussion of the Experience Corollary to see wherein our position differs from that of stimulus-response theory. So we prefer to state it the way we have — that two persons' psychological processes will be as similar as their constructions of experience.

One of the advantages of this position is that it does not require us to assume that it would take identical events in the lives of two people to make them act alike. Two people can act alike even if they have each been exposed to quite different phenomenal stimuli. It is in the similarity in the construction of events that we find the basis for similar action, and not in the identity of the events themselves. Again, as in the matter of learning, we think the psychologist can better understand his subjects if he inquires into the way in which they construe their stimuli than if he always takes his own construction of the stimuli for granted. In the words of our Modulation Corollary, we think psychologists need to use more permeable constructs in their own systems so that they can better subsume the variant constructions of their subjects.

Phenomenologically speaking, no two persons can have either the same construction or the same psychological processes. In that sense our Commonality Corollary would be unrealistic. But what we mean is this: to the extent that we can construe the constructions of two other people as being similar, we may anticipate that their psychological processes may also be construed as similar.

Terms

TO THE EXTENT. In our Individuality Corollary we committed ourselves to the view that persons differ from each other in their constructions of events. The Commonality Corollary may appear to imply a contradiction to this previous statement. But when we say that persons differ from each other we do not rule out the possibility that there may be certain respects in which persons can be construed as being like each other. To say that James differs from John is not to say that James and John have nothing in common. In fact, to say that two things differ from each other in every conceivable respect is to express the ultimate in particularism and to leave one's listener in a confused state of mind about the whole matter. It is also about as confusing to say that two things are like each other in every conceivable respect;

one is left wondering how they can then be considered as two distinct things.

What we have said in our Commonality Corollary does not contradict what we have assumed in our Individuality Corollary. By using the term, *to the extent*, we indicate that we are designating a totality of aspects in which the two persons' constructions of experience may be construed as similar. That there will still be many respects in which the two persons will retain their individuality goes without saying — our Individuality Corollary took care of that.

CONSTRUCTION OF EXPERIENCE. Experience, as we have defined it, is a matter of successively construing events. To construe experience, then, is to take stock of the outcome of this successive construing process. Thus, if two people take similar stock of their successive interpretations, their behavior will exhibit similar characteristics. The historical development of their thinking need not be similar — only the stock-taking need be similar. Hence it is not the similarity of experience which provides the basis for similarity of action, but similarity of their present construction of that experience.

By construction of experience we do not necessarily refer to highly verbalized interpretations. We keep reiterating this point. A person may construe his experience with little recourse to words, as, for example, in certain conditioned reflexes. Even those constructions which are symbolized by words are not necessarily similar just because the words are similar. Conversely, two persons may be using essentially the same constructions of their experience, although they express themselves in quite different terms.

Implications of the Commonality Corollary

It is an observed fact that certain groups of people behave similarly in certain respects. Some of these similarities are associated with similarities in their ages, some with similarities in what is expected of them by their associates, some with similarities in experience, and some with other kinds of constructions of similarity. Indeed, if we wish, we can approach the matter of similarities between persons from any one of a number of angles.

One of the common and interesting approaches to similarities and differences between persons is that taken from the standpoint of culture. Usually, as the term "culture" would imply, this means that we see persons grouped according to similarities in their upbringing and their environment. This, basically, means that cultural similarities and differences are understood in terms of stimulus-response theory.

Sometimes, however, culture is taken to mean similarity in what members of the group expect of each other. This is an interpretation of culture which is more commonly found among sociological than among psychological theories. Psychologists perhaps avoid this approach because it seems to require that one interpret the behavior of more than one person at a time; they prefer an approach which permits them to derive their system from observations of the individual man.

When one does understand culture in terms of similarity of expectations, he can proceed from that point in one of two directions. He can consider the expectations of others as stimuli to which each person is subjected; or he can understand cultural similarity between persons as essentially a similarity in what they perceive is expected of them. The latter approach throws the emphasis back upon the outlook of the individual person. This is, of course, the kind of approach one would be expected to make if he employed the psychology of personal constructs.

The similarity-of-expectations view of culture is also consistent with personal-construct theory from another angle. Our Fundamental Postulate assumes that a person's psychological processes are channelized by the ways in which he anticipates events. That makes the psychology of personal constructs an anticipatory theory of behavior. Some of the real events that one anticipates are the behaviors of other persons. Personal-construct theory would then understand cultural similarity, not only in terms of personal outlook rather than in terms of the impingement of social stimuli, but also in terms of what the individual anticipates others will do and, in turn, what he thinks they are expecting him to do.

In interpreting social behavior we are confronted with a spiraliform model. James anticipates what John will do. James also anticipates what John thinks he, James, will do. James further anticipates what John thinks he expects John will do. In addition, James anticipates what John thinks James expects John to predict that James will do. And so on! We are reminded of the famous illustration of the cat looking in the mirror. In complicated social situations, as in psychotherapy, for example, one may find himself looking at another person through such an infinite series of reflections.

Personal-construct theory approaches problems of the commonality of behavior primarily from the point of view of the individual person. Furthermore, it sees his point of view as an anticipatory one. It follows, then, that our approach to culture and group behavior is via the study of similarities and contrasts in a person's anticipations and the channels he constructs for making his predictions. We are interested, not only in the similarities in what people predict, but also in the similarities in their manner of arriving at their predictions. People belong to the same cultural group, not merely because they behave alike, nor because they expect the same things of others, but especially because they construe their experience in the same way. It is on this last similarity that the psychology of personal constructs throws its emphasis.

Sociality Corollary

Sociality Corollary: To the extent that one person construes the construction process of another, he may play a role in a social process involving the other person.

While a common or similar cultural background tends to make people see things alike and to behave alike, it does not guarantee cultural progress. It does not even guarantee social harmony. The warriors who sprang up from the dragon's teeth sown by Jason had much in common but, misconstruing each other's motives, they failed to share in a constructive enterprise and soon destroyed each other. In order to play a constructive role in relation to another person one must not only, in some measure, see eye to eye with him but must, in some measure, have an acceptance of him and of his way of seeing things. We say it in another way: the person who is to play a constructive role in a social process with another person need not so much construe things as the other person does as he must effectively construe the other person's outlook.

Here we have a take-off point for a social psychology. By attempting to place at the forefront of psychology the understanding of personal constructs, and by recognizing, as a corollary of our Fundamental Postulate, the subsuming of other people's construing efforts as the basis for social interaction, we have said that social psychology must be a psychology of interpersonal understandings, not merely a psychology of common understandings.

There are different levels at which we can construe what other people are thinking. In driving down the highway, for example, we stake our lives hundreds of times a day on our accuracy in predicting what the drivers of the oncoming cars will do. The orderly, extremely complex, and precise weaving of traffic is really an amazing example of people predicting each other's behavior through subsuming each other's perception of a situation. Yet actually each of us knows very little about the higher motives and the complex aspirations of the oncoming drivers, upon whose behavior our own lives depend. It is enough, for the purpose of avoiding collisions, that we understand or subsume only certain specific aspects of their construction systems. If we are to understand them at higher levels, we must stop traffic and get out to talk with them.

If we can predict accurately what others will do, we can adjust ourselves to their behavior. If others know how to tell what we will do, they can adjust themselves to our behavior and may give us the right of way. This mutual adjustment to each other's viewpoint takes place, in the terms of the theory of personal constructs, because, to some extent, our construction system subsumes the construction systems of others and theirs, in part, subsume ours. Understanding does not have to be a one-way proposition; it can be mutual.

For the touch and go of traffic it is not necessary for the motorists to have an extensive mutual understanding of each other's ways of seeing things but, within a restricted range and at the concrete level of specific acts represented by traffic, the mutual understandings must be precise. For the more complicated interplay of roles — for example, for the husband-and-wife interplay — the understanding must cover the range of domestic activities at least, and must reach at least a level of generality which will enable the participants to predict each other's behavior in situations not covered by mere household traffic rules.

One person may understand another better than he is understood. He may understand more of the other's ways of looking at things. Moreover, he may understand the other at a higher level of generality. Presumably, if this is true of a certain person with respect to a group of people whose ways of seeing things have some commonality, he is in a strategic position to assume a leadership relationship to the group. On the other hand, there may be still other factors which effectively deny him that opportunity.

A therapist-client relationship is one which exemplifies greater understanding on the part of one member than on the part of the other. As a therapist comes to subsume the client's construction system within his own, he becomes more and more facile in developing his own role in relation to the client. It then becomes possible for them to make progress jointly in a social enterprise.

Parenthetically it should be admitted that the therapist-client relationship can, in some instances, be effective with the client's understanding more about the therapist's construction system than the therapist understands about the client's. Some therapists conduct their interviews with so much elaboration of their own views that this kind of role relationship might easily be the outcome. Some clients try to manage the interplay of roles so that they can find out what the therapist thinks — as if that would help them get along in life — without letting the therapist in on what they think. If he accepts the flattery, the therapist may waste time confiding his views to the client.

Perhaps somewhat more legitimately, the therapist, in his relationship with the client, may carefully manage his own role and the constructions of experience which he permits the client to observe. In that way he may enable the client to develop a role under certain presumptions about the therapist. The therapist may tentatively present a carefully calculated point of view in such a way that the client, through coming to understand it, may develop a basis for understanding other figures in his environment with whom he needs to acquire skill in playing interacting roles. This is known as *role playing* in psychotherapy and there are many ways in which it may be effectively employed.

Definition of Role

In terms of the theory of personal constructs, a *role* is a psychological process based upon the role player's construction of aspects of the construction systems of those with whom he attempts to join in a social enterprise. In less precise but more familiar language, a role is an ongoing pattern of behavior that follows from a person's understanding of how the others who are associated with him in his task think. In idiomatic language a role is a position that one can play on a certain team without even waiting for the signals.

This definition of *role* lays emphasis upon several important points. First, like other patterns of behavior, it is assumed to be tied to one's personal construct system. This implies that it is anchored in the outlook of the role player and does not necessarily follow from his congregate relationship to other members of a group. It is a pattern of behavior emerging from the person's own construction system rather than primarily out of his social circumstances. He plays out his part in the light of his understanding of the attitudes of his associates, even though his understanding may be minimal, fragmentary, or misguided. This notion of role is, therefore, neither a typical stimulus-response notion nor a typical sociological notion. We believe it is essentially consistent with our Fundamental Postulate and with the various corollaries which have already been stated.

The second point to be emphasized is that this definition of role is not equivalent to the "self-concept" as used in some psychological systems. Seeing oneself as playing a role is not equivalent to identifying oneself as a static entity; but rather, as throughout the theory of personal constructs, the role refers to a process — an ongoing activity. It is that activity carried out in relation to, and with a measure of understanding of, other people that constitutes the role one plays.

The third point to be emphasized is that this definition ties up the role with a social process. While the concept of role is appropriate to a psychological system which is concerned with individual persons, it is defined herein so that it is dependent upon cognate developments within a group of two or more people. It is not enough that the role player organize his behavior with an eye on what other people are thinking; he must be a participant, either in concert or in opposition, within a group movement. This further restriction of the definition of a role places emphasis upon team membership on the part of the role player.

The fourth point to be emphasized is that, while one person may play a role in a social process involving the other person, through subsuming a version of that other person's way of seeing things, the understanding need not be reciprocated. Thus the one person is playing a role in a social process, but the the other is not playing a role in that social process. This is the way we have chosen to define *role*. It does not mean that the other person is not a factor to be taken into account in explaining the social process.

The fifth and final point to be emphasized is that this definition of role does not insist upon commonality in the construct systems of the people involved in the social process or in the persons specifically involved in playing roles. Commonality between construction systems may make it more likely that one construction system can subsume a part of another, but that fact is incidental rather than essential in those cases where roles are played between people who think alike and understand each other. Moreover, commonality can exist between two people who are in contact with each other without either of them being able to understand the other well enough to engage in a social process with him. The commonality may exist without those perceptions of each other which enable the people to understand each other or to subsume each other's mental processes. As in the case in psychotherapy in which the clinician identifies himself so closely with his client's way of seeing things that he cannot subsume the client's mental processes, the role the clinician plays becomes impoverished and the social process or the productive outcome of the clinician-client relationship comes to a standstill. The management of both transference and countertransference in psychotherapy is an example of the development of roles for both client and therapist.

We have made the point that for people to be able to understand each other it takes more than a similarity or commonality in their thinking. In order for people to get along harmoniously with each other, each must have some understanding of the other. This is different from saying that each must understand things in the same way as the other, and this delicate point has profound implications in psychotherapy. To the extent that people understand each other or, stated in the language of our theory, to the extent that their construction systems subsume each other, their activities in relation to each other may be called *roles,* a role being a course of activity which is played out in the light of one's understanding of the behavior of one or more other people.

Let us make sure, further, that we have not slighted the point that there is a difference between two people's holding the same construction system and two people's understanding each other so that they can play roles in relation to each other. Consider the differences in the characteristic approaches to life of men and women. None of us would claim, we believe, that men and women construe all aspects of life in the same way. And yet nature has provided us with no finer example of role relationships and constructive social interaction than in the sexes. If we look at the testimony of nature, we shall have to admit that it often takes a man to understand a woman and a woman to understand a man and there is no greater tragedy than the failure to arrive at those understandings which permit this kind of role interrelationship.

The Leadership Role

It is not intended to discuss all the implications of the Sociality Corollary at this point. However, it may be helpful to look at certain of its implications in order to suggest what impact this assumption might have in the field of psychology. For example, the Sociality Corollary has implications for the psychology of leadership which may prove useful. It will be necessary, however, first to clarify what is meant by "leadership." In studying groups sociometrically it appears that nominators may make their selections of "leaders" quite differently, depending upon their understanding of what the situation demands. If ingenuity and originality appear to him to be acquired, a nominator may choose one person. If defense of the group against an outside threat or a superordinate authority is believed to be needed, quite another kind of person may be chosen. If devotion to duty and housekeeping activities are required, still another may be selected. If individual members of the group are afraid their own freedom of action may be constricted if the group becomes tightly organized along certain lines, they may choose as leaders those who promise optimal permissiveness in the group structure. If the nominators feel keenly their interdependence upon each other, and therefore wish to mobilize the group, they may choose still another type of leader.

While prestige or status may be common to nearly all leadership, the psychologist will be badly fooled if he overlooks the variety of leadership patterns because they hold this one feature in common. A leader is one who performs any one of the variety of jobs which are popularly recognized as leadership jobs. He may do the job because of the expectancies with which he is surrounded; in that case, he may "perform better than he is able." Again, he may do the job with such originality that his "leadership" is recognized only in the pages of history.

Let us consider first what is involved in the leadership role of the mobilizing or rallying type of leader. The situation within which he operates tends to accelerate the social processes of the group as a whole, though it sometimes retards the social processes of subgroups or superordinate groups. The rallying leader's contribution to the acceleration of the group's social progress is dependent upon and proportional to his understanding of the relevant features in his colleagues' personal construction systems. By "understanding" we do not mean that he necessarily holds the common viewpoint, but rather that he has a way of looking at his colleagues' ideas that makes sense and enables him to predict their behavior. Of course, a commonality of viewpoint may, to a certain extent, make it easier for him to subsume parts of the construction systems of his colleagues within his own, but commonality is not a necessary prerequisite to subsuming.

Simply stated, the point is that one does not have to be like certain people in order to understand them, but he does have to understand them in certain respects in order to rally them. While this sentence may require some additional modifiers, it does express the central theme of what the psychology of personal constructs has to say about the rallying type of leadership.

In a somewhat different sense the Sociality Corollary provides inferences regarding other types of leadership. The ingenuity leader may not be playing a role in a social process, as we have defined *role* here, but the people who select him may be playing roles in a social process which involves him. In choosing him they are anticipating his contribution to the group and subsuming it within their own constructions of the part he ought to play.

The defending leader may not be called upon to perform an intragroup role; his role in a social process is played out primarily in relation to persons outside the group. The housekeeping leader may or may not be playing a role in the sense we have defined it. On the one hand, he may, like the ingenuity leader, be the one in relation to whom others play out their own roles in a social process. On the other hand, he may, as in the case of an effective executive secretary of an organization, understand the explicit and implicit policies of the group so well that he is able, without specific mandate, to act in each newly arising situation just as the group would want him to act.

The compromise leader need not play a role as we have defined it, and the role value of the participation of the people who select him may be minimal. Since his selection implies a slowing down of social process in the particular group with which his leadership is identified, perhaps so that other social processes will not be stifled, it is expected that his role will be constricted. To be sure, as some vice-presidents have done, he may surprise his electors and play out a role which generates more social progress than they bargained for.

Testing the Theory of Personal Constructs

Since a theory is an ad interim construction system which is designed to give an optimal anticipation of events, its life is limited by its period of usefulness. If this theory proves to be fertile in providing us with testable hypotheses and in suggesting new approaches to the problems psychologists face, it will have cleared its first hurdle. If, subsequently, it occurs that a considerable proportion of the hypotheses prove to be true, and many of the new approaches provide desired control over psychological events, the theory will have reached maturity. When its place is eventually taken by a more comprehensive, a more explicit, a more fertile and more useful theory, it will be time to relegate it to history.

It cannot be expected that we can accomplish any more than the partial clearing of the first hurdle in this presentation. An attempt will be made to show that the theory does provide us with some interesting new approaches to the problems psychologists face, particularly in the field of psychotherapy. Some hypotheses which are believed to be testable by more formal procedures will also be suggested. The establishment of real fertility in this respect, however, will depend upon what the readers of this manuscript come up with as a result of reading it.

SUMMARY OF ASSUMPTIVE STRUCTURE

Fundamental Postulate and Its Corollaries

FUNDAMENTAL POSTULATE: A person's processes are psychologically channelized by the ways in which he anticipates events.

CONSTRUCTION COROLLARY: A person anticipates events by construing their replications.

INDIVIDUALITY COROLLARY: Persons differ from each other in their constructions of events.

ORGANIZATION COROLLARY: Each person characteristically evolves, for his convenience in anticipating events, a construction system embracing ordinal relationships between constructs.

DICHOTOMY COROLLARY: A person's construction system is composed of a finite number of dichotomous constructs.

CHOICE COROLLARY: A person chooses for himself that alternative in dichotomized construct through which he anticipates the greater possibility for extension and definition of his system.

RANGE COROLLARY: A construct is convenient for the anticipation of a finite range of events only.

EXPERIENCE COROLLARY: A person's construction system varies as he successively construes the replications of events.

MODULATION COROLLARY: The variation in a person's construction system is limited by the permeability of the constructs within whose ranges of convenience the variants lie.

FRAGMENTATION COROLLARY: A person may successively employ a variety of construction subsystems which are inferentially incompatible with each other.

COMMONALITY COROLLARY: To the extent that one person employs a construction of experience which is similar to that employed by another, his psychological processes are similar to those of the other person.

SOCIALITY COROLLARY: To the extent that one person construes the construction processes of another, he may play a role in a social process involving the other person.

DAVID C. McCLELLAND

Toward a Theory of Motivation

1. THE AFFECTIVE AROUSAL MODEL

Our reservations with respect to contemporary motivation theory have led us to attempt to rough out proposals for an alternative theory which may now or ultimately meet some of these objections and handle the data at least as well as the other models discussed. We are well aware of the incompleteness, as of this writing, of our theoretical thinking, but we will attempt to state our views as precisely and forcefully as we can in the hope that we can stimulate more serious discussion and experimental testing of motivational theory. At several points we will be obliged to present alternative hypotheses, since we do not as yet have the data to decide between them. But we agree with Hull and others that the only way to make progress in a field is "to stick one's neck out" and to state implicit theoretical assumptions as explicitly as possible.

Our definition of a motive is this: *A motive is the redintegration by a cue of a change in an affective situation.* The word *redintegration* in this definition is meant to imply previous learning. In our system, all motives are learned. The basic idea is simply this: Certain stimuli or situations involving discrepancies between expectation (adaptation level) and perception are sources of primary, unlearned affect, either positive or negative in nature. Cues which are paired with these affective states, changes in these affective states, and the conditions producing them become capable of redintegrating a state (A) derived from the original affective situation (A), but not identical with it. To give a simple example, this means that if a buzzer is associated with eating saccharine the buzzer will in time attain the power to evoke a motive or redintegrate a state involving positive affective change. Likewise, the buzzer if associated with shock will achieve the power to redintegrate a negative affective state. These redintegrated states, which might be called respectively *appetite* and *anxiety*, are based on the primary affective situation but are not identical with it.

The term *change in affect* is used in two separate senses. It refers on the one hand to the fact that *at the time of arousal* of a motive, the affective

From *The Achievement Motive* by D. C. McClelland, J. W. Atkinson, R. A. Clark, and E. L. Lowell. Copyright © 1953. Reprinted by permission of Appleton-Century-Crofts, Educational Division, Meredith Corporation.

state which is redintegrated must be different from the one already experienced by the organism, and on the other hand to the *possibility* that *at the time of acquisition* of a motive, the affective state with which the cue gets associated must be undergoing a change. We are agreed that a "change in affect" at the time of arousal in the first sense must occur, but we see two possibilities on the acquisition side of the picture — one, that the association is with a *static* affective state; the other, that it is with a *changing* affective state. To elaborate this point further, the first alternative states simply that any cue associated with a situation producing affect will acquire the power to evoke a "model" of that situation (A') which will serve as a motive. The second alternative requires that the cue be associated with a *changing* state — of going from "shock" to "no shock" or from neutrality to pleasure, and so forth. The difference between the two possibilities is illustrated in the following diagram:

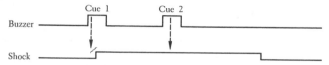

According to the first hypothesis, both cue 1 and cue 2 should be capable of evoking an avoidance motive, since they have both been paired with the affective state arising from shock. According to the second, alternative hypothesis, cue 2 should have weak or nonexistent motivating power since it has not been associated with a *change* in affect. It should be possible to determine which of these alternatives is correct by experimentation along these lines. Finally, it should be repeated that both hypotheses assume that the redintegrated affect *at the time of arousal* must represent a change over the present affective state of the organism.

In the discussion so far there has been some ambiguity as to just what is redintegrated — the affective state or change, the conditions which produced it, or both. Actually, the ambiguity reflects some uncertainty as to which alternative is correct and also some difficulty in expressing simply exactly what happens. By far the most likely possibility is that both the situation *and* the affect it produces are redintegrated. Thus the redintegrated "situation" defines the goal in the usual sense (e.g., sugar in the mouth), and the redintegrated "affect" (e.g., reaction to the sugar in the mouth) determines whether the goal is motivating or not. For the sake of simplicity, phrases like redintegrated "affective state" or "affective change" are used throughout this chapter to refer both to the affective reaction itself and the situation which produced it.

Two main questions connected with the concept of redintegrated affective state still remain to be answered. Why, first of all, should we have decided to base motives on affect? Secondly, how are we to determine the existence of affective arousal? It will be difficult to do complete justice to these questions, but a word on each may help indicate the progress of our thinking.

2. WHY AFFECT AS A BASIS FOR MOTIVES?

We have decided to base motives on affective arousal, following Young's lead (1949) for several reasons. In the first place, it seems apparent that the motive concept will be useful only if it has some kind of a limited base. That is, if all associations are motivating, then there seems no particular reason to introduce the concept of motivation to apply to a particular subclass of association. Thus the associations involved in forming motives must be in some way different from other types of associations. And we have chosen affective states as the basis for motives rather than biological needs or strong stimuli because of the limitations of those concepts already discussed. A more positive reason for choosing affective states as primary is that they are "obviously" important in controlling behavior, at least at the common-sense level. The hedonic or pleasure-pain view of motivation is certainly one of the oldest in psychological thinking and can be traced at least to Plato's *Protagoras*. Furthermore, in order to get motives in the laboratory we commonly pair cues with affective states resulting from shock, saccharine in the mouth, food deprivation, and the like. Operationally we manipulate states which we know subjectively will produce pleasure and pain when we work with motives.

Another reason for choosing affect as the basis for motives rather than tissue needs, etc., is the overwhelming evidence for the importance of selective sensitivity in guiding and directing behavior in lower animals. Tinbergen (1951) has collected dozens of cases which illustrate how special stimuli are required to release a particular "consummatory" response particularly in sub-mammalian species. Young (1949) has repeatedly called attention to the different palatability of various foods for the white rat. Weiner and Stellar (1951) have demonstrated unlearned salt preferences in the rat. And so forth. The list could easily be extended. The usual reaction by theorists to these facts is to assume that they are not characteristic of the human animal, which is obviously much more dependent on learning than on innate reactions to particular "releasing" stimuli. The difference is nicely highlighted by Ford and Beach (1951), who show how human sexual behavior is much less dependent than the behavior of lower animals on particular external signs and internal hormonal conditions.

But all of this seems no reason to assume a sharp discontinuity between man and other animals with respect to the factors controlling behavior. Rather we have been struck by the possibility that man's behavior may also be guided by selective sensitivity to particular kinds of situations. The difference may be one of degree rather than kind. With man the "releasing" situations may be much less specific than the dot on a gull's beak which releases pecking behavior of a gull chick, but they may exist just the same (Section 4). And the consummatory reactions elicited by such situations may also be much less specific and rigid than the pecking, fighting, courting responses shown in lower animals; in fact, the interesting possibility pursued here is that in man these specific overt reactions to "releasing" stimuli are attenuated and occur instead as diffuse reactions of the autonomic nervous system signifying what we usually call "affect." Thus our motivational system for man has been constructed to parallel the analysis of instinctive behavior in lower animals made by Tinbergen (1951) and others. Certain types of situations (Section 4) innately release reactions which are diffuse and covert in man rather than specific and overt, but which are consummatory in the same sense in that they ultimately exhaust themselves. These diffuse reactions are what we mean by affect, and they can be observed either through verbal reports and autonomic reactions, or inferred from approach and avoidance behavior, as we shall see in the next section. Man's advantage over lower animals lies precisely in the wider range of situations which will produce affect and in the lack of overt specificity of the affective reaction. Thus he can build a wide variety of motives on a much broader base, but to our mind it is essentially the same base as that which is responsible for guiding and directing the behavior of lower animals.

3. BEHAVIORAL EFFECTS OF AFFECTIVE AROUSAL

But how do we propose to define pleasure and pain or affective arousal? We certainly do not intend to fall into the trap of arguing that pleasurable sensations are those that lead to survival, and painful ones those that ultimately lead to maladaptation and death. This answer lands us back in the same difficulties that face the biological need theory of motivation. Let us first attempt to define affect by anchoring it on the behavioral side. It might seem more logical to consider first the antecedent conditions of affect (see Section 4) rather than its behavioral consequences, but the behavioral approach is more familiar because it is the one that has been customarily employed in attempts to measure affect or pleasure and pain (cf. Lindsley in Stevens, 1951). Thus, at a certain gross level, one can distinguish affective states from other states by the effects of autonomic activity — changes in respiration rate, in electrical skin resistance, in blood pressure, and the like. Thus one might initially state as a generalization that an affective state is present whenever the PGR shows a significant deflection, and that anyone who wants to establish a motive can simply pair cues with such deflections or the conditions which produced them. Autonomic accompaniments of emotions may not be perfect indexes of their presence, but they are sufficiently good to provide a very practical basis for deciding in a large number of cases that affective arousal has occurred.

Since autonomic measures apparently cannot be used at the present time to distinguish sensitively between positive and negative affective states, we will need to attack this problem in some other way. There are several possibilities. Among humans, expressive movements can readily be interpreted as indicating pleasant or unpleasant feeling states, particularly facial expressions (Schlosberg, 1952). Impromptu vocalizing seems also to be a good indicator of mood. Probably the most sensitive and frequently used index to hedonic tone is verbal behavior. If the person says "I dislike it," "I'm unhappy," or "it hurts," we take it as a sign of negative affect. If he says "I feel good," or "I like it," we take it as a sign of positive affect. One difficulty with these expressive signs is that they are not infallible. They can all be "faked," or changed by learning.

And what about animals? They can't talk, it would be difficult to try to interpret the facial expression of a rat or an elephant, and no one has made a careful study of animal vocalization patterns in response to pleasure and pain. In the case of some animals, certain innate response patterns are readily interpreted as signifying positive or negative affect — e.g., purring or spitting in the cat; licking, tail-wagging, or growling in the dog, and so on. More attention should be given to the study of the expressive signs of affect, but until it is, we must be satisfied with stopgap measures. Probably the most useful of these with adult animals is simple preference or approach behavior in contrast to avoidance behavior.

Sometimes there are reflex responses that are clearly approach or avoidance in nature — e.g., sucking, grasping, swallowing, spitting, vomiting, blinking — and in some instances they may provide direct evidence of positive or negative affective arousal. That is, eye-blinking in response to a puff of air, if accompanied by an autonomic response, would give evidence that affect was present and that this affect was negative in nature. Cues paired with the air puff would in time come to elicit an avoidance motive (as indicated by the presence of an avoidance *response* — the conditional or anticipatory eyeblink). But since reflexes are few in number and sometimes hard to classify as approach or avoidance (e.g., the knee jerk), better evidence for the existence of affective arousal is to be found in *learned* approach and avoidance behavior (locomotor, manual, verbal). There is an apparent circularity here, because what we are saying is that we can tell whether affective arousal occurred only after the organism has learned an approach or avoidance response in the service of a motive. Are we not first making a motive dependent on affective arousal and then saying we can find out whether affective arousal occurred if a motive has been formed which leads to approach or avoidance behavior? The answer is "Yes, we are," but the argument is not completely circular (cf. Meehl, 1950). Thus in one experiment we can determine that salty water leads to learned approach or preference behavior in the rat and we can then *infer* from this that it produces positive affective arousal. This inference (that salty water "tastes good" to the rat) can then be used as the basis for new learning experiments, theorizing, and so on. In this way we can gradually build up classes of objects, situations, response categories, or sensations which must produce affective arousal and then try to generalize as to what they have in common, as we have later on ... (Section 4). In brief, the notion here is to use autonomic responses to indicate the presence of affect and approach and avoidance (either learned or reflex) to distinguish positive from negative affect.

There is one misconception which may arise in connection with this definition that it is well to anticipate, however. The terms *approach* and *avoidance* must not be understood simply as "going towards" or "away from" a stimulus in a spatial sense. Thus "rage," when it goes over into attack, is an "avoidance" response, even though it involves "going towards" something. *Avoidance* must be defined in terms of its objective — to discontinue, remove, or escape from a certain type of stimulation and not in terms of its overt characteristics. Attack has, as its objective, removal of the source of stimulation in the same sense that withdrawal does. *Approach* must also be defined functionally — i.e., it is any activity, the objective of which is to continue, maintain, or pursue a certain kind of stimulation. Because of the ambiguity involved in using these terms, it might be better to substitute others like *stimulus enhancement* or *stimulus reduction*, but approach and avoidance have the advantage of common usage and if it is understood that they are used in a functional sense, difficulties should not arise in using them as the primary means of defining positive and negative affect on the response side. It is perhaps worth noting that Dearborn (1899) and Corwin (1921) came to the same decision long ago after recording involuntary "pursuit" (extension) and "withdrawal" (flexion) movements to pleasant and unpleasant stimuli, respectively.

3.1. Distinguishing the Effects of Affect and Motive

Analytically speaking, there are three events involved in the development of a motive, any of which may have observable and distinguishable behavioral effects. In order of occurrence, they are:

A. The situation producing affect
B. Redintegration of (A)
C. Response learned to (B)

We have discussed the problem of measuring the behavioral effects of A in the previous section. How can the effects of A and B be distinguished, if at all? The simplest assumption would seem to be the one that Hull made years ago (1931), to the effect that a cue paired with a goal response will evoke a fractional anticipatory portion of it. The notion behind this is that the redintegrated response is like the original but fractional in nature, that is, consisting of a portion of the total goal response which is perhaps less in intensity or duration. The difficulty with this idea has been discussed at some length by Mowrer (1950). In general, the objection is similar to the one made against the substitution hypothesis in conditioning experiments. That is, formerly it was commonly assumed that in conditioning the conditioned stimulus simply substituted for the unconditioned stimulus in evoking the unconditioned response. But, as Hilgard and Marquis (1940) point out, the conditioned response is in fact often quite different from the unconditioned response. It is not necessarily a miniature replica or fractional portion of the original unconditioned response. For example, there is evidence that the normal response in rats to the primary affective state produced by shock is squealing, defecating, and intense variable behavior whereas the normal response to anticipation of shock (e.g., to fear) is different, probably crouching (Arnold, 1945). The evidence that crouching is the normal response to fear is not conclusive, as Brown and Jacobs (1949) point out, because it can be eliminated by certain experimental procedures; but the probability is still fairly great that the response to fear differs in important ways from the response to shock. Therefore it would seem unwise at this state of our knowledge to assume that the fear response is just a partial copy of the shock response. At the phenomenological level, it seems that shock produces two distinguishable response elements — pain, which is the immediate reaction to shock, and fear, which is the anticipatory redintegration of the pain response. These two responses are clearly different. That is, if one's teeth are hurt by drilling in the dentist's chair, the sight of the chair may evoke a subjective feeling we label fear, but it does not evoke a "fractional" pain in the teeth.

When we consider the third event in the sequence of motive formation — namely, the responses learned to the redintegrated affect — the picture becomes even more complex. Our position is that the genotypic responses to redintegrated positive or negative affect are "functional" approach or avoidance. Thus from avoidance we can infer that negative affect has occurred if we lack a direct independent response definition of negative affect. But at the phenotypical level, the responses learned to redintegrated negative or positive affect may be very varied. A rat can be trained to run at as well as away from a shock (Gwinn, 1949). Rage and fear are genotypically avoidance responses, but phenotypically the former involves approach and the latter withdrawal. Similarly, love and contempt or scorn are genotypically similar in that they both involve attempts to maintain a source of stimulation, but phenotypically love involves "going towards" an object and scorn involves "keeping your distance" from the scorned object. A classification of emotions on a pleasant-unpleasant dimension and on an attentive-rejective one succeeds in ordering satisfactorily nearly all the facial expressions of emotion, according to Schlosberg (1952), a fact which tends to confirm our position that one must distinguish basically between positive and negative affect on the one hand and learned reactions to it, however classified, on the other. If the learned reactions are classified as to whether they phenotypically involve "going towards" or "away from" something, as they were approximately on Schlosberg's attentive-rejective dimension, then one gets a fourfold table in which Love, Contempt, Rage, and Fear represent the four major types of emotional reactions.

But obviously such classifications of phenotypic reactions can vary tremendously. The important points to keep in mind theoretically are (1) that they are surface modes of reaction with two basic objectives — to approach or maintain pleasure and to avoid or reduce pain, and (2) that they are acquired and hence take time to develop and show characteristic individual differences.

3.2. Measuring Motives through Their Effects

The fact that the learned reactions to motives may vary so much suggests that it may be difficult to identify motives through their effects. The first problem is to decide at what point the stream of behavior indicates the presence of a motive. It may be helpful to begin the analysis with a simple case in which the behavior produced by affect can be distinguished from that which reflects the subsequent redintegration of affect. Consider the startle reaction (Landis and Hunt, 1939). A pistol shot produces varied autonomic and reflex effects which are signs of affective arousal. The fact that this arousal is negative can be inferred after the longer latency "voluntary" avoidance responses appear which are signs of an avoidance motive cued off by the shot or its "startle" effects because of the former association of such cues with negative affect. A necessary inference from this is that the first time startle is elicited (as perhaps in the Moro reflex in infants), it should not produce the longer latency co-ordinated avoidance behavior which Landis and Hunt observed in adults.

This suggests that one of the important ways in which motivated behavior may be identified is in terms of the *co-ordination* of responses or in terms of some kind of a response *sequence*, which terminates when the organism arrives somewhere with respect to a source of affect. The terms *approach* and *avoidance* imply a sequence of responses which has a *goal* — e.g., arriving at or away from a situation producing affect. Perhaps the point can be clarified by referring to our response definitions of a motive in Table 1. The general definition is "goal-oriented free choice with habit and situational factors controlled." Under this we have placed approach and avoidance behavior, the only criterion one can use with animals, and the choice of certain "classes of goal-oriented thoughts" for inclusion in fantasy, the criterion we have used in measuring achievement motivation. These criteria are similar in implying choice responses with respect to a goal. We mean by the term *goal* here the same thing we meant when we were distinguishing between genotypic and phenotypic approach and avoidance, between the functional significance of an act (e.g., avoiding a stimulus) and the modality of the act itself (which may involve attacking the stimulus). The goal is the functional significance of the act. Let us be more specific. Any response an animal makes involves choice in a sense. Any succession of responses also involves co-ordination in the sense of alternation of effector pathways, and so on. But only when the succession becomes a sequence which results in approach to or avoidance of a situation can we argue that there is evidence for the existence of a motive.

In dealing with verbal responses in a story the problem is simpler. Many thoughts (e.g., "the boy is happy") indicate the presence of affect, but only

TABLE 1. Motive as a Hypothetical Construct Conceived as Based on Various Kinds of Antecedent Conditions and as Being Reflected in Various Types of Behavior

Possible *sources* of	MOTIVES	as reflected in *types of behavior*
1. Biologically defined survival needs—food deprivation, etc. (Hull)	"Survival model"	1. Adaptive responses which permit or promote survival (need reduction)
2. Stimulus intensity (Miller and Dollard)	"Stimulus intensity model"	2. (*a*) Increased response output (*b*) Improvement in performance (learning)
3. Stimulus patterns of particular sorts (*a*) Stimulus situations which evoke varying degrees of correspondence between expectancy and perception (Hebb) (*b*) Stimulus situations which evoke incompatible response tendencies producing frustration (Brown and Farber)	"Stimulus pattern model"	3. Response patterns (*a*) Organized direction of behavior, the relatedness of a series of acts (*c*) Distinctive response patterns measured in the brain, through autonomic effects, or in overt behavior
4. Cues paired with adaptation level discrepancies innately producing affect (McClelland, *et al.*)	"Affective arousal model"	4. Goal-oriented "free" choice with habit and situational factors minimized, known, or randomized (*a*) Approach-avoidance under the above conditions (*b*) Frequency with which classes of goal-oriented thoughts (R's) are chosen for inclusion in fantasy

those thoughts chosen for inclusion which imply affect in connection with a particular situation are evidence for the existence of a motive (e.g., "the boy wants to do a good job"). In this example, "wanting to do a good job" defines an end situation which would produce positive affect ... and the fact that the subject chooses to include such a statement is taken as evidence that he is motivated for achievement. That is, he has made a "goal-oriented" choice by making a statement about an achievement situation ("good job") which would inferentially produce positive affect (the boy "wants" it). Thus with such a measure of motivation we do not need the evidence of a co-ordinated though perhaps variable sequence of responses with a certain end, since the end ("good job") is directly stated, and it is this end state, with its accompanying affect rather than mere co-ordination, which seems to be the necessary criterion for deciding that behavior is showing evidence of the existence of motivation.

In short, in verbal behavior the "redintegrated affective situation" may be reflected directly and need not be inferred from a sequence of responses signifying approach and avoidance.

But why in the definition do we insist on "free" choice with certain factors controlled? The argument runs like this. Since general locomotor approach and avoidance are learned so early and so well in the life history of the organism, they can be utilized in normal animals to test the strength of a motivational association, provided the testing situation is a "free" one — provided the rats' "habits" are normal and provided the situation is a normal one for the rat. That is, it would be fair to test for the existence and strength of a rat's hunger motive by measuring the number of times he runs toward food as compared with other objects when placed on an open table top, provided his past experience has been "normal." But obviously if his past experience has not been normal — if he has lived in a vertical cage with no chance to walk in a horizontal dimension, if he has never had the opportunity to connect the sight of food with certain affective states (taste, reduction in hunger pangs), if he has been taught to run only when mildly hungry and to sit when very hungry — then the situation will not give a "fair" measure of his hunger motive. The number of times he ends up in the vicinity of the food could still be recorded in such cases, but it might be a measure of things other than hunger. It would measure hunger according to our argument if, and only if, it made use of a highly overlearned response (i.e., a "normal" habit) in a situation which did not clearly evoke incompatible responses (i.e., a "normal" situation).

In a sense, this is fairly similar to the state of affairs when a human being is telling a story in response to a picture. That is, for most subjects putting thoughts into words or verbalizing is a highly overlearned response. Furthermore, in the fantasy situation no particular set of responses is supposed to be perceived as especially appropriate. Fantasy is a "free" response situation, provided the picture is not too structured. It might not be for a certain class of persons, for professional writers, for example, because they may have learned a particular set of responses to use in such a situation, just as the rats who have been trained to sit still when hungry have learned a particular set of responses which prevent us from measuring their motivation in the usual way. But except for professional authors, individuals should have no particular set of verbal response tendencies which seem appropriate because of past experience with such situations. In contrast, if we ask a subject if he would like to get a good grade in a course, the fact that he answers "yes" is of no particular significance for diagnosing his achievement motivation, because we can assume that he will have learned that this is an appropriate response to such a question. Here the social reality or the modal cultural pattern determines his response. It is just for this reason that we prefer pictures which are not so structured as to elicit one particular response by common social agreement. We want the restraints on the free choice of responses by the subject reduced to a certain necessary minimum.

Furthermore, the fantasy situation is "free" because the testing conditions do not place any external constraints on the responses which are possible. Thus the subject can write about anything — about killing someone, committing suicide, touring the South Seas on a pogo stick, having an illegitimate child, and so forth. Anything is symbolically possible. Thus the choice of response patterns is not limited by what can be done under the conditions in which the motive strength is to be tested. Here our measure of human motivation has a great advantage over measures of animal motivation, but in both cases the problem is the same: to minimize or know the situational and habit determinants of behavior. This position fits into the general theoretical framework described elsewhere by McClelland (1951) in which he argues that behavior is determined by situational (perceptual) factors, by habit (memory) factors, and by motivational factors. It follows that if one wants a particular response to reflect motivation primarily, the strength of the other two determinants must either be known, minimized, or randomized. In the elementary state of our present knowledge, the best procedure would appear to be to use highly overlearned responses in "free" situations. There is, therefore, some theoretical justification for our empirical finding that motives can be measured effectively in imagination.

4. ANTECEDENT CONDITIONS FOR AFFECTIVE AROUSAL

Let us now focus our attention on the all-important problem of identifying the antecedent conditions which produce affective arousal. For if we know them, we are in a position, according to the theory, of knowing how to create a motive by pairing cues with those conditions, according to the principles discussed in section 5. Considering the antecedent conditions for affective arousal inevitably gets us into some ancient controversies over what causes pleasure and pain (McDougall, 1927; Beebe-Center, 1932; Dallenbach, 1939; Hebb, 1949). There is not the space here to review these controversies or to attempt to resolve them. Instead, we can only indicate what appears to us to be a promising approach to a general theory. This approach can only be outlined roughly here in the form of a series of propositions which seem promising to us but which will require experimentation and more detailed exposition in further publications.

4.1. Affective Arousal Is the Innate Consequence of Certain Sensory or Perceptual Events

It is probable (though not necessary) that the basic mechanism (see proposition 2) which gives rise to *sensory* pleasantness (e.g., sweetness) and unpleasantness (e.g., bitterness) is similar to that which gives rise to pleasantness-unpleasantness at a more complex perceptual level (pleasant music vs. dissonant music). In this connection we use the term *sensory* to refer roughly to simple variations in stimulus dimensions (e.g., stimulus intensity), whereas *perceptual* refers primarily to more complex variations in stimulus events.

4.2. Positive Affect Is the Result of Smaller Discrepancies of a Sensory or Perceptual Event from the Adaptation Level of the Organism; Negative Affect Is the Result of Larger Discrepancies

The salt curve in Figure 1 illustrates this postulated relationship from the hedonic reactions to increasing salt concentrations in the mouth. Fifty years ago it was a commonplace assumption that increasing sensory intensity in *any* modality produced a pleasantness-unpleasantness curve like this (Beebe-Center, 1932, p. 166). The new feature of such a curve for us is that, like Hebb, we would plot it not against increasing intensity as such but against size of discrepancy between the stimulus (perception) and the adaptation level of the organism (expectation). Such a modification has several advantages which we will enumerate, but among them is the fact that it brings the "discrepancy hypothesis" as to the source of affect within the realm of quantitative testing according to Helson's formulae (1948) for determining adaptation level and discrepancies from it. In the discussion which follows we have obviously leaned heavily on Helson's formulation of the concept of adaptation level.

4.3. Natural Adaptation Levels for Various Sensory Receptors Differ

Such a hypothesis is apparently essential to a discrepancy hypothesis because of the known fact that some receptors give rise most readily or "naturally" to pleasantness and others to unpleasantness. In Figure 1 the two curves for sweet and bitter sensations illustrate this point. Thus sugar appears to give rise to pleasurable sensations across the entire range of stimulus intensity. In terms of the discrepancy hypothesis, this suggests that a discrepancy from the natural adaptation level (AL) large enough to produce unpleasantness

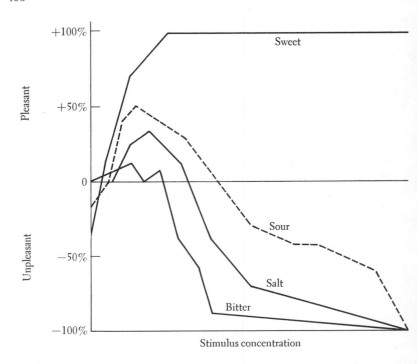

FIGURE 1. Preponderance of "pleasant" or "unpleasant" judgments in relation to the concentration of a sapid solution. The ordinate gives per cent "pleasant" minus per cent "unpleasant." The abscissa is proportional to the concentration, the full length of the baseline standing for 40 per cent cane sugar, for 10 per cent salt, and for .004 per cent quinine sulphate (all by weight). Data of R. Engel, after Woodworth, 1938.

is not possible. The bitter curve, on the other hand, is quite different: here nearly all intensities of stimulus concentration tested give rise to negative affect. The fact that the absolute threshold for sugar is considerably above what it is for bitter (Pfaffman in Stevens, 1951) suggests the following interpretation. The threshold for sweet is relatively high and the range of stimulation to which it is sensitive sufficiently narrow so that large discrepancies from AL which probably lies near the threshold are impossible. With bitter the threshold is so low that small fractions of the maximum concentration used in Figure 1 still represent fairly large discrepancies from an AL near the threshold. At this stage of our knowledge easy generalizations must be avoided, but it seems obvious even now that ultimately the natural AL for a receptor will turn out to be somewhere near its threshold (modified perhaps by the normal stimulation impinging on it) and that the size of the discrepancies which will yield positive and negative affect will be a joint rational function of the three constants in receptor functioning — the lower threshold, the upper threshold, and the Weber fraction.

What is clearly needed is a survey of all sensory qualities in terms of the discrepancy hypothesis as to what produces positive and negative affect. Such a survey cannot be attempted here both because of space limitations and because of the obvious complexity of some of the problems to be solved. Take pitch, for example. At first glance, it would look as if a few moments at the piano would easily disprove the discrepancy hypothesis. If two notes of small discrepancy in pitch, such as C and C-sharp, are played together in the middle pitch range, the effect is normally unpleasant; whereas if two notes farther apart in pitch, such as C and E, are played together, the effect is pleasant. Isn't this just the reverse of what our hypothesis would predict? It is, unless one considers the fact that two notes fairly close together produce a larger number of audible beats per second than two notes farther apart. It has long been recognized (Woodworth, 1938, p. 515) that unpleasantness is a function of these beats which represent discrepancies from an evenly pitched sound. Thus if size of discrepancy is measured in terms of "frequency of beats," it appears that the two tones close together are *more discrepant* than those farther apart and should therefore be more unpleasant. But this is only the beginning of what could be a thorough exploration of the esthetics of music according to this principle. Variables which appear to influence the pleasantness of combinations of tones, for example, include the absolute pitch of the two tones, the pattern of overtones, simultaneity vs. succession in sounding the two tones, and the like.

Or to take one more example — that of color. If our *AL* theory is correct, one would have to predict that dark-skinned peoples of the world would have different color *AL*'s from looking at each other than would light-skinned people. Consequently, the discrepancy in wavelength terms from the *AL*'s which should yield maximum pleasure in countries like India and the United States ought to be different. In these terms one might explain the fact that in India red is the most preferred color and white is the color of mourning, whereas in the United States blue-green is most preferred and black is the color of mourning (Garth, *et al.*, 1938). It is at least suggestive that nearly complementary skin color bases should produce complementary pleasant and unpleasant colors, but the most important point to note here is that our theory would argue for a *natural* basis for color preferences based on dominant or recurrent experiences rather than for a purely accidental basis subsequently reinforced by culture, as current thinking would appear to emphasize. Obviously such natural preferences can be changed by the culture or by the individual through particular experiences (e.g., there are plenty of American children who prefer red), but the point is that U.S. and Indian populations as groups should show different color preferences according to the principle that moderate discrepancy from different skin color *AL* bases will yield pleasure in colors of different wavelength composition.

These two examples should be sufficient to illustrate the deductive fertility of the discrepancy hypothesis and also the need for the kind of careful analysis of different sensory qualities which is beyond the scope of this introductory treatment.

4.4. A Discrepancy between Adaptation Level and a Sensation or Event Must Persist for a Finite Length of Time before It Gives Rise to an Hedonic Response

There are several reasons for making this assumption. In the first place, Beebe-Center and others have noted that certain types of sensations — e.g., taste, smell, pain — give rise to affective responses more readily than others — e.g., sight, hearing. A possible explanation for this fact would be "receptor lag" or "AL lag." That is, for the first group of sensations AL may change rather slowly, so that the discrepancy caused by a new stimulus will last long enough to give an hedonic report. In taste and smell, for instance, there appear to be purely "mechanical" reasons for the relative slowness with which previous concentrations of stimulator substances are changed by new substances. Thus a change might occur at one point in the receptor surface while the rest of the surface was still responding to earlier chemicals. In vision and hearing, on the other hand, the AL appears to respond rapidly to new sensations so that only major shifts in intensity will cause a discrepancy from AL to persist long enough to give rise to an hedonic response.

A second reason for the discrepancy-persistence hypothesis is that the hedonic j.n.d. seems to be larger than the sensory j.n.d. That is, in all modalities the discrepancies required to produce a just noticeable difference in hedonic tone seem to be larger than those required to produce a report of a difference in sensation. Unfortunately, adequate data on this point are apparently not available at present, although the problem is one that may be attacked easily experimentally. What is needed is a repetition of some of the standard psychophysics experiments in which hedonic judgments are called for under exactly the same conditions as judgments of *heavier, brighter, longer,* and so on. Usually these two types of judgments have been made separately. It would not be surprising if the hedonic j.n.d. turned out to be some function of the Weber fraction for each modality. The meaning of all this in terms of the present hypothesis is simply that a larger than just noticeable sensory difference is required to maintain a discrepancy over AL long enough to give rise to a just noticeable hedonic effect.

A third reason for the discrepancy-persistence hypothesis is simply to avoid making the whole of behavior affectively toned. After all, every sensory event might be considered, at least in some marginal sense, a discrepancy from some "expectation" and should therefore lead to some kind of affective arousal, were it not for some principle requiring a minimum degree of stability in the expectation or AL so that a discrepancy from it *could* persist. In short, the simple occurrence of an event is not sufficient to set up an AL such that any further modified occurrence of that same event will produce a discrepancy sufficient to cause affect. Rather the AL must be built up to a certain minimum level of stability through successive experiences, as in memory or psychophysical experiments, before discrepancies from it will produce affect. A case in point is provided by Hebb's young chimpanzee which did not fear a detached chimpanzee head until it had formed through experience a stable expectation of what a chimpanzee should look like (Hebb, 1949).

4.5. Discrepancies from Adaptation Level Will Give Rise to a Positive-Negative Affect Function in Either Direction along a Continuum

In many instances, events can differ from expectation only uni-directionally. Thus after the shape of the human figure has been learned, discrepancies can occur only in the direction of being less like the expected shape. But with many dimensions, particularly intensity, discrepancies are bi-directional and may have somewhat different affective consequences depending on their direction. For example, does a decrease of so many j.n.d.'s from an AL have the same hedonic tone as an increase of the same number of j.n.d.'s?

The simplest assumption is that the hedonic effect is the same regardless of the direction of the discrepancy. But the evidence for the assumption is not very convincing. It consists for the most part of some early experiments in esthetics such as the one summarized in Figure 2. Angier (1903) simply asked his subjects to divide a 160 mm line unequally at the most pleasing place on either side of the midpoint. The results in Figure 2 were obtained by averaging the frequencies of choices per 5 mm unit between 5–25 mm, 25–45 mm, 45–65 mm, 65–75 mm discrepancies, and plotting them with the actual frequencies for the 5 mm discrepancies on each side of the midpoint. Since Angier did not permit his subjects to choose the midpoint and since he forced them to make half of their judgments on either side of the midpoint, the data do not really test our hypothesis crucially. He should rather have let a large number of subjects choose any division points at all along the line. Still, Angier's introspective data from his subjects led him to conclude that "most of the subjects, however, found a *slight* remove from the center disagreeable" (1903, p. 550). Furthermore it is clear that his subjects did not like to divide the line near its extremities on either side. In short, there is evidence for the typical hedonic curve for descrepancies *in both directions* from the center which must be assumed to represent some kind of an AL based on symmetry, balance, and so forth. A similar bimodal preference curve for rectangles of different width-length ratios is reported by Thorndike (see Woodworth, 1938, p. 386), if the exactly balanced ratio of .50 is taken as the AL.

When an attempt is made to discover the same principle in the operation of sensory modalities, however, the situation becomes complex. Consider Alpert's data in Figure 3 as an example. The lower curve, which again is the

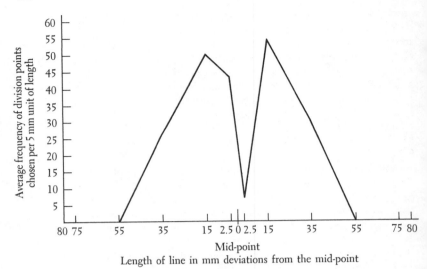

FIGURE 2.   Unequal division points of a straight line chosen as most pleasing. From Angier, 1903.

typical hedonic function for discrepancies from AL, was obtained in the following way. Subjects inserted one eye in a translucent "Ganzfeld" about the size of an egg cup. Around the outside of the cup, red lights were placed so as to produce inside it a diffuse red light covering the entire visual field and presumably stimulating largely only one set of receptors — the cones. In the center of the cup a small spot subtending about 18 degrees of visual arc was distinguishable from the rest of the field by a hazy dark line, produced by the fact that the spot was separately illuminated from behind. First the subject adjusted the illumination of the reddish spot until it matched the reddish "Ganzfeld" in all respects as closely as possible. Then the experimenter set a Variac which also controlled lamp voltage for the spot in such a way that if he switched off the "constant" lamp just adjusted by the subject and switched on the "variable" lamp for about two seconds, the subject got a glimpse of the spot as more or less intense than the surrounding "Ganzfeld." The subject made a judgment of pleasantness-unpleasantness on a scale of +3 to −3 *after* the "variable" lamp had been switched off and the "constant" lamp back on. Each subject made four judgments at each of the lamp voltage settings shown on the abscissa of Figure 3. The "spots" of different intensity were presented in random order four separate times. The procedure was duplicated for different illuminations of the "Ganzfeld" (i.e., for different adaptation levels). There were 10 subjects and the two curves in Figure 3 represent the average judgments of all of them under two adaptation level

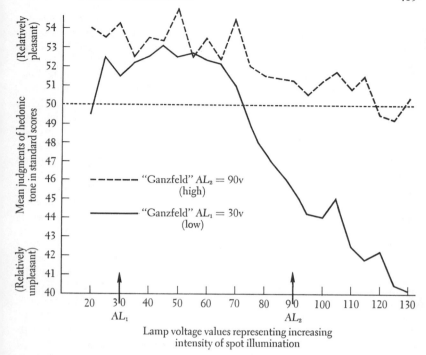

FIGURE 3. Hedonic tone judgments for discrepancies in spot illumination above and below low (AL₁) and high (AL₂) "Ganzfeld" illuminations. Red light, 10 subjects making 4 judgments at each lamp voltage value. Data from Alpert, 1953.

settings — one in which the "Ganzfeld" illumination was low ($<.5$ foot candles) and the other in which it was high (about 3 foot candles according to G.E. photometer). Each subject's judgments under all conditions were converted to a common scale of standard scores with a mean of 50 and an SD of 10. Thus the fact that the dotted line in Figure 3 is above 50 throughout most of its course means that most of the subjects' judgments in this condition were above their individual hedonic means *for the whole series of judgments* (including a series with a moderate AL not reproduced here).

Three conclusions can be drawn from Figure 3: (1) When the AL is low, and the receptors are close to the "resting" state, increases in stimulation produce first positive affect and then negative affect as postulated in Section 4.2. See solid line in Figure 3. (2) When the AL is high, well above the resting state, all increases in stimulation tend to produce negative affect and all decreases tend to produce positive affect. See dotted line in Figure 3. (3) There is no marked evidence in these curves either (a) for large decreases in stimulation leading to negative affect or (b) for stimulation around the

AL producing a neutral hedonic response. Neither (a) nor (b) should be considered as conclusive negative evidence, however. With respect to (a), common experience suggests that eating ice cream after drinking coffee is more painful than under normal conditions. On the surface, it would appear that this is because the low temperature of the ice cream represents a much larger discrepancy downwards from the heightened AL of the mouth or teeth produced by drinking coffee. But the problem is complicated by the fact that the heat and cold receptors may be different and related in an unknown way. That is, ice cream may not be a decrease in stimulation for warm receptors but an *increase* in stimulation for cold receptors. The virtue of using red illumination in the present experiment is that it presumably limits the effects of stimulation largely to one set of receptors — the cones. In short, the question of whether decreases in stimulation ever produce negative affect and of whether the hedonic curve is therefore alike on both sides of AL must be left open at the present time.

With respect to (b) there is a slight (though probably insignificant) dip in the lower hedonic curve for values of the spot which are close to those of the "Ganzfeld" AL. It can be argued that the reason the dip is not more striking is that at least two other AL's are operating in this situation. The first is the natural or physiological AL of the receptor which here and in other similar figures seems to lie somewhere around the threshold of the receptor. The illumination of the "Ganzfeld" was apparently close enough to this value for the lower curve in Figure 3 not to produce a major modification in its shape. The second AL is that produced by the *series* of spot stimuli of varying intensity. This can be calculated by Helson's formula (1947) to be equivalent to a lamp voltage value of around 63 volts, which is considerably *above* the "Ganzfeld" AL value and which may interact with it in some way to obscure further the dip in hedonic tone for values approximating AL. Generally speaking, the principle appears to hold for the lower curve if the AL is taken to be the physiological AL, and for the upper curve if the AL is taken to be the "Ganzfeld" value. Although both of these assumptions seem reasonable, once again the question must be considered open as to whether values approximating the AL always tend to take on a neutral hedonic tone, at least until we have more accurate ways of figuring out how AL's are shifted by exposure to various experiences.

4.6. Increases and Decreases in Stimulus Intensity Can Be Related to Motivation Only if Adaptation Level and Learning Are Taken into Account

Our view of motivation differs from Miller and Dollard's (1941) in two important ways. First, the effect of changes in stimulus intensity must always be referred to AL, and second, such changes produce affect immediately and motives only through learning. More specifically, an increase in stimulus intensity (a "drive" for Miller and Dollard) provides the basis for a motive only if it represents a large enough discrepancy from AL to produce positive or negative affect. It elicits a motive only if it or the situation producing it has been associated with such affect in the past. A decrease in stimulus intensity (a "reward" for Miller and Dollard) either provides the basis for an approach motive if it produces positive affect or removes the cues which have been redintegrating negative affect and thus eliminates an avoidance motive. Thus "drive" and "reward" in Miller and Dollard's sense are seen to be special cases of a more general theory.

Let us leave aside for the moment the question of whether motives or drives are always learned and look more closely at the question of the relation of stimulus intensity to AL. For us, it is not intensity per se which is important but discrepancy from AL. It follows that many strong stimuli will be unpleasant, but not all. It depends on over-all AL. Thus if a person is in dim illumination (bottom curve in Figure 3), a light with a lamp voltage value of 90 will produce marked negative affect; but if the illumination is already that bright, the same light will produce a rather indifferent response (upper curve in Figure 3). It is for this reason apparently that biting one's lips or otherwise hurting one's self helps relieve pain.

4.7. Changes in Adaptation Level, with Attendant Hedonic Changes, May Be Produced by Somatic Conditions

This is an obvious point and a few illustrations will serve to demonstrate its importance. The somatic conditions may be either chemical (hormonal) or neurological in nature. Pfaffman and Bare (1950) have demonstrated that the preferences for lower salt concentrations shown by adrenalectomized rats cannot be explained by a lowering of the *sensory* threshold of the nerves responding to salt. An explanation in our terms would simply be that the central AL has been lowered by chemical changes in the bloodstream so that lower salt concentrations on the tongue will produce a pleasurable discrepancy from it. That is, Pfaffman and Bare found that the lower concentrations had always produced action potentials in the gustatory nerve, although they did not produce preference behavior in the normal rat. The reason for this in our terms is that they were sufficiently near the normal AL not to evoke preference behavior. Figure 4, which is plotted from Harriman's data (1952), shows in detail what happens to salt preferences in adrenalectomized rats when salt has been removed from their diet. The solid curve shows the amount of salty water of different concentrations consumed by normal rats on a normal diet (including about 1 per cent salt) when they could choose between it and distilled water. The dotted curve shows the same results for the adrenalectomized animals on a salt-free diet.

The solid curve shows substantially the same relationship obtained for humans as presented in Figure 1 and it can be explained by the same assumptions — namely, that the AL for salt is somewhere below .3 per cent salt but above the absolute threshold for discrimination of salty from non-salty water which is at least as low as .01 per cent concentration of salt (Pfaffman and

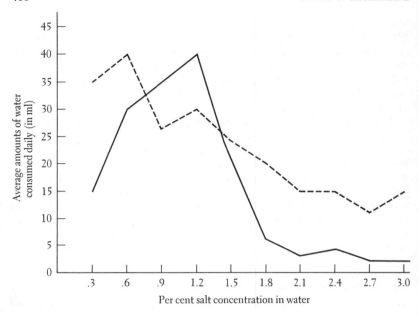

FIGURE 4. Data plotted from Harriman (1952) showing average amounts of salty water of different concentrations consumed by normal (solid line) and adrenalectomized rats (dotted line) on a salt-free diet.

Bare, 1950). The *AL* empirically is that concentration which a rat will not consistently approach or avoid as compared with distilled water. The dotted curve suggests that for the operated animals the *AL* has now moved to lower concentrations, so that a .3 per cent solution represents a "pleasurable" discrepancy whereas before it was relatively "neutral." The fact that formerly preferred concentrations (.9 per cent and 1.2 per cent) are now *less* preferred also supports the idea that the *AL* has been lowered, since these now represent larger (and therefore less pleasant) discrepancies from it. But how about the tail end of the dotted curve? Should not the adrenalectomized animals find the high salt concentrations even less pleasant than the normals, if their *AL* has been lowered? According to the discrepancy hypothesis they should, but these data are not conclusive evidence that they do not. That is, the operated animals may find the strong concentrations even more unpleasant than the normals do, but drink more of them in short "swallows" because the "after-taste" remains pleasant longer. In other words, if the salt solutions dissipate according to a negative decay function, there may be an appreciable time period after exposure to a strong concentration when the stimulus is pleasant, if the *AL* is low as in operated animals. Thus the operated animals may drink for the pleasant after-taste of strong concentrations; the normal animals may not because the dissipating solution reaches the higher AL sooner. At least the possibility is worth exploring.

In this fashion, changes in positive and negative affect resulting from the same stimulation on different occasions can be accounted for by chemical effects on AL. Such a hypothesis should be especially valuable in accounting for changes in the pleasurableness of sexual sensations accompanying certain hormonal cycles in lower animals (cf. Ford and Beach, 1951). Similarly Head's observations on the effects of thalamic lesions show that neurological damage can affect AL. Take this case, for example: "In one case a tube containing water at 38°C applied to the normal palm was said to be warm, but the patient cried out with pleasure when it was placed on the affected hand. His face broke into smiles and he said, 'Oh! that's exquisite,' or 'That's real pleasant'" (quoted in Beebe-Center, 1932, p. 391). Or another: "When a pin was lightly dragged from right to left across the face or trunk of one of the patients suffering from a lesion affecting the left side, she exhibited intense discomfort as soon as it had passed the middle line. Not only did she call out that it hurt more, but her face became contorted with pain. Yet careful examination with algesimeters showed that on the affected side her sensitivity to such stimulation was, if anything, slightly lowered" (Beebe-Center, 1932, p. 390). It is difficult to think about such findings in any other terms but some neurological effects on a central AL such that identical stimulations would produce different effects.

An interesting consequence of this proposition is that it suggests a reason why the sources of positive and negative affect may be different for different physiques. Thus if the AL for kinaesthetic sensations from large well-developed muscles is higher, it would be easy to understand why more activity would be required to get pleasurable discrepancies from the AL than for a weaker physique with lower kinaesthetic AL. In fact, one should argue that the amount of activity which produces pleasure for the mesomorphic physique (and consequently approach motives) might well produce too large a discrepancy, negative affect, and avoidance motives for the ectomorph. It might not be too far-fetched to attempt to account for the dominant sources of pleasure in each of Sheldon's somatotypes (1940) in terms of different AL's set up in different sensory modalities by different types of physiques. The argument would run something like this: The endomorph appears to get most of his pleasure from his gut because the AL for gut sensations is relatively high for such physiques and it takes gut sensations of greater intensity (or variety) to produce the discrepancies necessary for pleasure; the mesomorph appears to get most of his pleasure from his muscles because the AL for kinaesthetic sensations is relatively high and more variations in kinaesthetic sensations are required to give pleasure; the ectomorph appears to get more of his pleasure from minimal sensory stimulation because the AL for skin sensations is so low that moderate deviations from it give pleasure, and so forth. Such hypotheses are obviously incomplete and highly tentative, but they can certainly be tested experimentally and made more precise by isolating such physique types and determining their hedonic thresholds for various sensory qualities.

Finally, this proposition provides a basis for explaining Freud's libidinal development hypothesis, which has proven so fruitful clinically but so difficult to understand in terms of traditional "objective" theories of motivation. The explanation runs briefly as follows: "Erogenous zones" are skin areas where AL's are so low that relatively light tactual stimulation gives rise to sufficient discrepancies from AL to yield pleasure. If Freud is correct, it should be possible to demonstrate objectively that a constant tactual stimulus will give rise to pleasure responses in infants more readily in certain areas than in others. For the mouth, this seems well established, if the sucking response is taken as indicative of pleasure (i.e., because it is an approach response). For the anal and genital regions the facts are less well established. Freud's second hypothesis is that the erogenous sensitivity of these regions shifts as the child matures. In our terms, this simply means that changes in somatic conditions, produced here by maturation, modify AL's so that, as in the case of Head's patient, the same stimulus has a different hedonic effect. For example, the innate AL to mouth stimulation may increase with age so that touching the lips in the same way no longer yields pleasure and, at the same time, the anal region may become especially sensitive to tactual stimulation, and so on. The rise and fall in sensitivity of these various skin areas can certainly be measured behaviorally and understood in terms of physiologically produced changes in AL.

4.8. Changes in Adaptation Level, with Attendant Hedonic Changes, May Be Produced by Experience

This proposition opens up a whole new area that needs careful experimental exploration. We know some things but not nearly enough about how this happens. Thus Helson (1948) has demonstrated how an anchor or a series of stimuli can modify an AL in various modalities. His formulae even make assumptions as to the relative weights of background and figural stimulations in determining an AL produced by a series of stimuli. Furthermore, we know that hedonic judgments show the same type of central tendency, contrast, and assimilation effects that led Helson to formulate his notion of AL (Beebe-Center, 1932). This is as it should be, because as AL's shift in the "physical dimensions of consciousness" there should be corresponding shifts in hedonic reactions if they are a function of the size of discrepancies between new stimuli and the sensory AL. But the most clear-cut evidence we know of which demonstrates that the hedonic curve is shifted as a function of shifts in sensory AL is that which has already been presented in Figure 3 and discussed in Section 4.5. (See also Beebe-Center, 1932, p. 238.)

In the absence of more such data at a more complex level, we must work with qualitative observations to some extent. Take Hebb's treatment of the "fear of the strange" as a point of departure. "About the age of four months the chimpanzee reared in the nursery, with daily care from three or four persons only and seeing few others, begins to show an emotional disturbance at the approach of a stranger (Hebb and Riesen, 1943). The disturbance increases in degree in the following months. . . . Chimpanzees reared in darkness, and brought into the light at an age when the response (to a strange face) would be at its strongest, show not the slightest disturbance at the sight of either friend or stranger. *But* some time later, after a certain amount of visual learning has gone on, the disturbance begins to appear exactly as in other animals" (Hebb, 1949, pp. 244–45). He also reports that "a model of a human or chimpanzee head detached from the body" produces marked affective arousal in half-grown or adult chimpanzees but not in younger chimpanzees. From all this he concludes that "the emotional disturbance is neither learned nor innate: a certain learning must have preceded, but given that learning the disturbance is complete on the first appearance of certain stimulus combinations" (Hebb, 1949, p. 245). This is the crux of the matter as far as our theory of the conditions necessary for affective arousal (either positive or negative) is concerned. An *AL* must be built up in certain areas of experience (though it appears to be innately given for sense modalities) and then increasing discrepancies from that *AL* give rise first to positive and then to negative affect, as in Figure 1. *The AL may be acquired, the affective reactions to discrepancies from it are not*; they appear maximally the first time the discrepancy occurs and with less intensity thereafter because the new experience automatically interacts with the *AL*, changes it, and thereby reduces the discrepancy. Hence there is ultimate boredom or adaptation to pain or pleasure (satiation) as we shall see in a moment.

4.9. Events Can Differ from Expectations on a Variety of Dimensions

The example we have chosen from Hebb to illustrate the preceding point is important because, unlike the sensory *AL*'s which we have been discussing, it deals with changes in *patterns* of stimulation rather than with changes in *intensity* levels. Thus we have to expand the *AL* concept to include expectations about shapes (e.g., faces) or any other events that the organism has had occasion through past experience to build up expectations about. This expansion, while absolutely necessary for a complete theory, raises certain practical problems in defining the size of a discrepancy between expectation and perception — a variable which we must be able to determine quite precisely if we are going to be able to predict whether a given discrepancy will give rise to positive or negative affect.

Basically, the problem is one of isolating dimensions along which two events can differ and then attempting to define degrees of difference objectively. Thus the events can differ in intensity, extensity, clarity, quality, certainty, and so on, and traditional psychophysics gives us plenty of cues as to how degrees of difference along these dimensions can be determined. So far we have talked largely about intensity differences, but differences in quality (or similarity) can be treated the same way. Thus one would predict on the basis of the discrepancy hypothesis that an artificial language consisting of highly probably syllabic combinations would be more amusing than one consisting of highly improbable syllabic combinations, or that nonsense syllables that sounded like English (NOQ) would be more amusing than ones that didn't (VOQ). And so forth. The research along these lines that needs to be done appears almost limitless.

Most events, of course, can differ from expectation in a variety of ways. Suppose a rat runs down an alley, turns left, proceeds three or four steps further, finds and eats a food pellet of a certain size and consistency. If this series of events occurs with sufficient frequency, we argue that the rat has built up a chain of associations of high probability or certain "expectations" as to what will happen. But these expectations, redintegrated partially when the rat is placed in the maze, may fail to be exactly confirmed in a variety of ways. An obstacle may delay him so that it takes him longer to get to the food. We may substitute mash for a food pellet, or a large pellet for a small one. He may eat the food where it is or pick it up and carry it somewhere else to eat it. And so forth. According to the discrepancy hypothesis, certain predictions about this process can be made. So long as the animal is uncertain in his expectations (i.e., is still learning the habit), there will be a tendency to limit the variability of responses so as to increase the probability of expectations until events represent only moderate and hence pleasurable deviations from them. But once the habit is overlearned the animal will tend to introduce variations once more — now to *increase* uncertainty to a "pleasurable" level. In short, exactly confirming certain expectations produces boredom and a tendency to discontinue the act unless enough minor variations are permitted to produce positive affect. The evidence for this hypothesis from animal learning is considerable. Thus the tendency toward variability in routine behavior has been found by many learning psychologists and is perhaps best illustrated by Heathers' (1940) report that rats alternate the paths they choose to get food when either is equally good. They are apparently operating according to the same general principle when they prefer a path to food with a barrier in it to an unobstructed path to food (Festinger, 1943), or prefer seeds which are difficult to crack open to seeds which are not so difficult (Yoshioka, 1930). Other similar examples of "inefficient" preferences have been collected by Maltzman (1952). In these and other such cases, the rat may prefer what looks like an inefficient response because it involves minor variations from expectation along such dimensions as time delay, spatial location, size of expected object, nature of expected object, and so forth — variations which according to the discrepancy hypothesis should yield pleasure. Research on this problem has to be done with care because as soon as the modification is major (for example, when the time delay becomes too long), then, of course, negative affect results and the preference of the animal is reversed. To complicate the matter even more, one should know how certain, or overlearned, the expectations are before predicting the effects of variations from them. If the expectations are of low probability, then confirmation should produce negative affect as in "fear of the strange." If they are of moderate probability, precise confirmation should produce pleasure (as in reading a detective story or playing solitaire). If the expectations are of high probability, then precise confirmation produces boredom or indifference (as in reading over again the detective story one has just finished, to use Hebb's example). The hedonic effects of the interaction of degrees of certainty of an expectation on the one hand, and degrees of deviation of an event from that expectation on the other, have yet to be worked out experimentally, but there is no reason why they could not be, using either animal or human subjects.

4.10. Frustration Is a Source of Negative Affect

A special note is in order as to where the notion of frustration or conflict as a drive (Whiting, 1950; Brown and Barber, 1951) fits into this scheme. Frustration in their terms results essentially from competition of response tendencies in such a way that F (frustration) is increased by reducing the difference in strength between the two opposed tendencies and also by increasing the absolute strength of both of them. Such statements are completely in line with our assumptions, with some exceptions to be noted in a minute. That is, we too would argue that the more nearly equal in strength two response tendencies are, the more they would give rise to negative affect (F); because such competition means that if either response is made, the expectation based on the other is not confirmed; or that if neither is made, both are unconfirmed. Similarly, the effects of nonconfirmation should be greater, the greater the strength of the response tendency. There are two differences between our scheme and theirs, however: (1) We would argue that when the size of the discrepancy between the stronger and weaker response tendencies is large, there should be a stage when the competition of the weaker response tendency should give rise not to frustration but to pleasure, if the stronger tendency is confirmed. This would require a modification in their formula for computing F such that for a certain range of discrepancies between the two tendencies it would yield negative F values (signifying pleasure). (2) They treat F as if it were a drive, whereas in our terms F in itself is simply negative affect and does not become a motive until anticipations of it or by it are elicited.

4.11. The Achievement Motive Develops out of Growing Expectations

So far our scheme has been stated in fairly abstract form. A concrete example involving the development of the achievement motive may help explain its application in practice. Suppose a child is given a new toy car for Christmas to play with. Initially, unless he has had other toy cars, his expectations (or

AL's) as to what it will do are nonexistent, and he can derive little or no positive or negative affect from manipulating it until such expectations are developed. Gradually, if he plays with it (as he will be encouraged to by his parents in our culture), he will develop certain expectations of varying probabilities which will be confirmed or not confirmed. Unless the nonconfirmations are too many (which may happen if the toy is too complex), he should be able to build up reasonably certain expectations as to what it will do *and confirm them.* In short, he gets pleasure from playing with the car. But what happens then? Why doesn't he continue playing with it the rest of his life? The fact is, of course, that his expectations become certainties, confirmation becomes 100 per cent, and we say that he loses interest or gets bored with the car; he should get bored or satiated, according to the theory, since the discrepancies from certainty are no longer sufficient to yield pleasure. However, pleasure can be reintroduced into the situation, as any parent knows, by buying a somewhat more complex car, by making the old car do somewhat different things, or perhaps by letting the old car alone for six months until the expectations about it have changed (e.g., decreased in probability). So, if a child is to continue to get pleasure from achievement situations like manipulating toy cars, he must continually work with more and more complex objects or situations permitting mastery, since, if he works long enough at any particular level of mastery, his expectations and their confirmation will become certain and he will get bored. The situation is analogous to the experiments by Washburn, Child, and Abel (cf. Beebe-Center, 1932, p. 238) which show that pleasure decreases on successive repetitions of simple popular music, whereas it increases on successive repetitions of severely classical music. In the first instance, expectations or *AL*'s are readily formed and confirmed to the point of boredom, whereas they take much longer to form with classical music — so long in fact that some people never expose themselves to such music often enough to get pleasure from having them confirmed. Thus pleasure from anything — be it mastery, music, or modern art — depends on a moderate degree of novelty, which has to become ever greater as expectations catch up with it. But note that there are limits on this developmental process: not every child will develop a very high level achievement motive or esthetic appreciation motive. In the first place, there are limits placed by native intelligence: the possibilities of a toy car or a comic book may never be exhausted as far as a moron is concerned because they never become certain enough for him to be bored over trying them out. Thus one would expect some kind of a correlation between the mastery level involved in *n* Achievement for a given person and his intelligence.

In the second place, there are limits placed on the development of *n* Achievement by the negative affect which results from too large discrepancies between expectations and events. Thus Johnny may develop expectations as to what a model airplane or a solved arithmetic problem looks like, but he may be unable to confirm these expectations at all, or only very partially. The result is negative affect, and cues associated with these activities may be expected to evoke avoidance motives. To develop an achievement approach motive, parents or circumstances must contrive to provide opportunities for mastery which, because they are just beyond the child's present knowledge, will provide continuing pleasure. If the opportunities are too limited, boredom should result and the child should develop no interest in achievement (and have a low n Achievement score when he grows up). If the opportunities are well beyond his capacities, negative affect should result, and he may develop an avoidance motive as far as achievement is concerned. Since a fairly narrow range of circumstances will conspire to yield a high achievement approach motive, it would not be surprising to discover that individuals or groups of individuals in different cultures differ widely in the amount of achievement motivation they develop.

4.12. In Human Adults Adaptation Levels Are Numerous and Complex so That a Single Event May Have Several Hedonic Consequences

Take flunking out of school, for example. One might argue that if the student half expected it, he should feel pleasure since his expectation is confirmed. Although it is true that he may get some fleeting satisfaction from having predicted correctly, this is more than outweighed by the nonconfirmation of other expectations built up over his whole life history such as doing a good job, being a professional man, etc. So far we have been dealing largely with low level expectations and AL's taken one at a time for the sake of simplicity, but obviously in real life situations, after the person has matured, the calculus of pleasure and pain becomes exceedingly complex. Consider, for example, the traditional argument used against hedonic theories of motivation to the effect that adults at any rate frequently do things, out of a sense of duty or what not, which are distinctly unpleasant. What about the martyr, for example? Can he be seeking pleasure or avoiding pain? The answer is "yes," in the larger sense in which positive and negative affect are defined here. If a man builds up a conception of the Universe – an expectation of the way in which moral or spiritual laws govern it and his place in it – which is sufficiently firm and well defined, it may well be that the anticipated nonconfirmation of such an expectation through transgression of those laws would produce sufficient negative affect so that a man would choose the lesser negative affect of burning at the stake. One of the virtues of our view of motivation is precisely that it permits the development of new, high level motives as experience changes the person's expectations or adaptation levels. Whereas the rat or the child may be primarily governed by variations from sensory or simple perceptual expectations, the adult will be ruled by discrepancies in higher level cognitive structures (beliefs) which may lead to action in direct opposition to simple sensory pleasures and pains.

5. The Acquisition of Motives

Now that we have considered the possible antecedent conditions for affective arousal, what about the parallel problem of the antecedent conditions for motive formation? By our definition of a motive, the solution to this problem is straightforward. A motive is formed by pairing cues with affective arousal or with the conditions, just discussed, that produce affective arousal. These cues may be unconnected with affective arousal or they may be response-produced cues resulting from affective arousal. That is, the following sequence of events may occur:

Large discrepancy⟶Negative⟶Autonomic⟶Distinctive⋯⟶Avoidance
    from AL   affect   response   cues   motive

The first three links in this chain are unlearned (as indicated by solid arrows), but the last link is a learned association (as indicated by a broken arrow) based on previous pairings of such autonomic cues with negative affect. Thus the cues for setting off a motivational association may lie in the behavioral effects of the affect itself. Take Hebb's half-grown chimpanzees, for example. The sight of a detached plaster head produces negative affect that leads to diffuse autonomic responses which have been associated with negative affect in the past and which consequently evoke fear (the redintegrated portion of negative affect). Fear in turn elicits coordinated avoidance responses which continue until the situation which touched off the sequence changes — e.g., until the head is out of sight, or if that is impossible, until the animal "adapts" to it.

But the main point is that affect is the innate result of certain discrepancies between expectations and perceptions. A motive is the learned result of pairing cues with affect or the conditions which produce affect.

5.1. The Acquisition of Motives of Different Strength

Since motives are learned, the conditions for their acquisition that we must consider are largely those which are traditionally called the "laws of learning." That is, the strength of a motivational association should be a function of the same factors, such as contiguity, which have been assumed to govern the strength of any association. But what exactly is meant by the term *strength of a motive?* At least three meanings can be distinguished. Strength may refer to the likelihood or *probability* that a motive will be aroused by a particular cue; or it may refer to the *intensity* of the motive once aroused; or it may refer to the pervasiveness or *extensity* of the motive, by which is meant the variety of circumstances under which it will appear. Table 2 has been prepared to summarize very briefly the different variables which we believe will influence these three aspects of motive strength and also the response variables by which these aspects of motive strength may be most conveniently measured. As in Table 1 the sequence across the table from antecedent variable to hypothetical construct to response variable is not exact or exclusive.

TABLE 2. Motive Strength as a Hypothetical Construct Conceived as Varying in Three Dimensions, Each of Which Is Determined Primarily by Certain Antecedent Variables and Measured Primarily by Certain Response Variables

Antecedent variables influencing	Dimensions of MOTIVE STRENGTH	as reflected in the most relevant response variables
1. Frequency of association of cue with affective change	Motive Dependability	Probability that a choice response will occur per unit time
2. Contiguity between cue and affective change		
3. Rate of affective change		
4. Amplitude of affective change	Motive Intensity	Intensity of the choice response (Response amplitude, number of R's per unit time, latency or speed of R)
5. Variety of cues connected with affective change	Motive Extensity	Variety of cues eliciting R or resistance of choice response to extinction

Thus "rate of affective change" almost certainly influences motive intensity as well as motive dependability.

Most of the variables in the table are fairly self-explanatory and are drawn with one or two exceptions from prevailing theories of the factors which influence learning. Probably the simplest way to explain how they are all supposed to operate is to choose an hypothetical example which will illustrate each of them in turn. Let us take a frog as our experimental animal and place him in a water-filled container which is equipped with a platform onto which he can jump if he wants to. Let us further suppose that pouring hot water on a frog will evoke a negative affective change. Leaving aside for a moment the problem of how the frog acquired the instrumental response necessary for avoidance, we can further assume that the goal-oriented choice response we will be interested in observing here is whether or not he jumps out of the water onto the platform. As a conditioned stimulus we may use anything to which he is sensitive, say a light touch on the head. Now we begin the conditioning procedure and pair the touch on the head with a "shot" of hot water. The first two antecedent variables in the table then are the familiar conditioning variables, which state simply that the more frequently the cue (touch) is paired with the affective change (produced by hot water) and the more contiguous the association, the greater the probability that the motive will be aroused, as can be demonstrated by the greater frequency of the avoidance response of jumping onto the platform for a given number of taps on the head. The third variable, *rate of affective change*, is, on the other hand, a relatively unfamiliar one, although it has been used by Gwinn (1949) to explain certain effects of punishment in rats. What it states is that if the temperature in the water is changed slowly so that the affective change is spread out over time, it will produce a less dependable affective association. Or to turn this statement around, the more rapid the affective change, the more effective it is in producing a motivational association. There is little evidence that we know of which supports the importance of this variable directly, although it has seemed to us to follow logically from some of our other assumptions. That is, a slow change in water temperature would presumably raise the adaptation level so that the temperature increase from beginning to end would provide less discrepancy from *AL* at any given moment, and hence less negative affect, than would the same increase over a shorter period of time. By this interpretation, rate of change reduces to a special case of amplitude of the affective change, the next variable to be considered. That is, the more rapid the change, the greater the affect; and the greater the affect, the stronger the motive. Rate of change may also exert an influence indirectly through its effect on contiguity. Often the initial change in affect (as produced by an increase in temperature) provides cues that get associated by contiguity with further changes in affect (discomfort from the heat), but if the connection has been noncontiguous, as in slow changes in temperature, it will provide a more imperfect means of eliciting anticipatory negative affect.

The *amplitude of affective change* in our frog experiment could be controlled not only by rate of change but more simply by varying the temperature of the hot water. The assumption is that up to a certain point the hotter the water, the more vigorous would be the response to the conditioned stimulus (touch). The vigor of the response could be measured by the number of responses made per unit time (if he were blocked from escaping), by the latency of the avoidance response, by its speed, or by the strength of pull against a thread attached to some kind of recording instrument.

Our fifth variable, the variety of cues connected with affective change, also represents something of a new emphasis. The reason for its inclusion becomes quite apparent in the light of some recent studies by V. F. Sheffield (1949) and by McClelland and McGown (1953). These authors were interested in explaining why it was that extinction takes longer after partial reinforcement during learning. Both researches come to the conclusion that the reason for the delay in extinction is that some of the cues present during extinction were also present during acquisition in the partially reinforced group, namely, those cues resulting from non-reinforcement. This can be interpreted further as follows. It means in effect that the greater the similarity between the cues in the extinction and the acquisition conditions, the longer the extinction will take because the animal will find it harder to distinguish between extinction and acquisition conditions. In the ordinary learning experiment, where the animal has received 100 per cent reinforcement or reward, he is commonly extinguished under conditions of zero reinforcement. This constitutes such a major change in stimulating conditions that he can discriminate the difference without too much difficulty and learn that a different response is appropriate under such markedly changed conditions. But the perceptual difference between 50 per cent reinforcement in learning and zero reinforcement in extinction is not so large, and the animal should therefore take longer to make the discrimination and learn not to respond in extinction. To generalize this example a little, we can state that *the greater the variety of cues to which a response is attached, the harder it will be to extinguish it completely,* because the more difficult it will be to reinstate all the original cues and extinguish the response to them. Therefore, the more varied or irregular the conditions of acquisition, the more generalized the association will be and the harder it will be to extinguish it by any specific non-reinforcement. In our hypothetical frog experiment there are a number of ways in which the cue conditions during acquisition could be varied. We could use different conditioned stimuli (light and sound as well as touch); we could *vary* the time between the conditioned stimulus and unconditioned stimulus (hot water); we could sometimes fail to introduce the hot water after the conditioned stimulus (partial reinforcement), and so on. A rough measure of the generalized nature or extensity of the affective association is *the number of trials* it takes the animal to give up making the avoidance response completely when any particular conditioned stimulus is presented repeatedly without the unconditioned stimulus. That is, the more general the association, the harder it should be for the animal to discriminate the new situation (extinction) from the old (acquisition). So he should take more trials to extinguish. In passing it should be noted that, since "trials to extinction" measures primarily, though not exclusively, the *extensity* aspect of motive strength, it may not give exactly the same results as measures of other aspects of motive strength, such as strength of pull, latency, speed, and so forth.

Another, perhaps more direct, test of extensity of an association would be to explore the limits of the generalization gradients from some particular conditioned stimulus. Thus, one could certainly predict that the generalization gradients would be much wider for animals trained under a variety of conditions than those trained very regularly with a particular stimulus of a particular intensity, and so on.

These three aspects of motive strength are of great importance at the human level. We expect to find with further research that there are some subjects whose achievement motive is aroused by a great variety of cues. Other subjects may have achievement motives which are aroused only by very specific situations (e.g., playing cards, winning at football, making feminine conquests). People will also vary in the intensity as well as the extensity of their motives. Some will have an intense desire to succeed at cards, others only a mild desire in this area but an intense desire to get good grades in a course. It should be possib'e to plot for each individual a graph which would show the intensity of his achievement motive or achievement *interest*, in each of several different areas. Our present measure of *n* Achievement represents a kind of averaging out of these two variables so as to obtain one index for each person. Motive dependability is in a sense the primary aspect of strength, since a motive must be first aroused before its intensity and extensity can be measured. The best measure here seems to be the regularity with which a given cue, if repeated over and over again, will give rise to the achievement motive. Thus we might find some subjects who wanted to win at cards all the time; others only part of the time and some not at all. On the face of it, there seems no reason to assume that this variable is perfectly correlated with intensity. It is at least logically possible that a subject who is only occasionally aroused might, if aroused, show a very strong achievement motive. Conversely, a person who is always aroused by a particular situation might be aroused at a relatively low level of intensity. It is in these terms that some of the picture differences . . . can best be explained. To sum up, we expect to be able to measure independently at the human level the three aspects of motive strength theoretically distinguished here — e.g., dependability, intensity, and extensity. Motives also differ in kind as well as in strength, of course (see Section 6 . . .), so that the complete description of a motive will have four dimensions — quality (goal or scoring definition), extensity, intensity, and dependability.

6. TYPES OF AFFECTIVE CHANGE AND TYPES OF MOTIVES

As previously indicated, it is possible to distinguish two aspects of motives based on whether the choice response made involves approach or avoidance. These two types of behavior seem sufficiently different to warrant speaking of two different aspects of motivation. For one thing, Miller (1944), Clark (1952), and others have commonly assumed that approach and avoidance gradients differ markedly in slope. For another, we have found fairly convincing evidence in our own data for two aspects of the achievement motive, one of which seems characterized by defensiveness and a fear of failure, the other by increased instrumental striving and hope of success. Finally, if we consider the way in which motives are supposed to be learned, some should be acquired under circumstances in which pleasure results from successful achievement, whereas others should be acquired under circumstances in which negative affect results from failure.

In addition to these two basic aspects of motivation, there is at least the logical possibility of two other types which would result from other kinds of affective change. Thus the two types we have already mentioned might be thought of as resulting primarily from first, an increase in pleasure (an approach motive) and, second, from an increase in pain (an avoidance motive). But, at least theoretically, cues may also be associated with a decrease in pain or with a decrease in pleasure. One would expect the former to lead to approach behavior and the latter to avoidance behavior of a sort. At the present writing, however, there is very little evidence for the existence of either of these aspects of motivation, despite the current popularity of the notion that stimulus reduction is particularly important in motivation theory. Thus in a preliminary experiment Lee (1951) has shown that a cue paired with *onset* of shock will lead to intense avoidance behavior when presented in a new situation, whereas a cue associated with *offset* of shock will not lead to approach behavior, as it should, but to a somewhat less intense avoidance behavior. It may be that reduction in shock gains its apparent "rewarding" effect because it removes cues arousing an avoidance motive and not because it is in itself a positive goal. In common-sense language, a rat may learn to run off a charged grid not because the "safety box" attracts him (approach motive) but because the grid cues off an avoidance or fear motive which is no longer cued off in the safety box so that he stops running when he gets there. On the whole, however, further exploration of motives based on *decreases* in affective states is definitely called for.

7. BIOLOGICAL NEEDS AND MOTIVATION

There is undoubtedly [a connection between tissue needs and motivation] through the capacity of many biological needs to produce affective arousal. The species which have survived are probably those for which there is a fairly pronounced correlation between tissue needs and affective states.

Now according to our theory, how could we explain the fact that the longer an animal is deprived of food the more motivated he appears to become? Since most psychologists have been accustomed to thinking of biological need states as the primary sources of motivation, this is a very important question for us to discuss. In the first place, it is clear that in terms of our theory food deprivation does not produce a motive the first time it occurs. The lack of food in a baby rat or a baby human being will doubtless result in diffuse bodily changes of various sorts, but these do not constitute a motive until they are paired with a subsequent change in affect. More specifically, if the organism is to survive, the cues subsequent to food deprivation must always be associated with eating, and eating results in two types of affective change — pleasurable taste sensations, and relief from internal visceral tensions. Thus internal (or external) cues resulting from food deprivation are associated very early and very regularly in all individuals with positive affective change, and thus they become capable of arousing the hunger *motive* with great dependability. But this still does not explain why the motive gets stronger as food deprivation is increased from 10 hours to 24 or 36 hours. Several explanations for this are logically possible. For example, it could be argued that longer deprivation gives rise to distinctive cues which have been paired with greater subsequent changes in affect. Food tastes better after longer deprivation, and so on. As we have just pointed out, we consider amount of affective change one of the principles governing the strength of a motive. Another possible explanation is somewhat simpler than this. It is based on the assumption that as food deprivation increases, the cues to which it gives rise become more insistent (occur with greater frequency, and the like) and thus elicit with greater regularity the hunger motive. With lesser degrees of motivation, the hunger motive may be cued off occasionally but will yield its place from time to time to other associations. As the deprivation increases, the hunger association is cued off more and more regularly until it dominates the associative processes of the organism.

Such a way of thinking about the hunger motive throws light on several phenomena which have puzzled those who think of food deprivation itself as producing the hunger motive. It is one good explanation for the need to habituate animals in learning experiments, for example. According to this view, one of the consequences of habituation is to associate external cues (being picked up by the experimenter) with the affective changes resulting from eating, so that in time *the experimenter will become a dependable means of arousing the hunger motive.* The value of pre-feeding the animal can be explained in a similar manner. It has been found that if a hungry or thirsty rat is given a nibble of food or a few cc. of water before he starts working on an experimental day, he performs better and appears more motivated (Maltzman, 1952). This has seemed somewhat paradoxical to those who think of eating or drinking as producing a reduction in need or motivation. But in our view a bite to eat should also produce cues which arouse a motive based on past association of such cues with the pleasures of eating. In short, pre-feeding produces additional cues for arousing the food motive complex which in turn serves to make the animal perform slightly better.

What this adds up to is that we have redefined the whole problem of so-called primary and secondary drives. That is, from our point of view *all drives (motives) are learned.* Affective arousal, on which motives are based, is essentially primary (unlearned), although the adaptation levels which govern it can obviously be changed by experience. So the traditional distinction between *primary* (biological need) motives and *secondary* (learned or social) motives has disappeared. Instead, we may speak of primary and secondary motives if we like. Or we may even speak of primary and secondary motives, if it is understood that both involve learned associations but that the cues involved in the former are primarily biological rather than primarily social in nature. For example, after the food motive is learned, the cues which set it off occur as a result of body metabolism with great certainty and regularity; and in this sense they might be called primary cues as opposed to cues which occur less regularly as a result of social interaction and the like. But even this distinction seems somewhat confusing to us, since some social cues are also quite inescapable (e.g., those arising from the interaction of mother and child). And furthermore some biological cues (e.g., those resulting from certain autonomic responses) give rise to motives (fear) which are not ordinarily conceived of as "primary." In our opinion, it really seems somewhat preferable to discard the distinction between primary and secondary motives altogether.

REFERENCES

Angier, R. P. 1903. "The Aesthetics of Unequal Division," *Psychological Review* (Monogr. Suppl.), 4: 541–561.

Arnold, Magda B. 1945. "Physiological Differentiation of Emotional States," *Psychological Review*, 52: 35–48.

Beebe-Center, J. G. 1932. *The Psychology of Pleasantness and Unpleasantness*, New York: Van Nostrand.

Brown, J. S. and Farber, I. E. 1951. "Emotions Conceptualized as Intervening Variables — with Suggestions toward a Theory of Frustration," *Psychological Bulletin*, 48: 465–495.

———— and Jacobs, A. 1949. "The Role of Fear in the Motivation and Acquisition of Responses," *Journal of Experimental Psychology*, 39: 747–759.

Clark, R. A. 1952. "The Projective Measurement of Experimentally Induced Levels of Sexual Motivation," *Journal of Experimental Psychology*, 44: 391–399.

Corwin, G. H. 1921. "The Involuntary Response to Pleasantness," *American Journal of Psychology*, 32: 563–570.

Dallenbach, K. M. 1939. "Pain: History and Present Status," *American Journal of Psychology*, 52: 331–347.

Dearborn, G. V. N. 1899. "The Emotion of Joy," *Psychological Review* (Monogr. Suppl.), 2: No. 5.

Festinger, L. 1943. "Development of Differential Appetite in the Rat," *Journal of Experimental Psychology*, 32: 226–234.

Ford, C. S. and Beach, F. A. 1951. *Patterns of Social Behavior*, New York: Harper.

Garth, T. R., Moses, M. R., and Anthony, C. N. 1938. "The Color Preferences of East Indians," *American Journal of Psychology*, 51: 709–713.

Gwinn, G. T. 1949. "The Effects of Punishment on Acts Motivated by Fear," *Journal of Experimental Psychology*, 39: 260–269.

Harriman, A. E. 1952. "An Experimental Investigation into the Development of the Dietary Preference for Salt in Adrenalectomized Rats and into the Validity of the Processes Postulated to Account for the Manifestation of this Preference." Unpublished Ph.D. thesis. Cornell University.

Heathers, G. L. 1940. "The Avoidance of Repetition of a Maze Reaction in the Rat as a Function of the Time Interval between Trials," *Journal of Psychology*, 10: 359–380.

Hebb, D. O. 1949. *The Organization of Behavior*, New York: Wiley.

———— and Riesen, A. H. 1943. "The Genesis of Irrational Fears," *Bulletin of the Canadian Psychological Association*, 3: 49–50.

Helson, H. 1947. "Adaptation-level as Frame of Reference for Prediction of Psychophysical Data," *American Journal of Psychology*, 60: 1–29.

————. 1948. "Adaptation-level as a Basis of a Quantitative Theory of Frames of Reference," *Psychological Review*, 55: 297–313.

Hilgard, E. R. and Marquis, D. G. 1940. *Conditioning and Learning*, New York: Appleton-Century-Crofts.

Hull, C. L. 1931. "Goal Attraction and Directing Ideas Conceived as Habit Phenomena," *Psychological Review*, 38: 487–506.

Landis, C. and Hunt, W. A. 1939. *The Startle Pattern*, New York: Farrar & Rinehart.

Lee, W. A. 1951. "Approach and Avoidance to a Cue Paired with the Beginning and End of Pain." Unpublished MSS. Wesleyan University.

McClelland, D. C. 1951. *Personality*, New York: William Sloane Associates.

_____ and McGown, D. R. 1953. "The Effect of Variable Food Reinforcement on the Strength of a Secondary Reward," *Journal of Comparative and Physiological Psychology*, 46: 80–86.

McDougall, W. 1927. "Pleasure, Pain, and Conation," *British Journal of Psychology*, 17: 171–180.

Maltzman, I. 1952. "The Process of Need," *Psychological Review*, 59: 40–48.

Meehl, P. E. 1950. "On the Circularity of the Law of Effect," *Psychological Bulletin*, 47: 52–75.

Miller, N. E. 1944. "Experimental Studies of Conflict," in J. McV. Hunt (ed.) *Personality and the Behavior Disorders*, New York: Ronald Press.

_____ and Dollard, J. 1941. *Social Learning and Imitation*, New Haven: Yale University Press.

Mowrer, O. H. 1952. *Learning Theory and Personality Dynamics*, New York: Ronald Press.

Pfaffman, C. and Bare, J. K. 1950. "Gustatory Nerve Discharges in Normal and Adrenalectomized Rats," *Journal of Comparative and Physiological Psychology*, 43: 320–324.

Schlosberg, H. 1952. "The Description of Facial Expressions in Terms of Two Dimensions," *Journal of Experimental Psychology*, 44: 229–237.

Sheffield, V. F. 1949. "Extinction as a Function of Partial Reinforcement and Distribution of Practice," *Journal of Experimental Psychology*, 39: 511–526.

Sheldon, W. H., Stevens, S. S., and Tucker, W. B. 1940. *The Varieties of Human Physique*, New York: Harper.

Tinbergen, N. 1951. *The Study of Instinct*, London: Oxford, Clarendon Press.

Weiner, I. H. and Stellar, E. 1951. "Salt Preference of the Rat Determined by a Single Stimulus Method," *Journal of Comparative and Physiological Psychology*, 44: 394–401.

Whiting, J. W. M. 1950. "Effects of Conflict on Drive." Unpublished paper, available from the author.

Woodworth, R. S. 1938. *Experimental Psychology*, New York: Holt.

Yoshioka, J. G. 1930. "Size Preference of Albino Rats," *Journal of Genetic Psychology*, 37: 427–430.

Young, P. T. 1949. "Food-seeking Drive, Affective Process, and Learning," *Psychological Review*, 56: 98–121.

VII

Consistency Theory: Activation Version

The activation form of consistency theorizing emphasizes the match or mismatch between the level of bodily tension or activation that is customary for the person and that which actually exists at a given time. Consistency leads to quiescence, and inconsistency leads to attempts to modify the existing activation level in the direction of what is customary. If actual activation is *below* what is customary, then the attempt will be to *increase* the meaningfulness, intensity, or variety of stimulation. If actual activation is *above* what is customary, the opposite attempt will be made.

Statements about peripheral personality become possible through the additional assumption that the customary levels of activation for given persons differ on the basis of differences in previous experience. Thus, one can consider high activation types, who spend most of their time attempting to increase actual activation so as to match a high customary level, and low activation types, who do the opposite. This and other peripheral considerations are briefly considered in "Activation Theory and Personality," by Maddi and Propst.

SALVATORE R. MADDI
BARBARA SCOTT PROPST

Activation Theory and Personality

Activation theory is gradually replacing more restrictive drive theories and is becoming an integrative force felt in diverse fields of psychology. The personality field, however, has been little touched by activation theory, and it is to the correction of this lack that we wish to speak.

In order to establish rough ground rules for our enterprise, we shall briefly consider the nature of the personologist's interests. Basically, he wishes to identify and explain the way in which particular people lead their lives. This broadest of concerns carries at least three specific implications. The first is that the personologist's ideal is to identify and explain all the behavior that people can display. In trying to do this, he shows preference for data and concepts that are mental in the sense of referring to processes that are potentially — if not actually — represented in the person's consciousness. The second implication is that the personologist is concerned with long-term trends in functioning. And third, he is intrigued by differences between people in their typical functioning.

We will consider each of these three concerns of the personologist in our attempt to explicate the directions in which we think activation theory is most likely to influence the personality field. There are several versions of activation theory, and so we point out that the following relies heavily on the particular approach of Fiske and Maddi (1961).

IDENTIFICATION AND EXPLANATION
OF BEHAVIORAL POSSIBILITIES

In turning to the personologist's interest in the range of behavior that people can display, we will be asking about the contribution that activation theory can make to the descriptive classification of human behavior, and to the principles whereby the classified behavior can be understood. At present, activation theory seems best suited to description of a class of directional behavior involving increase or decrease in the experience of stimulation, and to the explanation of this class of behavior according to a homeostatic principle of motivation.

From the symposium: Some Determinants and Implications of Activation Level. American Psychol. Assoc., Philadelphia, Sept. 4, 1963.

In order to clarify what we mean, we will briefly consider the nature and determinants of activation. Fiske and Maddi identify the physiological side of activation with intensity of activity in a subcortical portion of the brain, and indicate that the mental side of activation is carried in such terms as "tension" and "emotionality." They assume that the physiological and mental sides of activation are both determined by the impact of stimulation, that is, by the meaningfulness, physical intensity, and variation of stimulation from exteroceptive, interoceptive, and cortical sources.

Having these definitions and relationships, it becomes possible to consider homeostasis. The two homeostatic principles current in activation theory involve considering levels of activation that are optimal for the performance of particular tasks, and levels of activation that are characteristic or typical of particular persons. It is the latter idea that is of most import for the personologist. According to Fiske and Maddi, the characteristic level of activation is a norm independent of the immediate demands upon the organism, and following the form during the day that Kleitman (1939) discussed as the waking portion of the sleep-wakefulness cycle. Having assumed the existence of a characteristic level of activation, the theorist can avail himself of the motivational implications of discrepancies between actual activation levels and levels typical for the various stages of the diurnal cycle. When activation is higher or lower than characteristic level, there will be a general tendency to modify the impact of stimulation so that activation level better approximates the norm. This, in abstract form, is the most ready contribution of activation theory to the classification and explanation of behavior. To reiterate, the descriptive category of functioning is impact-modifying behavior, that is, directional behavior aimed at increasing or decreasing the meaningfulness, physical intensity, and variation of stimulation. The motivational principle whereby this category of behavior is explained is the homeostatic tendency to reduce discrepancies between actual and characteristic levels of activation.

In order to make these abstract ideas more vivid, we will discuss them in terms that are closer to personal experience. This involves elaborating the mental side of activation — an elaboration that also makes activation theory more relevant to the personologist. Earlier, we said that the mental side of activation is emotionality. Now we add the assumption that mental representation of activation levels above and below the characteristic level takes the form of negative affect — mainly anxiety and pain in excessive motivation, and mainly boredom and apathy in insufficient activation. Further, the extremely impactful stimulus situation producing excessive activation would very likely be interpreted as overwhelming in intensity and threatening in meaning. The meagerly impactful stimulus situation producing insufficient activation would probably be interpreted as monotonous, weak in intensity, and trivial in meaning. We believe that further investigation of the mental side of activation is important because it may well be that the most effective impact-modifying behavior occurs when activation achieves clear representation in consciousness.

More detailed discussion of impact-modifying behavior is needed here. Since impact has been defined so broadly, we shall have to consider action, thought, and cognitive influences upon perception in order to be comprehensive. In the action sphere, impact can be decreased by such means as terminating one's physical proximity to an external stimulus situation, or relaxing the skeletal musculature, and increased by such means as precipitating closer contact between the sense receptors and external stimuli, or exercising the skeletal musculature. In the cognitive-perceptual sphere, impact can be decreased by becoming perceptually less sensitive, or by decreasing the imaginativeness and complexity of thought. This includes the processes that are usually called "defenses"; Freud once said that the defenses function to abolish stimuli. Impact can be increased in the cognitive-perceptual sphere by such means as becoming perceptually more sensitive, or by engaging more vigorously in imaginative and complex thought. To our way of thinking, attempts to increase and decrease impact serve the purely protective function of terminating the negative affect and disturbing interpretations of the environment associated with excessive and insufficient levels of activation.

But is all behavior a protective attempt to modify impact? For that matter, can the human being always be characterized as in a state of negative affect, alternating between anxiety and boredom? Introspection and reasoning both suggest that these questions must be answered negatively. The scheme for identifying and explaining behavior already discussed is fine as far as it goes, but it will not take the personologist far enough toward his ideal of considering all the behavioral possibilities open to people. Let us suggest a way in which the model might be changed to become more comprehensive.

Even though the assumption of something like a characteristic level is fairly common, we think it likely that negative affect, disturbing interpretations of the environment, and attendant impact-modifying behavior occur only when activation level is *very* high or *very* low. This suggests that it is more accurate to assume a characteristic *band* of activation rather than a level. Such a band has two important attributes, and so that we can convey them to you we ask that you visualize a continuum of activation running from absolute zero to an absolute maximum. The first important attribute of a person's band would be its range, or the amount of the continuum that it subsumes. The second attribute is the intensity of the band, or the height of the range along the continuum.

We expect that behavior aimed at modifying impact occurs only when activation level goes beyond the boundaries of the band. Behavior associated with activation levels anywhere within the band is not engaged in for the protective purpose of changing impact so as to terminate a negative affective state. But then what does determine behavioral choice within the band? Probably a number of things. The affective states associated with levels of activation within the band would most likely be positive, and can be summarized as feelings of well-being. One determining factor could be the tendency to continue a pleasurable affective state, but this factor would not provide a very precise explanation of behavioral choice within the band. The external situation would be contributing optimal impact and probably would be perceived as challenging and provocative, rather than threatening or trivial. This suggests that the demand characteristics of the surround would be another determinant of functioning. Still other determinants, though more internally grounded, would not be the kind associated with negative affective states and emergency measures. Rather, they would be factors such as interests, talents, and aesthetic taste. The behavior produced by these determinants might be descriptively classified as expressive, rather than impact-modifying.

Let us draw together the threads of our discussion by pointing out that we have roughly identified two broad, descriptive categories of behavior, and hinted at some subcategories of each. We have also suggested explanatory principles relevant to the behavioral categories. Although what we have done is by no means an exhaustive account of the behaviors that man can display, it is broad enough to show promise, and is rooted in activation theory.

Long-Term Trends in Functioning

Thus far, we have considered the immediate effects upon functioning of excessive, characteristic, and insufficient activation. Supplementing this approach with a consideration of functioning over much longer periods of time raises the topic of early and later developmental trends. In the following discussion, we will focus on the intriguing possibility that activation theory can provide a clear basis for explaining the later developmental trend called "psychological growth." At present, most personality theorists recognizing this phenomenon either simply assume it, or refer it to very vague explanatory principles such as self-actualization.

Although we shall not comment in detail, we assume that the early development of the range and intensity of the characteristic band involves a complex interaction between genetic predispositions and such aspects of the environment as its richness and its pattern of taboos and sanctions. Complex though the determination of the band may be, it probably becomes more and more stabilized during the early years, and is reasonably fixed in range and intensity at least by the time young adulthood is reached. A major reason for its fixity is that past experience accumulates through learning into principles of anticipatory functioning. The person comes to prefer and seek out the kinds of activities and situations that have yielded activation levels within the characteristic band, and to dislike and avoid activities and situations that have been associated with excessive or insufficient activation.

But the fixity of the characteristic band does not mean that the person's actual behavior would be unchanging. Quite the contrary, unchanging behavior would be inconsistent with the maintenance of characteristic activation. Consider some continuing behavioral process that starts within the characteristic range. As time goes on, the process may remain within the range, but it may also lead to activation levels that are too high or too low. If experience is repetitive, activation will become lower as time goes on (Fiske, 1961). One of the ideas that is most solidly supported by empirical findings is that there is gradual habituation — which would mean decreasing impact — to constant or repetitive stimulation (Walker, 1961). Behavioral processes continuing through time must be marked by variation in order to be very effective in maintaining characteristic activation. The probability of experiencing the necessary variation in one's future functioning can be maximized not only by developing a differentiated repertoire of actions, but also by developing a differentiated cognitive-perceptual system with which to construe and contemplate.

But here there is a danger for the person. Emphasis upon variation in functioning is accompanied by an increase in the risk of encountering too much impact. After all, the concrete outcomes of an orientation toward change cannot be very well anticipated. Thus, a behavioral process initially within the characteristic band may subsequently lead to excessive activation. This would happen most frequently when the change that occurred threatened to disconfirm the cognitive constructs or belief systems with which the person had theretofore functioned intimately. Crises in belief certainly would be states of excessive activation. If the necessity of maintaining activation within the characteristic band favors development of a repertoire of functioning that ensures adequate variation over time, so too does it favor parallel development of cognitive constructs that are generic enough to play an integrative role and be resistant to disconfirmation. Beyond the childhood years, our position provides a basis for explaining the long-term trend of behavior toward greater differentiation and integration, or psychological growth.

INDIVIDUAL DIFFERENCES

We have provided enough groundwork now to enable us to touch on the empirical implications of our position that are of deepest interest to the personologist. We refer, of course, to differences between people. In order to explicate differences, one must focus upon the dimensional or quantitative character of the concepts already mentioned. We will only scratch the surface by assuming that people can differ in the range and in the intensity of their characteristic bands of activation.

Consider the empirical implications of the first principle of difference. In observing people over a range of conditions that differed widely in impact potential, one would expect to find that the wider a person's characteristic band, the less he would show negative affect (both anxiety and boredom), interpretations of the environment as threatening or trivial, and impact-modifying behavior. Further, the wider his band, the more evidence there would be of feelings of well-being, and of behavior that is problem-centered and expressive of talents, tastes, and interests.

Now to the second principle of difference. In observing people over a range of conditions that differed widely in impact potential, one would expect to find that the higher a person's characteristic band, the less frequently he would express anxiety and interpretations of the environment as threatening, the more frequently he would express boredom and interpretations of the environment as trivial, and the more he would show impact-increasing rather than impact-decreasing behavior. The higher his band, the more would assessment of his repertoire of behaviors reveal an orientation toward variety expressed through cognitive and actional differentiation and a system of cognitive constructs that are generic and integrational.

In the empirical test of these predictions, the range and intensity of the characteristic band might be operationalized using measures of physiological functioning (cf. Duffy, 1962; Malmo, 1958). But even if the measurement of band range and intensity should prove impractical at present, the other ideas about the association of particular cognitive, perceptual, affective, and actional aspects of functioning could be assessed through multi-variate study. This would be a reasonable preliminary step in determining the accuracy and fruitfulness of our attempt to understand personality from the vantage point of activation theory.[1]

REFERENCES

Butler, J. M. and Rice, Laura N. "Adience, Self-Actualization, and Psychotherapy." In J. M. Wepman and R. W. Heine, eds. *Concepts of Personality.* Chicago: Aldine Press, 1963.

Duffy, Elizabeth. *Activation and Behavior.* New York: Wiley, 1962.

Fiske, D. W. "Effects of Monotonous and Restricted Stimulation." In D. W. Fiske and S. R. Maddi, *Functions of Varied Experience.* Homewood, Ill.: Dorsey Press, 1961.

Fiske, D. W. and Maddi, S. R. *Functions of Varied Experience.* Homewood, Ill.: Dorsey Press, 1961.

Kleitman, N. *Sleep and Wakefulness.* Chicago: University of Chicago Press, 1939.

Maddi, S. R. "Activation and the Need for Variety," *Counseling Center Discussion Papers.* University of Chicago, 9 (1963), no. 1.

Malmo, R. B. "Measurement of Drive: An Unsolved Problem in Psychology." In M. R. Jones, ed., *Nebraska Symposium on Motivation.* Lincoln, Neb.: University of Nebraska Press, 1958.

Welker, W. I. "An Analysis of Exploratory and Play Behavior in Animals." In D. W. Fiske and S. R. Maddi, *Functions of Varied Experience.* Homewood, Ill.: Dorsey Press, 1961.

[1] Since this paper was written there have been further theoretical and research developments, best summarized in: Maddi, S. R. *Personality theories: A comparative analysis,* Homewood, Ill.: Dorsey Press, 1968. Some of the relevant research papers are: Maddi, Propst, and Feldinger, "Three Expressions of the Need for Variety," *J. Pers.* 33 (1965): 82–98; Maddi and Andrews, *J. Pers.,* 34, (1966): 610–625; Pearson and Maddi, *J. Consult. Psychol.,* 30 (1966): 301–308.

VIII The Behavioristic Alternative

From the days of John Watson to modern times, behaviorism has represented a general approach in psychology. The position emphasizes overt, easily discernible acts (which are called responses) as the subject matter of the field, and attempts to explain these in terms of the stimuli that elicit them. Stimuli are considered to be predominantly of origin external to the organism, though some branches of behaviorism also consider internal stimuli, usually of a physiological sort. Behaviorism has had an extremely widespread influence on psychology, and for that reason if no other, it is sensible to include relevant readings here. But it is true that behaviorism has had relatively little to say about personality because the behavioristic emphasis on how stimuli come to elicit responses emphasizes the study of learning. In general, behaviorists have had much less to say about the content of man's inherent nature, and of the particular life-styles that persons bring with them to stimulus situations. This concern with "how" rather than "what" has meant that behaviorism has few implications for the core and periphery of personality, however sophisticated its views of the process of learning may be.

Two branches of behaviorism are important in American

psychology today. The more radical of the two is associated with
Skinner. This approach is presented and analyzed by Frankel, who
makes it clear that for Skinner behaviorism is actually an alternative
to personality theory. The emphasis is on how to explain acts of
the organism in terms of manipulable, external stimuli.
Psychological laws state the invariant effects that particular stimuli
have on particular responses. Individual differences in response to
situations merely define the psychologist's ignorance, and do not
demonstrate the importance of theorizing about personality. In
addition, one can be sure of understanding responses only when
they can be changed through some experimental manipulation.
Thus, the persistence of responses over situations — a phenomenon
so dear to the personologist's heart — is just another sign of
ignorance to the behaviorist.

A less radical form of behaviorism is represented by Berlyne.
Though he explicitly recognizes that behaviorism has little to say
about personality because of de-emphasis of individual differences
in favor of general stimulus-response laws, Berlyne does try to
accumulate what few theoretical and empirical implications there
are. You will notice that the theoretical statements about
individual differences are largely of a physiological rather than
mentalistic sort. Even the concept of habit, a major basis in
behaviorism for understanding why individual organisms may
respond differently to the ostensibly same stimulus situation, rests
on the process of conditioning, with no necessary implication of
mentation. Finally, you will find reviewed behavioristic research on
such topics as anxiety, conflict, repression, and aggression. Nothing
inherent in these topics marks them as behavioristic. Rather, they
represent the peculiar traditional link between psychoanalytic
thought and behaviorism. Dollard and Miller and other early
behaviorists saw the part of their task relevant to personality as
improving upon, or rendering more scientific, the intriguing work of
Freud. Parts of Freudian theory were discarded as untestable, and
other parts were redefined to emphasize measurement and learning.
This redefinition almost invariably involved removing the
mentalistic ring of Freudian concepts. The end result of this was to
permit the behaviorist to study such phenomena as conflict and
displacement in the laboratory, and to employ subhuman organisms
in such study. Many Freudians look on the behavioristic
reformulation of their ideas as a bastardization, specifically because

of the de-emphasis of mind and the alacrity with which simple laboratory and animal analogies are applied to the complexities of the human psyche.

MARVIN FRANKEL

Personality as a Response: Behaviorism

The object of this paper is to discuss some of the premises and concepts of Skinner's operant model as it relates to an understanding of the human personality. The guiding spirit of the operant model is its insistence on specifying the conditions under which behavior is observed. Using this approach, it becomes appropriate to ask ourselves under what conditions psychologists tend to speak of human beings in terms of their personality.

WHAT ARE WE IDENTIFYING WHEN WE IDENTIFY A PERSONALITY?

Psychologists often describe people in terms of their personalities. We are all familiar with personality characterizations such as paranoid, introverted, and extroverted. Such characterizations serve to prognosticate individual behavior. If we are told that Mr. X is a paranoid personality, we would expect him to be inappropriately sensitive to and suspicious of what other people think of him. Similarly, if we met someone described as an introverted personality, we would not expect him to be gregarious at a party. If characterizations of a personality are simply prognostications of behavior, can we say that a reference to a personality variable is no more than predicting the response to a stimulus? Can we say that suspiciousness as a response to an interpersonal situation is all that we mean by paranoia? The answer is negative, insofar as personality theorists would regard suspiciousness as a response that reflects, rather than is equivalent to paranoia. Further, when we are told that someone has a paranoid personality, we may presume that the suspicious response under observation is groundless and inappropriate to the interpersonal situation. The paranoid personality may think everyone is out to hurt him, but presum-

This article was prepared for this volume.

ably this is false. The suspiciousness of the paranoid is instead presumed to be a function of his own personality.

This example emphasizes a second characteristic of the conditions under which the psychologist employs personality constructs. The psychologist speaks of a personality type (paranoia) rather than just a response (suspiciousness) when he judges the response to be inappropriate to the situation. This is not merely the practice of the psychologist when making reference to psychopathological personalities. Consider the introverted personality. We observe that Mr. A is very quiet at a party. The host tells us that Mr. A has a terrible sore throat. A second person indicates some surprise, and adds that he thought Mr. A was simply a rather introverted personality. The characterization of Mr. A as having an introverted personality rests upon two explicit judgments. First is the judgment that an appropriate index of noise-making at parties is known by the psychologist, which permits him to ascertain whether the behavior of Mr. A is quieter than appropriate in a party context. Second, the person who employs the personality construct of "introversion" as an explanation of the behavior has implicitly given up the task of locating the stimulus controlling the behavior, inasmuch as "introversion" is not a stimulus but rather a characterization of people with response tendencies rendering them quiet. In contrast, the explanation that Mr. A is suffering from a throat ailment does not invoke a personality construct but instead designates a stimulus that is separate from, not an elaboration of, the response.

It appears to the Skinnerian that it is the very inability of the psychologist to identify the stimulus controlling the response under observation which leads him to invoke personality characteristics as a basis for explaining the behavior. Two examples of this propensity come easily to mind. Freud conceived of the death instinct as a result of his observation of World War I. It was apparently inconceivable to him that the "horrors of war" were appropriate responses to the dispute (stimuli) between nations. Consequently, Freud characterized the human personality as dominated by aggressive, destructive impulses in the service of the death instinct. Similarly, Rogers observed what he regarded as the tortuous efforts of the mentally ill to develop their personalities in the face of overwhelming obstacles. Failing to locate a stimulus which controlled such an effort, Rogers postulated an organismic tendency to actualize one's potential as characterizing human personality. These two examples strongly indicate that the more ignorant we are of the stimulus controlling the response, the more inclined we are to invent personality constructs. If, as we said above, Skinner insists on defining the task of psychology as that of specifying the stimulus conditions under which behavior is observed, then he evidently is not concerned with developing a theory of personality. Such theorizing would seem too much like a substitute for an identification of the stimulus conditions. But Skinner's concern with the experimental analysis of behavior does lead to an interest in responses that are at least functions of observable stimuli, if not "personality."

The Nature of Human Nature

Personality theorists frequently speculate on the nature of human nature. For Freud, instinctual conflict and ego defenses define the essence of the human personality. Hall and Lindzey (1970) go so far as to characterize the id as "the original system of personality." Jung viewed human nature as innately (archetypically) multifaceted, partaking of the social, religious, masculine, feminine, and animalistic. Rogers did not regard conflict as inherent in the human personality, but postulated instead that a core characteristic of man was his constant effort to actualize his potential.

Skinner (1968) quotes Breland (1961) to the effect that the operant psychologist does not presume that "the animal comes to the laboratory as a virtual tabula rasa, that species differences are insignificant, and that all responses are equally conditionable to all stimuli." However, Skinner's general focus is on the ways in which contingencies of reinforcement are associated with changes in response strength. On the subject of inherited characteristics, Skinner (1957) states that knowledge of genetic endowments may be useful insofar as they establish the limits within which behavior can be modified through reinforcement contingencies. But he does not concern himself further with the content of genetic endowments and species differences.

A Scientific Analysis of Behavior

If we came across a friend in the street and asked his destination, he might reply that he was hungry and consequently on his way to the grocery to purchase some food. For most of us such an explanation would be quite sufficient, because we recognize from experience that people often go to grocery stores when they are hungry. In other words, our friend's reason (hunger) is *coherently* related to his activity (going to the grocery). In general, the criterion of coherence determines our acceptance of or skepticism toward a given explanation. The standard against which an explanation is judged to be coherent inevitably rests with our own experience. Consequently, if our friend said that he was hungry and therefore going to the post office to purchase envelopes, we would respond with perplexity. Such an explanation would hardly be coherent according to our own experience. The criterion of coherence has largely determined the development of explanatory constructs in psychoanalytic theory. In fact, one might argue that the compelling nature of psychoanalytic theory emanated from Freud's sustained efforts to render the seemingly incoherent (slips of the tongue, memory lapses, dreams, and neuroses) understandable and coherent (Peters, 1958). Consider Freud's (1901) explanation of superstitious behavior.

Imagine that a black cat suddenly crosses the path of Mr. A. Being quite suspicious, Mr. A develops a sense of foreboding. This superstition presumably rests on the premise that black cats are dependably related to subsequent misfortune. For the person who does not share such a premise, Mr. A's fear doesn't make sense. For many of us the relationship between black cats and subsequent misfortunes is no more coherent than the rationale behind the purchase of envelopes when one is hungry. In his analysis, Freud (1960) attempts to show the "unconscious" reference for the fear — "Nervous persons afflicted with compulsive thinking and compulsive states . . . show very plainly that superstition originates from repressed, hostile, and cruel impulses. The greater part of superstition signifies fear of impending evil, and he who has frequently wished evil on others, but because of a good bringing up has repressed the same into the unconscious, will be particularly apt to expect punishment for such unconscious evil in the form of misfortune threatening him from without." The superstitious person "really" fears his own impulses which, if exercised without restraint, would cause the misfortune superstitiously attributed to the black cat.

Thus, in Freudian terms, an unrealistic, superstitious fear is rendered coherent when we learn its realistic source. A proper understanding of the unconscious inevitably leads to a realization of a latent unconscious rationality that transforms the bizarre into the commonplace. In addition to providing a coherent account of the seemingly incoherent, Freud specifies certain stimulus and response relationships that have eventuated in the behavior under consideration. In the area of superstitious behavior, Freud postulates the existence of certain instinctual stimuli (e.g., cruel and hostile impulses); external stimuli (e.g., "a good bringing up") as well as certain responses (e.g., repression and projection). These stimuli and responses are in the main covert and unobservable. The environmental stimulus suggested by the phrase "a good bringing up" implies in an approximate way child-rearing practices that censor the expression of covert aggressive impulses.

Skinner, however, believes that *prediction* and *control* (rather than coherence) are the only appropriate criteria for a scientific explanation of behavior. Prediction and control are achieved when the psychologist is able to demonstrate a *functional relationship* between *observable, manipulatable* stimuli and *observable* responses.

Skinnerians will not accept an explanation of a response that refers to *covert* unobservable stimuli such as an "unconscious" motive or process. Similarly, the empirical demonstration of an association between two events such as certain child-rearing practices and adult behavior represents at best a correlation rather than a functional analysis of behavior, because there has been no opportunity to manipulate child-rearing. In effect, then, a scientific explanation of behavior in the context of the operant model "is one which specifies the actual conditions which reliably produce the behavior to be explained." (Reynolds, 1968).

An Analysis of Stimuli and Responses

For an event to be classified as a stimulus it must be observable and manipulatable. For an event to be classified as a response it must be observable and subject to quantification. The operant psychologist distinguishes between two classes of response. When a response is regularly elicited by a stimulus as the result of the inherited characteristics of the organism, it is called an *unconditioned respondent*. If we were to change the diaper of an infant and accidentally stick him with a pin, he would probably start crying. Since the response of crying when pin-pricked is not the result of previous experience but the consequence of the inherited structure and capacities of the infant, it is an unconditioned respondent. When a previously neutral stimulus can elicit a response, it is called a *conditioned respondent*. The process whereby neutral stimuli function as conditioned eliciting stimuli is called *respondent conditioning*. Thus the sight of the pin may now cause the infant to cry.

Emotional behaviors often have respondent components. A slap across the face may elicit crying from a child. The sudden intrusion of an intense stimulus such as a loud sound may elicit a startle respondent. Respondent components of our emotions help to understand why people report a sense of being helpless about the way they feel. Sometimes people don't want to feel the way they do, but something (an eliciting stimulus) happened to them (elicited the emotion).

An early study by Watson and Raynor (1920) employed the following procedure for developing fear in an infant. The subject, an eleven-month-old infant, was introduced to furry animals such as a rat and a rabbit. Insofar as the infant did not fear the animals, they may be regarded as *neutral stimuli*. The experimenter struck a steel bar so as to produce a loud sound just as the infant was about to touch the rat. The infant drew back in fear. This event was repeated a few more times until the infant developed a fear of furry animals, so that the presentation of the once neutral stimulus led to crying and withdrawal. In this study, a neutral stimulus (furry animals) when paired with an aversive eliciting stimulus (loud sound) became an aversive conditioned eliciting stimulus resulting in the infant's crying (a respondent). In later years the subject may get very frightened whenever he is confronted by a furry object. A pyschoanalyst might speculate that the fear of furry items results from repressed cruel fantasies. But Watson and Raynor insist that the *necessary* and *sufficient* condition for establishing the fear was simple contiguity of an unconditioned eliciting stimulus and a neutral stimulus.

Although many of our actions are reflexive in nature, we must perform certain behaviors that we generally regard as voluntary. These behaviors are hardly voluntary in the sense of being independent of stimulus control. We may work five days because we will be paid a certain sum of money. If a sudden inflation made our salary insufficient to purchase a loaf of bread, many of us would stop working or look for another job. Most of our behavior is related to subsequent consequences. In fact, behavior is often "instrumental" in leading to the consequences. Such behavior comprises the second major class of responses, called *operant* responses. Opening a refrigerator is an operant response insofar as it is a function of subsequent stimuli (food). If the refrigerator were always empty we would not open refrigerator doors. The presence of the food increases the strength of the operant response. When a stimulus following an operant response increases the strength of the operant, it is called a *reinforcing stimulus*. The difference between a reinforcing stimulus and an *eliciting stimulus* is that the former always follows an operant response whereas the latter always precedes a respondent.

A reinforcer is said to be positive when the effect of the operant response is experimentally observed to "produce" the reinforcing stimulus. Food is therefore a *positive reinforcer* for opening refrigerator doors. In contrast, whenever the effect of an operant response is experimentally observed to "eliminate" a stimulus, that stimulus is called a *negative reinforcer*. Let us suppose that the infant is now six months old, and he has not forgotten that we stuck him with pins. If we discover that whenever we enter the room the infant turns to the wall, we might hypothesize that we were an aversive stimulus that negatively reinforced facing the wall. By regularly facing the wall in our presence, the child eliminates us from his visual field.

The operant psychologist also distinguishes between *unconditioned* and *conditioned* reinforcers. When it is assumed that the past training of the organism has not established the effectiveness of a reinforcer to increase the rate of an operant response, the stimulus is called an unconditioned reinforcing stimulus. In other words, the effectiveness of the reinforcement is not *presumed* to result from past conditioning, it is called an unconditioned reinforcer. Generally speaking, food and water are regarded as unconditioned reinforcers. We also seek objects that are not *immediately* relevant to food and drink. As we said before, the laborer works (operant response) for money. Students work in school to get good grades. We were not born with a need for money and grades. If we presented an infant with money enough to buy ten rattles he would evince little interest, for money is ineffective as a reinforcer when first presented. As the infant develops into a child, he will learn that when money is given to a grocer, food, candy, milk, and other reinforcers will materialize. A neutral stimulus (money) may subsequently function as a conditioned positive reinforcer when it has been present during the occurence of a positive reinforcer, which can be itself either an unconditioned or conditioned reinforcing stimulus. Similarly, neutral stimulus may subsequently function as a conditioned negative reinforcer when it is present during the occurrence of a negative reinforcer, where the latter may be either an unconditioned or conditioned reinforcing stimulus.

An excellent example of a conditioned reinforcement is the growing child's response to his mother. On the very first occasion, the infant does not respond any differently to the "mother" than to anyone else who may enter his room. In the course of experience, the infant may smile whenever his mother comes into the room. It may be argued that the mother has become a conditioned reinforcer as a result of the repeated pairing of her figure with other unconditioned positive reinforcers such as water, milk, and food.

Stimuli not only elicit and reinforce responses, but also supply information.

A stimulus that is informative is called a *discriminative stimulus*. In many ways our lives are controlled by discriminative stimuli. In our society some people perform duties that require uniforms, such as policemen. The uniform becomes a discriminative stimulus that occasions our asking aid. Medical students are known to walk with stethoscopes hanging from their white coats. Stethoscopes serve as discriminative stimuli for others, indicating that a doctor is walking by.

A stimulus may function as discriminative stimulus at one point in time and as conditioned reinforcer at another. In the presence of our mother (a discriminative stimulus) we may ask (an operant response) for money (a conditioned reinforcer). With the money in our hand (a discriminative stimulus) we may go (an operant response) to the grocer (a conditioned reinforcer) and ask (an operant response) the grocer (a discriminative stimulus) for candy (an unconditioned positive reinforcer). The discriminative stimulus must precede and accompany the operant response, whereas the conditioned reinforcer always follows the operant response.

A stimulus may serve as a discriminative stimulus for one person and a conditioned reinforcer for another. If Mr. Skinner wins the Nobel Prize he would have gained a conditioned reinforcer, which may serve as a discriminative stimulus for others, in that Mr. Skinner can provide conditioned reinforcers (important grants and positions) as a result of the influence signaled (discriminative stimulus) by the award-winning accomplishment.

Although stimuli and responses are discrete events, they are only relatively unique, having similarities. For example, when we were young, our parents and teachers were similar in that both instructed us. If our parents punished us when we failed to learn, it would not be surprising for us to be frightened of our teachers if we failed to learn our lessons. When "the reinforcement of a response in the presence of one stimulus increases the probability of responding not only in the presence of that stimulus but also in the presence of other stimuli" (Reynolds, 1967) we have an example of *stimulus generalization*. Stimulus generalization makes possible rapid learning that may be appropriate or inappropriate. If we extend our hands into one fireplace, stimulus generalization may inhibit the same response when we are confronted with another fireplace. On the other hand, fear of our teacher (from the example above) may inhibit responses that, if expressed, would eventuate in positive reinforcement. Responses also bear certain similarities to each other. If aggressiveness is positively reinforced by our parents, we might tend to do everything aggressively.

Response generalization may be of critical relevance for psychologists concerned with "personality." When we speak of a personality, we are detecting something about the nature of the response that cuts across various situations or stimuli. It would seem that compulsivity and obsessiveness are essentially response generalizations reified by the label "personality style." This reification tends to explain the response generalization as though it were caused by the personality style (he has a compulsive personality) when, as we have already discussed in the opening section, the "personality style" is the response that actually requires explaining. To explain a response (or personality) adequately is to show the contingencies of reinforcement that control that response. If someone were described as a masochistic personality, we would expect that person to behave in such a way that he does injury to himself. An operant may be a function of a positive or negative reinforcer. The operant, say of "masochistically" banging one's head against the wall may call attention to one's self (a positive conditioned reinforcer), or it may serve to keep people away (a negative conditioned reinforcer). We must show that the response (personality) at any given moment is in the service of reinforcing stimuli. This is accomplished by carefully analyzing the relation between an act and subsequent consequences (reinforcers).

THE OPERANT RESPONSE AS A FUNCTION OF CONTINGENCIES OF REINFORCEMENT

In a previous section we provided thumbnail descriptions of the way certain personality theorists characterized the nature of man. Such characterizations presume to tell us something about the nature of man's goals or destiny. There are nearly as many versions of that destiny as there are theorists, and each version is argued as if it were absolute truth. When one reads such theorizing one gets the sense of being sold something, some depiction of man in the quest of his destiny. The implication of all these grand views of man's destiny is that they express little more than the highly personal projections of the personality theorists. None of the presumed destinies are as concrete and mundane as having to defecate or puke, but rather imply something spectacular such as the sermon on the mount or a trip to the moon. The effort of personologists to characterize man does not seem to come from their empirical, scientific, or disciplinary knowledge, so much as from their idiosyncratic personal background. Yet it is never the facts of their personal background that are presented to defend the thesis, but instead technical sounding though ambiguous terms such as "propriate striving," "functional autonomy," "Imago," and "will to power."

Instead of pondering whether man is sacred or profane, reactive or proactive, Skinner believes that man is what man does. If you wish to say something useful about a man, then take a look and see what he is doing. From this it follows that man is composed more of what he does most than of what he does least. We can say that man is a waking animal because he is asleep for eight hours and awake for sixteen. For Skinner, the goals of man are the goals he is observed to pursue. Moreover, if we look closely, we will see that behavior doesn't lead to "goals" independent from the behavior. Instead, behavior leads to other behaviors. The behavior of walking to the kitchen leads to the behavior of drinking a glass of water. Man is engaged in a constant stream of behaviors. The more probable a behavior the more we can say that it constitutes the "destiny" of man. We have seen that most of our behavior can be conceptualized as a function of reinforcing consequences.

The above analysis has indicated that the consequence of one behavior is to make other behaviors possible. Thus, we can say that "the opportunity to engage in behavior which is currently highly probable is reinforcing." (Reynolds, 1969). For example, a child will do his chores if he is then permitted to go out to play. Many psychologists are interested in discovering why it is that one behavior is more probable at a given time and thus more reinforcing, but this question is irrelevant for Skinner. Undoubtedly, a biochemist should seek the biochemical mechanism that may account for the reinforcing effects of certain behaviors. However, Skinner argues that psychology has its own level of analysis, which is to show the various ways behavior is a function of reinforcement. The demonstration of lawful relationships between responses and contingencies of reinforcement constitute the scientific credibility of an experimental analysis of behavior.

To study the functional relationship between responses and stimuli, it is first necessary to identify a reinforcer for the organism at a particular time. Living organisms as complex as a pigeon or a man are engaged in so many different movements that it would be quite difficult to identify and control the reinforcing stimulus moment by moment in order to see what lawful relationships could be obtained. The answer to the dilemma is rather simple: The psychologist must employ a procedure that will assure that a stimulus will be reinforcing. It is for this reason that the pigeon (a frequent subject in operant conditioning experiments) is maintained at "eighty per cent of its free-feeding weight" (Reynolds, 1968). When the pigeon pecks at the proper stimulus, he generally receives only one pellet of food. This assures the "motive" of the pigeon to maintain the behavior of pecking. Motive simply refers to the antecedent procedure (maintenance of certain body weight, deprivation of food, water, etc.) that establishes the reinforcing properties of a stimulus.

The student may wonder why so much attention is paid to eating and food; certainly men occupy themselves with books, music, etc. Operant psychologists are well aware that literature and music constitute reinforcing stimuli. The point of a functional analysis is to show relations between responses and reinforcing stimuli. The relations demonstrated for one kind of reinforcer should hold true for another. The law of gravity is not differentially related to baseballs and ping-pong balls. If a child receives from his mother the money he asks to purchase a book, on subsequent occasions we may expect that he will make similar requests. If the request of the same child for a toy is also granted, we would expect on subsequent occasions that the child will make similar requests for toys. Having our requests fulfilled (reinforcement) increases the rate of the previous response regardless of what object (books or toys) constitutes the reference.

When behavior is reinforced every time it is emitted, we call this a *contin-*

uous schedule of reinforcement. Reinforcers are more often intermittent. By *intermittent reinforcement* we refer to the presentation of reinforcing stimuli when only some responses emitted are reinforced. As children we may have asked our parents if we could go outside to play every day only to find that on certain days we are given permission while on others such permission is not granted. Reinforcement may also be given only if we have already performed a number of responses. Such a schedule of reinforcement is called a *ratio schedule* because the experimenter establishes a rule whereby a ratio exists between the number of responses which must be emitted before reinforcement is provided. A mother may use ratio schedules of reinforcement when she tells her child that he will have to do all six of his chores every day before he is allowed to play with his friends. The ratio of reinforcement to chores is thus 6:1. A schedule of reinforcement can also relate to a time interval. The experimenter may prescribe that a certain duration of time must psss before reinforcement is provided. In public schools, recess comes generally only after a certain time period. Such reinforcement schedules are called *interval schedules.*[1]

Each reinforcement schedule has a differential effect on the acquisition, maintenance, and weakening of an operant response. Consider the following example. A child asks his father for money to buy bubble gum. Whenever he makes this request, he is given the money for the gum. Suppose that in the course of two months the child has received money two hundred times. When reinforcement follows an operant every time, the schedule is one of continuous reinforcement. Imagine now that another child makes the same requests for the same time period and the same number of times, but his father does not always grant the request. This is an *intermittent schedule of reinforcement.* Suppose the dentist subsequently tells both parents that their children must stop chewing bubble gum. The parents agree, and from that day on they refuse to grant the requests of their children. In operant terms, a previously rewarded operant response (asking for bubble gum) will undergo *extinction* as a result of non-reinforcement. Extinction refers to the procedure of continuous non-reinforcement which results in a lowering of response rate. Both children on discovering that their requests were going to be refused (non-reinforced) would suddenly begin asking more frequently. At first, non-reinforced trials result in a rise in the frequency of the operant. This observation has been confirmed in hundreds of experiments. It is also not uncommon in our experience to find ourselves trying harder after frustration. However, as the non-reinforcement of the operant response continues over trials, the weakening of the response manifests itself in lower and

[1] The present discussion is intended to be a very *bare* outline of *some* of the reinforcement contingencies utilized within the framework of the operant paradigm. The interested reader should consult the primary source material (e.g., Ferster and Skinner, 1957).

lower rates of responding, until finally it returns to its initial level (prior to first reinforcement), or disappears altogether. In our example, both children will gradually stop asking their parents for bubble gum. However, the child who had been reinforced on a continuous schedule will extinguish faster than the child who had been reinforced on an intermittent schedule. If we observe an individual seemingly struggling in vain, and we wonder how someone can work so hard when achieving so little reinforcement, we may speculate that a history of intermittent reinforcement for that individual affects the present drawn-out extinction process. Ironically, the very perserverance of an individual who has refused to give up and has inspired us with a sustained effort despite repeated failures may be at that moment undergoing extinction. When the response is no longer manifest, we may wonder why the person gave up "all of a sudden." If we had counted the rate of response we would have noted that the giving up was hardly sudden. Following a series of reinforced trials, a non-reinforced response does not become extinguished in a single (all of a sudden) trial.

The relevance of extinction to neurosis is rather obvious. The "neurotic" is typically someone who fails to relinquish old behaviors that in the judgment of the therapist, have outlived their usefulness. Such behaviors are sustained; novel behaviors are not attempted. An examination of the reinforcement history of such people would undoubtedly disclose that their parents provided a reinforcing stimulus infrequently enough to discourage extinction. Rogers has often pointed to the stubborn efforts of the neurotic in light of massive discouragement. He may have failed to note that it was precisely because of such general discouragement that seemingly few encouragements could sustain the "neurosis." Such a hypothesis is at least more testable than the postulation of "actualizing tendencies."

An Operant Analysis of Superstitious Behavior

It is instructive to draw comparisons between the approaches of two scientific models. Such comparison is especially educative when both scientific models have addressed themselves to the same problem. As it happens, the phenomenon of superstitious behavior has been the subject of analysis for Skinner as well as Freud. We have already presented Freud's explanation, and now it is Skinner's turn. Let us consider the case of Mr. B, who "knocks on wood" whenever he relates a fortunate incident. The operant of knocking on wood is under the control of a reinforcer, and yet *most of us* would regard such behavior as irrelevant to reinforcement. Most of us would not understand how knocking on wood can be relevant to mitigating subsequent misfortune or to sustaining the present good fortune. Yet superstitious behavior may continue over a period of many years without extinction. The first task for Skinner is to identify the reinforcing stimulus that shaped and sustains the behavior.

Let us say that a pigeon, maintained at 75 per cent of its body weight, is placed in an experimental chamber constructed so that a food hopper can be presented for five seconds at a time. If the "clock is arranged to present the food hopper at regular intervals *with no reference whatsoever to the bird's behavior*, operant conditioning usually takes place" (Skinner, 1961). Skinner (1961) describes the effects of such operant conditioning, "One bird was conditioned to turn counterclockwise about the cage, making two or three turns between reinforcements. Another repeatedly thrust its head into one of the upper corners of the cage. A third developed a 'tossing response,' as if placing its head beneath an invisible bar and lifting it repeatedly." Skinner observed that the responses were generally oriented to some aspect of the cage. The "effect of the reinforcement was to condition the bird to respond to some aspect of the environment rather than to merely execute a series of movements" (Skinner, 1961). Skinner interprets the experiments as demonstrating the development of superstitious behavior. The pigeon behaves to assure the reinforcement, although the reinforcement is not contingent upon a particular response. Will the "superstitious" behavior continue if food is no longer presented? When the time interval between reinforcements had been once every fifteen seconds, Skinner (1961) found that the pigeon continued to respond 10,000 times despite the absence of food. Skinner points to analogies in the human condition. The "accidental connections between a ritual and favorable consequences suffice to set up and maintain the behavior in spite of many unreinforced instances" (Skinner, 1961). In thus accounting for superstitious behavior, Skinner does not have recourse to covert stimuli and responses such as impulses, repression, and projection, but instead demonstrates through experimentation the conditions under which an organism will behave as if his actions were effective in determining the reinforcing consequences.

Skinner's model provides contrast to Freud's, in which coherency greatly determines the acceptability of one explanation rather than another. Freud (1959, p. 99) states clearly that only by assuming unconscious processes can the fragments of consciousness be rendered intelligible. Skinner insists that only when the experimenter succeeds in reliably developing the behavior through stimulus control is he entitled to declare that he has an explanation. Perhaps the best way to characterize the differences between the two positions would be to say that for Freud the proof of the pudding is in the recipe, whereas for Skinner the proof of the pudding is in the making of the pudding. Clearly, a recipe is irrelevant without a pudding, but it is equally clear that a pudding must have a recipe.

A Skinnerean Critique of Skinner's Operant Model

In the immediately preceding section I presented Skinner's experimental analysis of "superstitious" behavior. Originally I had written a draft in which

I used rather different examples of superstitious behavior than the one of Mr. B knocking on wood. I would like to present those illustrations now.

Mr. Smith goes to church every day. Once in church he removes his hat, slips to his knees and makes the sign of a cross upon his chest, whereupon he rises and walks towards a statue of a bearded man hanging from a cross. The man kneels again and moves lips. No words can be heard. Moments later the man walks behind a black curtain. Minutes later he emerges and walks out into the street to join the crowd. Meanwhile, in another country, at another time, we observe a number of men running around in a circle and clapping their hands while someone else sits and beats a drum. Every now and then the men fall to the ground in exhaustion while others quickly take their place. The constant running around, the patter of the drums, the exhaustion and the replacements all continue, until suddenly thunder is heard and rain starts to fall. The men look joyous and the drumbeat gets still more feverish. The men run in unison to a young anthropologist who sits there shaking his head and smiling. The natives shout: "We told you, we told you."

I decided against these illustrations for two reasons. First, I suspected that there are many potential readers who are in every way like Mr. Smith. The Mr. Smiths of the world might feel somewhat injured if they thought I regarded their behavior as well as the son of God a mere superstition and in the same class of behaviors as a rain dance taking place south of Pongo Pongo. They would say, "Rain dances are superstitious but prayers and Popes are something else again!" As I thought about it, I realized that superstitious behavior always seems to be something that someone else practices. How did Skinner know that bird was superstitious? Presumably because Skinner was outside the pigeon's universe, and thus was able to know that the ritualistic behavior of the pigeon was not instrumental in getting the pellet of food. But is it really possible to call one behavior superstitious and another behavior unsuperstitious within the framework of the operant model?

Let me make the point clearer through the use of a pigeon parable. Imagine that one of the pigeons, Max, begins to wonder whether it is necessary for him to walk in circles in order for the food to arrive. Max decides to perform an experiment and walks to another section of the cage, only to discover that the food is delivered. Shall he conclude that the reinforcement is unrelated to his behavior? He also might conclude that there are two behaviors related to the delivery of food. Max may try another experimental excursion to another part of the cage and once again discover that a pellet of food is delivered. He then might conclude either that his behavior is unrelated to the delivery of food or that three behaviors are related to the food. Suppose Max now decides to see whether doing nothing leads to the same result. He discovers that again food is delivered and again he is faced with the dilemma of deciding whether the *behavior of doing nothing* is related to food delivery or whether food delivery is unrelated to behavior. Suppose Max has access to a philosopher-pigeon, whom he asks for advice. He may say to the philosopher, "Food is a life and death matter and it comes at intervals so long as I am doing something. When I purposely *do nothing* it also comes. Must I worry about it or think about it at all?" The philosopher may reply, "The ways of the world are strange. Life is given and life is taken (reinforcement) both in the experimental chamber and back in the cage (present reinforcement and historical reinforcement contingencies), and it is difficult for us to comprehend the ways of our Lord, B. F. Skinner. Sometimes he is benevolent in the experimental chamber and sometimes he is not. It is a question of deciding ultimates. If what we do is irrelevant to life and death, then it becomes a problem to decide what is relevant to behavior and if anything can be 'relevant' in the context of a universe that remains ultimately beyond reach. The teachings of Skinner are clear about this — Man must assume control and behave as if his behavior is relevant to important goals. One of our prophets has developed a system whereby it would have been possible to kill many German men and women — because German men and women killed many Polish men and women. Thus the prophet, an American, developed a missile system carrying one of our own species to eventual destruction. The judgment of Skinner (1961, p. 426.02), as related in the book, is simply: 'The ethical question of our right to convert a lower creature into an unwitting hero is a peacetime luxury.' It is clear that Skinner is concerned with our species and more concerned with us than he appears to be with German men and women. So, in practical matters, one must assume there is a meaning, a reinforcement, to which our operants are directed."

Max may reply: "Philosopher, I take it you are not an atheist, but that you do believe there is a God, called Skinner, though his ways are inscrutable." The philosopher answers, "Yes, I do believe." "Are you not merely superstitious?" asks Max. The philosopher replies: "You come to me with a problem and I provide you with a solution which implies that inscrutability need not eliminate meaningfulness — go about your daily affairs as if things mattered, as Skinner suggests." Max walks away from the philosopher and ponders the solution. He doesn't want to be superstitious. He doesn't want to live as if anything he does matters, if it does not, in fact, matter. Max then hits upon a clever idea. "If my behavior is irrelevant (no God — no Skinner) then I may as well commit suicide or do nothing. However, if my behavior is relevant, then I must commit myself accordingly. It is also true that life would be better if behavior mattered. Since I will never understand, even if he 'is,' I will never know the solution to my problem. However, it makes sense to choose the alternative that would be better if true, and that alternative is to act *as if* my behavior were relevant to the consequences." Max then returns to his experimental chamber and continues his walking in circles.

Are we not all like Max insofar as we are inhabitants of a Skinner box? As inhabitants of a Skinner box, can any of us discover whether a given behavior is superstitious or non-superstitious? Skinner, the scientist, informs us that through the operation of contingencies of reinforcement our behavior is controlled. Skinner also informs us that the only relationship necessary to establish the effectiveness of a reinforcer is the "order and proximity of response and reinforcement." Such a formula does not allow for distinctions such as right and wrong, superstitious or non-superstitious unless these refer to receiving reinforcement after a response. Clearly, the pigeons accomplish this. They do get reinforced; therefore, they are as correct as they can be within the confines of an operant conditioning paradigm. Since reinforcement will always take place when the organism is doing one thing or another, there is no way for it to decide the relevance of its behavior to reinforcement.

The best the organism could hope to accomplish is to discover that the reinforcement is delivered on a certain time schedule, but this would require that the organism leave his universe and consult with the controlling network outside of his universe. By definition, such is not possible. At best, one may infer, deduce, or extrapolate that there must be a universal clock (interval schedule of reinforcement), and indeed, such deductions, inferences, and extrapolations on the parts of priests, medicine men, and philosophers take place. This is what Skinner calls superstitious behavior. He seems to think that science is free from such superstitions. If so it is also uninvolved in the nature of that "universal clock" that regulates the reinforcement schedule. In fact, scientists are as superstitious as anyone else. It is the scientist who has developed the extraordinary ritual of the scientific method in an effort to understand the nature of the universe or, as in the case of our pigeons, the nature of Skinner.

The scientist is searching for meaning in the form of laws. But what proof is offered that a law has been discovered? For the behaviorist, the ultimate criterion as to whether we know anything is contingent upon reinforcements. A law must be proven to have reinforcing consequences. To say we will discover other laws is to do nothing more than express the *faith* that we shall find behaviors that lead to reinforcing consequences. Of course, the Pope will also undoubtedly tell us that belief in Christ has reinforcing consequences, and further religiousity will lead to behaviors that lead to other reinforcements. We have already seen that "persevering" may become an interpretation of another person's behavior when he does not extinguish a response. If he is on an extinction schedule of non-reinforcement, then we would know whether such a response is wrong or right, but we can never know that unless we could get outside our universe. Thus, like our pigeons, we require *faith* to believe that behavior is relevant to the universal clock.

When Skinner writes an eassay concerning the ways in which the world operates and the ways in which it should operate, he is presuming to have an insight into the nature of that clock as a result of his scientific background. Skinner's statement (1961, p. 4) "Let us agree to start with, that health is better than sickness, wisdom better than ignorance, love better than hate, and productive energy better than neurotic sloth" ignores the implications of his own writings. It was Skinner who argued that one reinforcement is not better or worse than another. Reinforcements simply reinforce behavior. To say love is better than hate is to say nonsense, unless he adds that it is better to love X reinforcement than to hate Y reinforcement. This is absurd because loving or hating a reinforcement is contingent upon a history of other reinforcements or present contingencies. Thus, to hate or love a reinforcement is to love or hate the law of gravity. Yet Skinner writes as though knowledge of reinforcement affects the law of reinforcement.

In describing the evolution of social practices, Skinner writes: "As soon as man began to propose and carry out changes in practice for the sake of possible consequences, the evolutionary process must have accelerated." (1961, p. 4). How can man ascertain if consequences determine behaviors, when Skinner has insisted that man, whether he likes it or not, is controlled by reinforcing consequences? My knowledge of the law of gravity does not make that law more effective. Instead, my knowledge of the law of gravity may lead me to construct aeroplanes. Knowledge of reinforcement schedules only bears upon how we wish to control men (aeroplanes) in light of that knowledge.

Skinner has evolved a technology whereby he can get organisms to make movements directed towards aspects of the environment. He cannot tell us the meaning of these movements since "meaning" means nothing more than what the animal does. This is why Skinner places "superstitious" in quotes. In his description of the pigeon as tossing his head once again, the quotation marks around "tossing" appear. The quotation marks are used because Skinner knows he cannot know anything more than he observes. Skinner insists that by hunger, all he means is a pigeon's body weight, an operant response and the delivery of a reinforcing stimulus. Hunger is the operation leading to, and sustaining the eating of a reinforcing stimulus. Hunger must also be placed in quotation marks, for the pigeon may be nervous when he takes in the pellets. The word "hunger," like the word "superstition," is an interpretation of behavior. An interpretation of behavior is in reality a miniature theory insofar as it purports to describe the "meaning" of what is seen to be something else. But Skinner considers theory as an explanatory fiction at its worst, and irrelevant at its best. Yet he does not describe the movements of animals, but interprets such movements *as if* he had a theory. In fact, what Skinner is doing is anthropomorphizing in the guise of common sense (not uncommon systematic scientific observation) that the behavior, being "like" Webster's definition of superstition, undoubtedly is superstition. The effect is that superstition appears to be explained (explanatory fiction). Movements can be explained as exemplifying superstition only if Skinner provides a "theory" as to what constitutes superstitious and non-superstitious behavior, and then shows how the movements (evidence) relate to the interpretive descriptions (theories). In this way only is it possible to judge the adequacy of the evidence that superstitious behavior is indeed superstitious behavior. All human activity can be called superstitious insofar as we assume that it makes a difference whether we act or not. From this perspective, every experiment that Skinner ever performed is a study of superstitious behavior.

The only meaning that superstition can have is ignored by Skinner. That is, behavior that is inappropriately assigned to be relevant for determining or mitigating certain desirable and undesired consequences. To perform such a study, one would have to have the conceptual tools to define such terms as "inappropriate" and "appropriate." The closest Skinner comes to providing such a concept is his description of the discriminative stimulus. Behavior which is performed without regard to the discriminative stimulus would then constitute superstitious behavior. However, if behavior is performed without regard to a discriminative stimulus, then a discriminative stimulus is not a discriminative stimulus, for the latter is functionally defined. Since the operant model does not allow for more than the notation of movements, it remains a manual for control of movements. One can wonder what Skinner's appeal would be if he described only movements and did not add theoretical projections. Would the reader have the patience to project his own interpretations upon the movements or would he read someone like Freud who at least makes systematic projections? Skinner and Freud are similar in that both have an ingenious ability to take a unit of behavior and establish its meaning. Freud interprets dreams. Skinner interprets movements. The *undemonstrable conjectures* of Freud are perhaps no worse than the *meaningless movements* of Skinner.

I would like to return to a comment whereby we characterized Freud as emphasizing the recipe and Skinner the pudding, saying that, in matters of recipes and puddings, one without the other was rather meaningless. The efforts of Lundin (1970) to relate operant conditioning to personality and psychopathology make constant cross-references between Freud and Skinner. It is as though Freud points out the behavior, and operant researchers demonstrate its derivation. The operant psychologists are impotent to develop meaningful descriptions of movements unless they consult the recipe of other theories. In a sense then, one could say that insofar as Skinner has demonstrated psychoanalytic hypotheses, he has justified psychoanalytic theory.

REFERENCES

Ayllon, T. and Azrin, N., *The Token Economy*. Appleton-Century-Crofts, 1968.

Breland, K. and Breland, Marian, "The Misbehavior of Organisms," *American Psychologist*, 1961, 16: 681–684.

Ferster, C. B. and Skinner, B. F., *Schedules of Reinforcement*. Appleton-Century-Crofts, 1957.

Freud, S., (trans. J. Riviere), "The Unconscious" in *Collected Papers*, Vol. 4. Basic Books, 1959.

———, "The Psychopathology of Everyday Life" in *Standard Edition*, Vol. 6. London: Hogarth Press, 1960.

Hall, C. S. and Lindzey, G., *Theories of Personality.* John Wiley and Sons, Inc., 1970.

Reynolds, G. S., *A Primer of Operant Conditioning.* Scott, Foresman and Co., 1967.

Skinner, B. F., *Cumulative Record.* Appleton-Century-Crofts, 1961.

———, "The Phylogeny and Ontogeny of Behavior" in Endler, N., Boulter, L., and H. Osser, eds., *Contemporary Issues in Developmental Psychology.* Holt, Rinehart and Winston, 1968.

———, *Science and Human Behavior.* Macmillan, 1953.

Watson, J. B., and Raynor, R., "Conditioned Emotional Reactions," *J. exp. Psychol.,* 1920, 3:1–14.

DANIEL E. BERLYNE

Behavior Theory as Personality Theory

CHARACTERIZATION OF BEHAVIOR THEORY

It is extremely difficult to say exactly what "behavior theory" is and to delineate its boundaries. Is it a branch of psychology, a school of psychology, a theoretical position, a methodological approach? It is certainly not quite any of these, and yet it is all of them to some extent. What is the relation of behavior theory to the rest of psychology? In fact, what kinds of psychology, if any, lie outside its boundaries? All sorts of answers to these questions have been put forward at one time or another. There are those who have felt that behavior theory is destined to assimilate more and more of psychology as time goes on, so that everything in psychology will eventually be marked with its stamp, and the sooner the better. Others, of course, have felt that behavior theory is a transitory aberration whose pernicious influence will soon be seen for what it is and annihilated. Some have maintained that all psychologists are behavior theorists, but that some realize it and some do not; the implication is that those who are aware of what they are doing will do it better.

The term "behavior theory" has been used fairly interchangeably with the term "learning theory." "Learning theory" seems to have come into use rather

Reprinted from Edgar F. Borgatta and William W. Lambert, eds., *Handbook of Personality Theory and Research,* © 1968 by Rand McNally and Company, Chicago, pp. 630–682.

earlier, and some writers, notably Mowrer, have strongly favored it. Hull and Spence have preferred to speak of "behavior theory." There have been some not very happy attempts to distinguish between the theory of learning and "behavior theory" as the theory of performance, but, although, according to most theories, there are differences between the principles that determine the acquisition of habit-strength and those that determine the probability and vigor of responding, it is certainly impracticable to separate the two completely, let alone to assign them to two distinct bodies of theory. The term "behavior theory" is perhaps to be preferred, on the grounds that "learning theory" has come to encompass much more than a statement of the principles that govern learning. It has, for example, coalesced in large part with motivation theory. It has encroached on vast areas of social, abnormal, and developmental psychology. As the work of the ethologists (Tinbergen, 1951; Thorpe, 1956) has abundantly demonstrated, many of the principles governing learned behavior apply equally to unlearned or instinctive behavior. The content of this chapter may help the reader to decide whether or not behavior theory will eventually contain personality theory.

Behavior theory can safely be identified with the behaviorist movement and more particularly with its later or neo-behaviorist phase. So a brief review of the course of development through which this movement has gone seems called for at this point, if the positions of its contemporary exponents are to be understood.

The Early Behaviorism of J. B. Watson

Watson is now often regarded as a figure of fun, as a bogey-man, or as a straw man to use in attacking contemporary psychologists with behaviorist proclivities. Their position is often assumed to resemble his in all important respects. It is true that Watson wrote in a racy style, which was not conducive to meticulous phrasing and precise wording, and that he tended to be carried away by his iconoclastic fervor. He was not highly trained as a philosopher, and, in the 20th century, philosophy has become, if anything, more of a professionalized and esoteric vocation than in previous centuries. It has certainly become much more self-conscious about language, so that an amateur can hardly hope to enter that domain without showing himself for what he is as soon as he opens his mouth. Pulling Watson to pieces — laying bare the inconsistencies and oversights in his pronouncements — was, at one time, a favorite limbering-up exercise of philosophers, and an elementary one at that. Now we can arrive at a sounder evaluation and separate the wheat from the chaff in his contribution better than his contemporaries, and no doubt better than he himself, could have done.

Watson maintained that psychologists should no longer concern themselves with conscious mental events and should no longer rely on introspection as their prime source of data. The psychological Establishment of the time was bound to react to this as astronomers would do if told that, from now on, stars were no longer their business and that they must dispense with the telescope. From our present vantage-point, we can see that to follow Watson's advice means to preserve all the worthwhile problems of his predecessors, while evading much of the haze that sometimes enveloped them. Watson set off his revolution before psychologists became cognizant of the logical-empiricist philosophy-of-science movement, with its attempts at a sophisticated characterization of the aims of science and the kinds of linguistic formulae that it uses. But he saw the essential point that there is a great difference between the study of "public" or "intersubjective" phenomena, which are accessible to everybody's sense-organs so that a consensus about them can rapidly be reached, and the study of private, subjective experiences that everybody can, and no doubt should, pursue for his own benefit but that can hardly become part of a collective enterprise. He made rash and ultimately untenable statements with regard to the philosophical problems of body-mind relations. But he made us see that it is important for a psychologist to decide whether he is pursuing an explanation of behavior or an explanation of conscious experience. Confusion can hardly be avoided if the two are pursued together, and, unless one subscribes to the interactionist view that conscious experiences determine behavior, why should one want to pursue them together?

These lessons have, of course, not by any means permeated the whole of contemporary psychology. It is far from clear whether some current writers are trying to account for conscious experiences or for publicly observable responses. It is, in fact, far from clear that these writers themselves have decided which they would attempt. If it were not for vestiges of interactionism, why should there have been so much stir when stimuli appeared, in certain conditions, to evoke galvanic skin responses but not verbal responses?

Watson did not reject verbal reports once and for all from psychology. Indeed, he put onerous responsibilities on them himself, e.g., in his analysis of perception. Present-day social psychologists and psychophysicists would certainly be hard pressed if they were not allowed to listen to what subjects say. But our whole attitude to the verbal report has changed since Watson. We are now unlikely to hold that the verbal report gives a complete and thoroughly accurate specification of the processes within the subject that underlie his behavior.

We can now afford to smile superciliously at Watson's naïvete in believing that the brain works through structures very much like the spinal reflex arc, that all human behavior can have developed out of an inaugural stock of a few hundred specific innate reflexes and three innate emotional patterns through the operation of classical conditioning, at his truculent refusal to attach much importance to inherited individual differences, and at his insistence on belittling the differences between what human beings and lower animals can do. If, however, we disregard the literal content of much that he said, we can discern with more sympathy what he was really after. He was committing himself, and trying to commit psychology, to a strategy that had paid off in other branches of science, namely that of taking up the study of simple phenomena first and seeking in them clues that will later facilitate the study of more complex phenomena. He believed that the most elaborate and uniquely human activities must have grown, both phylogenetically and ontogenetically, out of the simplest adaptive response mechanisms and that they cannot be understood unless the process of development has been traced. He appreciated that, in any case, a scientific discipline has not completed its task unless it has related the complex to the simple and laid bare the common threads that string them together. He saw that, since most of the behavior of the higher mammals is learned, psychologists should give the highest possible priority to the task of working out the laws that govern learning.

A methodological position that, in its essentials, was the same as Watson's was being simultaneously established in Russia by Pavlov, extending the tradition founded by the 19th-century Russian physiologist, Sechenov. It is true that Pavlov turned to the study of behavior not for its own sake but as an indirect means of ascertaining what goes on in the brain. Nevertheless, he demonstrated the fruitfulness of carefully observing behavior and especially the modifications that combinations of environmental events impose on behavior.

The First Generation of Neo-Behaviorism

By the early 1930's, Watson's behaviorism had died while giving birth to an heir. The heir, while showing unmistakable signs of its parentage, has had enough individuality to deserve a name of its own, and it has accordingly been christened "neo-behaviorism." The event evidently received insufficient publicity, since many psychologists outside the family appear to believe either that behaviorism passed away long ago without issue or that the original bearer of the name is still hale. European psychologists, especially those working in the Soviet Union, are apt to see in Watson's ill-considered assertion that, given the response, it should be possible to predict the stimulus and vice versa the substance of contemporary "S-R behavior theory."

A publication that is often held to mark the changeover is Hull's (1929) article, "A Functional Interpretation of the Conditioned Reflex," which, in discussing the biological significance of familiar conditioning phenomena, strikes a new note in its emphases rather than in what it actually says. Tolman's book, *Purposive Behavior in Animals and Men* (1932), was the first large-scale contribution to neo-behaviorism, and he very definitely intended it to mark a breakaway. Holt, although a philosopher rather than a psychologist, gave the budding neo-behaviorist movement a substantial fillip with his book *Animal Drive and the Learning Process* (1931), and had, in fact, adumbrated some of the themes that were to characterize neo-behaviorism much earlier in his book *The Freudian Wish and Its Place in Ethics* (1915).

The principal differences between early behaviorism and the neo-behaviorism of the 1930's and 1940's can be summed up briefly as follows.

1. The neo-behaviorists were deeply influenced, directly or indirectly, by the logical-empiricist movement in philosophy, with its feeling that the boundaries of scientific activity and the scientific use of language need to be sharply delineated to avoid mutual interference between what lies inside them and what lies outside. Accordingly, the neo-behaviorists kept themselves aloof on the whole from such extra-scientific questions as the nature of conscious experiences, their relation to bodily events, and what it "means" to possess a mental process.

Either a mental event can possess no correlation at all with observable behavior – to outward view (even if aided by special recording equipment), the subject behaves in all respects as he would if the mental event were absent – or there is some degree of correlation or correspondence between mental events and overt behavior. In the former case, science, regarded as a social activity concerned with public phenomena, can have no interest in the mental events and could lose nothing by disregarding them. In the latter case, there must be a *logical equivalence* between statements about the mental events and statements about overt responses. In the new logic whose chief founders were Whitehead and Russell (1910–12), statements p and q are "logically equivalent" when p is true if and only if q is true. It follows that a set of statements about mental events can be replaced by a corresponding set of statements about overt responses without loss as far as the aims of science are concerned, i.e., with respect to antecedent and consequent conditions or, in other words, with respect to what the statements imply and are implied by. Whether statements that are logically equivalent in this way must be identical in "meaning" or "empirical content" is a contentious question that the neo-behaviorist psychologist can safely leave to the analytic philosopher.

In short, therefore, the neo-behaviorists took over the behaviorist methodology from Watson while holding aloof from his provocative stance over the nature of mind. They saw no reason to eschew verbal reports. They regarded verbal responses, including those elicited by questioning, as deserving of study like any others and perhaps especially valuable because of the unique potentialities for information transmission that their variety confers on them. They took care, however, not to regard a verbal report as a peephole affording a grandstand view of the subject's internal workings.

2. The neo-behaviorists were generally more interested than Watson or Watson's predecessors in the construction of systematic and rigorous theories. They were influenced by the lively discussions on the nature and desiderata of scientific theories that the logical-empiricist philosophers of science carried on in the 1920's and 1930's. They were self-conscious about their theorizing. Not only did they learn that they must make clear exactly what their theoretical statements mean in terms of empirical implications. They realized that

the onus was on them to demonstrate that they have any meaning at all of the sort in which science is interested.

3. The neo-behaviorists were fully aware that there is no one-to-one correspondence between stimulus conditions and response conditions. They recognized that the overt response depends jointly on the external stimulus situation and on conditions inside the organism. To take care of this difficulty, their theories tend to be replete with references to intervening variables, mediating processes, and implicit stimulus-producing responses, the function of all these devices being to make manageable the conceptual treatment of intricate input-output relations. Some neo-behaviorists, notably Skinner and his associates, have looked askance at all this talk about unobservable events inside the organism and at the constructs to which it has given rise, but even Skinner has been unable simply to list external stimulus conditions and specify the behavioral consequences of each. His early writings (e.g., 1938) mentioned such intervening variables as "reflex reserve," while his later works, particularly those dealing with human verbal behavior and cognate processes (1953, 1957), contain copious references to such hypothesized entities as "covert speech."

4. Most neo-behaviorists were intensely interested in motivational problems. This is partly because what we call motivational variables are obviously among the most important of the conditions whose variations cause changes in behavior when the external situation is held constant. But it was also part of an eagerness to place the facts about behavior in a biological setting, i.e., to show the relevance to biological adaptation of the characteristics of behavior that are disclosed.

5. This increased emphasis on the biological setting of behavior went together with a sharply reduced interest in its physiological underpinning. One of the few things that Watson took over unchanged from his introspectionist predecessors was the belief that to explain a psychological phenomenon means to relate it to the data of physiology. In the early 1930's, it became apparent that neurophysiology had so far contributed little to the understanding of learning, which was the neo-behaviorists' main preoccupation, so that there was no point in waiting for knowledge about the nervous system to catch up. The current view of science implied, furthermore, that there could be such a thing as an adequate theory of behavior making no reference to events in the nervous system. The psychologist would be carrying out his task quite adequately if he worked out the laws that enable responses to be predicted when pertinent facts about the external environment and the organism's internal condition are known. The internal condition (which, it seemed, need not be described in physiological terms) could be inferred either from previous behavior or from previous external stimulus conditions.

The neo-behaviorists had learned from Pavlov, Watson, and Thorndike to concentrate on the experimental study of learning as the best hope of placing psychology on a firm footing and, above all, of providing a language in which the various fields of psychology, including social psychology, developmental psychology, abnormal psychology, and the study of complex processes, can be discussed and interrelated. There was, however, an important difference in that early behaviorism placed its main hopes in the classical or Pavlovian conditioning paradigm. In contrast, the neo-behaviorists have set greater store by the kind of learning known as "instrumental conditioning" or "operant conditioning" or "selective learning."

Although there have been disputes over the precise relations between classical and instrumental conditioning, the latter appears to differ from the former insofar as it enables a new response pattern to be acquired, while classical conditioning is mainly a matter of associating old responses with new stimulus conditions. This is, however, something of an oversimplification, since the new response patterns must be put together out of components that were already in the organism's behavior repertoire and since the classically conditioned response, as has often been pointed out, is not always identical with what the unconditioned stimulus elicited. A more crucial distinction is perhaps to be found in the forms of reinforcement to which these two kinds of learning are susceptible: in both cases, the presence of a reinforcing agent is necessary to establish learning and ward off extinction, but in classical conditioning it takes the form of the unconditioned stimulus which originally evoked the response, and in instrumental conditioning it is a rewarding condition that closely follows the response.

The earliest experiments on instrumental conditioning may with some justification be held to be the puzzle-box experiments of Thorndike and the earliest experiments on maze learning in the rat, which were roughly contemporaneous with the first studies of classical conditioning in Pavlov's laboratory. Nevertheless, a number of experimenters working in different countries (e.g., Skinner, 1935, in the United States; Gridley, 1932, in England; Ivanov-Smolenski, 1927, in Russia; Miller and Konorski, 1928, in Poland) devised experimental situations that enabled the similarities and dissimilarities between classical and instrumental conditioning to be clearly shown.

The neo-behaviorists have never formed a coherent school, let alone a group subscribing to an explicit set of tenets. Those of the first generation seemed clearly more conscious of their disagreements than of any commonly held position. The points of dispute were, after all, interesting ones and stimulated feverish experimentation. Nevertheless, whereas the spokesmen of the various factions felt themselves to be poles apart, their opponents saw them as purveyors of slightly different brands of the same dubious product. Those who believe in the product's essential soundness can now recognize that, although the behavior theorists of the 1930's spent relatively little time marking out their areas of agreement, these were more extensive than they, in the heat of battle, were inclined to acknowledge.

The most prominent schism within the first echelon of neo-behaviorists was that between the "cognitive theorists" and "S-R theorists." The latter, when they accepted mediating processes (and some like Skinner have been vehemently averse to them), thought of them as implicit or internalized "responses," i.e., as derivatives of overt responses whose acquisition and performance follow essentially the same principles as those of overt responses. The cognitivists were somewhat more eager to find room for mediating processes and to conceive of these (expectations, cognitions, etc.) as subject to essentially different principles from those that apply to overt responses. The cognitivist mediating processes were thus closer in structure and content (to be precise, in "informational correspondence" — see Berlyne, 1965) to perceptual processes, whereas those of the S-R theorists came closer to motor processes.

There were other divisions within the S-R wing, bearing notably on the relations between classical and instrumental conditioning. For some, particularly Hull and his associates, all learning conformed to the instrumental pattern, while for others, particularly Guthrie, all learning was governed by contiguity and consisted essentially of classical conditioning. Some like Skinner and, for one period of his career, Mowrer maintained that classical and instrumental conditioning were two distinct kinds of learning applicable to different responses. In the Soviet Union, classical conditioning has always been taken as a model for learning in general, although it has been viewed rather flexibly. Pavlov had a theory of instrumental conditioning, which is little known in the West but was actually outlined in an article in the *Psychological Review* in 1932. He felt that contiguity learning could account for instrumental conditioning, provided that the formation of two-way connections between sensory and kinesthetic-motor areas of the cortex was accepted. Konorski (e.g., 1948) has, on the other hand, consistently emphasized the gulf between Type I (i.e., classical) and Type II (i.e., instrumental) conditioning.

Although neo-behaviorism has never denied its Watsonian parentage, and it would be disingenuous for it to do so, its origins were far from parthenogenetic. One far from insignificant contributor to it was psychoanalysis. As we shall see later in this chapter, efforts at synthesis between psychoanalysis and behavior theory took up a great deal of energy at one time. Quite apart from this explicit influence, there is no mistaking the similarity between the view of behavior, most clearly expressed in the writings of Hull and his followers, as a collection of devices for getting rid of internal or external disturbances and the motivational theory outlined by Freud at one stage in his career (1915).

McDougall's work also helped to make the neo-behaviorists realize, unlike Watson, that motivational questions must be faced. The neo-behaviorists were eager to crystallize within their theories the fruits of the thought and experimental work on motivation that began during the 1920's. This work and its continuation by the neo-behaviorists were inspired in no small measure by a desire to do what McDougall had shown to be necessary and yet overcome the objectionable features of his instinct theory. Tolman's book *Purposive Behavior in Animals and Men* (1932) was intended to show that behaviorists could accept McDougall's (1923) contention that "purposive" behavior has important characteristics marking it off sharply from reflex behavior and could handle the problems that goal-directedness raises in a manner fully consonant with the principles of behaviorism.

The influence of the American functionalism of the turn of the century (e.g., Dewey, 1896) is evident in the much greater importance that the neo-behaviorists, as compared with Watson, attached to chains of responses organized for the fulfillment of biological purposes.

Biases taken over from Gestalt psychology were most noticeable in the cognitivist wing (cf. Tolman's "sign-gestalt-expectations"), but some of the chief points on which the Gestalt school insisted were taken to heart to some extent by all the neo-behaviorists. Razran (1939) and Hull (1943) found quite congenial to learning theory the view that wholes or combinations have effects other than those of their components. They pointed to the substantial evidence that had been collected in both Russian and American laboratories for what they call "configural conditioning" or "patterning," such that an animal learns to perform a response to a combination of stimuli but to inhibit the response when the elements of the combination appear separately, or vice versa. Hull deliberately introduced his not too successful principle of "afferent neural interaction" to account for the special effects of combinations. The influence of Gestalt psychology was, however, most clearly evident in the wider connotation that neo-behaviorists began to give to the notion of a "stimulus." A "stimulus" came to mean virtually any kind of distinguishable property that can mark off a class of stimulus situations. We find, for example, Miller and Dollard (1941) recognizing that a response can become associated with a particular pitch of sound, with the existence of a difference in pitch between two sounds, with the direction of such a difference, with the extent of such a difference, etc.

The Second Generation of Neo-Behaviorism

Some marked changes in emphasis and atmosphere became apparent in the beginning of the 1950's. The first major publication sounding some of the new notes was Hebb's *The Organization of Behavior* (1949). The year 1949 was actually a remarkable one for psychology in many ways. It saw the appearance of the article by Moruzzi and Magoun (1949) that focused attention on the brain-stem reticular formation. This was the year when Shannon and Weaver's (1949) *The Mathematical Theory of Communication* presented the intellectual revolution of information theory to a potentially wide audience. It was also about then that investigators in the United States, the United Kingdom, and the Soviet Union had begun independently to treat exploratory behavior as a phenomenon worth intensive examination. All of these developments have left their stamp on the second phase of neo-behaviorism.

I was tempted to propose a new term, e.g., "ceno-behaviorism" (Greek *kainos*, recent), to denote the behaviorism of the 1950's and 1960's and to distinguish it from the neo-behaviorism of the 1930's and 1940's, but there have actually not been such violent breaks with the general aims and outlook of the first-generation neo-behaviorists as would justify this neologism. The changes that have occurred are simply of kinds that are to be expected as inquiry progresses, and they are certainly not comparable with those that divided the first neo-behaviorists from Watson. So it would be prudent to keep the term "ceno-behaviorism" for some more sweeping transformation that will undoubtedly come at the beginning of a future odd-numbered decade.

The main thing that marks off the work of contemporary neo-behaviorists from that of their predecessors is the abundant influence of new lines of inquiry that have taken shape outside the neo-behaviorist mainstream.

Among such sources of influence have been:

1. the cybernetic notion of gravitation towards a goal by negative feedback and correction of deviation,

2. the concepts and measures introduced by information theory,

3. the concepts, theoretical models, and research data supplied by computer simulation,

4. Piaget's findings and theoretical ideas concerning the development of perceptual and intellectual activities in the child,

5. experimental findings and theoretical ideas originated by Russian investigators of conditioning and of complex intellectual processes, these having been made available by the rapid growth of translation from Russian and of mutual contact between East and West that has occurred since the death of Stalin.

Behavior theories are, needless to say, not the only ones to have felt these influences. Psychologists not identified with the neo-behaviorist movement have, however, either confined their attention to circumscribed areas of interest opened up by these new trends or proposed, more or less, that psychology should be built up anew with one of these new approaches as its main foundation. Behavior theorists have, in contrast, confronted these new lines of investigation with the belief that the psychology of the past, including the behavior theory of the past, had some solid achievements to its credit. The most urgent need, it seems to them, is to establish some synthesis between the new complexities introduced by these recent developments and what was learned in the past with the help of established experimental techniques and theoretical concepts.

The most impressive contrast between present-day neo-behaviorism and the neo-behaviorism that existed before 1950 is in the attitudes of its proponents to neurophysiology. The first neo-behaviorist generation kept aloof — in some cases intransigently aloof — from reference to what might go on in the brain and were wont to use "neurologizing" as a defamatory term. Their recent successors have been faced with a veritable cloudburst of neurophysiological advances that has poured forth since shortly after World War II and shows no sign of abating. These advances were made possible by growing use of the electroencephalograph, supplemented before long by implanted recording and stimulating electrodes, micro-electrodes, stereotaxic instruments for aiming these electrodes at specific structures, and a variety of new techniques for recording and processing torrents of data. One of Hebb's avowed aims in his book *The Organization of Behavior* (1949) was to warn psychologists, and behavior theorists in particular, that, since they were last in touch with neurophysiology, that discipline had undergone changes with which they would do well to acquaint themselves. He argued that even those who proclaimed their indifference to brain function were, whether they realized it or not, apt to show the influence of outmoded neurophysiological conceptions. Insofar as his case rested on the accomplishments of neurophysiology before 1949, it may or may not have been found convincing. But within a few years, neurophysiological laboratories began to emit such a spate of significant new findings as must sooner or later break down any open-minded behavior theorist's skepticism regarding their pertinence to his interests. So present-day contributions to behavior theory are commonly formulated in terms that make contact with the latest neurophysiological discoveries. At the time of such headspinning flux, any hypothesis suggested by the latest neurophysiological picture is apt to require revision within a very short time. But there is no reason why this should matter. The attempt to keep up with the tide is exhilarating, and experimental techniques for testing any neuropsychological speculation either are available already or can confidently be expected before long. The old arguments of the 1930's and 1940's about the dispensability of physiological knowledge for the behavior theorist are as valid as ever. It is certainly possible to study relations between external events and observable behavior without any concern for what occurs in the brain, just as somebody who is unfamiliar with watches could arrive at a notion of what one does, and how its user can control it, by looking at the face and manipulating the crown. If, on the other hand, he professes to be interested in how a watch works but refuses to listen to what a friend who has succeeded in prying off the back has to tell him, he is being pigheaded.

There has been a feeling in some quarters that psychological and neurophysiological subject matters are fundamentally incapable of synthesis, because they represent different "levels of discourse." It has been held that psychology and physiology differ in that the latter breaks things down into smaller units. It would however, be hard to maintain that, say, a physiological condition of high arousal, with manifestations pervading the whole body, represents a finer scale of analysis than, say, the response of pressing a key with the right index finger, as in a traditional psychological experiment on reaction time. Some have felt that psychology, and especially behavior theory, should rigorously espouse a "black-box" point of view with the single-minded objective of analyzing relations between inputs and outputs. According to this view, reference to happenings in the brain is out of order, because it makes reference to processes that go on within the black box and are thus not embraced by that objective. This is surely a misunderstanding. Devices that provide us with clues to the working of the nervous system are not giving us a view of what is occurring within the black box. By definition, whatever occurs within the box is unobservable. As soon as an event becomes accessible to observation, it no longer belongs to the interior of the black box but to the output. Psychophysiological and neurophysiological recording techniques thus add to the outputs that the behavior theorist must take into account. And this information supplies additional guidance for our theoretical divagations by cutting down the number of alternative formulations that can be entertained, since the more numerous the outputs that must be predicted, the fewer the hypotheses regarding input-output relations that become tenable.

Apart from the reinstatement of brain physiology into a major advisory function, the latest phase of neo-behaviorism continues to show the traditional behaviorist biases with regard to content. Learning still has pride of place, although ethology has cautioned against underestimating the possible significance of unlearned behavior even in the higher mammals. There is still heavy reliance on animal experiments, with deliberate concentration on a few intensively studied species such as the rat and the pigeon, although the informative potentialities of human children and of computers are receiving more and more recognition.

However, despite the behaviorist insistence that it is best to start with the simplest phenomenon, behavior theorists are beginning to muster the confidence to attack the most complex symbolic processes. There is, in fact, an increasing readiness, both in the English-speaking countries and in the Soviet Union, to realize that there are vast differences between the simplest kinds of behavior of which animals and human beings are capable and the activities that we describe as "voluntary," "rational," and "accompanied by awareness." Yet recognition of the gulf between them does not preclude a naturalistic treatment of the differences or a search for principles common to them all. As another earnest of this willingness to face greater intricacies, let us note J. G. Taylor's book (1962), *The Behavioral Basis of Perception*, which, in aspiring to annex the domain of perception to behavior theory, revives some of the delicate problems regarding the function of consciousness that Watson and Lashley (1923) boldly took up, that Tolman (1932) toyed with, but that most neo-behaviorists steadfastly shunned.

Finally, the most recent neo-behaviorists have maintained their predecessors' concern for motivational problems, but several new doors have been opened by their steeply mounting interest in "intrinsic" or "collative" motivation. Earlier neo-behaviorists hoped to trace all behavior back to external annoyances or organic needs affecting tissues other than the sense organs and the nervous system. Now, it has become apparent that activities pursued "for

their own sake," without any practical consequences of an obvious and immediate nature, take up a large part of the time and energy of higher animals.
These activities appear to be self-motivating and self-reinforcing, which must
mean that the motivational factors to which they are subject depend on their
structure or, in other words, on the relations, harmonious or discordant, between simultaneous internal psychophysiological processes.

The attention of behavior theorists was first drawn to these matters by
experimental work on exploratory behavior and attention. Similar lessons have
been hammered home, in different guises, by recent trends in developmental
psychology, social psychology, attitude change, the psychology of thinking,
the psychology of humor, and aesthetics (Berlyne, 1960, 1963a, 1965).

The discrepant reactions that form the motivational basis for the kinds
of behavior in question arise largely from "collative" properties of stimulus
patterns, i.e., properties such as novelty, surprisingness, complexity, ambiguity,
vagueness, and puzzlingness. The operative element common to all these
properties may well be conflict, i.e., initiation of processes that would, if
completed without hindrance, lead to incompatible motor responses. Several
kinds of evidence point to a close relation between the motivational effects
of collative variables and the psychophysiological dimension of "arousal,"
which evidently depends on the degree of activity of the brain-stem reticular
formation and its modes of interaction with other brain structures. As close
affinities emerge between the new concept of "arousal" and the older concept
of "drive," which has for so many decades dominated the psychology of motivation, new light promises to be shed on the fundamentals of motivation
in general.

RELATIVE NEGLECT OF PERSONALITY
THEORY BY BEHAVIOR THEORISTS

Reasons for Neglect

It can hardly be overlooked that problems of personality have figured much
less prominently in the writings of the behavior theorists than in psychological
literature as a whole, although Pavlov and Watson, the joint founders of the
behaviorist current, were by no means tight-lipped on the topic.

One difficulty has been finding a conception of "personality" that would
cover everything with which psychologists have concerned themselves under
the aegis of that word. Most would agree to allot all study of individual
differences to personality theory, but some might object to this on the grounds
that "personality" implies some coherent pattern of individuality. Some matters that have at times been accepted as part of personality theory have no
direct bearing on individual differences at all. They relate rather to general
principles governing the nature and interrelations of the complex psychological processes contributing to the "integration" of the "self." Psychology
students have not infrequently been encouraged to feel that "personality"

is another name for those areas of psychology that are most "interesting," that have the widest immediate appeal. Writers can even be found who appear to be using the word "personality" simply as a pusillanimous substitute for what psychologists used to discuss without qualms as the "mind." For the purposes of this chapter, we had better simply identify "personality theory" as the theory of individual differences, while recognizing that this definition would not win universal assent.

Some of the reasons why behavior theory has neglected personality, in the sense of individual differences, are historical, which means that their validity for the present day would bear some reexamination. The behavior theorist has always committed himself to the goals of basic research and pure science, with all that they entail in the way of patience and relative aloofness from practical social problems. Most work on individual differences has, on the other hand, been actuated by the pressing needs of those engaged in clinical practice, education, or industry, which has all but equated it with applied psychology. There have therefore been the inevitable suspicions and disparagements that the ivory tower and the market place inspire in each other. Applied psychologists have, for example, been obliged to concern themselves with individual differences pertaining to extremely complex processes about which, the pure psychologist feels, little is known. One has only to think of the long-standing lack of contact between the theory of intelligence testing and the experimental psychology of thinking.

Further, behavior theorists have inherited from their empiricist and associationist forebears of previous centuries a bias towards environmentalism. Watson was evidently determined not to be outdone by any 17th-century *tabula rasa* theory, as witness his famous claim (1924) that any normal child can be turned into "any type of specialist I might select — doctor, lawyer, artist, merchant, thief, and yes, even make a man and a thief, regardless of his talents, penchants, tendencies, abilities, vocations and race of his ancestors." No neo-behaviorist has assumed this position, but the fact remains that behavior theorists spend most of their time studying learned behavior and feel that to understand the behavior of the higher mammals means, above all, to understand how learning works. Specialists in individual differences have, however, devoted much effort to considering and investigating how far personality may be predetermined by heredity. In recent years, the ethologists have made apparent the scope of elaborate unlearned behavior patterns in lower animals, and although it can hardly be doubted that such "instinctive" behavior is far less prominent in man than in the birds, fishes, and insects on which the ethologists have concentrated, the possibility that they play more part than we think in human life cannot be dismissed. Specialists in genetics (e.g., Hirsch, 1962; Darlington, 1963) have lately protested that hereditary factors may be responsible for characteristics of behavior that psychologists rarely consider from this angle. Nevertheless, the behavior theorist feels that personality theorists have all too often assumed something to be constitutional that is actually a product of learning and have, in any case, not paid nearly enough attention to the role of learning processes in the creation of individual differences.

Preoccupation with learning may lead one to disregard innate differences, which must seem the logical starting point to anyone who wishes to throw light on the dissimilarities among human beings. Nevertheless, interest in learning does not preclude interest in individual differences. One might well think that it must sooner or later compel attention to them. First, what is learned varies with the environmental conditions to which an individual is exposed and, since different individuals encounter different combinations of external stimulus conditions, they will inevitably acquire different behavior through learning. It has, in fact, been a commonplace among behavior theorists who have maintained contact with other social scientists that the contrasting child-rearing practices and economic circumstances that characterize different social groups must inevitably produce contrasting forms of learned behavior. Precisely because of the infinite variety that learning can exhibit, it has been difficult to find appropriate classificatory schemes to impose the necessary conceptual order on them, and this has certainly been an obstacle to progress in this direction. Secondly, individuals can differ in how they learn. Such differences might well be hereditary even though they affect behavior in conjunction with learning. Factors of this sort have long been discussed in Russia, but they have received little study, and most of what they have received has been recent, in the West.

This last point is connected with an issue of research strategy on which behavior theory is firmly committed to one side. It is perfectly obvious that human beings are different from one another in some respects but alike in other respects. The question is whether we should first look for statements that apply to all of them or whether we should first try to describe and explain their differences. The behavior theorist feels that research for common principles of human and animal behavior must take precedence. This, he would point out, is how scientific inquiry must proceed, and this is how other branches of science have had the spectacular successes that have so far eluded psychology. The urge to fashion order out of chaos and to catch sight of the homogeneities that underlie diversity has always been one of the mainsprings of the human quest for knowledge and understanding. Until we can see what individuals of a class or species have in common, we cannot hope to understand how their dissimilarities have come about or even to find the most fruitful way to describe and classify these dissimilarities.

The chemical elements, a behavior theorist would recall, are certainly distinct in behavior and in outward appearance, but could their differences have been described unless we were clear about the dimensions — color, density, melting point, etc. — along which any material substance can be located? Unless we had the general concept of a chemical reaction and knew the kinds of outcome that one could have, could we say anything worth saying about chemical behavior? Now physicists and chemists are in a position to relate the findings of chemistry to principles of atomic structure and quantum mechanics that are applicable to all atoms. The properties of the different elements can now be understood in terms of differences in the number of protons and neutrons in the nucleus, differences in the numbers of electrons occupying particular "shells," etc. Likewise embryology has advanced by working out the general scheme of development from zygote to mature adult that is followed by all sexually reproducing metazoa. Yet there are undoubted differences. For example, there are contrasts between the chordates, including vertebrates, and the echinoderms on the one hand and most invertebrates on the other hand. One of them relates to the location from which mesodermal cells begin to proliferate after gastrulation. Could such a difference have conceivably been characterized before the existence and nature of gastrulation, as something found throughout the animal kingdom apart from its very lowest phyla, were known?

It is true that this line of argument has limitations. Before the different properties of chemical elements could be related to universally applicable principles of atomic structure, their manifest differences had to be noted and recorded, which took a number of centuries before the modern study of the atom was begun. So when the behavior theorist feels ready to add personality differences to the phenomena that he aspires to explain and to utilize in predicting behavior, he must acknowledge his debt to those psychologists of other orientations who have done the spade-work of delineating personality differences.

The Place of Personality Traits in Behavior Theory

Hull (1945) felt the need to establish "a genuine junction between pure and applied psychology, which of late seem to be drifting farther and farther apart." He saw that a prerequisite of this aim was to find some way of handling inter-individual and inter-species differences within the bounds of "a strict quantitative natural-science approach to the theory of behavior." He offered the hypothesis that this could be achieved by "assuming that the *forms* of the equations representing the behavioral laws of both individuals and species are identical, and that the differences between individuals and species will be found in the empirical constants which are essential components of such equations."

In 1948, Spence introduced a useful and much discussed distinction between S-R and R-R laws, as they have come to be called. The former type of law takes the form of a statement or equation that identifies a response variable as a function of stimulus-variables. The latter type defines a response variable as a function of other response variables. In other words, the S-R law enables one to predict properties of behavior from a knowledge of stimulus conditions, whereas the R-R law enables one to predict one property of behavior from a knowledge of other properties of behavior or to predict how a subject will behave in one situation from how he has behaved in other situations. Now, it is clear that specialists in personality theory have expended the bulk of their effort on working out R-R laws. In attempting to disclose the fundamental dimensions of personality, they have had to ascertain what forms of behavior tend to be found together and what characteristics can be predicted from one another. They have accordingly made great use of correlational studies and techniques such as factor analysis for analyzing correlations among traits. They have contrived measuring instruments that can be used to diagnose psychological abnormalities or to specify the educational or occupational positions to which individuals are best suited. The use of such instruments depends on R-R laws that enable patterns of behavior in a wide range of everyday situations to be inferred from behavior in the test situation.

This has undoubtedly been a further factor tending to turn behavior theorists away from the study of personality. Experimental psychologists, and behavior theorists no less than others, have always given priority to the formulation of S-R laws. They are dissatisfied with R-R laws for a number of reasons. The R-R law expresses a correlation, and it has long been realized that the existence of a correlation does not identify a causal relation: if x is significantly correlated with y, x may determine y, y may determine x, they may both influence each other, or x and y may be determined by some third factor, z. If we think of the principal aims of science as control (in the sense of making particular events more or less probable than they would otherwise have been), prediction (in the sense of anticipating future events with a greater probability of being correct than if one were to guess at random), and explanation (the aim that is hardest to characterize and the one with regard to whose achievement it is hardest to obtain agreement), we can see that, whereas an S-R law must contribute to all three of these, the R-R law can contribute only to the second. Moreover, R-R laws can be deduced from an adequate set of S-R laws, but the converse is not true.

These arguments in favor of S-R laws are powerful, but some reservations must not be overlooked. As Cattell (1957) among others has pointed out, techniques like factor analysis that have traditionally been used to analyze intercorrelations of test scores and to reveal R-R laws can be used to analyze correlations between properties or events occurring in succession, such as stimulus variables and response variables. They can thus contribute to the formulation of S-R and R-R laws simultaneously. Moreover, an adequate behavior theory must yield R-R laws as well as S-R laws. Hull's theory (1943, 1951, 1952), for example, certainly incorporated both assumptions about S-R relations and assumptions about correlations among different response properties, particularly measures of response strength. During Hull's lifetime and since, a great deal of experimentation has been devoted to the testing of the S-R predictions, and little time has been spent in testing the R-R predictions.

Yet the latter stand in need of verification and many of them are, in fact, highly questionable.

In any case, the division of psychological laws into the S-R and R-R categories is an oversimplification. Contemporary psychologists, and especially behavior theorists, make copious use of "intervening variables," as we have noted. These are essentially mathematical devices to make cumbersome relations between inputs (stimulus-variables) and outputs (response-variables) conceptually manageable. There must be some sort of correspondence, but not necessarily a one-to-one correspondence, between values of these variables and conditions within the organism that are not directly observable. Spence recognizes this and mentions two additional types of psychological laws, the one (O-R laws) identifying response variables as functions of "organic variables" (i.e., "measurements of neuroanatomical or neurophysiological properties of the organism") and the other (S-O laws) identifying organic variables as functions of stimulus variables. Most psychological laws must surely be placed in a fifth category, containing what we may call "S,O-R laws," stating how response variables are determined jointly by stimulus and organic (i.e., intervening) variables.

A number of distinctions among the organic or intervening variables are worth drawing. First, we have what we might call *transient intervening variables* (O_T), whose values change within a matter of minutes or hours, e.g., motivational condition, emotional state, mood, degree of fatigue. A second important class is *age* (O_A): developmental psychology has the responsibility of providing laws of the O_A-R and the S,O_A-R types. It tells us, in other words, how the probabilities of certain kinds of behavior over a random sample of stimulus situations will vary from age to age, and it tells us how the probabilities of particular kinds of behavior in specifiable stimulus situations change with age. Thirdly, there are intervening variables whose values may change abruptly or gradually but can remain relatively fixed thereafter for many years (O_L). These represent the results of learning processes. They comprise what we call *habits*, but factors known by many other names, e.g., "attitude," "disposition," or "motive" often qualify for this category. Finally, we have variables that take on different values for different individuals but maintain the same values throughout the lifetime of one individual (O_C). These consist, of course, of *constitutional* or *congenital predispositions* to particular kinds of behavior. The variables of concern to personality theory must clearly include those of the last category. Many individual differences, however, i.e., acquired personality traits, belong to the third category, which is one reason why some behavior theorists have been led to doubt whether personality theory requires separate treatment, feeling it to be inseparable from the study of the formation and nature of learned behavior patterns in general. Be that as it may, we must recognize as the ultimate objective of behavior theory the formulation of laws that will enable the contribution of all of these kinds of variables in the determination of behavior to be taken into account. In other words, the only fully adequate laws of psychology will be of the S,O_T,O_A,O_L,O_C-R variety.

We shall now review the main bodies of work carried out within the behavior-theory movement that are relevant to personality theory. They can be divided from the outset into two groups. First, there are investigations concerned with factors, presumed to be mostly hereditary, that affect how an individual learns. Secondly, there are investigations concerned with differences in the learning experiences to which individuals have been exposed, creating differences in what they have learned.

INDIVIDUAL DIFFERENCES
IN LEARNING CAPACITY

Pavlov's Theory of Types of Nervous System

Although the concept of "behavior theory" is not current in the U.S.S.R., we shall begin with Russian work belonging to the Pavlovian tradition, because its general aims and methodology are fully consonant with those of Western behavior theory.

PAVLOV'S EARLY THEORY. In the two translated books, *Conditioned Reflexes* (1927, Lecture XVII) and *Lectures on Conditioned Reflexes* (1928, Chapter XL), Pavlov put forward a classification of "types of nervous system" that is fairly well known in the West. He describes four types of dogs, corresponding to the four types of human temperament in the Hippocratic scheme, representing different segments of a continuum going from extreme predominance of excitatory processes to extreme predominance of inhibitory processes.

At one pole, there is the highly "excitatory" dog, corresponding to the choleric temperament, which is aggressive and hard to discipline. Such dogs form positive conditioned associations easily but have difficulty in acquiring inhibitory associations. At the opposite pole, there is the "inhibitory" type, corresponding to the melancholic temperament, with a marked preponderance of inhibitory processes, as shown by the difficulty of establishing positive conditioned responses and the ease of training in inhibition. "Everybody who sees such an animal would immediately judge it a great coward." Between these two extreme types, there are the two "central" or "equilibrated" types, in which excitatory and inhibitory processes are less disproportionate in strength, so that such dogs are less prone to neurotic breakdown. Equilibrated dogs can, however, be divided into the "sanguine" type, with a slight preponderance of excitation, and the "phlegmatic" type, with slight preponderance of inhibition. Sanguine dogs are "extremely vivacious, always sniffing at everything, gazing at everything intently, and reacting quickly to the minutest sounds." They are satisfactory subjects for conditioning experiments as long as they receive a variety of stimuli in close succession. If left unstimulated for long, they are apt to become drowsy and go to sleep. The "phlegmatic" dog is, in contrast, "self contained and quiet — a persistent and steadfast toiler in life."

PAVLOV'S LATER THEORY. As time went on, Pavlov became more and more dissatisfied with this one-dimensional classification and, after his thinking on the subject had gone through several vicissitudes, arrived at a scheme (1935a, 1935b) that is not well known in the West but has been the accepted basis for most Soviet work on individual differences ever since. He now recognized three criteria by which nervous systems could be distinguished, namely, *strength, balance,* and *mobility.* Theoretically, a nervous system could be strong or weak; it could possess equilibrium between excitatory and inhibitory processes, disequilibrium with predominance of excitation, or disequilibrium with predominance of inhibition; it could have mobile or inert inhibitory processes. This means that there could be twenty-four different types, even if simple presence or absence of a particular property were noted. If differences of degree were introduced, the number of possible types would become, of course, much greater.

In spite of the theoretical admissibility of more numerous types, Pavlov continued to insist that most dogs fall clearly into one or other of four types, corresponding to the four temperaments of Hippocrates. His accounts of the differences separating these types had, however, undergone great changes since he formulated his earlier theory. He now identified the "choleric" with a *strong, unbalanced* nervous system, having a preponderance of excitation over inhibition, the "sanguine" type with a *strong, balanced, mobile* nervous system, the "phlegmatic" type with a *strong, balanced, inert* nervous system, and the "melancholic" type with a *weak* nervous system.

The *strength* of the nervous system is manifested by an animal's resistance to "passive" forms of inhibition. Western psychologists are generally familiar with the "active" or "internal" forms of inhibition that were fully described in the most familiar translated writings; this is the kind of inhibition responsible for extinction, differentiation, conditioned inhibition, and inhibition of delay. However, Pavlov also recognized "passive" inhibition, representing not simply temporary weakening of conditioned associations but temporary suppression of them by competing factors. An example of this is "external inhibition," which occurs whenever a novel, extraneous stimulus is presented at a time when an animal would otherwise be performing a conditioned response. In later writings (e.g., 1928), he attributed external inhibition to "negative induction" (i.e., the induction of inhibition in neighboring parts of the cerebral cortex when a strong excitatory process is generated at one locus) due to the powerful "orientation reaction" (i.e., exploratory and attentive activities) evoked by the extraneous stimulus. He also paid increasing attention to "transmarginal" or "supramaximal" inhibition. This is a protective process that intervenes when the nervous system is subjected to excess excitation, e.g., by inordinately intense, novel, or prolonged stimuli. It results in the paradoxical appearance of weaker responses to stronger conditioned stimuli (contravening the usual trend, which was called the "law of strength") or by the absence of any response at all to a stimulus productive of intolerable levels of excitation.

Pavlov (1935b) outlined the following procedures as methods for gauging the strength or weakness of the nervous system:

1. An attempt is made to establish a conditioned salivary response to the extremely loud sound of a rattle as well as to other, more moderate stimuli. Strong dogs will respond to the rattle as intensely, if not more intensely, as to the other stimuli. In weak dogs, the response to the rattle will be weaker or it will be absent altogether, and it may even give rise to a neurotic breakdown.

2. Excitatory processes are strengthened by starving the dog before the conditioning session begins. This will give rise to more pronounced conditioning responses than usual in animals of strong types, but it will diminish conditioned salivation in animals of the weak type.

3. The third technique (which has become the standard test for strength of the nervous system among Pavlov's successors studying animal behavior) depends on administration of caffeine, and this likewise heightens conditioned responses in strong nervous systems but produces decreased responding, indicative or supramaximal inhibition, in weak nervous systems.

4. The dog is conditioned to a conditioned stimulus which, in early trials, is followed by the presentation of food after a second or two. The delay is then increased to 20–30 seconds. In a strong nervous system, the amount of salivation will increase steadily from the onset of the stimulus to the moment when food is due, but, in weak nervous systems, there will be a steady decline in salivation or else irregular fluctuations.

Although imbalance could in principle take the form of either a deficiency of inhibition or a deficiency of excitation, Pavlov insisted that the latter was rarely if ever encountered; so estimating the degree of balance amounted to measurement of the *strength of inhibitory processes*. Pavlov described a number of ways of doing this:

1. An inhibitory conditioned stimulus is prolonged in order to ascertain the duration of inhibition that the nervous system can stand. If inhibitory processes are strong, unheralded prolongation of the stimulus up to 5–10 minutes will produce little or no disturbance. If inhibitory processes are weak, the continuation of a stimulus that has usually lasted 15 seconds for an additional 15 seconds may be seriously disruptive; a duration of 5 minutes, introduced even once, leads to a "collapse of all conditioned-reflex activity, in the form of a lasting neurosis."

2. According to Pavlov, both excitatory and inhibitory processes, having been set up in one location in the cerebral cortex, will first irradiate over

a wide expanse of cortical regions and then concentrate, producing opposite processes ("negative induction" and "positive induction" respectively) in adjacent regions. Animals with strong inhibitory processes will show great capacity for rapid and narrow concentration. So if a positive conditioned stimulus is presented shortly after a negative or inhibitory stimulus, an unbalanced nervous system, weak in inhibition, will show an inhibitory after-effect, whereas strength of inhibition will be manifested through positive induction, i.e., the positive stimulus will evoke a more intense response than usual.

3. A nervous system that is weak in inhibition will form inhibitory associations slowly, and they will always be somewhat unstable.

4. An unbalanced nervous system will be unable to develop inhibitory associations if attempts are made to establish these concurrently with positive conditioned responses.

5. In an animal with an unbalanced nervous system, anything more than a small dose of a bromide will cause conditioned-reflex activity to disappear, whereas animals with stronger inhibitory processes will withstand larger doses.

The *mobility* factor had been little studied when Pavlov wrote the article (1935b) whose content we are reviewing. But he mentions three ways in which degree of mobility might be measured.

1. If the conditioned stimulus is made to act for a long time before the unconditioned stimulus appears, an inert nervous system will have difficulty in forming a delayed conditioned response; the necessity of changing over from inhibition to excitation at the appropriate moment will exceed its capacity.

2. The inert nervous system has difficulty in responding appropriately when a positive conditioned stimulus closely follows a negative conditioned stimulus or vice versa. The process of excitation or inhibition induced by the first stimulus tends to persist during the application of the second. One particularly effective test is to subject the animal to a situation in which the same conditioned stimulus is presented four times consecutively, being reinforced with food after the last of the four presentations. The inert nervous system is unable to refrain from salivation at the first three presentations and then to salivate during the fourth. Animals with low mobility will likewise be disturbed by a "change in stereotype," i.e., a change in the habitual order of presentation of a series of intermingled positive and negative stimuli. The change may cause all conditioned salivary responses to disappear for days, whereas the dog with high mobility will regularly respond or not respond to a stimuli, as appropriate, despite the order in which they appear.

3. If a positive conditioned stimulus is to be turned into a negative one, by ceasing to pair it with the unconditioned stimulus, or vice versa, the mobile nervous system will acquire the new association quickly and easily whereas the inert nervous system will do so slowly and imperfectly.

MORE RECENT WORK WITH DOGS. During a visit to the Pavlov Institute of Experimental Psychology at Kol'tushi near Lenigrad, in 1961, the writer found the study of individual differences in dogs continuing to be assiduously pursued. A conversation with Professor Krasuski disclosed that the caffeine test is now the standard procedure for measuring strength, and attempting to turn positive into negative conditioned stimuli and vice versa is the usual method for measuring mobility. There is no one procedure in use for measuring balance, but, in general, the ease of establishing differential and other inhibitory associations is examined. The bromide test for inhibitory processes and the sudden replacement of a positive by a negative conditioned stimulus or vice versa as a test for mobility have both been given up as insufficiently reliable.

In a recent article, Krasuski (1963) describes 48 types of dogs that his investigations have led him to distinguish. He recognizes four levels of "strength," depending on the dose of caffeine that is necessary to produce supramaximal inhibition, and three levels of "balance," depending on the ratio of the amplitude of response to a differential stimulus and the amplitude of response to a positive conditioned stimulus. "Mobility" has four levels: when a positive conditioned stimulus is turned into a negative one and vice versa, the changeover may be successful or unsuccessful, and the reversal of effect may be equal or unequal for the two stimuli involved. Finer distinctions can be made with regard to the "mobility" dimension by taking into account exactly how effective the changeover is for the two stimuli, how permanent it is, and how many trials are required to establish it. In this way, a tenfold classification can be made along the "mobility" dimension, resulting in 120 types.

One topic of concentration at Kol'tushi is the role of genetic factors in the determination of type of nervous system. It had been found that environment could modify behavior so as to produce behavior characteristic of a particular type. For example, dogs reared in restricted environments behave like animals with weak nervous systems even if born of strong parents. They do not actively investigate novel stimuli but show arrested movement and widespread inhibition (what Pavlovians called the "passive-defensive reflex"). The findings of Melzack (1954) and Melzack and Scott (1957), who likewise studied differences in emotional behavior between normally reared and restricted dogs, may be compared.

Similarly, nutrition makes a difference. If better-than-usual food is fed to the mother during pregnancy and to the offspring for the first year of life, strength will be increased in both constitutionally strong and constitutionally weak individuals. Nevertheless, the next generation will revert to type, showing that these environmentally induced changes have simply masked constitutional characteristics.

Experiments were under way to ascertain whether heredity effects in underlying strength and mobility are dominant or recessive. It was conjectured that they must be recessive, since weak or inert nervous systems are maladaptive.

Then, physiological correlates of the Pavlovian traits were under investigation. It had been found that mobile adults are more generally active, as shown by a stabilimeter test, than inert dogs, and balanced slightly more active than unbalanced, but there was little difference between strong and weak animals. In strong dogs, inflammation of the skin induced by cantharides or by ultra-violet rays occurs more rapidly, the effects of ACTH are more pronounced, and abscesses are produced much more slowly by turpentine. This suggests that, in strong animals, the corrective reactions of the body are prompter and more efficient.

EXTENSION TO HUMAN BEINGS. Among Pavlov's students, the pioneers in applying conditioned-response techniques to human subjects were Krasno-gorski and Ivanov-Smolenski. Both specialized in child subjects, but they made use of different experimental techniques. Krasnogorski devised a variant of the original salivary conditioning technique used with dogs. The uncondi-tioned stimulus consisted of an edible substance, usually some sort of cran-berry puree, delivered into the child's mouth through a spout. The responses investigated consisted of mechanically recorded masticatory movements and the secretion of saliva, collected through a metal device placed in the child's mouth. Ivanov-Smolenski and his followers originated a "motor-conditioning" procedure. The response consisted of pressing a rubber bulb, connected with a kymograph by means of a rubber tube so that the slightest variations in pressure could be registered, and the unconditioned stimulus consisted of hearing the word "Press!" uttered by the experimenter. Inhibitory associations were set up by having the experimenter say "Don't press!" immediately after the presentation of the stimuli that were to be negative. Various events — visual, auditory, etc. — were used as conditioned stimuli in both laboratories.

Both Krasnogorski (1958) and Ivanov-Smolenski (Briks, 1956) applied their conditioning methods to the investigation of individual differences in chil-dren. In Ivanov-Smolenski's laboratory, the method of free association to verbal stimuli was also tried out. Four types of children, corresponding to the four types of nervous system figuring in Pavlov's later classificatory scheme, were found to exist in both laboratories.

The descriptions given by Krasnogorski and by Briks were in agreement with each other and with Pavlov's descriptions of the corresponding types of dogs, except for a few details. For example, Briks writes that children of the weak type are characterized by an absence of generalization whereas Kras-nogorski mentions "generalized irradiation" and "reduction in processes of concentration" as typical of them. In general, however, both writers depict the strength of the nervous system as manifested by a resistance to passive forms of inhibition and a capacity for connected speech of high quality. Kras-nogorski mentions emotional reactions, signifying relative lack of dominance by the cortex of subcortical centers, as an additional manifestation of weak-ness, as well as the proneness to neurotic symptoms mentioned by Pavlov. Strength of excitatory and inhibitory processes is revealed through the speed with which positive or negative associations are established, stability of these associations, and response latency. Children of the choleric (strong, unbalanced) type tend to give several words as a response in the free-association test and to engage in motor activity at the same time. Mobility is shown by the capacity to change abruptly from inhibition to excitation, e.g., when a prolonged conditioned stimulus is at last accompanied by the unconditioned stimulus.

Rabinovich (1961) has related Pavlov's concept of mobility to that adopted by the St. Petersburg University school of physiologists led by Vvedenski and Ukhtomski. Vvedenski regarded mobility as a matter of the number of electrical "oscillations" that neural tissue can support within a unit of time. Rabinovich measures mobility with the help of an apparatus that presents a light repeatedly for a brief period. The subject is instructed to turn off the light with a switch before it goes off by itself. By varying the frequency with which the light appears, the rate at which the subject can respond is ascertained.

Rogov *et al.* (1964) have related the Pavlovian typology to vasomotor reactions. Their investigations indicate that strong balanced individuals have plethysmograms with steady base-lines and that both their conditioned and unconditioned vasoconstrictions (cold being the unconditioned stimulus) are high in amplitude and stable. When the nervous system is strong but unbalanced, the base-line is wavy, and conditioned and unconditioned vasomotor reflexes fluctuate in amplitude. Subjects with weak nervous systems have flat base-lines; their unconditioned reflexes are "inert and small," while their conditioned reflexes are slight and unstable.

The most thoroughgoing effort to study human individual differences with the guidance of Pavlov's classificatory concepts was headed by Teplov (1956, 1961) at the Institute of Psychology of the Academy of Pedagogical Sciences in Moscow. An extremely helpful compilation of material in English on the work of this group and on the development of the Pavlovian approach to individual differences has appeared under Gray's (1965) editorship. Teplov deliberately rejected the motor-conditioning method adopted by Ivanov-Smolenski, following Pavlov's criticism that this method must involve the intervention of thought processes, as the child tries to puzzle out what is required of him in this situation, and thus does not represent typical conditioning. There is actually evidence (Paramanova, 1956) that this is true of older children, whereas, at about the age of three, a direct conditioned association between the conditioned stimulus and motor response is set up. There are some interesting and striking differences, e.g., in latency, stability, and speed of forming associations, between the two cases.

At any rate, Teplov argued in favor of involuntary responses as indices of the characteristics in which he was interested. His group relies heavily on the "conditioned proto-chemical reflex" discovered by Dolin. The unconditioned response is the decrease in visual sensitivity brought on by brief exposure to an intense, uniform patch of light. If an auditory stimulus is immediately coupled with exposure to the light, it may come to evoke a conditioned rise in threshold. All the standard conditioning phenomena can, it is claimed, be detected and measured with this method. Other procedures are used to supplement it, and more recently, conditioned EEG alpha blocking, with a flashbulb light as the unconditioned stimulus and a tone as the conditioned stimulus, has been used.

The assumption that the processes under study can be accounted for in terms of Pavlov's dimensions and the assumption that the various aspects of behavior regarded as indices of a particular dimension are actually intercorrelated seem to call for statistical tests. Recently, members of Teplov's group have begun to make use of the kinds of statistical techniques that Western psychologists would apply in these circumstances. They have examined the hypothesis that " 'strength' of a nervous system is correlated with low reactivity, hence with low sensitivity to peripheral stimulation" (Nebylitsyn, Rozhdestvenskaia, and Teplov, 1960), finding that persons with strong nervous systems (ascertained by measuring supermaximal inhibition, with or without caffeine, in a conditioned-photochemical-response situation) have significantly higher visual and auditory absolute thresholds. Significant positive correlations have been found among certain measures of EEG activity assumed to be indices of balance, e.g., the speed with which alpha waves return after the presentation of a tone alone or of a tone that has been paired with light, the rapidity with which repeated presentation of a tone produces extinction, duration of alpha blocking to the tone before or after conditioning, and the speed with which differentiation between tones of two pitches is set up (Nebylitsyn, 1961). A Thurstone-type factor analysis of intercorrelations among 21 suspected indices of strength of nervous system (Rozhdestvenskaia, Nebylitsyn, Borisova, and Ermolaeva-Tomina, 1960) revealed a factor on which thirteen of the measures have significant loadings. On the other hand, four indices, relating to amplitude and speed of extinction of vasomotor orientation reactions, which have traditionally been regarded by Pavlovians as indices of strength, had small loadings on the first factor but high loadings on the second factor, identified with balance. A more recent factor analysis of 18 EEG variables (Nebylitsyn, 1963) produced four centroid factors. The first three were identified with "balance," "excitatory strength," and "alpha-reactivity" respectively, while the fourth was found difficult to interpret and left unnamed.

Finally, Teplov and his collaborators have attempted to identify the general psychological characteristics that go together with the variables on which the type of nervous system depends, which means extending the Pavlovian theory of individual differences to the elucidation of temperament (Leites, 1956). Strength of excitatory processes is said to go together with a capacity to handle complex materials perceptually and intellectually, as well as with ability to withstand prolonged tension and to recover quickly from fatigue. Persons with strong inhibitory processes tend to concentrate their attention effectively, terminate and restrain their activities where appropriate, write and speak concisely, and generally exercise self-control. Weakness in both excitation and inhibition means inability to concentrate, lack of capacity for intellectual work, lack of initiative and perseverance. The signs of a balanced nervous system include placidity, freedom from impetuousity in thought, speech, and action, and immunity to neurotic disturbance. High mobility implies adaptiveness and flexibility in rapidly changing conditions. Teplov's group recognizes, however, that innate properties of the nervous system interact with learning to produce "character," so that "genotypes" must not be confused with "phenotypes."

Later findings led Teplov (1963) to the conclusion that the strength of excitatory processes and the strength of inhibitory processes should be recognized as separate traits rather than lumped together under the label of "strength of nervous system" in accordance with the traditional practice. Furthermore, factor-analytic data compelled him to distinguish two kinds of lability, one pertaining to the ease with which excitatory stimuli can become inhibitory and vice versa, the other to the speed with which neural processes are set off and arrested.

Nebylitsyn (1966), Teplov's successor, now regards equilibrium as a "secondary property of the nervous system," depending on primary properties (strength, mobility, dynamism) of both excitation and inhibition. Dynamism is now regarded as a separate parameter, distinct from strength. It is reflected in the speed with which conditioned (excitatory or inhibitory) connections are formed and in the magnitude and rate of extinction of EEG desynchronization and of the components of the orientation reaction.

PSYCHOLOGICAL ABNORMALITIES. One of Pavlov's most celebrated contributions to personality theory is his inauguration of the study of experimental neurosis. In *Conditioned Reflexes* (1927), he tells of a number of ways in which behavior apparently analogous to human neurotic breakdowns can be induced in dogs. They comprise (1) exposure to a stimulus midway between a positive conditioned stimulus (a circle) and a differential inhibitory stimulus (an ellipse), (2) the use of an excessively intense electric shock as a conditioned stimulus reinforced with food, (3) the sudden replacement of a positive conditioned stimulus (24 tactual stimulations per minute) by an inhibitory stimulus (12 tactual stimulations per minute), (4) extreme prolongation of the conditioned stimulus (a buzzer) before delivery of food, (5) training in extremely difficult discriminations, (6) exposure to "powerful and unusual stimuli" due to a flood.

It is evident that individual dogs will vary widely in susceptibility to experimental neurosis and in the kinds of behavior shown when experimental neurosis occurs. In accordance with his first typology, Pavlov began with the view that neurosis is most likely in animals representing extreme preponderance of excitation (the choleric type) or extreme preponderance of inhibition (the melancholic type). In the former, neurosis meant a loss of inhibitory associations and violent motor activity, which he compared with neurasthenia. Dogs at the opposite extreme showed weakening of excitatory associations and abnormal immobility, which he compared with hysteria (Pavlov, 1928, p. 375).

Later, his typology changed, as we have seen, and, in the final years of his life, he became intensely interested in psychological abnormality. He spent a great deal of time observing human patients exhibiting various disorders and attempting to interpret their symptoms with reference to his concepts (Pavlov, 1941; Ivanov-Smolenski, 1954). He still regarded choleric and melancholic nervous systems as those most prone to psychopathological disorders, regarding imbalance and weakness as relatively maladaptive properties. He related these two types, in fact, to Kretschmer's *cyclothymia* and *schizothymia* respectively.

In *schizophrenia,* he noted an intense susceptibility of the cerebral cortex to passive inhibition producing, in extreme cases, symptoms like mutism and catatonia. Through disinhibition and positive induction, older processes which had long been subject to inhibition are restored. Infantile behavior and automatism appear, or unconditioned postural reflexes may be liberated from cortical control to produce catalepsy. Focal disturbances at various points in the cortex create disintegration. *Paranoia* results from pathological inertness of excitation together with a decline in active inhibitory processes, which are responsible for correction of tendencies to delusion in normal persons. As for *manic-depressive psychosis,* there was held to be extreme excitation in the manic phase, with an insufficiency of the "abating and restorative process" that normally comes from supramaximal inhibition.

In interpreting neurotic syndromes, Pavlov refers to an additional dimension of personality that he came to recognize as he turned his attention late in life to human behavior. "Life," he writes, "definitely uses two categories of people — artists and thinkers.... The artists ... comprehend reality as a whole, as a continuity, as a complete living reality, without any divisions, without any separation. The other group, the thinkers, pull it apart, kill it, so to speak, making out of it a temporary skeleton and then only gradually putting it together anew occasionally ..." (Pavlov, 1941, pp. 113–114). The character of the thinker reveals dominance of the "second signal system" (i.e., verbal behavior and responses to verbal stimuli) over "the first signal system" (i.e., behavior involving nonverbal stimuli and responses), whereas, in the artist, the first signal system is on top.

Pavlov regarded *neurasthenia* as the kind of disturbance to which dogs and human beings with weak or unbalanced nervous systems are liable, but he distinguished a "hypersthenic" form, with a preponderance of excitation, from a "hyposthenic" form, with a preponderance of inhibition, as well as cases in which periods of excitation and activity alternate with periods of "weakness and temporary wear." Then, in addition, there are the two uniquely human conditions of *psychasthenia* and *hysteria,* representing accentuations of the "thinking" and "artistic" types respectively. Psychasthenia may include compulsive actions and obsessive thoughts, showing, in their perseveration, psychological inertness with inadequate inhibition, but there may also be obsessive fears (phobias) and inabilities to act, which means that inhibition has overstepped normal bounds. Hysteria involves inhibition of particular functions or of widespread systems of conditioned associations (e.g., amnesias). Subcortical functions may be manifestly out of control due to weakness of the higher parts of the central nervous system. Hysterics are prone to suggestion and to hypnotism, in which a focus of excitation is allowed free play as potentially interfering processes are disabled through negative induction.

Pavlov, as well as his collaborators and successors, paid some attention to therapeutic measures. He recommended administration of bromide as a means of strengthening inhibitory processes and thus overcoming either pathologically inert excitation or unbalanced conditions in which inhibition is unduly overwhelmed by excitation. Prolonged narcosis and other conditions conducive to rest were widely used for the treatment of cases in which the protective effects of supramaximal inhibition, whose restorative power Pavlov continually stressed, were deficient. In the early years of conditioned-response research, a period of respite from experimentation had been found the best way to deal with dogs suffering from an excess of inhibition (Pavlov, 1927, p. 317).

Eysenck and the Maudsley Group

TAXONOMIC STUDIES. Early in his research career, Eysenck (1947, 1952a) was a personality theorist in the tradition of Spearman and Burt, believing that the highest priority should be assigned to taxonomic problems and that factor analysis and related statistical techniques form the most valuable aids to their solution. His first major study (1947) was one in which information about the presence of symptoms and other traits and about previous life-history was collected for 700 neurotic patients in a military hospital and the data were factor-analyzed. The outcome was the identification of two major personality factors labeled *neuroticism* and *introversion-extraversion*. The Maudsley Medical Questionnaire and, later, the Maudsley Personality Inventory (MPI) and Eysenck Personality Inventory (EPI) were subsequently published as means of measuring these factors.

Neuroticism was conceived as a dimension on which neurotics have higher scores than normal persons. It seemed to be close to the "*w*" factor that Webb (1915) had introduced in the early days of factor analysis and described as "prominent on the 'character' side of mental activity," reflecting "persistence of motives," "consistency of action resulting from deliberate volition or will"; low "*w*" corresponds, of course, to high neuroticism. Persons tending towards the two poles of the introversion-extraversion dimension were characterized as follows (Eysenck, 1947): "(a) the introvert has a more subjective, the extravert a more objective outlook; (b) the introvert shows a higher degree of cerebral activity, the extravert a higher degree of behavioral activity; (c) the introvert shows a tendency to self-control (inhibition), the extravert a tendency to lack of self-control." Introverts high in neuroticism tended to develop "dysthymic" disorders, i.e., anxiety state, obsessive-compulsive neurosis, or reactive depression, whereas hysterics and psychopaths appeared to be high in neuroticism and extraversion.

A review of the previous literature on personality classification (Eysenck, 1953) showed that, despite wide differences in the kinds of data collected and in methods of analysis, dimensions close to neuroticism and introversion-extraversion had emerged time after time under different names. Sometimes investigators appeared to have discovered the same factor space with the reference vectors rotated. At other times, typologies had been suggested that could readily be related to Eysenck's two-dimensional scheme. For example, the fourfold Hippocratic classification that so many psychologists of recent times (including Pavlov) have felt unable to reject has been assimilated by Eysenck (1963a) by identifying the melancholic type with unstable (i.e., relatively neurotic) introverts, the choleric type with unstable extraverts, the phlegmatic type with stable introverts, and the sanguine type with stable extraverts.

Studies subjecting normal and psychologically abnormal subjects to a variety of experimental situations have brought to light several significant differences separating neurotics from normal individuals and introverts from extraverts. As this work proceeded, it became apparent that a third dimension, labeled *psychoticism* since it distinguished psychotics from both neurotics and normals, should be added (Eysenck, 1952a; S. B. G. Eysenck, H. J. Eysenck, and Claridge, 1960).

PERSONALITY AND CONDITIONING. In the mid-1950's, Eysenck became committed to the enterprise of relating differences in personality to concepts of behavior theory, with the aim of giving personality theory a firm footing in general psychology (1955, 1957). After turning to the works of Pavlov and Hull for guidance he formulated a *Postulate of Individual Differences* stating that:

> Human beings differ with respect to the speed at which excitation and inhibition are produced, the strength of excitation and inhibition produced, and the speed at which inhibition is dissipated. These differences are properties of the physical structures involved in making stimulus-connections (Eysenck, 1957).

He added a *Typological Postulate*, according to which

> Individuals in whom excitatory potential is generated slowly and in whom excitatory potentials so generated are relatively weak, are thereby predisposed to develop extraverted patterns of behavior and to develop hysterical-psychopathic disorders in cases of neurotic breakdown; individuals in whom excitatory potential is generated quickly and in whom excitatory potentials so generated are strong, are thereby predisposed to develop

introverted patterns of behavior and to develop dysthymic disorders in case of neurotic breakdown. Similarly, individuals in whom reactive inhibition is developed quickly, in whom strong reactive inhibitions are generated, and in whom reactive inhibition is dissipated slowly, are thereby predisposed to develop extraverted patterns of behavior and to develop hysterical-psychopathic disorders in case of neurotic breakdown; conversely, individuals in whom reactive inhibition is developed slowly, in whom weak reactive inhibitions are generated, and in whom reactive inhibition is dissipated quickly, are thereby predisposed to develop introverted patterns of behavior and to develop dysthymic disorders in case of neurotic breakdown.

It was deduced from these postulates that introverts will acquire conditioned responses more quickly than extraverts and take longer to show extinction when a conditioned response ceases to be reinforced.

The hypothesis that extraverts have more inhibition than introverts must seem rather paradoxical, since introverts are generally thought of as more "inhibited," i.e., more reserved and restrained, less likely to express themselves easily or to behave impulsively. Eysenck overcomes this difficulty by postulating that the introvert is more "socialized." He has learned more effectively than the extravert to conform to social norms and to avoid behavior that might incur social disapproval. He has a relative preoccupation with "social duties, ethics, guilt, and similar moral notions." In his opinions on moral, social, and political matters, he is apt to be "tender-minded," i.e., to be governed by ethical and religious ideals and to be opposed to overgratification of sexual and aggressive impulses (Eysenck, 1954, 1957). Since moral training and socialization depend largely on the acquisition of instrumental avoidance responses and conditioned fear responses, the presumption is that the introvert's superior aptitude for rapid and effective conditioning will make him acquire these behavior patterns to a fuller degree than the extravert. Thus, "a smaller degree of reactive inhibition" makes for "a greater degree of social inhibition." The proneness of the dysthymic, or introverted neurotic, to anxiety is claimed as corroboration of this hypothesis.

The postulate of individual differences was tested in two experiments performed by Franks. The first of them (1956) showed the frequency of conditioned eyeblink responses during conditioning and subsequent extinction to be significantly higher for dysthymics than for hysterics. GSR was also recorded and yielded the same results. Normal subjects came between the two neurotic groups in eyelid responses but were not significantly different from hysterics. They were quite close to the hysterics in GSR incidence. The second experiment (1957a) used non-neurotic subjects throughout. The number of conditioned eyeblink responses was found to be significantly higher in introverts than in extraverts but not significantly related to neuroticism.

CRITICISMS AND QUERIES. Eysenck (e.g., 1957) claimed strong support for his Postulate of Individual Differences from Franks's findings, as well as from investigations of other forms of behavior, e.g., kinesthetic figural after-effects and dark adaptation. His position underwent, however, a number of quite vituperative attacks (e.g., Hamilton, 1959; Lykken, 1959; Storms and Sigal, 1958), to which Eysenck retorted no less forthrightly (1959b, 1959c, 1960b).

Some criticisms were aimed at ambiguities in Eysenck's assertions. They brought up such questions as which of several possible parameters descriptive of excitatory and inhibitory processes are to be regarded as crucial, whether more frequent responses during conditioning can be said to indicate a high rate of conditioning, whether dysthymics may have shown more conditioned blinking because they were more reactive from the start. With regard to these points, Eysenck could be defended on the grounds that he was opening up new and long overdue lines of research and that what was needed at that juncture was a set of hypotheses precise enough to indicate empirical relations worthy of investigation but imprecise enough to be progressively filed down as research progressed. That a strategy of gradual zeroing-in may be conducive to the advancement of science can be justified on information-theoretic grounds (Broadbent, 1956; Berlyne, 1964).

More substantive questions were, however, raised as well:

1. Differences in the rate at which inhibition is accumulated should affect the ease of acquiring any kind of learned response. Should it not first have been established that subjects tend to be consistently high or low in conditionability and resistance to extinction over a wide variety of conditioning situations? Campbell (1938) failed to find significant correlations between measures of the strength of conditioned eyeblink and patellar reflexes. Davidson, Payne, and Sloane (1964) examined conditioned finger-withdrawal responses and GSRs to a tone, with electric shock as the unconditioned stimulus, and found a negligible correlation between the strengths of the two kinds of conditioned response. If there is not a general factor of conditionability, might not the differences between introverts and extraverts observed by Franks be restricted to eyelid conditioning? Davidson, Payne, and Sloane obtained no significant correlations between any of their conditioning measures and either neuroticism or extraversion.

On the other hand, significant tendencies for extravert normals and alcoholics to show less GSR conditioning have been found by Vogel (1960, 1961). Franks (1956), it will be remembered, obtained more GSR conditioning from dysthymics than from hysterics, and Halberstam (1961) obtained a comparable difference between subjects scoring high on the Psychasthenia and Hysteria scales, respectively, of the MMPI.

Willett (1960) found a significant negative correlation between extraversion and salivary-conditioning scores in a pilot experiment, but, in a large-scale study conducted subsequently, only a small, insignificant negative correlation was obtained. There was an insignificant negative correlation between extraversion and the rate of progress towards probability matching in a binary guessing situation, while a "spatial-conditioning" procedure, designed to find out how far sound would be wrongly localized in the direction of a simultaneously presented light, yielded a significant negative correlation between extraversion and tendency to perceive the sound displaced towards the light. Willett concludes, however, that these last two tasks did not represent true conditioning. It cannot, however, be denied that they measured either learning in the experimental situation or the effectiveness of previous learning, and the Postulate of Individual Differences should presumably apply to learning in general. Nevertheless, there may well have been all sorts of complicating factors in these less automatic forms of behavior.

2. Do dysthymics and hysterics form suitable criterion groups for introversion and extraversion respectively? Might they not differ in other respects that could account for the differences that distinguish them in eyeblink conditioning? Hysterics have been found to occupy intermediate positions between dysthymics and normals on measures of neuroticism in studies by Claridge and Herrington (1960) and Sigal, Star, and Franks (1958). Might dysthymics and hysterics differ in drive level, which would certainly be expected to affect rate of conditioning? Has the predicted difference between introverts and extraverts been established in normal populations?

Some of the force of these questions was removed by Franks's (1957a) experiment in which introverted normals performed more conditioned eyeblinks than extraverted normals. However, Willett (1960) cites four experiments, including his own, in which correlations between extraversion in normal subjects and eyeblink conditioning were examined. He notes that Franks (1957a) was the only experimenter to find a significant correlation in the predicted direction.

Two more recent experiments (Spence and Spence, 1964; Franks, 1963b) could be added to those that failed to confirm Franks's original finding to a statistically significant extent. Eysenck (1965) has since reviewed studies relating level of conditioning to extraversion. He reports a significant confirmation of his hypothesis in six out of eleven partial-reinforcement eyeblink-conditioning studies, in two out of four continuous-reinforcement eyeblink-conditioning studies, and in five out of nine GSR-conditioning studies. No significant differences or correlations in the opposite direction are reported, and all but one of the nonsignificant correlations specified are negative. He discusses variations in procedure that might account for those results that fail to demonstrate a negative relation between conditioning and extraversion. Franks (1963b), in a recent article summing up the current status of this line of research, reviews several attitudinal and other factors that are known to affect conditioning scores in human subjects and whose independent fluctuations must tend to lessen correlations between conditioning measures and measures of basic personality factors.

3. Willett expresses doubt that the MPI is a satisfactory instrument for measuring extraversion, mentioning that differences between extraverts and introverts in experimental tasks have sometimes turned out to be more clear-

cut when subjects are placed in these two categories on the basis of ratings of behavior rather than of MPI scores alone. A study by Franks, Holden, and Phillips (1961) revealed that ratings by external observers and self-ratings in the form of answers to items from the MPI were reliably correlated in normal subjects. In an abnormal population, external ratings, while showing a high inter-judge reliability, tended to be uncorrelated with MPI self-ratings. Eysenck and Eysenck (1963) have recently acknowledged that the extraversion scale derived from the MPI can be regarded as measuring two oblique factors with a .5 correlation between them and reflecting "impulsiveness" and "sociability" respectively. These are reminiscent of the two forms of extraversion that Guilford and Guilford (1934) differentiated some time ago. So there is clearly room for more progress to be made in analyzing the introversion-extraversion dimension and in devising measure for it.

4. The one distinguishing mark of internal inhibition (Pavlov, 1927) or reactive inhibition (Hull, 1943) is the fact that it dissipates, producing spontaneous recovery, after a rest. Is not therefore reminiscence (the improvement in performance that appears immediately after a rest period) the crucial test of the postulate of individual differences? Should not Franks have brought back his subjects after, say, an interval of 24 hours and measured spontaneous recovery if he wished to demonstrate decisively that differences of inhibitory potential were responsible for his findings? Franks (1963a) has found that subjects performing more conditioned eyeblink responses during training are likely to have higher reminiscence scores. He did not compare introverts and extraverts in this study, but some corroboration is provided for the assumption that differences in performance during conditioning reflect differences in the quantity of inhibition accumulated.

RECENT DEVELOPMENTS. Since the publications that embroiled him in these controversies, Eysenck and his associates have conducted further studies from which they claim further substantiation of their taxonomic scheme (Eysenck, Eysenck, and Claridge, 1960; Eysenck and Claridge, 1962), making use of the new technique of canonical variate analysis. They have, moreover, come to rely on pursuit-rotor and other skilled manual tasks, rather than on conditioning, in seeking empirical support for their hypotheses. Eysenck (1962) cites twenty investigations using techniques of this kind, some, but not all, of which verify that extraverted normal subjects show greater reminiscence. Claridge (1960) confirmed expectations derived from the hypothesis that hysterics are more susceptible to inhibition than dysthymics, obtaining from them a poorer over-all performance and a steeper decline in a vigilance task, greater reminiscence in a pursuit-rotor task, and shorter-lasting after-effects of fixating a rotating spiral.

Complications have arisen, however, with respect to the role of differences in drive or arousal. Eysenck and his colleagues (Eysenck and Maxwell, 1961) were compelled, as their work with the pursuit-rotor continued, to recognize the validity of a theory originally presented by Kimble (1949), according to

which there must be a close relation between drive level and the amount
of inhibition that is acquired. According to the theory, amount of inhibition
is limited by the fact that subjects give themselves brief rest pauses whenever
inhibition reaches a critical level and thus prevent inhibition from going
higher. The critical level — the maximum amount of inhibition that will be
tolerated — is, in its turn, held to vary directly with the level of drive. In
view of evidence for processes of this kind, Eysenck has recently (1962) modified his Postulate of Individual Differences. He now maintains that extraverts
generate reactive inhibition more quickly than introverts and dissipate it more
slowly but that they do not necessarily accumulate more inhibition.

As Eysenck (1962) concedes, we might expect introverts to have higher
prevailing levels of drive, since most motivation in human beings must be
secondary or acquired motivation and introverts, being more conditionable,
should be more susceptible to the kinds of conditioning that engender secondary drive. Evidence that dysthymics exceed hysterics in their prevailing
level of drive or arousal has come from Claridge's (1960) study, already mentioned, from an investigation of sedation threshold (Claridge and Herrington,
1960), and from an investigation of performance on a paced five-choice serial
reaction-time task (Claridge, 1961). Claridge suggests that the "excitation-
inhibition balance assumed to underlie the dimension of extraversion" may
undergo shifts dependent on arousal level. "If this were true," he writes, "then
it would mean that, for example, the lower arousal (excitation) level in hysterics would result in a relatively speedier growth of inhibition in these patients than would be predictable from their position on the extraversion-
introversion continuum."

PHYSIOLOGICAL SPECULATIONS. Guided by a study of Wenger's (1948),
showing that persons diagnosed as neurotics significantly surpass normals on
a number of indices of sympathetic-nervous-system activity, Eysenck proposes the identification of his neuroticism factor with "automatic lability,"
meaning predominance of sympathetic functions. He concludes from this
that neurotics are distinguished from normals by a higher level of drive.
This may be a slightly precarious step, since, although there is some evidence
(see Berlyne, 1960, 1963a; Malmo, 1959) that indices of sympathetic activity
are increased by some recognized drive conditions, it has by no means been
established that high sympathetic activity always means a rise in drive with
all its connotations. There is some apparent tendency for states of high drive
to be experienced and reported as unpleasant. Neurotics are frequently un-
happier than normals, but are they always? The *"belle indifférence"* of the
hysteric is well-known, and some unpleasant states, e.g., depressions, may well
go together with lowered drive. Injections of adrenalin, which produce most
of the manifestations of high sympathetic activity, may in some conditions
give rise to euphoria (Schachter and Singer, 1962).

As for the introversion-extraversion dimension, Eysenck (1963a, p. 7) asks
"Is it possible to locate any structure within the nervous system which may

be responsible for individual differences in these mysterious processes of exci-tation and inhibition? I would suggest that the ascending reticular formation may fit this prescription reasonably well." This speculation is supported by studies suggesting that stimulant drugs shift behavior in an introverted direc-tion, whereas depressive drugs, e.g., amytal, have the opposite effect. For example, d-amphetamine sulfate raises performance during eyeblink condi-tioning and slows down extinction, while amytal depresses performance and hastens extinction (Franks and Trouton, 1958; Eysenck, 1963b).

This physiological interpretation raises some interesting questions. The two orthogonal dimensions of neuroticism and introversion-extraversion are assumed to depend on sympathetic activity and reticular activity respectively. There is evidence that the sympathetic nervous system and the reticular for-mation normally act in close concert (Bonvallet, Dell, and Hiebel, 1954; Bloch and Bonvallet, 1960; Harris, 1958). Positive correlations have been found between measures of sympathetic activity and measures of EEG activation (the most direct indices of reticular-system activity available in the intact organism) when subjects are stimulated (Darrow et al., 1942; Sherman and Jost, 1942). On the other hand, these correlations have been reported as negative when subjects are awake but unstimulated (Darrow, Pathman, and Kronenberg, 1946), and a variety of evidence has recently been accumulating to show that the electrocortical manifestations of high arousal, dependent on the reticular formation, and the vegetative manifestations of high sympa-thetic activation, dependent on the hypothalamus, are separable (Feldman and Waller, 1962; Lacey, 1966).

EYSENCK AND PAVLOV. To relate Eysenck's classificatory scheme to Pavlov's is difficult. As Eysenck has repeatedly pointed out, his view of introversion-extraversion as a dimension characterized by relative predominance of excita-tion and inhibition fits, and was in fact partly inspired by, Pavlov's early (1927) theory of individual differences. But as we have seen, Pavlov later felt obliged to abandon this linear model and to postulate three factors that can vary independently, viz., the strength of excitatory processes, the strength of inhib-itory processes (these two determining "strength" and degree of "balance"), and degree of mobility. He made use of these three criteria, for example, to explain the four Hippocratic types, whereas Eysenck identifies them with the four quadrants marked out by the two axes corresponding to his principal dimensions. Pavlov later believed that individuals with a predominance of inhibition are not common, so that balance became essentially a matter of whether inhibitory processes are commensurate with excitatory processes or not. Finally, we recall that, according to Eysenck, dysthymics and hysterics differ in their locations along the extraversion-introversion dimension, which means, according to his hypotheses, that they differ in susceptibility to inhibi-tion and maybe in arousal also. Pavlov, on the other hand, depended on the thinker-artist dichotomy to account for the contrasts between psychasthenia (which Eysenck would presumably include under dysthymia) and hysteria.

There surely must be some way of integrating what is valid in Pavlov's and Eysenck's contributions, especially since the Pavlovians have recently taken to factor analysis and Eysenck has come to lay more and more stress on learning processes as the best indicators of what lies behind personality differences.

Both introversion (Eysenck, 1963) and weakness of nervous system (Gray, 1965) have been equated with relatively high arousability, which suggests a close affinity between the two. It is noteworthy that, according to Eysenck's statements, introverts are more prone than extraverts to find stimulation excessive and therefore distressing. Similarly, the Pavlovians regard high susceptibility to supramaximal inhibition and to the "passive defensive reflex," both processes affording protection against excessive excitation, as the prime distinguishing marks of the weak type. Introverts, according to Eysenck's account, form conditioned eyeblink and GSR responses rapidly, but there is so far no demonstration that they are particularly quick at acquiring "appetitive" conditioned responses, with pleasant or rewarding forms of reinforcement, such as conditioned salivary responses. The eyeblink is clearly an action that wards off irritating external stimulation, whereas the GSR is a component of the orientation reaction and thus an index of momentarily increased arousal. Eysenck (1967) has, in fact, recently identified his extraversion factor with the Pavlovian strength factor on the basis of evidence that he has collected. He finds, for example, that introverts, like "weak" individuals, have lower absolute sensory thresholds and are more prone to supramaximal inhibition. Rozhdestvenskaia (1966) has found that subjects with stronger nervous systems show more signs of fatigue and inhibition in the course of performing monotonous mental work. This seems at first sight surprising in view of the conception of the strong nervous system as one with a superior "working capacity." But it fits in with Eysenck's evidence that "strong" individuals are more extraverted and that extraverts are particularly susceptible to reactive inhibition and boredom.

On the other hand, there would seem to be some resemblance between the individual with an unbalanced nervous system and an individual with high neuroticism. It was recognized quite early by Pavlov's school (see Ivanov-Smolenski, 1952) that experimental neuroses can be produced most easily in the unbalanced type. Furthermore, we have Nebylitsyn's (1964) review of reasons for believing that, in the unbalanced nervous system, the brain-stem arousal system is subject to comparatively weak restraint by the cerebral cortex, while Eysenck believes that high-neuroticism subjects are characterized by chronically high drive. Nebylitsyn stressed the role of the reticular formation in this regard, but he might well have considered the possible importance of the hypothalamus and the autonomic processes dependent on it, especially in view of the recent contributions cited above.

To sum up, a view that might be worth investigating further is that the stable (high-neuroticism) or unbalanced individual is high in prevailing level of arousal, while the introvert or weak individual is high in arousability, i.e., in the ease with which his arousal can be increased. These two attributes could be more or less independent of each other. However, it is hardly necessary to say that the ultimate truth is unlikely to be so simple.

As for the psychoticism dimension, might this approximate Pavlov's mobility dimension? Eysenck (1952a, p. 217), summing up his findings, states that psychotics are "less fluent, . . . perform poorly in mirror drawings, show slower oscillation on the reversal of perspective test, are slow in tracing with a stylus, . . ." This sounds as if these traits might well have something to do with low mobility. Mirror drawing, in particular, involves abandoning one set of habits and replacing them with another set, which resembles the process of turning a positive stimulus into a negative stimulus or vice versa that is the main Pavlovian test for mobility. Pavlov mentioned "inertia" as a characteristic of psychotic behavior patterns, and Eysenck (1962) concludes, on the basis of studies of reminiscence in psychotics, that psychotics dissipate inhibition very slowly. He mentions the *"general slowness* of psychotics," i.e., their inability to adjust to environmental conditions gradually, which is likewise similar to the Pavlovian notion of inertia. Payne and Hewlett (1960), in a factor-analytic study of thought-disorder tests, found psychotics to be differentiated significantly from neurotics and normals by a "retardation" factor, manifested by slowness in a variety of intellectual, perceptual, and motor tasks. Rabinovich (1961), using the test of mobility mentioned earlier . . . , found the maximum rate of responding to be much lower in schizophrenics than in normal subjects.[1]

Spence and the Iowa Group

Since the beginning of the 1950's, Spence, J. A. Taylor, and their students have been engaged in a series of experiments (summed up by Spence, 1956, and Taylor, 1956), designed to test some of the assumptions about drive embodied in the Hull-Spence theory. Anxiety is the drive on which they have chosen to concentrate, and, instead of the more usual procedure of experimentally manipulating the drive level, they have sought to compare groups of subjects to whom different degrees of anxiety can be presumed to exist naturally. Their instrument for distinguishing high-anxiety from low-anxiety subjects has been the Taylor Manifest Anxiety Scale (MAS) (Taylor, 1953). This consists of items from the Minnesota Multiphasic Personality Inventory (MMPI) judged by clinical practioners to indicate anxiety. So, although this research is not aimed primarily at the understanding of personality differences

[1] G. S. Claridge (*Personality and Arousal.* London and New York: Pergamon, 1967) has proposed an alternative interpretation after studying arousal processes in psychiatric disorders. He identifies introversion-extraversion with an "arousal modulation" dimension, to which a "tonic arousal" dimension is orthogonal. Neuroticism (obsessoid-hysteroid) and psychoticism (cycloid-schizoid) dimensions are orthogonal to each other and oblique to the other two.

but rather at the furtherance of basic behavior theory, it investigates correlates of individual differences, using a personality test and a personality variable, anxiety, that has long been of interest to personality theorists.

The predictions tested have been derived from the postulated multiplicative influence of drive on response strength (reaction potential): an increase in drive (D) is assumed to entail an increase in the strength (E) of all instigated responses by a certain proportion (Spence, 1956, p. 147, adapted from Hull, 1943). It follows that an increase in drive will raise the difference in strength between any two responses by the same proportion, since $kE_1 - kE_2 = k(E_1 - E_2)$.

The effects of an increase in drive on learning will depend on how complex the situation is, and particularly on how the "correct" responses, i.e., the response to be learned, stands in relation to competing responses. If the correct response is instigated virtually alone or at least stands higher than its competitors from the start, the number of reinforced trials necessary for it to reach the criterion of mastery should be less when drive is higher. If, on the other hand, the correct response is intially in competition with erroneous responses of comparable strength or is even overshadowed by them, it will take longer under higher drive to make up the leeway and attain the required degree of predominance.

These predictions have been confirmed with fair consistency in several experimental situations. Blinking is a response with a high rate of spontaneous occurrence, and it has no serious competitors as a reaction to a puff of air. So we should expect high-anxiety subjects to acquire a conditioned eyeblink response more rapidly than low-anxiety subjects, which has been found repeatedly to be the case (e.g., Spence and Taylor, 1951; Taylor, 1951). When, however, some tendency for errors to replace correct responses can be expected, as in stylus-maze learning (Farber and Spence, 1953), verbal-maze learning (Taylor and Spence, 1952) and paired-associate verbal learning (Ramond, 1953), high anxiety has been found, as predicted, to slow down learning. In one informative crucial experiment on serial nonsense-syllable learning by Montague (1953), high-anxiety subjects performed better with lists composed of items with low mutual similarity and high association value and worse with lists whose items had high mutual similarity and low association value.

As Spence and Taylor have acknowledged, there are two possible interpretations of the characteristics underlying difference in MAS scores. High-anxiety subjects may differ from low-anxiety subjects in having a higher prevailing level of anxiety drive most of the time regardless of environmental conditions. On the other hand, high-anxiety subjects may be subjects whose level of anxiety drive receives a larger increment when they are exposed to threat. The latter interpretation is favored by the fact that speed of salivary conditioning apparently bears no relation to anxiety level (Bindra, Patterson, and Strzelecki, 1955) and by the results of experiments (Lucas, 1952; Gordon and Berlyne, 1954) in which the performance of high-anxiety subjects in verbal-learning tasks deteriorated when fear of failure was introduced in them but not otherwise.

The Iowa group has accumulated an impressive measure of corroboration for its hypotheses, but their theoretical analyses have by no means won universal assent. Among the alternatives mooted have been the following:

1. Child (1954) lays stress on interfering responses, evoked by internal anxiety stimuli, which impede performance of their correct response. Mandler and Sarason (1952) obtained some evidence for the existence of such responses in studies comparing test performance of subjects with high and low scores on a measure of test anxiety. It is conceivable that complex tasks, which, unlike eyeblink conditioning, present a threat of failure, may produce such interfering responses in high-anxiety subjects and that these may be responsible for their inferior performance.

2. Several investigators, particularly Bélanger and his students, have provided indications that the strength of a learned response does not increase monotonically with drive level but rather reaches a maximum and then declines as drive rises above an optimum point (e.g., Ducharme and Bélanger, 1961; Bélanger and Feldman, 1962). The hypothesis that the decline is due to the emergence of competing responses has been tested by Dufresne-Tassé (1963), but the findings tend to refute it. It seems quite possible that the optimum level of drive is lower for more complex tasks, and this may have had something to do with the difficulties that such tasks present for high-anxiety subjects.

3. The most vehement counterblast against the Iowa position has been set off by Eysenck (1957). Having found that MAS score is positively correlated with both neuroticism and introversion, he suggests that the greater susceptibility to eyeblink conditioning of high-anxiety subjects simply reflects the higher conditionability of introverts, attributable to their lower capacity for acquiring reactive inhibition.

In support of his criticism, Eysenck cites Franks's (1956) finding that, whereas dysthymic neurotics acquire conditioned eyeblinks more easily than normal subjects, hysteric neurotics acquire them less readily. Since in his view, neurotics in general have a higher drive level than normals, both neurotic groups should, he maintains, show more conditioning than normals if Spence's hypotheses about the role of drive are valid. Although Eysenck refers to this as a "crucial" experiment (p. 115), the argument depends on Eysenck's assumption that prevailing drive level is the main thing that distinguishes high-neuroticism from low-neuroticism individuals. As we have already noted, this may be called in question. Further, as Eysenck (1962) has conceded, introverts can be expected to have higher levels of at least acquired drives than extraverts because of their superior conditionability. So a difference in drive may well contribute to the differences in the behavior of introverts and extraverts in eyeblink conditioning.

Eysenck even goes so far as to dispute the long-established principle that response strength in the conditioning situation is affected by drive. He cites an experiment by Franks (1957b), in which subjects who had abstained from eating, drinking, and smoking for 18 hours before the experimental session were found not to differ from control subjects in eyeblink conditioning and subsequent extinction. This result is rather surprising, since there is a large body of literature (see Brown, 1961; Kimble, 1961) showing the strength of a variety of learned responses to increase with the level of drive, relevant or irrelevant. Brown gives reasons why Franks's experiment may not have constituted a fair test of the hypothesis.

On the other hand, Eysenck's argument that the MAS test is not a very satisfactory instrument for the purpose to which it was applied, since its score is likely to reflect several different things, is well taken and has been posed by other writers also. Manipulation of anxiety, which is not difficult to contrive, might have yielded less equivocal answers to the questions that actuated the Iowa experiments.

Spence and Spence (1964) have recently retaliated with a study in which the number of conditioned eyeblink responses was positively correlated with MAS scores and with the MPI neuroticism scale but bore no significant relation to either the MPI extraversion scale or the MMPI hysteria scale. They point out that the practice of the Iowa group is to exclude, or study separately, the records of subjects who tend to give responses of a "voluntary form." The failure of Eysenck's group to follow this practice would, they claim, depress the correlation between MAS scores and measures of conditioning.

Reviewing eyelid-conditioning experiments performed in his own laboratory and elsewhere, Spence (1964) has found differences in favor of high-anxiety Ss appearing in 21 out of 25 independent comparisons, the majority being sufficiently significant. Whether or not a significant difference emerged has depended, he suggests, on the number of Ss, the presence or absence of "voluntary-form" responders, the degree of experimental naivete of Ss, and "the extent to which the experimental situation is designed to arouse some degree of apprehensiveness."

DIFFERENCES IN WHAT HAS BEEN LEARNED

In the laboratories directed by Pavlov and Eysenck, interest has focused on characteristics of the nervous system that determine how quickly and in what manner learned responses will be acquired. The differences uncovered by these studies appear to be genetically determined in large part. In Spence's laboratory, it has been shown that anxiety or, at any rate, something reflected in MAS scores affects ease of learning in various situations, but there has been no commitment to a position on whether or not hereditary differences are involved.

The studies that we shall take up now have been directed at differences in behavior resulting from different environmental conditions to which individuals have been exposed in the past and which have caused them to learn different things. It is a familiar truism that one of the ways in which learned behavior contrasts with unlearned behavior, and one source of its advantages over unlearned behavior, is the fact that, when external conditions vary from one member of a species to another, the response patterns adopted to cope with them can vary accordingly. Yet learned responses are of interest to personality theory only when they are relatively broad in scope and are manifest in a wide sample of an individual's behavior. The fact that one animal has learned to go left in a T-maze while another has learned to go right or the fact that one person has mastered a particular skill or learned a certain poem off by heart is not in itself regarded as a feature of personality.

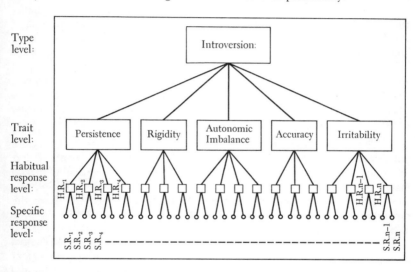

FIGURE 1. Hierarchical organization of levels of behavior. Reproduced with permission from H. J. Eysenck: *Dimensions of Personality*. London: Routledge, 1947.

How the theory of learning, and especially the S-R or neo-associationist conception of learning, fits in with the interests of personality theorists can, however, be seeen from the hierarchical scheme (Fig. 1) that Eysenck (1947) has presented to reflect the basic notions on which factor analysis depends. The figure shows four levels. As one ascends from the lowest to the highest level, smaller correlations are found but larger samples of behavior are involved. The lowest or *specific-response* level stands for the particular responses that a subject makes in specific stimulus situations. The next or *habitual-response* level represents the close similarities that exist among the ways in which a subject responds when confronted with similar stimulus situations, making it relatively easy to predict how he will behave in that kind of situation in future once one knows how he has behaved in such a situation once. The *trait* level represents the correlations that exist between responses performed in a variety of distinct but related situations, e.g., "persistence" means a relatively high correlation between duration of effort in different tasks even though the stimuli with which the subject is faced in the two tasks and the forms of response required of him may be very dissimilar. Finally, there is the highest or *type* level, representing the correlations that exist among virtually all facets of an individual's behavior in all the situations in which he finds himself, so that, if he behaves, say, in a manner characteristic of introverts in one situation, an observer can infer something about how he is likely to behave in any other situation that could be specified.

The two highest levels are, of course, those that interest personality theorists. There have been bitter controversies over the precise meaning of the factors, corresponding to traits and types, that are revealed by factor analysis, some maintaining that they are merely classificatory devices while others argue that there must be a unitary causal agent underlying each of them. To revert to learned behavior, it is undoubtedly true that, on knowing that a subject has performed response R_A in a stimulus situation, S_1, it is often possible to infer that he will perform R_B in S_2 and R_C in S_3. There are presumably three ways in which this could come about:

1. The three stimulus-response associations may be inherited (if they are unlearned) or facilitated (if they are learned) by a common genetic factor or by correlated genetic factors. Thus membership of a particular species means possession of a particular combination of unlearned (instinctive, species-specific) patterns of behavior. Similarly, hereditary susceptibility to the rapid development of inhibitory processes will influence properties of a wide assortment of learned stimulus-response associations.

2. Many recent writers (see Berlyne, 1965, ch. 7) have suggested that, when a subject goes through a learning experience, it is not acquiring a particular response, to be performed in a particular kind of situation, but something like a "rule" or "principle" that is manifested by the performance of a number of different responses in different situations, all having something structural in common. An alternative, but currently less popular, way of making the same point is to say that there is a tendency to widespread stimulus-response generalization.

3. A number of specific learned responses may have been acquired quite separately and independently of one another, and yet they may tend to occur together not because of the way that the nervous system is constituted but because of the way that the external environment is constituted. If the world is so made that individuals who have one kind of experience are likely also to have another kind of experience, then there will be a correlation between attributes of the behavior, appearing in different stimulus situations, to which these experiences give rise.

4. Some forms of learning may occur with an extraordinarily wide capacity for stimulus generalization.

Of these four cases, the first is evidently the one to which Pavlov and Eysenck have attached importance. Little of concern to personality theory other than vague talk has so far issued from a consideration of the second case, and we must presumably await advances in the study of higher forms of learning before any more can be expected. The third and fourth cases cover the phenomena to which the investigators we are about to review have given their attention.

A large part of the Freudian contribution to the theory of personality appertains to the fourth case. Psychoanalytic theories of psychosexual development, of defense mechanisms, and of character formation rested on the claim that emotional attitudes and motor patterns are much more widely generalizable than was formerly apparent. Feelings, wishes, and actions that emerge in response to the crises of early childhood, relating to satisfaction and frustration of fundamental biological needs, were held to transfer to an immense range of stimulus conditions encountered in later life. These conditions are ones that possess links, sometimes extremely remote, with the original critical situations, through resemblances, through being among their incidental accompaniments, or indirectly through chains of words or thoughts. This psychoanalytic view is thus, in principle, fully in tune with the notions of primary and secondary stimulus generalization, first-order and higher-order conditioning. The only point at issue is whether, in fact, generalization can span such vast distances. Dollard and Miller (1950) argue that generalization may well run riot and follow trivial resemblances and associations within the realm of the "unverbalized," which they identify with a Freudian "unconscious." When intellectual processes are in charge of behavior, a restriction of generalization to "rational" resemblances and associations is, they hold, assured mainly by processes of secondary generalization and discrimination that work through verbal labels.

Motivation Theory

The advent of neo-behaviorism brought with it a keen interest in motivational processes, a predilection for relatively elaborate (and therefore relatively versatile) theoretical structures with copious reference to inferred internal mediating processes, and a feeling of readiness to confront human behavior in its full complexity. Psychologists identifying themselves with this current inevitably found themselves turning to problems that Freud had been the first, or one of the first, to raise and about which psychoanalysts have been much more to say than any other group of psychological thinkers. The Institute of Human Relations at Yale University was expressly set up to foster interaction among diverse lines of inquiry into human behavior, and, in the 1930's, Hull presided over a series of seminars at which the ideas of prominent social theorists were critically examined. The participants included a most impressive sample of those who bore responsibility for the subsequent course of behavior theory. It was only natural that the prospect of establishing a synthesis between the kind of psychology represented by Hull and the kind represented by Freud should be irresistibly alluring. There were such obvious points of contact right from the start, and what union could be more propitious than that between the rich insights of psychoanalysis and the methodological fastidiousness of behavior theory?

It has often been asserted that Freud was primarily interested in understanding behavior, even though he might have thought of himself as a student of mental processes, conscious and unconscious. His pleasure principle had much in common with the law of effect that assumed larger and larger responsibilities as the wide scope of the instrumental-conditioning paradigm came to be appreciated. Both could, after all, be traced back to the hedonism of the 18th and 19th centuries and earlier. The reality principle, according to which the older child and adult tempered the pursuit of pleasure with a sense of expediency, evidently depicted the operation of the laws of effect when a great deal of discrimination learning had taken place.

The view that behavior is motivated by uncomfortable drive states, resulting from conditions of biological need or disturbances of homeostasis, came close to the view that Freud had developed, i.e., in his article on "Instincts and Their Vicissitudes" (1915). There, he held behavior to be initiated either by *Reize* (stimuli) or by *Triebe* (commonly translated "instincts" but actually etymologically related to the English word "drive"), holding the only differences between these two kinds of disturbance to be that the former are external in origin and intermittent, whereas the latter are internal and recurrent. At this stage, he represented behavior as a collection of devices for keeping stimulation, whether external or internal, to a minimum and thus maintaining or restoring quiescence. Hull's postulate (1943), according to which responses are reinforced when followed by "the diminuation of the receptor discharge characteristic of a need" had much the same implications. The similarity became even closer when Miller and Dollard (1941) replaced need-reduction by drive-reduction, a change in which Hull acquiesced (1951), although many critics of the drive-reduction position have failed to notice the far-reaching differences this made. Miller and Dollard maintained that a drive is nothing but a strong stimulus. In fact, every stimulus was held to have a drive property in proportion to its intensity. So reinforcement became a matter of reducing net stimulation for them, as for Freud in his middle period.

Secondary Motivation

The links between behavior theory and Freudian theory became firmer as the theory of secondary motivation was developed.

SECONDARY REINFORCEMENT. The principle of *secondary reinforcement* postulated that neutral stimuli accompanying primary rewards (i.e., conditions in which primary drives are reduced) would acquire a conditioned reward-value in their own right. This principle had much in common with Freud's account of how external events or thoughts associated, by contiguity or by similarity, with biological gratifications would become objects of cathexis and sources of symbolic or substitute satisfaction.

FEAR. Even more to the point was the concept of "anxiety" or "fear" as a *secondary* (or *acquired*) *drive*. Mowrer (1939) offered a stimulus-response analysis of the biological and psychological role of anxiety, pointing out the convergences between the view that had grown out of the experimental study of learning and the view at which Freud eventually arrived (e.g., 1926). Both Mowrer (1940b) and Miller (1941, 1948) applied the theory of secondary drive to the analysis of avoidance learning in the rat. "Anxiety," as Mowrer called it, or "fear" as Miller called it, was assumed to be evoked as a consequence of conditioning by any stimulus (warning signal) that has habitually preceded or accompanied pain. The avoidant response, which, if performed during the interval between the onset of the warning signal and the delivery of an electric shock, averts the shock, was assumed to be reinforced by reduction of the secondary drive.

It was recognized that relatively little human behavior, at least in civilized societies, is controlled by primary drives and primary rewards alone. Secondary drives and secondary reinforcement will virtually always be playing some part, whether alone or in conjunction with primary drives and rewards. Fear has been by far the most thoroughly investigated of all presumed secondary drives, and this is justified by the pervasive part that learned fear must play in all departments of human behavior. Social motives, such as the desire for acceptance as a member of a group, for prestige and power, for money, must presumably contain at least a large admixture of fear. Fear reduction, it is argued, must be responsible for the reinforcement of learning to inhibit actions that are followed by punishment, for the learning of an action governed by foresight in the sense of anticipation of consequences delayed by more than a few minutes, for learning to adhere to group mores and to ethical principles. In this way, many personality traits, both normal and abnormal, can be interpreted as behavior patterns that have been learned because of their effectiveness in relieving or preventing fear. They may do this by affording access to stimulus conditions indicative of safety and thus conditioned to some kind of relaxation response or by terminating or forestalling the impact of stimuli conditioned to a fear response.

AGGRESSION. The next most important secondary drive, especially in relation to social interaction and personality, is *anger* or *aggressiveness*. Despite the publicity given to Freud's emphasis on sexual motivation, it has been pointed out (e.g., Mowrer and Kluckhohn, 1944) that Freud saw many neurotic symptoms and other irrational forms of behavior as defences against aggressive impulses and all the adverse consequences that their expression would entail.

A treatise on the principles governing aggressive behavior was published under the title *Frustration and Aggression* in 1939. Its authors — Dollard, Doob, Miller, Mowrer and Sears — were five leading figures among Hull's younger associates and constituted the nucleus of what came to be called the "Yale group." The first half of the book is concerned with laying down some basic postulates about aggressive behavior, all hinging on the basic assumption, as stated on the first page, that "aggression is always a consequence of frustration." The strength of instigation to aggression was held to depend on (1) the strength of instigation to the frustrated response, (2) the degree of interference with the frustrated response, and (3) the number of frustrated response sequences. Direct expression of aggressiveness, being frequently punished, is subject to inhibition. This inhibition leads to indirect expression, with either the object or the form of the aggressive behavior changed. Experiments using a heterogeneous assortment of situations to test predictions from the theory were reported, and a great deal of space was devoted to the relations between aggressive components of personality and the experiences typical of childhood and adolescence in various societies. A few years earlier, Seward (1945a, 1945b, 1945c, 1946) had drawn on conditioning principles to predict how experiences of success and failure in fighting would give rise to dominant and submissive behavior patterns, and he had performed a series of experiments with rats that contributed relevant data.

The determinants of aggressive behavior have received a high degree of attention from experimenters. Berkowitz (1962) and Buss (1961) have written books reviewing the findings that have accrued to date. As was to be expected, the simple formulations that guided early work on this topic have proved inadequate. In particular, many writers have found reason to doubt that frustration always gives rise to aggression or that aggression results only from frustration. There have, in fact, been suggestions from animal experiments that aggressive behavior can be innately evoked by a variety of aversive or punishing stimuli (e.g. Ulrich and Azrin, 1962).

CONFLICT AND FRUSTRATION. The two outstanding pioneers in the study of neurotic behavior, Pavlov and Freud, both came, despite their vastly different approaches, to underline the etiological role of conflict. Pavlov regarded "collision" between excitatory and inhibitory processes as the principal cause of neurotic breakdown, whereas Freud's theory went through a number of stages, culminating in his emphasis on conflict between the ego and the id, with the super-ego joining in sometimes on the one side and sometimes on the other (Freud, 1923; Fenichel, 1945).

Lewin (1935) realized that conflicts of a less spectacular nature must be a recurrent feature of normal everyday life and have effects on behavior that are important even though they may not have the duration and gravity of neurosis. He distinguished three special cases of conflict and deduced what kind of behavior would result from each. First, there is the situation in which a subject finds himself between two attractive objects or regions. Conflict of this sort is resolved relatively easily and quickly, since approach toward one attraction is in itself often sufficient to give it predominance. Secondly, the subject may find himself between two repulsive objects or regions, and the consequences are then more serious: he will have a tendency to "go out of the field," i.e., to move away from both of them, or, if this is prevented by a barrier of some nature, he will remain trapped midway between the two. Thirdly, the subject may find himself within sight of a region that has both attractive and repulsive qualities; he is then likely to advance part of the way towards this region and then to remain at this distance, unable to approach nearer or to retreat (Lewin, 1931, 1935). Lewin pointed out, however, that what behavior actually emerges will depend not only on the type of conflict but also on the relative strength of the attractive and repulsive forces in the situation.

N. E. Miller (1944, 1951) built on Lewin's theory of conflict and translated it into the language of behavior theory. Besides the three types of conflict — approach-approach, avoidance-avoidance, and approach-avoidance — described by Lewin, Miller recognized a fourth important type. This was the double approach-avoidance conflict, which occurs when a subject finds himself between two regions, each of them having attractive and repulsive aspects. He laid down four postulates, viz., (1) that the strength of the tendency to approach a positive incentive increases with nearness to it, (2) that the strength of the tendency to avoid a negative incentive increases with nearness to it, (3) that the strength of the avoidance tendency diminishes with increasing distance more steeply than that of the approach tendency, and (4) that the strength of an approach or an avoidance tendency at a given distance from the incentive object varies directly with the strength of the relevant drive. From these postulates, which paralleled assumptions formulated by Lewin in his own peculiar terminology, a number of predictions regarding behavior in conflict situations were deduced. Since Miller's theory was first presented, it has given rise to a large mass of experimental work, which has provided substantial confirmation for both the postulates and some of the predictions derived from them (Miller, 1959).

Since, whenever an organism is in conflict, the two competing response tendencies cannot complete themselves as each of them would if it were acting alone, frustration of at least one may result. Frequently, both response tendencies and their corresponding motives will be frustrated. In addition, it seems likely that conflict itself will be a source of discomfort and drive. This being so, an organism will need to acquire behavior patterns that are capable of averting or resolving conflict, and many personality traits can be explained as behavior patterns that have been learned thanks to the reinforcement value of conflict reduction. In recent years, the concept of conflict has been broadened by recognizing the possibility of incompatibilities among implicit response-tendencies, including those of a perceptual or symbolic nature. The assumption that conflict is in itself an aversive or drive-raising condition has proved especially promising for the study of stimulus-seeking, attentive, and intellectual behavior patterns. For reviews of relevant literature, see Berlyne (1960, 1963a, 1964).

Although conflict must entail frustration, frustration can occur without conflict, if one defines it as a state of affairs in which an instigated response is prevented from completing itself, e.g., because some external condition required for its completion is missing (see Rosenzweig, 1944). Amsel (1958, 1962) has built up a powerful theory, centering round the hypothesis that stimulus conditions associated with frustration (by which he means absence of an expected reward) will produce an increase in drive and emotional disturbance. This theory, which has prompted a great deal of experimental work, explains why lack of reward sometimes leads to the abandonment of an accustomed response but sometimes favors prolonged persistence. It has been applied mainly to animal behavior, but its applicability to behavior patterns that shape human personalities is obvious.

Brown and Farber (1951) proposed a quantitative conceptualization of conflict (although they called it "frustration") as the principal determinant of emotion. They postulated that its degree will be greater (1) the more nearly equal two competing response stimuli are in strength, and (2) the greater their absolute strength. Berlyne (1954), extending this treatment to cases where three or more response tendencies may be in conflict and to cases where competing response-tendencies may be less than fully incompatible, added (3) a number of competing response-tendencies and (4) degree of compatibility, as determinants of degree of conflict. The list of four determinants thus produced has proved suggestive for the theoretical analysis and experimental investigation of collative motivation in general and, in particular, of the forms of curiosity that underlie exploratory and epistemic behavior (see Berlyne, 1960, 1963a). Further, they make fruitful contact with concepts belonging to information theory (Berlyne, 1957) and with the list of factors on which the degree of "cognitive dissonance" (Festinger, 1957), a concept that has been highly influential in recent social psychology, is held to depend.

Temporal Integration

Mowrer and Ullman (1945) have drawn attention to, and analyzed, the problems that arise from the fact that responses commonly have several consequences, some of which are immediate and some of which occur after a considerable delay. There is reason to believe that the direct reinforcing effect of a reward declines steeply as the time interval between the response and the rewarding event increases, reaching zero if the delay is longer than a few seconds (Spence, 1947). Much the same probably applies to the inhibiting effects of punishment. On the other hand, rewards and punishments can be

effective after much longer delays if some intermediary stimulus with secondary reward value or conditioned fear-inducing power, as the case may be,
occurs immediately after the response and can thus act as a representative
of the impending, but temporally remote consequences. Particularly in human
life, a response will often have immediate consequences that are rewarding
but long-term consequences that are punishing or vice-versa. The long-term
consequences will more often than not, be more serious than the immediate
consequences, and yet the reinforcement-gradient principle (Hull, 1943) will
tend to give them much less weight in determining how the organism will
behave. In fact, they will have no weight at all unless an intermediary stimulus
can bridge the gap. In human beings, such intermediary stimuli will prepon-
derantly be internal and result from implicit symbolic responses. Thoughts
about the uninviting prospect of a penurious old age may induce a man to
contribute to a pension plan, and, although there will be no monetary return
for several decades, immediate reinforcement will be furnished by relief from
fear and the secondary reward-value of the knowledge that a retirement income is assured.

Mowrer and Ullman carried out an experiment with rats to illustrate some
of the factors that are involved. The limited symbolic capacities of the rat
make it necessary to provide an external stimulus representing a delayed
consequence, but the authors took care to underline the analogies between
the behavior shown by some of the rats in their experiment and human personality disorders. In their experiment, food pellets were delivered into a
trough but, if the food was eaten within 3 seconds of its appearance, the rat
was condemned to receive an electric shock. For different groups, the shock
was administered at the end of the 3-second "taboo period," 3 seconds after
its end, and 9 seconds after its end. In all cases, a buzzer sounded from the
time the food appeared until the end of the taboo period. After the first
day or two, most rats in the first two groups learned to refrain from eating
until it was safe to do so. This was designated "normal" behavior. But a
minority of animals engaged in "delinquent" behavior, i.e., eating during the
taboo period, and suffered the punishment when it became due, or "neurotic"
behavior, i.e., not eating at all. In the third group, the one with the longest
delay of punishment, most rats behaved "delinquently."

What Mowrer and Ullman called "integrative learning," i.e., learning that
takes short-term and long-term consequences into account in proportion to
their intrinsic importance, has obviously much in common with what Freud
called the "reality principle," which he held to govern behavior once a child
became capable of "reality testing" and "delay of gratification."

Bixenstine (1956) has carried further the work of Mowrer and Ullman.
In his experiments, rats in an experimental group had not only a danger signal
during the taboo period (a blinking light that appeared whenever they came
within 3 inches of the trough) but also, in case they ate during the taboo
period, a second stimulus (a steady light) that remained on until 3 seconds

before the punishment was due and was then replaced by the blinking light which lasted until the punishment was administered. A control group was deprived of the blinking light immediately before punishment, so that there was no stimulus condition accompanying both the "delinquent" act and the imminence of shock. The experimental group showed appreciably more integrative learning than the control group, even when the taboo period lasted for 40 seconds and the shock was delayed for 110 seconds after the taboo period terminated.

Eysenck (1963b) has compared performance in Mowrer and Ullman's situation of rats belonging to emotional and non-emotional strains, which he likens respectively to human beings high and low in neuroticism. He found non-integrative responses to be more frequent in more emotional rats, "delinquent" reactions (which Eysenck prefers to call "psychopathic reactions") were commoner than "neurotic" reactions (which he prefers to call "dysthymic reactions"). When the shock was made more intense, "integrative" reactions became more frequent in both strains. Eysenck predicts that when ways of placing rats along the introversion-extraversion dimension have been devised, introverted rats will turn out to be more prone to "dysthymic" reactions and extraverted rats more prone to "psychopathic" reactions in these conditions.

Sidman and Boren (1957) have demonstrated how a stimulus that warns of impending punishment can be more intolerable than the punishment itself. When rats are able to choose between terminating a visual stimulus associated with shock, at the expense of suffering a shock, and preventing shock, at the expense of prolonging the stimulus, there is a tendency for them to prefer the former. Kamin (1956) had earlier shown that a running response would be learned by rats whether it led to avoidance of shock without termination of a stimulus associated with shock or to termination of the stimulus without avoidance of the shock.

Defence-Mechanisms and Other Adaptive Behavior Patterns

One of the most celebrated and piquant parts of Freud's contribution was his description of "defence-mechanisms" or devices for staving off anxiety. They served to protect the subject against exposure to situations or thoughts that were productive of anxiety, e.g., by preventing the expression in action or in consciousness of forbidden impulses. They were apt to become so pervasive and distinctive as to constitute major ingredients of personality. Neurotic and psychotic symptoms amounted to exaggerated variants of these defence-mechanisms.

As means of allaying or averting anxiety, defence-mechanisms were easily recognized as complex avoidance responses, and it was impossible to overlook the linkages between Freud's conception of them and the more recently launched theory of fear (anxiety) as a secondary drive supplying the main motivation for avoidance conditioning. So in the 1940's, one major objective of behavior theorists was to show how the occurrence of the kinds of behavior that Freudians attributed to defence-mechanisms could be inferred from principles of learning. Support for these analyses was drawn from animal experiments, either already in the literature or expressly designed for this purpose, in which apparently analogous behavior patterns were observed. The simplicity of the organisms under study and the experimentally controlled conditions could presumably afford a more reliable view of the underlying processes and the determining factors to supplement descriptions and interpretations of everyday human reactions. Books given over in large part to discussions of this kind were written by Dollard and Miller (1950), Masserman (1943), Mowrer (1950), and Sears (1943). Psychotherapy, concerned basically in Freudian terms, was analyzed as a special kind of learning process by these writers and by Shoben (1949). Others who showed interest in reconciling elements of Freudian theory with behavior theory were Guthrie (1938), Skinner (1953), and Tolman (1942), although this was not a primary target of experimental research for them.

FIXATION AND REGRESSION. Freud (1916–17) indicated a close relation between *fixation* and *regression* with the help of an apt analogy. "If you think of a migrating people who have left large numbers at the stopping-places on their way, you will see that the foremost will naturally fall back upon those positions when they are defeated or when they meet with an enemy too strong for them. And again, the more of their number they leave behind in their progress, the sooner will they be in danger of defeat" (Freud, 1920). This view could easily be translated into the language of behavior theory. When one behavior pattern is given up in favor of another as the result of extinction or counter-conditioning, the earlier pattern will not be obliterated but merely inhibited (Mowrer and Kluckhohn, 1944). The subject will possess a hierarchy of responses, ordered according to their strength, with the most recently acquired response on top if it has received sufficient reinforcement to supplant its predecessors. If this response, in its turn, meets with frustration or inhibition, the consequent reduction in its strength may relegate it to a lower position in the hierarchy, with the result that a previously abandoned response becomes uppermost and reemerges. The more strongly reinforced the earlier responses were, the more serious the competition they will offer, the more precarious the hegemony of the most recently acquired response, and the more easily it can be weakened to the point of being submerged.

Sears (1943) was able to cite a large number of pertinent animal experiments and several factors that, according to established principles of learning, should affect the degree to which instrumental responses can resist inhibition. "Object fixation," as distinct from "instrumental act fixation," could be interpreted in terms of the conditioning processes that produce secondary reward-value.

A number of studies had apparently shown that an animal is particularly apt to become stereotyped in its behavior when it has just been punished. Maier (1949) reported a series of experiments in which rats were subjected to an insoluble discrimination problem in a Lashley jumping-stand and developed an astonishingly consistent habit of jumping in one direction repeatedly, which was extremely difficult to eliminate even if the conditions of the experiment changed. He concluded from the phenomenon of "fixation" that frustration released behavior from the normally operating laws of motivation and reinforcement and transferred it to the control of an altogether different kind of mechanism. A number of writers, notably Mowrer (1950), Wilcoxon (1952), and Eglash (1954), objected to this conclusion. They pointed to the probable role of intermittent reinforcement (which is known to generate extraordinary resistance to extinction) in an insoluble-problem situation and of the reinforcement that the response of jumping in any direction would receive through termination of the electric shock, air blast or prodding with whose help Maier forced his rats to leave the stand.

Experiments by Farber (1948) and Whiteis (1956) verified implications of the hypothesis that removal from cues associated with pain provides reinforcement through fear-reduction and thus accounts for the peculiar strength that punished locomotor responses often exhibit. More recently, experiments by Amsel and Ward (1965) show how conditioning to internal cues connected with frustrative non-reward can contribute to persistence. Experiments with rats by Mowrer (1940) and Whiting and Mowrer (1943) demonstrated a tendency to regress to an earlier response when the more effective or less strenuous response that has replaced it is weakened by punishment, nonreward or a physical barrier. Child and Waterhouse (1952, 1953) discussed the more complicated kind of regression, sometimes known as "primitivation," that frustration may engender in the child (Barker, Dembo, and Lewin, 1941). They argued that this kind of regression, taking the form of a qualitative decline to a point characteristic of immaturity, is due to interference from responses associated with frustration.

IMITATION AND IDENTIFICATION. Experiments designed to find out whether animal learning can be speeded up by *imitation* have been performed since the beginning of the 20th century, and although their findings have been open to debate, evidence for imitative learning in primates seems fairly good. For reviews, see Miller and Dollard (1941) and Masserman (1943). A Russian experimenter, Pen (1934), showed that 10–year–old children could acquire a response (pressing a rubber bulb when a bell sounded), and also show conditioned inhibition (withholding the response when a white light accompanied the bell), as a result of imitation. They would respond correctly on seeing another person demonstrate the response, after witnessing the demonstration, and even when the stimuli and manipulanda were changed somewhat. In the West, the behavior-theoretic analysis of imitation was initiated by Miller and Dollard (1941), whose experiments showed that rats and children would learn to perform responses observed in a model, that this imitative behavior conformed to acknowledged principles of learning, and that, once an imitative habit had been acquired, it would be generalized to other situations, other responses, and other models. Differential reinforcement could bring about discrimination, so that certain models were imitated but not others.

Mowrer (1950) discussed the more far-reaching forms of imitation that Freud had in mind when he introduced the concepts of *identification* and *introjection*. The relations between imitation and identification have been vigorously argued over ever since. If a useful distinction is to be made, it would seem that the word "identification" should be used when extensive sectors of behavior, as distinct from isolated response sequences, are taken over from the model and when implicit responses — attitudes, values, etc. — are taken over as well as overt behavior. There will, in such cases, be what Piaget (1945) has called "deferred imitation," i.e., performance of responses characteristic of the model when the model is no longer present. When these conditions are met, we come close to what social psychologists have frequently called "role-playing." It can be expected to occur only when stimuli coming from behavior characteristic of the model have an intrinsic or secondary reward-value in their own right, so that the behavior in question is not reinforced solely by some extrinsic reward whose attainment it facilitates.

Lair (1949) has recommended a distinction between "developmental identification" or identification with liked persons, i.e., persons productive of stimulation with secondary rewarding properties, and "defensive identification" or identification with a person at whose hands punishment or frustration is being suffered, i.e., a person in whose place one would prefer to be (the "identification with the aggressor" of Anna Freud, 1936).The role of identification, especially with one or the other parent, in the formation of personality and the conditions that favor it have received copious discussion (e.g., Sears, 1957; Whiting, 1959, 1960). Bandura, Ross, and Ross (1963) found that children are more likely to imitate adults who control the dispensation of reward rather than those who are recipients, thus corroborating some of the theories of identification that have been propounded (e.g., Whiting, 1960) and rebutting others. The growing mass of experimental work on imitation and identification in animal and human subjects has been reviewed by Mowrer (1960) and by Bandura (1962).

REPRESSION. Shaw (1946) worked out a stimulus-response analysis of repression. Thoughts associated with actions that have incurred social disapproval come to evoke anxiety. Stimuli habitually preceding such thoughts thus come to act as warning signals, and the response of inhibiting, or not entertaining, a frightening thought will be learned as an instrumental avoidance response, reinforced by anxiety-reduction. Essentially the same interpretation was given by Dollard and Miller (1950).

REACTION FORMATION. In the course of one of his experiments concerned primarily with regression, Mowrer (1940a) observed behavior that he regarded as an instance of reaction formation. Rats that had been accustomed to press a pedal as a means of terminating electric shocks began to receive a shock from the pedal whenever they pressed it. Mowrer reports: "After discovering that the pedal was charged, these animals would frequently *retreat* from the pedal end of the apparatus soon after they began to feel the grill shock, i.e., as soon as they began to have an impulse to press the pedal. In effect, they were thus *running away from the pedal because they wanted to go toward and touch it.*"

DISPLACEMENT. Miller (1948b) has presented a rather ambitious theory of displacement. A response will, it is predicted, undergo displacement to some target other than its original one, if the original target is absent or if the aiming of the response at the original target is inhibited by fear. In the former case, the displacement target will be whichever object, out of those that are available, most resembles the original target. In the second case, there will be conflict. Miller deduced, with the help of the kind of diagram shown in Figure 2 that the displacement target would bear some intermediate degree of resemblance to the original target. This diagram is reminiscent of those that Miller had used in his analysis of approach-avoidance conflict. There is, however, the difference that the horizontal axis of the diagram illustrating the theory of conflict represents a set of points ordered according to their

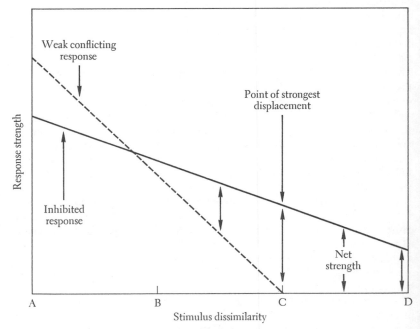

FIGURE 2. N. E. Miller's Theory of Displacement. Reproduced from N. E. Miller: "Theory and Experiment Relating Psychoanalytic Displacement to Stimulus-Response Generalization. *J. abnorm. soc. Psychol.*, 1948, 43, 155–178.

spatial or temporal distance from the goal-object, while, in the diagram illustrating the theory of displacement, the horizontal axis represents a set of alternative goal-objects ordered according to their degree of resemblance to the original goal-object. In approach-avoidance conflict, it was predicted that the subject would take up a location corresponding to the point at which the gradients crossed, but, when displacement occurred, the object chosen as displacement target would correspond to the point at which the distance of the approach gradient above the avoidance gradient is at a maximum. As with conflict, the changes that would occur if the approach or avoidance gradient were raised or lowered, i.e., if the drive motivating the response (e.g., aggressiveness) or the fear leading to its inhibition were heightened or moderated, can be deduced from the diagram.

Various implications of the theory have received experimental support (reviewed by Miller, 1959). Brush *et al.* (1952) extended Miller's theory of displacement in a direction of greater mathematical rigor, linking it with the Bush-Mosteller mathematical model for learning (1951). It is interesting that, like several other phenomena characteristic of learned behavior, a tendency to displacement is prominent among the unlearned "instinctive" or "species-specific" behavior patterns studied by the ethologists (Tinbergen, 1951): frustration (absence of the normal goal-object) or conflict causes consummatory responses to be directed towards unusual targets, including, at times, no target at all ("vacuum activity" or "explosion activity") or else to be replaced by responses appropriate to a quite different drive from the one that is aroused.

REFERENCES

Amsel, A. "The Role of Frustrative Nonreward in Noncontinuous Reward Situations." *Psychol. Bull.*, 1958, 55: 102–119.
———. "Frustrative Nonreward in Partial Reinforcement and Discrimination Learning: Some Recent History and a Theoretical Extension." *Psychol. Rev.*, 1962, 69: 306–328.
———, and Ward, J. S. "Frustration and Persistence: Resistance to Discrimination Following Prior Experience with the Discriminanda." *Psychol. Monogr.*, 1965, 79, No. 4.
Bandura, A. "Social Learning through Imitation." In M. R. Jones (Ed.), *Nebraska Symposium on Motivation*, 1962. Lincoln: Univer. of Nebraska Press, 1962. 211–269. (a)
———, Ross, D., and Ross, S. A. "A Comparative Test of the Status Envy, Social Power, and Secondary Reinforcement Theories of Identificatory Learning." *J. abnorm. soc. Psychol.*, 1963, 67: 527–534.
Barker, R. G., Dembo, Tamara, and Lewin, K. "Frustration and Regression: An Experiment with Young Children." *Univer. Ia. Stud. Child Welf.*, 1941, 18 (Whole No. 386).
Bélanger, D., and Feldman, S. M. "Effects of Water Deprivation upon Heart Rate and Instrumental Activity in the Rat." *J. comp. physiol. Psychol.*, 1962, 55: 220–225.
Berkowitz, L. *Aggression: A Social Psychological Analysis.* New York: McGraw-Hill, 1962.
Berlyne, D. E. "A Theory of Human Curiosity." *Brit. J. Psychol.*, 1954, 45: 180–191.

_____. "Uncertainty and Conflict: A Point of Contact between Information-Theory and Behavior-Theory Concepts." *Psychol. Rev.*, 1957, 64: 329–339.

_____. *Conflict, Arousal, and Curiosity.* New York: McGraw-Hill, 1960.

_____. "Exploratory and Epistemic Behavior." In S. Koch (Ed.), *Psychology: A Study of a Science.* Vol. 5. New York: McGraw-Hill, 1963. (a)

_____. "Emotional Aspects of Learning." *Annu. Rev. Psychol.*, 1964, 15: 115–142.

_____. *Structure and Direction in Thinking.* New York: Wiley, 1965.

Bindra, D., Patterson, A. L., and Strzelecki, J. "On the Relation between Anxiety and Conditioning." *Canad. J. Psychol.*, 1955, 9: 1–6.

Bixenstine, V. E. "Secondary Drive as a Neutralizer of Time in Integrative Problem Solving." *J. comp. physiol. Psychol.*, 1956, 49: 161–166.

Bloch, V., and Bonvallet, M. "Le déclenchement des réponses électrodermales à partir du système réticulaire facilitateur." *J. Physiol.*, Paris, 1960, 52: 25–26.

Bonvallet, M., Dell, P., and Hiebel, G. "Tonus sympathique et activité électrique corticale." *EEG Clin. Neurophysiol.*, 1954, 6: 119–144.

Briks, Z. N. ["Experimental Investigations of the Typological Characteristics of the Higher Nervous Activity in School Age Children."] *Trudy Inst. Vys. Nerv. Deiat. Pavlova*, 1956, 2: 149–174. English translation in *The Central Nervous System and Behavior.* Bethesda, Md.: U.S. Public Health Service, 1960.

Broadbent, D. E. "The Concept of Capacity and the Theory of Behaviour." In C. Cherry (Ed.), *Information Theory.* New York: Acad. Press Inc., 1956.

Brown, J. S. *The Motivation of Behavior.* New York: McGraw-Hill, 1961.

_____, and Farber, I. E. "Emotions Conceptualized as Intervening Variables with Suggestions Toward a Theory of Frustration." *Psychol. Bull.*, 1951, 38: 465–495.

Brush, F. R., Bush, R. R., Jenkins, W. O., John, W. F., and Whiting, J. W. M. "Stimulus Generalization after Extinction and Punishment: An Experimental Study of Displacement." *J. abnorm. soc. Psychol.* 1952, 47: 633–640.

Bush, R. R., and Mosteller, F. "A Mathematical Model for Simple Learning." *Psychol. Rev.*, 1951, 58: 313–323.

Buss, A. H. *The Psychology of Aggression.* New York: Wiley, 1961.

Campbell, A. A. "The Interrelations of Two Measures of Conditioning in Man." *J. exp. Psychol.*, 1938, 22: 225–243.

Cattell, R. B. *Personality and Motivation Structure and Measurement.* Yonkers, N.Y.: World, 1957.

Child, I. L. "Personality." *Annu. Rev. Psychol.*, 1954, 5: 149–170.

_____, and Waterhouse, I. K. "Frustration and the Quality of Performance: I. A Critique of the Barker, Dembo, and Lewin Experiment." *Psychol. Rev.*, 1952, 59: 351–362.

_____, and Waterhouse, I. K. "Frustration and the Quality of Performance: II. A Theoretical Statement." *Psychol. Rev.*, 1953, 60: 127–139.

Claridge, G. "The Excitation-Inhibition Balance in Neurotics." In H. J. Eysenck (Ed.), *Experiments in Personality.* Vol. 1. *Psychodiagnostics and Psychodynamics.* London: Routledge & Kegan Paul, 1960.

_____. "Arousal and Inhibition as Determinants of the Performance of Neurotics." *Brit. J. Psychol.*, 1961, 52: 53–63.

_____, and Herrington, R. N. "Sedation Threshold, Personality, and the Theory of Neurosis." *J. ment. Sci.*, 1960, 106: 1568–1583.

Darlington, C. D. "Psychology, Genetics, and the Process of History." *Brit. J. Psychol.*, 1963, 54: 293–298.

Darrow, C. W., Jost, H., Solomon, A. P., and Mergener, J. C. "Autonomic Indications of Excitatory and Homeostatic Effects in the Electroencephalogram." *J. Psychol.,* 1942, 14: 115-130.

———, Pathman, J., and Kronenberg, G. "Level of Autonomic Activity and Electroencephalogram." *J. exp. Psychol.,* 1946, 36: 355-365.

Davidson, P. O., Payne, R. W. and Sloane, R. B. "Introversion, Neuroticism, and Conditioning." *J. abnorm. soc. Psychol.,* 1964, 68: 136-143.

Dewey, J. "The Reflex Arc Concept in Psychology." *Psychol. Rev.,* 1896, 3: 357-370.

Dollard, J., Miller, N. E., Doob, L. W., Mowrer, O. H., and Sears, R. R. *Frustration and Aggression.* New Haven: Yale Univer. Press, 1939.

Dollard, J., and Miller, N. E. *Personality and Psychotherapy.* New York: McGraw-Hill, 1950.

Ducharme, R., and Bélanger, D. "Influence d'une stimulation électrique sur le niveau d'activation et la performance." *Canad. J. Psychol.,* 1961, 15: 61-68.

Dufresne-Tassé, C. "La compétition des réponses et l'activité instrumentale." Unpublished doctoral dissertation, Univer. of Montreal, 1963.

Eglash, A. "Fixation and Inhibition." *J. abnorm. soc. Psychol.,* 1954, 49: 241-245.

Eysenck, H. J. *Dimensions of Personality.* London: Routledge, 1947.

———. *The Scientific Study of Personality.* New York: Macmillan, 1952. (a)

———. *The Structure of Human Personality.* London: Methuen, 1953.

———. *Psychology of Politics.* London: Routledge, 1954.

———. "A Dynamic Theory of Anxiety and Hysteria." *J. ment. Sci.,* 1955, 101: 28-51.

———. *The Dynamics of Anxiety and Hysteria: An Experimental Application of Modern Learning Theory to Psychiatry.* London: Routledge & Kegan Paul, 1957.

———. "Anxiety and Hysteria: A Reply to Vernon Hamilton." *Brit. J. Psychol.,* 1959, 50: 64-69. (b)

———. "Scientific Methodology and the Dynamics of Anxiety and Hysteria." *Brit. J. med. Psychol.,* 1959, 32: 56-63. (c)

———. "Eysenck on Lykken." *Cont emp. Psychol.,* 1960, 5: 106-107. (b)

———. "Reminiscence, Drive and Personality — Revision and Extension of a Theory." *Brit. J. soc. clin. Psychol.,* 1962, 1: 127-140.

———. "Biological Basis of Personality." *Nature,* 1963, 199: 1031-1034. (a)

———. "Emotion as a Determinant of Integrative Learning: An Experimental Study." *Beh. Res. & Therapy,* 1963, 1: 197-211. (b)

———. "Extraversion and the Acquisition of Eyeblink and GSR Conditioned Responses." *Psychol. Bull.,* 1965, 63: 258-270.

———, and Claridge, G. "The Position of Hysterics and Dysthymics in a Two-Dimensional Framework of Personality Dimension." *J. abnorm. soc. Psychol.,* 1962, 64: 46-55.

———. *The Biological Basis of Personality.* New York: Charles C. Thomas, 1967.

———, and Maxwell, A. E. "Reminiscence as a Function of Drive." *Brit. J. Psychol.,* 1961, 52: 43-52.

Eysenck, S. B. G., and Eysenck, H. J. "The Validity of Questionnaire and Rating Assessments of Extraversion and Neuroticism, and Their Factorial Stability." *Brit. J. Psychol.,* 1963, 54: 51-62.

———, Eysenck, H. J., and Claridge, G. "Dimensions of Personality, Psychiatric Syndromes, and Mathematical Models." *J. ment. Sci.,* 1960, 106: 581-589.

Farber, I. E. "Response Fixation under Anxiety and Non-Anxiety Conditions." *J. exp. Psychol.,* 1948, 38: 111-131.

————, and Spence, K. W. "Complex Learning and Conditioning as a Function of Anxiety." *J. exp. Psychol.*, 1953, 45: 120-125.

Feldman, S. M., and Waller, H. J. "Dissociation of Electrocortical Activation and Behavioral Arousal." *Nature*, 1962, 196: 1320-1322.

Fenichel, O. *The Psychoanalytic Theory of Neurosis.* New York: Norton, 1945.

Festinger, L. *Theory of Cognitive Dissonance.* Evanston, Ill.: Row, Peterson, 1957.

Franks, C. M. "Conditioning and Personality: A Study of Normal and Neurotic Subjects." *J. abnorm. soc. Psychol.*, 1956, 52: 143-150.

————. "Personality Factors and the Rate of Conditioning." *Brit. J. Psychol.*, 1957, 48: 119-126. (a)

————. "Effect of Food, Drink, and Tobacco Deprivation on the Conditioning of the Eyeblink Response." *J. exp. Psychol.*, 1957, 53: 117-120. (b)

————. "Ease of Conditioning and Spontaneous Recovery from Experimental Extinction." *Brit. J. Psychol.*, 1963, 54: 351-358. (a)

————. "Personality and Eyeblink Conditioning Seven Years Later." *Acta. Psychol.*, 1963, 21: 295-312. (b)

————, Holden, E. A., and Phillips, M. "Eysenck's 'Stratification' Theory and the Questionnaire Method of Measuring Personality." *J. clin. Psychol.*, 1961, 17: 248-253.

————, and Trouton, D. "Effects of Amobarbital Sodium and Dexamphetamine Sulphate on the Conditioning of the Eyeblink Response." *J. comp. physiol. Psychol.*, 1958, 51: 220-222.

Freud, Anna. *Das Ich und die Abwehrmechanismen.* Vienna: Internationaler Psychoanalytischer Verlag, 1936. [*The Ego and the Mechanisms of Defense.* London: Hogarth, 1937.]

Freud, S. "Triebe und Triebschicksale." *Inter. Z. f. ärztl. Psycholanal.*, 1915, 3: 84-100. [Instincts and Their Vicissitudes. In *Collected Papers*, Vol. IV. London: Hogarth, 1925.]

————. *A General Introduction to Psychoanalysis.* New York: Boni and Liveright, 1920 (Trans. of Freud, 1916-1917.)

————. *Das Ich und das Es.* Vienna: Internationaler Psychoanalytischer Verlag, 1923. *The Ego and the Id.* London: Hogarth, 1927.

————. *Hemmung, Symptom und Angst.* Vienna: Internationaler Psychoanalytischer Verlag, 1926. [*Inhibitions, Symptoms and Anxiety.* London: Hogarth, 1936.]

Gordon, W. M., and Berlyne, D. E. "Drive-Level and Flexibility in Paired-Associate Nonsense-Syllable Learning." *Quart. J. exp. Psychol.*, 1954, 6: 181-185.

Gray, J. A. *Pavlov's Typology.* New York: Macmillan, 1965.

Grindley, G. C. "The Formation of a Simple Habit in Guinea-Pigs." *Brit. J. Psychol.*, 1932, 23: 127-147.

Guilford, J. P., and Guilford, R. B. "An Analysis of the Factors in a Typical Test of Introversion-Extroversion." *J. abnorm. soc. Psychol.*, 1934, 28: 377-399.

Guthrie, E. R. *The Psychology of Human Conflict.* New York: Harper, 1938.

Halberstam, J. L. "Some Personality Correlates of Conditioning, Generalization, and Extinction." *Psychosom. Med.*, 1961, 23: 67-76.

Hamilton, V. "Eysenck's Theories of Anxiety and Hysteria: A Methodological Critique." *Brit. J. Psychol.*, 1959, 50: 48-63.

Harris, G. W. "The Reticular Formation, Stress, and Endocrine Activity." In H. H. Jasper *et al.* (Ed.), *Reticular Formation of the Brain.* Boston: Little, Brown, 1958.

Hebb, D. O. *The Organization of Behavior.* New York: Wiley, 1949.

Hirsch, J. "Individual Differences in Behavior and Their Genetic Basis." In E. L. Bliss (Ed.), *Roots of Behavior.* New York: Harper, 1962.

Holt, E. B. *The Freudian Wish and Its Place in Ethics.* New York: Holt, 1915.

_____. *Animal Drive and the Learning Process.* Vol. I. New York: Holt, 1931.

Hull, C. L. "A Functional Interpretation of the Conditioned Reflex." *Psychol. Rev.,* 1929, 36: 498–511.

_____. *Principles of Behavior.* New York: Appleton-Century-Crofts, 1943.

_____. "The Place of Innate Individual and Species Differences in a Natural-Science Theory of Behavior." *Psychol. Rev.,* 1945, 52: 55–60.

_____. *Essentials of Behavior.* New Haven: Yale Univer. Press, 1951.

_____. *A Behavior System.* New Haven: Yale Univer. Press, 1952.

Ivanov-Smolenski, A. G. "On the Methods of Examining the Conditioned Food Reflexes in Children and in Mental Disorders." *Brain,* 1927, 50: 138 (4).

_____. *Essays on the Pathophysiology of the Higher Nervous Activity.* Moscow: Foreign Langs. Publ. House, 1954.

Kamin, L. J. "The Effects of Termination of the CS and Avoidance of the US on Avoidance Learning." *J. comp. physiol. Psychol.,* 1956, 49: 420–424.

Kimble, G. A. "An Experimental Test of a Two-Factor Theory of Inhibition." *J. exp. Psychol.,* 1949, 39: 15–23.

_____. *Hilgard and Marquis' Conditioning and Learning.* (2nd ed.) New York: Appleton-Century-Crofts, 1961.

Konorski, J. *Conditioned Reflexes and Neuron Organization.* New York: Cambridge Univer. Press. 1948.

Krasnogorski, N. I. *Vysshaia nervnaia deiatel'-nost' rebenka* [*The Higher Nervous Activity of the Child*]. Leningrad: Medgiz, 1958.

Krasuski, V. J. ["Method of Estimating Properties of Nervous Processes in Dogs, Accepted by the Laboratory of Physiology and Genetics of Higher Nervous Activity Types."] *Zh. Vys. Nerv. Deiat.,* 1963, 13: 165–176.

Lacey, J. I. "Somatic Response Patterning and Stress: Some Revisions of Activation Theory." In M. H. Appley & R. Trumbull (Eds.), *Psychological Stress: Issues in Research.* New York: Appleton-Century-Crofts, 1967.

Lair, W. S. "Psychoanalytic Theory of Identification." Unpublished doctoral dissertation, Harvard Univer., 1949.

Leites, N. S. ["An Attempt at Psychological Characterization of Temperaments."] In B. M. Teplov (Ed.), *Tipologicheskie osobennosti vysshei nervnoi deiatel'nosti cheloveka* [*Typological Characteristics of Higher Nervous Activity in Man*]. Moscow: Acad. Pedag. Sci., 1956.

Lewin, K. "Environmental Forces in Child Behavior and Development." In C. Murchison (Ed.), *A Handbook of Child Psychology.* Worcester, Mass.: Clark Univer. Press. 1931.

_____. *A Dynamic Theory of Personality.* New York: McGraw-Hill, 1935.

Lucas, J. D. "The Interactive Effects of Anxiety, Failure and Intra-Serial Duplication." *Amer. J. Psychol.,* 1952, 65: 59–66.

Lykken, D. T. "Turbulent Complication." *Cont. emp. Psychol.,* 1959, 4: 377–379.

McDougall, W. *Outline of Psychology.* New York: Scribner, 1923.

Maier, N. R. F. *Frustration, the Study of Behavior without a Goal.* New York: McGraw-Hill, 1949.

Malmo, R. B. "Activation: A Neurophysiological Dimension." *Psychol. Rev.*, 1959, 66: 367–386.

Mandler, G., and Sarason, S. B. "A Study of Anxiety and Learning." *J. abnorm. soc. Psychol.*, 1952, 47: 166–173.

Masserman, J. H. *Behavior and Neurosis: An Experimental Psychoanalytic Approach to Psychobiological Principles.* Chicago: Univer. of Chicago Press, 1943.

Melzack, R. "The Genesis of Emotional Behavior: An Experimental Study of the Dog." *J. comp. physiol. Psychol.*, 1954, 47: 166–168.

Melzack, R., and Scott, T. H. "The Effects of Early Experience on the Response to Pain." *J. comp. physiol. Psychol.*, 1957, 50: 155–161.

Miller, N. E. "An Experimental Investigation of Acquired Drives." *Psychol. Bull.*, 1941, 38: 5–34.

———. "Experimental Studies in Conflict." In J. McV. Hunt (Ed.), *Personality and the Behavior Disorders.* Vol. I. New York: Ronald, 1944.

———. "Studies of Fear as an Acquirable Drive: I. Fear as Motivation and Fear-Reduction as Reinforcement in the Learning of New Responses." *J. exp. Psychol.*, 1948, 38: 89–101. (a)

———. "Theory and Experiment Relating Psychoanalytic Displacement to Stimulus-Response Generalization." *J. abnorm. soc. Psychol.*, 1948, 43: 155–178. (b)

———. "Learnable Drives and Rewards." In S. S. Stevens (Ed.), *Handbook of Experimental Psychology.* New York: Wiley, 1951.

———. "Liberalization of Basic S-R Concepts: Extension to Conflict Behavior, Motivation, and Social Learning." In S. Koch (Ed.), *Psychology: A Study of a Science.* Vol. 2. New York: McGraw-Hill, 1959.

———, and Dollard, J. *Social Learning and Imitation.* New Haven: Yale Univer. Press, 1941.

Miller, S., and Konorski, J. "Sur une forme particulière des réflexes conditionnels." *C. R. Soc. biol.*, 1928, 99: 1,155–1,157.

Montague, E. K. "The Role of Anxiety in Serial Rote Learning." *J. exp. Psychol.*, 1953, 45: 91–96.

Moruzzi, G., and Magoun, H. W. "Brain Stem Reticular Formation and the Activation of the EEG." *EEG Clin. Neurophysiol.*, 1949, 1: 455–473.

Mowrer, O. H. "A Stimulus-Response Analysis of Anxiety and Its Role as a Reinforcing Agent." *Psychol. Rev.*, 1939, 46: 553–565.

———. "An Experimental Analogue of 'Regression,' with Incidental Observations on 'Reaction Formation.'" *J. abnorm. soc. Psychol.*, 1940, 35: 56–87. (a)

———. "Anxiety Reduction and Learning." *J. exp. Psychol.*, 1940, 27: 497–516. (b)

———. *Learning Theory and Personality Dynamics.* New York: Ronald Press, 1950.

———. *Learning Theory and the Symbolic Processes.* New York: Wiley, 1960.

———, and Kluckhohn, C. "Dynamic Theory of Personality." In J. McV. Hunt (Ed.), *Personality and the Behavior Disorders.* Vol. I. New York: Ronald, 1944.

———, and Ullman, A. D. "Time as a Determinant in Integrative Learning." *Psychol. Rev.*, 1945, 52: 61–90.

Nebylitsyn, V. D. ["Some Electroencephalographic Indices of the Equilibrium of Neural Processes."] *Doklady Akad. Pedag. Nauk.*, 1961, 2: 115–120.

———, Rozhdestvenskaia, V. I., and Teplov, B. M. "Concerning the Interrelation between Absolute Sensitivity and Strength of the Nervous System." *Quart. J. exp. Psychol.*, 1960, 12: 17–25.

————. "The Electroencephalographic Study of the Characteristics of Strength of Nervous System and Balance of Neural Processes in Man Using Factor Analysis." In B. M. Teplov (Ed.), *Tipologicheskie osobennosti vysshei nervnoi deiatel'nosti cheloveka* [*Typological Peculiarities of Higher Nervous Activity in Man*]. Vol. III. Moscow: Acad. Pedag. Sci., 1963.

————. ["Cortico-Reticular Relations and Their Role in the Structure of Properties of the Nervous System."] *Vop. psikhol.* 1964, 1: 1–24.

————. "Some Questions Relating to the Theory of Properties of the Nervous System." *Proc. XVIII Int. Cong. Psychol.,* 1966.

Orlansky, H. "Infant Care and Personality." *Psychol. Bull.,* 1949, 46: 1–48.

Paramanova, N. P. ["On the Formation of the Two Signal Systems in the Normal Child."] In A. R. Luriia (Ed.), *Problemy vysshei nervnoi deiatel'nosti normal'nogo i anomal'nogo rebenka* [*Problems of the Higher Nervous Activity of the Normal and Abnormal Child*]. Vol. I. Moscow: Acad. Pedag. Sci., 1956.

Pavlov, I. P. *Conditioned Reflexes.* Oxford: Oxford Univer. Press, 1927.

————. *Lectures on Conditioned Reflexes.* New York: International, 1928.

————. "The Reply of a Physiologist to Psychologists." *Psychol. Rev.,* 1932, 39: 91–126.

————. "The Conditioned Reflex." In *Conditioned Reflexes and Psychiatry.* New York: International, 1941. First published 1935. (a)

————. "General Types of Higher Nervous Activity in Animals and Man." In *Selected Works.* Moscow: Foreign Lang. Publ. House, 1955. First published 1935. (b)

Payne, R. W., and Hewlett, J. H. G. "A Thought Disorder in Psychotic Patients." In H. J. Eysenck (Ed.), *Experiments in Personality,* Vol. II, *Psychodiagnostics and Psychodynamics.* London: Routledge & Kegan Paul, 1960.

Pen, R. M. ["The Formation of New Conditioned Connections through Imitation."] In A. G. Ivanov-Smolenski (Ed.), *Na puti k izucheniia vysshikh form neirodinamiki rebenka* [*Towards the Study of the Higher Forms of Neurodynamics in the Child*]. Moscow: Medgiz, 1934.

Piaget, J. *La formation du symbole chez l'enfant,* Neuchâtel & Paris: Delachaux & Niestlé, 1945. [*Play, Dreams and Imitation in Childhood,* New York: Norton, 1951.]

Rabinovich, M. ["Electrophysiological Analysis of the Activities in Different Layers of the Cortex during the Formation of a Conditioned Reflex."] *Zh. Vys. Nerv. Deiat.,* 1961, 11: 463–473.

Ramond, C. K. "Anxiety and Task as Determiners of Verbal Performance." *J. exp. Psychol.,* 1953, 46: 120–124.

Razran, G. H. S. "Studies in Configural Conditioning: I. Historical and Preliminary Experimentation." *J. gen. Psychol.,* 1939, 21: 307–330.

Rogov, A. A., Gorlanova, T. T., Kantorovich, M. M., and Kovaleva, N. T. "Changes in Vascular Conditioned Reflexes in Man as a Function of Typological Features of the Nervous System." *Zh. Vys. Nerv. Deiat.,* 1964, 14, No. 4 (Translation in *Sov. Psychol. Psychiat.,* 1965, 3: 25–28.)

Rosenzweig, S. "An Outline of Frustration Theory." In J. McV. Hunt (Ed.), *Personality and the Behavior Disorders,* Vol. I. New York: Ronald, 1944.

Rozhdestvenskaia, V. I., Nebylitsyn, V. D., Borisova, M. N., and Ermolaeva-Tomina, L. B. ["A Comparative Study of Different Indices of Strength of Nervous System in Man."] *Vop. Psikhol.,* 1960, 6 (5): 41–56.

Rozhdestvenskaia, V. I. "A Study of Mental Capacity for Work in Relation to Typological Characteristics of the Nervous System." *Proc. XVIII Int. Cong. Psychol.,* 1966.

Schachter, S., and Singer, J. E. "Cognitive, Social and Physiological Determinants of Emotional State." *Psychol. Rev.*, 1962, 69: 379–399.

Sears, R. R. *Survey of Objective Studies of Psychoanalytic Concepts.* New York: Social Science Research Council, 1943.

———. "Identification as a Form of Behavioral Development." In D. B. Harris (Ed.), *The Concept of Development.* Minneapolis: Univer. of Minnesota Press, 1957.

Seward, J. P. "Aggressive Behavior in the Rat. I. General Characteristics, Age and Sex Differences." *J. comp. Psychol.*, 1945, 38: 175–197. (a)

———. "Aggressive Behavior in the Rat. II. An Attempt to Establish a Dominance Hierarchy." *J. comp. Psychol.*, 1945, 38: 213–224. (b)

———. "Aggressive Behavior in the Rat. III. The Role of Frustration." *J. comp. Psychol.*, 1945, 38: 225–238. (c)

———. "Aggressive Behavior in the Rat. IV. Submission as Determined by Conditioning, Extinction, and Disuse." *J. comp. Psychol.*, 1946, 39: 51–76.

Shannon, C. E., and Weaver, W. *The Mathematical Theory of Communication.* Urbana: Univer. of Illinois Press, 1949.

Shaw, F. "A Stimulus-Response Analysis of Repression and Insight in Psychotherapy." *Psychol. Rev.*, 1946, 53: 36–42.

Sherman, M., and Jost, H. "Frustration Reactions of Normal and Neurotic Persons." *J. Psychol.*, 1942, 13: 3–19.

Shoben, E. J. "Psychotherapy as a Problem in Learning Theory." *Psychol. Bull.*, 1949, 46: 366–392.

Sidman, M., and Boren, J. J. "The Relative Aversiveness of Warning Signal and Shock in an Avoidance Situation." *J. abnorm. soc. Psychol.*, 1957, 55: 339–344.

Sigal, J. J., Stark, K. H., and Franks, C. M. "Hysterics and Dysthymics as Criterion Groups in the Study of Introversion-Extroversion." *J. abnorm. soc. Psychol.*, 1958, 57: 143–148.

Skinner, B. F. "Two Types of Conditioned Reflex and a Pseudo-Type." *J. gen. Psychol.*, 1935, 12: 66–77.

———. *The Behavior of Organisms: An Experimental Analysis.* New York: Appleton-Century-Crofts, 1938.

———. *Science and Human Behavior.* New York: Macmillan, 1953.

———. *Verbal Behavior.* New York: Appleton-Century-Crofts, 1957.

Spence, K. W. "The Role of Secondary Reinforcement in Delayed Reward Learning." *Psychol. Rev.*, 1947, 54: 1–8.

———. "The Postulates and Methods of 'Behaviorism.' " *Psychol. Rev.*, 1948, 55: 67–78.

———. *Behavior Theory and Conditioning.* New Haven: Yale Univer. Press, 1956.

———. "Anxiety (Drive) Level and Performance in Eyelid Conditioning." *Psychol. Bull.*, 1964, 61: 129–139.

———, and Spence, J. T. "Relation of Eyelid Conditioning to Manifest Anxiety, Extraversion, and Rigidity." *J. abnorm. soc. Psychol.*, 1964, 68: 144–149.

———, and Taylor, J. A. "Anxiety and Strength of the UCS as Determiners of the Amount of Eyelid Conditioning." *J. exp. Psychol.*, 1951, 42: 183–188.

Storms, L. H., and Sigal, J. J. "Eysenck's Personality Theory with Special Reference to 'The Dynamics of Anxiety and Hysteria.' " *Brit. J. med. Psychol.*, 1958, 31: 228–246.

Taylor, J. A. "The Relationship of Anxiety to the Conditioned Eyelid Response." *J. exp. Psychol.*, 1951, 41: 81–92.

————. "A Personality Scale of Manifest Anxiety." *J. abnorm. soc. Psychol.*, 1953, 48: 285–290.

————. "Drive Theory and Manifest Anxiety." *Psychol. Bull.*, 1956, 53: 303–320.

————, and Spence, K. W. "The Relationship of Anxiety Level to Performance in Serial Learning." *J. exp. Psychol.*, 1952, 44: 61–64.

Taylor, J. G. *The Behavioral Basis of Perception.* New Haven: Yale Univer. Press. 1962.

Teplov, B. M. (Ed.), *Tipologicheskie osobennosti vysshei nervnoi deiatel'nosti cheloveka* [*Typological Characteristics of Higher Nervous Activity in Man*]. Moscow: Acad. Pedag. Sci., 1956.

————. *Problemy individual'nykh razlichii* [*Problems of Individual Differences*]. Moscow: Acad. Pedag. Sci., 1961.

————. "New Data in the Study of the Characteristics of the Nervous System in Man." In B. M. Teplov (Ed.), *Tipologicheskie osobennosti vysshei nervnoi deiatel'nosti cheloveka* [*Typological Peculiarities of Higher Nervous Activity in Man*]. Vol. III. Moscow: Acad. Pedag. Sci., 1963.

Thorpe, W. H. *Learning and Instinct in Animals.* London: Methuen; Cambridge, Mass.: Harvard Univer. Press, 1956.

Tinbergen, N. *The Study of Instinct.* Oxford: Clarendon Press, 1951.

Tolman, E. C. *Purposive Behavior in Animals and Men.* New York: Appleton-Century, 1932.

————. *Drives toward War.* New York: Appleton-Century, 1942.

Ulrich, R. E., and Azrin, N. H. "Reflexive Fighting in Response to Aversive Stimulation." *J. exp. anal. Behav.*, 1962, 5: 511–520.

Vogel, M. D. "The Relation of Personality Factors to GSR Conditioning of Alcoholics: An Exploratory Study." *Canad. J. Psychol.*, 1960, 14: 275–280.

————. "GSR Conditioning and Personality Factors in Alcoholics and Normals." *J. abnorm. soc. Psychol.*, 1961, 63: (2), 417–421.

Watson, J. B. *Behaviorism.* New York: W. W. Norton & Co., Inc., 1924.

Webb, E. "Character and Intelligence." *Brit. J. Psychol.*, *Monog. Supp.*, 1915, 1, part 3.

Wenger, M. A. "Studies of Autonomic Balance in Army Air Forces Personnel." *Comp. Psychol.*, *Monogr.*, 1948, 19: 1–111.

Whiteis, U. E. "Punishment's Influence on Fear and Avoidance." *Harv. Educ. Rev.*, 1956, 26: 360–373.

Whitehead, A. N., and Russell, B. *Principia Mathematica.* Cambridge: Cambridge Univer. Press, Vol. I, 1910; Vols. II & III, 1912.

Whiting, J. W. M. "Sorcery, Sin, and the Superego." In M. R. Jones (Ed.), *Nebraska Symposium on Motivation*, 1959. Lincoln: Univer. of Nebraska Press, 1959, 174–195.

————. "Resource Mediation and Learning by Identification." In I. Iscoe and H. W. Stevenson (Eds.), *Personality Development in Children.* Austin: Univer. of Texas Press, 1960, 112–126.

————, and Mowrer, O. H. "Habit Progression and Regression — a Laboratory Study of Some Factors Relevant to Human Socialization." *J. comp. Psychol.*, 1943, 36: 229–253.

Wilcoxon, H. C. " 'Abnormal Fixation' and Learning." *J. exp. Psychol.*, 1952, 44: 324–333.

Willett, R. A. "Measures of Learning and Conditioning." In H. J. Eysenck (Ed.), *Experiments in Personality*, Vol. II, *Psychodiagnostics and Psychodynamics.* London: Routledge & Kegan Paul, 1960.

IX

Research, Measurement, and Psychotherapy

No book of readings is sufficient to provide an introduction to as vast and amorphous a field as personality, but this one does show you something of the various theoretical alternatives there are, and includes as many basic articles as possible, regardless of when they were written. Theoretical readings are important because they let you know what the field is about, and what its concepts, problems, and issues are. But justice has not been done to the concrete activities of personologists. Important among these activities are the measurement or assessment of personality, the performance of personality research, and the practice of psychotherapy. I cannot hope to do justice to these topics in fewer pages than it has taken to come this far, but I will at least attempt to make some general statements about each of the topics and to place them in relation to the readings included here.

THE PRACTICE OF PSYCHOTHERAPY

Very frequently, personality theories include the basis for distinguishing between psychopathology and health. Techniques of psychotherapy tend to spring up as aids in changing a psychopathological state to something more nearly approaching mental health. It is understandable that the form of psychotherapy associated with a personality theory would reflect the distinction between health and the illness that is involved.

In personality theories expressing the psychosocial conflict model, the ideal peripheral personality, which indicates that which is considered mental health, stresses inhibiting action and consciousness to comply with the requirements of organized, harmonious social living. For Freud (see Chapter II), the ideal meant maximizing instinctual gratification while simultaneously minimizing punishment and guilt, a feat to be accomplished by expressing and being conscious of only those implications of the instincts that are acceptable to society. Defenses are present in this ideal personality type called the "genital character," but they distort the instincts minimally and are therefore called "sublimation." There are psychopathologies associated with each of the so-called pregenital character types. These psychopathologies are either extreme forms or breakdown products of the pregenital character types. The psychopathologies associated with the oral character type are psychoses, specifically the schizophrenias, expressing as they do primitivity, dependency, interpersonal inability, and retreat into fantasy. Associated with the anal character type is the obsessive-compulsive neurosis, with its inordinate emphasis on control and feelings of unworthiness. Hysterical neuroses and other sexual disorders like homosexuality are generally thought to be related to the phallic or Oedipal character type. In all these disorders, the defenses are so strong and crippling that very little instinctual gratification is possible and a normal life is precluded.

In the attempt to move persons toward the genital character type, with its emphasis on sublimation rather than more crippling defenses, Freud advocated the technique of psychotherapy called "psycho-analysis" (Freud, 1924). In this, the patient free associates, screening nothing from expression. He also scrutinizes his dreams for whatever insights they can give into what has been repressed. The therapist helps by providing analytic tools (or habits of thought) for this self-scrutiny, and by making interpretations of the patient's verbalizations that are designed to help him understand the roots of current problems in the oral, anal, or phallic fixations of the past. By these procedures, the therapist hopes to weaken the grip of the debilitating defenses, and start the patient on the road to constructive sublimations, i.e., to maximizing instinctual gratification while minimizing punishment and guilt. But defenses there must always be, and avoidance of the regulatory function of society would, if possible, be undesirable.

Theories expressing the intrapsychic conflict model are similar to the above in implications for psychopathology and psychotherapy. But they deviate from the psychosocial conflict theories in being more optimistic and granting more power to the person's consciousness (see Chapter III). Indeed, Rank's (1947) form of therapy was called "will therapy" to show that the patient had to take his life in his own two hands. The ideal peripheral personality, or artist, is one who can express his individuality in a manner that others can accept, respect, and admire. The artist is a natural leader, and is not described in the language of defense. But he does have to accommodate by virtue of the fact that although he wishes to be an individual he cannot risk complete social isolation, for his nature is in part communal. Probably some defensiveness is necessary, though Rank is unclear about this. The neurotic type is clearly considered psychopathological, because he has suppressed his communal side, or the fear of life. Therapy functions to encourage him to recognize his need for approval and admiration, without removing completely his already too overplayed need for individuality. The type called the "average man" should really be considered psychopathological as well, for Rank respects him even less than the neurotic. Therapy with the average man would focus on building up will, which is the self-realization relevant to individuality that has been suppressed.

Will therapy is similar to psychoanalysis insofar as it employs free association and interpretation, focuses upon the past, and is designed to help the patient accommodate to conflict, believing its transcendence to be impossible. But it deals with many more kinds of content than the merely sexual, is somewhat more future-oriented, and considers the ideal state to be less defensive in nature.

You will recall that the ideal personality type in the actualization fulfillment model stresses transcendence of the limiting effects of conventional society in order to express more fully the one great force that resides in the genetic blueprint. Rogers' characteristics of the fully functioning person exemplify this model well (see Chapter IV). They include openness to experience, organismic valuing, existential living, creativity, and an absence of conditions of worth. The maladjusted or psychopathological person shows the opposites of these characteristics, and the task of psychotherapy is to aid in their removal. The therapy, called "client-centered counseling" (Rogers, 1959), utilizes unconditional positive regard (or total acceptance) of the patient by the therapist. Just providing this free climate for growth is considered enough, for the actualizing tendency is inherent in the organism and its genetic blueprint. Soon, defenses will drop away, as will conditions of worth, and the patient will trust his intuitions, avoid heavy-handed preconceived plans, and function in novel ways. The therapist under no condition gives interpretations, for this would indicate a lack of respect for the patient and substitute external meanings for the internal ones he should be pursuing.

Once again, there is similarity between Rogerian therapy and the therapies associated with the perfection fulfillment model. In the latter, the ideal personality type is considered undefensive, individualistic, and self-reliant, whereas psychopathology is the opposite of these (see Chapter V). And the therapy of such perfection fulfillment theorists as Adler (1924) reflects these similarities to Rogerian therapy in its employment of techniques to express respect for and acceptance of the patient. But perfection fulfillment theories do not specify unmitigated individuality as the ideal. Instead, they advocate some overall, common view of the perfect life. It is understandable, therefore, that Adlerian therapy would be somewhat more directive than Rogerian, somewhat more concerned that the patient come to appreciate the finest things in life. The Adlerian therapist will often exhort and encourage the patient to overcome feelings of inferiority and strive for something better. But he will try to do this in a manner that is minimally manipulative and expresses the high value he puts on the patient's attempt to transcend conventional society.

In general, the consistency model does not produce elaborate psychotherapies, mainly because it makes relatively little of the distinction between psychopathology and mental health (see Chapters VI and VII). Consistency theories do recognize that people make mistakes and fail because of them to obtain what they wish or what would be good for them. But there is little basis in these theories for conceiving mistakes as self-perpetuating. Thus, it is understandable that whatever therapies exist here are mainly techniques for aiding the patient to get the necessary information whereby he can correct former mistakes.

Kelly's (1955) cognitive dissonance form of the consistency model employs what is called "fixed role therapy." Having listened to the patient's complaints about how his life is not what he wishes and how he is beset by anxiety and uncertainty, the therapist plans an elaborate role for the patient to play. The role is designed to help the patient obtain just the kind of information that will help him build or alter his construction system so that anxiety and uncertainty can be better avoided. The patient goes off and plays the role as capably as he can, and from that point on, therapy involves discussions with the therapist about the nature of ensuing experience. Gradually, as a function of the inflow of new information, the patient begins to change in the desired directions. The content of the role designed by the therapist, like the content of the patient's construction system when he comes for help, may be anything. Thus not only the personality theory but the therapy as well expresses Kelly's emphasis on constructive alternativism.

As you can see, the therapies associated with various theories and models of personality seem to have clear differences in aim and techniques. Which are best? Much research has been done on the merits of particular psychotherapies and on their comparison (e.g., Stollak, Guerney and Rothberg, 1966; Shlien, 1968; Gottschalk and Auerbach, 1966; Ford and Urban, 1963). This does not mean, however, that any clear answer has emerged so far. Indeed, one authority (Eysenck, 1965) claims that research shows that no kind of psychotherapy is more effective than the mere passage of time. Perhaps it is safest to say that most therapies seem to help a little, if practiced by skilled therapists on conscientious patients. But the relative merits of the therapies seem far outweighed by the skill of the therapists. In addition, the suspicion is growing that skilled therapists from different schools of therapy function in a remarkably similar way, regardless of differences in their theories. But even if the little good that is being done comes out of the general wisdom of experienced therapists more than out of their theories, this does not mean that we could not devise some theory that would work better. After all, it is hardly true that all patients are aided in therapy, or even that a substantial number of patients are changed radically.

Although it is not possible to say at this time which therapies are best, there do seem to be prevailing differences in popularity. Still very popular is psychoanalysis, though its practice and aims have changed considerably since Freud's day. Modern psychoanalysis is expressive of ego psychology, which means that there is less emphasis on conflict and defense as being necessary and more emphasis on reason and consciousness. With the decrease in reliance on classical Freudian precepts, the practice of psychoanalysis has become much more variable from one therapist to another. Often the techniques and aims of psychoanalysts differ so markedly that one wonders whether there is any longer a single tradition. Nonetheless, the heterogeneous practice called "psychoanalysis" is still quite popular among practitioners.

Of late, the popularity of actualization fulfillment therapies has risen sharply. Rogerian therapy, regarded as close to unethical twenty years ago, is now widely accepted. Indeed, the current emphasis on sensitivity training and confrontation groups is largely an outgrowth of actualization ideas. It is no accident that Maslow and Rogers have been very active in this movement.

Also very popular now is the conditioning therapy associated with the radical, Skinnerian branch of behaviorism (e.g., Ullmann and Krasner, 1965; Wolpe, 1958; Goldiamond and Dyrud, 1968). In this therapy, the practitioner accepts the patient's statement of concrete, behavioral goals and attempts to bring about their realization by a strict, overtly manipulative regimen of rewards and punishments applied to responses. Since behavior therapy involves few substantive assumptions, it is difficult to compare it to the others. Nonetheless it seems to have more in common with consistency therapies, such as that of Kelly, than with psychoanalytic or actualization therapies.

The Measurement or Assessment of Personality

It goes without saying that statements about peripheral personality are intended to provide a basis for understanding persistent differences among persons. A major practical use of personality theories has been the assessment or diagnosis of peripheral personality. This use has spurred the development of a wide variety of tests and interviews designed to elicit the necessary information. Sometimes the theory involved dictated the form and content of the assessment procedure. But all too frequently, the assessment procedure was devised on other grounds and then fitted to the theory, with uncertain relevance.

A major tool of assessment has been the interview, either in the form of specific questions to which elaborate answers are solicited, or in a less structured form involving questions so broad as to serve mainly to stimulate the interviewee to talk. Both forms of the interview permit the interviewer to ask additional questions based on the answers given to previous questions. Given that the content of the questions is relevant to the theory concerned, all personality theorists would find interviews germane to assessment. Indeed, many theorists (e.g., Freud, Sullivan, Rank, Angyal, Adler, Allport and Fromm) saw the interview as the assessment procedure of choice.

The major objection to the interview was raised by methodologists, who thought it an unrigorous procedure. There is no guarantee, in an interview, that information obtained from several interviewees is comparable, because the same questions may not have been asked. Further, there is no very consistent and straightforward way of transforming interview responses into scores so that numerical comparisons among interviewees can be made. Science has always required quantification of data in order to progress. More generally, the potentially great impact of the interviewer's mood, attitude, and even sex, on the interviewee's responses is rarely scrutinized and, even when studied, difficult to determine. It is even possible, in such a freewheeling assessment procedure, that the interviewer will actually influence the interviewee so that the responses obtained will conform to prior expectation. Szasz (1961) elaborated this possibility when he argued that the disorder called "hysteria" (almost never diagnosed in men) is really a fiction or creation of the male psychiatrist's imagination, expressing his derogatory, sterotyped view of femininity.

Recognizing the possibly limited reliability and validity of the interview, psychologists set about developing what they hoped were more foolproof procedures. The two main classes of procedure are the unstructured (or "projective") test and the structured (or "objective") test. In the unstructured test, a standard set of ambiguous stimuli are presented to the subject and his task is to structure them for the tester. In doing this, the subject presumably "projects" his own personality onto the stimuli, a process facilitated by their ambiguity. The structured test, by contrast, employs a standard set of very specific and unambiguous stimuli (usually questions) to which the subject must respond in some simple, specified manner (e.g., by answering "true" or "false"). Whereas the unstructured test deals with fantasies, the structured test seems to deal with "objective" descriptions of self.

The two most popular unstructured procedures are the *Rorschach Test* (Rorschach, 1942), comprised of a series of ink blots to be identified by the subject in his own way, and the *Thematic Apperception Test* (Murray, 1943), in which the subject composes stories for a series of ambiguous pictures involving human beings. The Rorschach Test seems to have been developed independently of any specific personality theory, though it is commonly used these days by psychoanalytically oriented personologists. But it cannot be said to be a rigorous, point-for-point operationalization of Freud's position. In contrast, the Thematic Apperception Test was developed by Murray specifically to aid in diagnosing the various needs he theorized to exist in people.

In general, many personality theorists consider unstructured tests relevant assessment procedures. But few develop and elaborate this relevance in a specific, rigorous way. One of the few is the *Blacky Test* (Blum, 1949), a variant of the Thematic Apperception Test devised in order to be especially relevant to psychoanalytic theory. In this procedure, meant to be used on children, a family of dogs is depicted in situations reminiscent of the conflicts associated with the various stages of psychosexual development (e.g., oral, anal, phallic). Thus, psychoanalytic assessment is rendered less ambiguous — though not necessarily more valid — by the existence of this procedure. McClelland (1958) regards unstructured tests as especially relevant to his position, because he believes motives to be most clearly displayed in fantasy productions. According to him, fantasy is influenced neither by habits nor role-playing behavior. He has tailored the Thematic Apperception Test to his purposes, providing one of the most rigorous operationalizations of a statement on the periphery of personality that exists in the personality field. Maddi (1968) has proceeded similarly for the same reason.

The structured or self-description procedure has, if anything, been more popular in personology than the unstructured procedure. One reason for this is that the structured test is shorter and easier to administer and score. Another reason is that structured procedures have greater reliability. In other words, a subject's response to a structured procedure at one time is a better predictor of what his response will be to the same procedure at another time. Thus, the structured procedure would seem to be getting at some consistent disposition in the person, whereas one can be less certain of this with an unstructured procedure. Of course, personologists who rely on unstructured techniques regard the reliability of structured techniques as spurious, as produced by the directive, manipulative form of the questions rather than a pre-existing personality characteristic. This argument has raged for a long time. In any event, a final reason for the reliance on structured procedures is that some personologists (e.g., Allport, Kelly) believe that the best way to know what a person is like and will do is to ask him directly. Such personologists do not celebrate unconscious processes in their personality theories. In general, the greater the presumed importance of the unconscious, the greater will be the reliance on unstructured assessment procedures.

Several general, structured tests of personality have achieved popularity. Among them are the *Minnesota Multiphasis Personality Inven-*

tory (Dahlstrom and Welsh, 1960), the *California Psychological Inventory* (Gough, 1957), the *Activities Index* (Stern, 1958), the *Edwards Personal Preference Schedule* (Edwards, 1963), and the *Sixteen Personality Factor Questionnaire* (Cattell and Stice, 1957). The first and last of these are not really specific to any personality theory. The first has been mainly useful for identifying psychopathology and the second was developed in a strictly empirical, non-theoretical way. The others have all been influenced in large degree by Murray's theorizing about needs. The enormous influence this theorist has had on personality tests is readily understandable when you realize that he is virtually alone in having offered an elaborate, comprehensive statement on the periphery of personality. It is the periphery that conceptualizes individual differences, and, of course, the aim of a personality test is to identify such differences.

A few structured tests have special relevance to theories other than that of Murray, though they have not achieved such wide use as those mentioned above. Rogerians have made considerable use of a procedure for assessing the discrepancy between how you see yourself and what you would like to be (Butler and Haigh, 1954). This self-ideal discrepancy is obtained by a procedure in which the subject sorts various statements about himself first in terms of the degree to which they describe him, and then in terms of his ideals. The size of discrepancy is considered indicative of maladjustment. Recently (Shostrom, 1966), a structured test designed to identify peripheral personality as construed by Maslow has been offered. In connection with his theory, Kelly (1955) devised an unusual assessment procedure called the *Role Repertory Test*. The subject is asked to think of groups of three people important in his life (e.g., mother, father, and favorite teacher) and to indicate how two of them are similar to each other but different from the third. As you can see, the subject gives what Kelly defines as a construct in responding. Many groups of three people are mentioned, and the result is a mapping of the content and organization of the subject's construction system.

At this time, it would be hazardous to state strong conclusions about which assessment approaches are the most advantageous. Certainly structured tests are more reliable than unstructured tests, but it is possible that the reliability of the former is forced rather than genuine. Further, reliability is important mainly because it limits how valid a test can be. In the extreme, a test with no reliability at all will yield scores on the basis of chance alone. And how can chance scores tell you anything you want to know about a person's personality and its influence on his behavior? But once reliability is above zero, one can learn something about the personalities measured even when the test may not be fully satisfying (McClelland, 1958). This line of argument shifts the question of which are the most advantageous approaches to a consideration of validity. For present purposes, the kind of validity of importance is the degree to which a test produces results that seem to operate in a fashion consistent with the personality theory guiding the test development. This has been called "construct validity" (Cronbach and Meehl, 1955). But once we scrutinize the construct validity of the available tests, it becomes apparent that we have not yet reached the point where clear, definitive conclusions can be reached. It will take some time yet before the conflicting research claims of validity and non-validity are investigated sufficiently to be resolved.

At the moment, psychology is in the situation where there are strong advocates of unstructured testing and equally strong advocates of structured testing. Of late, the advocates of structured testing have developed considerable theorizing and technology to increase the ability to use test questions to identify individual differences (e.g., Fiske, 1963, 1966; Loevinger, 1966, 1955; Fiske and Pearson, 1970). The methodological sophistication of this movement represents a potentially influential force in personology.

But it is not entirely clear that one must conclude in favor of either unstructured or structured tests. After all, on the face of it, the two approaches elicit different kinds of information. McClelland (1958) has argued cogently that the fantasies elicited by unstructured procedures may be the most valid and pure source of information about motives and relatively unconscious processes. He contends that structured tests, with their emphasis on specific, even pointed, questions about the self may be most useful in eliciting information about the façade a person presents to others, especially those in authority. This kind of information is clearly relevant to a personologist, but it is also clearly different from that which can be obtained in fantasy. In supporting his position, McClelland (1958) points to research on achievement concerns when these concerns are measured in fantasy; the resulting scores predict degree of striving and risk-taking. In contrast, achievement concerns measured in questionnaires (1) do not correlate with fantasy measures, and (2) predict susceptibility to suggestion and public valuation of achievement, but do not predict striving and risk-taking. Consistent with his argument is the emergent literature on test-taking attitudes. It seems that whenever a set of questions is given to a subject, his resulting scores will almost always include not only true answers but also some contribution from his attempt to avoid personal threat by giving the tester what he seems to want. Two important forms of this image-maintenance are the tendency to respond in a socially desirable fashion and the tendency to agree with any statement (e.g., Crowne and Marlowe, 1964; Cronbach, 1946). So much have these tendencies bedeviled structured attempts at measurement that we now see the emergence of tests which, though structured, include some very elaborate technology to attempt purification (e.g., Jackson, 1965). But if McClelland is right, then perhaps we should be using both structured and unstructured approaches to assessment and conclude from each only what seems most certain.

PERSONALITY RESEARCH

Another major activity of personologists is to conduct research. The research may have the aim of investigating directly the validity of a particular personality theory or it may be more concerned with understanding some phenomenon (e.g., suicide) to which personality theory would seem to make some contribution. Understandably, the latter kind of research is generally less relevant to the direct, deductive evaluation of theory. Sometimes the data on the phenomenon are collected before some theoretical interpretation of them is developed. Such post-hoc functioning should never be regarded as a test of a theory, however stimulating for future research and theorizing the work may have been.

Mainly, personality research seeks to determine the relationship of responses to each other. McClelland might determine subjects' scores on a fantasy measure of need for achievement and see in what manner these scores relate to the degree of risk taken in a performance task. In such correlational research, the personologist hopes to understand how characteristics of personality influence behavior. Less frequently, experimental rather than correlational research is undertaken. Generally, the aim of experimental studies in personality is to determine the effects on behavior of certain levels of personality characteristics by creating them in an artificial but controllable fashion.

The present research on peripheral personality is critically reviewed by Maddi (1968). Mentioning a few examples here may help provide an idea of the work being done. Of relevance to psychoanalytic theory,

Blum (1949) has employed the Blacky Test in construct validity studies of peripheral personality. By intercorrelating the various scores obtained from the Blacky Test itself, Blum has identified patterns of responses conforming somewhat to the Freudian character types. In addition, studies relating Blacky Test scores to behavioral variables external to the test have yielded promising results (Blum and Hunt, 1952). There are also experimental studies of psychoanalytic theory (e.g., Sarnoff 1951, 1960), in which particular defenses are aroused by experimental means and the effects of so doing are then observed on various revelant behaviors. The large body of research on perceptual defense and vigilance (see Eriksen, 1963; MacKinnon and Dukes, 1962) is relevant not only to psychoanalytic theory but also to the other theories explicitly employing the concept of defense. It is a complex, even frustrating body of research, yielding no simple conclusions.

Murray is one of the personologists included in this book who has conducted his own research. It typically employs few subjects and not only interviews but also structured and unstructured tests, in an attempt to achieve comprehensive understanding of the individual personalities involved (e.g., Murray, 1938; 1963). As mentioned before, much contemporary research utilizing general tests of personality — either to validate them directly, or to use them to determine the personalistic contribution to other phenomena — has some relevance for Murray's theory, as it inspired the personality variables studied.

A substantial body of related studies has been done on the Rogerian idea of self-ideal discrepancy. Butler and Haigh (1954) and others (e.g., Chodorkoff, 1954a; 1954b) contend that not only large but also small self-ideal discrepancies are evidence of defensiveness. Research also suggests that the larger the self-ideal discrepancy, the greater the ineptitude for living (e.g., Turner and Vanderlippe, 1958; Rosenberg, 1962), and the less one can accept and respect others (e.g., Suinn, 1961; Medinnus and Curtis, 1963). The findings seem generally consistent with Rogerian theory.

Of general relevance to Maslow's theory, with its emphasis on democratic values as indications of mental health, are the many studies relating measures of authoritarianism and dogmatism to other behavioral variables (e.g., Adorno, Frenkel-Brunswick, Levinson and Sanford, 1950; Rokeach, 1960). As is well known, however, the impurity of measures of authoritarianism has plagued this whole line of research (e.g., Hyman and Sheatsley, 1954; Peabody, 1966), however exciting its results. Finally, Shostrom's (1966) inventory of self-actualization seems to have produced correlational evidence supporting such of Maslow's views as that psychopathology is different from, and creativity similar to, actualization (Fox, Knapp & Michael, 1968; Guinan & Foulds, 1970).

Allport's own research has focused mainly on expressive movements (e.g., Allport and Vernon, 1933), a valuable emphasis even though it is not central to his formal personality theorizing. Perhaps more relevant is the recent research studying the differences in living between people who feel in control of their fate as opposed to those who feel externally controlled. This research on "internal vs. external locus of control" (proactive vs. reactive behavior, Allport would say) was stimulated originally by Rotter (1954). Studies (e.g., Gore and Rotter, 1963; Strickland, 1965) have demonstrated that persons having an internal locus of control tend to influence what their lives are like whereas those with an external locus of control are passively manipulated by circumstances.

Until recently, Fromm had done little systematic research himself and had not stimulated much research by others. But now there are two large-scale studies of relevance. One is Kenniston's (1966) investigation of alienated college students, who should clearly express the characteristics described by Fromm under the marketing orientation. Kenniston's work finds some support for this view. The other is an anthropological study of a Mexican village, in which evidence is found for the existence of several Frommian character orientations (Fromm & Maccoby, 1970).

McClelland has performed and stimulated much research concerning his position on the needs for achievement, affiliation, and power. These needs are measured with a modified form of the Thematic Apperception Test, and the resulting scores are correlated with a wide range of other behavioral variables. I cannot hope to summarize all the findings here and refer you instead to other reviews (e.g., Atkinson, 1958; McClelland, 1961). It does seem clear, though, that people high in need for achievement work harder on tasks on which performance can improve as a function of skill development, but fail to work harder on tasks where performance involves chance (see McClelland, 1961). In addition (McClelland, 1958), people high in need for achievement tend to take moderate rather than high or low risks, once again indicating a preference for a situation in which their skill can show to good advantage. Because a high need for achievement should express itself in entrepreneurial behavior, McClelland (1961) studied the relationship between the average level of that need (as reflected in children's literature) in a large number of societies and their rate of economic growth. Through some complicated analyses, he demonstrated this expected effect. Economic growth is high in societies high in achievement need. Research on the other needs has not been so extensive.

Maddi and his associates have conducted research relevant to the activation consistency position. The studies are similar methodologically to those of McClelland. The need for variety is measured with a modified form of the Thematic Apperception Test and the scores are correlated with other behavioral variables. This research (e.g., Maddi, Propst and Feldinger, 1965; Maddi and Andrews, 1966) has distinguished three forms of need for variety on the grounds of activeness-passiveness and internal vs. external orientation in the search for stimulation. Some construct validity has been obtained, but the picture is far from complete.

Finally, examples of behavioristic research relevant to personality are included in Berlyne's paper. This work is not representative of the Skinnerian tradition, but this tradition has understandably done little personality research.

Many personality theories seem to have their own body of research and researchers. How can one evaluate the relative merits of the research and the validity of the theories it is supposed to be demonstrating? This is an arduous and complex task, calling for detailed inquiry into the methodological adequacy of the studies and the degree to which their design is really germane to the underlying theory. Such evaluation is impossible here, but I have tried to do it elsewhere (Maddi, 1968). In that attempt, I have also pinpointed the issues separating the conflict, fulfillment, and consistency theories of personality, and amassed research in a manner that bears on the eventual resolution of the issues. Once the issues are resolved, it will be possible to determine which are the most promising leads in personality theorizing.

When all this is said and done, an extensive and somewhat ill-defined body of research considered relevant to personality remains. This research is directed at particular phenomena of common sense interest rather than the investigation of formal theory. There is no simple way of summarizing this research since it is quite diverse in its conception and implications. Useful readings in finding out about it are Klein, Barr, and Wolitsky (1967), Wiggins (1968), and Adelson (1969).

REFERENCES

Adelson, J. "Personality." In P. H. Mussen and M. R. Rosenzweig, eds., *Annual Review of Psychology*. Palo Alto: Annual Reviews, 1969.

Adler, A. *The Practice and Theory of Individual Psychology*. New York: Harcourt, Brace, 1924.

Adorno, T. W.; Frenkel-Brunswick, Else; Levinson, D. J.; and Sanford, R. N. *The Authoritarian Personality*. New York: Harper, 1950.

Allport, G. W. and Vernon, P. E. *Studies in Expressive Movement*. New York: Macmillan, 1933.

Atkinson, J. W., ed., *Motives in Fantasy, Action and Society*. Princeton: Van Nostrand, 1958.

Blum, G. S. "A Study of the Psychoanalytic Theory of Psychosexual Development." *Genet. Psychol. Monogr.*, 39 (1949): 3–99.

Blum, G. S. and Hunt, H. F. "The Validity of the Blacky Pictures." *Psychol. Bull.*, 49 (1952): 238–250.

Butler, J. M. and Haigh, G. V. "Changes in the Relation between Self-Concepts and Ideal-Concepts Consequent upon Client-Centered Counseling." In C. R. Rogers and R. F. Dymond, eds., *Psychotherapy and Personality Change*. Chicago: University of Chicago Press, 1954.

Cattell, R. B. and Stice, G. F. *Sixteen Personality Factor Questionnaire*. rev. ed., Champaign, Ill.: Inst. Pers. Abil. Test., 1957.

Chodorkoff, B. "Adjustment and the Discrepancy between Perceived and Ideal Self." *J. clin. Psychol.*, 10 (1954): 266–268. (a)

———. "Self-Perception, Perceptual Defense, and Adjustment." *J. Abnorm. Soc. Psychol.*, 49 (1954): 508–512. (b)

Cronbach, L. J. "Response Sets and Test Validity." *Educ. Psychol. Measmt.*, 6 (1946): 475–94.

Cronbach, L. J. and Meehl, P. E. "Construct Validity in Psychological Tests." *Psychol. Bull.*, 52 (1955): 281–302.

Crowne, D. P. and Marlowe, D. *The Approval Motive: Studies in Evaluative Dependence*. New York: Wiley, 1964.

Dahlstrom, W. G. and Welsh, G. S. *An MMPI Handbook*. Minneapolis: University of Minnesota Press, 1960.

Edwards, A. L. *Edwards Personal Preference Schedule*. New York: Psychol. Corp., 1963.

Eriksen, C. W. "Perception and Personality." In J. M. Wepman and R. W. Heine, eds., *Concepts of Personality*. Chicago: Aldine, 1963.

Eysenck, H. J. "The Effects of Psychotherapy." *Intern. J. Psychiat.*, 1 (1965): 97–144.

Fiske, D. W. "Problems in Measuring Personality." In J. M. Wepman and R. W. Heine, eds., *Concepts of Personality*. Chicago: Aldine, 1963.

———. "On the Coordination of Personality Constructs and Their Measurement." *Hum. Develpmt.*, 9 (1966): 74–83.

Fiske, D. W. and Pearson, Pamela. "Theory and Techniques of Personality Measurement." In P. H. Mussen and M. R. Rosenzweig, eds., *Annual Review of Psychology*. Palo Alto: Annual Reviews, 1970.

Ford, D. H. and Urban, H. B. *Systems of Psychotherapy: A Comparative Study*. New York: Wiley, 1963.

Fox, J., Knapp, R. and Michael, W. Assessment of Self Actualization of Psychiatric Patients: Validity of the Personal Orientation Inventory. *Educat. Psychol. Measmt.*, 28 (1968): 565–569.

Freud, S. "Papers on Technique." In *Collected Papers*. London: Hogarth Press, 1924, Vol. II.

Fromm, E. and Maccoby, M. *Social Character in a Mexican Village*. Englewood Cliffs, N.J.: Prentice-Hall, 1970.

Goldiamond, I. and Dyrud, J. E. "Some Applications and Implications of Behavior Analysis for Psychotherapy." In J. M. Shlien, ed., *Research in Psychotherapy*. Wash., D.C.: Amer. Psychol. Assn., 1968, Vol. III.

Gore, P. M. and Rotter, J. B. "A Personality Correlate of Social Action." *J. Pers.*, 31 (1963): 58–64.

Gottschalk, L. A. and Auerbach, A. H., eds., *Methods of Research in Psychotherapy*. New York: Appleton-Century-Crofts, 1966.

Gough, H. C. *Manual: California Psychological Inventory*. Palo Alto: Consult. Psychologists Press, 1957.

Guinan, J. and Foulds, M. "Marathon Group: Facilitator of Personal Growth?" *J. counsel. Psychol.*, 17 (1970): 145–149.

Hyman, H. H. and Sheatsley, P. B. " 'The Authoritarian Personality' — a Methodological Critique." In R. Christie and Marie Jahoda, eds., *Studies in the Scope and Method of "the Authoritarian Personality."* New York: Free Press, 1954.

Kelly, G. A. *The Psychology of Personal Constructs*. New York: Norton, 1955, Vol. I.

Keniston, K. *The Uncommitted: Alienated Youth in American Society*. New York: Harcourt, Brace, 1966.

Klein, G. S.; Barr, Harriet L.; and Wolitsky, D. L. "Personality." In P. R. Farnsworth, Olga McNemar, and Q. McNemar, eds., *Annual Review of Psychology*. Palo Alto: Annual Reviews, 1967.

Loevinger, J. "Some Principles of Personality Measurement." *Educ. Psychol. Measmt.*, 15 (1955): 3–17.

_____. "The Meaning and Measurement of Ego Development." *Amer. Psychologist*, 21 (1966): 195–206.

Mackinnon, D. W. and Dukes, W. "Repression." In L. Postman, ed., *Psychology in the Making*. New York: Knopf, 1962.

Maddi, S. R. *Personality Theories: A Comparative Analysis*. Homewood, Ill.: Dorsey Press, 1968.

Maddi, S. R. and Andrews, Susan. "The Need for Variety in Fantasy and Self-Description." *J. Pers.*, 34 (1966): 610–625.

Maddi, S. R.; Propst, Barbara S.; and Feldinger, I. "Three Expressions of the Need for Variety." *J. Pers.*, 33 (1965): 82–98.

McClelland, D. C. "The Measurement of Motivation." In J. W. Atkinson, ed., *Motives in Fantasy, Action and Society*. Princeton: Van Nostrand, 1958.

_____. *The Achieving Society*. Princeton: Van Nostrand, 1961.

Medinnus, G. R. and Curtis, F. J. "The Relation between Maternal Self-Acceptance and Child Acceptance." *J. Counsel. Psychol.*, 27 (1963): 542–544.

Murray, H. A. *Explorations in Personality*. New York: Oxford, 1938.

_____. *Thematic Apperception Test*. Cambridge, Mass.: Harvard University Press, 1943.

_____. Studies of Stressful Interpersonal Disputations. *Amer. Psychologist*, 18 (1963): 28–36.

Peabody, D. "Authoritarianism Scales and Response Bias." *Psychol. Bull.*, 65 (1966): 11–23.

Rank, O. *Will Therapy and Truth and Reality*. New York: Knopf, 1947.

Rogers, C. R. "A Theory of Therapy, Personality, and Interpersonal Relationships, as Developed in the Client-Centered Framework." In S. Koch, ed., *Psychology: A Study of a Science*. New York: McGraw-Hill, 1959, Vol. 3.

Rokeach, M. *The Open and Closed Mind*. New York: Basic Books, 1960.

Rorschach, H. *Psychodiagnosis*. 2nd ed. Translated by Lemkan and Kronenberg. New York: Grune & Stratton, 1942.

Rosenberg, L. A. "Idealization of Self and Social Adjustment." *J. Consult. Psychol.*, 26 (1962): 487.

Rotter, J. B. *Social Learning and Clinical Psychology*. New York: Prentice-Hall, 1954.

Sarnoff, I. "Identification with the Aggressor: Some Personality Correlates of Anti-Semitism among Jews." *J. Pers.*, 20 (1951): 199–218.

————. "Reaction Formation and Cynicism." *J. Pers.*, 28 (1960): 129–143.

Shlien, J. M., ed., *Research in Psychotherapy*. Wash., D.C.: Amer. Psychol. Assn., 1968, Vol. III.

Shostrom, E. L. *Personal Orientation Inventory: An Inventory for the Measurement of Self-Actualization*. San Diego: Educational and Industrial Testing Service, 1966.

Stern, G. G. *Preliminary Record: Activities Index — College Characteristics Index*. New York: Syracuse University Psychol. Res. Center, 1958.

Stollak, G. E.; Guerney, B., Jr.; and Rothberg, M., eds., *Psychotherapy Research: Selected Readings*. Chicago: Rand McNally, 1966.

Strickland, Bonnie R. "The Prediction of Social Action from a Dimension of Internal-External Control." *J. Soc. Psychol.*, 66 (1965): 353–358.

Suinn, R. M. "The Relationship between Self-Acceptance and Acceptance of Others: A Learning Theory Analysis." *J. Abnorm. Soc. Psychol.*, 63 (1961): 37–42.

Szasy, T. S. *The Myth of Mental Illness*. New York: Hoeber, 1961.

Turner, R. H., and Vanderlippe, R. H. "Self-Ideal Congruence as an Index of Adjustment." *J. Abnorm. Soc. Psychol.*, 57 (1958): 202–206.

Ullman, L. P. and Krasner, L., eds., *Case Studies in Behavior Modification*. New York: Holt, Rinehart, and Winston, 1965.

Wiggins, J. S. "Personality Structure." In P. R. Farnsworth, M. R. Rosenzweig, and Judith T. Polefka, eds., *Annual Review of Psychology*. Palo Alto: Annual Reviews, 1968.

Wolpe, J. *Psychotherapy by Reciprocal Inhibition*. Stanford: Stanford University Press, 1958.